ACTIVE
SERVER PAGES
Solutions

Al Williams
Kim Barber
Paul Newkirk

CORIOLIS

President, CEO
Keith Weiskamp

Publisher
Steve Sayre

Acquisitions Editor
Stephanie Wall

Marketing Specialist
Tracy Schofield

Project Editor
Toni Zuccarini Ackley

Technical Reviewer
Brian Kierstead

Production Coordinator
Meg E. Turecek

Cover Designer
Jody Winkler

Layout Designer
April Nielsen

CD-ROM Developer
Robert Clarfield

Active Server Pages Solutions

Limits Of Liability And Disclaimer Of Warranty
The author and publisher of this book have used their best efforts in preparing the book and the programs contained in it. These efforts include the development, research, and testing of the theories and programs to determine their effectiveness. The author and publisher make no warranty of any kind, expressed or implied, with regard to these programs or the documentation contained in this book.

The author and publisher shall not be liable in the event of incidental or consequential damages in connection with, or arising out of, the furnishing, performance, or use of the programs, associated instructions, and/or claims of productivity gains.

Trademarks
Trademarked names appear throughout this book. Rather than list the names and entities that own the trademarks or insert a trademark symbol with each mention of the trademarked name, the publisher states that it is using the names for editorial purposes only and to the benefit of the trademark owner, with no intention of infringing upon that trademark.

The Coriolis Group, LLC
14455 North Hayden Road
Suite 220
Scottsdale, Arizona 85260

480/483-0192
FAX 480/483-0193
http://www.coriolis.com

Library of Congress Cataloging-in-Publication Data
Williams, Al, 1963–
     Active server pages solutions / by Al Williams, Kim Barber, and Paul Newkirk.
          p.   cm.
     ISBN 1-57610-608-X
     1. Active server pages.   2. Web servers--Computer programs.   I. Barber, Kim, 1953–.
II. Newkirk, Paul.   III. Title.
TK5105.8885.A26 W57 2000
005.2'76 — dc21   00-025156

CIP

Printed in the United States of America
10 9 8 7 6 5 4 3 2 1

14455 North Hayden Road • Suite 220 • Scottsdale, Arizona 85260

Dear Reader:

Coriolis Technology Press was founded to create a very elite group of books: the ones you keep closest to your machine. Sure, everyone would like to have the Library of Congress at arm's reach, but in the real world, you have to choose the books you rely on every day *very* carefully.

To win a place for our books on that coveted shelf beside your PC, we guarantee several important qualities in every book we publish. These qualities are:

- *Technical accuracy*—It's no good if it doesn't work. Every Coriolis Technology Press book is reviewed by technical experts in the topic field, and is sent through several editing and proofreading passes in order to create the piece of work you now hold in your hands.

- *Innovative editorial design*—We've put years of research and refinement into the ways we present information in our books. Our books' editorial approach is uniquely designed to reflect the way people learn new technologies and search for solutions to technology problems.

- *Practical focus*—We put only pertinent information into our books and avoid any fluff. Every fact included between these two covers must serve the mission of the book as a whole.

- *Accessibility*—The information in a book is worthless unless you can find it quickly when you need it. We put a lot of effort into our indexes, and heavily cross-reference our chapters, to make it easy for you to move right to the information you need.

Here at The Coriolis Group we have been publishing and packaging books, technical journals, and training materials since 1989. We're programmers and authors ourselves, and we take an ongoing active role in defining what we publish and how we publish it. We have put a lot of thought into our books; please write to us at **ctp@coriolis.com** and let us know what you think. We hope that you're happy with the book in your hands, and that in the future, when you reach for software development and networking information, you'll turn to one of our books first.

Keith Weiskamp
President and CEO

Jeff Duntemann
VP and Editorial Director

Look For These Other Related Books From The Coriolis Group:

HTML Black Book
by Steven Holzner

Java Black Book
by Steven Holzner

Visual Basic 6 Black Book
by Steven Holzner

XML Black Book
by Natanya Pitts-Moultis and Cheryl Kirk

Also Recently Published By Coriolis Technology Press:

Windows 2000 Systems Programming Black Book
by Al Williams

Windows 2000 Registry Little Black Book
by Nathan Wallace

Windows 2000 Security Little Black Book
by Ian McLean

Windows 2000 Reducing TCO Little Black Book
by Robert E. Simanski

Windows 2000 Mac Support Little Black Book
by Gene Steinberg and Pieter Paulson

For my entire family, but especially my wife Pat.
—Al Williams

To my lovely wife of 26 years, Sherrie.
—Kim Barber

For my wife Lisa and daughter Brynna.
—Paul Newkirk

&

About The Authors

Al Williams is the author of many popular programming books including *MFC Black Book*, *Developing ActiveX Web Controls* (both from Coriolis), and many others. Al frequently speaks at industry conferences and his columns appear each month in *Web Techniques* magazine. A long-time consultant and instructor, Al has worked on everything from tiny embedded systems to mainframe computers on projects ranging from plastic manufacturing to the International Space Station. In Al's sparse spare time, he enjoys amateur radio and science fiction.

Kim Barber has several years experience developing and teaching computer programming courses as well as training courses on HTML and Active Server Pages development. Kim had a career in the U.S. Army as an intelligence analyst and retired from military service in 1993. Shortly after leaving the military, Kim began working at CompuServe Interactive Services and has held positions as technical training manager and project manager. Kim has been an avid pilot for 26 years and currently co-owns a Piper Cherokee 6. Other interests include tropical and marine fish-keeping, astronomy, bass fishing, and his big-screen TV. Kim also enjoys starting multiple "fix-up" projects at home, but rarely completes them.

Paul Newkirk is a Project and Process Manager for UUNET Product Engineering. His current charge is to improve software development practices, such as introducing and systematizing formal code reviews and improving requirements gathering. He has over 13 years experience working with software development teams, including documenting systems and network software for companies such as CompuServe, Bell Labs, and UUNET, an MCI WorldCom Company; training development and coordination (teaching HTML and running a five-day Web camp); and creating or consulting on many corporate intranet and extranet Web sites.

Acknowledgments

When you watch a TV show or a movie, you always think of the actors. However, the actors are really a small part of a TV show. Behind the scenes are directors, writers, camera operators, lighting specialists, and a host of people who make it possible for the actors to be seen and heard.

Books are much like that. This book has three names on the cover, but that's because there isn't space enough for all the people who have put so much into the project. People like Toni Zuccarini Ackley, Chuck Hutchinson, Meg Turecek, April Nielsen, Jody Winkler, and Robert Clarfield. These are the people who make it possible for us to talk to you and we appreciate them.

Since this book was a team effort, there are some people each of us would like to thank individually:

Thanks to Kim and Paul for agreeing to have another round of deadlines with me. Of course, my family is used to them, but thanks go to them as well. I'm afraid I'm unable to thank Madison and Sassy (our two dogs). Their contribution was limited to barking at the UPS man and forcing me to watch where I roll my chair.
—Al Williams

I would like to acknowledge Al Williams for his continued support and confidence.
—Kim Barber

Thanks go to Al Williams for letting me work with him on another book, where I am challenged to continue to learn more about technology and also learn a lot from his patience and good humor at dealing with people on deadlines. Most importantly, I want to note my appreciation to my wife and daughter, whose understanding and support make it all possible.
—Paul Newkirk

Contents At A Glance

Table Of Contents

Introduction

Only a few inventions in history have had the impact of the World Wide Web. Oddly enough, nearly all of these inventions involved communications. In the Middle Ages, for example, books were rare and jealously guarded. The effort required to copy a book by hand was extraordinary—especially when so few people were literate. Of course, why should people learn to read when there are practically no books? The idea of a public library where practically anyone could check out a book and take it home was ridiculous.

Around 1450, Johannes Gutenberg devised a system for printing with moveable type. This was a new idea in Europe, although it was old hat in China. In almost no time, the printing press spread across Europe. Soon, books were plentiful and affordable, fostering enormous changes in politics, religion, education, and economies. Too bad Gutenberg didn't make enough money out of the press to pay his bills. Only a handful of other inventions have had such a widespread and long-lasting effect.

The television was another world-altering invention. Educator, babysitter, and entertainer—television is a major part of modern life and has changed the way we look at the world.

Of course, both of these inventions have a price. For every play written by Shakespeare, there are hundreds of comic books and romance novels. For every "Sesame Street," there is a "South Park." Mass media have often been vehicles for spreading harmful propaganda. Sure, television makes us better informed and more worldly, but it has also reduced the effectiveness of the electoral process. There is no free lunch.

Is the Web the 21st century printing press and television? It seems likely. Already, media analysts are touting *convergence*—the joining of television and Internet. I think it is more likely that the Internet will consume television, much in the same way that television largely consumed radio a few decades ago.

One of the most attractive—and potentially dangerous—features of the Internet is that it reduces the barriers for ordinary people to create mass media. When you read something in a book or see something on TV, it might be wrong—you certainly don't want to believe everything you see. However, when you see a news anchor reading something on CNN, you know that if it is wrong, it had to fool many people to get on the news. On the Web, anyone with a computer and a modem can publish to a potential audience of millions.

I have often said that the Web reminds me of what would happen if you blew up the Library of Congress. You'd be surrounded by fragments of information. Some of the fragments might be the truth. Others might be from works of fiction. How do you tell them apart?

The sad truth is that people make judgments based on appearance. The trick on the Web is to make your fragments of information more compelling than the other fragments. You can do that by making your site active. Movies sell better than books with photographs, after all. Better still, make your site interactive so that it draws the user. That's exactly what this book is about. By using scripting you can build powerful interactive Web pages that stand out in the crowd. An interactive site not only attracts new visitors, but it keeps them on your site longer and increases repeat visits as well.

Why This Book Is For You

All three of us have been involved, in some way, in teaching Web development (as well as actually doing it). We became so frustrated trying to find a book that covered what we were teaching that we decided to write one.

What does this mean to you? It means that in this book you'll find a holistic approach to Web development with Active Server Pages. Practical examples show you how today's sites run and how you can get the same results quickly and easily.

This book is a great way to get started with Active Server Pages if you are:

♦ A Web author who wants an easy way to process forms and add interactivity

♦ A Web programmer who wants to simplify back-end development

♦ A database developer wanting to move to the Web

♦ Someone who manages or supervises any of the above people

In addition, if you are just getting started, you'll find information in the appendixes to help you get started in Web development in general. If you have Visual Basic or Java skills, you'll learn how you can extend your Web sites using these programming languages in two special chapters that show you how to build your own ASP components.

The Details

Of course, not every chapter is for everyone. If you are already writing ASP pages, you might find some material more relevant to your projects than others. Here's an overview of what you'll find in each chapter:

♦ *Chapter 1: The World Wide Why*—This chapter provides an overview of why you want and need Active Server Pages.

♦ *Chapter 2: Jump Right In*—We're big believers that the best way to learn something is to jump right in and do it. With that in mind, this chapter starts you right out with a practical project (a currency converter). Although this chapter glosses over some of the fine points, you'll pick them up in later chapters.

♦ *Chapter 3: Server-Side Scripting In VBScript*—Although Chapter 2 gets you started quickly, it doesn't cover a lot of detail. This chapter fills in all the blanks—at least, the blanks that involve VBScript.

♦ *Chapter 4: Server-Side Scripting In JavaScript*—JavaScript is another popular option for scripting. Remember, on the server the language you use is mostly a matter of personal taste. If you are looking for fast results, you can probably choose to read either Chapter 3 or Chapter 4, depending on which language you want to use.

♦ *Chapter 5: Server-Side Objects*—Regardless of what language you use, Microsoft provides built-in and ancillary objects that provide much of the power of Active Server Pages. For example, if you want to read data from a form, you'll need the **Request** object. Altering the HTML output requires the **Response** object. Moreover, external objects allow you to access databases, link pages, and perform other sophisticated tasks.

♦ *Chapter 6: The Client Connection*—Server-side scripting can only do so much. Certain techniques require you to work with client-side script, as well. This chapter shows you how to apply what you know about server-side script to the client environment and mix both technologies to develop a complete solution.

♦ *Chapter 7: Database Access*—The hottest Web sites contain data. Sites that serve up news, catalog pages, or even messages are likely to build on top of a database system. This chapter shows you how to use server-side objects to interact with nearly any SQL database.

♦ *Chapter 8: Remembering Users*—Another important feature that many Web sites use is personalization. To personalize the user's visit, you'll need to identify users and remember information about them. This chapter shows you how using several different techniques.

♦ *Chapter 9: Advanced Tools*—Many developers use Microsoft FrontPage or Visual InterDev to develop Web sites. Luckily, these tools will work well with Active Server Pages, and this chapter will show you how to apply ASP to either tool.

♦ *Chapter 10: Ideas To Use And Reuse*—One way to increase productivity in any programming language is to make reusable modules. Then you, or another programmer, can easily incorporate these modules into other projects. This chapter shows you how.

- *Chapter 11: Custom Server Objects*—If you are comfortable with Visual Basic (or would be willing to learn it), you can create your own server-side objects easily. This chapter contains several examples that you can use to get started.

- *Chapter 12: Your Own Client-Side Objects*—Another task that Visual Basic can handle is creating custom client-side objects. Of course, for maximum browser compatibility, you might prefer to use Java to run programs in the browser. Either way, this chapter will get you started and show you several practical examples.

- *Chapter 13: Other Choices*—ASP and IIS are not the only games in town. This chapter will show you how you can run ASP on other platforms (including Apache), and outline tools that are comparable to ASP (for example, PHP and JSP).

- *Chapter 14: ASP Cookbook*—This is the best chapter to turn to if you want to quickly cut and paste code into your existing project. Here you'll find practical tasks ready to insert into your Web site. Some of the material is consolidated from other chapters, other material (like the message posting scripts) appears only in this cookbook chapter.

- *Chapter 15: Where To On The Web*—This chapter wraps up the main portion of the book and gives us a chance to speculate on the future of ASP and Web development.

- *Appendix A: A Case Study*—This chapter contains a complete case study that converts an existing HTML Web site into a dynamic ASP Web site, complete with database access, advertisements, personalization, and more.

- *Appendix B: Introduction To HTML*—If you need a refresher on some of the finer points of HTML, you'll find it in this appendix.

- *Appendix C: Advanced HTML*—If you commonly use an editor to create forms, tables, and frames, you might find some of the information in this appendix useful.

- *Appendix D: DHTML In Depth*—Dynamic HTML (DHTML) allows you to do more processing on the client so your server-side scripts can be leaner and more efficient. Several chapters integrate DHTML with server-side script, but they assume you already understand DHTML. If you need a quick jumpstart on this relatively new technology, you'll want to read this appendix.

- *Appendix E: Design Considerations*—This book is for programmers and by programmers. If you didn't know that, you could probably guess from the aesthetics of most of the examples. In this appendix, Paul shows you some good and bad Web sites and provides plenty of design and style guidance so your site can look as good as it works.

What Do I Need?

To work with the bulk of the examples in this book, you will need some sort of Web server that supports ASP. Microsoft's Personal Web Server will do for most of the projects. You can also use Microsoft's Internet Information Server (IIS), or any other server that has ASP installed.

In a few examples, you'll need more advanced server software (for example Microsoft Site Server or equivalent). However, these examples make up a very small percentage of the total number of examples.

Several chapters contain material on Microsoft FrontPage or Visual InterDev. There are also chapters that deal with Java and Visual Basic. You can get the full benefit of this book without any of these tools, but you will need these if you want to follow the specific material that relates to them. However, if you skip this material, you won't miss any information on ASP development.

Get On With It

So why are you still here? Jump right in to Chapter 1, and get started with ASP development now.

Chapter 1
The World Wide Why

Paul Newkirk

This chapter provides an overview of the growth of the Web and describes why everyone who wants to be a player (whether as programmer, graphic designer, or Web wizard) will have to master Web scripting and active content. This chapter provides an insider's view not only of the history of the Web but also of the transitions in the industry, the latest and most significant of which is active Web content. Scripting, in its various forms, will help you meet and exceed the rapidly expanding expectations of Web surfers. If you already know the history, how Web scripting fits into the future, and why you want active content, skip ahead to the chapters that will help you become an expert in this pivotal technology. Of course, even if you're a seasoned veteran, you might get some new insights into the Web and Web scripting from this chapter.

You can script a Web page in many ways. As you might guess, this book focuses on Active Server Pages (ASP). Currently, ASP works with Microsoft's Internet Information Server (IIS), but other Web servers may soon support it. Although this book is mostly about ASP, you'll find you have to do some scripting on the user's computer to get the job done. Therefore, you'll also find a great deal of information about client-side scripting in JavaScript and VBScript. Armed with these tools (and a good understanding of HTML), you'll be ready to conquer the Web.

Even Grandma Has A URL

By now, it is a foregone conclusion that the Web is here to stay, and everyone wants to be on it. Grandparents are getting email addresses, nearly every commercial in any medium (radio, TV, print) contains a reference to a Web page, and most "talking head" announcers have gone beyond sounding ill-informed when giving a URL ("That's at HTTP..., say, wait a minute folks, what is the rest of this stuff?") to where the terminology is so common that they reel it off deadpan, seemingly without a second thought. In a restaurant in San Diego where I was attending a convention, my waitress, after finding out I was a professional geek, started telling me about the multimedia system for which she had just plunked down two grand. She had a vague idea what the numbers were (one number we figured out was the amount of RAM she had) but no idea what they meant (yet she happily spent a large chunk of change to get there). Friends and neighbors who used to have no interest are now keenly signing up, and some have used whatever tools they can find to create rudimentary Web pages.

Days Of Change

For those of us who have been in the industry for some time, these continue to be heady and exciting times. Not only has the consumer base and popular recognition changed and exponentially expanded, but, as anyone who can still remember surfing the Net using only tools such as FTP, Telnet, or RN (an old-fashioned news reader) will tell you, the Net has drastically changed, and it continues to do so at fundamental levels. That change is what this book is about.

From Democracy To "Corpocracy"

Back when *the Net* became *the Web*, there was something excitingly democratic about this change. All of a sudden, you didn't have to wear suspenders and tie-dyed shirts and grunt over a command-line interface to play on the Net. The Web was graphical, and all that command-line stuff was hidden behind the scenes (for the most part). Perhaps even more democratic than that, the standard currency of the Web (HTML) was a text markup language that almost anyone could understand, so almost anyone could have a Web page. Even more enjoyable was that the playing field was level. Billy Bob's page on exciting facts about minnow gills was just as big, spiffy, and accessible as the pages created by companies with 200,000 employees.

But, the field is shifting, and with the corporate assault on Web territory, the bar is being lifted higher and higher. Key words now include *professionalism* and *added value*.

In the old days, a Web site put out by a one-person part-time business had the potential to look every bit as good as one put out by a Fortune 500 corporation. That is no longer true. It is no longer good enough just to stand out and to try to attract and retain visitors. Today's successful sites must first meet the bar of expected professionalism. Second, they must provide the added value that sets them apart from their rivals.

A Note About Wall Street

Since we first began writing about the Internet, the Net has changed, and the Web has fundamentally changed the face of American and world business. Because this change is so drastic, it is almost hard to know where to start describing it. When I first started writing about the Web, predicting that every business would soon have a Web page was pretty easy. You could even glimpse some of the future by seeing how Web businesses would uproot and shake up existing businesses (for example, consider Amazon.com). But, the effect of the Web is so much deeper and more ingrained. The very word (well, acronym) *IPO*, which stands for *Initial Public Offering*, is commonplace nowadays. Over the last year, most developers in the technical world have wondered whether they should give up their existing jobs in mainstream businesses (such as phone companies or insurance companies) to join or create Internet startup businesses. The stories are legion of friends or relatives once or twice removed who ran off to work for some startup.com or other and now own a million-dollar house overlooking San Francisco Bay. Some of these companies have no tangible assets (like a steel mill would) nor positive revenue streams or even products on shelves somewhere, yet they are worth more than existing businesses with all these things.

I have an uncle who invests his retirement money partly in Internet funds, and an 87-year-old aunt who asked me to try to explain Y2K (I tried; it didn't get through). On the one hand, an insider knows that many of the Internet startups won't be around 10 years from now, and if we hit an economic downturn, the shakedown might be violent. On the other hand, a lot of money from traditional sources is going into this new industry. This money, instead of being made available to build blast furnaces and paper mills, is being made available to build new technology. These changes are very exciting and indicate a huge investment in the future—a different future than you might have imagined.

This new way of thinking is already changing some of the cornerstones of business. Traditional companies such as Sears and Chevron have been taken off market indexes and replaced by technology companies. As a result of these changes and growth, new laws may be written to make sure this growth doesn't get out of hand. Merrill Lynch, one of the last big holdouts, finally reversed itself and said it would offer online trading. Those with the Internet know-how lead the companies; those who said "we will never do that" get brushed aside into the dust bucket of history like so many Neville Chamberlains. Furthermore, for Merrill Lynch and many others, these changes do not just mean a new division or a new product line; going to online trading (rather than being left behind) immediately and wholly undercuts the fundamental principles of the way they do business (centered around brokers). Who needs brokers, you might ask, when you can find all that information on the Web and make all your trades yourself? You can bet a lot of people in that industry are watching what they must know is, to some extent, the end of an era and a way of doing business.

The Web has become so much more than just an online catalog or a reference page that every company must have. It has become deeply imbedded into the economy and even our culture—so much so that new laws are being generated to govern it and protect us from it. Whereas some see a bubble, others see the birth of a new economic era that they liken to the boom days of steel or railroads.

Big companies (and the big company wannabes) are pouring money into their Web sites and finding they have to make their sites bigger and better to compete, raising the bar for everyone searching for cost-effective ways to make their sites just a little bit better. And, the key words don't just include *bigger and better*; the new word is *discovery*—discovery of that added value that the joining of their company and this medium uniquely lets them provide. That discovery—whether it is new reporting, new access, or new sales channels—is driving new revenue streams. And that discovery is powered by Web scripting.

Upward And Onward From Plain HTML

Now that the first-generation Web has stabilized, we are well into the next stage of the Web's evolutionary development: Web scripting and active content. Using HTML is fine for static pages if all you want to do is put up documents and pictures—a magazine or book, if you will—on your computer screen (with very nice linking capabilities). However, with regrets to Billy Bob's minnow page and all its wonderful friends, the big boys are here now, and they are using programming to make Web pages not only stand out but also leap ahead by fully exploiting the competitive possibilities of the medium.

Just like a command-line interface to the Net looked ancient compared to the Net using Mosaic's browser, plain HTML pages are beginning to look as archaic next to the jazzed-up sites using active content and scripting. Even the neat tricks of HTML, like image maps, seem pretty poor when compared to buttons that become active when you drag your mouse pointer over them.

As Microsoft belatedly noticed the Web (and hurriedly made up for it), the technical battle-ground has moved from the PC-based environment to the Web-based environment. If you are a Web wizard (a description that can span a lot of definitions, depending on whom you ask), a programmer, or someone who wants to join in the fun, Web scripting is the main tool you will need to master to stay ahead.

Web And Net Changes

The charm of the early Internet was the myriad sites where volunteers published things that interested them. You could find sites containing guitar chord progressions in ASCII for every song known to humanity. (How these people found the time to put up this information is amazing.) As the *Net* became the *Internet*, most of those long-tenured and popular sites were shut down one by one as people from the real world began to pay attention and perceive a need to stake out and defend turf there (such as attorneys representing recording music copyright holders). The latest similar change is the wholesale migration to the Net by programmers, graphic designers, database specialists, "marketroids," and any other main-stream corporate specialists.

From the first time I used a browser (early Mosaic), I was told how I could include sound and video. Adding these features was a cool idea, but no one at that time had anything more than a speaker good for a few beeps every now and then. Now, people have sound cards, speakers, and AVI players (and you don't have to be an expert in setting up MIME types to use them). In fact, the majority of the Web surfing population today probably doesn't even remember the days when computers didn't have stereo sound built in. People from the visual and musical worlds have been jumping in to add their expertise with bouncy buttons, sounds, and visual effects that sometimes make you think the fake, amazing, and overly simple "computer" representations in Hollywood films aren't as far-fetched as you originally thought.

After all, what good is looking at simple text pages when you have a multithousand-dollar computer on your desk? What good is the medium if you can't push the potential of your PC and the limitations of the networks to the extent that they (and your imagination) let you?

Pivotal Questions Updated

In a book I wrote a few years ago, the *Active Server Pages Black Book*, I asked the following questions:

♦ How much of the future Web is going to have some kind of subscription basis for use, and what will the model for that system be?

♦ What kinds of tools and development environment will software developers, hackers, Web wizards, and graphic designers use to take us warp speed into the future?

The first question is much easier to answer today. Although it is clear that the advertising revenue of some sites is still insufficient to support their Web presence, few have rushed to the other model. And, although it is true that some sites featuring material ranging from X-rated subjects to specialty data providers place virtual bouncers at their doors to collect entry fees, this approach is the exception rather than the norm or even the expected norm. It is unclear when the advertising model will improve enough to support the costs of *all* who want to provide Web sites. The current advertising model can support smaller sites with fewer employees, but it cannot cover the salaries, vacations, bonuses, 401(k) plans, office rent, and Fourth of July parties for the entire staff of a *New York Times* or ABC. Until it can, larger-site managers will continue to have to decide whether to take a loss, reduce content, or find innovative ways to draw in extra sources of revenue.

Some of the more innovative of these approaches have been methods of *co-branding* or *co-marketing*. For example, if you place a link on your Web site to a book on Amazon's site, and Amazon sells a copy based on your Web referral, you get a cut. Or, rather than look at all the manufacturers one by one for a pair of winter shoes, you can go to Yahoo! Shopping and quickly get to a specialized list of vendors that sell winter shoes. I am not sure if Yahoo! makes extra revenue off their preferred listing, but a company called goto.com does, earning revenue from vendor placement on their site and from the more traditional advertising at the top of the page.

One last innovative example for generating extra revenue—other than the egregious selling of personal data—is a sort of reselling of existing resources. In this case, for example, a company like eBay has the mechanisms in place for conducting online auctions and follow-up financial transactions. If your great aunt dies and leaves you an enormous collection of antique cups and saucers, which you have no intention of dusting around for the next 60 years, you can fairly easily create part of an auction site on your own home page (storing the pictures of the items) and link them into eBay's auction and billing mechanisms by filling out a few forms. Instantly, you become an online auction house, and you pay eBay a cut for not having to figure out the stuff that it has already figured out (such as how to handle an auction on the Web and how to bill for it). eBay can generate even more (non-ad) revenue from you by providing you extra services or placement (on key pages, for example).

The second question posed at the beginning of this section is still a lot easier to answer. With strict programming on one end of the spectrum (in languages such as C, C++, Pascal, and COBOL) and HTML on the other, a vibrant new middle ground is expanding rapidly like never before. That middle ground is scripting. Although you can use traditional languages for scripting, newer scripting languages are continuing to evolve and become more powerful and easier to use at the same time. These languages and the scripting done with them are at the very foundation of the Web and fundamentally drive its exploding value.

The currency of programmers, Web wizards, and graphic artists is now Web scripting. Although scripting has always been used to add that little extra bit of functionality to the Web (often CGI scripts using Perl), the new wave is something much more exciting. It encompasses new languages, new tools, and ever-increasing new capabilities within the browsers, servers, and languages themselves.

Plain HTML Ignores And Excludes The Web's Potential

If the Web remained just a method to display text (as it would with just HTML), with only a few odd programming gadgets (such as counters and so on) thrown in for good measure, the Web would probably exclude at least two-thirds of its potential. Only so many publishers and companies want to make documents available. The real power of the Web is (and will continue to be) hooking it up to databases and creating custom applications that let you do any kind of business you want.

The ability to search through databases for information on the Web adds another layer of people who have valid business reasons to be on the Web (people who have data, not just documents, for sale). The ability to alter those databases adds two more large layers (traditional retail businesses and industries that depend on exchanging information electronically, whether internally or externally). For example, on one hand, every merchant will be doing business on the Web; on the other, corporations with large, diverse sales forces will be using Web browsers to get leads, log sales, and fill out customer orders (instead of using proprietary systems). "So, you want to order $20,000 worth of pharmaceuticals? Let me enter your order on our Web page, get confirmation we have it in stock, and get you the shipping date."

Then, there is that unknown element for businesses new to the Web: They either will enhance their profit margin by exploiting the potential of the Web in new ways, or they will create profit centers by satisfying the demands created in this new arena. This area is the most exciting and is what has driven the acronym *IPO* into such a wide popular parlance. It is also what has made millionaires out of so many people who work for companies that, in many cases, have no income stream or products—yet.

Web Scripting Is The Answer

Web scripting is the medium that will let you meet all the current and future needs hinted at in this chapter. Simply stated, you must become a master of Web scripting to solve today's and tomorrow's problems, to push the envelope, and to stay competitive. The sooner you do it, the better for you and your company.

This book, of course, covers ASP scripting. Is scripting the only answer? No. But, it may be the best answer available today. ASP runs with Internet Information Server (IIS) and Personal Web Server (PWS). Microsoft gives both of these products away. That means you can easily get started using ASP with no investment (if you already run Windows). Although it is free, ASP is fairly robust and scalable. You can write an example on your laptop computer and deploy it on a giant NT Web server with little difficulty.

When you get used to writing active pages, you won't ever be satisfied with ordinary, static Web pages again. More importantly, your users are already dissatisfied with them. In academia, the battle cry is "Publish or perish!" On the new Web, it might well be "Interact or perish!"

Where Do You Jump In?

Even if you take the time to learn what all the acronyms and tools and funny "product groups" are (for example, what does ActiveX contain—a product, a language, a frame of mind?), how do you pick which ones to master? Should you master them all? Perhaps most important, where do you get solid real-world examples that you can use today?

The truth is, if you sat down and took the time to learn Java, Visual Basic, VBScript, JavaScript, JScript, OLE, COM, CGI, ActiveX, Server Side Includes, ISAPI, DHTML, Perl, and so on one by one, even in 21-day increments, you would be left foolishly in the dust. The technology would pass you by, and you wouldn't have time for anything else.

So, how do you understand and keep track of it all? How do you quickly pick and choose between the languages, technologies, and tools while making informed decisions? How do you find out about the tips, tricks, techniques, and gotchas without trudging through and finding out the hard way firsthand? How do you get *the edge* without having to read every white paper and readme file in existence? Trust me, even in white papers and help files, little, hidden, apparently harmless notes are often really camouflaged warnings or notices.

The world would be a much simpler place if companies just used a more clearly and explicitly stated "this feature doesn't work very well" with a follow-up enumeration of the places where the feature will bite you. It's not as if you won't find out anyway.

Start With An Expert Who Has Done It Before

One of my favorite technical questions I have been asked is, "How do I learn X-Windows?" If you have a Unix background, the answer is like a lot of things in Unix (and life): It's a little complex. First, borrow someone else's profile or environment configuration file. Second, figure out what each of the pieces is doing. Finally, start modifying the pieces you understand and try to make them do what you want them to do (when you have a feel for it). If you're lucky, you can ask a patient guy next door to answer your tough questions when you get stuck. Strange as this concept may seem, the Internet and, by extension, the Web have strong roots in Unix and the Unix mentality. The best (fastest and sometimes only) way of learning has been to start poking around and asking the guy next door some questions—that is, unless a couple of the guys next door happened to have sifted through all the documentation, paid all the dues and taken all the hard knocks firsthand, organized the resultant information, and put it all together in a handy book.

Fortunately, that is what you have in this book. So many things in the computer business are best learned by "osmosis." You can soak up the information from someone who has already driven up the learning curve. In this book, you'll see the examples that capture what my co-authors and I have learned about this technology.

What HMTL Gave Us

HTML gave us text, graphics, links, movies, sound, colors, tables, and even forms (although, to do anything with forms, you had to do some scripting). HTML is based on 30-year-old technology (GML and then SGML), and even with pretty colors and backgrounds and table layouts, "straight" HTML pales in comparison to the effect and power of scripted pages. After all, a scripted page is just HTML with something extra.

What HMTL With Early Scripting Gave Us

Early scripting (for example, CGI) gave us the following:

- Image maps
- Forms to collect data and submit that data to the server
- Counters
- Rough access to databases
- Some custom applications

Although these features are certainly good, it is difficult to do everything using the unwieldy programs and Perl scripts you usually use with CGI, which is a lot like Tinkertoys.

Some people have built working computers that can play tic-tac-toe with nothing but Tinkertoys. However, you don't want to do that. It is too much work for the average person.

What You Get With Modern Scripting

CGI and other early scripting gave us ways to broaden the horizon of the Web, but the current tools give vastly different capabilities:

- Buttons that change when you pass the mouse pointer over them
- Pages that know who you are and remember things about you
- Pages that respond to your actions by dynamically changing
- Pages that are dynamically generated to reflect, for example, changing information
- Easier access to databases
- "Libraries" of predefined objects that make your life easier
- Predefined objects that do not require you to learn all the underlying technology
- More modern development environments
- Special sound and video effects (going to a movie instead of a magazine stand)
- The ability to easily create "applications" for the Web with program flow and logic

This book contains examples such as a restaurant reservation page and the infamous Elvis sighting page, which has been used in training classes all over the country. These examples show not only how two-dimensional the HTML-based Web looks next to the Active content-based Web, but also all the important points for using the same technology to meet your own needs. If plain HTML is like 1950s black-and-white TV, Active content is circa 1990s home theatre with surround sound.

Languages You Can Learn For Scripting

When you decide to do scripting, you will need to make decisions regarding the scripting language, whether you want your script to run on the client or the server, and so on. Most of these decisions have the potential to cut off certain segments of your audience. For example, if you choose to do client-side scripting using VBScript, you shut out a large number of people because Netscape Navigator doesn't do VBScript without an add-in. This book will help you make the best decisions.

You can essentially use any language for Web scripting (Perl, C, C++, FORTRAN, and so on) as long as you know how to hide it in a control or otherwise integrate it with the browser or server. However, modern script languages that are built into the browser and server (such as VBScript and JavaScript) are better integrated and much easier to use.

This book uses primarily VBScript and JavaScript in its examples: VBScript because it is an easy-to-use scripting language and JavaScript because it is universally recognizable. On the server side, the examples use Microsoft's ASP scripting, usually with VBScript (although ASP will support JScript). These tools are all easily accessible and widely used to create exciting, dynamic Web sites.

What Do You Have To Learn?

Scripting isn't for grandma—at least not most people's grandmas. You have to learn how to use HTML and HTML forms. A solid understanding of advanced HTML is useful. You can also use Dynamic HTML (DHTML) in many cases. You have to understand what procedures, arrays, objects, data types, and operators are. You also have to learn the choices you need to make to get your job done for your audience. This book is the best place to start learning.

Gratuitous Roswell Rumor

You will no doubt notice that this chapter spared you the obligatory, normal, chronological, and acronym-filled history of the Internet/Web. If you want one, search the Net (these histories usually go like this: ARPA, DARPA, Urbana-Champaign, CERN, boom!). Instead, I decided to include a gratuitous rumor about some history I made up. In my version, the whole thing was stolen from an alien ship recovered at Roswell, New Mexico, by the U.S. Air Force. For grins, tell some friends. Act serious. Silly rumor-mongering can certainly be more fun than recanting the real history (yet again). As an example, explain to Web newbies, with a straight face, "Yeah, the TCP/IP protocol and distributed network topology really came from some books found by the Air Force on an alien ship in New Mexico." Maybe someday the rumor will even get back to me ("Son, is it true that the Internet is really alien technology?") or will be reported in the tabloids.

If nothing else, have some fun with Web scripting and this book. The challenges and opportunities in this new and quickly changing environment are exciting, fun, and certainly never dull.

Chapter 2
Jump Right In

Kim Barber

Do you remember learning to drive? (If you don't drive, you can consider this a rhetorical question.) You had probably seen people drive your entire life. You may even have had textbook instruction in driver's education class. But nothing prepared you for really getting behind the wheel.

No textbook can teach you the feel of the wheel or the feedback from the brake. If you learned on a standard transmission, you had to get the rhythm of the clutch yourself—not from a book.

If you are like most people, you would prefer do something rather than just read about it. With that point in mind, this chapter allows you to just jump right into scripting with a quick, simple project. Later chapters will provide more details, but this chapter will give you a quick start.

Setting Up Your Computer For Development

To experiment with Active Server Pages, you need some sort of Microsoft Web server. You might also be able to find an extension for other Web servers (such as Apache or Netscape) from the ActiveScripting Organization (**www.activescripting.com**).

In this book, however, we will assume you are using a Microsoft server. Many of the examples will run on Microsoft's Personal Web Server (PWS). Microsoft includes PWS with many products (including some copies of Internet Explorer and many development tools). You can also download PWS for free from **www.microsoft.com/ie/pws**.

For the purposes of development, PWS is like a simplified version of Internet Information Server (IIS). IIS is part of Windows NT and 2000 server-level operating systems. If you are using Windows 95, 98, or a workstation version of Windows NT or Windows 2000, you need to use PWS.

A few examples in this book (mostly those that pertain to the Microsoft Personalization System) require Microsoft's Site Server edition of IIS (which is sometimes known as Commerce Server).

After you've started running a Web server that supports ASP, you don't really need much else other than a Web browser and a text editor. In this book, we will assume you are running Internet Explorer as a Web browser. However, most of the examples will work on Netscape Navigator or, for that matter, on any Web browser. One advantage of Active Server Pages is that the code runs on the server; therefore, your browser isn't of much importance. However, some of the examples in this book demonstrate how to integrate with client-side script. Some of these examples will require Internet Explorer because Navigator doesn't handle VBScript (without a special plug-in from NCompass—**www.ncompasslabs.com**).

Using a text editor is the simplest way to write the Web pages that contain Active Server scripts. However, a text editor usually doesn't offer much help with writing HTML. Many editors available for purchase or for free allow you to easily manipulate HTML pages. However, be careful that these editors do not corrupt your server-side script by mistaking it for a comment or an illegal HTML tag.

Of course, Microsoft offers several high-powered development environments for HTML and server-side scripts. Microsoft FrontPage offers a visual environment for developing Web sites that is similar to a word processor. Visual InterDev offers many of the same features but is more oriented toward programmers. Both tools fully support ASP scripts. You can read more about these tools in Chapter 9.

If you would prefer to use a regular text editor, you can use Notepad, although you'll find that it lacks certain key features. In particular, Notepad doesn't display the current line number, which makes it hard to track down error messages. A free editor that is much more capable than Notepad is PFE (Programmer's File Editor), available at **www.lancs.ac.uk/ people/cpaap/pfe**.

A Simple Project

Consider a simple Web page that converts currency values (see Figure 2.1). It might be part of a travel-related site or a banking site. It might even be part of an e-commerce site with many international customers.

This type of Web page is usually a nightmare to create and maintain. You need some sort of processing (usually a Perl script). Also, currency values fluctuate constantly, making frequent changes necessary.

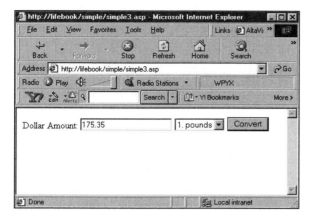

Figure 2.1
A currency conversion application.

How Can ASP Help?

The Web page in Figure 2.1 is just an HTML form. The processing all occurs in the script. If you know Perl and you are comfortable with CGI programming, you're all set. However, dealing with CGI is often a hassle even if you know Perl. A script can be difficult to install, hard to debug, and can get out of sync with its associated form easily.

The purpose of using ASP is to replace these arcane scripts with simple programs that integrate smoothly with HTML. In Perl, you have to output any HTML you want directly. ASP allows you to mix HTML and script steps together.

If you know JavaScript, you can use it to write ASP scripts. You may find it easier, however, to use VBScript (which is similar to Basic). You can even buy add-on scripting engines that support a Perl-like script language, if you prefer.

A Simple ASP Script

Consider this file:

```
<HTML>
<HEAD>
<TITLE>A simple test</TITLE>
</HEAD>
<BODY>
<P>It is <%= now %></P>
<%
  result = 73*16
  tmp = result * 3 + 472
  answer = result*1.25
```

```
%>
<P>Here is the answer:
<%= answer %>
</P>
</BODY>
</HTML>
```

This file appears to be an ordinary HTML document with the exception of the odd tags that contain percent signs. These special tags cause the Web server to execute the script these tags contain. The server doesn't normally examine files for these tags, however. If you want to make the script execute, the file must have an .ASP extension.

Conceptually, here's what happens:

1. A user requests a document with an .ASP extension.
2. The server intercepts the request and locates the document.
3. The server begins copying the document's contents to the browser.
4. Everywhere the server finds server-side script, it processes the script, possibly writing the script's result to the browser. In no case does the server send the script itself to the browser.

The **<%=** tag causes one script statement to execute and places the result in the outgoing HTML stream. If the tag doesn't have the equal sign, the server quietly executes the script (although specific commands in the script may write to the HTML output).

The first script element in the preceding example displays the current time and date (current at the server's location, of course). VBScript uses the **now** keyword to retrieve the current date and time.

The second element calculates a few simple math expressions and stores them for later use. The final piece of script displays one of the results calculated.

Too Simple?

The math in the script example isn't very interesting. The results depend on constants preprogrammed into the script. To create the currency conversion page, you need input from the user (data provided by the form).

Luckily, reading a value from a form is easy. The server provides several objects that allow you to interact with it in some way. One of these objects, the **Request** object, allows you to read data provided by a form.

Now look at Listing 2.1, which contains a stripped-down version of the original form. Notice that the form's action is simple.asp (which appears in Listing 2.2). The form has one text input field, **amount**.

In Listing 2.2, the script uses **Request("amount")** to read the value the user entered. The simple script converts the dollar value entered into pounds (British money, not weight). The conversion factor is hard-coded into the script, so you have to change the script every time the exchange rate changes.

Listing 2.1   The simplified form.

```
<HTML>
<HEAD><TITLE>Simple Currency Conversion</TITLE></HEAD>
<BODY>
<FORM ACTION=simple.asp METHOD=POST>
Dollar Amount: <INPUT TYPE=TEXT NAME=Amount><BR>
<INPUT TYPE=SUBMIT VALUE=Convert>
</FORM>
</BODY>
</HTML>
```

Listing 2.2   Processing the form.

```
<HTML>
<HEAD><TITLE>Results</TITLE></HEAD>
<BODY>
<% ' Function to format currency
   function DFormat(s)
   Dim s1
   Dim n
   s1 = (s*100+.49)\1   ' convert to rounded whole cents
   s1 = s1/100          ' back to dollars
   if s1-s1\1=0 then    ' if whole dollars
    s1=s1 & ".00"       ' just put .00
   else
    s1=s1 & "0"         ' some # of cents so add 0
    n=Instr(s1,".")     ' find decimal point
    s1=left(s1,n+2)     ' cut off after two decimal points
   end if
   DFormat = s1
   end function
%>

$<%= DFormat(Request("Amount")) %>

is
&pound;<%= DFormat(Request("Amount")*.895) %><BR>
Thanks for using the Simple converter.
</BODY>
</HTML>
```

Notice all the code in the **<% %>** brackets that defines a function named **DFormat**. This function formats a number so that it has two places after the decimal point. The idea is simple: The function converts the amount to cents (by multiplying by 100) and uses integer division (the **** operator) to truncate the result to an integer. The function then divides by 100. This operation results in a number with zero, one, or two digits after the decimal point. If no digits appear after the decimal point, the function adds a decimal point and two 0 characters.

The other possibility is that the number has either one or two digits following the decimal point. In either case, the function appends a 0 to the number. This action results in a number with two or three digits following the point. The function then truncates the result after two places to prevent the program from showing results like 1.5 instead of 1.50.

If you don't exactly follow the logic behind **DFormat**, don't worry. You'll read more about constructing functions in later chapters. For now, just focus on the lines that use the **DFormat** function.

You might wonder what the purpose of the word **£** is in Listing 2.2. It represents the pound sign (that is, the British currency symbol). You can name many symbols in this fashion. For example, **©** is the copyright symbol and ** ** represents a nonbreaking space (a space that the browser is not allowed to alter).

HTML Or Script?

The final result of all this code appears in the form shown in Figure 2.1. Notice that the ASP script is really part program and part HTML file. The general format is like an HTML file, but you can embed scripts into the file.

If you try to run this example yourself, you might get tripped up by a common pitfall. When you are experimenting with HTML, it is common to just create a file and point your browser at the file on your hard drive to view it. That approach doesn't work with ASP files. For ASP files to operate correctly, you must read them via a Web server.

As an example, suppose you're running Microsoft's Personal Web Server (PWS) on your local PC. The server's main directory is at c:\InetPub\wwwroot. You can't point your browser to c:\inetpub\wwwroot\simple.htm. Instead, you must access the file through the server (for example, http://localhost/simple.htm). Just remember to access the file via whatever Web server you are using. Of course, your Web server also has to support ASP files, and your administrator has to enable ASP scripting.

External Objects

In the preceding example, the script used the **Request** object to read fields from the input form. This object is part of the Web server. However, some objects are external to the server. (Although they may ship with the server software, they are not part of the actual server.)

Suppose you want to place the conversion factor in a file. This way, people who really don't understand Web programming can update the conversion factor. If the value is in a separate file, they cannot alter your original program.

To place the conversion factor in a file, you need to use an external object. In this case, the object's name is **Scripting.FileSystemObject**. This object allows you to open and create text files on the server's file system. When you create or open a file, it creates another object (a **textstream** object).

Objects can have properties, methods, and events:

♦ *Properties* are like variables; your script can set them and read them (at least, in theory— some properties might be read-only or write-only). For example, the **Textstream** object has an **AtEndOfStream** property. This property is read-only and reads **True** when your program reaches the end of the file. Some properties contain simple values (like this one, which is a Boolean value). Others contain another object. For example, the **Scripting.FileSystemObject** object has a property named **Drives**. This property returns a collection object that allows you to obtain a list of legal drive names. A *collection* is a special object that acts like an array with some special capabilities.

♦ *Methods* are like subroutine calls that affect the object or request some action from an object. For example, the **Scripting.FileSystemObject** object has an **OpenTextFile** method that allows a script to open an existing file for reading. The **Textstream** object contains a **Close** method that you can call when you no longer want the file open.

♦ *Events* allow objects to signal your script when something interesting happens. For example, an object might use an event to alert your script that an error occurred or that a user clicked on the component. The file objects you'll use in this example don't have any events.

Integrating Objects In Your Development

The key to understanding scripting is to recognize that the scripting language interacts with objects to perform useful tasks. With ASP scripts, some objects are built into the server, and others you can create in your script. Client-side scripts have a similar set of objects, both built-in and external, that work with the Web browser.

Creating custom objects is well within reach of most programmers (see Chapters 11 and 12). If you decide to create such objects, you will need a deeper understanding of objects. However, to simply use objects in scripts, you really need to understand only a few basic concepts.

An *object*, stated simply, is a piece of code that represents some entity. For example, the **Server** object represents the Web server, and the **Request** object represents the request the Web browser sent to the server.

Each object has a public interface. Programs (like Web scripts) can access objects only via this public interface. If the object changes (for example, after a software update), it must still support the documented public interface. That way, programs don't care how the object works—only that it does.

The objects you will use have three elements that make up their public interface: properties, methods, and events. Some objects have many properties, methods, and events; others have only a few. Objects provide only the elements necessary for their operation. In other words, one object might have only properties, whereas another might have only properties and methods; that is perfectly legal.

Working With A File

When you have knowledge of how the file system objects work, reading the conversion factor from a file is a simple matter. The only missing piece of the puzzle is how to create the objects you need. In the earlier example, you didn't need to create an object because the **Request** object is always present as part of the server. Before you can use the file system objects, however, you have to create them. The **Textstream** object, of course, is a byproduct of calling the **OpenTextFile** method of the **Scripting.FileSystemObject** object. However, you're still left with the question of how to get the **Scripting.FileSystemObject** object.

To create arbitrary objects, you need to use another object built into the server. This object represents the server, and not surprisingly is named **Server**. Like **Request**, the **Server** object is always present. It contains several methods and properties, but the one of interest here is **CreateObject**. This method allows you to create arbitrary objects.

The following example reads the conversion factor from a file:

```
Dim factor
set f = Server.CreateObject("Scripting.FileSystemObject")
set ts = f.OpenTextFile("c:\factor.txt")
factor=ts.ReadLine
ts.Close
```

Of course, then the script that displays the calculated result looks like this:

```
<%= DFormat(Request("Amount")*factor) %>
```

You can find the complete form and script in Listings 2.3 and 2.4. Having the form and the script can lead to problems. If you make changes that affect both, you must be sure that you don't use a new version of one file with an older version of another file.

Listing 2.3   The modified form.

```
<HTML>
<HEAD><TITLE>Simple Currency Conversion</TITLE></HEAD>
<BODY>
<FORM ACTION=simple1.asp METHOD=POST>
Dollar Amount: <INPUT TYPE=TEXT NAME=Amount><BR>
<INPUT TYPE=SUBMIT VALUE=Convert>
</FORM>
</BODY>
</HTML>
```

Listing 2.4   Processing with a file.

```
<HTML>
<HEAD><TITLE>Results</TITLE></HEAD>
<BODY>
<% ' Function to format currency
   function DFormat(s)
   Dim s1
   Dim n
   s1 = (s*100+.49)\1   ' convert to rounded whole cents
   s1 = s1/100          ' back to dollars
   if s1-s1\1=0 then    ' if whole dollars
    s1=s1 & ".00"       ' just put .00
   else
    s1=s1 & "0"         ' some # of cents so add 0
    n=Instr(s1,".")     ' find decimal point
    s1=left(s1,n+2)     ' cut off after two decimal points
   end if
   DFormat = s1
   end function

' read conversion factor from file
Dim factor
set f = Server.CreateObject("Scripting.FileSystemObject")
set ts = f.OpenTextFile("c:\factor.txt")
factor=ts.ReadLine
ts.Close

%>

$<%= DFormat(Request("Amount")) %>

is
&pound;<%= DFormat(Request("Amount")*factor) %><BR>
Thanks for using the Simple converter.
</BODY>
</HTML>
```

Joining Form And Script

One point that should be apparent to you now is that the key to everything is understanding the objects you use to manipulate the environment. The more you know about objects, the more you can accomplish.

Suppose you knew a way to tell whether a script received any form data. You could create a script that made use of this information. If no form data exists, you can assume that a user just browsed to the script. In that case, the script can show the form.

The form is essentially the same as in the earlier examples, with one important twist: The form's action points back *to the very same script that displayed the form*. In other words, the form submits data to itself.

When the submission occurs, the script detects that form data does exist. In that case, the script can perform the processing. In this way, the form and its associated script can reside in a single file.

The trick is to use a special value of the **Request** object that tells you how much data is available. Reduced to skeletal form, your script could look like this:

```
<HTML>
<BODY>
<% if Request("content_length")=0 then %>
<!-- display form -->
<% else %>
<!-- process form -->
<% end if %>
</BODY>
</HTML>
```

You might wonder what would happen if the user submitted the form without entering any data. Would the script become confused and display the form again? No. Even if the user doesn't enter any data, the act of submitting a form generates some input (the input field names, for example).

You can find the entire integrated form in Listing 2.5. You'll notice that other than the surrounding **if** statement, the listing is just a merge of the two files shown in Listings 2.3 and 2.4.

Listing 2.5   An integrated form.

```
<HTML>
<BODY>
<% if Request("content_length")=0 then %>
<!-- display form -->
<FORM ACTION=simple2.asp METHOD=post >
```

```
Dollar Amount: <INPUT TYPE=TEXT NAME=Amount><BR>
<INPUT TYPE=SUBMIT VALUE=Convert>
</form>
<% else %>
<!-- process form -->
<% ' Function to format currency
   function DFormat(s)
   Dim s1
   Dim n
   s1 = (s*100+.49)\1   ' convert to rounded whole cents
   s1 = s1/100          ' back to dollars
   if s1-s1\1=0 then    ' if whole dollars
    s1=s1 & ".00"       ' just put .00
   else
    s1=s1 & "0"         ' some # of cents so add 0
    n=Instr(s1,".")     ' find decimal point
    s1=left(s1,n+2)     ' cut off after two decimal points
   end if
   DFormat = s1
   end function

' read conversion factor from file
Dim factor
set f = Server.CreateObject("Scripting.FileSystemObject")
set ts = f.OpenTextFile("c:\factor.txt")
factor=ts.ReadLine
ts.Close

%>

$<%= DFormat(Request("Amount")) %>

is
&pound;<%= DFormat(Request("Amount")*factor) %><BR>
Thanks for using the Simple converter.
<% end if %>
</BODY>
</HTML>
```

More Fun With Files

What if you want to handle more than one type of currency? The original form contains a selection box that allows the user to pick the type of currency he or she wants to convert. If you are reading the conversion factor from a file, you need to generate this selection box using script from information in the file.

Creating a selection list in plain HTML is simple enough:

```
<SELECT NAME=ConvertTo>
<OPTION VALUE=Pounds:1.80>Pounds
<OPTION VALUE=Yen:128>Yen
<OPTION VALUE=Pesos:820>Pesos
</SELECT>
```

The script can read the value of the selection box by reading **Request("ConvertTo")**. The value in this case contains both the currency and the conversion rate. The conversion code can split this value apart using the string functions **Mid**, **Left**, and **Instr**. The **Mid** function returns a substring starting at a particular position of the string. The **Left** function returns a specified number of characters from a string starting at the leftmost character. **Instr** searches a string from a particular substring and returns the substring's position. Consider this fragment of code:

```
cvt2=Request("ConvertTo")
factor=Mid(cvt2,Instr(cvt2,":")+1)
cvt2=Left(cvt2,Instr(cvt2,":")-1)
```

When this code executes, **factor** contains the conversion rate, and **cvt2** contains the name of the currency. There is no need to read the file in this case because the form passes the correct conversion factor. Of course, you need to construct the selection list by reading the file.

You can find the code that performs this operation in Listing 2.6. The program opens the file (just as before). Then, the **while** statement forms a loop that executes until the end of the file (indicated by the **atEndOfStream** property). Inside the loop, the program reads a line from the file and picks it apart using **Instr** and **Left**. Then, it constructs the appropriate **<OPTION>** statement (adding a **SELECTED** clause to the first item). The **wend** statement closes the loop, causing the program to repeat the loop until the program reaches the end of the file. A common idea is to use a few lines of script in a loop to generate many lines of HTML.

Listing 2.6 Programmatically creating the selection box.
```
<HTML>
<BODY>

<% if Request("content_length")=0 then %>
<!-- display form -->
<FORM METHOD=POST ACTION=simple3.asp>
Dollar Amount: <INPUT TYPE=TEXT NAME=Amount>
<SELECT NAME=ConvertTo>
<%
  dim ln
```

```
  dim cname
  dim lineno
  lineno = 0
  set f = Server.CreateObject("Scripting.FileSystemObject")
  set ts = f.OpenTextFile("c:\factors.txt")
  while NOT ts.atEndOfStream
    lineno=lineno+1
    ln=ts.ReadLine
    cname=Left(ln,Instr(ln,":")-1)
%>
<OPTION
<% if lineno=1 then %>
<%= " SELECTED " %>
<% end if %>
VALUE="<%= ln %>"> <%= lineno & ". " & cname %>
<%
  wend
 ts.Close
%>
</SELECT>
<INPUT TYPE=SUBMIT VALUE=Convert>
</FORM>
<% else %>
<!-- process form -->
<% ' Function to format currency
  function DFormat(s)
  Dim s1
  Dim n
  s1 = (s*100+.49)\1  ' convert to rounded whole cents
  s1 = s1/100         ' back to dollars
  if s1-s1\1=0 then   ' if whole dollars
   s1=s1 & ".00"      ' just put .00
  else
   s1=s1 & "0"        ' some # of cents so add 0
   n=Instr(s1,".")    ' find decimal point
   s1=Left(s1,n+2)    ' cut off after two decimal points
  end if
  DFormat = s1
  end function
  cvt2=Request("ConvertTo")
  factor=Mid(cvt2,Instr(cvt2,":")+1)
  cvt2=Left(cvt2,Instr(cvt2,":")-1)
%>

$<%= DFormat(Request("Amount")) %>
```

```
is
<%= DFormat(Request("Amount")*factor) & " " & cvt2 %><BR>
Thanks for using the Simple converter.
<% end if %>
</BODY>
</HTML>
```

Converting An Existing Web Site To ASP

When you're just starting out with ASP, you often have to convert an existing Web site to use ASP. For the most part, converting a regular HTML file into an ASP file is as simple as renaming the file to end with the .ASP extension instead of the .HTML or .HTM extensions. Just because the ASP file doesn't have any script in it yet doesn't mean it isn't an ASP page.

However, you need to be aware of a few pitfalls. Suppose your site contains two files: DEFAULT.HTM and PAGE1.HTM. If you rename these files to DEFAULT.ASP and PAGE1.ASP, you break any hyperlinks from one page to the other. That means you have to change any hyperlinks so that they don't point to the HTM version of the file.

This problem is usually quite obvious if you rename the files. If you copy the files, however, you wind up with both DEFAULT.ASP and DEFAULT.HTM (as well as two copies of the PAGE1 file). Then, everything seems to work until you try to change the ASP file and realize that you are not really viewing it in the browser when you click on a link.

If you use a tool such as FrontPage or Visual InterDev, you won't have this problem. You can just rename the page, and the tool asks whether you want to fix all potentially broken hyperlinks. If you answer yes, the program automatically makes the correct changes.

Another consideration is your start page. Your server may be set to look for a particular file name (for example, DEFAULT.HTM or INDEX.HTM) as the start page. If you rename your page to DEFAULT.ASP, the server might not be able to find the default page. Your server's administration program allows you to set the name of the default file, and you (or your system administrator) will have to change it if you have this problem. Most servers allow you to specify a set of names for the default page, and the server searches until it finds one of these names. If your server already searches for files with an .ASP extension, you won't have a problem.

So What's It All About?

You'll learn more details about scripting later, of course. However, you should know that scripts can be as simple as the ones shown here. You need to understand only the basic syntax of the scripting language (VBScript in this case) and the objects available to you. For the purpose of scripting, you need to know the properties, methods, and events that these objects provide.

If you are more comfortable with Java, you might prefer to use JavaScript instead of VBScript. However, for most people, JavaScript, with its case sensitivity and rigid syntax rules, is harder to use than VBScript. When you're writing script that runs on a browser, JavaScript is preferred because both Internet Explorer and Netscape Navigator recognize it. (VBScript is generally available only with Internet Explorer.) However, for server scripts, you don't have to worry about compatibility; as long as your server supports VBScript, you don't have to worry about the browser in use.

Another important idea is how information flows from browser to server and back again. Each time the browser loads a page from the server, it issues a request. The server sends back a response. In the simplest case, the browser issues a request when the user enters a URL or clicks on a hyperlink. If the request is for a simple HTML file, the server simply sends the file to the browser (potentially accompanied by headers that contain information about the document). If the request is for a file that contains script (an ASP file), the server processes the script to generate the response.

When the user submits a form, the process gets more interesting. The **<FORM>** tag has an **ACTION** clause. When the user submits the form, the browser issues a request to the URL specified in the clause. Along with the usual information sent in a request, the browser also sends the data the user entered in the form. The server then processes this data (normally in an ASP script named in the **ACTION** clause) to formulate the response.

If you understand these fundamentals—basic syntax, objects, and the request-and-response cycle—you are well on your way to mastering Active Server Page scripting. You do need to know a few more details, of course. You also should add other techniques such as client-side scripting and custom object creation to your repertoire. You'll read more about those techniques in later chapters.

This chapter shows you a glimpse of what lies ahead. If you are eager to get started, this simple project can serve as an interesting basis for self-exploration.

Chapter 3
Server-Side Scripting In VBScript

Kim Barber

S erver-side script is a good choice when you can't, or don't want to, depend on your user having a browser that supports client-side scripting, or when you need access to sophisticated server components. VBScript is frequently a familiar and easy-to-learn language that you can use to get started writing server-side script right away.

VBScript is a scripting language that allows you to write programs that are embedded in Web pages. With VBScript, you can create rich, dynamic, interactive Web content. Because VBScript is interpreted, the host environment must have the correct software to execute the code. In the case of server-side script, Internet Information Server (IIS) interprets the code. With client-side script, the Web browser must be VBScript aware. Microsoft Internet Explorer has this capability built in, but many browsers require a plug-in to interpret VBScript.

In the preceding chapter, you had a whirlwind tour of scripting and Active Server Pages. In this chapter, you'll find out more details and study server-side scripting with more rigor. In Chapter 6, you'll see client-side script and how it compares to server-side script.

What Is VBScript?

VBScript, a subset of Visual Basic for Applications, is a Microsoft technology that adds scripting capability to Web pages. Portability is a primary consideration, so Microsoft omitted platform-specific features. Therefore, Windows-specific features such as Dynamic Data Exchange, the clipboard, and many other advanced features are not available in VBScript. If you have programmed in Visual Basic, you know that it uses a main form window to contain your program. This, too, is absent from VBScript. Instead, VBScript programs run as part of the Web server, browser, or some other scripting host.

VBScript has very limited I/O capabilities. This limitation results primarily from security concerns. VBScript does not have access to resources, such as the printer and disk I/O, on the client computer.

What Is An Active Server Page?

Before jumping into VBScript, let's briefly discuss Active Server Pages. An *Active Server Page* is a page that contains server-side script and, possibly, HTML. Active Server Pages can also push client-side script out to the client, so you might have a mix of client and server script commands intermixed with HTML. Active Server Pages have the file-name extension .ASP. When a client requests a file with an .ASP extension, IIS passes the file to the scripting engine for processing. The server processes any server-side script and passes any script output, as well as any HTML, to the client.

You can use Active Server pages to perform a variety of tasks. For example, you can determine the brand and version of the browser and dynamically generate output based on the browser's capabilities. You can also create customized and personalized pages based on the user's preferences and interests.

You can write server-side script in a number of languages, provided that the server has the appropriate scripting engine. The default language for IIS is VBScript; a JavaScript engine is also available (JavaScript is covered in Chapter 4). It is worth mentioning that other scripting languages are available for other Web servers. For example, PHP works with many servers (see **www.php.net**), and you can even find a PHP version that works with IIS. However, for the purposes of this book (which is, after all, *Active Server Pages Solutions*), you'll look exclusively at ASP scripting.

How To Write An Active Server Page

This example shows a fairly common application of Web pages. Listing 3.1 displays an HTML form to collect sales information and calculate a commission on the basis of sales. To do so, the form posts the sales figure to a page on the server to perform the necessary calculation. Listing 3.1 is an interesting use of Active Server Pages. Rather than post the sales data to a different page, the form posts the data to itself. To use this listing, however, you need some information from Chapter 5.

The **Request** object provides access to data in the HTTP Request Header, and the **Response** object provides access to data in the HTTP Response Header. Listing 3.1 uses the **Request** object to determine whether there is data. If data is not present, this must be a request to show the form. If data is present, the script should process it. The **Request** object then retrieves the sales amount value. Next, the script makes a function call to calculate the commission. The **Response** object then outputs the result. You'll learn more about all these objects in Chapter 5.

Listing 3.1 Typical use of server-side script.

```
<%@ LANGUAGE="VBSCRIPT" %>
<!-- Not purely necessary, but a good idea to include -->

<%
Function CalcCommission(Sales)
    Commission = 0
    If Sales <= 1000 Then
        Commission = .05
    ElseIf Sales > 1000 And Sales <= 5000 Then
        Commission = .10
    ElseIf Sales > 5000 And Sales <= 10000 Then
        Commission = .15
    Else
        Commission = .20
    End If
    CalcCommission = Commission * Sales
    End Function
%>

<HTML>
<HEAD>
<TITLE>Listing 3.1 Server-Side Script</TITLE>
</HEAD>
<BODY>
<H2>Acme Commission Calculator</H2>

<% If Request("CONTENT_LENGTH") = 0 Then %>
<!-- If no data, then show form -->
    <FORM NAME=calc METHOD=POST ACTION="3-1.asp"> <!-- post to self -->
    Enter sales amount:<INPUT TYPE=TEXT NAME="sales"><BR>
    <INPUT TYPE=SUBMIT VALUE="Calculate">
    <INPUT TYPE=Reset VALUE="Clear">
    </FORM>
<% Else %>  <!-- data detected, so do calculations -->
<%
    Comm = CalcCommission(Request.Form("sales"))
    Response.Write("Your commission is: $" & Comm)
%>
<% End If %>

</BODY>
</HTML>
```

Advantages And Disadvantages

Server-side script has several advantages; of course, one advantage is that it can be browser-independent. Because only HTML is sent to the browser, you don't have to worry about whether the client supports scripting, unless you're also sending client-side script in the output stream. Server-side script is generally easier and faster to write and maintain than CGI executables. You can make modifications to your code (which is conveniently in the same file as your HTML), and the changes will take effect immediately with no need to recompile. Your source code is not visible to the user, thus allowing you to protect your intellectual property and the results of your hard work.

Server-side script can also use *components*, which are objects that execute on the server. Components perform tasks that would otherwise be difficult or impossible to do. IIS provides several components, and you can write your own for additional functionality (see Chapter 11). You'll learn more about the components that IIS provides in Chapter 5. You can also use server-side script to access data sources, maintain persistent variables, and more.

Using server-side script poses only a few disadvantages. One disadvantage is that it places additional work on the server, and poorly written code can significantly affect server performance. Server-side script doesn't have much support for user interfaces. You can't use **MsgBox**, **Prompt**, and **Alert**, for example. Instead, most scripts use HTML forms to gather information. Also, you must have access to a server to develop and test your code. Preferably, you have access to IIS, but you can write and test many things using Personal Web Server (PWS).

Show Me The Code

Before going any further, let's take a look at a very simple example of server-side VBScript. Many books on programming contain the very familiar "Hello World" example. There is an unwritten rule that any text on programming must contain this example. Although I can't validate this rumor, I've heard that the inclusion of this example is a primary consideration in selecting textbooks for computer science departments in universities. Well, just to make sure I'm not violating any implied laws, Listing 3.2 shows the classic Hello World example.

Listing 3.2   A server-side VBScript Hello World program.

```
<HTML>
<HEAD>
<TITLE>Hello World Example</TITLE>
<% ="Hello World" %>
</HEAD>
<BODY>
</BODY>
</HTML>
```

As you can see, Listing 3.2 is a fairly typical HTML file. In this example, the script is placed in the **<HEAD>** section. This isn't a requirement, though. Because the page includes server-side script only, you can also write it as follows:

```
<% ="Hello World" %>
```

That's all that would be necessary.

You might be asking yourself what the characters **<%** and **%>** are. They are script delimiters. Server-side script is generally enclosed within delimiters whether or not it is mixed with HTML. The **<SCRIPT>** tag is also used as a script delimiter.

How To Use <% %> Delimiters

Server-side script is often embedded between **<%** and **%>** delimiters. The scripting engine processes script embedded in these delimiters on the server. You can't nest script delimiters inside each other, but you can use as many separate pairs of the tags as you need. Single statements as well as groups of statements can be placed within them.

The following is an example of a single VBScript statement in delimiters:

```
<% fontsize = 5 %>
```

As you can see, this example is just a typical VBScript statement, except that the delimiters tell the server to execute the code.

The following example shows more than one statement inside a single set of delimiters:

```
<%
    Dim Commission, Sales
    Commission = .05
    Sales = 10000
    If Sales > 5000 Then Commission = .10
%>
```

The equal sign (=) is used to output the value of an expression. The following statement places the value of the variable **Commission** into the HTML output stream:

```
<% = Commission %>
```

Because you can use as many script delimiters as you need, you can easily mix server-side script and HTML. Listing 3.3 mixes the two to output text in font sizes from 1 through 7.

Listing 3.3   Mixing server-side script and HTML.

```
<% For fontsize = 1 to 7 %>
    <FONT SIZE=<% =fontsize %>>
    Server-side script!<BR>
    </FONT>
<% Next %>

<HTML>
<HEAD>
<TITLE>Listing 3.3 Server-Side Scripting</TITLE>
</HEAD>
<BODY>

</BODY>
</HTML>
```

Figure 3.1 shows the result of viewing this page in Internet Explorer.

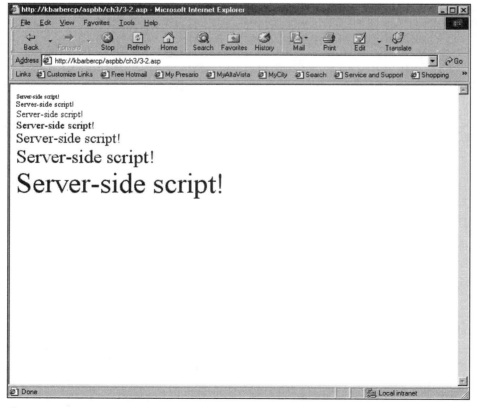

Figure 3.1
Output generated by server-side script.

How To Use The <SCRIPT> Delimiter

In addition to the script delimiters, you can also embed server-side script in the **<SCRIPT>** tag. When you use the **<SCRIPT>** tag, you must include the **RUNAT** attribute, which you set to **Server**. Listing 3.4 uses the **<SCRIPT>** tag to do the same as Listing 3.3.

Listing 3.4   Using the <SCRIPT> tag with server-side script.

```
<SCRIPT LANGUAGE=VBScript RUNAT=Server>
For fontsize = 1 to 7
     Response.Write("<FONT SIZE=" & fontsize & ">")
     Response.Write("Server-side script!<BR></FONT>")
Next

</SCRIPT>
<HTML>
<HEAD>
<TITLE>Listing 3.4 Using the <SCRIPT> Tag</TITLE>
</HEAD>
<BODY>

</BODY>
</HTML>
```

The **<SCRIPT>** tag isn't the only difference in this example. Notice that the script and HTML aren't mixed as they were in the previous example. Instead, the code places HTML in the output stream using the **Response** object, which is an intrinsic Active Server component that allows you to send output to the client. In this example, it's functionally equivalent to the **=** character that Listing 3.3 uses. You'll learn more about the **Response** object in Chapter 5.

How To Specify The Default Language

VBScript is the default language for server-side script. The default language for a page is easily set to a different language, like this:

```
<%@ LANGUAGE="JavaScript" %>
```

You are not allowed to place any other elements within this delimiter pair. Also, you must insert a space between the @ character and **LANGUAGE**.

The Web site administrator can set the default language on a more permanent basis by using the Microsoft Management Console to alter the properties for the application. Because every application can have its own default language, it is a good idea to explicitly specify the language your script expects using the @ command mentioned earlier. That way, your script will work as expected even if you move it between dissimilar projects.

Code in delimiters and the **<SCRIPT>** tag executes immediately, unless the code is within a procedure body (for example, a **SUB** or a **FUNCTION**).

VBScript Comments

Many of the examples in this chapter use comments that you likely will use in your script. VBScript comments can be entered anywhere in the script and are ignored by the VBScript interpreter. There are two methods for inserting comments: the **Rem** keyword and the apostrophe ('). The **Rem** keyword is typically used at the beginning of a line:

```
Rem Comments are ignored by the interpreter
```

Rem can also follow a program statement but must be separated from the statement with a colon (:):

```
Dim intCounter          : Rem Declaring a variable
```

At least one space character must be placed between **Rem** and the comment.

You can also use an apostrophe at the beginning of a line or on the same line as a program statement:

```
Dim intCounter          'Declaring a variable
```

Data Types

Many programming languages, including Visual Basic, support multiple data types, such as integer, string, floating-point, Boolean, and so on. However, VBScript has only one data type: the *variant*. The variant data type can contain different types of data, depending on how it is used. The different data types represented by the variant are referred to as *subtypes*. Table 3.1 shows the various subtypes, and Table 3.2 shows the conversion subtypes you will encounter.

Usually, any kind of data can be stored in a variant and will work as it should for the type of data it contains. If a numeric value is stored in a variant, VBScript assumes that it is a number and handles it accordingly. A string value placed in a variant is treated as a string.

VBScript automatically performs subtype conversions when necessary. Suppose you store a numeric value in a variant and want to use it as a string. VBScript will convert the numeric value in memory and perform the specified operation. Listing 3.5 shows a couple of examples of automatic type conversion.

Table 3.1   VBScript variant subtypes.

Subtype	Meaning
Boolean	True or false
Byte	Integer in the range of 0 to 255
Currency	Numeric value in the range of –922,337,203,685,477.5808 to 922,337,203,685,477.5808
Date (Time)	Number representing a date between January 1, 100, and December 31, 9999
Double	Double-precision, floating-point number in the range of –1.79769313486232E308 to –4.94065645841247E-324 for negative values; 4.94065645841247E-324 to 1.79769313486232E308 for positive values
Empty	Uninitialized; the value is either 0 for numeric variables or a zero-length string for string variables
Error	Error number
Integer	Integer in the range of –32,768 to 32,767
Long	Integer in the range of –2,147,483,648 to 2,147,483,647
Null	Intentionally contains no valid data
Object	An object
Single	Single-precision, floating-point number in the range of –3.402823E38 to –1.401298E-45 for negative values; 1.401298E-45 to 3.402823E38 for positive values
String	A variable-length string up to approximately 2 billion characters in length

Table 3.2   VBScript conversion functions.

Function	Returns Subtype
Asc(*string*)	Integer ANSI character code of the first letter in the string
CBool(*expression*)	Boolean
CByte(*expression*)	Byte
CCur(*expression*)	Currency
CDate(*date*)	Date
CDbl(*expression*)	Double
Chr(*charcode*)	String
CInt(*expression*)	Integer
CLng(*expression*)	Long
CSng(*expression*)	Single
CStr(*expression*)	String
Hex(*number*)	String
Oct(*number*)	String

Listing 3.5   Automatic data type conversion.

```
<HTML>
<HEAD>
<TITLE>Listing 3.5</TITLE>

<% ="25" + 75 %>
```

```
<% ="<BR>" %>
<% ="25" & 75 %>

</HEAD>
<BODY>

</BODY>
</HTML>
```

The first statement outputs the numeric value 100. Because the **+** operator indicates arithmetic (operators are discussed later), VBScript temporarily converts the string "25" to a number and then performs the arithmetic operation.

The statement

```
<% ="<BR>" %>
```

sends the HTML **
** tag to insert a blank line.

The third statement performs string concatenation with the **&** operator. In this case, VBScript converts the integer 75 to a string value and appends it to the string "25". What would result from the following?

```
<% ="VBScript" + 75 %>
```

In this case, VBScript generates a "type-mismatch" error because the string "VBScript" can't be converted to a numeric value.

However, sometimes you need to explicitly convert a variant from one subtype to another. VBScript provides several conversion functions to perform this task. For example, a variant contains a string value representing the date "December 1, 1999". You need to increment this date by two weeks to display a due date for your library Web application. You could do so by using the **CDate** conversion function as follows:

```
<% =CDate("December 1, 1999") + 14 %>
```

However, a better way to do so is to use one of VBScript's date functions.

Note

VBScript date functions are described later in the chapter in Table 3.19.

Variables

It's good to know that VBScript uses the variant data type to contain a wide variety of data, but how is this data referenced in script? You can reference data items by storing them in variables. A variable is simply a location in memory that has been given a name and whose contents can be changed. Assigning a name to a memory location creates a variable. You determine a meaningful name for the variable, and VBScript takes care of the details of associating the name with a memory location. Data is then placed in the variable and subsequently accessed through the variable name.

Let's revisit the Hello World program. This time, the program stores the greeting in a variable. Listing 3.6 shows the revised program.

Listing 3.6   A revised Hello World program.

```
<% strGreeting = "Hello World" %>
<% =strGreeting %>
```

The first statement declares the variable **strGreeting** and assigns a string value to it. The assignment operator (=) is used to assign values to variables. The = statement then outputs the contents of the variable.

Declaring Variables

Variables can be declared either *implicitly* or *explicitly*. You implicitly declare a variable by simply using it, as in Listing 3.2. You explicitly declare a variable using the **Dim** statement. The following statement explicitly declares the **strGreeting** variable:

```
Dim strGreeting
```

Notice that, unlike Visual Basic, a VBScript **Dim** statement includes no type information because all variables are variants. You can explicitly declare multiple variables in the same statement by separating the variable names with a comma:

```
Dim strGreeting, strName
```

Declaring variables explicitly is a very good idea. Implicit declaration can cause problems. For example, if a variable name is misspelled, VBScript thinks it is a different variable. This can easily produce unexpected results in your program. You can force explicit variable declaration in your program by including the **Option Explicit** statement in the script. If you include this statement and later try to implicitly declare a variable, VBScript will generate a "Variable is undefined" error message.

You should include **Option Explicit** as the first statement inside the **<SCRIPT>** body, as shown in Listing 3.7. Also, the **Option Explicit** statement affects only variable declarations within the same script body. If the document contains multiple scripts, each script must include the **Option Explicit** statement to force explicit variable declaration within each script.

Listing 3.7   Using the Option Explicit statement.

```
<%
        Option Explicit
        Dim strGreeting

        strGreeting = "Good morning"      ' this is okay
        strName = "Mr. Phelps"           ' implicit declaration not allowed
%>
```

Naming Variables

VBScript has a few rules that apply to variable names:

♦ Names must begin with an alphabetic character.

♦ Names can't contain periods, spaces, and some special characters, such as #, ~, and /.

♦ Names can't be longer than 255 characters.

♦ Names must be unique in the scope in which they are declared (scope is discussed in the next section).

♦ Reserved words (for example, **if**, **option**, **for**, **dim**, and so on) can't be used as variable names.

In addition to these rules are some other considerations in naming variables. VBScript is not case sensitive, as some languages are. Therefore, **LastName** and **lastname** are equivalent. Also, variable names should be descriptive of the value they contain or of their use. This way, the code is easier to read when you come back to it in six months or when someone else must maintain the code. Variable names such as **i** and **fn** are certainly more cryptic than, say, **Count** and **FileName**.

It is also a good idea to adopt some sort of naming convention. Using such conventions not only improves the readability of your code but also adds consistency. Programmers often use mixed cases, such as **EmployeeID** and **CalculatePayment**, when assigning names. Prefixing the variable name to indicate the subtype it contains is also a good practice. Table 3.3 shows some of the more common subtype prefixes.

Table 3.3   Common subtype prefixes.

Prefix	Subtype
dbl	Double
err	Error
int	Integer
lng	Long
obj	Object
str	String

Variable Scope

Scope refers to where a variable is available for use within a script. The two levels of scope in VBScript are *script level* and *procedure level*.

A variable has script-level scope when it is declared outside any procedures. A script-level variable can be used anywhere in the script after the variable is declared and is useful for maintaining information that is required throughout the script. Script-level variables are similar to *global* variables in other languages, such as C. It is good practice to declare script-level variables at the top of the script.

Variables declared within a procedure have procedure-level scope and are available only within the procedure. Procedure-level variables are also known as *local* variables.

The variable-naming rule that names must be unique in the scope in which they are declared means that you can use the same variable name at both the script and the procedure level (although doing so is a bad idea because using the same name can be very confusing). Also, a given variable name can be used in multiple procedures (a common occurrence). Listing 3.8 shows the use of script- and procedure-level variables. Don't worry about the details of procedures right now because they are discussed later in this chapter.

Listing 3.8   Script-level and procedure-level variables.

```
<%
Option Explicit
Dim VarA                          ' script-level variables
Dim VarB

VarA = 5
VarB = 10

Sub SomeProcedure()
        Dim VarA                  ' procedure-level variable

        VarA = 15
        VarB = 20
End Sub

SomeProcedure()                   ' call the procedure
%>

<% =VarA %>                       ' still equals 5
<% =VarB %>                       ' now equals 20
```

Private And Public

Script-level variables are public by default, which means that they are available in all scripts in all currently loaded documents. However, VBScript provides two replacements for the **Dim** statement that allow you to change the default. The **Private** statement creates variables that are available only in the script that declares them. The **Public** statement is used to explicitly declare variables that are available to all scripts (the same as using **Dim**). You can use **Private** and **Public** only at the script level.

Lifetime

Variable *lifetime* refers to the amount of time a variable exists. Script-level variables exist from the time they are declared until the script finishes running. Procedure-level variables exist from the time they are declared until the procedure is finished executing.

VBScript Variant Functions

VBScript provides several functions that return information about variants. Table 3.4 lists the available functions.

IsArray

The **IsArray** function determines whether a variable is an array (you'll read about arrays in the next section). The function shown here returns a Boolean of **TRUE** if the variable is an array and **FALSE** if it isn't:

```
<%
Dim intCount
Response.Write IsArray(intCount)          ' returns FALSE
%>
```

IsDate

IsDate determines whether VBScript can convert a variable or expression to a date. The variable or expression must be in the format of a valid date, as shown in the following:

```
<%
Dim DateDue
DateDue = "12/15/99"
Response.Write IsDate(DateDue)            ' returns TRUE
%>
```

Table 3.4   VBScript variant functions.

Function	Returns
IsArray	Boolean indicating whether a variable is an array.
IsDate	Boolean indicating whether a variable can be converted to a date.
IsEmpty	Boolean indicating whether a variable has been initialized.
IsNull	Boolean indicating whether a variable is **Null**.
IsNumeric	Boolean indicating whether a variable can be evaluated as a number.
IsObject	Boolean indicating whether a variable references an OLE Automation object.
TypeName	String that provides subtype information.
VarType	Value indicating the variant subtype.

IsEmpty

IsEmpty returns **TRUE** if the variable is uninitialized or set to **Empty**. Variables are empty when you declare them or explicitly set them to **Empty**:

```
<%
Dim DateDue
Response.Write IsEmpty(DateDue)        ' returns TRUE
DateDue = "12/15/99"
Response.Write IsEmpty(DateDue)        ' returns FALSE
DateDue = Empty
Response.Write IsEmpty(DateDue)        ' returns TRUE
%>
```

IsNull

IsNull returns **TRUE** if the variable is set to a **Null** value. This value isn't the same as **Empty**, which means that the variable hasn't been initialized. **Null** means that the variable contains no valid data. Variables must be set to **Null** explicitly:

```
<%
Dim DateDue
Response.Write IsNull(DateDue)        ' returns FALSE
DateDue = Empty
Response.Write IsNull(DateDue)        ' returns FALSE
DateDue = Null
Response.Write IsNull(DateDue)        ' returns TRUE
%>
```

IsNumeric

IsNumeric returns **TRUE** if the variable can be evaluated as a number. This function is frequently used to determine whether a user entered a valid number:

```
<%
Quantity = "Hi"
if not IsNumeric(Quantity) then
     Response.Write "Please re-enter Quantity"
end if
%>
```

IsObject

IsObject returns **TRUE** if the variant contains an object reference.

TypeName

TypeName returns a string that provides the name of the variant subtype contained in a variable. Table 3.5 contains the possible return values and their descriptions.

Table 3.5   TypeName result strings.

Return	Description
Boolean	Boolean value
Byte	Byte value
Currency	Currency value
Date	Date or time value
Decimal	Decimal value
Double	Double-precision floating-point value
Empty	Uninitialized
Error	Error
Integer	Integer value
Long	Long integer value
Nothing	Object variable does not refer to an object
Null	Not valid data, variable set to **Null**
Object	Generic object
object type	Type name of an object
Single	Single-precision floating-point value
String	String value
Unknown	Unknown object type

VarType

VarType returns a value that indicates the subtype of a variable. Table 3.6 contains the possible values returned and the VBScript constant names for each variable type value. Constants are variables, but their values cannot be changed. VBScript defines many constants. Their names always begin with **vb**. You'll see how to create user-defined constants later in this chapter.

The **VarType** function does not actually return 8192 for an array. VBScript supports only arrays of variants, so this function always returns 8204, which is equal to 8192 plus the value for the variant type. However, **VarType** returns the appropriate value for individual array elements.

Table 3.6   VarType return values.

Value	Constant	Description
0	**vbEmpty**	Uninitialized
1	**vbNull**	Contains no valid data
2	**vbInteger**	Integer
3	**vbLong**	Long
4	**vbSingle**	Single-precision floating-point number
5	**vbDouble**	Double-precision floating-point number
6	**vbCurrency**	Currency

(continued)

Table 3.6   VarType return values *(continued).*

Value	Constant	Description
7	**vbDate**	Date
8	**vbString**	String
9	**vbObject**	Automation object
10	**vbError**	Error
11	**vbBoolean**	Boolean
12	**vbVariant**	Variant (used only with arrays of variants)
13	**vbDataObject**	Data-access object
17	**vbByte**	Byte
8192	**vbArray**	Array (added to type of array)

Arrays

Unlike *scalar* variables, which can hold only one value, *array* variables can hold multiple values. These variables are useful for storing data items of related information.

You declare arrays by using the **Dim** statement. You use it just as you do with scalars, except that array variables use parentheses following the variable name. The following statement declares an array variable, **arrFavoriteLinks**, that will store a collection of favorite hyperlinks:

```
Dim arrFavoriteLinks(9)
```

The value in parentheses specifies the number of items the array can store. The preceding statement declares an array that can contain 10 items, or *array elements*. Why 10? Arrays in VBScript are *zero-based*, which means that the first element in the array is element zero (0). Therefore, the number of array elements the array can contain is the number in parentheses plus one. The element number is often referred to as the array *subscript* or *index*.

You reference individual elements in an array by specifying the element number in parentheses. Listing 3.9 assigns a value to the first element in our favorite-hyperlinks array and then displays the value stored there using the **Response.Write** function.

Listing 3.9   Referencing array elements.
```
<%
Dim arrFavoriteLinks(9)

arrFavoriteLinks(0)  = "http://www.al-williams.com"
Response.Write arrFavoriteLinks(0)

%>
```

You also can specify the array subscript by using a variable of subtype integer. This statement references an array element using a variable:

```
n = 0
arrFavoriteLinks(n) = "http://www.al-williams.com"
```

Arrays can contain only data items of the same type. Of course, VBScript has only the variant type, which can hold a variety of subtypes. You therefore can store strings, integers, doubles, and so on in the same array. Take a look at the following:

```
arrMenuItem(0) = "Large Pizza"
arrMenuItem(1) = 14.75
```

Now, **arrMenuItem(0)** contains a string, and **arrMenuItem(1)** contains a floating-point value.

Multidimensional Arrays

The array **arrFavoriteLinks(9)** is a *one-dimensional* array. *Multidimensional* arrays are arrays with more than one dimension. Suppose you want to store descriptive text with the URL. You do so by declaring the array as a two-dimensional array—conceptually, an array of rows and columns. A multidimensional array is declared like a one-dimensional array, with a size specifier for each dimension, separated by commas. VBScript allows arrays of up to 60 dimensions. However, arrays with more than three dimensions are seldom useful and always confusing.

The following statement declares a two-dimensional array of 10 rows and 2 columns:

```
Dim arrFavoriteLinks(9,1)
```

Values are assigned to the two-dimensional array as follows:

```
arrFavoriteLinks(0,0) = "http://www.al-williams.com"
arrFavoriteLinks(0,1) = "Al Williams Consulting"
```

These statements assign the URL to the first row and first column of the array. The first row, second column stores the text.

Listing 3.10 shows the use of a multidimensional array to output a list of favorite hyperlinks. Notice how **Response.Write** is used to mix script and HTML and send it back to the client as plain old HTML. This example is just what you need to output your hyperlinks.

Listing 3.10   Using multidimensional arrays.

```
<%
Dim arrFavoriteLinks(9,1)

arrFavoriteLinks(0,0) = "http://www.al-williams.com"
arrFavoriteLinks(0,1) = "Al Williams Consulting"
arrFavoriteLinks(1,0) = "http://www.coriolis.com"
```

```
arrFavoriteLinks(1,1) = "The Coriolis Group"
arrFavoriteLinks(2,0) = "http://www.microsoft.com/vbscript/"
arrFavoriteLinks(2,1) = "Microsoft's VBScript Site"

Response.Write "<A HREF=" & arrFavoriteLinks(0,0) & ">"
Response.Write arrFavoriteLinks(0,1) & "</A>"
Response.Write "<BR>"

Response.Write "<A HREF=" & arrFavoriteLinks(1,0) & ">"
Response.Write arrFavoriteLinks(1,1) & "</A>"
Response.Write "<BR>"

Response.Write "<A HREF=" & arrFavoriteLinks(2,0) & ">"
Response.Write arrFavoriteLinks(2,1) & "</A>"
%>
```

Figure 3.2 shows the browser displaying the list. The script stores the URLs for the hyperlinks in the first column of the array and the text in the second column. Then, **Response.Write**

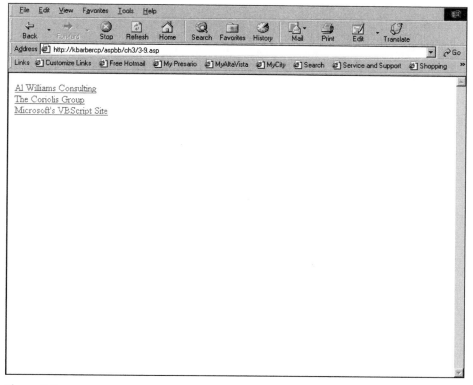

Figure 3.2
A multidimensional array of hyperlinks displayed in the browser.

outputs the hyperlink in HTML. The browser interprets the string and displays it as a hyperlink. Notice that the **Response.Write** method is also sending pure HTML in this example (notice the lines that write the **
** tag).

Dynamic Arrays

The **arrFavoriteLinks** array is a *fixed-size* array. After you declare its size, that size doesn't change. You can resize *dynamic* arrays as necessary during script execution by increasing the size of the array to hold more data or decreasing it if space is no longer needed. You can also resize both one- and multidimensional dynamic arrays. However, you'll encounter a limitation when using multidimensional dynamic arrays, as you'll see shortly.

You use the **Dim** statement to declare both static and dynamic arrays. You can tell a dynamic array declaration from a fixed-size one because the size of a dynamic array isn't specified. Instead, the parentheses are empty. The following statement declares a dynamic array:

```
Dim arrFavoriteLinks()
```

Private and **Public** are also used to declare a dynamic array. The following statement declares a private dynamic array:

```
Private arrFavoriteLinks()
```

You can also declare dynamic arrays by using the **ReDim** statement, in which case you must specify an initial size as follows:

```
ReDim arrFavoriteLinks(9)
```

You can resize dynamic arrays by using **ReDim** and specifying the new size in parentheses. Your program can make the array larger by specifying a larger number or smaller by specifying a smaller number. Be careful when you're resizing dynamic arrays because the array elements are initialized by default to **Empty** when the array is resized. Sometimes you want this behavior. If you want the contents of the array to remain, include the **Preserve** keyword in the **ReDim** statement. The following statement resizes the array without losing the array contents:

```
ReDim Preserve arrFavoriteLinks(20)
```

This approach works well when you must increase the array size. However, when reducing the array size, you'll lose all the data that lies beyond the new array boundary.

You can also resize multidimensional arrays. You can modify the size of each dimension as well as add and remove dimensions. The following statements declare a one-dimensional dynamic array and then resize the array to make it two-dimensional:

```
Dim arrFavoriteLinks()
ReDim arrFavoriteLinks(10)
...
ReDim arrFavoriteLinks(9,1)
```

One limitation you must remember when working with multidimensional dynamic arrays is that **Preserve** works only if the last dimension is being changed. If a dimension other than the last dimension is resized, or if you are adding or removing dimensions, you cannot use **Preserve**. In that case, VBScript discards all the array data.

VBScript Array Functions And Statements

VBScript provides several functions and statements that work with arrays. The VBScript array features are shown in Table 3.7.

The Array Function

Some languages allow you to initialize arrays during declaration. For example, the following C statement declares an array of integers and fills the first three locations with 1, 2, and 3:

```
int somevariable[ ] = {1,2,3};
```

VBScript can't initialize arrays However, you can accomplish almost the same result by using the **Array** function, which returns a variant containing an array:

```
Dim somevariable
somevariable = Array(1,2,3)
```

The variable **somevariable** is now a variant that contains an array of variants. You can access the individual array elements as usual.

The Erase Statement

The **Erase** statement reinitializes fixed-size arrays and releases dynamic array memory. The elements of a fixed-size array are still accessible after **Erase** but are set to their initial values of zero for numeric arrays, zero-length strings ("") for string arrays, and

Table 3.7	**VBScript array functions and statements.**
Keyword	**Action**
Array	Returns a variant that contains an array.
Dim	Declares variables.
ReDim	Resizes array variables.
Erase	Reinitializes fixed-size arrays. Frees memory used by dynamic arrays.
IsArray	Returns a Boolean indicating whether a variable is an array.
LBound, UBound	Returns the lower and upper limits of an array dimension.
Private, Public	Declares private and public variables.

nothing for arrays of objects. Dynamic arrays must be declared again with **ReDim** before the array can be accessed:

```
Erase somevariable
```

The IsArray Function

The **IsArray** function allows you to determine whether a variable is an array. The function returns a Boolean of **TRUE** if the variable is an array and **FALSE** if it isn't:

```
Dim c
Response.Write IsArray(c)          ' returns FALSE
c = Array(1,2,3)
Response.Write IsArray(c)          ' returns TRUE
```

The LBound And UBound Functions

The **LBound** function returns the lowest subscript of an array, which is always zero in VBScript (but not always in Visual Basic). The **UBound** function returns the highest subscript of the array. As an option, you can specify an array dimension in both functions:

```
Dim arrFavoriteLinks(9,1)
' returns upper bound for first dimension (9)
Response.Write UBound(arrFavoriteLinks)
' returns upper bound for second dimension (1)
Response.Write UBound(arrFavoriteLinks, 2)
```

Constants

Variables provide a way to store values that may change as the program executes. It's often convenient to store values that do not change. Suppose you are writing a program that makes many calculations using the value of pi (π), which is about 3.1415967. You could simply type this number wherever it is needed, but typing it would be no fun and full of errors for those of us who are typing challenged. Alternatively, you could assign it to a variable and use the variable throughout the program. This approach would be easier and less error prone, but it still has a disadvantage. Because it is a variable, its value can be changed, and if it is changed (by accident, of course), calculations using the variable will produce erroneous results.

You can use *constants* in expressions as if they were variables, but you can't change their values. Constants provide the convenience of referencing unchanging values by name without the possibility of accidentally changing the values. Constants can also provide some level of self-documentation if you use meaningful names. You can declare a constant by using the **Const** statement like this:

```
Const PI = 3.1415967
```

The standard naming rules that apply to variables also apply to constants. You can't use variables, expressions with operators, intrinsic VBScript functions, or user-defined functions in constant declarations.

Tip

Programmers commonly use all-uppercase names to distinguish constants from variables.

By default, script-level constants are public and procedure-level constants are private. You can declare script-level constants explicitly public or explicitly private, as shown here:

```
Private Const PI = 3.1415967
```

VBScript defines many constants to specify colors, dates and times, date formats, comparisons, and more. These constants are documented on the Microsoft VBScript Web site at **http://msdn.microsoft.com/scripting/vbscript/**.

Operators

Operators form expressions that perform calculations, comparisons, and logical operations. VBScript has a complete set of operators that you will use extensively in all but the simplest programs. The three classifications of operators are:

♦ *Arithmetic*—These operators perform mathematical calculations.

♦ *Comparison*—These operators evaluate two expressions and compare them to see whether they are, for example, equal or not equal.

♦ *Logical*—Logical operators perform operations with Boolean or binary values; they are often used with comparisons to form compound comparisons.

Arithmetic Operators

Arithmetic operators allow you to perform arithmetic on one or more variables. Table 3.8 contains the VBScript arithmetic operators.

The string concatenation operator is not actually an arithmetic operator; rather, it fits with arithmetic operators in order of operator precedence. You also can use the addition operator to perform string concatenation, but its use for this is sometimes confusing when reading code and can lead to ambiguities. For example, consider this code:

```
s="10"
s1=s+9
```

Should **s1** equal 19? Or should it equal 109? The answer isn't clear. Therefore, you should always use **&** to join strings.

Table 3.8   Arithmetic operators.

Operator	Operation	Description	Syntax
^	Exponentiation	Raises a number to the power of the exponent	c = a ^ b
*	Multiplication	Multiplies two numbers	c = a * b
/	Division	Divides two numbers, returns a floating-point value	c = a / b
\	Integer division	Divides two numbers, returns an integer	c = a \ b
mod	Modulo arithmetic	Divides two numbers, returns only the remainder	c = a mod b
+	Addition	Adds two expressions	c = a + b
-	Subtraction*	Finds the difference between two expressions	c = a - b
&	String concatenation	Joins two string expressions	c = a & b

* Also used for unary negation, to change the sign of the value of an expression.

Comparison Operators

Comparison operators compare two expressions. The operators usually return **TRUE** or **FALSE**. If either expression is null, then the operator returns **Null**. You'll find a list of comparison operators in Table 3.9.

The **Is** operator does not directly compare two objects. Rather, it compares two object references to determine whether they both refer to the same object. This is a subtle distinction. Suppose you have two objects that contain a string. The **Is** operator will return **FALSE** if the objects are different, even if they happen to contain the same string. The only way **Is** will return **TRUE** is when you present it with two object variables that genuinely refer to the exact same object.

Logical Operators

Logical operators evaluate one or more logical expressions and return a **TRUE** or a **FALSE** result. These operators can also perform a bitwise evaluation and return a numeric result if the two expressions are numeric values. Table 3.10 lists the logical operators.

Table 3.9   Comparison operators.

Operator	Operation	TRUE If
=	Equality	expression1 = expression2
<>	Inequality	expression1 <> expression2
<	Less than	expression1 < expression2
>	Greater than	expression1 > expression2
<=	Less than or equal to	expression1 <= expression2
>=	Greater than or equal to	expression1 >= expression2
Is	Object reference comparison (see text)	object_ref1 Is object_ref2

Table 3.10   Logical operators.

Operator	Operation	Syntax	Expression1	Expression2	Result
Not	Logical negation	result = Not expression1	TRUE		FALSE
			FALSE		TRUE
			Null		Null
And	Logical conjunction	result = expression1 And expression2	TRUE	TRUE	TRUE
			TRUE	FALSE	FALSE
			TRUE	Null	Null
			FALSE	TRUE	FALSE
			FALSE	FALSE	FALSE
			FALSE	Null	FALSE
			Null	TRUE	Null
			Null	FALSE	FALSE
			Null	Null	Null
Or	Logical disjunction	result = expression1 Or expression2	TRUE	TRUE	TRUE
			FALSE	FALSE	TRUE
			TRUE	Null	TRUE
			FALSE	TRUE	TRUE
			FALSE	FALSE	FALSE
			FALSE	Null	Null
			Null	TRUE	TRUE
			Null	FALSE	Null
			Null	Null	Null
Xor	Logical exclusion	result = expression1 Xor expression2	TRUE	TRUE	FALSE
			TRUE	FALSE	TRUE
			FALSE	TRUE	TRUE
			FALSE	FALSE	FALSE
Eqv	Logical equivalence	result = expression1 Eqv expression2	TRUE	TRUE	TRUE
			TRUE	FALSE	FALSE
			FALSE	TRUE	FALSE
			FALSE	FALSE	TRUE
Imp	Logical implication	result = expression1 Imp expression2	TRUE	TRUE	TRUE
			TRUE	FALSE	FALSE
			TRUE	Null	Null
			FALSE	TRUE	TRUE
			FALSE	FALSE	TRUE
			FALSE	Null	TRUE
			Null	TRUE	TRUE
			Null	FALSE	Null
			Null	Null	Null

Operator Precedence

VBScript frequently evaluates operators in an order different than they appear in your program. The *order of precedence* rules determine which operators have priority over other operators. First, arithmetic operators are evaluated, then comparison operators, and then logical operators. There is also an order of precedence within the arithmetic and logical categories. Comparison operators have equal precedence, so VBScript evaluates them from left to right.

Tables 3.8 and 3.10 list the arithmetic and logical operators in their order of precedence. Some of the arithmetic operators have equal precedence. Multiplication, division, and integer division have equal precedence, as do addition and subtraction. Operators with a high precedence are evaluated before lower-precedence operators. Operators with equal precedence are evaluated left to right. Because multiplication has higher precedence than addition, the expression

```
10 + 2 * 3
```

results in 16, not 36, just as it does in standard mathematics.

You can override the standard order of precedence by enclosing operations in parentheses. Operations in parentheses take precedence over those not in parentheses, and normal precedence is maintained within parentheses. Parentheses can be nested to further control the order of operation, and operations within the innermost parentheses are evaluated first.

The following statements illustrate how operator precedence is controlled using parentheses:

```
A = 1 * 2 + 6 / 3
A = 1 * (2 + 6) / 3
```

These statements produce different results. In the first example, the product of 1 * 2 is added to the result of 6 / 3, and yields 4. In the second example, the sum of 2 + 6 is multiplied by 1 and then divided by 3, and yields 2.667.

Controlling The Flow

You could write a very modest VBScript program using only the information you already have. However, robust applications require much more than the very basics of VBScript. Most programs make decisions and follow an execution path as a result of those decisions. These decisions frequently depend on the value of a variable or on other factors, such as the setting of a radio button or other HTML control. VBScript comes equipped with a fairly complete package of conditional statements (discussed in the next section) that you use to add decision-making capability to programs. Conditional statements evaluate a condition and specify statements to execute on the basis of whether the condition is true or false.

Most applications also execute some lines of code repeatedly. If you need to initialize a 100-element array to a specific value using only the information covered so far, you would have a bit of work on your hands. You could use 100 assignment statements or use the **Array** function with a 100-element argument list, neither of which is desirable. VBScript provides looping statements that are used to execute lines of code a specific number of times or while a condition is true or false.

Conditional Statements

Conditional statements allow programs to make decisions and execute specific lines of code on the basis of the value of a condition. The ability to make decisions and act on them increases your program's "IQ." VBScript supports the following conditional statements:

+ **If…Then**
+ **If…Then…Else**
+ **If…Then…ElseIf**
+ **Select Case**

If…Then

The **If…Then** statement, by far the most common conditional statement, executes a statement or statements if a condition evaluates to true:

```
If condition Then
     statement(s) to execute
End If
```

If the condition evaluates to true, the block of statements between the **If…Then** statement and the **End If** statement executes. The **End If** statement marks the end of the code block. Program execution jumps to the first line of code following the **End If** statement if the condition is false. If you need only one statement to execute, you can omit the **End If** as long as you write the entire statement on one line like this:

```
If condition Then statement
```

Listing 3.11 shows the use of **If…Then**. In this example, a block of code executes if the value of a variable is greater than or equal to $10,000.00.

Listing 3.11   The If…Then statement.
```
<%
Dim Sales, Commission

Commission = .05
Sales = 12500.00   'in real life this would be a computed value
If Sales >= 10000.00 Then
```

```
        Commission = .10
        Response.Write "You're doing well!"
End If
%>
```

*If you are used to using Visual Basic, you might type **End If** as one word instead of
two. Typing as one word is permissible with Visual Basic because the VB editor
automatically converts **EndIf** to **End If**. However, when writing script, you may be
using a regular text editor that does not do this conversion. Therefore, be sure to
include the space between **End** and **If** so that your scripts will work properly.*

If...Then...Else

The **If...Then...Else** statement provides an alternative. One block of statements executes if
the condition is true, and another block executes if the condition is false:

```
If condition Then
        statements(s) to execute if true
Else
        statement(s) to execute if false
End If
```

Listing 3.12 uses **If...Then...Else** to evaluate the **Sales** variable and displays an alternate
message if **Sales** is less than an expected value.

Listing 3.12   The If...Then...Else statement.
```
<%
Option Explicit
Dim Sales, Commission

Commission = .05
Sales = 12500.00
If Sales >= 10000.00 Then
        Commission = .10
        Response.Write "You're doing well!"
Else
        Response.Write "You need to work harder."
End If
%>
```

If...Then...ElseIf

If...Then...ElseIf evaluates several conditions:

```
If condition1 Then
        statements(s) to execute if condition1 is true
```

```
ElseIf condition2 Then
    statement(s) to execute if condition2 is true
ElseIf condition3 Then
    statement(s) to execute if condition3 is true
Else
    statement(s) to execute if none of the above is true
End If
```

Listing 3.13 uses **If...Then...ElseIf** to evaluate possible values of the variable **Sales** and sets the value for **Commission** on the basis of that value. The **Else** statement is used as the default if none of the conditions evaluate to true, which in this case occurs when the value of **Sales** is less than $1,000.

Listing 3.13   Using If...Then...ElseIf.

```
<%
Option Explicit
Dim Sales, Commission

If Sales >= 10000 Then
    Commission = .20
ElseIf Sales >= 5000 Then
    Commission = .15
ElseIf Sales >= 1000 Then
    Commission = .10
Else
    Commission = .05
End If
%>
```

You'll often use logical operators with conditional statements to further define the evaluation. Listing 3.14 uses the **And** logical operator to determine whether **Sales** is within a specific range.

Listing 3.14   Using logical operators in conditional statements.

```
<%
Option Explicit
Dim Sales, Commission

If Sales < 1000 Then
    Commission = .05
ElseIf Sales >= 1000 And Sales < 5000 Then
    Commission = .10
ElseIf Sales >= 5000 And Sales < 10000 Then
    Commission = .15
```

```
Else
    Commission = .20
End If
%>
```

Listing 3.14 gives the same result as 3.13 but also shows how logical operators are used to define possible conditions. However, in this example, Listing 3.13 is more efficient.

Select Case

You use the **Select Case** statement to execute one of many groups of statements depending on the value of an expression. You use **Case Else** to specify statements to execute if the program finds no match. Here is the syntax for **Select Case**:

```
Select Case expression
Case condition1
    statement(s) to execute
Case condition2
    statement(s) to execute
. . .
Case Else
    statement(s) to execute if no match
End Select
```

Listing 3.15 uses **Select Case** to evaluate the possible values of **Commission** and set the variable **Bonus** accordingly.

Listing 3.15   Using Select Case.

```
<%
Option Explicit
Dim Sales, Commission, Bonus

Select Case Commission
Case .05
    Bonus = 0
Case .10
    Bonus = 500
Case .15
    Bonus = 1000
Case .20
    Bonus = 1500
Case Else
    Response.Write "Invalid Commission Value"
End Select
%>
```

Looping

You can use *looping* statements to execute selected lines of code repeatedly. VBScript has looping statements that can repeat lines of code a specific number of times or while or until a condition is true. The four loop statements in VBScript are as follows:

♦ **For...Next**

♦ **For Each...Next**

♦ **Do...Loop**

♦ **While...Wend**

For...Next

The **For...Next** loop executes a block of statements a specific number of times. You specify a *counter* variable to control the number of times the loop is repeated. The value of this variable increases (or decreases) automatically each time the loop repeats.

The **For...Next** loop has the following syntax:

```
For counter_variable = start_value To end_value
    statement(s) to execute
Next
```

Tip
*Visual Basic allows you to optionally specify the counter variable after **Next**. Specifying it this way improves code readability. However, it is not allowed in VBScript. You must not put anything after the **Next** statement.*

The counter variable is an integer that you must declare explicitly if you specified **Option Explicit**. The starting and ending values are variables or literal expressions that specify the number of times the loop is repeated. The counter variable automatically increments by one each time the loop executes, and the loop ends when the counter variable is equal to or greater than the ending value. The **Next** statement marks the end of the loop.

Listing 3.16 uses the **For...Next** loop to output an array of favorite hyperlinks.

Listing 3.16   Using the For...Next loop.

```
<%
Option Explicit
Dim arrFavoriteLinks(9, 1)
Dim intCounter

For intCounter = 0 To 9
    Response.Write "<A HREF=" & arrFavoriteLinks(intCounter,0) & ">"
    Response.Write arrFavoriteLinks(intCounter,1) & "</A>"
```

```
        Response.Write "<BR>"
Next
%>
```

Using the **Step** keyword, you can specify an increment other than one. You can even specify a negative step value to decrement the counter. The following lines of code display the favorite-links array backward:

```
For intCounter = 9 To 0 Step -1
    Response.Write "<A HREF=" & arrFavoriteLinks(intCounter,0) & ">"
    Response.Write arrFavoriteLinks(intCounter,1) & "</A>"
    Response.Write "<BR>"
Next
```

The **Exit For** statement is used to exit the loop early:

```
For intCounter = 0 To 9
    if IsEmpty(arrFavoriteLinks(intCounter, 0)) Then Exit For
    Response.Write "<A HREF=" & arrFavoriteLinks(intCounter,0) & ">"
    Response.Write arrFavoriteLinks(intCounter,1) & "</A>"
    Response.Write "<BR>"
Next
```

This example uses the **IsEmpty** function to test array elements. If **IsEmpty** returns **TRUE**, then **Exit For** executes and the loop ends.

For Each...Next

The **For Each...Next** loop executes a block of code for each element in an array or *collection*. A collection is an object that contains related objects, such as all the controls in an HTML form. Here is the syntax for the **For Each...Next** statement:

```
For Each item In array_or_collection
    statement(s) to execute
Next
```

item is a variable that references each item in *array_or_collection*, which is the name of an array or collection. The statements within the loop execute once for each item, and the loop terminates when no more items appear in the array or collection. You can use the **Exit For** statement to exit from the loop early.

Listing 3.17 uses **For Each...Next** to search for a string in the favorite-links array. The script uses the **InputBox** function to get a search string from the user. The **InputBox** function displays a dialog box and waits for the user to input text into a text box and click on the OK button. It returns the contents of the text box to the script. The variable **arrItem** references each item in **arrFavoriteLinks** in turn. As the loop repeats for each item, the program compares **arrItem** to **strSearchString**. If a match occurs, the program sets the Boolean variable **blnFound** to **TRUE** and terminates the loop.

For Each...Next doesn't automatically maintain a counter variable, so **intIndex** is used to keep track of the number of times the loop repeats. It's useful in this example to increment **intIndex** at the end of the loop because the variable is used later as an array subscript. Therefore, **intIndex** will equal the correct subscript if the routine finds the search string.

Listing 3.17   Using the For Each...Next loop.

```
<%
Option Explicit
Dim arrFavoriteLinks(9)
Dim strSearchString
Dim arrItem, intIndex
Dim blnFound

arrFavoriteLinks(0) = "Al Williams Consulting"
arrFavoriteLinks(1) = "The Coriolis Group"
arrFavoriteLinks(2) = "Microsoft's VBScript Site"

strSearchString = "The Coriolis Group"

For Each arrItem in arrFavoriteLinks
    If arrItem =  strSearchString Then
        blnFound = TRUE
        Exit For
    End If
    intIndex = intIndex + 1
Next

If blnFound Then
    Response.Write arrFavoriteLinks(intIndex)
Else
    Response.Write "Search string not found."
End If
%>
```

Do...Loop

Do...Loop repeats a block of statements while or until a condition is true. **Do...Loop** can use two different keywords: **While** and **Until**. **While** causes the loop to repeat while a condition is true, and **Until** causes the loop to repeat until a condition is true. In either case, the condition may be evaluated either at the beginning or at the end of the loop. The statements in the loop always execute at least once when the evaluation is made at the end. **Exit Do** is used to break out of the loop before the condition is met.

The **Do...Loop** is used with **While** in either of the following ways:

```
Do While condition_is_true
    statement(s) to execute
Loop

Do
    statement(s) to execute
Loop While condition_is_true
```

The **Do...Loop** is used with **Until** in either of the following ways:

```
Do Until condition_is_true
    statement(s) to execute
Loop

Do
    statement(s) to execute
Loop Until condition_is_true
```

Listing 3.18 demonstrates how to use the **Do...Loop** with the **Until** keyword to output the **arrFavoriteLinks** array.

Listing 3.18   The Do...Until loop.

```
<%
Option Explicit
Dim arrFavoriteLinks(9, 1)
Dim intIndex

arrFavoriteLinks(0,0) = "http://www.al-williams.com"
arrFavoriteLinks(0,1) = "Al Williams Consulting"
arrFavoriteLinks(1,0) = "http://www.coriolis.com"
arrFavoriteLinks(1,1) = "The Coriolis Group"
arrFavoriteLinks(2,0) = "http://www.microsoft.com/vbscript/"
arrFavoriteLinks(2,1) = "Microsoft's VBScript Site"

intIndex = 0
Do Until IsEmpty(arrFavoriteLinks(intIndex, 0))
    Response.Write "<A HREF=" & arrFavoriteLinks(intIndex,0) & ">"
    Response.Write arrFavoriteLinks(intIndex,1) & "</A>"
    Response.Write "<BR>"
    intIndex = intIndex + 1
Loop
%>
```

While...Wend

The **While...Wend** loop is an old-fashioned way to write a loop that repeats while a condition is true. This loop is much like the **Do...Loop** (and you can replace it with one). The **While...Wend** loop's condition must be evaluated at the beginning of the loop, as you can see in the following syntax:

```
While condition_is_true
     statement(s) to execute
Wend
```

VBScript Procedures

There are times when your program must perform certain tasks many times. Perhaps you are writing a program that calculates the distance between several pairs of geographic coordinates and displays the results graphically. Rather than enter the program statements each time the calculation and drawing are needed, you could place the necessary code in *procedures*. A procedure is a block of code that is called to perform a specific task. Each time the program needs to make the calculation, a call is made to the appropriate procedure.

VBScript supports two types of procedures: *subroutines* and *functions*. Subroutines perform a specific task but don't return a result. Functions also perform a specific task and do return a result. If you want to calculate the distance between two coordinates, for example, you would probably use a function because you want the procedure to return a result. Some procedures take *arguments*, or *parameters*, which are pieces of information that a procedure uses in, for example, the two geographic coordinates in a distance calculation function.

Most of your VBScript programs will include procedures to perform calculations, verify form data, build pages dynamically, and so on. You will also write procedures to respond to *events*. An event is an action that the system generates to inform your program that something interesting has happened. For example, the **Application_OnEnd** event occurs when a server-side script application quits. You can have your program respond to this event by writing an *event procedure*. The system will then call this procedure when the event occurs.

Subroutines

A subroutine is a procedure that performs an action but doesn't return a result. You can define a subroutine by embedding the necessary program statements between the **Sub** and **End Sub** statements. The **Sub** statement also assigns a name to the subroutine. Subroutine names follow the same naming rules as variables do.

The following subroutine displays a message:

```
Sub ShowMessage
     Response.Write "VBScript is fun!"
End Sub
```

This subroutine has the name **ShowMessage**. Like variables, procedures are public by default but can be declared either **Public** or **Private**:

```
Private Sub ShowMessage
```

Subroutine names can optionally include empty parentheses:

```
Sub ShowMessage()
```

However, parentheses are required for subroutines that take arguments.

You can call subroutines in a variety of ways, depending on whether they take arguments. Because **ShowMessage** doesn't take an argument, you can call it in any of the following ways:

```
ShowMessage          ' no arguments
ShowMessage()        ' empty argument list
Call ShowMessage     ' Call statement and no arguments
Call ShowMessage()   ' Call statement with empty argument list
```

As you can see, you also have the option to use the **Call** statement, in which case you must enclose any arguments in parentheses.

Passing Arguments

You can define arguments for your subroutines by including an *argument list* in parentheses. The following redefines **ShowMessage** to take a single argument containing the message to display:

```
Sub ShowMessage(strMessage)
     Response.Write strMessage
End Sub
```

The argument **strMessage** is simply a variable that will contain the value passed to the subroutine. It has local scope (that is, it is visible only within **ShowMessage**). Now that **ShowMessage** has an argument, you can call it in any of the following ways:

```
ShowMessage "Hello"
ShowMessage("Hello")
Call ShowMessage("Hello")
```

You can define procedures that take multiple arguments by separating the arguments with a comma in the argument list. Listing 3.19 defines a subroutine that displays the array of favorite hyperlinks. The subroutine takes an array containing the hyperlinks and an integer containing the size of the array as arguments. Compare this example to Listing 3.10, which does the same thing. Clearly, Listing 3.19 is more efficient to write because the output code appears only once. It will also be easier to change the format of the output or to add more items using Listing 3.19.

Listing 3.19   Using a subroutine with multiple arguments.

```
<%
Option Explicit
Dim arrFavoriteLinks(9, 1)

arrFavoriteLinks(0,0) = "http://www.al-williams.com"
arrFavoriteLinks(0,1) = "Al Williams Consulting"
arrFavoriteLinks(1,0) = "http://www.coriolis.com"
arrFavoriteLinks(1,1) = "The Coriolis Group"
arrFavoriteLinks(2,0) = "http://www.microsoft.com/vbscript/"
arrFavoriteLinks(2,1) = "Microsoft's VBScript Site"

Sub ShowLinks(arrLinkArray, intCount)
Dim intIndex
     for intIndex = 0 to intCount
          if IsEmpty(arrFavoriteLinks(intIndex,0)) Then Exit Sub
          Response.Write "<A HREF=" & arrLinkArray(intIndex,0) & ">"
          Response.Write arrLinkArray(intIndex,1) & "</A>"
          Response.Write "<BR>"
     Next
End Sub

Call ShowLinks (arrFavoriteLinks, UBound(arrFavoriteLinks))
%>
```

Listing 3.19 also uses the **IsEmpty** function to check the contents of the array. If the array element is empty, a call to **Exit Sub** immediately exits the subroutine. You can use **Exit Sub** to prematurely end a subroutine and **Exit Function** to terminate a function.

Changing The Argument Value

VBScript allows your programs to pass variables to procedures *by value* or *by reference*. When a variable is passed by value, VBScript makes a private copy of the variable for the procedure. The procedure can change the value of the variable locally but not the value of the original variable.

If you need to change the value of a variable within a procedure so that the caller sees this change, you must pass the variable by reference. When a variable is passed by reference, VBScript allows the procedure to alter the original variable. If you pass by value, the procedure can modify only its private copy of the variable. By default, VBScript passes arguments by value. You can explicitly use either method by using the **ByVal** and **ByRef** keywords.

Listing 3.20 contains two subroutines that calculate the square of a number. The program passes the number to the subroutine **SqByVal** by value. The value of the variable changes only locally, and the original value remains unchanged outside the subroutine. The program passes the number to the subroutine **SqByRef** by reference. Changes made to the variable are retained when the subroutine finishes executing.

Listing 3.20   Passing arguments by value and by reference.

```
<%
Option Explicit
Dim lngNumber

Sub SqByVal(ByVal x)
    x = x * x
End Sub

Sub SqByRef(ByRef x)
    x = x * x
End Sub

lngNumber = 5
Call SqByVal(lngNumber)
Response.Write lngNumber              ' lngNumber still equals 5
Response.Write "<BR>"
Call SqByRef(lngNumber)
Response.Write lngNumber              ' lngNumber now equals 25
%>
```

Functions

Functions are very similar to subroutines, but a function can return a value, whereas a subroutine can't. You define functions by using the **Function** and **End Function** statements:

```
Function Sq(x)
    function statement(s)
End Function
```

Functions return values by assigning a value to the function name within the function body. Listing 3.21 contains a function that returns the square of a number.

Listing 3.21   A VBScript function that squares a number.

```
<%
Option Explicit
Dim lngNumber
Dim lngResult
```

```
lngNumber = 5

Function Sq(x)
     Sq = x * x
End Function

lngResult = Sq(lngNumber)
%>
```

Function calls normally appear in expressions:

```
Response.Write Sq(lngNumber)
```

You also can use a function on the right side of an assignment statement (see Listing 3.21).

Event Procedures

VBScript makes it easy to write procedures that respond to events, which is very useful. You can define an *event procedure* as you would any other procedure. The only difference is that event procedures have special names. Event procedure names consist of the name of the control and the name of the event joined by the underscore character:

```
Sub object_EventName
    Code
End Sub
```

You'll see how to use server-side event procedures in Chapter 5.

Method Procedures

Method procedures are procedures belonging to objects. Many objects expose these procedures for use in applications. You saw examples of this when you used the **Write** method of the **Response** object to output HTML to the browser. You can call method procedures by specifying the object name and method name and joining them with a period:

```
object.method
```

Here's how it's done in practice:

```
Response.Write
```

Most intrinsic server-side objects have methods you can call. You'll read more about server-side objects in Chapter 5.

Dealing With Errors

Let's face it: Errors happen. The programmer's job is to anticipate errors and write code to prevent errors from crashing the program. You can use several strategies to prevent many runtime errors. You can add data validation routines to all sections of code where there is a possibility of an incorrect value causing an error (for example, a divide-by-zero error). Another strategy is to use VBScript's capability to instruct the interpreter not to halt when an error occurs.

Handling Errors In VBScript

VBScript provides the capability to prevent the program from crashing when a fatal error occurs. The **On Error Resume Next** statement tells the interpreter to ignore the error and continue executing on the next statement following the one in which the error occurred. Keep in mind that this statement doesn't handle the error; rather, it simply tells the program to salute and continue to march.

The following statements show the use of **On Error Resume Next**:

```
Rate = 18
Periods = 0
On Error Resume Next
PeriodicRate = Rate / Periods
program execution resumes here
. . .
```

On Error Resume Next is automatically reset when you call another procedure. Therefore, you should include it in all routines that might be susceptible to errors.

The **Err** Object

The **Err** object contains information about runtime errors and, in combination with **On Error Resume Next**, offers a powerful way to handle errors. When an error occurs, the properties of the **Err** object are set to information that identifies the error as well as information that you can use to handle the error. Table 3.11 lists the **Err** object properties. You can find the **Err** object's methods in Table 3.12.

Table 3.11   Err object properties.

Property	Returns Or Sets A
Description	String describing the error
HelpContext	Context ID for a topic in a help file
HelpFile	Path to a help file
Number	Number specifying the error
Source	The name of the application or object that generated the error

Table 3.12 **Err object methods.**

Method	Description
Clear	Clears the setting of the **Err** object properties
Raise	Generates a runtime error

The **Raise** method is useful during debugging to test error-handling routines. It is also useful if you want to cause an error that will be visible to another part of the program. The **Raise** method uses the following syntax:

```
Err.Raise(number, source, description, helpfile, helpcontext)
```

Listing 3.22 uses the **On Error Resume Next** statement with the **Err** object to trap and handle an error.

Listing 3.22   Using On Error Resume Next with the Err object.

```
<%
Dim Rate
Dim PeriodicRate
Dim Periods

Sub ErrorHandler(num, desc, src)
    Response.Write "Error: " & num & ": " & desc & " generated by " & src
End Sub

On Error Resume Next
Rate = 18
Periods = 0
PeriodicRate = Rate / Periods
If Err.number <> 0 Then
    Call ErrorHandler(Err.number, Err.description, Err.source)
End If
%>
```

After the division operation executes, the program examines the value of **Err.number**. If it is nonzero, there is an error, in which case the program calls a routine to handle the error. The subroutine **ErrorHandler** simply displays some of the properties of the **Err** object. A real program might use a much more sophisticated error-handling routine.

Basic Data Validation

Data validation routines are frequently a large part of a program for a number of reasons, one of which is to prevent errors. Assume for a moment that you are writing a program that calculates loan payments. The user enters the annual interest rate and the number of payment periods. The program must divide the annual interest rate by the number of payments to calculate the interest rate per period. If the user enters a zero for the number of periods, a divide-by-zero error will result. To prevent this problem, the program should check the user's input to determine whether the period is zero. If it is, the user is prompted to reenter the number of periods. Listing 3.23 shows how you might write this validation code using VBScript.

Listing 3.23   Validating data to prevent a runtime error.

```
<%
Dim Rate
Dim PeriodicRate
Dim Periods

Function ValidatePeriods
    ValidatePeriods = -1
    If Periods = 0 Then
        ValidatePeriods = 0
    End If
End Function

If Not ValidatePeriods Then
    Response.Write "Please reenter the number of periods."
Else
    PeriodicRate = Rate / Periods
End If
%>
```

Listing 3.23 uses a function, **ValidatePeriods,** to check the value entered by the user. If the user entered 0, **ValidatePeriods** returns 0; otherwise, it returns –1. If the function returns 0, the program message instructs the user to reenter the number of periods.

Sometimes, basic data validation isn't enough error prevention. Other problems can occur and cause your program to produce unexpected results or just crash. You therefore can use VBScript's **On Error Resume Next** statement to deal with potential error situations.

Debugging Active Server Pages

Web pages containing server-side script can be inconvenient—at best—to debug. Until recently, no debugger was available. Without a debugging tool, you have to resort to sending the values of variables and properties to the browser. Often, this approach doesn't provide all the information you need, and it's difficult to trace code execution.

Debugging server-side scripts is now much easier with the Microsoft Script Debugger. At first, you could debug only client script. Beginning with IIS 4, you can now debug server-side script.

Before you can debug server-side script, though, you must create an Active Server application. An application is a virtual directory marked as an application, and all the files and directories in the virtual directory are part of the application. You use the IIS Internet Service Manager program to create applications. You must also use the Internet Service Manager to enable server-side debugging.

How To Create An Active Server Application With IIS

This example shows you how to create an Active Server application using IIS 4 Internet Service Manager. In addition to creating the application, you'll also enable server-side script debugging. This example assumes that a directory named myapp already exists and is a child directory of the IIS root directory \inetpub\wwwroot:

1. From the Start menu, select Programs | Microsoft Internet Information Server | Internet Service Manager. This menu choice might be different on your computer, depending on the installation. Choosing this command runs the Microsoft Management Console (see Figure 3.3).

2. Right-click on myapp, and then select Properties to display the myapp Properties dialog (see Figure 3.4). As you can see, you can set several properties for any given application.

3. To create the application, click on the Create button in the Application Settings section. Then, enter "myapp" in the Name text box. Also, make sure to select Script in the Permissions settings.

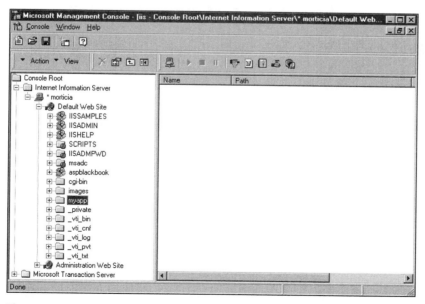

Figure 3.3
The Microsoft Management Console.

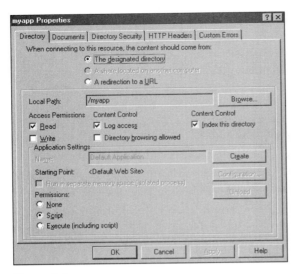

Figure 3.4
IIS's Properties dialog box for myapp.

4. To enable server-side script debugging, click on the Configuration button. This displays the Application Configuration dialog box (see Figure 3.5).

5. Select the App Debugging tab of the Application Configuration dialog box (shown in Figure 3.6), which allows you to set debugging options. Select the Enable ASP Server-side Script Debugging option. This allows IIS to enter the Microsoft Script Debugger

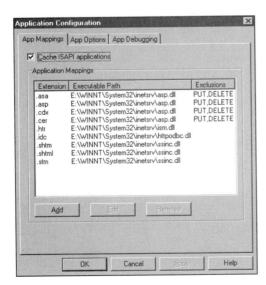

Figure 3.5
The Application Configuration dialog box.

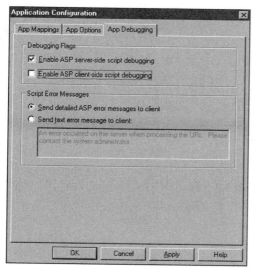

Figure 3.6
Enabling server-side script debugging.

when processing server-side scripts. You'll want to turn off this feature when you place your application into production.

6. Click on Apply, and click on OK to close this dialog. Then, click on Apply, and click on OK to close the myapp Properties dialog.

The application is now created with debugging enabled.

How To Create An Active Server Application Using Personal Web Server

You can use the Microsoft Personal Web Server (PWS) to write Active Server Pages. Most of the functionality of Active Server Pages is available in PWS; however, server-side script debugging isn't. Creating an Active Server application in PWS is very straightforward. This example assumes that a directory named myapp already exists and is a child directory of \inetpub\wwwroot:

1. Start the Personal Web Server Manager by selecting Start | Programs | Microsoft Personal Web Server | Personal Web Manager. You should now see the Personal Web Manager, as shown in Figure 3.7.

2. Click on the Advanced icon to see the options shown in Figure 3.8.

3. Now, click on Add. You will see the Add Directory dialog box, as shown in Figure 3.9.

4. Make sure Read, Execute, and Scripts are checked. Click on the Browse button, and expand the Inetpub directory. Next, expand wwwroot and then select myapp.

5. Click on OK twice, and you're done!

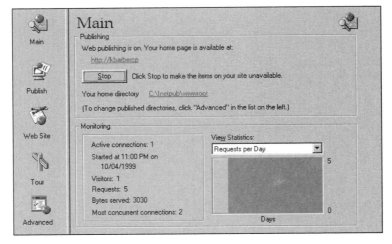

Figure 3.7
Personal Web Manager.

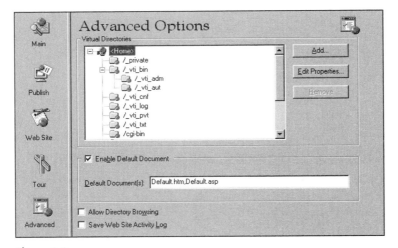

Figure 3.8
Advanced options.

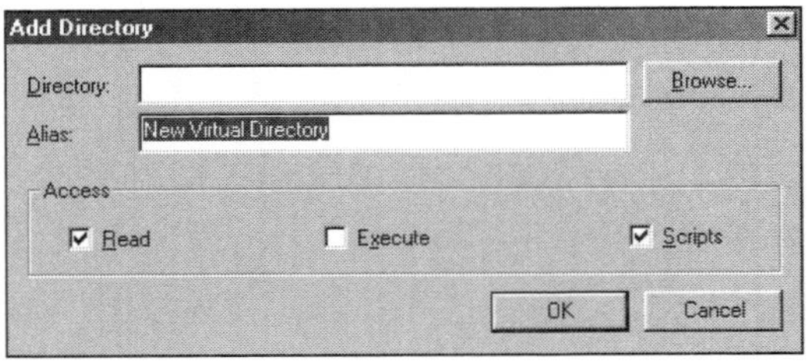

Figure 3.9
The Add Directory dialog box.

How To Debug Server-Side Script Using The Microsoft Script Debugger

Before you can use the Microsoft Script Debugger, you must enable server-side script debugging in the IIS software. Refer to "How To Create An Active Server Application Using Personal Web Server" earlier in this chapter to see how to enable debugging. Additionally, debugging on a remote machine isn't supported; therefore, you must debug on the server locally.

In this example, you'll see how to invoke the debugger, view variable and form element values, set breakpoints, and step through a script.

Starting The Debugger

To start debugging, request the page from the server—in this case Listing 3.1. Then, start the debugger from the Start menu. Figure 3.10 shows the debugger with the Running Documents and Command Window windows open. If these are not already open, you can bring them up by using the View menu.

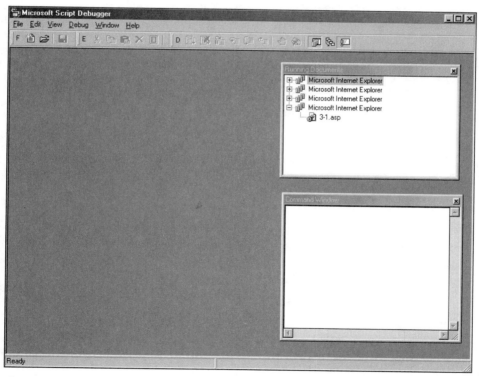

Figure 3.10
The Microsoft Script Debugger.

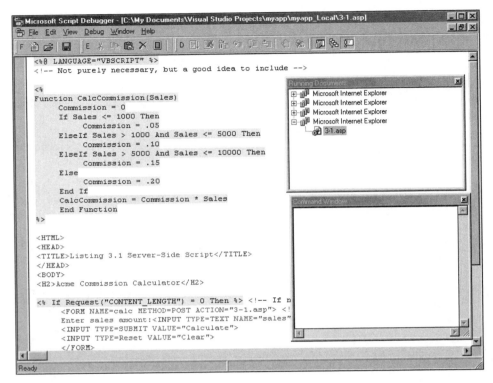

Figure 3.11
Server-side script source listing.

In the Running Documents window, you can see 3-1.asp. Double-clicking on this file displays the script source (see Figure 3.11). The Script Debugger is read-only, so you'll have to use another editor to make changes.

Setting Breakpoints

You can set a breakpoint by placing the cursor on the line where you want it and pressing F9. You can also select the Toggle Breakpoint icon (open hand) on the toolbar. Conversely, you can clear an existing breakpoint by placing the cursor on the line and pressing F9 (or the Toggle Breakpoint icon). You can also select the Clear All Breakpoints icon (open hand with a red X) on the toolbar to remove all breakpoints at once.

Figure 3.12 shows the debugger with a breakpoint set at the line that defines the form. You can tell there is a breakpoint at this line because a solid red circle appears in the left margin, and the line is highlighted red.

To begin debugging, return to the browser and reload the page. When the page reloads, the script executes up to (but not including) the line with the breakpoint. When the debugger encounters the breakpoint, script execution halts, and focus returns to the debugger.

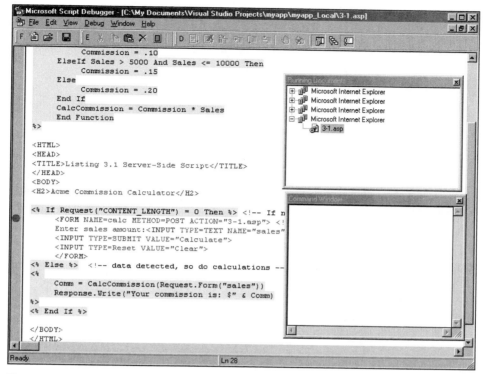

Figure 3.12
Setting breakpoints.

Figure 3.13 shows the script source in the debugger. Now you can see an arrow pointing to the line where the breakpoint stopped the script. This arrow indicates the next line to execute.

You can step through the program line by line using Step Into (F8), Step Over (Shift+F8), and Step Out (Ctrl+Shift+F8), which also have corresponding buttons on the toolbar:

- *Step Into (F8)*—This executes the next line of script. It allows you to follow the script line by line. If the next line is a procedure call, execution is followed into the procedure.
- *Step Over (Shift+F8)*—This steps over procedure calls. The called procedures are executed, but the debugger doesn't step through them.
- *Step Out (Ctrl+Shift+F8)*—This is used when **Step Into** stepped into a procedure and you want to step out of it and proceed to the next line following the procedure call.

If you press F8, the current line executes, and program flow continues on the line following the **End If** statement. Pressing F8 again causes you to return to the browser display. Now, you can enter a sales value and click on the Calculate button. Focus then switches back to the debugger, and the arrow appears on the line following the end of the **CalcCommission** function.

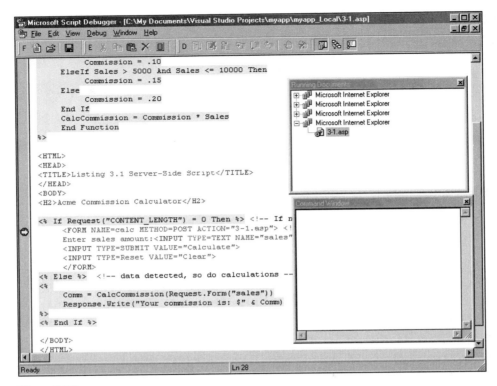

Figure 3.13
The arrow points to the next line to be executed.

You can use the Command Window to examine the value of a variable or property. To do so, click on the Command Window, and enter "?" followed by the item you want to examine. Figure 3.14 shows the value of the **sales** element displayed in the Command Window.

If you continue to press F8, you'll step through the program and see the **CalcCommission** function execute. Eventually, program flow will return you to the browser, where you'll see the result displayed.

You can also change the value of a variable during the debugging session. For example, if you want to change the value of the variable **Sales** to 5000 in the **CalcCommission** function, you can do so by entering the following statement in the Command Window:

```
Sales = 5000
```

The script uses the new value until it finishes executing or something else changes the value.

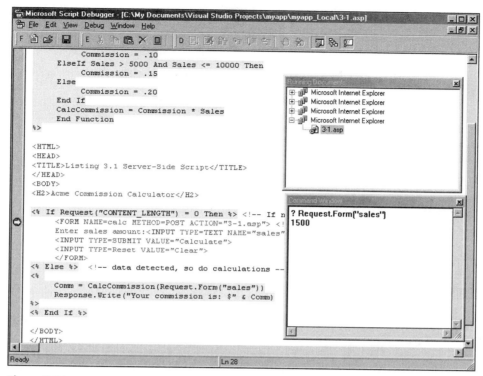

Figure 3.14
The Command Window.

The Microsoft Script Debugger isn't as rich with features as the Visual Basic or Visual C++ debugger, but it's certainly much better than the alternative (embedding output statements in your program, for example).

VBScript Quick Reference

The tables in this section contain a quick reference to the features available in VBScript.

Table 3.13   Array handling quick reference.

Keyword	Description	Syntax
Array	Returns a variant that contains an array.	**x = Array(argument list)**
Dim	Declares a variable and allocates memory.	**Dim x(dimensions)**
Erase	Reinitializes fixed size array, releases dynamic array memory.	**Erase x**
IsArray	Returns a Boolean indicating whether a variable is an array.	**IsArray(x)**

(continued)

Table 3.13   Array handling quick reference *(continued)*.

Keyword	Description	Syntax
LBound	Returns the lower limit of an array dimension (always 0).	**LBound(x[,*dimension*])**
Private	Declares a private variable.	**Private x(*dimensions*)**
Public	Declares a public variable.	**Publix x(*dimensions*)**
Redim	Declares a dynamic array and reallocates memory.	**Redim [Preserve] x(*dimensions*)**
UBound	Returns the upper limit of an array dimension.	**UBound(x,[,*dimension*])**

Table 3.14   Assignment operators quick reference.

Keyword	Description	Syntax
=	Assigns the value of a literal or expression to a variable.	**x = 10**
Set	Assigns an object reference to a variable.	**Set x = *object***

Table 3.15   Comments quick reference.

Keyword	Description	Syntax
'	Begins a comment.	**' *comment***
Rem	Begins a comment line.	**Rem *comment***

Table 3.16   Constants and literals quick reference.

Keyword	Description	Syntax
Empty	Indicates an uninitialized variable.	**x = Empty**
Nothing	Releases an object variable reference.	**Set x = Nothing**
Null	Indicates a variable contains no valid data.	**x = Null**
TRUE, FALSE	Boolean values −1 and 0, respectively.	**x = TRUE**

Table 3.17   Control flow quick reference.

Keyword	Description	Syntax
Do...Loop	Loops while or until a condition is true.	**Do While x < 10 *statements* Loop** **Do *statements* Loop While x < 10** **Do Until x = 10 *statements* Loop** **Do *statements* Loop Until x = 10**
For...Next	Repeats a loop a specified number of times.	**For x = 1 to 10 *statements* Next**
For Each...Next	Repeats statements for each element in an array or collection.	**For Each x in y *statements* Next**
If...Then...Else	Conditionally executes statements.	**If *true* then *statements* Else *statements* End If**

(continued)

Table 3.17   Control flow quick reference (continued).

Keyword	Description	Syntax
Select Case	Executes one of several groups of statements.	Select Case x Case *value1 statements* Case *value2 statements* . . . End Case
While...Wend	Repeats a loop while a condition is true.	While x < 10 *statements* Wend
With	Executes a block of statements on an object.	With *object, statements* End With

Table 3.18   Conversion functions quick reference.

Keyword	Description	Syntax
Abs	Returns the absolute value of a number.	Abs(x)
Asc, AscB, AscW	Returns the ANSI character code of the first letter in a string.	Asc("x")
Chr, Chrb, ChrW	Returns the character for the specified character code.	Chr(65)
CBool	Returns a subtype Boolean.	CBool(x)
CByte	Returns a subtype Byte.	CByte(x)
CCur	Returns a subtype Currency.	CCur(x)
CDbl	Returns a subtype Double.	CDbl(x)
CInt	Returns a subtype Integer.	CInt(x)
CLng	Returns a subtype Long.	CLng(x)
CSng	Returns a subtype Single.	CSng(x)
CStr	Returns a subtype String.	CStr(x)
DateSerial	Returns a subtype Date.	DateSerial(*month, day, year*)
DateValue	Returns a subtype Date.	DateValue(*date string*)
Fix	Returns the integer portion of a number.	Fix(*number*)
Hex	Returns a string representing a hexadecimal value.	Hex(*number*)
Int	Returns the integer portion of a number.	Int(*number*)
Oct	Returns a string representing an octal value.	Oct(*number*)
Round	Returns a number rounded to a specified number of decimal places.	Round(*number* [,*numberofdecimalplaces*])
Sgn	Returns an integer indicating the sign of a number.	Sgn(*number*)
TimeSerial	Returns a subtype Date containing the time.	TimeSerial(*hour, minute, second*)
TimeValue	Returns a subtype Date containing the time.	TimeValue(*time string*)

Table 3.19   Date and time functions quick reference.

Keyword	Description	Syntax
Date	Returns the system date.	**Date**
DateAdd	Returns a date to which a time interval has been added.	**DateAdd(*interval, number, date*)**
DateDiff	Returns the number of intervals between two dates.	**DateDiff(*interval, date1, date2* [,*firstdayofweek*[,*firstweekofyear*]])**
DatePart	Returns the specified part of a date.	**DatePart(*interval, date* [,*firstdayofweek*[,*firstweekofyear*]])**
DateSerial	Returns a subtype Date.	**DateSerial(*month, day, year*)**
DateValue	Returns a subtype Date.	**DateValue(*date string*)**
Day	Returns a number representing the day of the month.	**Day(*date expression*)**
Hour	Returns a number (0 to 23) representing the hour.	**Hour(*time expression*)**
Minute	Returns a number (0 to 59) representing the minute.	**Minute(*time expression*)**
Month	Returns a number representing the month.	**Month(*date expression*)**
Now	Returns the current date and time.	**Now**
Second	Returns a number (0 to 60) representing the second.	**Second(*time expression*)**
Time	Returns a subtype Date containing the system time.	**Time**
TimeSerial	Returns a subtype Date containing the time.	**TimeSerial(*hour, minute, second*)**
TimeValue	Returns a subtype Date containing the time.	**TimeValue(*time string*)**
Weekday	Returns a number representing the day of the week.	**Weekday(*date* [,*firstdayofweek*])**
Year	Returns a number representing the year.	**Year(*date expression*)**

Table 3.20   Declaration statements quick reference.

Keyword	Description	Syntax
Class	Declares and defines a class.	**Class *name, definition* End Class**
Const	Declares a constant.	**Const PI = 3.14159**
Dim	Declares a variable.	**Dim x**
Function	Declares a function.	**[Private] [Public] Function *name*[(*arguments*)] *statements* End Function**
Private	Declares a private variable.	**Private x**
Property Get	Declares the name, properties, and code that form a procedure and returns the property value.	**Property**

(continued)

Table 3.20   Declaration statements quick reference *(continued)*.

Keyword	Description	Syntax
Property Let	Declares the name, properties, and code that form a procedure and assigns the value of a property.	**Property**
Property Set	Declares the name, properties, and code that form a procedure that sets an object reference.	**Property**
Public	Declares a public variable.	**Public x**
ReDim	Declares a dynamic array variable.	**ReDim [Preserve] x(*dimensions*)**
Sub	Declares a subroutine.	**[Private] [Public] Sub *name*[(*arguments*)]**

Table 3.21   Error handling quick reference.

Keyword	Description	Syntax
On Error	Enables an error handling routing.	**On Error Resume Next**
Err	Object containing information about the last error.	**Err[.*property or method*]**

Table 3.22   Input and output functions quick reference.

Keyword	Description	Syntax
InputBox	Displays a prompt and waits for input.	**InputBox(*prompt*[,*title*][,*default*] [,*xpos*][,*ypos*][,*helpfile,context*])**
LoadPicture	Returns a picture object.	**LoadPicture(*picture_name*)**
MsgBox	Displays a message and waits for a button click.	**MsgBox(*prompt*[,*buttons*][,*title*] [,*helpfile, context*])**

Table 3.23   Math functions quick reference.

Keyword	Description	Syntax
Atn	Returns the arctangent of a number.	**Atn(x)**
Cos	Returns the cosine of an angle.	**Cos(x)**
Exp	Returns a number raised to a power.	**Exp(x)**
Log	Returns the logarithm of a number.	**Log(x)**
Randomize	Initializes the random number generator.	**Randomize [*number*]**
Rnd	Returns a random number less than 1.	**Rnd [(*number*)]**
Sin	Returns the sine of an angle.	**Sin(x)**
Sqr	Returns the square root of a number.	**Sqr(x)**
Tan	Returns the tangent of an angle.	**Tan(x)**

Table 3.24 Operators quick reference.

Keyword	Description	Syntax
+	Addition	**a + b**
-	Subtraction	**a - b**
	Negation	**- a**
^	Exponentiation	**a^b**
Mod	Modulus arithmetic	**a Mod b**
*	Multiplication	**a * b**
/	Division	**a / b**
\	Integer division	**a \ b**
&	String concatenation	**a & b**
=	Equality	**a = b**
<>	Inequality	**a <> b**
<	Less than	**a < b**
<=	Less than or equal to	**a <= b**
>	Greater than	**a > b**
>=	Greater than or equal to	**a >= b**
Is	Object reference equivalence	**obj1 Is obj2**
And	Logical conjunction	**a And b**
Or	Logical disjunction	**a Or b**
Xor	Logical exclusion	**a Xor b**
Eqv	Logical equivalence	**a Eqv b**
Imp	Logical implication	**a Imp b**

Table 3.25 Objects and object functions quick reference.

Keyword	Description	Syntax
CreateObject	Returns a reference to an automation object.	**CreateObject(*objectclassname*)**
Dictionary	Stores key/item pairs.	**Set *objvar* = CreateObject("Scripting.Dictionary")**
Err	Contains information about the last error.	**Err[.*property or method*]**
FileSystemObject	Provides access to the file system (server-side only).	**Set *objvar* = CreateObject("Scripting.FileSystemObject")**
GetObject	Returns a reference to an ActiveX object.	**GetObject([*path*] [,*class*])**
TextStream	Provides sequential access to a file.	**TextStream.[*property or method*]**

Table 3.26 Options quick reference.

Keyword	Description	Syntax
Option Explicit	Forces explicit variable declaration.	**Option Explicit**

Table 3.27   Procedures quick reference.

Keyword	Description	Syntax
Call	Calls a procedure.	**Call** *FunctionName*
Function	Declares a function.	**[Private] [Public] Function** *name*[(*arguments*)] *statements* **End Function**
Sub	Declares a subroutine.	**[Private] [Public] Sub** *name*[(*arguments*)]

Table 3.28   Script engine ID functions quick reference.

Keyword	Description	Syntax
ScriptEngine	Returns a string describing the scripting language in use.	**ScriptEngine**
ScriptEngineBuildVersion	Returns the build number.	**ScriptEngineBuildNumber**
ScriptEngineMajorVersion	Returns the major version number.	**ScriptEngineMajorVersion**
ScriptEngineMinorVersion	Returns the minor version number.	**ScriptEngineMinorVersion**

Table 3.29   String functions quick reference.

Keyword	Description	Syntax
Asc	Returns the ANSI character code of the first letter in a string.	**Asc(***char***)**
AscB	Used with byte data, returns the first byte.	**AscB(***string***)**
AscW	Returns the Unicode (wide) character code.	**AscW(***char***)**
Chr	Returns the character for the specified character code.	**Chr(***code***)**
ChrB	Returns a byte instead of a character, which might be one or two bytes.	**ChrB(***code***)**
ChrW	Accepts a Unicode (wide) character code, returns a char.	**ChrW(***code***)**
Filter	Returns a filtered array containing a subset of a string array.	**Filter(***inputstrings, value*[,*include*[,*compare*]]**)**
FormatCurrency	Returns a string formatted as a currency value.	**FormatCurrency(***string* [,*decimalplaces*[,*inclleadingzero* [,*useparenthesis*[,*groupdigits*]]]]**)**
FormatDateTime	Returns a string formatted as a date or time value.	**FormatDateTime(***date*[,*format*]**)**
FormatNumber	Returns a string formatted as a number.	**FormatNumber(***string* [,*decimalplaces*[,*inclleadingzero* [,*useparenthesis*[,*groupdigits*]]]]**)**

(continued)

Table 3.29   String functions quick reference *(continued)*.

Keyword	Description	Syntax
FormatPercent	Returns a string formatted as a percentage.	**FormatPercent(***string* **[,***decimalplaces***[,***inclleadingzero* **[,***useparenthesis***[,***groupdigits***]]]])**
Instr	Returns the position of the first occurrence of one string in another.	**Instr([***start,***]***string1,string2* **[,***compare***])**
InstrB	Same as **Instr** but uses byte data. Returns the byte position.	
InstrRev	Returns the position of the first occurrence of one string in another, beginning from the end.	**InstrRev(***string1, string2***l [,***start***[,***compare***]])**
Join	Returns a string constructed by joining substrings in an array.	**Join(***list***[,***delimiter***])**
Len, LenB	Returns the number of characters in a string or the number of bytes required to store a variable.	**Len(***string or variable***)**
LCase	Returns a string that has been converted to lowercase.	**LCase(***string***)**
Left, LeftB	Returns the specified number of characters beginning from the left.	**Left(***string, number***)**
LTrim	Returns a string without leading spaces.	**LTrim(***string***)**
Mid, MidB	Returns the specified number of characters.	**Mid(***string, start***[,***number***])**
Replace	Returns a string in which a specified substring has been replaced a specified number of times.	**Replace(***string,stringtoreplace, replacewith***[,***start***[,***count* **[,***compare***]]])**
Right, RightB	Returns the specified number of characters beginning from the right.	**Right(***string, number***)**
RTrim	Returns a string without trailing spaces.	**RTrim(***string***)**
Space	Returns a string consisting of the specified number of spaces.	**Space(***number***)**
Split	Returns an array containing the specified number of substrings.	**Split(***string***[,***delimiter***[,***count* **[,***compare***]]])**
StrComp	Returns a value indicating the result of a string comparison.	**StrComp(***string1,string2***[,***compare***])**
String	Returns a character string of a specified character of the length specified.	**String(***number,character***)**
StrReverse	Returns a reversed string.	**StrReverse(***string***)**
Trim	Returns a string without leading or trailing spaces.	**Trim(***string***)**
UCase	Returns a string that has been converted to uppercase.	**UCase(***string***)**

Table 3.30   Variant functions quick reference.

Keyword	Description	Syntax
IsArray	Boolean indicating whether a variable is an array.	**IsArray(x)**
IsDate	Boolean indicating whether a variable can be converted to a date.	**IsDate(x)**
IsEmpty	Boolean indicating whether a variable has been initialized.	**IsEmpty(x)**
IsNull	Boolean indicating whether a variable is null.	**IsNull(x)**
IsNumeric	Boolean indicating whether a variable can be evaluated as a number.	**IsNumeric(x)**
IsObject	Boolean indicating whether a variable references an OLE Automation object.	**IsObject(x)**
TypeName	String that provides subtype information.	**TypeName(x)**
VarType()	Value indicating the variant subtype.	**VarType(x)**

Chapter 4
Server-Side Scripting In JavaScript

Kim Barber

J avaScript, which is an *object-based* scripting language developed
by Netscape, allows you to add features to Web pages and write
programs that reside inside Web pages. Syntactically, it is similar
to Java but is not a subset of it. JavaScript has a rich feature set
that provides a very good environment for developing client and
server applications and is well suited for quick development and
easy maintenance of relatively small programs, such as those typically found in Web applications.

It also is an interpreted language, so the host environment (the
Web server) must have a JavaScript scripting engine to execute
the code. Both Internet Information Server (IIS) and Personal
Web Server (PWS) natively support JavaScript.

This chapter covers most of JavaScript's language details. You'll
find a couple of different implementations of JavaScript, so let's
address this issue before jumping into the code.

JavaScript, JScript, ECMAScript?

Netscape developed JavaScript, and, not surprisingly, Microsoft
developed its own implementation of the language, called JScript.
As you might guess, the two implementations share many common features, but each has additional features that are intended
to "enhance" the language. Although these enhancements are
great for marketing, they can be a source of frustration for developers who must create Web pages that can be displayed in the
most popular browsers.

To make the language compatible across multiple platforms, Netscape, Microsoft, and other vendors worked with the European Computer Manufacturers Association (ECMA) to develop a standard scripting language for the Internet. The specification uses JavaScript as its basis and is known as ECMA-262, or ECMAScript. The ECMA-262 specification is available at **www.ecma.ch/stand/ecma-262.htm**. Documentation for the Microsoft and Netscape versions is available on each company's Web site.

Although most of this chapter focuses on the features of the language supported by the ECMA-262 standard, mention is made of nonstandard features as well.

A Classic Programming Example

Before going any further, let's take a look at a simple example of a JavaScript program. You saw an example of the classic "Hello World" program in VBScript in Chapter 3. Listing 4.1 shows what it looks like in JavaScript.

Listing 4.1 Simple JavaScript.

```
<HTML>
<HEAD>
<TITLE>Hello World</TITLE>
<%@ LANGUAGE="JavaScript" %>
<%
    Response.Write("Hello World");
%>
</HEAD>
<BODY>
</BODY>
</HTML>
```

As you can see, Listing 4.1 is a fairly typical HTML file. In this example, the script resides in the **<HEAD>** section. Placing it in this section isn't a requirement, though. Because the page includes only server-side script, you can also write it as follows:

```
<%@ LANGUAGE="JavaScript" %>
<% Response.Write("Hello World"); %>
```

That's all that would be necessary.

You can place JavaScript code practically anywhere in an HTML document, although it is often placed in the **<HEAD>** section. Your ASP files sometimes won't even include **<HEAD>** and **<BODY>** sections, however. Rather, they will just include script and possibly some HTML mixed in.

How To Use The <% %> Delimiters

Server-side script is often embedded between <% and %> delimiters. The scripting engine processes script embedded in these delimiters on the server. You can't nest script delimiters inside each other, but you can use as many separate pairs of the tags as you need. You can place single statements as well as groups of statements within them.

The following is an example of a single JavaScript statement in delimiters:

```
<% fontsize = 5; %>
```

As you can see, this example is just a typical JavaScript statement, except that the delimiters tell the server to execute the code.

The following example shows more than one statement inside a single set of delimiters:

```
<%
    var Commission, Sales;
    Commission = .05;
    Sales = 10000;
    if (Sales > 5000)
    Commission = .10;
%>
```

The equal sign (=) is used to output the value of an expression. The following statement places the value of the variable **Commission** into the HTML output stream:

```
<% =Commission %>
```

Because you can use as many script delimiters as you need, you can easily mix server-side script and HTML. Listing 4.2 mixes the two to output text in font sizes from 1 through 7.

Listing 4.2   Mixing server-side script and HTML.
```
<%@ LANGUAGE="JavaScript" %>
<% var fontsize; %>
<% for (fontsize=1; fontsize<=7; fontsize++) { %>

    <FONT SIZE=<% =fontsize %>>
    Server-side script!<BR>
    </FONT>
<% } %>

<HTML>
<HEAD>
<TITLE>Listing 4.2 Server-Side Scripting</TITLE>
```

```
</HEAD>
<BODY>

</BODY>
</HTML>
```

Figure 4.1 shows the result of viewing this page in Internet Explorer.

How To Use The **<SCRIPT>** Delimiter

As with VBScript, you can also embed server-side script in the **<SCRIPT>** tag. When you use the **<SCRIPT>** tag, you must include the **RUNAT** attribute, which you set to **Server**. The following example uses the **<SCRIPT>** tag to do the same as Listing 4.1.

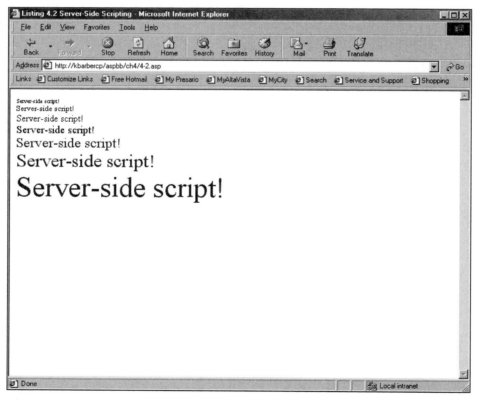

Figure 4.1
The script from Listing 4.2 displayed in the browser.

```
<SCRIPT LANGUAGE=JavaScript RUNAT=Server>

for (fontsize = 1; fontsize <= 7; fontsize++) {
    response.write("<FONT SIZE=" + fontsize + ">")
    response.write("Server-side script!<BR></FONT>")
}
</SCRIPT>
<HTML>
<HEAD>
<TITLE>Using the SCRIPT Tag</TITLE>
</HEAD>
<BODY>

</BODY>
</HTML>
```

The **<SCRIPT>** tag isn't the only difference in this example. Notice that the script and HTML aren't mixed as they were in the previous example. Instead, the code places HTML in the output stream using the **response** object, which is an intrinsic Active Server component that allows you to send output to the client. In this example, it's functionally equivalent to the = character that Listing 4.1 uses. You'll learn more about the **response** object in Chapter 5.

Code in delimiters and the **<SCRIPT>** tag executes immediately, unless the code is within a procedure body (for example, a **SUB** or a **FUNCTION**).

How To Specify The Default Language

VBScript is the default language for server-side script. Because you are using JavaScript, you must specify a new default language. You can easily set the default language for a page to a different language, like this:

```
<%@ LANGUAGE="JavaScript" %>
```

You are not allowed to place any other elements within this delimiter pair. Also, you must insert a space between the @ character and **LANGUAGE**.

The Web site administrator can set the default language on a more permanent basis by using the Microsoft Management Console to alter the properties for the application. Because every application can have its own default language, it is a good idea to explicitly specify the language your script expects using the @ command mentioned earlier. That way, your script will work as expected even if you move it between dissimilar projects.

Language Details

The following sections of this chapter focus on many of the details of JavaScript. If you have experience using C, C++, or Java, you'll be familiar with much of this discussion. The following are a couple of useful tidbits of information:

♦ JavaScript is case sensitive. This is quite different from VBScript (covered in Chapter 3), which is not case sensitive.

♦ The use of semicolons at the ends of lines is optional but recommended.

Variables

JavaScript variables are the same as variables in other languages. Simply stated, they are placeholders in memory where data is stored. A variable name is assigned to the place-holder, and the data stored there is referenced by the name.

JavaScript variable names must comply with a few simple rules:

♦ The first letter must be a character, an underscore (_), or a dollar sign ($).

♦ The name can't be a reserved word.

♦ The name can't contain certain characters, such as a period.

As I mentioned earlier, JavaScript is case sensitive. This point is important to remember because, to JavaScript, **Grossincome** and **GrossIncome** are different variables.

Declaring Variables

Variables are declared either *implicitly* or *explicitly*. You declare variables explicitly by using the **var** statement like this:

```
var Hours;
```

You also can declare multiple variables in the same statement by separating the variable names with a comma, as shown here:

```
var Hours, Wage;
```

Hours and **Wage** are now declared but are *undefined*. Variables are undefined until a value has been assigned. In fact, JavaScript has a data type, Undefined, that it gives to declared but uninitialized variables. A variable is initialized when a value is assigned:

```
Hours = 40;
Wage = 23.50;
```

Simply using a new variable declares it implicitly. The following statement implicitly declares the variable **GrossIncome**:

```
GrossIncome = Hours * Wage;
```

Usually, you can declare variables either implicitly or explicitly. However, it is considered good programming practice to declare variables explicitly using the **var** keyword. Also, getting into the habit of explicitly declaring variables generally improves the readability of the program. You need to remember only one rule: Variables that are local to a function must be declared explicitly with the **var** statement.

Variable Scope And Lifetime

Variable *scope* refers to where within a script a variable is available. JavaScript variables have two levels of scope: *global* and *local*. Global variables are declared outside functions and are available throughout the script. Also, variables declared inside functions without using the **var** statement are global. Local variables are declared inside functions using the **var** statement and are visible only within the function in which they are declared.

Variable *lifetime* refers to the amount of time a variable exists. Global variables exist from the time they are declared until the script finishes running. Local variables exist from the time they are declared until the function finishes executing.

Data Types

JavaScript is a *loosely typed* language; that is, you don't specify the data type in a variable declaration as you do in Java and C++. You can store values of any type in a variable, and JavaScript will handle it appropriately. If a number is placed in the variable, it is treated as a number. If a string is stored, it is treated as a string. JavaScript is also clever enough to automatically convert data when an expression contains both numbers and strings. In this case, JavaScript temporarily converts the numeric values to strings in memory:

```
var a_string = "150", result;
result = a_string * 2;          // result = 300
```

The first statement defines a string variable containing the value "150". The second statement multiplies the string value by 2. To perform this task, JavaScript temporarily converts the string in memory to a number and then performs the operation. The numeric result is placed in **result**. String concatenation is another good example of JavaScript's capability to convert data types automatically:

```
var a_number = 456, a_string = "123", result;
result = a_string + a_number;   // result = "123456"
```

JavaScript uses the + operator for both addition and string concatenation. Because the preceding statement "adds" a number to a string, JavaScript assumes that you want to perform a concatenation operation, so it converts **a_number** temporarily to a string and stores the string result in **result**.

JavaScript is factory equipped with six data types:

♦ *string*—This data type is a sequence of characters enclosed in single or double quotation marks.

♦ *number*—JavaScript supports integer and floating-point numbers. Numbers are represented as base 10 (decimal), base 8 (octal), or base 16 (hexadecimal). Octal numbers begin with 0 and contain the digits 0 through 7. Hexadecimal numbers begin with 0x and contain the digits 0 through 9 and the characters A through F. Octal and hexadecimal numbers can be negative but can't contain a decimal point. Exponential numbers are indicated with the letter *e* or *E* in decimal and octal numbers.

♦ *boolean*—This data type contains **true** or **false**, which equals 1 or 0, respectively.

♦ *object*—This data type is a collection of properties and methods.

♦ *null*—This data type indicates no value.

♦ *undefined*—When you declare a variable but don't provide a value for it, it uses the *undefined* value.

JavaScript has four primitive types: number, boolean, string, and function. These are not called primitive types because they have a Neanderthal-like appearance and behavior. Instead, they are called primitives because they contain a single value that is easily manipulated by the interpreter. The interpreter manipulates number and boolean types *by value* and string and function types *by reference*. Accessing data by value and by reference is covered later in this chapter.

JavaScript also has a number of built-in objects (covered in the next section). Object types are more sophisticated in that they contain an arbitrary number of properties and methods. Because object types vary in size, they are not as easily manipulated by the interpreter as primitives are. Therefore, they are manipulated by *reference*. You might be wondering why strings and functions are considered primitives because they do not have a fixed size. JavaScript views them as primitives because they are not objects.

Wrapper Objects

So, what's the difference between a primitive and an object? Objects can have properties and methods. However, JavaScript has a corresponding object type for each primitive type. Therefore, JavaScript has **number, boolean, string**, and **function** objects. These objects contain the same primitive data item, as well as properties and methods to operate on the data item, and are used as *wrapper objects* around the primitive types.

Listing 4.3 shows how wrapper objects give primitive types object-like behavior.

Listing 4.3   A JavaScript wrapper object in action.

```
<%@ LANGUAGE="JavaScript" %>
<%
var a_string, new_string;
var len;

a_string = "JavaScript is cool!";

new_string = a_string.toUpperCase();  // new_string = JAVASCRIPT IS COOL!
a_string.toUpperCase();               // a_string still = JavaScript is cool!

len = a_string.length;                // len = 16

%>
```

Listing 4.3 declares three variables and assigns **a_string** a string value. The **String** object's method **toUpperCase** returns a string converted to all uppercase characters. The statement

```
new_string = a_string.toUpperCase();
```

uses **a_string** in an object context, applies the **toUpperCase** method to the value stored in the variable, and stores the resulting uppercase string in **new_string**. The next statement retrieves the **String** object's **length** property and places it in **len**.

JavaScript automatically creates a temporary wrapper object when a primitive type is used as an object. In the preceding example, the object created is a string wrapper that contains the value of the simple variable as well as the **String** object's properties and methods. The value of the original variable is not affected, but you have access to the functionality of the object.

The reverse is also true. JavaScript converts the value of objects to their corresponding primitive type when they are used as primitives, as in the following statements:

```
var a_string;
var a_string_obj = new String("JavaScript is ");
a_string = a_string_obj + "Cool!";
```

This example declares a string object and assigns it a value. The last statement performs string concatenation using the **String** object and the string primitive.

JavaScript's capability to treat primitives as objects is convenient and frequently more efficient than using an object type. The next section covers the built-in JavaScript objects, several of which have a corresponding primitive type.

JavaScript Objects

JavaScript is an object-based language, so it is not surprising that JavaScript supplies several built-in objects in addition to the primitive types. JavaScript has objects that conform to the ECMA-262 standard and objects that are specific to Microsoft's implementation. Netscape's JavaScript also has objects specific to its implementation.

The following sections describe JavaScript objects that conform to the ECMA-262 standard. Microsoft's implementation offers several additional objects to provide drive and file access (server-side scripting only) and other special-purpose functions.

It is also easy to create your own objects to provide needed functionality. You'll see how to roll your own objects and to extend the built-in objects in Chapter 10.

JavaScript Arrays And The **Array** Object

An *array* stores a collection of related data items and can hold multiple values. The **Array** object provides support for arrays in JavaScript. Because JavaScript is loosely typed, arrays can hold any type of data.

You use the **var** keyword to declare an array. The following statement declares an array variable, **SalesRegion**, which will store sales data for four regions:

```
var SalesRegion = new Array(3);
```

The operator **new** creates a new object, in this case an **Array** object. The value in parentheses specifies the array size. This statement declares an array that can contain four items, or *array elements*. Arrays in JavaScript are *zero-based*, which means that the first element in the array is element 0 (zero). Therefore, the number of array elements that the array can contain is the number in parentheses plus 1. The element number is referred to as the array *index*.

Specifying the element number in brackets ([]) references individual elements in an array. A string is stored in the first array element as follows:

```
SalesRegion[0] = "East";
```

You can also declare an array without specifying an initial size like this:

```
var SalesRegion = new Array();
```

In this example, **SalesRegion** has a size of zero, but you can still assign values to any array element, and JavaScript will automatically adjust the size (array size is stored in the **length** property). The statement

```
SalesRegion[0] = "East";
```

assigns a value to the first array element and adjusts the **length** property to 1. JavaScript arrays are *sparse*, meaning that array indices need not be contiguous. Assuming that the next assignment statement is

```
SalesRegion[3] = "South";
```

length is adjusted to 4. The **length** property does not equal the number of elements in the array but instead is equal to 1 plus the highest element defined in the array. What about elements 1 and 2? They are still available, but they are undefined at this time.

You initialize arrays during declaration by specifying the values in parentheses instead of specifying the array size. The **length** property is then determined on the basis of the number of values provided. The following declaration initializes the **SalesRegion** array:

```
var SalesRegion = new Array("East", "West", "North", "South");
```

Arrays And Objects

Arrays and objects are the same thing in JavaScript. You can prove this fact by using the **typeof** operator:

```
Response.Write (typeof(SalesRegion));
```

The **typeof** operator returns the type of the expression in parentheses and returns **object** for arrays as well as objects.

Because an array is an object, it can have properties. This means that you can use nonnumeric indexes as properties. Arrays are also indexed with property names. Continuing with the **SalesRegion** example, consider these statements:

```
var SalesRegion = new Array();
SalesRegion.East = 200;
SalesRegion.West = 350;
SalesRegion.North = 180;
SalesRegion.South = 225;
```

This sequence declares the array, gives it properties indicating the various regions, and assigns values to each property. These statements reference the array properties by using dot notation. You can also access named elements of an array by placing the name string in brackets. This notation is similar to using associative arrays in languages such as AWK and Perl:

```
SalesRegion["East"] = 200;
```

However, you can't reference properties with a numerical index. The statement

```
SalesVol = SalesRegion[0];
```

does not assign a value to **SalesVol** because **SalesRegion[0]** is undefined.

You'll notice a subtle but important difference between using dot notation and using property names in brackets. The property name is an identifier when dot notation is used and as such must be defined in advance. When used in brackets, the property name is a string. Strings can be manipulated at runtime, so property names can be defined dynamically while the program is executing. You have already seen that array elements can be added at any time and that the size of the array is automatically adjusted. This, coupled with the ability to generate property names at runtime, gives the user a very flexible and powerful capability. Objects used in this manner are called *associative arrays*. Using these arrays, you can assign values to arbitrary strings dynamically. This feature is very powerful. For example, you could define a phone book array that easily transforms names into phone numbers.

Multidimensional Arrays

JavaScript does not provide direct support for multidimensional arrays. However, you can simulate multidimensional arrays by defining arrays of arrays. Listing 4.4 defines an array of arrays to contain the following information on each of the four sales regions: region name, city, state, and sales volume.

Listing 4.4   Using an array of arrays to simulate multidimensional arrays.
```
<%@ LANGUAGE="JavaScript" %>
<%
var SalesRegion = new Array();
var i, j;

    for (i = 0; i <= 3; i++)
      SalesRegion[i] = new Array();

    SalesRegion[0][0] = "East";
    SalesRegion[0][1] = "New York";
    SalesRegion[0][2] = "NY";
    SalesRegion[0][3] = 200;

    SalesRegion[1][0] = "West";
    SalesRegion[1][1] = "Los Angeles";
    SalesRegion[1][2] = "CA";
    SalesRegion[1][3] = 350;

    // and so on
%>
```

The **for** statement is a loop structure (covered later in this chapter), and you'll be familiar with it if you have experience with C, C++, or Java. The **for** loop is used here to iterate through the **SalesRegion** array and assign an **Array** object to each array element.

The statement

```
SalesRegion[0][0] = "East";
```

assigns the region name to the first element of the first **SalesRegion** array element. The next three statements assign the city, state, and sales volume values to the remaining three elements of the first **SalesRegion** array element. These steps are repeated for the rest of the **SalesRegion** array.

You can also implement this example using an associative array of associative arrays. Listing 4.5 uses associative arrays this way to store the sales region information.

Listing 4.5   Using an associative array of associative arrays.

```
<%@ LANGUAGE="JavaScript" %>
<%
var SalesRegion = new Array();
var SalesVol;

   SalesRegion.East = new Array();
   SalesRegion.East.City = "New York";
   SalesRegion.East.State = "NY";
   SalesRegion.East.Vol = 200;

   SalesRegion.West = new Array();
   SalesRegion.West.City = "Los Angeles";
   SalesRegion.West.State = "CA";
   SalesRegion.West.Vol = 350;

   // and so on
%>
```

Listing 4.5 defines elements of the **SalesRegion** array using property identifiers. The region property of each array is given the name of the region and assigned an array. Each region's array is then given properties for the various pieces of information that will be stored, and each property is assigned a value. After initializing the properties, you could use the statement

```
SalesVol = SalesRegion.West.Vol;
```

to retrieve the value of the **SalesRegion.West.Vol** property and place it in **SalesVol**.

Listing 4.6 is another example of the flexibility of associative arrays. This example uses an array of associative arrays.

Listing 4.6   Using an array of associative arrays.

```
<%@ LANGUAGE="JavaScript" %>
<%
var SalesRegion = new Array();
var SalesVol;
var i;

   for (i = 0; i <= 3; i++)
     SalesRegion[i] = new Array();

   SalesRegion[0]["Region"] = "East"
   SalesRegion[0]["City"] = "New York";
   SalesRegion[0]["State"] = "NY";
   SalesRegion[0]["Vol"] = 200;

   SalesRegion[1]["Region"] = "West";
   SalesRegion[1]["City"] = "Los Angeles";
   SalesRegion[1]["State"] = "CA";
   SalesRegion[1]["Vol"] = 350;

   // and so on
   SalesVol = SalesRegion[0].Vol;
   SalesVol = SalesRegion[1]["Vol"];
%>
```

Another way to simulate multidimensional arrays is to build composite string keys using a character as a separator. Consider this example:

```
ary["10:3"]=0
```

This statement doesn't really place anything on the tenth row and third column; rather it simply associates a value with the string "10:3". However, if your program consistently uses this notation, it appears to create a two-dimensional array. Of course, you could easily add even more dimensions using the same technique.

Array Object Properties

Table 4.1 shows the **Array** object's properties.

Table 4.1   The Array object properties.

Property	Description	Syntax
constructor	Specifies the object's constructor function	arr.constructor;
length	Indicates the highest element in the array	arr.length;
prototype	Contains a reference to the object's prototype	arr.prototype;

The **constructor** property returns the function that created the object. This property is a member of every object that has a *prototype*, which is an object that defines the properties, methods, and constants for a class of objects. You use the **constructor** property as follows:

```
var Greeting = new String("Hello World!");
var Result = Greeting.constructor;
if (Result == String)
   Response.Write("It's a String!");
```

The **length** property returns a value equal to 1 plus the highest element in the array. It does not always mean the number of elements in the array because array elements are not always contiguous. The following statement retrieves the **length** property:

```
var SalesRegion("East", "West", "North", "South");
var UBound = SalesRegion.length;      // UBound equals 4
```

The **length** property is also used to set the highest element in the array. If the new value is less than the previous value, the array is truncated, and data in elements higher than the previous value is lost. If the new value is greater than the previous value, the array expands, and the new elements are undefined. For example, the statement

```
SalesRegion.length = 6;
```

adds two elements to the **SalesRegion** array.

You use the **prototype** property to define the properties, methods, and constants for a class of objects. All intrinsic JavaScript objects have a **prototype** property. New instances of the object inherit the features of the object. This property extends the functionality of an existing class of objects within the scope of the current script. The **prototype** property adds a **count** method to the **Array** object. The **count** method returns the number of elements that actually are in an array.

Array Object's Methods

Table 4.2 shows the **Array** object's methods.

Table 4.2   The Array object's methods.

Method	Description	Syntax
concat	Combines two arrays	**arr3 = arr1.concat(arr3);**
join	Converts array elements to a string	**arr2 = arr1.join(*separator*);**
reverse	Reverses the array elements	**arr.reverse();**
slice	Returns a section of the array	**arr2 = arr1.slice(*start*[,*stop*]);**
sort	Sorts the array elements	**arr.sort([*compare function*]);**
toString	Returns a comma-separated string of the array elements	**arr2 = arr1.toString();**
valueOf	Returns a comma-separated string of the array elements	**arr2 = arr1.valueOf();**

The **concat** method combines two arrays and returns a new array containing the two original ones. The method doesn't change the original arrays unless you name one of them on the left side of the assignment operator:

```
var SalesRegion = new Array("East", "West", "North", "South");
var NewRegion = new Array("Hawaii", "Alaska");
var AllRegions = SalesRegion.concat(NewRegion);
```

The **join** method converts array elements to a string and joins them. You pass a *separator* argument to specify the character used between the elements. If you omit the separator argument, the method uses a comma to separate the elements. The statements

```
var arr1 = new Array("1", "2", "3");
var arr2 = arr1.join("");
```

set **arr2** to the string "123".

The **reverse** method reverses the elements of the array. If the array is sparse, the method creates elements to fill in the missing elements:

```
var arr1 = new Array("a", "b", "c");
arr1.reverse();
```

The **slice** method returns a section of the array. This method takes an argument to specify a zero-based starting position and optionally takes a zero-based ending position. If you omit the starting position, **slice** copies to the end of the array. For example, imagine that you have this declaration

```
var arr1 = new Array("a", "b", "c", "d", "e", "f");
```

followed (eventually) by this statement:

```
arr2 = arr1.slice(1);
```

The result will be to copy from the second element of **arr1** to the end of the array. The statement

```
arr2 = arr1.slice(1, 4);
```

copies from the second element up to (but not including) the fourth element. If a negative value is specified for the starting position, that value is used as an offset from the end.

The **sort** method sorts the array elements. The **sort** method takes an optional argument of type **function** to specify the sort order. The method sorts the array in ascending order if the argument is omitted. The following statements define and sort an array in ascending order:

```
var arr1 = new Array("a", "f", "e", "b", "d", "c");
arr1.sort();
```

To sort the array in a different order, you can provide a comparison function as an argument. The comparison function takes two arguments and returns a value as follows:

♦ <0—The first argument is less than the second argument.

♦ 0—Both arguments are equivalent.

♦ >0—The first argument is greater than the second argument.

Listing 4.7 first sorts an array in ascending order and then sorts it in descending order using the function **compare** to compare the arguments.

Listing 4.7   Using the sort method.

```
<%@ LANGUAGE="JavaScript" %>
<%
var arr1 = new Array(12, 51, 32, 10, 16);

    function compare(a,b) {
         return b - a;
    }
    arr1.sort();            // sort ascending
    arr1.sort(compare);     // sort descending
%>
```

The toString method returns a comma-separated string type containing the array elements:

```
var arr1 = new Array("a", "f", "e", "b", "d", "c");
var arr2 = arr1.toString();
```

The **valueOf** method returns a comma-separated **string** object containing the array elements. The method converts the array elements to strings and concatenates them:

```
var arr1 = new Array(1,4,3,6,7);
var arr2 = arr1.valueOf();
```

The **valueOf** method acts like the **toString** method, except it returns an object.

The **Boolean** Object

The **Boolean** object creates a Boolean value and is also the wrapper object for the boolean primitive type. It is useful for converting non-Boolean values to Boolean values. The statement

```
var bln = new Boolean(true);
```

creates a **Boolean** object with a value of **true**. If the value is not specified, it is **false**.

Boolean Object Properties

Table 4.3 shows the **Boolean** object's properties.

Boolean Object Methods

Table 4.4 shows the **Boolean** object's methods.

The **Date** Object

The **Date** object provides several functions for getting and setting date and time values. You define a **Date** object like this:

```
var theDate = new Date();
```

Here, the **Date** object supplies the current date and time, and the script stores it in **theDate**. The declaration

```
var theDate = new Date("Nov 23, 1997 22:49:00");
```

specifies a date string to initialize **theDate**. You can also specify a number, which represents the number of milliseconds since January 1, 1970:

```
var theDate = new Date(880000000000);
```

The preceding statement initializes **theDate** to "Wed Nov 19 23:26:40 Eastern Standard Time 1997". You can also use this format:

```
var theDate = new Date(year, month, date[, hour[, minute[, second[,ms]]]])
```

Table 4.5 shows the descriptions for the arguments used in the preceding syntax.

The **Date** object is also used as a function. It returns the current date and time:

```
var theDate = Date();
```

Table 4.3   The Boolean object's properties.

Property	Description	Syntax
constructor	Specifies the object's constructor function	bln.constructor;
prototype	Contains a reference to the object's prototype	bln.prototype;

Table 4.4   The Boolean object's methods.

Method	Description	Syntax
toString	Returns a string representation	bln.toString();
valueOf	Returns a string representation	bln.valueOf();

Table 4.5   Date object constructor optional arguments.

Argument	Description
year	The year in the format 1999
month	The month expressed as an integer from 0 to 11
date	The date expressed as an integer from 1 to 31
hour	The hour expressed as an integer from 0 to 23
minute	The minutes expressed as an integer from 0 to 59
second	The seconds expressed as an integer from 0 to 59
ms	The milliseconds expressed as an integer from 0 to 999

What Is UTC?

Coordinated Universal Time (UTC) refers to the time as set by the World Time Standard and is, for practical purposes, equivalent to Greenwich Mean Time (GMT). Many of the **Date** object methods set or return time values in UTC.

You might wonder why the acronym is *UTC* instead of *CUT*. The International Telecommunications Union selected this acronym as a compromise because English-speaking groups wanted to use *CUT*, but French-speaking groups wanted to use *TUC* to reflect the French definition.

Date Object Properties

The **Date** object has the **constructor** and **prototype** properties, which are used as described earlier in Table 4.1.

Date Object Methods

The **Date** object has several methods for getting and setting date and time values. Table 4.6 shows descriptions of the available methods.

Table 4.6   Date object methods.

Method	Description	Syntax
getDate	Returns the day of the month (1 to 31)	theDate.getDate();
getDay	Returns the day of the week (0 to 6)	theDate.getDay();
getFullYear	Returns the year	theDate.getFullYear();
getHours	Returns the hours (0 to 23)	theDate.getHours();
getMilliseconds	Returns the milliseconds past the second (0 to 999)	theDate.getMilliseconds();
getMinutes	Returns the minutes past the hour (0 to 59)	theDate.getMinutes();
getMonth	Returns the month (0 to 11)	theDate.getMonth();
getSeconds	Returns the seconds past the minute (0 to 59)	theDate.getSeconds();

(continued)

Table 4.6 Date object methods *(continued)*.

Method	Description	Syntax
getTime	Returns the time in milliseconds since midnight January 1, 1970	theDate.getTime();
getTimezoneOffset	Returns the difference in minutes between Coordinated Universal Time (UTC) and time on the host computer	theDate.getTimezoneOffset();
getUTCDate	Returns the UTC day of the month (1 to 31)	theDate.getUTCDate();
getUTCDay	Returns the UTC day of the week (0 to 6)	theDate.getUTCDay();
getUTCFullYear	Returns the UTC year	theDate.getUTCFullYear();
getUTCHours	Returns UTC hours (0 to 23)	theDate.getUTCHours();
getUTCMilliseconds	Returns the number of milliseconds past the second according to UTC (0 to 999)	theDate.getUTCMilliseconds();
getUTCMinutes	Returns the number of minutes past the hour according to UTC (0 to 59)	theDate.getUTCMinutes();
getUTCMonth	Returns the UTC month (0 to 11)	theDate.getUTCMonth();
getUTCSeconds	Returns the number of seconds past the minute according to UTC (0 to 59)	theDate.getUTCSeconds();
getVarDate	Returns the **VT_DATE***	theDate.getVarDate();
getYear	Returns the years past 1900	theDate.getYear();
setDate	Sets the numeric date	theDate.setDate(*date*);
setFullYear	Sets the year	theDate.setFullYear(*year*[,*month*[,*date*]]);
setHours	Sets the hours	theDate.setHours(*hours*[,*mins*[,*secs*[,*millisecs*]]]);
setMilliseconds	Sets the milliseconds	theDate.setMilliseconds(*millisecs*);
setMinutes	Sets the minutes	theDate.setMinutes(*mins*[,*secs*[,*millisecs*]]);
setMonth	Sets the month	theDate.setMonth(*month*[,*date*]);
setSeconds	Sets the seconds	theDate.setSeconds(*secs*[,*millisecs*]);
setTime	Sets the time and date	theDate.setTime(*millisecs*);
setUTCDate	Sets the numeric UTC date	theDate.setUTCDate(*date*);
setUTCFullYear	Sets the UTC year	theDate.setUTCFullYear(*year*[,*month*[,*date*]]);
setUTCHours	Sets the UTC hours	theDate.setUTCHours(*hours*[,*mins*[,*secs*[,*millisecs*]]]);
setUTCMilliseconds	Sets the UTC milliseconds	theDate.setUTCMilliseconds(*millisecs*);
setUTCMinutes	Sets the UTC minutes	theDate.setUTCMinutes(*mins*[,*secs*[,*millisecs*]]);
setUTCMonth	Sets the UTC month	theDate.setUTCMonth(*month*[,*date*]);

(continued)

Table 4.6   Date object methods *(continued)*.

Method	Description	Syntax
setUTCSeconds	Sets the UTC seconds	theDate.setUTCSeconds(*secs* [,*millisecs*]);
setYear	Sets the years past 1900	theDate.setYear(*years*);
toGMTString	Converts the date to a string using GMT format	theDate.toGMTString();
toLocalString	Converts the date to a string using the current locale format	theDate.toLocalString();
toUTCString	Converts the date to a string according to UTC format	theDate.toUTCString();
toString	Returns a string representation of the date	theDate.toString();
valueOf	Returns the milliseconds since 1 Jan 70	theDate.valueOf();

* You use **getVarDate** when you're working with objects that work with dates in the **VT_DATE** format

The **Date** object has two static methods: **parse** and **UTC**. You don't call them against a particular object because they are static. Instead, you call them using the class name like this:

```
Date.parse(argument);
Date.UTC(arguments);
```

The **parse** method parses a date string and returns the number of milliseconds between midnight January 1, 1970, and that date.

The **UTC** method returns the number of milliseconds between January 1, 1970, UTC and the specified date. The **UTC** method uses this syntax:

```
Date.UTC(year,month,day[,hours[,mins[,secs[,millisecs]]]]);
```

The **Function** Object

A *function* is a block of code that performs a specific task and can return a result. Functions are given names that they are called by throughout a program. Some functions take arguments containing values that the functions use to do their jobs. A function that calculates and returns a payment, for example, would accept arguments specifying the principal, interest rate, and number of payments.

JavaScript uses functions extensively and even has a primitive function type. The **Function** object is a wrapper object for the primitive type and is also used to create new functions. You'll read about creating user-defined functions later in this chapter, but you no doubt have an inquiring mind and want to know. Therefore, take a look at the following statements, which create a function that calculates and returns the square of a number:

```
function sqr(x) {
   return x * x;
}.
```

The keyword **function** is used to declare a function. This function is named **sqr** and takes one argument, **x**, which contains the value to operate on. The **return** statement returns the result to the caller.

Function Object Properties

The **Function** object has two properties in addition to the **constructor** and **prototype** properties. Table 4.7 contains descriptions of them.

The **arguments** property is an array that contains the arguments passed to the function. Because it is an array, the **length** property is used to determine the number of arguments passed. Using the **sqr** function as an example, the statement

```
sqr.length;
```

returns the number of arguments passed to the function, which is 1. The following statement returns the argument value:

```
sqr.arguments[0];
```

The **length** and **arguments** properties are useful within functions to determine whether the correct number of arguments was passed and within writing functions that work with a variable number of arguments.

The **caller** property contains a reference to the function that called the current function. The value of **caller** is **null** when the function is called from the script's top level.

The **arguments** and **caller** properties are defined only while the function is executing.

Function Object Methods

Table 4.8 shows the **Function** object's methods, which you are already familiar with: **toString** and **valueOf**.

Table 4.7   The Function object's properties.

Property	Description	Syntax
arguments	An array that contains the arguments passed to the function	**fctn.arguments[*n*];**
caller	Contains a reference to the caller function	**fctn.caller;**

Table 4.8   The Function object's methods.

Method	Description	Syntax
toString	Returns a string representation of the entire function	**fctn.toString();**
valueOf	Returns the entire function	**fctn.valueOf();**

The **Global** Object

The **Global** object contains all global methods. It is an intrinsic object, and you'll never create a variable of this type because JavaScript creates it for you. You can use the **Global** object's properties and methods without referencing the object itself.

Global Object Properties

Table 4.9 shows descriptions of the **Global** object's properties.

The **NaN** (Not a Number) value is returned when a mathematical operation returns an error or undefined result. For example, the **parseInt** method converts a string to its equivalent numerical value. The function returns **NaN** if the string does not form a legal number. Consider the following statements:

```
var somenum;
somenum = parseInt("Hello");
```

The variable **somenum** equals **NaN** after the call to **parseInt**. You can't use **NaN** in comparisons directly. Instead, you can use the **isNaN** function to evaluate for the **NaN** value. If an expression is equal to **NaN**, **isNaN** returns **true**:

```
if (isNaN(somenum))
// statement(s) to execute
```

The **Infinity** and **-Infinity** values are returned when a positive or negative number is larger than the largest representable type.

Global Object Methods

Table 4.10 shows the **Global** object's methods.

Table 4.9   The Global object's properties.

Property	Description
NaN	Indicates a value cannot be evaluated as a numeric value
Infinity	Indicates a value is larger than the largest representable value

Table 4.10   The Global object's methods.

Method	Description	Syntax
escape	Applies HTML encoding to the specified string	escape(*charstring*);
eval	Executes the specified code string	eval(*codestring*);
isFinite	Evaluates a number for **NaN** or **Infinity**	isFinite(*number*);
isNaN	Returns **true** if a value equals **NaN**	isNaN(*value*);
parseFloat	Converts a string value to a floating-point value	parseFloat(*string*);
parseInt	Converts a string value to an integer value	parseInt(*string*[,*radix*]);
unescape	Returns a string without HTML encoding characters	unescape(*charstring*);

The **escape** method applies HTML encoding rules to the specified character string. This method is useful when a script is dynamically constructing URL query strings:

```
theURL = "http://www.diningclub.com?"
+ escape("FavRestaurant=Luigi's Pizza Parlor and Pub");
```

After this statement executes, **theURL** contains the following string:

```
"http://www.diningclub.com?FavRestaurant
%3DLuigi%27s%20Pizza%20Parlor%20and%20Pub"
```

The **unescape** method performs the opposite task of removing HTML encoding:

```
theURL = unescape(theURL);
```

The **eval** method evaluates a specified code string that can contain any number of JavaScript statements separated by semicolons. The statements

```
theURL = "http://www.diningclub.com?" +
    "FavRestaurant=Luigi's Pizza Parlor and Pub";
codestring = "theURL = escape(theURL)";
eval(codestring);
```

assign a JavaScript statement to **codestring** and pass the string to the **eval** method, causing HTML encoding to be applied to the string stored in **theURL**.

isFinite returns **true** if the specified number is any value other than **Infinity**, **-Infinity**, or **NaN**.

The **parseInt** and **parseFloat** functions convert strings to integer and floating-point numbers if the specified strings begin with characters that form numbers. If the strings cannot be converted to numeric values, both methods return **NaN**. Also, **parseInt** has an optional argument *radix*, which specifies the base of the number in *string*. *radix* is a value between 2 and 36 and can also be specified as hexadecimal ("0xnnn") or octal ("0nnn"). The following statements contain expressions that can be converted:

```
parseInt("10");
parseInt("10.5");              // returns 10
parseInt("10 Hello");         // returns 10
parseFloat("10.5");
parseFloat("10.5 World");     // returns 10.5
```

The Math Object

The **Math** object provides math functions through several methods and properties. It is like the **Global** object in that it is not created with the **new** operator and its methods and properties are directly available.

Math Object Properties

Table 4.11 shows the **Math** object's properties.

Math Object Methods

Table 4.12 shows descriptions of the **Math** object's methods.

The **Number** Object

The **Number** object provides properties that are used as numeric constants and is the wrapper object for the number primitive type.

Table 4.11   The Math object's properties.

Property	Description	Syntax
E	Base of natural logarithms, approximately equal to 2.71828	Math.E
LN2	Natural logarithm of 2, approximately equal to .069314	Math.LN2
LN10	Natural logarithm of 10, approximately equal to 2.30258	Math.LN10
LOG2E	Base 2 logarithm of *e*, approximately equal to 1.44269	Math.LOG2E
LOG10E	Base 10 logarithm of *e*, approximately equal to .43429	Math.LOG10E
PI	Constant π, approximately equal to 3.14159	Math.PI
SQRT1_2	1 divided by the square root of 2, approximately equal to .70710	Math.SQRT1_2
SQRT2	Square root of 2, approximately equal to 1.41421	Math.SQRT2

Table 4.12   The Math object's methods.

Method	Description	Syntax
abs	Absolute value	Math.abs(*number*);
acos	Arccosine	Math.acos(*number*);
asin	Arcsine	Math.asin(*number*);
atan	Arctangent	Math.atan(*number*);
atan2	Angle from the X axis to a point	Math.atan2(*x, y*);
ceil	Rounds a number up	Math.ceil(*number*);
cos	Cosine	Math.cos(*number*);
exp	Computes e^x	Math.exp(*number*);
floor	Rounds a number down	Math.floor(*number*);
log	Natural logarithm	Math.log(*number*);
max	Returns the larger of two values	Math.max(*n1, n2*);
min	Returns the smaller of two values	Math.min(*n1, n2*);
pow	Computes x^y	Math.pow(*base, exponent*);
random	Returns a random number between 0 and 1	Math.random()
round	Returns a numeric expression rounded to the nearest integer	Math.round(*number*)
sin	Sine	Math.sin(*number*);
sqrt	Square root	Math.sqrt(*number*);
tan	Tangent	Math.tan(*number*);

Number Object Properties

In addition to the **constructor** and **prototype** properties, the **Number** object has the properties shown in Table 4.13.

Number Object Methods

Table 4.14 shows the **Number** object's methods.

The **Object** Object

The **Object** object serves as the "mother of all objects" in JavaScript. That is, all objects derive from **Object**. Therefore, its properties and methods are properties and methods available to all other JavaScript objects.

Object Object Properties

Table 4.15 shows descriptions of the **Object** object's properties.

You use the **prototype** property to define the properties, methods, and constants for a class of objects. All intrinsic JavaScript objects have a **prototype** property. New instances of the object inherit the features of the object. This property extends the functionality of an existing class of objects within the scope of the current script.

Table 4.13   The Number object's properties.

Property	Description	Syntax
MAX_VALUE	Maximum representable value	**Number.MAX_VALUE;**
MIN_VALUE	Minimum representable value	**Number.MIN_VALUE;**
NaN	Indicates an expression returned a nonnumeric value	**Number.NaN;**
NEGATIVE_INFINITY	Indicates a negative value is more negative than the largest representable number	**Number.NEGATIVE_INFINITY;**
POSITIVE_INFINITY	Indicates a value is larger than the largest representable number	**Number.POSITIVE_INFINITY;**

Table 4.14   The Number object's methods.

Method	Description	Syntax
toString	Returns a string representation of a number	**toString(*number*);**
valueOf	Returns the numeric value of a number	**valueOf(*number*);**

Table 4.15   The Object object's properties.

Property	Description	Syntax
constructor	Specifies the object's constructor function	**Object.constructor;**
prototype	Contains a reference to the object's prototype	**Object.prototype;**

How To Create Objects

JavaScript is an object-based language that provides several built-in objects. Additionally, JavaScript makes it easy to create your own objects.

The simplest method of creating an object is to declare it using the **Object** object. The statement

```
var myobj = new Object();
```

declares an object variable, but one of little use. You can think of objects as collections of methods and properties. The object **myobj** is empty; that is, it has no properties or methods.

However, you can add properties to **myobj** by assigning it a value like this:

```
myobj.name = "John";
```

Now, **myobj** has a **name** property. You also add methods in the same manner:

```
// define the method
function showname() {
    Response.Write(this.name);
}

// assign the method to the object
myobj.show = showname;
myobj.name = "John";
// now invoke the method
myobj.show();
```

Although this method of creating an object is easy, it does pose a slight problem. You must repeat the steps for every object that you want to use. So, if you want 10 objects just like **myobj**, you need to repeat the same steps 10 times to initialize each new object. Wouldn't it be easier to define one object and declare objects that would automatically have all properties and methods? You bet, and you can do so by using a constructor.

Listing 4.8 shows the use of the **prototype** and **constructor** properties. The code defines a constructor function for a very simple object, **MyObject**, which has just one property, **someProp**. The code adds the method **showme** to all instances of this object using the **prototype** property. Then, it defines the variable **MyObject** and sets **someProp** to the string "JavaScript is cool!". Finally, the code calls the **showme** method to output the property value.

Listing 4.8   Using the prototype and constructor properties.

```
<%@ LANGUAGE="JavaScript" %>
<%
  // define a constructor function
  function MyObject(someProp) {this.someProp = someProp;}

  // give it a method
  MyObject.prototype.showme = new Function("Response.Write(this.someProp);");

  // create one
  var myobj = new MyObject("JavaScript is cool!");

  myobj.showme();

  Response.Write("<BR>");                   // send a carriage return
  Response.Write(MyObject.prototype);       // outputs [object Object]
  Response.Write("<BR>");
  Response.Write(myobj.constructor);        // outputs function
MyObject(someProp)
%>
```

Object Object Methods

Table 4.16 shows descriptions for the **Object** object's methods.

The **regular expression** Object

Regular expressions are patterns of characters used in pattern matching and substitution. The JavaScript regular expressions follow the Perl model. The **regular expression** object stores patterns that are used when searching strings. Either these patterns are passed to a string method, or a string is passed to a **regular expression** method.

The **RegExp** object contains information about the last regular expression search and is updated automatically by the **regular expression** object and **String** object methods. You'll learn more about the **RegExp** object in the next section.

The **RegExp** object supports two syntaxes:

```
var regexpr = /pattern/[switch];
var regexpr = new RegExp("pattern"[,"switch"]);
```

Table 4.16   The Object object's methods.

Method	Description	Syntax
toString	Returns a string representation of the object	**Object.object();**
valueOf	Returns the object primitive	**Object.valueOf();**

The *pattern* argument is required and specifies the regular expression pattern to use. The *switch* argument is optional and is one of the following:

♦ **i**—Ignore case

♦ **g**—Global search for all occurrences

♦ **gi**—Global search, ignore case

You use the first syntax if you know the search pattern when you write the script. You use the second syntax when the search pattern is unknown or subject to change.

regular expression Object Properties

Table 4.17 shows descriptions of the **regular expression** object's properties.

All the **regular expression** properties are read-only, except for **lastIndex**.

regular expression Object Methods

Table 4.18 shows descriptions of the **regular expression** object's methods.

The **compile** method converts the search pattern to a format that results in faster execution. You can invoke this method explicitly, if you like. You can skip this step, but if you are performing many searches with the same pattern, compiling it can increase performance. JScript automatically compiles search patterns when the script loads if you use the following syntax:

```
var regexpr = /pattern/[switch];
```

However, if the expression is a string, compilation occurs for each search, as in this example:

```
var regexpr = new RegExp("pattern"[,"switch"]);
```

Table 4.17   regular expression object properties.

Property	Description	Syntax
global	Indicates whether the global switch was used	**regexpr.global;**
ignorecase	Indicates whether the ignore case switch was used	**regexpr.ignorecase;**
lastIndex	Specifies where to begin the next search	**regexpr.lastIndex;**
source	Indicates the regular expression pattern	**regexpr.source;**

Table 4.18   regular expression object methods.

Method	Description	Syntax
compile	Compiles a pattern to an internal format	**regexpr.compile(*pattern*);**
exec	Executes a search	**regexpr.exec(*string*);**
test	Tests for a match	**regexpr.test(*string*);**

The **exec** method executes a search on the specified string. If no match is found, it returns **null**; if one or more matches are found, it returns an array and updates the **RegExp** object.

The **test** method checks to see whether a pattern exists. If one does exist, the method returns **true**; if it doesn't exist, it returns **false**. The **test** method does not update the **RegExp** object.

Listing 4.9 shows the use of the first syntax to search for the pattern */JavaScript/*.

Listing 4.9   Using the regular expression object.

```
<%@ LANGUAGE="JavaScript" %>
<%
var regexpr = /JavaScript/gi;
var result;

   result = regexpr.exec("Programming in JavaScript is fun!");

   Response.Write(result + "<BR>");          // pattern found
   Response.Write(result.length + "<BR>");   // it's an array and has
                                             // a length property
   Response.Write(result.lastIndex + "<BR>");
%>
```

Listing 4.10 shows the use of the second syntax.

Listing 4.10   Using an alternate syntax with the regular expression object.

```
<%@ LANGUAGE="JavaScript" %>
<%
var regexpr = new RegExp("JavaScript", "gi");
var result;

   result = regexpr.exec("Programming in JavaScript is fun!");

   Response.Write(result + "<BR>");        // pattern found
   // it's an array and has a length property
   Response.Write(result.length + "<BR>");
   Response.Write(result.lastIndex + "<BR>");
%>
```

The **RegExp** Object

JavaScript stores information on regular expression pattern searches in the **RegExp** object. This object has only properties, and the search methods of **regular expression** objects as well as **String** objects update **RegExp**. The **RegExp** object is always available; you don't need to create it.

RegExp Object Properties

The **RegExp** object has several read-only properties that store information on regular expression pattern searches. Table 4.19 shows descriptions of the **RegExp** object's properties.

The **String** Object

The **String** object has several methods to format, manipulate, and search strings. Many of the **String** object's methods format strings in HTML. This object is also the wrapper object for the string primitive type. The **String** object's methods and properties are available with string primitives, string literals, and string objects:

```
var str = "JavaScript";
var len;
len = str.length;
len = "JavaScript".length;
```

String Object Properties

Table 4.20 shows descriptions of the **String** object's properties.

Table 4.19   RegExp object properties.

Property	Description	Syntax	Optional Syntax
$1 ... $9	Specifies the nine most recent matches	RegExp.$1;	
index	Indicates where the first match begins	RegExp.index;	
input	Contains the string on which a search was performed	RegExp.input;	RegExp.$_
lastIndex	Indicates where the last match begins	RegExp.lastIndex;	
lastMatch	Contains the substring from the last match	RegExp.lastMatch;	RegExp.$&;
lastParen	Specifies the last parenthesized substring match	RegExp.lastParen;	RegExp.$+;
leftContext	Specifies the string up to the most recent match	RegExp.leftContext;	RegExp.$';
multiline	Indicates whether searching across multiple lines	RegExp.multiline;	RegExp.$*
rightContext	Specifies the string following the most recent match	RegExp.rightContext;	RegExp.$'

Table 4.20   String object properties.

Property	Description	Syntax
length	Returns the length of the string	str.length;
prototype	Contains a reference to the string object prototype	str.prototype;

String Object Methods

Table 4.21 shows non-HTML-related methods. Table 4.22 shows descriptions of the methods that format strings in HTML.

Table 4.21 String object methods.

Method	Description	Syntax
charAt	Returns the nth character from a string	str.charAt(*n*);
charCodeAt	Returns the Unicode value for the specified character	str.charCodeAt(*n*);
concat	Returns the concatenation of two strings	str1.concat(*str2*);
fromCharCode	Returns a string created from a series of Unicode values	String.fromCharCode(*code1, code2, ...*)
indexOf	Finds the first occurrence of a substring in a string	str.indexOf(*substring*[, *startindex*]);
lastIndexOf	Finds the last occurrence of a substring in a string	str.lastIndexOf(*substring*[, *startindex*]);
match	Searches a string	str.match(*regexpr*);
replace	Replaces text found with a regular expression	str.replace(*regexpr, newtext*);
search	Searches for a regular expression match	str.search(*regexpr*);
slice	Returns a segment of a string	str.slice(*start*[,*end*]);
split	Removes a regular expression from a string	str.split(*regexpr*);
substr	Returns a substring	str.substr(*start*[,*length*];
substring	Returns a substring	str.substring(*start, end*);
toLowerCase	Returns the string in lowercase	str.toLowerCase();
toUpperCase	Returns the string in uppercase	str.toUpperCase();
toString	Returns a string object	str.toString();
valueOf	Returns the string value	str.valueOf();

Table 4.22 String object HTML formatting methods.

Method	Description	Syntax	Equivalent HTML
anchor	Adds an HTML anchor	str.anchor(*name*);	<A>*name*</A>
big	Makes the string big	str.big();	<BIG>*string*</BIG>
blink	Makes the string blink	str.blink();	<BLINK>*string*</BLINK>
bold	Makes the string bold	str.bold();	<B>*string*</B>
fixed	Makes the string fixed width	str.fixed();	<TT>*string*</TT>
fontcolor	Sets the string's font color	str.fontcolor(*color*);	<FONT COLOR=*color*>
fontsize	Sets the font size	str.fontsize(*n*);	<FONT SIZE=*n*>
italics	Makes the string italic	str.italics();	<I>*string*</I>
link	Adds a hyperlink to the string	str.link(*URL*);	<A HREF=*URL*>*string*</A>
small	Makes the text small	str.small();	<SMALL>*string*</SMALL>

(continued)

Table 4.22   String object HTML formatting methods (continued).

Method	Description	Syntax	Equivalent HTML
strike	Strikes through the string	str.strike();	\<STRIKE\>*string*\</STRIKE\>
sub	Makes a string subscript	str.sub();	\<SUB\>*string*\</SUB\>
sup	Makes a string superscript	str.sup();	\<SUP\>*string*\</SUP\>

JavaScript Operators

Operators are used to form expressions that perform calculations, comparisons, and logical operations. JavaScript has a complete range of operators that are extensively used in all but the simplest programs. You'll be familiar with JavaScript operators if you have programmed in C, C++, or Java. JavaScript has four classifications of operators: arithmetic, comparison, logical, and bitwise.

Arithmetic Operators

Arithmetic operators perform basic arithmetic operations on one or more variables. Also, some math operations in JavaScript, such as exponentiation, are performed using the **Math** object. Table 4.23 shows JavaScript's arithmetic operators.

Comparison Operators

Comparison operators compare expressions and return **true** or **false**. JavaScript comparison operators fall into three general categories: relational, equality, and identity. Numbers, strings, and Booleans are compared by value. Objects, arrays, and functions are compared by reference on the basis of whether they refer to the same object. Table 4.24 shows JavaScript's comparison operators.

When performing relational operations, JavaScript tries to convert both expressions into numbers. However, if both expressions are strings, a lexicographical string comparison is performed. In the case of equality operations, JavaScript tries to convert the expressions to

Table 4.23   JavaScript arithmetic operators.

Operator	Operation	Description	Syntax
-	Unary negation	Returns the negative value of an expression	a = -b;
++	Increment	Increments the value by 1	a++; or ++a;*
--	Decrement	Decrements the value by 1	a--; or --a;*
*	Multiplication	Multiplies two numbers	a = b * c;
/	Division	Divides two numbers	a = b / c;
%	Modulo arithmetic	Divides two numbers returning the remainder	a = b % c;
+	Addition	Adds two numbers**	a = b + c;
-	Subtraction	Finds the difference between two numbers	a = b - c;

** **a++/a--** increments/decrements but returns the original value; **++a/--a** increments/decrements the value and returns the new value.*

** The + operator is also used in string concatenation operations.

Table 4.24 JavaScript comparison operators.

Operator	Operation	True If
<	Less than	**expression1 < expression2**
>	Greater than	**expression1 > expression2**
<=	Less than or equal to	**expression1 <= expression2**
>=	Greater than or equal to	**expression1 >= expression2**
==	Equality	**expression1 == expression2**
!=	Inequality	**expression1 != expression2**
===	Identity	**expression1 === expression2**
!==	Nonidentity	**expression1 !== expression2**

strings, numbers, or Booleans if the expressions are different. Identity operators perform the same as equality operators except that no type conversion is done.

Logical Operators

Logical operators evaluate one or more logical expressions and return **true** or **false**. These operators are frequently used with comparison operators to evaluate multiple expressions. Table 4.25 shows JavaScript's logical operators.

Bitwise Operators

Bitwise operators perform low-level bit manipulation on integer values. These operators perform two general functions: logical operations on individual bits and shifting bits left or right. Table 4.26 shows the available bitwise operators.

The bitwise shift operators are useful for performing fast multiplication and division. Shifting bits left performs multiplication such that shifting left 1 bit multiplies by 2, shifting left 2 bits multiplies by 4, and so on. The number of places to shift left is an integer in the range of 1 through 31. As bits shift to the left, JavaScript fills the "vacated" positions on the right with zeros.

Table 4.25 JavaScript logical operators.

Operator	Operation	Syntax	Expression1	Expression2	Result
!	Logical negation	**result = !expression1**	True		False
			False		True
&&	Logical conjunction	**result = expression1 && expression2**	True	True	True
			True	False	False
			False	True	False
			False	False	False
||	Logical disjunction	**result = expression1 || expression2**	True	True	True
			True	False	True
			False	True	True
			False	False	False

Table 4.26   JavaScript bitwise operators.

Operator	Description	Syntax
<<	Left shift	a = b << *n*
>>	Right shift	a = b >> *n*
>>>	Unsigned right shift	a >>> *n*
~	**Not**	a = ~b
&	**And**	a = b & c
^	**Xor**	a = b ^ c
|	**Or**	a = b | c

Shifting bits right performs division in the same manner as shifting left performs multiplication. As bits shift right, the positions on the left are filled with the topmost bit of the original operand. This operation has the effect of preserving the number's sign. If you shift a negative number right, the result is still a negative number. The unsigned shift right operator fills the vacated positions on the left with zeros.

Be careful not to confuse the negation operator (~) with the logical negation operator (!). The ~ operator flips all the bits in a number, making the ones into zeros and vice versa. The ! operator simply returns **true** if a Boolean expression is false and **false** if the expression is true.

Assignment Operators

The assignment operator (=) assigns the value of the expression on the right side of the operator to the left side of the operator. The assignment operator expects a variable, an object property, or an array element to be on the left side, as in this example:

```
a = b * 2;
```

JavaScript, like C, C++, and Java, lets you use compound assignment statements. This shortcut allows you to combine other operators with the assignment operator. The assignment operator is always the second operator when you use this syntax. The statement

```
a += 2;
```

is equivalent to

```
a = a + 2;
```

You can use compound assignments with arithmetic, logical, and bitwise operators.

A Few More JavaScript Operators

JavaScript has a few miscellaneous operators that defy classification.

The Conditional Operator

The conditional operator is the only ternary (three-operand) operator in JavaScript. The conditional operator uses the following syntax:

```
op1 ? op2 : op3;
```

The value of the first operand must be a Boolean value and is typically the result of some comparison. If the value of the first operand is **true**, the operator returns the value of the second operand. If the value of the first operand is **false**, the operator returns the value of the third operand. The following statement sets **result** to the value of **a** or **b**, whichever is larger:

```
result = a > b ? a : b;
```

The conditional operator performs the same function as the **if...else** statement (discussed later in this chapter) but is more concise and can be used inside an expression.

The typeof Operator

The **typeof** operator returns a string indicating the type of an expression. The following are the possible return values:

♦ **boolean**

♦ **function**

♦ **number**

♦ **object**

♦ **string**

♦ **undefined**

The **typeof** operator has the following syntax:

```
typeof var;
typeof(var);
```

The new Operator

You have already seen examples of the **new** operator in this chapter. The **new** operator creates new objects using the syntax

```
new constructor[(argument list)];
```

where **constructor** is the object's constructor function. The **new** operator works by first creating a new object without any defined properties. It then calls the object constructor function and optionally passes arguments to the constructor. The constructor can then initialize the new object using the keyword **this**. The following statement defines a new string object:

```
var newstring = new String("I'm a string object!");
```

The delete Operator

The **delete** operator deletes variables, object and object properties, and arrays and array elements by undefining them. Unlike the C++ **delete**, it does not actually free up the memory associated with the variable or object being deleted. JavaScript has automatic garbage collection, so the **delete** operator doesn't need to free memory. Here's how you use **delete**:

```
delete expression;
```

The void Operator

The **void** operator evaluates an expression and returns **undefined**. This operator is useful when you want to evaluate an expression but not return the value:

```
void expression;
```

The Comma Operator

The comma operator (**,**) evaluates multiple expressions sequentially. The statement

```
Response.Write("The Comma operator "),
str="is little used.",Response.Write(str);
```

is equivalent to these statements:

```
Response.Write("The Comma operator ");
str="is little used.";
Response.Write(str);
```

The resulting return value is whatever the last expression returns. You won't use the comma operator much, except in **for** loops, which you will read about shortly.

Operator Precedence

Operators are evaluated in a predetermined *order of precedence*. Often, this order of precedence is different than the order in which you write the operators. Arithmetic operators have a higher precedence than comparison operators, which have a higher precedence than assignment operators. There is also an order of precedence within some of the operator categories. Operators with equal precedence are evaluated left to right.

JavaScript evaluates operators in the following order, highest to lowest:

- *Call, member*— ., [], ()
- *Unary, object creation/deletion*— **++**, **--**, **~**, **!**, **typeof**, **new**, **void**, **delete**
- *Multiplication, division, modulo division*— *****, **/**, **%**

- *Addition, subtraction, string concatenation—* **+, -, +**
- *Bitwise shifting—* **>>, <<, >>>**
- *Relational—* **<, <=, >, >=**
- *Equality, identity—* **==, !=, ===, !==**
- *Bitwise and, exclusive or, or——* **&, ^, |**
- *Logical and, or—* **&&, ||**
- *Conditional—* **?:**
- *Assignment—* **+, +=, -=, /=, %=, <<=, >>=, >>>=, &=, ^=, |=**

You can override the standard order of precedence by enclosing operations in parentheses. Operations in parentheses take precedence over those not in parentheses, and normal precedence is maintained within parentheses. Nesting parentheses further controls the order of operation, and operations within the innermost parentheses are evaluated first.

The following statements illustrate how operator precedence and parentheses work:

```
A = B * C + D / E
A = B * (C + D) / E
```

These statements produce different results. In the first example, the product of B * C is added to the result of D / E. In the second example, the sum of C + D is multiplied by B and then divided by E. For a more numeric example, consider the following:

```
10 + 2 * 2
```

The correct result is 14 (not 24) because **+** has a higher precedence than **+**. This example, of course, obeys the standard rules of mathematics.

Controlling Program Flow

Most programs make decisions and perform different operations as a result. The program often makes these decisions on the basis of a variable's or object property's value. A program's capability to make decisions and execute code accordingly is provided by *conditional statements*. Conditional statements evaluate a condition and specify statements to execute as a result of the evaluation.

Programs commonly execute a block of code repeatedly, for example, to initialize an array. *Looping statements* provide a way for a program to repeat statements a specific number of times or while a condition is **true** or **false**.

Conditional Statements

Programs make decisions using conditional statements. The capability to make decisions and execute statements on the basis of decisions is useful in all but the most basic programs. JavaScript has the following conditional statements:

- if
- if...else
- switch

The if And if...else Statements

The **if** statement evaluates a condition and executes a statement or group of statements if the condition is **true**:

```
if (condition == true) {
    statement(s) to execute
}
```

If the condition is **true**, the statements inside the curly braces ({}) are executed. If you have only one statement, you don't need to use the braces, but including them is still a good practice. Listing 4.11 shows the **if** statement in action.

Listing 4.11   The if statement.

```
<%@ LANGUAGE="JavaScript" %>
<%
var Sales, Commission;

    Commission = .05;
    Sales = 12500.00;

    if (Sales >= 10000.00)
      Commission = .10;
%>
```

You can also specify statements to execute on both a **true** condition and a **false** condition. The **else** clause specifies statements to execute if the condition is **false**:

```
if (condition == true) {
    statements to execute
}
else {
    statements to execute
}
```

Listing 4.12 uses the **else** clause to execute a statement when the condition is **false**.

Listing 4.12   Using the else clause in an if statement.

```
<%@ LANGUAGE="JavaScript" %>
<%
var Sales, Commission;

    Commission = .05;
    Sales = 12500.00;

    if (Sales >= 10000.00)
      Commission = .10;
    else
      Response.Write ("You need to work harder.");
%>
```

It is very common to combine an **if** statement with a relational operator to further define the condition. Listing 4.13 uses relational operators with the **if** statement to determine whether a value is within a range.

Listing 4.13   Using relational operators in an if statement.

```
<%@ LANGUAGE="JavaScript" %>
<%
var Sales, Commission = 0.0;

    if (Sales < 1000.00)
      Commission = .05;
    else if (Sales >= 1000.00 && Sales < 5000.00)
      Commission = .10;
    else if (Sales >= 5000.00 && Sales < 10000.00)
      Commission = .15;
    else {
      Commission = .20;
      Response.Write ("Wow! Great job!");
    }
%>
```

The switch Statement

The **switch** statement executes one of several blocks of statements on the basis of an expression's value. A statement block executes when the expression value matches a label, which is specified by the **case** clause. The **default** clause specifies statements to execute when no match exists.

The **switch** statement uses the following syntax:

```
switch (expression) {
  case label:
    statements to execute
```

```
    case label:
      statements to execute
    default:
      statements to execute
}
```

You can find an example of the **switch** statement in Listing 4.17 later in this chapter.

Loop Statements

Loops execute selected lines of code repeatedly. JavaScript has loop statements that repeat program statements a specific number of times or while a condition is true. Of course, by using the logical negation operator (!), you can easily reverse the sense of any loop statement to make it repeat while a condition is false. The following are the loop statements:

♦ **for**

♦ **for...in**

♦ **while**

♦ **do...while**

The for Statement

The **for** statement executes a block of statements a specific number of times. This statement uses an integer counter variable to control the number of times the loop is repeated, and it modifies the counter variable each time through the loop.

The **for** statement uses this syntax:

```
for (init_counter; test_counter; increment/decrement_counter) {
    statements to execute
}
```

The loop initializes the counter variable before the loop begins and tests it at the beginning of each iteration. The loop repeats as long as the test returns **true**. You don't need the braces if only one statement is in the loop, but it is a good habit to include them anyway.

The following statement sets each element in an array to zero:

```
for (counter = 0; counter < 10; counter++)
    somearray[counter] = 0;
```

You use the comma operator (,) to handle more than one counter variable in a **for** statement. This is one of the most common uses of the comma operator. The following statements show the use of the comma operator in a **for** statement:

```
for (i = 0, j = 10; i < 10; i++, j++)
    Response.Write (i + " " + j);
```

Although it is common to increment or decrement the loop counter as the last clause in the **for** loop, you can use any legal expression. For example, if you want the counter to increase by 10 on each iteration, you could write this line:

```
for (x=0,y=0;x<100;x+=10,y+=10)
```

The for...in Statement

The **for...in** statement executes the loop one time for each element in an array or for each property in an object:

```
for (var in object) {
    statements to execute
}
```

var is the name of a variable, an array element, or an object property. *object* is the name of an object or an array.

Arrays have a **length** property that returns the highest array index plus 1. JavaScript arrays can be sparse, so the **length** property might not return the actual number of array elements. Listing 4.14 uses **for...in** to count the actual number of elements in an array.

Listing 4.14   Using for...in to count array elements.
```
<%@ LANGUAGE="JavaScript" %>
<%
var Count = 0;
var SomeArray = new Array(10);

    // statements to initialize the array

    for (i in SomeArray)
      Count++;
%>
```

Listing 4.15 shows how to use **for...in** to iterate through an object's properties.

Listing 4.15   Iterating through an object's properties.
```
<%@ LANGUAGE="JavaScript" %>
<%
var Place = new Object;
var Prop;

    Place["City"] = "Columbus";
    Place["State"] = "OH";
    Place["Zip"] = "43220";
```

```
   for (Prop in Place)
      Response.Write(Prop + ": " + Place[Prop] + "<BR>");
%>
```

The while Statement

The **while** statement executes a loop while a condition is true:

```
while (condition==true)
   statements to execute
```

The following statements use the **while** statement to output array element values:

```
var Count = 0;
var SomeArray = new Array(10);

// statements to initialize the array

while (count < 10) {
   Response.Write(SomeArray[count]);
   Count++;
}
```

The do...while Statement

The **do...while** statement works much like the **while** statement, except that the body of the loop is executed at least once. It is executed because the statement doesn't evaluate the condition until the end of the loop:

```
do {
   statements to execute
} while (expression);
```

The following statements perform the same function as the previous example but with the **do...while** statement:

```
var Count = 0;
var SomeArray = new Array(10);

// statements to initialize the array

do {
   Response.Write(SomeArray[Count]);
   Count++;
} while (Count < 10);
```

The break And continue Statements

The **break** statement causes a loop to exit early. Listing 4.16 searches an array for a value and breaks out when it finds a match.

Listing 4.16   Using the break statement.

```
<%@ LANGUAGE="JavaScript" %>
<%
var SomeArray = new Array(10);
var SearchItem;
var Found = false;

    // statements to initialize SomeArray
    // and SearchItem

    for (i = 0; i < 10; i++) {
      if (SearchItem == SomeArray[i]) {
         Found = true;
         break;
      }
}
%>
```

You'll recall that the **switch** statement also uses the **break** statement, as shown in Listing 4.17.

Listing 4.17   Using break in the switch statement.

```
<%@ LANGUAGE="JavaScript" %>
<%
var Commission = .0;
var Bonus = 0;

    switch (Commission) {
      case .05:
         Bonus = 0;
         break;
      case .10:
         Bonus = 500.00
         break;
      case .10:
         Bonus = 1000.00
         break;
      case .20:
         Bonus = 1500.00
         break;
      default:
```

```
          Response.Write ("Invalid Bonus value");
   }
   %>
```

The **continue** statement stops the current iteration of the loop and starts a new one. The following example uses the **for** statement to sum the values of an array. If an array element is not a number, **continue** immediately starts a new iteration, as you can see here:

```
<%@ LANGUAGE="JavaScript" %>
<%
var a = new Array(10);
var asum;

   for (i = 0; i < 10; i++)
     a[i] = i;

   a[7] = "I'm not a number anymore.";
   asum = 0;
   for (i = 0; i < 10; i++) {
     if (isNaN(a[i]))
         continue;
     asum += a[i];
   }
%>
```

Functions

Most programs include sections of code that perform specific tasks and are used many times. Such sections of code in JavaScript are *functions*. Functions are blocks of code that perform a specific task for the rest of the program. Functions can accept arguments, accept values used by the function, and return a result.

JavaScript provides several built-in functions and also allows you to define your own functions. Functions are a major part of JavaScript programming and are even a type of data. Because a function is a data type, it can be assigned to a variable, an object property, or an array element and can be passed as an argument to another function. JavaScript also has a **Function** object, which is a wrapper object around the primitive function type.

Defining Functions

Defining a function is straightforward. A function definition consists of the **function** keyword, the name of the function, any arguments, and the statements that constitute the function body:

```
function name(argument1, argument2, ...) {
   function statements
}
```

The following statements define a function that calculates the square of a number:

```
function sqr(x) {
   return x * x;
}
```

Argument **x** contains the value to square. The **return** statement returns the specified value (in this case, the result of the calculation) to the caller.

The statement

```
sqr(5);
```

calls the **sqr** function with 5 as the argument; **sqr** will return 25. However, in this example, there is nothing to accept the returned value. Functions that return values are typically used in expressions on the right side of an assignment statement, as shown here:

```
result = sqr(5);
area = Math.PI * sqr(radius);
```

By Value Vs. By Reference

JavaScript functions can manipulate arguments *by value* and *by reference*. When you pass a variable by value to a function, JavaScript actually passes a copy of the variable to the function. The function can change the value locally without changing the original value.

When you pass a variable by reference, JavaScript sends the function the variable's address in memory. The function can change the value stored at that address, and the change persists even after the function returns.

Some languages let you specify how to pass arguments, but JavaScript doesn't. Rather, JavaScript passes numbers and Booleans by value and passes objects and arrays by reference. Strings and functions are primitive types like numbers and Booleans, but their length can vary. Therefore, JavaScript passes them by reference, too.

The Function Constructor

In addition to defining functions with the **function** keyword, you can create functions by using the **new** statement and specifying the **Function** object like this:

```
var sqr = new Function("x", "return x * x;");
```

This method uses the **Function** object constructor to create the function. The constructor takes any number of string arguments. The last string that is specified defines the function body.

Using the constructor is convenient when you are defining a method for an object. The following statements, for example, declare an object variable **loan** and assign it a method that calculates a payment:

```
var loan = new Object;
var payment
loan.pmt = new Function("I", "P", "Amt", "return I / P * Amt;");
payment = loan.pmt(.07, 12, 200000);
```

Exception Handling

Let's face it, program errors are a fact of programming life. Many factors can cause errors to happen: a coding error, I/O failure, and communications errors, just to name a few. It's our responsibility to do the best we can to anticipate potential errors and provide some means of handling them gracefully. This makes better code, which is certainly less embarrassing. How many times have you hit a Web page just to see a script error? This is frustrating and most often avoidable. The bad thing is that you see errors on many large sites.

Until recently, JavaScript didn't have a nice, structured way of handling errors. This situation has changed because, beginning with version 5, JavaScript has built-in exception handling using the **try...catch** statement.

It's easy to imagine what this statement does: **try** to do something and if an exception occurs, **catch** it. Here is what it looks like:

```
try {
    // the try block contains the code to execute
}
catch (exception) {
    // the catch block contains code to execute
    // if there is an exception
}
```

The code in the **try** block is executed, and if all goes well, program execution jumps past the **catch** block and resumes on the line immediately following it. If an exception occurs in the **try** block, execution stops on the offending line, and the code in the **catch** block is executed. **exception** is a variable that contains information about the error.

Most objects are designed to inform you of exceptions by raising an error. Assume you want to use a server component called **myobject** (server components are covered in later chapters). The following syntax creates an instance of **myobject**:

```
var myobj = Server.CreateObject("myobject");
```

If **myobject** doesn't exist on the server, you'll see something like this

```
Server object error 'ASP 0177 : 800401f3'
Server.CreateObject Failed
/test1/except.asp, line 5
800401f3
```

in your browser window. By putting the same statement in a **try...catch** block, you can prevent this situation from happening:

```
try {
    var myobj = Server.CreateObject("myobject");
}
catch (exception) {
    // code to handle the exception
}
```

The preceding code keeps the script from crashing, but it doesn't handle the error. You still have to do something about that. JavaScript allows you to write your own exception hander so that your program can take action to deal with the situation. The following example shows how this is done:

```
// define an exception object
function myException(ErrNum, ErrDesc) {
    this.ErrorNumber = ErrNum;
    this.ErrorDescription = ErrDesc;
}

// define a function to raise the exception
function ThrowException() {
    exception = new myException(1, "user defined exception");
    // raise the exception
    throw exception;
}

// now make it happen
try {
    ThrowException();
}
catch (exception) {
    if (exception instanceof myException)
        Response.Write("Exception occurred with myException");
}
%>
```

In the preceding example, **myException** defines an exception object. **ThrowException** creates an instance of **myException** and sets the error number and description properties. The JavaScript **Throw** statement, which generates an error condition that can be handled by the **try...catch** statement, is used to raise the exception. Program execution passes to the **catch** part of **try...catch**, and the **instanceof** operator is used to see whether the error is an instance of **myException**. If so, the specified action is taken. You can easily test for other exception objects as well.

What happens if the error is caused by something else? If something else causes an error, and you aren't checking for it (perhaps because you aren't even aware of it), you still need to deal with it. You do so by throwing the exception again, like this:

```
if (exception instanceof myException)
    Response.Write("Exception occurred with myException");
else
    throw exception;
```

This example passes to the next higher level exception handler.

Adding robust exception handling to your Web applications clearly requires additional effort, but it is well worth it.

JavaScript Quick Reference

Most of the time you need to quickly find out if a language supports a certain feature. So for your convenience, the JavaScript features are listed in Table 4.27.

Table 4.27 JavaScript quick reference.

Category	Keyword/Feature	JScript	JavaScript	ECMAScript
Array support	**Array**	✔	✔	✔
	concat	✔		✔
	dimensions	✔		
	getItem	✔		
	join	✔	✔	✔
	lbound	✔		
	length	✔	✔	✔
	reverse	✔	✔	✔
	slice	✔		
	sort	✔	✔	✔
	toArray	✔		
	ubound	✔		
	VBArray	✔		
Collections	**Drives**	✔		
	Files	✔		
	Folders	✔		

(continued)

Table 4.27 JavaScript quick reference *(continued).*

Category	Keyword/Feature	JScript	JavaScript	ECMAScript
Comments	/*...*/	✔	✔	✔
	//	✔	✔	✔
Conditional compilation	@cc_on	✔		
	Conditional_Compilation_Variables	✔		
	@if statement	✔		
	@set statement	✔		
Constants	Infinity	✔	✔	✔
	NaN	✔	✔	✔
	null	✔	✔	✔
	true, false	✔	✔	✔
	undefined	✔	✔	✔
Control flow	break	✔	✔	✔
	continue	✔	✔	✔
	do...while	✔		
	for	✔	✔	✔
	for...in	✔	✔	✔
	if...else	✔	✔	✔
	Labeled	✔		
	return	✔	✔	✔
	switch	✔		
	while		✔	
	with	✔	✔	✔
Date/Time	Date	✔	✔	✔
	getDate	✔	✔	✔
	getDay	✔	✔	✔
	getFullYear	✔		✔
	getHours	✔	✔	✔
	getMilliseconds	✔		✔
	getMinutes	✔	✔	✔
	getMonth	✔	✔	✔
	getSeconds	✔	✔	✔
	getTime	✔	✔	✔
	getTimeZoneOffset	✔	✔	✔
	getUTCDate	✔		✔
	getUTCDay	✔		✔
	getUTCFullYear	✔		✔
	getUTCHours	✔		✔
	getUTCMilliseconds	✔		✔
	getUTCMonth	✔		✔
	getUTCSeconds	✔		✔
	getVarDate	✔		
	getYear	✔	✔	✔

(continued)

Table 4.27   JavaScript quick reference *(continued).*

Category	Keyword/Feature	JScript	JavaScript	ECMAScript
Date/Time	parse	✔	✔	✔
	setDate	✔	✔	✔
	setFullYear	✔		✔
	setHours	✔	✔	✔
	setMilliseconds	✔		✔
	setMinutes	✔	✔	✔
	setMonth	✔	✔	✔
	setSeconds	✔	✔	✔
	setTime	✔	✔	✔
	setUTCDate	✔		✔
	setUTCFullYear	✔		✔
	setUTCHours	✔		✔
	setUTCMilliseconds	✔		✔
	setUTCMonth	✔		✔
	setUTCSeconds	✔		✔
	setYear	✔	✔	✔
	toGMTString	✔	✔	✔
	toLocaleString	✔	✔	✔
	toUTCString	✔		✔
	UTC	✔	✔	✔
Declaration	function	✔	✔	✔
	new	✔	✔	✔
	var	✔	✔	✔
Enumeration	Enumerator	✔		
	atEnd	✔		
	item	✔		
	moveFirst	✔		
	moveNext	✔		
File and file system objects	Dictionary	✔		
	Drive	✔		
	File	✔		
	Folder	✔		
	FileSystemObject	✔		
	TextStream	✔		
Function support	Function	✔	✔	✔
	arguments	✔	✔	✔
	caller	✔	✔	
	length	✔		✔
Global methods	Global	✔		✔
	assign		✔	
	escape	✔	✔	✔
	eval	✔	✔	✔

(continued)

Table 4.27 JavaScript quick reference *(continued).*

Category	Keyword/Feature	JScript	JavaScript	ECMAScript
Global methods	isFinite	✔	✔	✔
	isNaN	✔	✔	✔
	parseFloat	✔	✔	✔
	parseInt	✔	✔	✔
	toString	✔	✔	✔
	unescape	✔	✔	✔
	valueOf	✔	✔	✔
Math	Math	✔	✔	✔
	abs	✔	✔	✔
	acos	✔	✔	✔
	asin	✔	✔	✔
	atan	✔	✔	✔
	atan2	✔	✔	✔
	ceil	✔	✔	✔
	cos	✔	✔	✔
	E	✔	✔	✔
	exp	✔	✔	✔
	floor	✔	✔	✔
	LN2	✔	✔	✔
	LN10	✔	✔	✔
	log	✔	✔	✔
	LOG2E	✔	✔	✔
	LOG10E	✔	✔	✔
	max	✔	✔	✔
	min	✔	✔	✔
	PI	✔	✔	✔
	pow	✔	✔	✔
	random	✔	✔	✔
	round	✔	✔	✔
	sin	✔	✔	✔
	sqrt	✔	✔	✔
	SQRT1_2	✔	✔	✔
	SQRT2	✔	✔	✔
	tan	✔	✔	✔
Numbers	Number	✔	✔	✔
	MAX_VALUE	✔	✔	✔
	MIN_VALUE	✔	✔	✔
	NaN	✔	✔	✔
	NEGATIVE_INFINITY	✔	✔	✔
	POSITIVE_INFINITY	✔	✔	✔
Object support	Object	✔	✔	✔
	assign		✔	

(continued)

Table 4.27   JavaScript quick reference *(continued).*

Category	Keyword/Feature	JScript	JavaScript	ECMAScript
Object support	constructor	✔	✔	✔
	new	✔		✔
	prototype	✔		✔
	this	✔	✔	✔
	toString	✔		✔
	valueOf	✔	✔	✔
Objects	Array	✔	✔	✔
	Boolean	✔	✔	✔
	Date	✔	✔	✔
	Enumerator	✔		
	Function	✔	✔	✔
	Global	✔		✔
	JavaArray		✔	
	JavaClass		✔	
	JavaMethod		✔	
	JavaObject		✔	
	JavaPackage		✔	
	Math	✔	✔	✔
	Number	✔	✔	✔
	Object	✔	✔	✔
	Packages		✔	
	RegExp	✔		
	Regular Expression	✔		
	String	✔	✔	✔
	VBArray	✔		
Operators	=	✔	✔	✔
	OP=	✔	✔	✔
	+, -	✔	✔	✔
	%	✔	✔	✔
	*, /	✔	✔	✔
	==, !=	✔	✔	✔
	<, <=	✔	✔	✔
	>, >=	✔	✔	✔
	===, !==	✔		
	&&, ||, !	✔	✔	✔
	&, |, ~, ^	✔	✔	✔
	<<, >>	✔	✔	✔
	>>>	✔	✔	✔
	?:	✔	✔	✔
	,	✔	✔	✔
	--, ++	✔	✔	✔
	delete	✔		✔

(continued)

Table 4.27 JavaScript quick reference *(continued).*

Category	Keyword/Feature	JScript	JavaScript	ECMAScript
Operators	typeof	✔	✔	✔
	void	✔	✔	✔
Script Engine identification	ScriptEngine	✔		
	ScriptEngineBuildVersion	✔		
	ScriptEngineMajorVersion	✔		
	ScriptEngineMinorVersion	✔		
String support	String	✔	✔	✔
	anchor	✔	✔	
	big	✔	✔	
	blink	✔	✔	
	bold	✔	✔	
	charAt	✔	✔	✔
	charCodeAt	✔		✔
	concat	✔		
	fixed	✔	✔	
	fontcolor	✔	✔	
	fontsize	✔	✔	
	fromCharCode	✔		✔
	indexOf	✔	✔	✔
	italics	✔	✔	
	lastIndexOf	✔	✔	
	length	✔	✔	✔
	link	✔	✔	
	match	✔		
	replace	✔		
	search	✔		
	slice	✔		
	small	✔	✔	
	split	✔	✔	✔
	strike	✔	✔	
	sub	✔	✔	
	substring		✔	
	sup	✔	✔	
	toLowerCase	✔	✔	✔
	toUpperCase	✔	✔	✔

Chapter 5
Server-Side Objects

Kim Barber

ActiveX server objects and installable components provide a great deal of functionality and enhancements that you can easily use in your Web applications. These server objects make it easy to perform necessary tasks, and the installable components make it easy to add some interesting and powerful features, such as database access.

One of the primary advantages to server-side scripting is the access it provides to ActiveX server objects and components. Internet Information Server (IIS) and Personal Web Server (PWS) provide built-in objects and installable components that you can use for a wide variety of tasks. Using the built-in objects, you can maintain state, perform per-application and per-user initialization, access information passed to and from the server in the Hypertext Transfer Protocol (HTTP) **Request** and **Response** headers, access information about the server, and more. Using the installable components, you can access files on the server, determine the client browser's capabilities, access databases, implement dynamic content and advertising, and much more. Additionally, you can install third-party components and write your own.

ActiveX server objects and components don't have a user interface. They normally perform all user input/output (I/O) via the HTML stream. Therefore, I/O is based on the capabilities of HTML, the target browsers, whether you're also using client-side script, and whether you're also using, for example, ActiveX controls and Java applets.

This chapter introduces you to ActiveX objects and components. As with everything associated with Web development, you can find up-to-the-minute details on Web sites that provide information on this topic, such as **http://msdn.microsoft.com**. Also, IIS 5 and PWS optionally install complete documentation that can help you as you begin to develop your own code.

What Is A Web Application?

First, you need to understand what a *Web application* is. A Web application consists of a virtual directory and all the files and directories belonging to that directory. A Web application starts when the first user requests any page in the application and ends when the server is shut down or when the application is unloaded with the IIS Service Manager.

You also need to understand *user sessions*. The server automatically creates a session when users request their first page in the application and exists until it times out or is explicitly abandoned. The purpose of a session is to provide state for a single user. You manage applications and sessions using script and the events and objects the server provides.

The Global.asa File

Global.asa is an optional file that, as its name implies, is used globally by the application. You can have only one Global.asa file, and it lives in the application root directory. This file specifies scripts and objects that have application or session scope. It contains no content; rather, it's used mainly to manage the application and user sessions. It typically contains script to declare objects, declare and maintain global variables, maintain state, and process application and session events. *Application events* apply to information shared by all users, whereas *session events* apply to individual users.

Application Events

Application events have application-wide scope, and all users share them. You might use an application event to maintain a hit counter, for example. Application events have access to the **Application** and **Server** objects (described later in this chapter). The two application events are:

♦ **Application_OnStart**

♦ **Application_OnEnd**

Application_OnStart occurs before the first user session is created and defines what happens when the application starts. **Application_OnEnd** occurs when the application quits.

The following script defines a hit counter in the **Application_OnStart** event code:

```
Sub Application_OnStart
    Application("hits") = 0
End Sub
```

Of course, this hit counter resets to zero each time the server or the application restarts. To increment the counter, a page could include this ASP code:

```
<% Application("hits")=Application("hits")+1 %>
```

Session Events

Session events have session-wide scope and manage individual user sessions. For example, you can use session events to set user preferences or perform initialization and cleanup of data that applies to the session (a shopping cart, perhaps). Session events have access to all the ActiveX server objects. The two session events are:

♦ **Session_OnStart**

♦ **Session_OnEnd**

Session_OnStart occurs when the server creates a new session and processes any script prior to loading the first page. **Session_OnEnd** occurs when the session times out after a predetermined period or a when a script explicitly abandons it.

The following event procedure increments the site's hit counter when a new user session is created. Additionally, it defines a session variable that contains a visitor number:

```
Sub Session_OnStart
    Application("hits") = Application("hits") + 1
    Session("visitor") = Application("hits")
End Sub
```

Listing 5.1 contains all the script for the sample Global.asa file. At this point, the code doesn't attempt to handle **Application_OnEnd** and **Session_OnEnd**.

Listing 5.1   The Global.asa file.

```
<SCRIPT LANGUAGE=VBScript RUNAT=Server>

Sub Application_OnStart
    Application("hits") = 0
End Sub

Sub Session_OnStart
    Application("hits") = Application("hits") + 1
    Session("visitor") = Application("hits")
End Sub

</SCRIPT>
```

Putting Global.asa To Work

Listing 5.2 contains a Global.asa file with scripts that manage the application's hit counter, user information, and cookies. Additionally, it uses the **FileSystemObject** to access disk files on the server.

The **Application_OnStart** event handler creates a hit counter variable. The value of the hit counter variable is saved to disk in the **Session_OnStart** event handler. The **Application_OnStart** event handler checks for the presence of this file in case the server is being restarted. **Application_OnStart** also checks for a file that stores the most recent customer number. This value is used to assign customer numbers to cookies.

The code in the **Session_OnStart** event handler increments the hit counter and assigns this value to a visitor variable for the individual session. The script then writes the value of the visitor variable to the hit counter file. Then, the script checks to see whether a cookie was sent as part of the HTTP request. If it was not, the code assumes that this is a new visitor. Therefore, the script increments the customer number variable and assigns the new number as a cookie. Also set are the customer status (0 for a new customer) and the cookie's **Expires** property. To keep permanent track of the number, the code updates the customer number file with the new value. Finally, a session variable receives the customer number for future use during the session.

Listing 5.2   Counting hits with the Global.asa file.

```
<SCRIPT LANGUAGE=VBScript RUNAT=Server>

Sub Application_OnStart
    Application("hits") = 0
    Application("cust_num") = 0
    fname = Server.MapPath("/ch5") + "\hits.txt"
    Set fs = Server.CreateObject("Scripting.FileSystemObject")
    Set out = fs.OpenTextFile(fname, 1, FALSE, FALSE)
    Application("hits") = out.ReadLine
    out.close
    fname = Server.MapPath("/ch5") + "\cust_num.txt"
    Set fs = Server.CreateObject("Scripting.FileSystemObject")
    Set out = fs.OpenTextFile(fname, 1, FALSE, FALSE)
    Application("cust_num") = out.ReadLine
    out.close
End Sub

Sub Application_OnEnd
    ' do any necessary cleanup
End Sub
```

```
Sub Session_OnStart
    Application.Lock
    Application("hits") = Application("hits") + 1
    Session("visitor") = Application("hits")

    fname = Server.MapPath("/ch5") + "\hits.txt"
    Set fs = Server.CreateObject("Scripting.FileSystemObject")
    Set out = fs.CreateTextFile(fname, TRUE, FALSE)
    out.WriteLine(Session("visitor"))
    out.close

    If Request.Cookies("CustomerID")("Cust_Num") = Empty Then
        Application("cust_num") = Application("cust_num") + 1
        Response.Cookies("CustomerID")("Cust_Num") = Application("cust_num")
        Response.Cookies("CustomerID")("Status") = 0
        Response.Cookies("CustomerID").Expires = #December 31, 1999#
        fname = Server.MapPath("/ch5") + "\cust_num.txt"
        Set fs = Server.CreateObject("Scripting.FileSystemObject")
        Set out = fs.CreateTextFile(fname, TRUE, FALSE)
        out.WriteLine(Request.Cookies("CustomerID")("Cust_Num"))
        out.close
    End If
    Application.Unlock
    Session("cust_num") = Request.Cookies("CustomerID")("Cust_Num")
End Sub

Sub Session_OnEnd
    ' do any necessary cleanup
End Sub
</SCRIPT>
```

Listing 5.3 uses the cookie's **Status** value, which contains the script for the default page. If the status is 0, the page redirects the customer to the new member registration page. If the status is not 0, the redirection points to the site's home page.

Listing 5.3   The default page.

```
<%@ LANGUAGE="VBSCRIPT" %>
<%
If Request.Cookies("CustomerID")("Status") = 0 Then
    Response.Redirect "5-8.asp"
Else
    Response.Redirect "5-4.asp"
End If
%>
```

```
<HTML>
<HEAD>
<TITLE>The Default Page</TITLE>
</HEAD>
<BODY>
</BODY>
</HTML>
```

Listing 5.4 contains the script for the site's home page. Returning customers automatically see this page. This simple example retrieves the customer's name and favorite cuisine information from the cookie and displays a welcome message.

Listing 5.4   The site's home page.

```
<%@ LANGUAGE="VBSCRIPT" %>
<%
    fname = Request.Cookies("CustomerID")("fname")
    lname = Request.Cookies("CustomerID")("lname")
    cuisine = Request.Cookies("CustomerID")("cuisine")
%>

<HTML>
<HEAD>
<TITLE>Community Dining Club Home Page</TITLE>
</HEAD>
<BODY>

<FONT COLOR=BLUE>
<H1 ALIGN=CENTER>Community Dining Club</H1>
</FONT>
<FONT SIZE=4 COLOR=BLUE>
Welcome back <% =fname & " " & lname %>!<P>
</FONT>
</BODY>
</HTML>
```

Object Declarations

You are not required to declare intrinsic server objects, such as the **Application** and **Session** objects, before you reference them in script. You must, however, declare other objects, such as installable components, before referencing them. You can declare objects that have application or session scope in the Global.asa file or in any script in the application.

You use the **<OBJECT>** tag to declare objects in Global.asa:

```
<OBJECT RUNAT=Server SCOPE=Scope ID=Identifier
  {PROGID=ProgID | CLASSID=ClassID}>
```

SCOPE is either **Application** or **Session** (or you can omit the **SCOPE** clause for a page-level object). **ID** is a unique identifier used to reference an instance of an object, and **PROGID** is a class identifier for the object and is usually in the following format:

```
[Vendor.]Component[.Version]
```

The following **<OBJECT>** tag declares an instance of the **AdRotator** component:

```
<OBJECT RUNAT=Server SCOPE=Application ID=MyAds PROGID="MSWC.AdRotator">
</OBJECT>
```

Alternatively, you can use the object's **CLASSID** to identify the object like this:

```
<OBJECT RUNAT=Server SCOPE=Application ID=MyAds
CLASSID="CLSID:1621F7C0-60AC-11CF-9427-444553540000"></OBJECT>
```

You also have the option of declaring objects in the documents where they are used. The **Server** object (discussed later in this chapter) provides the **CreateObject** method, which can create an object instance. If you use this method, the object's scope is limited to the current file (unless you store it in an application or session variable). Also, there's a slight performance penalty because the object is instantiated immediately. When you use the **<OBJECT>** tag in Global.asa, the object isn't instantiated until a script references it.

ActiveX Server Objects

Internet Information Server provides a number of built-in objects that have a significant amount of functionality. Using these objects, you can access information coming from and going to the user, manage sessions, and access properties and methods on the server.

The built-in server objects are:

- ◆ **Application**
- ◆ **ObjectContext**
- ◆ **Request**
- ◆ **Response**
- ◆ **Server**
- ◆ **Session**

You need not instantiate these objects before using them. Generally, the built-in objects are almost always available, except as noted previously. Only the **Application** and **Session** objects are available in the **Application_OnStart** and **Application_OnEnd** event handlers.

The **Application** Object

You use the **Application** object to share information among all users. You have already seen some use of this object because the **Application_OnStart** and **Application_OnEnd** events belong to it. Also, the hit counter in Listing 5.1 is stored in the **Application** object.

Methods

Because all users of your application share the **Application** object, you can use two methods to prevent multiple users from modifying information at the same time. These methods appear in Table 5.1.

The hit counter example is a good candidate for these methods because you don't want several users trying to increment the counter at the same time. You can modify the code in the **Session_OnStart** event to do this:

```
Sub Session_OnStart
    Application.Lock
    Application("hits") = Application("hits") + 1
    Application.Unlock
    Session("visitor") = Application("hits")
End Sub
```

This problem of multiple users trying to increment the counter at the same time occurs because the script may run concurrently for multiple users. For example, suppose the hit count is currently 122. User A's script reads the value and adds one to it. Then, the operating system preempts the thread for user A and begins user B's thread. User B's thread performs the same steps, reading 122 and adding one to it. User B's thread then stores the new value (123) before the A thread resumes. When it does, it also stores 123 in the application variable. This means you miss one count. This problem can also occur when the server uses multiple processors. Using **Lock** and **Unlock** prevents it from happening.

Collections

Two collections in the **Application** object contain items such as variables and objects. Information stored in these collections has application scope and is available throughout the application. Table 5.2 lists the **Application** object collections.

Table 5.1   Application object methods.

Method	Description
Lock	Prevents other users from modifying object properties
Unlock	Allows other users to modify object properties

Table 5.2 Application object collections.

Collection	Description	Syntax
Contents	Contains items that have been added to the object	**Application.Contents(*key*)**
StaticObjects	Contains objects created with the **<OBJECT>** tag that have application scope	**Application.StaticObjects(*key*)**

The **Contents** collection contains all items added through script, except objects defined with the **<OBJECT>** tag. *key* specifies the name of the item. Using the hit counter, the following statement retrieves the counter's value:

```
t_hits = Application.Contents("hits")
```

You do not have to specify the **Contents** collection explicitly. The following statement produces the same result:

```
t_hits = Application("hits")Events
```

The **Application** object has only two events and you are already familiar with them: **Application_OnStart** and **Application_OnEnd**.

The **ObjectContext** Object

You can use the **ObjectContext** object with Microsoft Transaction Server to commit or abort a transaction.

Methods

Table 5.3 describes the **ObjectContext** object's two methods.

SetComplete doesn't specifically complete the transaction. The transaction will complete when all the involved script components call **SetComplete**. Generally, you don't have to call **SetComplete** because it is assumed if none of the related script components call **SetAbort**.

Events

The **ObjectContext** object's events are listed in Table 5.4.

Table 5.3 ObjectContext methods.

Method	Description
SetComplete	Indicates that the script isn't aware of any reason for the transaction not to complete
SetAbort	Aborts the transaction

Table 5.4   ObjectContext events.

Event	Description
OnTransactionCommit	Fires after the transaction commits
OnTransactionAbort	Fires when the transaction is aborted

The **Request** Object

You use the **Request** object to retrieve values passed from the user. This object is very useful because you can get the values sent from HTML forms or pull data directly out of the query string. Also, you can use this object to access several server environment variables. You will use the **Request** object frequently in your Web applications.

Methods

The one method in the **Request** object is the **BinaryRead** method, which is used to read the data sent from the user as part of an HTTP **POST** request and to store it in an array. Because form data is sent as a **POST** request, you can get form data with this method. However, if you do so, subsequent attempts to read the data from the **Form** collection will cause an error.

Properties

The **Request** object has one property: **TotalBytes**. This property specifies the total number of bytes being sent by the client. The following script uses **TotalBytes** and the **BinaryRead** method to read the data and to store it in an array:

```
<%
mybytes = Request.TotalBytes
myarray = Request.BinaryRead(mybytes)
%>
```

Collections

You can use several collections in the **Request** object to access server environment information, cookie data, client certificate information, and data sent in forms and query strings. Table 5.5 lists the **Request** object collections.

Table 5.5   Request object collections.

Collection	Contents
ClientCertificate	The values stored in the client certificate fields
Cookies	Cookie values
Form	Form element values
QueryString	Variable values sent in the HTTP query string
ServerVariables	Environment variable values

If a Secure Sockets Layer (SSL) protocol is in use, the **ClientCertificate** collection will contain the values stored in the certification fields. The Web server must be configured to request client certificates before you can use this collection. This collection is used as follows:

```
Request.ClientCertificate(key[subfield])
```

key specifies the name of the certification field and can be the following:

- **Certificate**—A string containing the entire certificate content
- **Flags**—Flags that provide additional client certificate information:
  - **ceCertPresent**—Indicates that a certificate is present
  - **ceUnrecognizedIssuer**—Indicates that the last certification in the chain is unknown
- **Issuer**—A string containing a list of subfield values that contain information about the certificate's issuer
- **SerialNumber**—A string containing the certification serial number
- **Subject**—A string containing subfield values that contain subject information of the certificate
- **ValidFrom**—Specifies the date when the certificate became valid
- **ValidUntil**—Specifies the date when the certificate expires

Tip

You must have the client certificate include file in your Active Server Pages if you use these flags. For VBScript, the include file is cevbs.inc. For JavaScript, the include file is cejavas.inc. The include files should be in the \Inetpub\ASPSamp\Samples directory.

Optionally, you can use subfield parameters with the **Issuer** and **Subject** keys. You specify the subfield by suffixing the key parameter with the following suffixes:

- **C**—Country of origin
- **CN**—User's common name (for use with the **Subject** key only)
- **GN**—A given name
- **I**—Set of initials
- **L**—Locality
- **O**—Company or organization name
- **OU**—Name of the organizational unit
- **S**—State or province
- **T**—Title of the person or organization

Using the **Cookies** collection, you can retrieve the values of cookies sent in the HTTP request. The following statement retrieves the value of a cookie named **CustomerID**:

```
t_custid = Request.Cookies("CustomerID")
```

The **Cookies** collection has an optional attribute—*key*—that you use to retrieve values from cookie dictionaries. Assuming that **CustomerID** is a dictionary with three keys— **FirstName**, **LastName**, and **AccountNumber**—you would use the following syntax to retrieve the customer's account number:

```
t_acctnum = Request.Cookies("CustomerID")("AccountNumber")
```

If you access a cookie dictionary without specifying the key, all the keys are returned as a single query string. For example, the statement

```
t_custid = Request.Cookies("CustomerID")
```

returns

```
FirstName=thefirstname&LastName=thelastname&AccountNumber=theaccountnumber
```

The **Cookies** collection has one optional attribute—**HasKeys**—that returns **TRUE** if the cookie is a dictionary and **FALSE** if it isn't. This attribute is referenced as follows:

```
t_amiacookie = Request.Cookies("CustomerID").HasKeys
```

You can use the **Form** collection to retrieve the values of form elements passed by an HTTP **POST** request. This collection contains all the values a user entered into a form and submitted. The following syntax is used:

```
Request.Form(element)[(index)] | [.Count]
```

element specifies the name of the form element being accessed. The **Count** attribute returns the number of data items in the element. *index* is an optional parameter that you use to access one of multiple form element values and is in the range of 1 to **Count**. For example, if you have a form element named **fish** that contains five values, you would access the third value as follows:

```
t_fish = Request.Form("fish")(3)
```

If you reference a form element that has multiple values and you don't specify an index, all the values are returned in a comma-delimited string.

The following example consists of two listings. Listing 5.5 contains an HTML document with a form that collects pay data from the user. When the user clicks on the Submit button, the form posts its data to the script in Listing 5.6, which retrieves the form data and calculates and displays the gross pay.

Listing 5.5   An input form.

```
<HTML>
<HEAD>
<TITLE>Listing 5.5</TITLE>
</HEAD>
<BODY>

<FORM METHOD=POST ACTION="5-6.asp">
<PRE>
Hours Worked: <INPUT TYPE=TEXT NAME="hours">
Hourly Wage:  <INPUT TYPE=TEXT NAME="wage">
<INPUT TYPE=SUBMIT VALUE="Calculate">
</PRE>
</FORM>

</BODY>
</HTML>
```

Listing 5.6   Retrieving values with the Form collection.

```
<HTML>
<HEAD>
<TITLE>Listing 5.6</TITLE>
</HEAD>
<BODY>

<%
   t_hours = Request.Form("hours")
   t_wage = Request.Form("wage")
   t_pay = t_hours * t_wage

  Response.Write("Gross pay: " & t_pay)
%>

</BODY>
</HTML>
```

The **Response** object, which is discussed later, is used to send output to the HTML stream. The **Request** object will give you a break if you don't like to type. Specifying the **Form** collection is optional. The statement

```
Request("hours")
```

also works.

The **QueryString** collection lets you retrieve the values of variables in an HTTP query string. The **QueryString** collection contains all the information passed as a parameter after the ? in a URL or from a form if the action is **GET**. **QueryString** uses this syntax:

```
Request.QueryString("variable")[(index) | [.Count]
```

variable specifies the name of the variable name in the HTTP query string. *index* is an optional parameter that you use to access one of multiple values for a variable. **Count** returns the number of variables in the collection.

The following HTML defines a hyperlink to a page called calcpay.asp and appends the hour and wage information as a query string to the URL:

```
<A HREF="calcpay.asp?hours=40&wage=10">Calculate Pay</A>
```

The following script in calcpay.asp uses the **QueryString** collection to retrieve the values and calculate the gross pay:

```
<%
     t_hours = Request.QueryString("hours")
     t_wage = Request.QueryString("wage")
     t_pay = t_hours * t_wage
%>
```

The **QueryString** collection is very useful if you need to retrieve values directly from a query. Using the pay calculator as an example, the following script retrieves the variable name and value from the query string:

```
<%
For Each item in Request.QueryString
     Response.Write(item + " " + Request.QueryString(item) + "<BR>")
Next
%>
```

You can use this method to retrieve name-value pairs without knowing anything about the query string.

The **ServerVariables** collection is useful for retrieving the values of several predefined environment variables. You'll find the variables in Table 5.6.

As you can see, the **ServerVariables** collection provides access to a lot of useful information. **CONTENT_LENGTH** is especially useful when you're processing forms. Using this variable, you can use the same document to collect information from the user and process the information. You can omit the collection name when using the **Request** object. If you do, IIS searches the collections in the following order: **QueryString**, **Form**, **Cookies**, **ClientCertificate**, and **ServerVariables**.

Table 5.6   The ServerVariables collection.

Variable	Description
ALL_HTTP	All HTTP headers sent by the client
ALL_RAW	All HTTP headers in raw form
APPL_MD_PATH	The metabase path for the application
APPL_PHYSICAL_PATH	The physical path for the application
AUTH_PASSWORD	The value in the client's authentication dialog box
AUTH_TYPE	The authentication method used to validate users
AUTH_USER	The raw authenticated username
CERT_COOKIE	A unique ID for the client certificate
CERT_FLAGS	Bit 0 is set if the client certificate is present; bit 1 is set if the certifying authority isn't valid
CERT_USER	The issuer of the client certificate
CERT_KEYSIZE	The size of the SSL key in bits
CERT_SECRETKEYSIZE	The number of bits in the private key
CERT_SERIALNUMBER	The serial number of the client certificate
CERT_SERVER_ISSUER	The issuer of the server certificate
CERT_SERVER_SUBJECT	The subject field of the server certificate
CERT_SUBJECT	The subject of the server certificate
CONTENT_LENGTH	The content length provided by the client
CONTENT_TYPE	The data type sent by the client
GATEWAY_INTERFACE	The version of the CGI specification in use by the server
HTTP_HeaderName	The value stored in the header specified by **HeaderName**
HTTPS	**ON** if the request came from a secure SSL channel; **OFF** if it came from a nonsecure channel
HTTPS_KEYSIZE	The size in bits of the SSL key
HTTP_SECRETKEYSIZE	The size in bits of the server certificate private key
HTTPS_SERVER_ISSUER	The issuer of the server certificate
HTTPS_SERVER_SUBJECT	The subject of the server certificate
INSTANCE_ID	The ID of the current instance is IIS
INSTANCE_META_PATH	The metabase path for the current instance of IIS
LOCAL_ADDR	The address on which the request came in
LOGON_USER	The NT account the user is logged into
PATH_INFO	Path information provided by the client
PATH_TRANSLATED	A version of **PATH_INFO** with any necessary virtual-to-physical mapping
QUERY_STRING	The query string
REMOTE_ADDR	The IP address of the machine making the request
REMOTE_HOST	The name of the host making the request
REMOTE_USER	The username sent by the user
REQUEST_METHOD	The method used (for example, **POST** and **GET**)
SCRIPT_NAME	The virtual path to the executing script
SERVER_NAME	The server's host name, DNS alias, or IP address
SERVER_PORT	The port number where the request was sent

(continued)

Table 5.6   The ServerVariables collection *(continued)*.

Variable	Description
SERVER_PORT_SECURE	Contains 1 if on a secure port; 0 if not on a secure port
SERVER_PROTOCOL	The name and version of the request information protocol
SERVER_SOFTWARE	The name and version of the server software
URL	The base URL

The **Response** Object

The **Response** object provides access to the information sent in the HTTP **Response** header. You can use the **Response** object to create cookies, control caching, write content to the HTTP output stream, and perform several other functions.

Methods

Table 5.7 contains the **Response** object methods. In practice, you'll use only a few of them (notably **Write**).

AddHeader doesn't replace any existing header information with the same name; rather, it adds a new HTTP header. Normally, you don't need to use this method because other **Response** object methods usually provide all the functionality you need. **AppendToLog** appends a specified string to the end of the Web server log. **BinaryWrite** sends the specified data without any character conversion to the HTTP output stream. This method is useful for writing binary data, such as images.

The **Clear** method erases any buffered HTML output in the response body. You must be sure to set **Response.Buffer** to **TRUE** before using this method, or an error will occur. **End** causes the server to stop processing the ASP file and flush the buffer. Set **Response.Buffer** to **FALSE** to prevent the output from being returned. **Flush** will return an error if **Response.Buffer** is not **TRUE**. The **Redirect** method causes the browser to try to connect to the specified URL and automatically generates a response body containing the redirect URL. Additionally, it sends the following explicit header:

```
HTTP/1.0 302 Object Moved Location URL
```

Table 5.7 Response object methods.

Method	Description
AddHeader	Adds an HTML header
AppendToLog	Appends a string of up to 80 characters to the Web server log file
BinaryWrite	Writes the specified information to the HTTP output stream
Clear	Erases any buffered HTML output
End	Stops processing of the HTML file and returns the result
Flush	Sends buffered output immediately
Redirect	Causes the browser to try connecting to another URL
Write	Writes a string to the HTTP output stream

The **Write** method writes a string to the HTTP output stream and is generally equivalent to the = character used to send output in server-side script delimiters (<%...%>).

Properties

You'll find the list of **Response** object properties in Table 5.8.

You use the **Buffer** property to specify whether to buffer output. If **Buffer** is set to **TRUE**, the server will not send a response until all the scripts in the current page are finished executing or until **Flush** or **End** is called. **FALSE** is the default setting. You use **CacheControl** to override the **Private** default value. Proxy servers can cache ASP output if you set this property to **Public**. **Charset** appends the name of the character set to the **Response** object content-type header. **ContentType** is set to a string in the HTTP format **type/subtype**.

The **Expires** property controls when a page is reloaded. If the user refreshes a page before the specified time elapses, the page is read from the browser's cache. If it is refreshed after the time elapses, the page is reloaded. In some cases, you might want the user to get a new page every time he or she requests it. For example, the page might display the current outdoor temperature. To cause this to happen, set **Expires** to zero.

ExpiresAbsolute specifies a date and time for when a cached page expires. If the user returns before then, the cached page is displayed. **IsClientConnected** indicates whether the client has disconnected from the server. The **Pics** property adds a value to the **pics-label Response** header. You can use the **Status** property to specify the value of the HTTP status returned by the server. The status string consists of a three-digit number followed by a brief description.

Collections

The **Response** object has only one collection: **Cookies**. You use the **Cookies** collection to set cookie values. If the cookie doesn't exist, you create it with the following syntax:

```
Response.Cookies(name)[(key) | .attribute] = "value"
```

Table 5.8   Response object properties.

Property	Description
Buffer	Specifies whether to buffer output
CacheControl	Overrides the **Private** default value
Charset	Appends the character set name to the HTTP content-type header
ContentType	Specifies the HTTP content type for the response
Expires	Specifies the length of time before a cached page expires
ExpiresAbsolute	Specifies the date and time when a cached page expires
IsClientConnected	Indicates whether the client has disconnected from the server since the last **Response.Write**
Pics	Adds a value to the **Response** header **pics-label** field
Status	Specifies the value of the HTTP status line returned by the server

If you want to create a cookie dictionary, you specify the *key* name and assign it a value. For example, the following creates a cookie with two keys:

```
Response.Cookies("CustomerID")("LastName") = "Smith"
Response.Cookies("CustomerID")("FirstName") = "John"
```

The **Server** Object

The **Server** object provides access to properties and methods on the server. The methods provided are mainly utility functions.

Methods

Table 5.9 describes the methods available with the **Server** object.

You use **CreateObject** to create an instance of a server component, such as **AdRotator**. Recall from the discussion on Global.asa that you can also create an instance of a server component by using the **<OBJECT>** tag. The server immediately instantiates objects created with **CreateObject**. If you use the **<OBJECT>** tag, the server doesn't actually create the object until a script uses it.

The statement

```
<% Set myad = Server.CreateObject("MSWC.AdRotator")%>
```

sets **myad** to reference an instance of the **AdRotator** component.

Objects created with **CreateObject** have page scope by default. If you need an object to have application or session scope, create it by using the **<OBJECT>** tag, and specify the scope or store the object in an application or session variable. The following statement creates an instance of the **AdRotator** component with session scope:

```
<OBJECT RUNAT=Server SCOPE=Session
  ID=myad PROGID="MSWC.AdRotator">
</OJBECT>
```

Table 5.9   Server object methods.

Method	Description
CreateObject	Creates an instance of a server component
HTMLEncode	Applies HTML encoding to the specified string
MapPath	Returns the physical path for the specified relative path
URLEncode	Applies URL encoding to the specified string

HTMLEncode is used to apply HTML encoding to a string. This method is frequently useful if you want to display unparsed HTML tags in the browser display. For example, the line

```
<% s=Server.HTMLEncode("This is the <OBJECT> tag.") %>
```

sets variable **s** to:

```
This is the &It;OBJECT&gt; tag.
```

MapPath is useful if you need to write to disk and don't know, or don't want to know, what the physical path is. To illustrate this method, you can revise the sample Global.asa file to save the hit counter to disk. Listing 5.7 contains the revised script.

Listing 5.7   Using the MapPath method.
```
<SCRIPT LANGUAGE=VBScript RUNAT=Server>
Sub Application_OnStart
    Application("hits") = 0
    fname = Server.MapPath("/ch5") + "\hits.txt"
    Set fs = Server.CreateObject("Scripting.FileSystemObject")
    set out = fs.OpenTextFile(fname, 1, FALSE, FALSE)
    Application("hits") = out.ReadLine
    out.close
End Sub

Sub Session_OnStart
    Application.Lock
    Application("hits") = Application("hits") + 1
    Application.Unlock
    Session("visitor") = Application("hits")
    fname = Server.MapPath("/ch5") + "\hits.txt"
    Set fs = Server.CreateObject("Scripting.FileSystemObject")
    set out = fs.CreateTextFile(fname, TRUE, FALSE)
    out.WriteLine(Session("visitor"))
    out.close
End Sub

</SCRIPT>
```

In the **Application_OnStart** event handler, the **MapPath** method is used to assign the physical path with a file name to the variable **fname**. **MapPath** converts the logical application path, which on my computer is http://localhost/Ch5, to the physical path, which is C:\inetpub\wwwroot\Ch5. The **FileSystemObject** component creates the file where the program will store the hit value. You'll read more about the **FileSystemObject** later in this chapter.

The **Session_OnStart** event handler updates hits.txt every time the server creates a new session.

URLEncode applies URL encoding to the specified string. This method is frequently useful if you are building HTTP query strings dynamically. Whenever the browser sends a string in a query string, it encodes spaces and other characters with special characters. This encoding is necessary for successfully transmitting the string.

The **Session** Object

The **Session** object is very similar to the **Application** object, the primary difference being that you use the **Session** object to manage information on individual user sessions. A **Session** object is created when a user who doesn't already have a session accesses a page in the application. The object persists until it times out or is explicitly abandoned.

The **Session** object is a good place to store information about the user, including his or her color preferences, whether the client browser can display graphics or use ActiveX controls, and so on.

Methods

The **Session** object has only one method. The **Abandon** method destroys the session and all data maintained by the **Session** object for the session. By default, a user session lasts for 20 minutes (see the **Timeout** property in Table 5.10). If 20 minutes pass without the user requesting or refreshing a page, the session goes away. You can force the session to close earlier by calling **Abandon**:

```
Session.Abandon
```

Properties

The **Session** object has the properties listed in Table 5.10.

CodePage is a character set that varies, depending on the language in use. For example, 1252 is the code page for English. An **LCID** uniquely identifies the language in use.

SessionID returns a unique identifier for each user. Don't store this ID for later use because it is valid only for the duration of the session.

Table 5.10   Session object properties.

Property	Description
CodePage	Specifies the character set code page
LCID	Specifies the locale identifier
SessionID	Returns a unique session identifier for the user
Timeout	Specifies the timeout period in minutes for the session

By default, sessions last for 20 minutes. If the user hasn't requested or refreshed a page after 20 minutes, the session goes away. You can change the 20-minute default by assigning a different value to the **Timeout** property like this:

```
Session.Timeout = 10
```

This statement causes the timeout to occur in 10 minutes. You can also change the timeout by using the IIS Service Manager or by changing the Registry.

Collections

The **Session** object has two collections: **Contents** and **StaticObjects**. They function the same for user sessions as they do for the **Application** object. The **Contents** collection contains all the items defined for the session except those defined with the **<OBJECT>** tag. The **StaticObjects** collection contains objects defined with the **<OBJECT>** tag that have session scope.

Events

The **Session** object has the **Session_OnStart** and **Session_OnEnd** events. These events are described in the section "The Global.asa File."

Conclusion

The ActiveX server objects provide the functionality that you need to manage the application and user sessions. Being able to tap into the HTTP **Request** and **Response** headers gives you substantial power to retrieve and manage user input and to return output.

Although some of the server objects have obscure purposes, you'll find that many of the methods in **Response** and **Request** are crucial for handling forms. When you are accustomed to using them, variables in the **Session** and **Application** objects are very handy as well.

ActiveX Components

ActiveX components are installable components that run on the server as part of the Web application. They are based on the Microsoft Component Object Model (COM), which is a standard that defines how programs can create and use binary objects (as opposed to, for example, C++ or Java objects, which are objects only at the source code level). Server components generally provide functionality that is routinely needed, such as database and file access. For the purposes of this book, you'll use ActiveX components only with Web pages, but you can also use them in many other types of applications, such as Visual Basic or C++ programs.

You can include server components in your application using two methods. The first method uses the **Server** object **CreateObject** method like this:

```
<% Set myadd = Server.CreateObject("MSWC.AdRotator") %>
```

The second method uses the **<OBJECT>** tag, as follows:

```
<OBJECT RUNAT=Server SCOPE=Application ID=myads PROGID="MSWC.AdRotator">
</OBJECT>
```

The first method causes the object to be instantiated immediately, and the scope of the object is limited to the document in which it is declared. When the second method is used, the object isn't instantiated until it is referenced in script, at which time it has either application or session scope. Therefore, you can reference the object anywhere it's in scope.

The remainder of this chapter introduces you to many of the components provided with IIS 5 and PWS.

The **AdRotator** Component

Advertising is the traditional way to generate revenue from the Web. Many sites display ads and provide links to advertisers' Web sites. The **AdRotator** component makes it very easy to do so. This component automates the display of different advertisements each time the user opens or reloads a page and will optionally jump to the specified Web site when the user clicks on the ad. Using the **AdRotator** component requires three files: the ASP file that displays the ad, the Rotator Schedule file that manages the ads, and a redirection file that takes care of jumping to the advertiser's Web site (and possibly logging the hit).

The Rotator Schedule File

The **AdRotator** component uses a Rotator Schedule file to maintain information that it uses to manage and display the various ads. The Rotator Schedule file contains the details of each ad, including the size of the ad's display area, the percentage of time the ad is displayed, the image to display, and the advertiser's URL.

The Rotator Schedule file has two sections. The first section is optional and contains information that pertains to all ads in the schedule. The second section specifies information for each ad. An asterisk (*) separates the two sections. If you omit the first section, place an asterisk in the first line of the file.

The first section can take any of the optional parameters in Table 5.11.

The second section of the Rotator Schedule file contains up to four parameters for each ad. Table 5.12 lists the available parameters.

If the advertiser doesn't have a Web site, enter a hyphen (-) for the **adHomePageURL**. **impressions** specifies the relative percentage of time an ad is displayed. The total for all ads in the file should be 100. Keep in mind that the component selects ads at random, using the **impressions** number as a guide.

Table 5.11   Optional Rotator Schedule file parameters.

Parameter	Description
Border	Thickness of the border around the ad; default is 1
Height	Height of the display area in pixels; default is 60
Redirect	Path to the file that implements redirection
Width	Width of the display area in pixels; default is 440

Table 5.12   Available advertisement parameters.

Parameter	Description
adHomePageURL	Location of the advertiser's home page
adURL	Location of the ad image file
impressions	The percentage of time an ad is displayed
text	Alternate text for nongraphical browsers

The Redirection File

You must supply a Redirection file to send the user to the advertiser's Web site. This file generally includes the following line of script that parses the query string sent by the **AdRotator** object:

```
<% Response.Redirect(Request.QueryString("URL")) %>
```

The GetAdvertisement Method

The **AdRotator** component has one method—**GetAdvertisement**—that retrieves the next ad from the Rotator Schedule file.

An AdRotator Component Example

The new member registration page (see Listing 5.8) uses the **AdRotator** component to display advertising that changes when the page loads (or reloads). This example contains only three ads: Al's Mexican Palace, Paul's China Garden, and Kim's Steak House. When the user clicks on the ads, he or she sees the appropriate Web page.

Listing 5.8   The new member registration page.

```
<%@ LANGUAGE="VBSCRIPT" %>
<% Response.Expires = 0 %>
<% Set myad = Server.CreateObject("MSWC.AdRotator") %>
<% =myad.GetAdvertisement("5-9.txt") %>

<HTML>
<HEAD>
<TITLE>New Member Registration</TITLE>
</HEAD>
<BODY>
<H2 Align=Center>New Member Registration</H2>
<HR SIZE=5 WIDTH=90%>
```

```
<P ALIGN=CENTER>
<TABLE>
<TD>
<PRE>
<FORM METHOD=POST ACTION="5-15.asp">
<B>First Name:  </B><INPUT TYPE=TEXT NAME="firstname">
<B>Last Name:   </B><INPUT TYPE=TEXT NAME="lastname">
<B>Address1: </B><INPUT TYPE=TEXT NAME="addr1">
<B>Address2:  </B><INPUT TYPE=TEXT NAME="addr2">
<B>City:   </B><INPUT TYPE=TEXT NAME="city">
<B>State:   </B><INPUT TYPE=TEXT NAME="state" MAXLENGTH=2 SIZE=2>
<B>Zip:   </B><INPUT TYPE=TEXT NAME="zip" MAXLENGTH=10 SIZE=10>
<B>Area Code/Phone: </B><INPUT TYPE=TEXT NAME="code" MAXLENGTH=3 SIZE=3>
<INPUT TYPE=TEXT NAME="phone" MAXLENGTH=7 SIZE=7>

<B>Preferred Cuisine: </B><SELECT NAME="cuisine" SIZE="1">
                          <OPTION VALUE="1">American
                          <OPTION VALUE="2">Chinese
                          <OPTION VALUE="3">French
                          <OPTION VALUE="4">German
                          <OPTION VALUE="5">Greek
                          <OPTION VALUE="6">Indian
                          <OPTION VALUE="7">Italian
                          <OPTION VALUE="8">Japanese
                          <OPTION VALUE="9">Seafood
                          <OPTION VALUE="0">Other
                          </SELECT>

<INPUT TYPE=SUBMIT VALUE="Register"> <INPUT TYPE="RESET" VALUE="Clear">
</PRE>
</FORM>
</TD>
</TABLE>
</P>
</BODY>
</HTML>
```

Notice the equal sign (=) preceding the call to **GetAdvertisement** in Listing 5.8. It is necessary but easy to forget. If you forget to include this character, the component will not display the ad. Instead, it will generate all the HTML required, and the server will throw it away.

The **AdRotator** component uses a Rotator Schedule file to maintain information about the ads. Listing 5.9 contains the code for this file. The **GetAdvertisement** method retrieves the information from the Rotator Schedule file.

Listing 5.9   The Rotator Schedule file.

```
--------------- Rotator Schedule --------------------
REDIRECT 5-10.asp
width 440
height 60
border 0
*
als.bmp
http://kbarbercp//aspbb2ed/ch5/als.asp
Enjoy Al's authentic Mexican food!
34
pauls.bmp
http:// kbarbercp//aspbb2ed/ch5/pauls.asp
Hunan is Paul's specialty!
33
kims.bmp
http:// kbarbercp//aspbb2ed/ch5/kims.asp
Huge Texas style steak!
33
```

Listing 5.10 contains the script that implements the redirection to the advertiser's Web site.

Listing 5.10   The Redirect file.

```
<%@ LANGUAGE="VBSCRIPT" %>
<!-- Note: Could redirect to a local page that counts the hit and
redirects to the sponsor's URL. -->
<% Response.Redirect(Request.QueryString("URL")) %>
```

The Browser Capabilities Component

The **Browser Capabilities** component provides information about the client browser's capabilities. When the client browser connects to the Web server, it sends an HTTP **Request** header, which sends a variety of information about the browser. One piece of information it sends—the **User-Agent** header—is a string that contains the browser name and version. You can use this information to send output that is customized according to the client's capabilities. For example, you don't want to send client-side VBScript to a browser that doesn't support it.

The **Browser Capabilities** component compares the **User-Agent** header to header entries in a special file, Browscap.ini, which is on the server in the directory \WINNT\system32\ inetsrv in NT Server and \WINDOWS\SYSTEM\inetsrv on PWS in Windows 98. This file contains information on the capabilities supported by various browsers, identified by the **User-Agent** header. It is important to realize that the server doesn't really know what the browser can or can't do; it knows only what the Browscap.ini file says about a given **User-Agent** string. The following is a sample browser definition:

```
; browscap.ini
[Netscape 3.0]
browser=Netscape
version=3.0
majorver=#3
minorver=#0
frames=TRUE
tables=TRUE
cookies=TRUE
backgroundsounds=FALSE
vbscript=FALSE
javascript=TRUE
ActiveXControls=FALSE

[Mozilla/3.0b5 (Win95; I)]
parent=Netscape 3.0
platform=Win95
```

The first line is a comment, which is indicated by a semicolon. The **User-Agent** identifier is enclosed in brackets and is followed by the definitions for that browser. You can make changes to this file to add or remove capabilities and complete definitions.

browser is an optional parameter that specifies the HTTP **User-Agent** header of a browser to use as a parent browser. **parent** allows the second browser definition to inherit from the first. Inherited properties remain set unless they are overwritten in the browser definition.

Table 5.13 lists some of the possible entries in Browscap.ini.

Table 5.13   Possible Browscap.ini entries.

Property	Description
ActiveXControls	Indicates whether ActiveX controls are supported
backgroundsounds	Indicates whether background sounds are supported
beta	Indicates whether the browser is beta software
browser	Indicates the name of the browser
cdf	Indicates whether the browser supports the Channel Definition Format
cookies	Indicates whether cookies are supported
frames	Indicates whether frames are supported
Javaapplets	Indicates whether Java applets are supported
javascript	Indicates whether JavaScript is supported
platform	Indicates the platform the browser runs on
tables	Indicates whether tables are supported
vbscript	Indicates whether VBScript is supported
version	Indicates the version number of the browser

Using The Browser Capabilities Component

The **Browser Capabilities** component provides information about the capabilities of the client browser. It uses the **User-Agent** header passed in the HTTP **Request** header to search for browser data in the Browscap.ini file. If a match is found, the component assigns entries in Browscap.ini to the object variable's properties. You can use this information to customize output on the basis of the browser in use.

Listing 5.11 contains script to display the browser's capabilities in an HTML table.

Listing 5.11   Using the Browser Capabilities component.

```
<%@ LANGUAGE="VBSCRIPT" %>
<% Set bc = Server.CreateObject("MSWC.BrowserType") %>
<HTML>
<HEAD>
<TITLE>Browser Capabilities</TITLE>
</HEAD>
<BODY>
<H3>The following is a list of properties of your browser:</H3>
<TABLE BORDER=1>
<TR><TD>Browser Type</TD><TD><%= bc.browser %></TD>
<TR><TD>What Version</TD><TD><%= bc.version %></TD>
<TR><TD>Major Version</TD><TD><%= bc.majorver %></TD>
<TR><TD>Minor Version</TD><TD><%= bc.minorver %></TD>
<TR><TD>Beta</TD><TD><%= bc.beta %></TD>
<TR><TD>Platform</TD><TD><%= bc.platform %></TD>
<TR><TD>Frames</TD><TD><%= bc.frames %></TD>
<TR><TD>Tables</TD><TD><%= bc.tables %></TD>
<TR><TD>Cookies</TD><TD><%= bc.cookies %></TD>
<TR><TD>Background Sounds</TD><TD><%= bc.backgroundsounds %></TD>
<TR><TD>ActiveX Controls</TD><TD><%= bc.ActiveXControls %></TD>
<TR><TD>VBScript</TD><TD><%= bc.vbscript %></TD>
<TR><TD>JavaScript</TD><TD><%= bc.javascript %></TD>
<TR><TD>Java Applets</TD><TD><%= bc.Javaapplets %></TD>
</TABLE>
</BODY>
</HTML>
```

The **Content Linking** Component

Most Web pages contain links to other pages on the same site, and managing these links can sometimes be a bit of work. If your Web application consists of several pages with Next and Previous links, you often need to make changes to multiple pages as pages are added to or removed from the application.

The **Content Linking** component simplifies keeping track of these links by managing them as though the Web pages were pages in a book. Using this component, you can include jumps to the next or previous Web page in a list of URLs you create that automatically changes when your content changes. Better still, you can write script to handle the previous and next linking and include this one file in each page. Another possibility is to use the content linking component to automatically generate an index for your site.

The Content Linking List File

The **Content Linking** component references a Content Linking List file that contains a list of the linked Web pages. This file contains a line of information for each URL in the list. Only two pieces of information are necessary: the URL and a description. This information is separated by one Tab, and the line ends with a hard return (Enter):

```
Web page URL <Tab> description [<Tab> comment]<Enter>
```

You can also include an optional comment. Be careful, though. The component insists that you separate the fields using a real Tab character and not some number of blank spaces. Depending on the text editor you use, you might have to do something special to insert an actual Tab.

The *Web page URL* is the relative, or virtual, URL of the Web page. You can't use absolute URLs, such as those that begin with **http:**, **//**, or ****.

Methods

The **Content Linking** component provides methods to move through and retrieve information from the Content Linking List file. These methods are listed in Table 5.14.

Table 5.14 Content Linking component methods.

Method	Description
GetListCount	Returns the number of items in the list file
GetListIndex	Returns the index of the current page in the list
GetNextDescription	Returns the description of the next page in the list
GetNextURL	Returns the URL of the next page in the list
GetNthDescription	Returns the description of the nth page in the list
GetNthURL	Returns the URL of the nth page in the list
GetPreviousDescription	Returns the description of the previous page in the list
GetPreviousURL	Returns the URL of the previous page in the list

Using The Content Linking Component

The **Content Linking** component makes it easy to manage links among pages in your Web application. It uses a text file, the Content Linking List, to maintain a list of URLs in the order you want them navigated. The **Content Linking** component provides methods to move through the list file. You can also build an index using the content linking component.

Listing 5.12 contains an ASP file that implements the **Content Linking** component. It uses the Content Linking List file to build an HTML unordered list of hyperlinks.

Listing 5.12   Using the Content Linking component.

```
<%@ LANGUAGE="VBSCRIPT" %>
<% Set NextLink = Server.CreateObject("MSWC.NextLink") %>

<HTML>
<HEAD>
<TITLE>Content Linking Component</TITLE>
</HEAD>
<BODY>
<% count = NextLink.GetListCount("5-13.txt") %>
<% i = 1 %>
<UL>
<% Do While(i <= count) %>
<LI><A HREF="<% =NextLink.GetNthURL("5-13.txt",i) %>">
<% =NextLink.GetNthDescription("5-13.txt",i) %></A>
<% i = i + 1 %>
<% Loop %>
</UL>
</BODY>
</HTML>
```

Listing 5.13 contains the Content Linking List file with the URLs and descriptions of the three pages used in this example.

Listing 5.13   The Content Linking List file.

```
als.asp   Al's Mexican Palace
kims.asp  Kim's Steak House
pauls.asp  Paul's China Garden
```

Listing 5.14 contains script that is useful to include in each page listed in the list file. The script implements Previous and Next links on all the pages. To make it look a little better, this example uses graphics to add Previous and Next pointers. You can put this code in one file and use the **#include** directive to include it in the pages, as shown here:

```
<!-- #include file =  "5-14.inc" -->
```

Listing 5.14   A handy include file.

```
<% Set NextLink = Server.CreateObject("MSWC.NextLink") %>
<A HREF="<% =NextLink.GetPreviousURL("10-13.txt") %> ">
<IMG SRC="u_prev_3.gif"></A>
<A HREF="<% =NextLink.GetNextURL("10-13.txt") %> ">
<IMG SRC="u_next_3.gif"></A>
<HR>
<A HREF="link.asp">Return to table of contents</A>
```

The **Database Access** Component

The **Database Access** component uses Active Data Objects (ADOs) to provide access to information stored in Open Database Connectivity (ODBC) data sources. You can easily add database access to your Web applications using ADO, which consists of an object model with the following objects:

♦ **Command**—Defines a specific command that can be executed against a data source

♦ **Connection**—Represents an open connection to a data source

♦ **Error**—Contains details pertaining to data access errors

♦ **Field**—Represents a column of data within a **Recordset**

♦ **Parameter**—Represents a parameter or argument associated with a parameterized **Command**

♦ **Property**—Represents a characteristic of an ADO object that is defined by the provider

♦ **Recordset**—Represents the set of records returned from a query

This chapter provides an introduction to ADO and uses only the **Connection** and **Recordset** objects to read and write to a database.

The Connection Object

A **Connection** object represents a unique connection to a data source. This object has several properties and methods that the underlying database may or may not support. Table 5.15 contains the **Connection** object properties. The **Connection** object's methods appear in Table 5.16.

The Recordset Object

The **Recordset** object is the main interface to the data. It represents the set of records from a table or the results of a command that has been executed. **Recordset** objects are constructed using records (rows) and fields (columns). The **Recordset** object references a single record at a time in the current record set.

Table 5.15   Connection object properties.

Property	Description
Attributes	References one or more attributes of an object
ConnectionString	Contains information used to establish a connection to a data source
CommandTimeout	Specifies how long to wait while executing a command before timing out
DefaultDatabase	Specifies the default database
IsolationLevel	Specifies the level of isolation
Mode	Specifies the available permissions for modifying data in a connection
Provider	Specifies the provider's name
Version	Indicates the ADO version number

Table 5.16   Connection object methods.

Method	Description
BeginTrans	Begins a new transaction
Close	Closes an open object and dependent objects
CommitTrans	Saves changes and ends the transaction
Execute	Executes the specified query, SQL statement, or stored procedure
Open	Opens a connection to a data source
RollbackTrans	Cancels any changes and ends the transaction

The following script generates a record set from the data source **custdb**:

```
<%
Set Conn = Server.CreateObject("ADODB.Connection")
Conn.Open "custdb"
Set RS = Conn.Execute("SELECT * FROM custinfo")
%>
```

You can also create **Recordset** objects without using a previously defined **Connection** object. You do so by passing a connection string with the **Open** method. The following is an example:

```
<%
Set RS = Server.CreateObject("ADODB.Recordset")
RS.Open "SELECT * FROM custinfo","custdb",3,3
%>
```

The **Open** method uses the following syntax:

```
recordset.Open source, ActiveConnection,CursorType,LockType
```

The ADO still creates a **Connection** object in the previous example but doesn't assign it to a variable. If you're assigning multiple **Recordset** objects over the same connection, you should explicitly create a **Connection** object. Otherwise, ADO creates a new **Connection** object for each **Recordset** object.

The **Recordset** object has two collections: **Fields** and **Properties**. The **Fields** collection consists of **Field** objects, each corresponding to a column in the record set. You can refer to a **Field** object by its **Name** property or by its number, as in this example:

```
RS.Fields.Item(0)
RS.Fields.Item("CustomerID")
RS.Fields(0)
RS.Fields("CustomerID")
RS("CustomerID")
```

The **Properties** collection consists of **Property** objects. Each **Property** object corresponds to a characteristic of the ADO object specific to the provider. The following example displays the property names of a **Connection** object:

```
<%
Set Conn = Server.CreateObject("ADODB.Connection")
Conn.Open "custdb"
%>
<% For I = 0 to Conn.Properties.Count - 1 %>
<% =Conn.Properties(I) %>
<BR>
<% Next %>
```

The **Recordset** object's properties are listed in Table 5.17. Table 5.18 lists the **Recordset** object's methods.

Table 5.17   Recordset object properties.

Property	Description
AbsolutePage	Specifies to which page to move for a new record
AbsolutePosition	Specifies the ordinal position of a **Recordset** object's current record
ActiveConnection	Specifies to which **Connection** object the specified **Command** or **Recordset** object belongs
BOF	Indicates that the current record position is before the first record
Bookmark	Returns a bookmark that identifies the current record or sets the current record to the record identified by a valid bookmark
Cachesize	Specifies the number of records that are cached locally in memory
CursorLocation	Specifies the location of the cursor engine
CursorType	Specifies the cursor type
EditMode	Specifies the editing status of the current record
EOF	Indicates the current record position after the last record
Filter	Specifies a filter
LockType	Specifies the type of locks placed on records during editing
MarshalOptions	Specifies which records are to marshal back to the server
MaxRecords	Specifies the maximum number of records to return to a record set
PageCount	Specifies the number of pages of data the object contains
PageSize	Specifies the number of records constituting one page
RecordCount	Specifies the current number of records in the object
Source	Indicates the source of data or the name of the object or application that generated an error
State	Indicates the object's current state
Status	Indicates the current record's status with respect to batch updates or bulk operations

Table 5.18 Recordset object methods.

Method	Description
AddNew	Creates a new record
CancelBatch	Cancels a pending batch update
CancelUpdate	Cancels changes made to the current record or to a new record prior to calling the **Update** method
Clone	Creates a duplicate **Recordset** object from an existing object
Close	Closes an open object and dependent objects
Delete	Deletes the current record
GetRows	Retrieves multiple records into an array
Move	Moves the position of the current record
MoveFirst	Moves to the first record
MoveLast	Moves to the last record
MoveNext	Moves to the next record
MovePrevious	Moves to the previous record
NextRecordset	Clears the current object and returns the next record set by advancing through a series of commands
Open	Opens a cursor
Requery	Updates the record set by reexecuting the query
Resynch	Refreshes the data in the current object
Supports	Determines whether a specified object supports a specified type of functionality
Update	Saves changes made to the current record
UpdateBatch	Writes all pending batch updates

Using The Database Access Component

The **Database Access** component uses ADO to access ODBC data sources. The ADO makes it very easy to write to and update databases. The following example uses ADO to write new member information to a Microsoft Access database named custdb.mdb.

The new member registration page shown in Listing 5.8 earlier in the chapter contains a form that collects information from the user. The **ACTION** attribute specifies Listing 5.15 as the page to post the form data to.

The script in Listing 5.15 first creates a **Connection** object and then assigns it to **Conn**. The **Open** method opens a connection to the data source. **custdb** is the Data Source Name (DSN) that references the database.

The script creates a **Recordset** object and assigns it to **RS**. Then, the program uses the record set to open a connection to the table **custinfo**, which holds all the data entered into the HTML form as well as the customer number and status (from the user's cookie).

Each field in the **custinfo** table receives values from the form. The **Request** object accesses the values posted to this page. When the program places data in the fields of the **Recordset** variable, it effectively places them in the database (subject to an **Update** call, of course).

After the program writes to the database and closes the connection, it updates the user's cookie with the additional information from the form.

Listing 5.15   Using Active Data Objects.

```
<%@ LANGUAGE="VBSCRIPT" %>
<%
set Conn = Server.CreateObject("ADODB.Connection")
Conn.Open "custdb"
Set RS = Server.CreateObject("ADODB.Recordset")
Conn.BeginTrans
RS.Open "custinfo",Conn,3,3
RS.AddNew
RS("fname") = Request("firstname")
RS("lname") = Request("lastname")
RS("addr1") = Request("addr1")
RS("addr2") = Request("addr2")
RS("city") = Request("city")
RS("state") = Request("state")
RS("zip") = Request("zip")
RS("area") = Request("code")
RS("phone") = Request("phone")
RS("cuisine") = Request("cuisine")
RS("cnum") = Request.Cookies("CustomerID")("cust_num")
RS.Update
Conn.CommitTrans
RS.Close
Conn.Close

Response.Cookies("CustomerID")("fname") = Request("firstname")
Response.Cookies("CustomerID")("lname") = Request("lastname")
Response.Cookies("CustomerID")("cuisine") = Request("cuisine")
Response.Cookies("CustomerID")("Status") = 1
%>
<HTML>
<HEAD>
<TITLE>New Member</TITLE>
</HEAD>
<BODY>
Member Registered
</BODY>
</HTML>
```

Listings 5.16 and 5.17 show how to access a specific record in the database. Listing 5.16 consists of a simple HTML document in which the user enters a customer number. The script posts that value to Listing 5.17, which does the lookup and displays the record.

Listing 5.16   A simple HTML form.

```
<HTML>
<HEAD>
<TITLE>Find Customer</TITLE>
</HEAD>
<BODY>


<H2 ALIGN=CENTER>Find Customer</H2>
<PRE>
<FORM METHOD=POST ACTION="5-17.asp">
Customer Number: <INPUT TYPE=TEXT NAME="cust_num">
                 <INPUT TYPE=SUBMIT VALUE="Find">
</FORM>
</PRE>
</BODY>
</HTML>
```

Listing 5.17   Searching with Active Data Objects.

```
<%@ LANGUAGE="VBSCRIPT" %>
<%
Set Conn = Server.CreateObject("ADODB.Connection")
Conn.Open "custdb"
queryString = "SELECT * FROM custinfo WHERE cnum = " & _
     "'" & Request("cust_num") & "'"
Set RS = Conn.Execute(queryString)
%>


<HTML>
<HEAD>
<TITLE>Customer Lookup</TITLE>
</HEAD>
<BODY>
<H2 ALIGN=CENTER>Find Customer</H2>
<TABLE BORDER=1>
<TR>
<% For i = 0 to RS.Fields.Count - 1 %>
<TD><B><% =RS(i).Name %></B></TD>
<% Next %>
</TR>
<% Do While Not RS.EOF %>
<TR>
<% For i = 0 to RS.Fields.Count - 1 %>
<TD VALIGN=TOP><% =RS(i) %></TD>
<% Next %>
</TR>
<%  RS.MoveNext
```

```
        Loop
        RS.Close
%>
</TABLE>
</BODY>
</HTML>
```

Listing 5.17 assigns an SQL query string to the variable **queryString** and passes the string to the **Connection** object's **Execute** method. You can access the results of the query using the record set variable **RS**, which will contain the complete set of records resulting from the query. In this example, it should return only one record, assuming that a record is found, because the customer number should be a unique value. The script in the document body is written to display all the records contained in a record set object in an HTML table.

The **File Access** Component

The **File Access** component uses the **FileSystemObject** to provide access to the file system on the server. You can use the **FileSystemObject** to create, read from, and write to disk files. The **FileSystemObject** has numerous methods for general use with VBScript and JavaScript, but only two are of interest here:

- **OpenTextFile**—Opens the specified file
- **CreateTextFile**—Creates the specified file

The **FileSystemObject** appears earlier in this chapter during the discussion of the Global.asa file. There, it creates the hit counter's text file. The following script creates and writes to the file:

```
Set fs = Server.CreateObject("Scripting.FileSystemObject")
Set out = fs.OpenTextFile(fname, 1, FALSE, FALSE)
Application("hits") = out.ReadLine
out.close
```

OpenTextFile uses the following syntax:

```
object.OpenTextFile(fname[,iomode][,create][,format])
```

The optional parameter *iomode* can indicate **ForReading** (1) or **ForAppending** (2). *create* specifies whether the object can create a new file if one doesn't already exist. *format* specifies the **Tristate** value to indicate the format of the opened file and can be one of the following:

- **TristateTrue**—Opens the file as Unicode
- **TristateFalse**—Opens the file as ASCII (default)
- **TristateUseDefault**—Opens the file using the system default

CreateTextFile uses the following syntax:

```
object.CreateTextFile(fname,[overwrite][,unicode])
```

overwrite is an optional value that indicates whether the object can overwrite an existing file (the default is **FALSE**). *unicode* is also optional. It indicates whether the file uses Unicode (16-bit characters). The default is **FALSE**, which causes the file to use ASCII (or ANSI, if you prefer).

Both these methods return a **TextStream** object, which provides the actual file access. The **TextStream** object has the methods listed in Table 5.19.

The **TextStream** object has the properties listed in Table 5.20.

The **Content Rotator** Component

The Content Rotator component rotates an HTML content string each time a page is read. Similar to the Ad Rotator component, the Content Rotator component uses a secondary file called the Content Schedule file. The Content Schedule file contains the HTML that will be displayed.

This component has two methods: **ChooseContent** reads a string from the schedule file; **ChooseAllContent** reads all the content strings in the schedule file.

Table 5.19   TextStream object methods.

Method	Description
Close	Closes the file
Read	Reads a specified number of characters
ReadAll	Reads all the characters from a file
ReadLine	Reads the next line
Size	Returns the size of the file in bytes
Skip	Skips a specified number of characters
SkipLine	Skips the next line
Write	Writes a string to a file
WriteBlankLines	Writes empty lines
WriteLine	Writes a string followed by a new-line character

Table 5.20   TextStream object properties.

Property	Description
AtEndOfLine	Returns **TRUE** if the file pointer is at the end of the line
AtEndOfStream	Returns **TRUE** if the file pointer is at the end of the file
Column	Returns the column number of the current character position
Line	Returns the current line number

The Content Schedule file is a text file that contains the strings and the relative weight of each string. The syntax for the schedule file is as follows:

```
%% [#weight][//comments]
String
```

weight is an optional parameter and can be in the range of 0 to 10000. The default weight is 1, and an error will be generated if the total weight of all strings is greater that 10000.

comments are also optional and are preceded by //.

String is one or more lines of HTML, and can include images, sounds, hyperlinks, and other HTML. Anything between a block of %% characters is considered one string. The following is an example:

```
---- theContent.txt ----
%% #5 // Example Content Schedule File
Dining out is fun!
%%
<H2>New Member Registration Form</H2>
```

The following script creates an instance of the **Content Rotator** component and displays one string from the schedule file named content.txt:

```
<%
    Set mobj = Server.CreateObject("MSWC.ContentRotator")
    Response.Write mobj.ChooseContent("content.txt")
%>
```

The **Counters** Component

You can use the **Counters** component to maintain various counters. For example, you can count the number of times your Web site is visited, a hyperlink is selected, and so on. The counters are global, so after you create them, they are available across the entire Web site. All counters are stored in a text file called counter.txt.

The **Counters** component has four methods, as shown in Table 5.21.

Table 5.21   Counters component methods.

Method	Description
Get	Returns the value of the specified counter
Increment	Increments the specified counter by 1
Remove	Removes the specified counter
Set	Sets the value of the specified counter

To use this component, you create it one time in the Global.asa file, as follows:

```
<OBJECT RUNAT=Server SCOPE=Application ID=myCounter PROGID="MSWC.Counters">
</OBJECT>
```

The following statement sets the value of counter **hits** to zero. The counter is created and set to the specified value if it doesn't exist:

```
Counter.Set("hits", 0)
```

The following statements increment the counter and display its value:

```
Counter.Increment("hits")
Response.Write(Counter.Get("hits"));
```

Just like the **Set** method, the **Increment** method creates the counter if it doesn't exist but sets it to 1.

You can remove a counter from the Counters.txt file by using the **Remove** method like this:

```
Counter.Remove("hits")
```

The **Page Counter** Component

The **Page Counter** component keeps track of the number of times a specific page has been accessed. This component uses another object, the **Central Management** object, to record the number of hits for each page in an application.

Unlike the **Counters** component, which keeps counts on an application-wide basis, the **Page Counter** component maintains counts only on pages where it is used. To use the component, you must create an instance of it on each page you want to track.

Table 5.22 lists the **Page Counter** methods.

The following code creates an instance of **Page Counter**, increments the hit count, displays the page hits, and then resets the count to zero:

```
<%
    Set myObj = Server.CreateObject("MSWC.PageCounter")
    myObj.PageHit()
    Response.Write("This page has been hit " & myObj.Hits & " times.")
    myObj.Reset()
%>
```

Table 5.22 Page Counter component methods.

Method	Description
Hits	Returns the number of times the specified URL has been accessed
PageHit	Increments the hit count
Reset	Sets the count for the specified page to zero

The **Logging Utility** Component

The **Logging Utility** component allows you to write script that reads the IIS log. Possible uses might be to display log records and custom reports in a Web page.

Table 5.23 lists the **Logging Utility** methods.

You must specify the IIS log file name in the **OpenLogFile** method. By default, the file is opened for reading; you can open it for writing as follows:

```
var.OpenLogFile(file, 2)
```

The **CloseLogFiles** method will close all files, all files open for reading, or all files open for writing. You specify which files to close by passing an argument with one of the following values:

- 1—Closes files open for reading
- 2—Closes files open for writing
- 3—Closes all open files

The **Logging Utility** component has several properties, as shown in Table 5.24.

Note that these properties must be enabled in IIS logging before this component can return their values.

Table 5.23 Logging Utility component methods.

Method	Description
AtEndOfLog	Returns **TRUE** if all records have been read
CloseLogFiles	Closes log files
OpenLogFile	Opens the specified log file
ReadFilter	Reads records filtered by date and time
ReadLogRecord	Reads the next log record
WriteLogRecord	Writes a record to the log file

Table 5.24 Logging Utility component properties.

Property	Description
BytesReceived	The bytes received
BytesSent	The bytes sent

(continued)

Table 5.24   Logging Utility component properties *(continued)*.

Property	Description
ClientIP	The client's IP address
Cookie	The client's cookie
CustomFields	An array of custom headers
DateTime	The GMT date and time
Method	The HTTP method
ProtocolStatus	The protocol status
ProtocolVersion	The HTTP protocol version
Referer	The referrer URL
ServerIP	The server IP address
ServerName	The server name
ServerPort	The port number
TimeTaken	The total processing time
URIQuery	The parameters passed in the request
URIStem	The target URL
UserAgent	The client's **UserAgent** string
UserName	The user's name
Win32Status	The Win32 status code

Using The Logging Utility Component

Listing 5.18 shows how you can use the Logging Utility component to read selected records from a daily IIS log and display the values in an HTML table. This example uses the log file for November 4, 1999, which on my server is in the c:\winnt\system32\logfiles\w3svc3\ directory.

Listing 5.18   Reading an IIS log.

```
<%@ Language=VBScript %>
<% Response.Expires = 0 %>
<%
   set myobj = Server.CreateObject("MSWC.IISLog")
   myobj.OpenLogFile("c:\winnt\system32\logfiles\w3svc3\ex991104.log")

%>

<H1> The Logging Utility </H1>

<TABLE BORDER>
<TR><TH>DateTime</TH><TH>ClientIP</TH><TH>URIStem</TH>
<%
While Not myobj.AtEndOfLog()
   myobj.ReadLogRecord()
%>
<TR>
<TD><% Response.Write(myobj.DateTime) %></TD>
```

```
<TD><% Response.Write(myobj.ClientIP) %></TD>
<TD><% Response.Write(myobj.URIStem) %></TD>

<%
Wend
    myobj.CloseLogFiles(32)
%>
</TABLE>
```

Chapter 6
The Client Connection

Kim Barber

This book is about Active Server Pages and active server scripting. You can write sophisticated Web applications that perform a great deal of processing on the server and return plain old HTML to the client. At some time, though, you might be able to write Web applications that perform most, or all, of the work on the client.

You might use client-side scripting if you are sure the client supports it and all the functionality you need. A good example is an intranet in which a standard browser is used. Client-side scripting lets you offload a lot of processing from the server and place it on the client.

Client-side scripting provides the capability to incorporate application-like behavior in your Web pages. Many tasks that once required processing on the server now can be done on the client. This reduces both the number of trips to the server and the workload placed on the server. For example, a single Web page can request user input, perform calculations or some other processing, and output the results. Using the CGI approach would require two HTML pages and a CGI script or executable on the server to perform the same task.

The capability to perform calculations on the client is a relatively small but powerful aspect of client-side scripting. For example, client-side scripts can be used to process HTML forms and perform data validation. These scripts ensure that form data is complete and correct prior to submitting the data to the server. Your script code can respond to user actions, such as clicking on an HTML button control, by executing blocks of code you define.

Your code then can interact with HTML elements. For example, you can set the values of text controls and the radio button and checkbox settings. Scripts also can control the appearance and behavior of ActiveX controls and Java applets by setting properties and calling methods. If all these capabilities aren't enough, client-side scripts can interact with the browser itself.

This chapter describes how script, or code, is embedded in HTML documents and explains many of the features provided by Internet Explorer. Examples will show you how scripts interact with HTML forms and intrinsic HTML controls, how to attach scripts to events, and how to control ActiveX controls and Java applets.

Chapters 3 and 4 cover VBScript and JavaScript and show these languages in use as server-side scripts. Using these scripting languages, you also can write programs that are embedded in HTML documents and processed by the browser. In addition, you can combine both client-side and server-side scripting in a single document. You'll see an example in this chapter. Because client-side script is interpreted, the Web browser must be aware of the scripting language in use. Microsoft Internet Explorer has built-in VBScript and JavaScript interpreters.

Show Me The Code

Before going any further, let's take a look at a very simple example of client-side VBScript. Many books on programming contain the familiar "Hello World" example. There is a good reason for this: The "Hello World" example shows you the basics of a program in a given language. Listing 6.1 shows a client-side VBScript example.

Listing 6.1   A client-side VBScript "Hello World" program.

```
<HTML>
<HEAD>
<TITLE>Hello World</TITLE>
<SCRIPT LANGUAGE=VBScript>
<!--
     MsgBox "Hello World"
-->
</SCRIPT>
</HEAD>
<BODY>
</BODY>
</HTML>
```

As you can see, Listing 6.1 is a fairly typical HTML file. VBScript is embedded in the HTML with the **<SCRIPT>** tag, which is used to include client-side script in HTML documents. This tag is paired, meaning it requires the **</SCRIPT>** ending tag, and the script code is placed within this tag pair. Like many HTML tags, the **<SCRIPT>** tag has attributes that allow you to modify the tag's behavior. Because browsers can support many different languages, the **LANGUAGE** attribute is used to specify the scripting language. **SRC** is another useful attribute. You can use **SRC** to specify the URL of a file that contains the script source code. This is convenient if you use the same script in several files. Also, an HTML document can contain multiple scripts in different languages.

The VBScript **MsgBox** function displays the output. Figure 6.1 shows how this page as displayed in Internet Explorer 5. In this example, the function takes the string "Hello World" as an argument and displays it. It also provides an OK button for the user to click to continue. The **MsgBox** function can take other arguments to specify both the buttons to include and the caption to display at the top of the box. Also, notice the use of the HTML comment tags: **<!--** and **-->**. It's a very good idea to place script code within comment tags because some browsers don't support client-side scripting. Browsers that don't support scripting ignore script placed within comment tags. If you don't use comment tags, a browser that doesn't understand script simply displays the code as text, which might confuse the user.

You can place script code anywhere in an HTML document, although normally you place it in the **<HEAD>** section. The exception to this general rule occurs when you need to include inline script in the **<BODY>** section. You generally place script here to respond to events, such as a button click, or when you want script to generate HTML. The point to remember is that code must be defined before it is referenced. The browser processes script code as the page is loaded. Code that isn't part of a procedure or inline event-driven code is executed immediately.

Figure 6.1
"Hello World" in Internet Explorer 5.

Advantages Of Client-Side Scripting

You can add logic to a Web page in many ways. However, client-side scripting poses some distinct advantages:

♦ *Processing on the client*—Processing can be performed on the client, thereby reducing the number of trips to the server and the workload placed on the server. Processing this way also improves the user's experience because the Web pages are more responsive.

♦ *Interactive*—You can create pages that involve the user by requesting information and displaying responses using functions provided by the scripting language. Web pages can also respond to user actions, such as clicking on a button or selecting or changing a form element.

♦ *Access to ActiveX controls and Java applets*—Client-side script can control the appearance and behavior of ActiveX controls and Java applets. You therefore can add a very high level of richness and functionality to Web pages.

♦ *Access to the browser*—Client-side script can interact with the browser itself and with the document contained within the browser.

Disadvantages Of Client-Side Scripting

Like most things, especially in programming, there are often disadvantages to consider as well as advantages. Two of the more significant disadvantages of client-side scripting are:

♦ *Browser dependency*—Client-side script is useful only if the user's browser supports it. Microsoft's Internet Explorer is the only browser that currently supports VBScript without a plug-in. Both Internet Explorer and Netscape support JavaScript.

♦ *Source viewable on client*—Just like HTML, client-side script code can be viewed on the client. As a result, you share your hard work and intellectual property with the world.

A Trio Of Scripting Tips

You'll find the following three tips useful when using VBScript or JavaScript.

Using <NOSCRIPT>

Protecting your script code with HTML comments is good practice. By using comments, you can prevent older browsers from displaying your code as plain text. However, that doesn't allow you to take a different action for those browsers. In this case, the **<NOSCRIPT>** tag comes in handy. It allows you to provide other information when the browser doesn't understand the **<SCRIPT>** tag. It also works when a script is in an unknown language or when the user disables scripts. Consider this example:

```
<SCRIPT TYPE="vbscript">
  <!--
  Sub myfunction ()
```

```
  .  .  .
    End Sub
    -->
</SCRIPT>
<NOSCRIPT>
<P>
Please go get a real browser at <A HREF=http://the.browsercompany.com>
The Browser Co.</A>
</NOSCRIPT>
```

This example works because script-aware browsers know to ignore everything between **<NOSCRIPT>** and **</NOSCRIPT>** unless they purposely ignored the previous script. Older browsers don't understand **<NOSCRIPT>**, so they ignore it and process everything between the two tags.

Setting Script Language

According to the HTML 4 documentation, you can use the **<META>** tag to set a default scripting language (instead of doing it each time you use the **<SCRIPT>** tag on a page). You do so by including a line like the following in the **<HEAD>**:

```
<META HTTP-EQUIV="Content-Script-Type" CONTENT="text/vbscript">
```

The HTML 4 specification also allows you to set the script type using the **TYPE** modifier like this:

```
<SCRIPT TYPE=text/vbscript>
```

This example works in IE 5 and Navigator.

Ending A Script

The HTML 4 specification specifically requires browsers to end a script at the first sign of any tag that starts with **</** followed by a letter. So although you usually use **</SCRIPT>** to end a tag, technically, anything that resembles an end tag should work. This is a problem when you write things like

```
document.write("<B>Bold</B>");
```

because the script language should end when it sees the **</B>** tag. Currently, Internet Explorer and Navigator don't follow the specification in this case; you must end the script with a **</SCRIPT>** tag. But, other browsers might not. To be safe, you should write the preceding using a backslash escape character (for JavaScript, anyway):

```
document.write("<B>Bold<\/B>");
```

This example has the same effect but doesn't confuse the scripting engine.

How To Use Script With HTML Forms

The code in Listing 6.2 creates a Web page that allows people to join the Community Dining Club. This fictitious Web site is for people who enjoy dining out. It offers the convenience of learning about participating restaurants and making reservations online. New club members can use the form created in this listing to register. This example illustrates how VBScript works with the form's elements, performs basic data validation, and responds to control events.

Listing 6.2   Using VBScript with an HTML form.

```
<HTML>
<HEAD>
<TITLE>New Member Registration</TITLE>
<SCRIPT LANGUAGE="VBScript">
<!--
Sub cmdSubmit_OnClick()


    Dim TheForm
    Set TheForm = Document.RegistrationForm

    If Len(TheForm.firstname.Value) = 0 Then
        MsgBox "Please enter your first name.", vbOKOnly, "First Name"
        TheForm.firstname.Focus

    ElseIf Len(TheForm.lastname.Value) = 0 Then
        TheForm.lastname.value = _
            InputBox ("Please enter your last name.", "Last Name")
        If Len(TheForm.lastname.Value) <> 0 Then TheForm.addr1.Focus
    ElseIf Len(TheForm.addr1.Value) = 0 Then
        MsgBox "Please enter your address.", vbOKOnly, "Address1"
        TheForm.lastname.Focus
    ElseIf Len(TheForm.city.Value) = 0 Then
        MsgBox "Please enter the city.", vbOKOnly, "City"
        TheForm.city.Focus

    ElseIf Len(TheForm.state.Value) <> 2 Then
        MsgBox "Please enter the 2-letter state abbreviation.", _
            vbOKOnly, "State"
        TheForm.state.Focus
        TheForm.state.Select

    ElseIf Len(TheForm.zip.Value) < 5 Then
        MsgBox "Please enter a valid ZIP code.", vbOKOnly, "ZIP Code"
        TheForm.zip.Focus
        TheForm.zip.Select
```

```
        ElseIf Len(TheForm.code.Value) <> 3 _
        Or Not IsNumeric(TheForm.code.Value) Then
            MsgBox "Please enter a valid area code.", vbOKOnly, "Area Code"
            TheForm.code.Focus
            TheForm.code.Select
        ElseIf Len(TheForm.phone.Value) <> 7 _
        Or Not IsNumeric(TheForm.phone.Value) Then
            MsgBox "Please enter a valid phone number.", vbOKOnly, "Phone Number"
            TheForm.phone.Focus
            TheForm.phone.Select

        ElseIf TheForm.cuisine.SelectedIndex = 0 Then
            MsgBox "Please let us know what your favorite cuisine is.", _
                vbOKOnly, "Cuisine"
            TheForm.cuisine.Focus

        End If
End Sub
-->
</SCRIPT>
</HEAD>
<BODY>
<H1 Align=Center>Community Dining Club</H1>
<H2 Align=Center>New Member Registration</H2>
<HR SIZE=5 WIDTH=90%>
<PRE>
<FORM NAME="RegistrationForm">
<B>First Name:        </B><INPUT TYPE=TEXT NAME="firstname">
<B>Last Name:         </B><INPUT TYPE=TEXT NAME="lastname">
<B>Address1:          </B><INPUT TYPE=TEXT NAME="addr1">
<B>Address2:          </B><INPUT TYPE=TEXT NAME="addr2">
<B>City:              </B><INPUT TYPE=TEXT NAME="city">
<B>State:             </B><INPUT TYPE=TEXT NAME="state" MAXLENGTH=2 SIZE=2>
<B>Zip:               </B><INPUT TYPE=TEXT NAME="zip" MAXLENGTH=10 SIZE=10>
<B>Area Code:         </B><INPUT TYPE=TEXT NAME="code" MAXLENGTH=3 SIZE=3>
<B>Phone:             </B><INPUT TYPE=TEXT NAME="phone" MAXLENGTH=7 SIZE=7>

<B>Preferred Cuisine: </B><SELECT NAME="cuisine" SIZE="1">

                        <OPTION VALUE="1">American
                        <OPTION VALUE="2">Chinese
                        <OPTION VALUE="3">French
                        <OPTION VALUE="4">German
                        <OPTION VALUE="5">Greek
                        <OPTION VALUE="6">Indian
                        <OPTION VALUE="7">Italian
```

```
                              <OPTION VALUE="8">Japanese
                              <OPTION VALUE="9">Other
                              </SELECT>
<INPUT TYPE=BUTTON NAME="cmdSubmit" VALUE="Submit">
<INPUT TYPE="RESET" VALUE="Clear">
</PRE>
</FORM>
</BODY>
</HTML>
```

The document defines a form to collect user information in the **<BODY>** section. When the user clicks on the Submit button, VBScript calls the event procedure **cmdSubmit_OnClick**. This procedure checks the form to ensure that the required data is available and, in some cases, valid.

First, **cmdSubmit_OnClick** declares the variable **TheForm** and then sets it to reference the form **RegistrationForm**. The **Document** object (discussed later) contains subobjects that correspond to each form in the document. You can access the form elements using a statement such as this:

```
document.RegistrationForm.firstname.Value
```

However, assigning a variable to reference the form reduces typing and makes the code easier to read. Because **TheForm** references an object, you must use the **Set** statement to make the assignment.

The remainder of the procedure validates the input. The first test checks the length of **firstname**'s **Value** property. If it is equal to zero, the code displays a message box asking the user to enter his or her first name. Then, the code calls the text box control's **Focus** method to place the cursor back in the text box.

If nothing appears in **lastname**, the user can enter his or her last name in response to a prompt from the **InputBox** function. Although this behavior is inconsistent with the rest of the script, it shows that HTML control properties are easy to change programmatically. When the new name is in place, the code rechecks the **Value** property and moves the focus to the next control.

If the information entered for **state** is not two characters, the program asks the user to enter a two-character abbreviation. Then, the program calls the text box control's **Select** method to highlight any text already there. The user can then easily overtype the incorrect information.

Finally, the code checks the **SelectedIndex** property of the selection control to determine whether the user selected a preferred cuisine. The **SelectedIndex** property is set to the value of the selected item or to zero if nothing is selected.

How To Use Script With ActiveX Controls

ActiveX control properties are set in HTML using the **<PARAM>** tag when the page is loaded. The property settings are otherwise static, unless the control itself is changing them. Properties, methods, and events exposed by ActiveX controls can be accessed using script and can be used programmatically. Therefore, the control's behavior can be modified dynamically.

Listing 6.3 "spruces up" the Community Dining Club New Member Registration page with a spinning billboard. The script uses two controls that Microsoft supplies with Internet Explorer: Label and Timer. The Label control displays text. You can change the control's properties to set the font, angle, and other display characteristics. The Label control also has several events and one method, but you don't need them for this example. The user never sees the Timer control in the browser. The timer's only purpose is to fire a **Timer** event at a specified interval. Each time the script detects a **Timer** event, it spins the text by changing the label's properties. VBScript is the glue that connects these two controls. Through VBScript, the Timer control affects the characteristics of the Label control.

Listing 6.3   Controlling ActiveX controls with VBScript.

```
<HTML>
<HEAD>
<TITLE>New Member Registration</TITLE>
<SCRIPT LANGUAGE=VBScript>
    Dim Angle
    Dim Message, MsgNo

    Randomize
    Message = Array("Join Today!", "Fine Dining!", "Impress Friends!", _
                            "Save Money!", "Be Cool!")
    MsgNo = 0
    ColorNo = 1
    Angle = 0

    Sub IeTimer_Timer
        IeLabel.Caption = Message(MsgNo)
        IeLabel.Angle = Angle
        Angle = Angle + 5
        If Angle > 360 Then
            Angle = 0
            MsgNo = MsgNo + 1
            If MsgNo > 4 Then MsgNo = 0
            ChangeColor
        End If
    End Sub
```

```
Sub ChangeColor
    IeLabel.ForeColor = Rnd * 16777215
End Sub

Sub cmdSubmit_OnClick()
    Dim TheForm
    Set TheForm = Document.RegistrationForm

    If Len(TheForm.firstname.Value) = 0 Then
        MsgBox "Please enter your first name.", vbOKOnly, "First Name"
        TheForm.firstname.Focus
    ElseIf Len(TheForm.lastname.Value) = 0 Then
        TheForm.lastname.value = _
        InputBox ("Please enter your last name.", "Last Name")
        If Len(TheForm.lastname.Value) <> 0 Then TheForm.addr1.Focus
    ElseIf Len(TheForm.addr1.Value) = 0 Then
        MsgBox "Please enter your address.", vbOKOnly, "Address1"
        TheForm.lastname.Focus
    ElseIf Len(TheForm.city.Value) = 0 Then
        MsgBox "Please enter the city.", vbOKOnly, "City"
        TheForm.city.Focus
    ElseIf Len(TheForm.state.Value) <> 2 Then
        MsgBox "Please enter the 2-letter state abbreviation.", _
          vbOKOnly, "State"
        TheForm.state.Focus
        TheForm.state.Select
    ElseIf Len(TheForm.zip.Value) < 5 Then
        MsgBox "Please enter a valid ZIP code.", _
        vbOKOnly, "ZIP Code"
        TheForm.zip.Focus
        TheForm.zip.Select
    ElseIf Len(TheForm.code.Value) <> 3 _
    Or Not IsNumeric(TheForm.code.Value) Then
        MsgBox "Please enter a valid area code.", vbOKOnly, "Area Code"
        TheForm.code.Focus
        TheForm.code.Select
    ElseIf Len(TheForm.phone.Value) <> 7 _
    Or Not IsNumeric(TheForm.phone.Value) Then
        MsgBox "Please enter a valid phone number.", _
        vbOKOnly, "Phone Number"
        TheForm.phone.Focus
        TheForm.phone.Select
    ElseIf TheForm.cuisine.SelectedIndex = 0 Then
        MsgBox "Please let us know what your favorite cuisine is.", _
          vbOKOnly, "Cuisine"
        TheForm.cuisine.Focus
```

```
          End If
      End Sub
</SCRIPT>
</HEAD>
<BODY>

<H1 ALIGN=Center>Community Dining Club</H1>
<H2 ALIGN=Center>New Member Registration</H2>
<HR SIZE=5 WIDTH=90%>

<OBJECT ID="IeTimer" WIDTH=39 HEIGHT=39
 CLASSID="CLSID:59CCB4A0-727D-11CF-AC36-00AA00A47DD2">
    <PARAM NAME="Interval" VALUE="50">
</OBJECT>

<TABLE>
<TD>
<OBJECT ID="IeLabel" WIDTH=150 HEIGHT=150
 CLASSID="CLSID:99B42120-6EC7-11CF-A6C7-00AA00A47DD2">
    <PARAM NAME="Caption" VALUE=" ">
    <PARAM NAME="Angle" VALUE="0">
    <PARAM NAME="Alignment" VALUE="4">
    <PARAM NAME="Mode" VALUE="1">
    <PARAM NAME="FillStyle" VALUE="0">
    <PARAM NAME="ForeColor" VALUE="#000000">
    <PARAM NAME="BackColor" VALUE="#C0C0C0">
    <PARAM NAME="FontName" VALUE="Arial">
    <PARAM NAME="FontSize" VALUE="14">
    <PARAM NAME="FontItalic" VALUE="0">
    <PARAM NAME="FontBold" VALUE="1">
    <PARAM NAME="FontUnderline" VALUE="0">
    <PARAM NAME="FontStrikeout" VALUE="0">
    <PARAM NAME="TopPoints" VALUE="0">
    <PARAM NAME="BotPoints" VALUE="0">
</OBJECT>
</TD>
<TD>
<PRE>
<FORM NAME="RegistrationForm">
<B>First Name:      </B><INPUT TYPE=TEXT NAME="firstname">
<B>Last Name:       </B><INPUT TYPE=TEXT NAME="lastname">
<B>Address1:        </B><INPUT TYPE=TEXT NAME="addr1">
<B>Address2:        </B><INPUT TYPE=TEXT NAME="addr2">
<B>City:            </B><INPUT TYPE=TEXT NAME="city">
<B>State:           </B><INPUT TYPE=TEXT NAME="state" MAXLENGTH=2 SIZE=2>
<B>Zip:             </B><INPUT TYPE=TEXT NAME="zip" MAXLENGTH=10 SIZE=10>
```

```
<B>Area Code:        </B><INPUT TYPE=TEXT NAME="code" MAXLENGTH=3 SIZE=3>
<B>Phone:            </B><INPUT TYPE=TEXT NAME="phone" MAXLENGTH=7 SIZE=7>

<B>Preferred Cuisine: </B><SELECT NAME="cuisine" SIZE="1">
                          <OPTION VALUE="1">American
                          <OPTION VALUE="2">Chinese
                          <OPTION VALUE="3">French
                          <OPTION VALUE="4">German
                          <OPTION VALUE="5">Greek
                          <OPTION VALUE="6">Indian
                          <OPTION VALUE="7">Italian
                          <OPTION VALUE="8">Japanese
                          <OPTION VALUE="9">Other
                          </SELECT>

<INPUT TYPE=BUTTON NAME="cmdSubmit" VALUE="Submit">
<INPUT TYPE="RESET" VALUE="Clear">
</PRE>
</FORM>
</TD>
</TABLE>

</BODY>
</HTML>
```

Figure 6.2 shows the page in Internet Explorer 5. The script first performs some initialization by seeding the random number generator with the **Randomize** statement. The random number generator is used in the **ChangeColor** subroutine to set the text color. The billboard will cycle through five messages that are stored in the **Message** array (which is initialized using the **Array** function).

VBScript calls the event procedure **IeTimer_Timer** when the Timer control fires the **Timer** event. The procedure sets the Label control's **Caption** property from the **Message** array and sets the **Angle** property from a variable. The script increments the **Angle** variable and checks to see whether it is greater than 360 degrees. If it is, the code resets the angle to zero and increments **MsgNo** so that the next message will appear on the next **Timer** event. A call to **ChangeColor** then changes the text color. **ChangeColor** simply sets the Label control's **ForeColor** property to a random color.

The Timer control resides in the body of the HTML document. The **Interval** property specifies the time in milliseconds between calls to the **Timer** event. The document sets the **Interval** property to 50, which results in a rapidly spinning billboard.

The Label control and HTML form are inside a table so that the control appears next to the form. Notice that the Label control has several properties, but you need only the **Caption** and **ForeColor** properties.

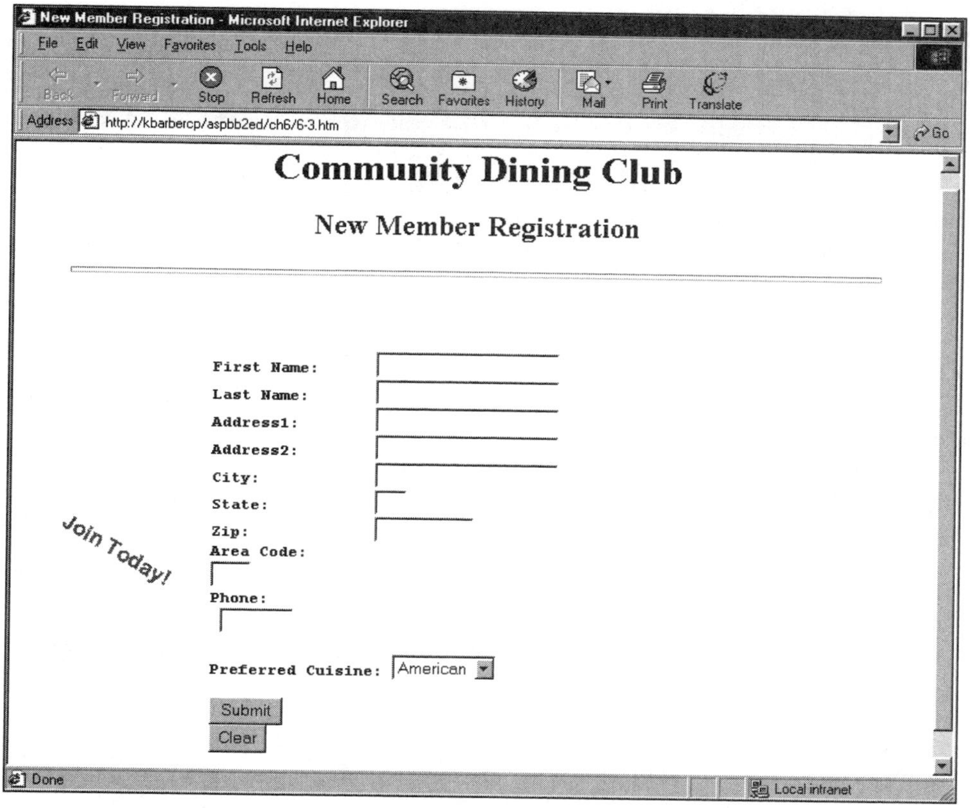

Figure 6.2
The New Member Registration page.

The Dynamic HTML Object Model

If anything stands out as a general theme in Active Server Pages, it's objects. Objects used on the server include intrinsic server objects and installable components. Objects used on the client include HTML controls, ActiveX controls, and Java applets.

You should not be surprised to learn, then, that an HTML document is simply an object. Like any object, an HTML document has properties, methods, and events. The Web browser exposes documents (as well as itself) through a structured set of objects referred to as the *Dynamic HTML Object Model*. You use client-side scripting to access and manipulate objects belonging to this model.

Remember that you can't directly manipulate these objects from the server. However, you can use server-side script to write client-side code—the code that the server generates and then executes on the client and that can manipulate the browser's objects.

The Dynamic HTML Object Model is part of the browser and provides a way to access and manipulate the browser and the documents it contains. The object model defines and exposes several objects through which browser elements and functionality are accessed. In addition, one object provides access to documents and their contents.

Before you look at the objects themselves, consider how a browser such as Internet Explorer operates. Figure 6.3 shows Internet Explorer's structure. The actual browser application, IEXPLORE.EXE, is a relatively small executable that functions as a container for the **WebBrowser** object: SHDOCVW.DLL.

The **WebBrowser** object provides the browser's basic capabilities, such as navigation, refreshing pages, printing, and so on. This object doesn't display anything. To display an HTML page or other resource, it creates an ActiveX object from the appropriate document server. The document server actually displays the document. This allows the browser to display not only HTML pages but other documents as well, such as Word files (because Word is an ActiveX document server). Internet Explorer, then, can display any document that has an ActiveX document server.

Internet Explorer uses the Microsoft HTML viewer, MSHTML.DLL, to display HTML pages. The HTML viewer is an ActiveX server that displays HTML documents. It also provides client-side scripting. Figure 6.4 shows how the HTML viewer implements client-side scripting.

When a page contains the **<SCRIPT>** tag, the HTML viewer loads the scripting engine to execute the script. If the document specifies VBScript, the viewer loads VBSCRIPT.DLL. For JScript or JavaScript, the viewer loads JSCRIPT.DLL. The HTML viewer then passes the code in the **<SCRIPT>** tag to the scripting engine.

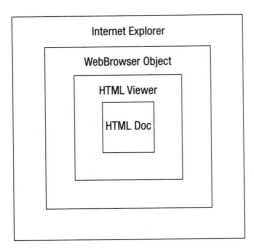

Figure 6.3
Internet Explorer's structure for displaying HTML documents.

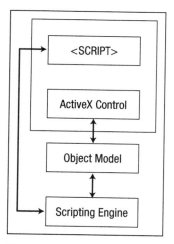

Figure 6.4
Client-side scripting in MSHTML.DLL.

The HTML viewer also exposes objects that client-side script accesses. These objects include those embedded in the document with the **<OBJECT>** and **<APPLET>** tags as well as browser objects and objects of the loaded document. These objects constitute the Dynamic HTML Object Model, and the HTML viewer exposes the object model to scripting.

The following section provides an overview of the objects and their properties, collections, methods, and events. You can find detailed information on the Microsoft Web site at **http://msdn.microsoft.com/workshop/c-frame.htm#/workshop/author/default.asp**.Netscape Navigator uses a similar object model; information on the Netscape implementation is available at **home.netscape.com/eng/mozilla/3.0/handbook/javascript/index.html**.

The Object Hierarchy

The object model consists of a hierarchy of seven objects and one collection (see Figure 6.5). Some of the objects also contain other objects.

Tip

This section provides a brief description of each of the objects. You'll find reference tables to the objects and their properties, collections, methods, and events throughout this chapter.

The **window** Object

The **window** object is the top-level object; it represents the browser's window. You access all other objects through the **window** object. In other words, the **window** object owns all the other browser objects. You are not limited to one **window** object, though. If a document

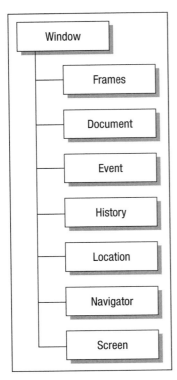

Figure 6.5
The object model hierarchy.

consists of frames, each frame has a **window** object. The main window's object contains a **frames** collection. This collection contains the **window** objects that correspond to the frames.

Although this point is somewhat confusing, an object named **window** represents the top-most window in the browser. It is an object of the **window** class. However, other **window** objects might have different names.

You access **window** object properties like this:

```
window.propertyname
```

If you are using the main window, you don't even have to specify the object, as shown here:

```
propertyname
```

The **window** object's properties are displayed in Table 6.1. Its collections are shown in Table 6.2, its methods in Table 6.3, and its events in Table 6.4.

Table 6.1 window object properties.

Property	Description	Syntax
clientInformation	Returns the **navigator** object	*winobj*.clientInformation.appCodeName
closed	Indicates whether the window is closed	*winobj*.closed
defaultStatus	Specifies the default message in the status bar	*winobj*.defaultStatus = *status*
dialogArguments	Returns the variable of array of variables passed to the modal dialog window	*winobj*.dialogArguments
dialogHeight	Specifies the height of the dialog window	*winobj*.dialogHeight = *height*
dialogLeft	Specifies the left coordinate of the dialog window	*winobj*.dialogLeft = *coord*
dialogTop	Specifies the top coordinate of the dialog window	*winobj*.dialogTop = *coord*
dialogWidth	Specifies the width of the dialog window	*winobj*.dialogWidth = *width*
document	Represents the HTML document in a window	document.*member*
event	Represents the state of an event	*winobj*.event.*member*
history	Represents the browser history list	history.*member*
length	Returns the number of frames in a window	*winobj*.length
location	Contains information about the current URL	location.*member*
name	Specifies the name of a window or frame	*winobj*.name = *name*
navigator	Contains information about the browser	navigator.*member*
offscreenBuffering	Specifies whether to use off-screen buffering	*winobj*.offscreenBuffering = *boolean*
opener	Specifies a reference to the window that created the current window	*winobj*.opener
parent	Returns the parent object	*winobj*.parent
returnValue	Specifies the return value from a modal dialog window	*winobj*.returnValue
screen	Represents information about the client's screen and rendering capabilities	screen.*member*
self	References the current window	*winobj*.self
status	Specifies the status bar message	*winobj*.status
top	Specifies the top-most window	*winobj*.top

Table 6.2 window object collections.

Collection	Description	Syntax
frames	Contains a collection of currently defined **window** objects	*obj*.frames(*index*)

Table 6.3 window object methods.

Method	Description	Syntax
alert	Displays an alert dialog box	*winobj*.alert(*optional message*)
blur	Causes an object to lose focus and fires the **onblur** event	*obj*.blur()
clearInterval	Cancels the interval set by **setInterval**	*winobj*.clearInterval(*intervalID*)
clearTimeout	Cancels the timeout set by **setTimeout**	*winobj*.clearTimeout(*timeoutID*)
close	Closes the current window	*winobj*.close()
confirm	Displays a confirm dialog box	*winobj*.confirm(*optional message*)
execScript	Executes a script defined with the *expression* argument	*winobj*.execScript(*expression, language*)
focus	Causes a control to receive focus	*obj*.focus()
navigate	Navigates to the specified URL	*winobj*.navigate(*URL*)
open	Opens a new document	*winobj*.open([*URL*[,*name*[,*features*[,*replace*]]]])
prompt	Displays a prompt dialog box	*winobj*.prompt([*message*[,*inputDefault*]])
resizeBy	Changes the window's dimensions by the specified x and y relative offsets	*winobj*.resizeBy(*x, y*)
resizeTo	Sets the window's dimensions to the specified size	*winobj*.resizeTo(*x, y*)
scroll	Scrolls the window to the specified offsets at the upper-left corner	*winobj*.scroll(*x, y*)
scrollBy	Scrolls the window relatively by the specified offsets	*winobj*.scrollBy(*x, y*)
scrollTo	Scrolls the window to the specified offsets at the upper-left corner	*winobj*.scrollTo(*x, y*)
setInterval	Repeatedly evaluates an expression at the specified interval in milliseconds	*winobj*.setInterval(*expression, msec*[,*language*])
setTimeout	Evaluates an expression after the specified interval has elapsed	*winobj*.setTimeout(*expression, msec*[,*language*])
showHelp	Displays a help file	*winobj*.showHelp(*URL*[,*contextID*])
showModalDialog	Creates and displays a modal dialog box	*winobj*.showModalDialog(*URL*[, *arguments*[,*features*]])

Table 6.4   window object events.

Event	Description
onbeforeunload	Fires prior to a page being unloaded
onblur	Fires when the object loses input focus
onerror	Fires when a scripting error occurs
onfocus	Fires when the object receives input focus
onhelp	Fires when the user selects Help or presses F1
onload	Fires when the object is loaded
onresize	Fires when the object is resized
onscroll	Fires when the scroll box is repositioned
onunload	Fires just prior to a page being unloaded

The frames Collection

The **frames** collection is the only collection in the **window** object. This collection contains a collection of all the **window** objects defined by a document or window. You access all **window** objects other than the top-most window through the **frames** collection.

If the document has a **<BODY>** tag, the **frames** collection contains one **window** object for each **IFRAME** element. If the document contains the **<FRAMESET>** tag, the **frames** collection contains one **window** object for each **<FRAME>** tag.

Specifying individual elements in the collection accesses frame windows. In VBScript, you use parentheses as follows to access elements:

```
frames(0)                    // the current window
parent.window.frames(0)      // the parent window's first frame
top                          // references the top-most window
```

For JavaScript, you use square brackets instead, like this:

```
frames[0]
```

Table 6.5 shows the **frames** collection's properties, and Table 6.6 shows its methods.

Table 6.5   frames collection properties.

Property	Description	Syntax
length	Returns the number of elements in the collection	*winobj*.**length**

Table 6.6   frames collection methods.

Method	Description	Syntax
item	Returns a collection of elements	*elm* = *obj*.**item**(*index*[,*subindex*])

How To Use The *window* Object

Listings 6.4 through 6.7 are modifications of the Community Dining Club New Member Registration page that you saw earlier. It now consists of four pages: Listing 6.4 defines a frameset to contain the other three pages, Listing 6.5 displays the heading, Listing 6.6 displays the billboard, and Listing 6.7 collects and validates new member registration information.

Listing 6.5 contains the function **window_onload**, which the browser calls when the **window** object fires the **onload** event. This function is like an ordinary JScript function, and the statement immediately following the function definition calls it. There is another way to respond to the **onload** event, as you'll see in a moment. The **window_onload** function sets background and text colors using the **document** object of the loaded document.

Listing 6.6 also responds to the **window** object's **onload** event but in a more direct way, using the **FOR** and **EVENT** attributes of the **<SCRIPT>** tag. This event handler sets the background and text colors of the document as well as the initial text color of the ActiveX Label control. Rather than use the ActiveX Timer control to periodically update the label, the page uses the **window** object's **setInterval** method. This method evaluates an expression at the specified interval. In this case, it calls the function **update_billboard** every second. The **update_billboard** function updates the Label control's **Caption** and **ForeColor** properties.

Listing 6.7 also responds to the **onload** event to set background and text colors. The page also has script that sets the **defaultStatus** property to a string that displays the page's purpose. The script that validates the new member information changes the **defaultStatus** property.

Listing 6.4   The frameset page.

```
<!-- The frameset document -->
<HTML>
<HEAD>
<TITLE>Listing 6.4 Frameset</TITLE>
</HEAD>
<FRAMESET FRAMEBORDER=0 SCROLLING=NO ROWS="10%, 10%, *">
    <FRAME scrolling=no src="6-4_head.htm" name="header">
    <FRAME scrolling=no src="6-4_bill.htm" name="billboard">
    <FRAME src="6-4_reg.htm" name="register">
</FRAMESET>
</HTML>
```

Listing 6.5   The header page.

```
<HTML>
<HEAD>
<TITLE>Listing 6.5 Header</TITLE>
<SCRIPT LANGUAGE=JavaScript>
<!--
```

```
function window_onload() {
    document.body.bgColor="DARKBLUE";
    document.body.text="ALICEBLUE";
}

onload = window_onload;
// -->
</SCRIPT>
</HEAD>
<BODY>

<H2 ALIGN=CENTER>Community Dining Club</H2>

</BODY>
</HTML>
```

Listing 6.6   The billboard page.

```
<HTML>
<HEAD>
<TITLE>Listing 6.6 Billboard</TITLE>
<SCRIPT FOR="window" EVENT="onload" LANGUAGE=JavaScript>
<!--
    document.body.bgColor="ALICEBLUE";
    document.body.text="YELLOW";
    IeLabel.ForeColor=0x00FFFF;
// -->
</SCRIPT>

<SCRIPT LANGUAGE=JavaScript>
<!--
var MsgNo, ColorNo;
var Message = new Array("Join Today!", "Fine Dining!",
"Impress Friends!", "Save Money!", "Be Cool!");

MsgNo = 0;
ColorNo = 1;

setInterval("update_billboard()", 1000);

function update_billboard() {
    IeLabel.Caption = Message[MsgNo];
    MsgNo += 1;
    if (MsgNo > 4)
        MsgNo = 0;
    IeLabel.ForeColor = Math.random() * 16777215;
}
```

```
// -->
</SCRIPT>
</HEAD>
<BODY>
<P ALIGN=CENTER>
<OBJECT ID="IeLabel" WIDTH=150 HEIGHT=25
 CLASSID="CLSID:99B42120-6EC7-11CF-A6C7-00AA00A47DD2">
     <PARAM NAME="Caption" VALUE=" ">
     <PARAM NAME="Angle" VALUE="0">
     <PARAM NAME="Alignment" VALUE="4">
     <PARAM NAME="Mode" VALUE="1">
     <PARAM NAME="FillStyle" VALUE="0">
     <PARAM NAME="ForeColor" VALUE="#000000">
     <PARAM NAME="BackColor" VALUE="#C0C0C0">
     <PARAM NAME="FontName" VALUE="Arial">
     <PARAM NAME="FontSize" VALUE="14">
     <PARAM NAME="FontItalic" VALUE="0">
     <PARAM NAME="FontBold" VALUE="1">
     <PARAM NAME="FontUnderline" VALUE="0">
     <PARAM NAME="FontStrikeout" VALUE="0">
     <PARAM NAME="TopPoints" VALUE="0">
     <PARAM NAME="BotPoints" VALUE="0">
</OBJECT>
</P>
</BODY>
</HTML>
```

Listing 6.7   The new member registration page.

```
<HTML>
<HEAD>
<TITLE>Listing 6.7 Member Registration</TITLE>
<SCRIPT FOR="window" EVENT="onload" LANGUAGE=JavaScript>
<!--
     document.body.bgColor="WHITE";
     document.body.text="BLUE";
// -->
</SCRIPT>

<SCRIPT LANGUAGE=JavaScript>
<!--
     defaultStatus="Community Dining Club New Member Registration";

//-->
</SCRIPT>

<SCRIPT FOR="cmdSubmit" EVENT="onclick" LANGUAGE=JavaScript>
```

```
<!--
    var TheForm;
    TheForm = document.RegistrationForm;

    defaultStatus = "Validating";

    if (TheForm.firstname.value.length == 0) {
        alert("Please enter your first name.");
        TheForm.firstname.focus();
    }
    else if (TheForm.lastname.value.length == 0) {
        TheForm.lastname.value = prompt("Please enter your last name.");
        if (TheForm.lastname.value.length != 0)
            TheForm.addr1.focus();
    }
    else if (TheForm.addr1.value.length == 0) {
        alert("Please enter your address.");
        TheForm.addr1.focus();
    }
    else if (TheForm.city.value.length == 0) {
        alert("Please enter the city.");
        TheForm.city.focus();
    }
    else if (TheForm.state.value.length != 2) {
        alert("Please enter the 2-letter state abbreviation.");
        TheForm.state.focus();
    }
    else if (TheForm.zip.value.length < 5) {
        alert("Please enter a valid ZIP code.");
        TheForm.zip.focus();
        TheForm.code.select();
    }
    else if (TheForm.code.value.length != 3 || isNaN(TheForm.code.value)) {
        alert("Please enter a valid area code.");
        TheForm.code.focus();
        TheForm.code.select();
    }
    else if (TheForm.phone.value.length != 7 || isNaN(TheForm.phone.value)) {
        alert("Please enter a valid phone number.");
        TheForm.phone.focus();
        TheForm.phone.select();
    }

// -->
</SCRIPT>
</HEAD>
```

```
<BODY>
<H2 Align=Center>New Member Registration</H2>
<HR SIZE=5 WIDTH=90%>

<P ALIGN=CENTER>
<TABLE>
<TD>
<PRE>
<FORM NAME="RegistrationForm">
<B>First Name:        </B><INPUT TYPE=TEXT NAME="firstname">
<B>Last Name:         </B><INPUT TYPE=TEXT NAME="lastname">
<B>Address1:          </B><INPUT TYPE=TEXT NAME="addr1">
<B>Address2:          </B><INPUT TYPE=TEXT NAME="addr2">
<B>City:              </B><INPUT TYPE=TEXT NAME="city">
<B>State:             </B><INPUT TYPE=TEXT NAME="state" MAXLENGTH=2 SIZE=2>
<B>Zip:               </B><INPUT TYPE=TEXT NAME="zip" MAXLENGTH=10 SIZE=10>
<B>Area Code/Phone: </B><INPUT TYPE=TEXT NAME="code" MAXLENGTH=3 SIZE=3>
                        <INPUT TYPE=TEXT NAME="phone" MAXLENGTH=7 SIZE=7>

<B>Preferred Cuisine: </B><SELECT NAME="cuisine" SIZE="1">
                        <OPTION VALUE="1">American
                        <OPTION VALUE="2">Chinese
                        <OPTION VALUE="3">French
                        <OPTION VALUE="4">German
                        <OPTION VALUE="5">Greek
                        <OPTION VALUE="6">Indian
                        <OPTION VALUE="7">Italian
                        <OPTION VALUE="8">Japanese
                        <OPTION VALUE="9">Other
                        </SELECT>

<INPUT TYPE=BUTTON NAME="cmdSubmit"
VALUE="Submit"> <INPUT TYPE="RESET" VALUE="Clear">
</PRE>

</FORM>
</TD>
</TABLE>
</P>
</BODY>
</HTML>
```

The **document** Object

The **document** object represents the page in the current browser window. The **document** object provides access to the elements contained in the page and specifies information about the document through the object's properties. The **document** object also takes care of processing events and exposes events to script.

The **document** object's properties are shown in Table 6.7. Its collections are displayed in Table 6.8, its methods are displayed in Table 6.9, and its events are displayed in Table 6.10.

Table 6.7 document object properties.

Property	Description	Syntax
activeElement	Identifies the element that has focus	*docobj*.activeElement
alinkColor	Specifies the color of the active link	*docobj*.alinkColor[=*color*]
bgColor	Specifies the background color	*docobj*.bgColor[=*color*]
charset	Specifies the document's character set	*docobj*.charset[=*charset*]
cookie	Specifies a string value of a cookie	*docobj*.cookie[=*cookie*]
defaultCharset	Specifies the document's default character set	*docobj*.defaultCharset[=*charset*]
domain	Specifies the document's security domain	*docobj*.domain[=*domain*]
expando	Specifies whether variables can be created within an object	*docobj*.expando[=*boolean*]
fgColor	Specifies the document's text color	*docobj*.fgColor[=*color*]
lastModified	Returns the document's last-modified date, if supplied	*docobj*.lastModified
linkColor	Specifies the color of the document links	*docobj*.linkColor[=*color*]
location	Specifies information on the current URL	*docobj*.location[=*location*]
parentWindow	Returns the document's **window** object	*docobj*.parentWindow
readyState	Specifies the current state of an object being downloaded	*docobj*.readyState
referrer	Returns the URL of the previous location	*docobj*.referrer
selection	Returns the action selection title	*docobj*.selection
url	Specifies the current document's URL	*docobj*.url[=*url*]
vlinkColor	Specifies the color of visited links	*docobj*.vlinkColor[=*color*]

Table 6.8 document object collections.

Collection	Description	Syntax
all	Returns a reference to a collection of the document's elements	*docobj*.all([*index*])
anchors	Returns a collection of the document's **<A>** elements	*docobj*.anchors([*index*])
applets	Returns a collection of the document's **<APPLET>** objects	*docobj*.applets([*index*])
children	Returns a collection of the document's children	*docobj*.children([*index*])
embeds	Returns a collection of the document's **<EMBED>** elements	*docobj*.embeds([*index*])
forms	Returns a collection of the document's **<FORM>** elements	*docobj*.forms([*index*])

(continued)

Table 6.8   document object collections *(continued).*

Collection	Description	Syntax
frames	Returns a collection of the document's **window** objects	*docobj*.**frames**([*index*])
images	Returns a collection of the document's **<IMG>** elements	*docobj*.**images**([*index*])
links	Returns a collection of the document's **<A>** elements that have an **HREF** attribute, and all **<AREA>** elements	*docobj*.**links**([*index*])
plugins	Serves as an alias for the **embeds** collection	*docobj*.**plugins**([*index*])
scripts	Returns a collection of the document's **<SCRIPT>** elements	*docobj*.**scripts**([*index*])
stylesheets	Returns a collection of the document's **stylesheet** objects	*docobj*.**stylesheets**([*index*])

Table 6.9   document object methods.

Method	Description	Syntax
clear	Clears the document's contents	*docobj*.**clear**()
close	Closes the output stream	*docobj*.**close**()
createElement	Creates an element object for the specified tag	*docobj*.**createElement**(*tag*)
createStyleSheet	Creates a style sheet	docobj.**createStyleSheet**([*url*[,*index*]])
elementFromPoint	Returns the element at the specified coordinates	*docobj*.**elementFromPoint**(x,y)
execCommand	Executes a command over the selection or text range	*docobj*.**execCommand**(*Cmd* [,*UserInterface*[,*Value*]])
open	Opens an output stream for **write** and **writeln** methods	*docobj*.**open**(*mimetype*[,*replace*])
queryCommandEnabled	Returns whether a command can be executed	*docobj*.**queryCommandEnabled**(*cmd*)
queryCommandIndeterm	Returns whether a command is in the indeterminate state	*docobj*.**queryCommandIndeterm**(*cmd*)
queryCommandState	Returns the command's current state	*docobj*.**queryCommandState**(*cmd*)
queryCommandSupported	Returns whether the command is supported	*docobj*.**queryCommandSupported**(*cmd*)
queryCommandText	Returns the string associated with the command	*docobj*.**queryCommantText**(*cmd*)
queryCommandValue	Returns the current value of the command **ShowHelp**	*docobj*.**queryCommandValue**(*cmd*)
write	Writes an HTML expression to the document	*docobj*.**write**(*exp*)
writeln	Writes an HTML expression followed by a carriage return	*docobj*.**writeln**(*exp*)

Table 6.10   document object events.

Event	Description
onafterupdate	Fires after data is transferred from the element to the data provider
onbeforeupdate	Fires before data is transferred from the element to the data provider
onclick	Fires when the left mouse button is clicked
ondblclick	Fires when the left mouse button is double-clicked
ondragstart	Fires when the user starts to drag a selection
onerrorupdate	Fires when the **onbeforeupdate** event handler has canceled the data transfer
onhelp	Fires when the user presses F1 or the browser Help key
onkeydown	Fires when a key is pressed
onkeypress	Fires when a key is pressed
onkeyup	Fires when a key is released
onmousedown	Fires when a mouse button is pressed
onmousemove	Fires when the mouse is moved
onmouseout	Fires when the mouse pointer is moved out of an element
onmouseover	Fires when the mouse pointer is moved over an element
onmouseup	Fires when a mouse button is released
onreadystatechange	Fires when an object's ready state changes
onrowenter	Fires when the current row changes and new data is available
onrowexit	Fires when the data source control is changing the current row
onselectstart	Fires at the beginning of an element selection

How To Use The document Object

Now, check out Listing 6.8, which is similar to Listing 6.7, except that it uses the **document** object's **forms** collection to reference the **RegistrationForm** elements. The **forms** collection contains all the forms in the document. This example uses only one form, so it is referenced in JScript at index 0 like this:

```
forms[0]
```

You can access the individual form elements by using the **forms** collection's **item** method, which also takes a zero-based index to reference form elements.

Listing 6.8   Using the document object.

```
<!-- The registration page -->
<HTML>
<HEAD>
<TITLE>Listing 6.8 Member Registration</TITLE>
<SCRIPT FOR="window" EVENT="onload" LANGUAGE=JavaScript>
<!--
    document.body.bgColor="WHITE";
    document.body.text="BLUE";
// -->
</SCRIPT>
```

```
<SCRIPT LANGUAGE=JavaScript>
<!--
    defaultStatus="Community Dining Club New Member Registration";

//-->
</SCRIPT>

<SCRIPT FOR="cmdSubmit" EVENT="onclick" LANGUAGE=JavaScript>
<!--

    defaultStatus = "Validating";

    if (forms[0].item(0).value.length == 0) {
        alert("Please enter your first name.");
        forms[0].item(0).focus();
    }
    else if (forms[0].item(1).value.length == 0) {
        forms[0].item(1).value = prompt("Please enter your last name.");
        if (forms[0].item(1).value.length != 0)
            forms[0].item(1).focus();
    }
    else if (forms[0].item(2).value.length == 0) {
        alert("Please enter your address.");
        forms[0].item(2).focus();
    }
    else if (forms[0].item(4).value.length == 0) {
        alert("Please enter the city.");
        forms[0].item(4).focus();
    }
    else if (forms[0].item(5).value.length != 2) {
        alert("Please enter the 2-letter state abbreviation.");
        forms[0].item(5).focus();
    }
    else if (forms[0].item(6).value.length < 5) {
        alert("Please enter a valid ZIP code.");
        forms[0].item(6).focus();
        forms[0].item(6).select();
    }
    else  if (forms[0].item(7).value.length != 3 ||
        isNaN(forms[0].item(7).value)) {
        alert("Please enter a valid area code.");
        forms[0].item(7).focus();
        forms[0].item(7).select();
    }
    else if (forms[0].item(8).value.length != 7 ||
        isNaN(forms[0].item(8).value)) {
        alert("Please enter a valid phone number.");
```

```
            forms[0].item(8).focus();
            forms[0].item(8).select();
      }

// -->
</SCRIPT>
</HEAD>
<BODY>
<H2 Align=Center>New Member Registration</H2>
<HR SIZE=5 WIDTH=90%>

<P ALIGN=CENTER>
<TABLE>
<TD>
<PRE>
<FORM NAME="RegistrationForm">
<B>First Name:        </B><INPUT TYPE=TEXT NAME="firstname">
<B>Last Name:         </B><INPUT TYPE=TEXT NAME="lastname">
<B>Address1:          </B><INPUT TYPE=TEXT NAME="addr1">
<B>Address2:          </B><INPUT TYPE=TEXT NAME="addr2">
<B>City:              </B><INPUT TYPE=TEXT NAME="city">
<B>State:             </B><INPUT TYPE=TEXT NAME="state" MAXLENGTH=2 SIZE=2>
<B>Zip:               </B><INPUT TYPE=TEXT NAME="zip" MAXLENGTH=10 SIZE=10>
<B>Area Code/Phone: </B><INPUT TYPE=TEXT NAME="code" MAXLENGTH=3 SIZE=3>
                        <INPUT TYPE=TEXT NAME="phone" MAXLENGTH=7 SIZE=7>

<B>Preferred Cuisine: </B><SELECT NAME="cuisine" SIZE="1">
                        <OPTION VALUE="1">American
                        <OPTION VALUE="2">Chinese
                        <OPTION VALUE="3">French
                        <OPTION VALUE="4">German
                        <OPTION VALUE="5">Greek
                        <OPTION VALUE="6">Indian
                        <OPTION VALUE="7">Italian
                        <OPTION VALUE="8">Japanese
                        <OPTION VALUE="9">Other
                        </SELECT>

<INPUT TYPE=BUTTON NAME="cmdSubmit" VALUE="Submit">
<INPUT TYPE="RESET" VALUE="Clear">
</PRE>

</FORM>
</TD>
</TABLE>
</P>
</BODY>
</HTML>
```

The **event** Object

The **event** object provides several items of information regarding the event being processed. The browser sets the **event** object's properties, most of which are read-only.

You also can use the **event** object to cancel an event's default behavior and to prevent additional event handlers from being executed. The Dynamic HTML Object Model allows events to bubble up through the document hierarchy. The element that generates an event processes it first. Then, the element's parent processes it. Then, the parent's parent element gets a chance. This process continues until the **document** object receives the event. You can even write your own event handlers to process events for several elements and then use the **event** object to cancel the default behavior of bubbling events up the hierarchy.

Table 6.11 shows the **event** object's properties, and Table 6.12 shows its collections.

Table 6.11   event object properties.

Property	Description	Syntax
altkey	Returns the state of the Alt key	*event*.**altkey**
button	Returns which mouse button was pressed, if any	*event*.**button**
cancelBubble	Specifies whether the current event should bubble up	*event*.**cancelBubble[=*bool*]**
clientX, clientY	Returns the relative positions of the mouse click	*event*.**clientx**
ctrlKey	Returns the state of the Ctrl key	*event*.**ctrlKey**
fromElement	Returns the element being moved from	*event*.**fromElement**
keyCode	Specifies the Unicode key code associated with the key event	*event*.**keycode[=*code*]**
offsetX, offsetY	Returns container-relative positions	*event*.**offsetX**
reason	Returns the status of data transfer for a data source object	*event*.**reason**
returnValue	Specifies the return value from an event	*event*.**returnValue[=*bool*]**
screenX, screenY	Returns coordinates relative to screen size	*event*.**screenX**
shiftKey	Returns the state of the Shift key	*event*.**shiftKey**
srcElement	Returns the element that fired the event	*event*.**srcElement**
srcFilter	Returns the filter object that fired the **onfilterchange** event	*event*.**srcFilter**
toElement	Returns the element being moved to	*event*.**toElement**
type	Returns the event name or scripting language for the **event** object and the **script** object	*event*.**type**
x, y	Returns the position of the mouse click relative to an element	*event*.**x**

Table 6.12   event object collections.

Collection	Description	Syntax
bookmarks	Returns a collection of ADO bookmarks	*event*.**bookmarks**
boundElements	Returns a collection of page elements bound to a data set	*event*.**boundElements**

How To Use The event Object

Listing 6.9 shows the new member registration page, which now contains a very simple example of using the **event** object. The **event** object contains a variety of data on the event being processed. Also, the Dynamic HTML Object Model uses an event model that allows events to bubble up through the object hierarchy. Events are first processed by the element firing the event and then by each of the parent elements up to the **document** object.

To illustrate event bubbling, this page has two new statements. First, look at the member registration page. The **alert** method displays a message containing the name of the element that fired the event—in this case, the **cmdSubmit** button. The event then bubbles up to the document's object level. The **document** contains an **onclick** handler that also displays the name of the element. If you click anywhere in the document except on the Submit button, the document's **onclick** event handler fires. You can prevent the **cmdSubmit onclick** event from bubbling up to the document level by adding the statement

```
event.cancelBubble = true;
```

inside the button's **onclick** event handler.

Listing 6.9   Using the event object.

```
<!-- The registration page -->
<HTML>
<HEAD>
<TITLE>Listing 6.9 Member Registration</TITLE>
<SCRIPT FOR="window" EVENT="onload" LANGUAGE=JavaScript>
<!--
     document.body.bgColor="WHITE";
     document.body.text="BLUE";
// -->
</SCRIPT>

<SCRIPT LANGUAGE=JavaScript>
<!--
     defaultStatus="Community Dining Club New Member Registration";

//-->
</SCRIPT>

<SCRIPT FOR="document" EVENT="onclick" LANGUAGE=JavaScript>
<!--
     alert ("Now at document level: " + event.srcElement.name);
//-->
</SCRIPT>

<SCRIPT FOR="cmdSubmit" EVENT="onclick" LANGUAGE=JavaScript>
<!--
```

```
        defaultStatus = "Validating";
        alert ("Now at element level: " + event.srcElement.name);

        if (forms[0].item(0).value.length == 0) {
            alert("Please enter your first name.");
            forms[0].item(0).focus();
        }
        else if (forms[0].item(1).value.length == 0) {
            forms[0].item(1).value = prompt("Please enter your last name.");
            if (forms[0].item(1).value.length != 0)
                forms[0].item(1).focus();
        }
        else if (forms[0].item(2).value.length == 0) {
            alert("Please enter your address.");
            forms[0].item(2).focus();
        }
        else if (forms[0].item(4).value.length == 0) {
            alert("Please enter the city.");
            forms[0].item(4).focus();
        }
        else if (forms[0].item(5).value.length != 2) {
            alert("Please enter the 2-letter state abbreviation.");
            forms[0].item(5).focus();
        }
        else if (forms[0].item(6).value.length < 5) {
            alert("Please enter a valid ZIP code.");
            forms[0].item(6).focus();
            forms[0].item(6).select();
        }
        else if (forms[0].item(7).value.length != 3 ||
            isNaN(forms[0].item(7).value)) {
            alert("Please enter a valid area code.");
            forms[0].item(7).focus();
            forms[0].item(7).select();
        }
        else if (forms[0].item(8).value.length != 7 ||
            isNaN(forms[0].item(8).value)) {
            alert("Please enter a valid phone number.");
            forms[0].item(8).focus();
            forms[0].item(8).select();
        }

// -->
</SCRIPT>
</HEAD>
<BODY>
```

```
<H2 Align=Center>New Member Registration</H2>
<HR SIZE=5 WIDTH=90%>

<P ALIGN=CENTER>
<TABLE>
<TD>
<PRE>
<FORM NAME="RegistrationForm">
<B>First Name:        </B><INPUT TYPE=TEXT NAME="firstname">
<B>Last Name:         </B><INPUT TYPE=TEXT NAME="lastname">
<B>Address1:          </B><INPUT TYPE=TEXT NAME="addr1">
<B>Address2:          </B><INPUT TYPE=TEXT NAME="addr2">
<B>City:              </B><INPUT TYPE=TEXT NAME="city">
<B>State:             </B><INPUT TYPE=TEXT NAME="state" MAXLENGTH=2 SIZE=2>
<B>Zip:               </B><INPUT TYPE=TEXT NAME="zip" MAXLENGTH=10 SIZE=10>
<B>Area Code/Phone: </B><INPUT TYPE=TEXT NAME="code" MAXLENGTH=3 SIZE=3>
                        <INPUT TYPE=TEXT NAME="phone" MAXLENGTH=7 SIZE=7>

<B>Preferred Cuisine: </B><SELECT NAME="cuisine" SIZE="1">
                        <OPTION VALUE="1">American
                        <OPTION VALUE="2">Chinese
                        <OPTION VALUE="3">French
                        <OPTION VALUE="4">German
                        <OPTION VALUE="5">Greek
                        <OPTION VALUE="6">Indian
                        <OPTION VALUE="7">Italian
                        <OPTION VALUE="8">Japanese
                        <OPTION VALUE="9">Other
                        </SELECT>

<INPUT TYPE=BUTTON NAME="cmdSubmit"
VALUE="Submit"> <INPUT TYPE="RESET" VALUE="Clear">
</PRE>

</FORM>
</TD>
</TABLE>
</P>
</BODY>
</HTML>
```

The **history** Object

You use the **history** object to move forward and backward through the browser's history list. This object is exceedingly simple, with only one property and three methods, as shown in Tables 6.13 and 6.14.

Table 6.13 history object properties.

Property	Description	Syntax
length	Returns the number of elements in the history list	*history*.length

Table 6.14 history object methods.

Method	Description	Syntax
back	Loads the previous URL	*history*.back()
forward	Loads the next URL	*history*.forward()
go	Loads the specified URL	*history*.go(*integer* | *urlstring*)

The **location** Object

You can access and manipulate the URL of the current page by using the **location** object. This object provides access to individual sections of the URL and to the entire URL. The complete URL is in the **href** property. The object also picks apart the URL into properties, such as **hostname** and **pathname**. Changing any property of the **location** object causes the browser to load a new URL.

Table 6.15 shows the **location** object's properties, and Table 6.16 shows its methods.

How To Use The location Object

When completed, the new member registration page needs a location to which to send the form data. Listing 6.10 modifies the registration page to use the **location** object to bundle the form data into a query string and send it to a page that will further process it, such as

Table 6.15 location object properties.

Property	Description	Syntax
hash	Specifies the section of the **href** attribute following the #	*loc*.hash[=*hash*]
host	Specifies the host:port section of the URL	*loc*.host[=*host*]
hostname	Specifies the host name section of the URL	*loc*.hostname[=*hostname*]
href	Specifies the entire URL	*loc*.href[=*url*]
pathname	Specifies the file or object path	*loc*.pathname[=*pathname*]
port	Specifies the port number in the URL	*loc*.port[=*port*]
protocol	Specifies the URL access protocol	*loc*.protocol[=*protocol*]
search	Specifies the section of the URL following the ?	*loc*.search[=*querystring*]

Table 6.16 location object methods.

Method	Description	Syntax
assign	Sets the current location to the specified URL	*loc*.assign(*url*)
reload	Reloads the current page	*loc*.reload([*bool*])
replace	Replaces the current document with the specified document	*loc*.replace(*url*)

writing it to a database. All the work takes place inside the validation script. The script defines a few variables: **data_ok** is a Boolean that signals when the data is valid and ready for forwarding, and **submit_url** contains the name of the page that will receive the data— 6-10_mbr.asp. This page is an Active Server Page, thus the .asp extension. Active Server Pages contain script that executes on the server. Finally, the **query_string** variable holds the name/value pairs that the form sends to the Active Server Page.

If a data item is invalid, **data_ok** is set to **false**, and the user must reenter the data. When all the data is valid, the script constructs **query_string** from the form elements. The script uses a **for** loop that iterates through the **forms** collection for this form. The script appends each form item's **name** and **value** properties to **query_string**. An HTML query string's name/value pairs are separated with +, so the script must also insert this character in **query_string** after each name/value pair. When the loop completes, **query_string** has an extra + on the end. The script removes this unnecessary character by using the JScript **string** object's **substr** method. Finally, the script appends **query_string** to **submit_url** to construct the URL with the query string.

Changing any of the **location** object's properties causes the browser to load the new URL. Assigning **submit_url** to the **location** object accesses 6-10_mgr.asp with the new member data.

Listing 6.10   Using the **location** object.

```
<!-- The registration page -->
<HTML>
<HEAD>
<TITLE>Listing 6.10 Member Registration</TITLE>
<SCRIPT FOR="window" EVENT="onload" LANGUAGE=JavaScript>
<!--
     document.body.bgColor="WHITE";
     document.body.text="BLUE";
// -->
</SCRIPT>

<SCRIPT LANGUAGE=JavaScript>
<!--
     defaultStatus="Community Dining Club New Member Registration";

//-->
</SCRIPT>

<SCRIPT FOR="cmdSubmit" EVENT="onclick" LANGUAGE=JavaScript>
<!--
     var data_ok = true;
     var submit_url = "6-10_mbr.asp";
     var query_string = "?";
```

```
defaultStatus = "Validating";

 if (forms[0].item(0).value.length == 0) {
     data_ok = false;
     alert("Please enter your first name.");
     forms[0].item(0).focus();
 }
 else if (forms[0].item(1).value.length == 0) {
     data_ok = false;
     forms[0].item(1).value = prompt("Please enter your last name.");
     if (forms[0].item(1).value.length != 0)
         forms[0].item(1).focus();
 }
 else if (forms[0].item(2).value.length == 0) {
     data_ok = false;
     alert("Please enter your address.");
     forms[0].item(2).focus();
 }
 else if (forms[0].item(3).value.length == 0) {
     forms[0].item(3).value = " ";
 }
 else if (forms[0].item(4).value.length == 0) {
     data_ok = false;
     alert("Please enter the city.");
     forms[0].item(4).focus();
 }
 else if (forms[0].item(5).value.length != 2) {
     data_ok = false;
     alert("Please enter the 2-letter state abbreviation.");
     forms[0].item(5).focus();
 }
 else if (forms[0].item(6).value.length < 5) {
     data_ok = false;
     alert("Please enter a valid ZIP code.");
     forms[0].item(6).focus();
     forms[0].item(6).select();
 }
 else if (forms[0].item(7).value.length != 3 ||
     isNaN(forms[0].item(7).value)) {
     data_ok = false;
     alert("Please enter a valid area code.");
     forms[0].item(7).focus();
     forms[0].item(7).select();
 }
 else if (forms[0].item(8).value.length != 7 ||
         isNaN(forms[0].item(8).value)) {
```

```
        data_ok = false;
        alert("Please enter a valid phone number.");
        forms[0].item(8).focus();
        forms[0].item(8).select();
    }

    if (data_ok) {
        for (i = 0; i < forms[0].length - 2; i++) {
            query_string += forms[0].item(i).name + "="
                + forms[0].item(i).value + "+";
        }
        query_string = query_string.substr(0, query_string.length-1);
        submit_url += query_string;
        location = submit_url;
    }

// -->
</SCRIPT>
</HEAD>
<BODY>
<H2 Align=Center>New Member Registration</H2>
<HR SIZE=5 WIDTH=90%>

<P ALIGN=CENTER>
<TABLE>
<TD>
<PRE>
<FORM NAME="RegistrationForm">
<B>First Name:       </B><INPUT TYPE=TEXT NAME="firstname">
<B>Last Name:        </B><INPUT TYPE=TEXT NAME="lastname">
<B>Address1:         </B><INPUT TYPE=TEXT NAME="addr1">
<B>Address2:         </B><INPUT TYPE=TEXT NAME="addr2">
<B>City:             </B><INPUT TYPE=TEXT NAME="city">
<B>State:            </B><INPUT TYPE=TEXT NAME="state" MAXLENGTH=2 SIZE=2>
<B>Zip:              </B><INPUT TYPE=TEXT NAME="zip" MAXLENGTH=10 SIZE=10>
<B>Area Code/Phone:  </B><INPUT TYPE=TEXT NAME="code" MAXLENGTH=3 SIZE=3>
                        <INPUT TYPE=TEXT NAME="phone" MAXLENGTH=7 SIZE=7>

<B>Preferred Cuisine: </B><SELECT NAME="cuisine" SIZE="1">
                        <OPTION VALUE="1">American
                        <OPTION VALUE="2">Chinese
                        <OPTION VALUE="3">French
                        <OPTION VALUE="4">German
                        <OPTION VALUE="5">Greek
                        <OPTION VALUE="6">Indian
```

```
                              <OPTION VALUE="7">Italian
                              <OPTION VALUE="8">Japanese
                              <OPTION VALUE="9">Other
                              </SELECT>

<INPUT TYPE=BUTTON NAME="cmdSubmit" VALUE="Submit">
<INPUT TYPE="RESET" VALUE="Clear">
</PRE>

</FORM>
</TD>
</TABLE>
</P>
</BODY>
</HTML>
```

The **navigator** Object

The **navigator** object provides information about the client browser, such as the application name and version number. Table 6.17 shows the **navigator** object's properties, Table 6.18 shows its collections, and Table 6.19 shows its methods.

The **screen** Object

The **screen** object provides information about the client's screen and rendering capabilities. It is useful when you want to create a new window and set height and width, choose images to display, and so on. Table 6.20 shows the **screen** object's properties.

Table 6.17   navigator object properties.

Property	Description	Syntax
appCodeName	Returns the code name of the browser	*nav.***appCodeName**
appMinorVersion	Returns the application's minor version value	*nam.***appMinorVersion**
appName	Returns the browser's name	*nav.***appName**
appVersion	Returns the browser's version	*nav.***appVersion**
browserLanguage	Returns the browser's language	*nav.***browserLanguage**
connectionSpeed	Returns the session's connection speed	*nav.***connectionSpeed**
cookieEnabled	Returns whether client-side cookies are enabled	*nav.***cookieEnabled**
cpuClass	Returns the client's CPU class	*nav.***cpuClass**
onLine	Returns whether the system is in the global offline mode	*nav.***onLine**
platform	Returns the client's platform	*nav.***platform**
systemLanguage	Returns the system's default language	*nav.***systemLanguage**
userAgent	Returns the client's HTTP user-agent header	*nav.***userAgent**
userLanguage	Returns the current user language	*nav.***userLanguage**
userProfile	Provides methods to request read access to a user's profile	*nav.***userProfile.***method*

Table 6.18   navigator object collections.

Collection	Description	Syntax
mimeTypes	Provided for compatibility, returns an empty collection for IE	*nav*.mimeTypes
plugins	Provided for compatibility, returns an empty collection for IE	*nav*.plugins

Table 6.19   navigator object methods.

Method	Description	Syntax
javaEnabled	Returns whether Java is enabled	*nav*.javaEnabled()
taintEnabled	Returns whether data tainting is enabled	*nav*.taintEnabled()

Table 6.20   screen object properties.

Property	Description	Syntax
availHeight	Returns the working height of the system's screen	*scrn*.availHeight
availWidth	Returns the working width of the system's screen	*scrn*.availWidth
bufferDepth	Specifies an off-screen bitmap buffer	*scrn*.bufferDepth[=*bufferdepth*])
colorDepth	Returns the bits-per-pixel value used for colors	*scrn*.colorDepth
height	Returns the vertical screen resolution	*scrn*.height
updateInterval	Specifies the screen's update interval	*scrn*.updateInterval[=*msec*])
width	Returns the horizontal screen resolution	*scrn*.width

How To Use The screen And navigator Objects

Listing 6.11 uses the **screen** and **navigator** objects to retrieve information about the client browser. This example shows how to access this information, but it does not use that information for anything. Listing 6.12 shows an additional page that the registration page opens. The new page simply displays some of the client application information.

Listing 6.11   Using the screen object.

```
<!-- The registration page -->
<HTML>
<HEAD>
<TITLE>Listing 6.11 Member Registration</TITLE>
<SCRIPT FOR="window" EVENT="onload" LANGUAGE=JavaScript>
<!--
    document.body.bgColor="WHITE";
    document.body.text="BLUE";


// -->
</SCRIPT>
```

```
<SCRIPT LANGUAGE=JavaScript>
<!--
    var appName = navigator.appName;
    var appVersion = navigator.appVersion;
    var userAgent = navigator.userAgent;
    var screenHeight = screen.height;
    var screenWidth = screen.width;
    var screenAvailHeight = screen.availHeight;
    var screenAvailWidth = screen.availWidth;
    var screenColorDepth = screen.colorDepth;

    defaultStatus="Community Dining Club New Member Registration";

    open("6-12.htm", null, "toolbar=0,location=0,status=0,menubar=0");
//-->
</SCRIPT>

<SCRIPT FOR="cmdSubmit" EVENT="onclick" LANGUAGE=JavaScript>
<!--
    var data_ok = true;
    var submit_url = "7-7_mbr.asp";
    var query_string = "?";

    defaultStatus = "Validating";

    if (forms[0].item(0).value.length == 0) {
        data_ok = false;
        alert("Please enter your first name.");
        forms[0].item(0).focus();
    }
    else if (forms[0].item(1).value.length == 0) {
        data_ok = false;
        forms[0].item(1).value = prompt("Please enter your last name.");
        if (forms[0].item(1).value.length != 0)
            forms[0].item(1).focus();
    }
    else if (forms[0].item(2).value.length == 0) {
        data_ok = false;
        alert("Please enter your address.");
        forms[0].item(2).focus();
    }
    else if (forms[0].item(3).value.length == 0) {
        forms[0].item(3).value = " ";
    }
    else if (forms[0].item(4).value.length == 0) {
        data_ok = false;
```

```
            alert("Please enter the city.");
            forms[0].item(4).focus();
        }
    else if (forms[0].item(5).value.length != 2) {
        data_ok = false;
        alert("Please enter the 2-letter state abbreviation.");
        forms[0].item(5).focus();
    }
    else if (forms[0].item(6).value.length < 5) {
        data_ok = false;
        alert("Please enter a valid ZIP code.");
        forms[0].item(6).focus();
        forms[0].item(6).select();
    }
    else if (forms[0].item(7).value.length != 3 ||
        isNaN(forms[0].item(7).value)) {
        data_ok = false;
        alert("Please enter a valid area code.");
        forms[0].item(7).focus();
        forms[0].item(7).select();
    }
    else if (forms[0].item(8).value.length != 7 ||
        isNaN(forms[0].item(8).value)) {
        data_ok = false;
        alert("Please enter a valid phone number.");
        forms[0].item(8).focus();
        forms[0].item(8).select();
    }

    if (data_ok) {
        for (i = 0; i < forms[0].length - 2; i++) {
            query_string += forms[0].item(i).name + "="
                + forms[0].item(i).value + "+";
        }
        query_string = query_string.substr(0, query_string.length-1);
        submit_url += query_string;
        location = submit_url;
    }

// -->
</SCRIPT>
</HEAD>
<BODY>
<H2 Align=Center>New Member Registration</H2>
<HR SIZE=5 WIDTH=90%>
```

```
<P ALIGN=CENTER>
<TABLE>
<TD>
<PRE>
<FORM NAME="RegistrationForm">
<B>First Name:        </B><INPUT TYPE=TEXT NAME="firstname">
<B>Last Name:         </B><INPUT TYPE=TEXT NAME="lastname">
<B>Address1:          </B><INPUT TYPE=TEXT NAME="addr1">
<B>Address2:          </B><INPUT TYPE=TEXT NAME="addr2">
<B>City:              </B><INPUT TYPE=TEXT NAME="city">
<B>State:             </B><INPUT TYPE=TEXT NAME="state" MAXLENGTH=2 SIZE=2>
<B>Zip:               </B><INPUT TYPE=TEXT NAME="zip" MAXLENGTH=10 SIZE=10>
<B>Area Code/Phone: </B><INPUT TYPE=TEXT NAME="code" MAXLENGTH=3 SIZE=3>
                        <INPUT TYPE=TEXT NAME="phone" MAXLENGTH=7 SIZE=7>

<B>Preferred Cuisine: </B><SELECT NAME="cuisine" SIZE="1">
                        <OPTION VALUE="1">American
                        <OPTION VALUE="2">Chinese
                        <OPTION VALUE="3">French
                        <OPTION VALUE="4">German
                        <OPTION VALUE="5">Greek
                        <OPTION VALUE="6">Indian
                        <OPTION VALUE="7">Italian
                        <OPTION VALUE="8">Japanese
                        <OPTION VALUE="9">Other
                        </SELECT>

<INPUT TYPE=BUTTON NAME="cmdSubmit" VALUE="Submit">
<INPUT TYPE="RESET" VALUE="Clear">
</PRE>

</FORM>
</TD>
</TABLE>
</P>
</BODY>
</HTML>
```

Listing 6.12   Accessing client statistics.

```
<!-- The client statistics page-->
<HTML>
<HEAD>
<TITLE>Listing 6.12 Client Stats</TITLE>
</HEAD>
```

```
<SCRIPT LANGUAGE=JavaScript>
<!--
     var appName = navigator.appName;
     var appVersion = navigator.appVersion;
     var userAgent = navigator.userAgent;
     var screenHeight = screen.height;
     var screenWidth = screen.width;
     var screenAvailHeight = screen.availHeight;
     var screenAvailWidth = screen.availWidth;
     var screenColorDepth = screen.colorDepth;

     document.write(appName + "<BR>");
     document.write(appVersion + "<BR>");
     document.write(userAgent + "<BR>");
     document.write(screenWidth + " x " + screenHeight + "<BR>");

//-->
</SCRIPT>
<SCRIPT FOR="close" EVENT="onclick" LANGUAGE=JavaScript>
<!--
     window.close();
//-->
</SCRIPT>
<BODY>

<INPUT TYPE=BUTTON NAME="close" VALUE="Close me">
</BODY>
</HTML>
```

Chapter 7

Database Access

Kim Barber

It's hard to think of the Web today without thinking of data access. True, many Web sites display information without accessing some sort of database. However, the majority of significant Web sites do perform some level of database access. I'm sure you can think of several sites you visit that present information from a database. Examples that I immediately think of are online shopping, banking, email, search engines, information services such as CompuServe and America Online, and more. The Web truly is information at your fingertips, and most of it comes from databases.

This chapter shows you how to use Microsoft technologies to implement database access in your Web pages. These technologies and the strategy behind them are known collectively as *Universal Data Access*. You'll see how to access databases with server-side processing only, as well as how to manipulate data remotely on the client. The latter is done using a combination of client-side and server-side scripting.

Universal Data Access

Universal Data Access (UDA) is Microsoft's strategy for providing organization-wide access to information. The goal is to provide high-performance access to any data on any platform from any client. UDA gives you access to several relational and nonrelational data formats via Microsoft Data Access Components.

UDA is based on the Component Object Model (COM), a well-known and used object technology; it allows you to use a variety of languages and tools. As a result, you can develop business solutions using tools that you are already familiar with.

Microsoft Data Access Components

UDA is implemented via Microsoft Data Access Components (MDAC). MDAC consists of high-performance, easy-to-use component technologies that include the following:

- *OLE DB*—A low-level data interface that supports relational and nonrelational data sources
- *Active Data Objects (ADO)*—A high-level programming interface that uses OLE DB
- *Open Database Connectivity (ODBC)*—A single interface that allows access to several different database management systems (DBMS)

These technologies are the subject of this chapter. Remote Data Service (RDS) is another technology covered here. RDS is an ADO service that provides remote client-side data access (remoting). This feature improves performance by reducing the number of round trips to the server.

OLE DB

OLE DB consists of COM interfaces that provide a standard method for accessing databases in a program. These COM interfaces provide a low-level object-based way to access most database formats, both relational and nonrelational. OLE DB is efficient—both fast and with low memory requirements.

OLE DB uses OLE DB *providers* to allow your applications to access and manipulate data. It also uses ODBC to access relational databases. Actually, OLE DB consists of three types of components:

- *Data providers*—To contain and expose data; for example, SQL databases, spreadsheets, email files, and so on
- *Data consumers*—To use the data; examples are ADO, VB, and VBScript
- *Services*—To process and transport the data and to enhance the data provider's functionality

OLE DB contains the following objects:

- **Command**—Executes commands, such as queries
- **Data Source**—Provides functions that identify the data provider; also initializes a connection to the data source and verifies user permissions
- **Enumerator**—Searches for **Data Source** objects and enumerators on a system
- **Error**—Contains error information
- **Rowset**—Represents the data; created from a **Command** or **Session** object

♦ **Session**—Defines the object's actions

♦ **Transaction**—Used to commit or abort transactions

♦ **View**—Defines a subset of the rows and columns from a rowset

As a Web application developer, you probably won't use these objects directly. Rather, you will employ ADO to use them indirectly.

ODBC

ODBC is another interface that you can use to access databases from your applications. ODBC uses drivers to interface an application to a specific DBMS. Database vendors typically provide ODBC drivers for their specific databases. Because ODBC uses a single interface to access any database, an application using ODBC calls can access data stored in any ODBC-compliant database.

You really don't have to worry too much about using ODBC in your Web applications because you'll be using ADO. Most likely, all you will have to do is select the right driver when you set up an ODBC database for use. Of course, you'll also have to specify the database to use. You do so from the Control Panel by selecting the ODBC Data Sources icon. This chapter uses a Microsoft Access database, so you'll need the Microsoft Access driver on your system if you want to experiment with the examples.

Active Data Objects

Active Data Objects (ADO) is a collection of high-level automation interfaces used to implement database access in applications. ADO uses OLE DB providers to access a data source's functionality. One provider accesses ODBC drivers. Because ADO uses OLE DB providers, you can access a variety of data sources.

ADO is small, efficient, and easy to use. You can use ADO with several programming languages, such as VB, VBScript, Java, and JavaScript. Because you can use VBScript and JavaScript in Web pages, you can easily use ADO on the Web.

The ADO object model consists of a collection of objects that expose properties, methods, and events needed to work with a data source. Figure 7.1 shows the ADO objects and their collections. The sections that follow describe these objects and properties, methods, and events. Later, you'll see several programming examples.

The **Connection** Object

The **Connection** object represents a unique connection to a data source. This object has several properties and methods that the underlying database may or may not support. This object encapsulates the OLE DB **Data Source** and **Session** objects. Tables 7.1, 7.2, and 7.3 list the **Connection** object's properties, methods, and events, respectively.

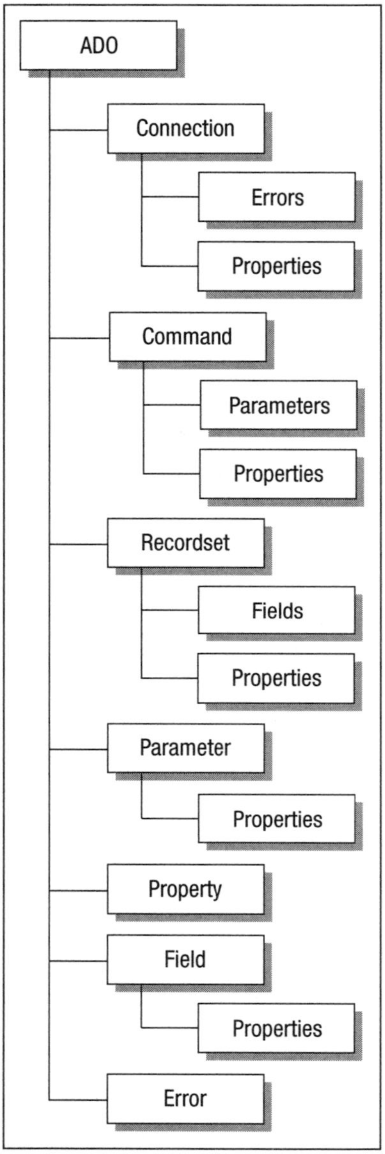

Figure 7.1
The ADO object model.

Table 7.1   Connection object properties.

Property	Description
Attributes	References one or more attributes of an object
CommandTimeout	Specifies how long to wait while executing a command before timing out

(continued)

Table 7.1   Connection object properties *(continued)*.

Property	Description
ConnectionString	Contains information used to establish a connection to a data source
ConnectionTimeout	Specifies how long to wait before terminating a connection attempt
CursorLocation	Indicates the location of the cursor service
DefaultDatabase	Specifies the default database
IsolationLevel	Specifies the level of isolation
Mode	Specifies the available permissions for modifying data in a connection
Provider	Specifies the provider's name
State	Indicates whether the object is open or closed
Version	Indicates the ADO version number

Table 7.2   Connection object methods.

Method	Description
BeginTrans	Begins a new transaction
Cancel	Cancels a pending asynchronous method call
Close	Closes an open object and dependent objects
CommitTrans	Saves changes and ends the transaction
Execute	Executes the specified query, SQL statement, or stored procedure
Open	Opens a connection to a data source
OpenSchema	Returns database schema information from the provider
RollbackTrans	Cancels any changes and ends the transaction
Save	Saves the record set in a file or stream object

Table 7.3   Connection object events.

Event	Description
BeginTransComplete	Fired when the **BeginTrans** method is finished
CommitTransComplete	Fired when the **CommitTrans** method is finished
ConnectComplete	Fired after the connection starts
Disconnect	Fired after a connection ends
ExecuteComplete	Fired after a command finishes executing
InfoMessage	Fired when a warning occurs during a connection
RollbackTransComplete	Fired when the **RollbackTrans** method is finished
WillConnect	Fired before a connection starts
WillExecute	Fired just before a pending command executes

The **Connection** object also has two collections: the **Errors** collection and the **Properties** collection. The **Errors** collection contains **Error** objects created because of a provider-related error. The **Properties** collection contains the **Property** objects for an instance of an object.

The **Command** Object

The **Command** object contains the command to be executed on a data source. Typical commands are SQL statements to retrieve data from a data source, or add, delete, or modify data in the data source. This object encapsulates the OLE DB **Command** structure.

The **Command** object doesn't have events but does have properties, methods, and collections. Table 7.4 lists the **Command** object's properties. Table 7.5 lists its methods.

The **Command** object has two collections: the **Parameters** collection and the **Properties** collection. The **Parameters** collection contains all the parameters of a **Command** object. The **Properties** collection contains all the **Property** objects for an instance of an object.

The **Recordset** Object

The **Recordset** object is the main interface to data. It represents the set of records from a table or the results of a command that has been executed. **Recordset** objects are constructed using records (rows) and fields (columns). The **Recordset** object references a single record at a time in the current record set. This object encapsulates the OLE DB **Rowset** object.

Table 7.6 lists the **Recordset** object's properties. Table 7.7 lists the **Recordset** object's methods. Table 7.8 lists the **Recordset** object's events.

The **Recordset** object has a **Fields** and a **Properties** collection. The **Fields** collection contains all the **Field** objects in a record set or **Recordset** object. The **Properties** collection contains the **Property** objects for an instance of an object.

Table 7.4   Command object properties.

Property	Description
ActiveConnection	Indicates the **Connection** object that a specified **Command**, **Recordset**, or **Record** object belongs to
CommandText	Indicates the command text that will be executed on a provider
CommandTimeout	Specifies how long to wait on a command execution before terminating
CommandType	Specifies the type of a **Command** object
Name	Specifies the name of an object
Prepared	Specifies whether to save a compiled copy of a command before execution
State	Indicates whether an object is open or closed

Table 7.5   Command object methods.

Method	Description
Cancel	Cancels a pending asynchronous method call
CreateParameter	Creates a new **Parameter** object with specified properties
Execute	Executes a query, SQL statement, or stored procedure specified in the **CommandText** property

Table 7.6   Recordset object properties.

Property	Description
AbsolutePage	Specifies to which page to move for a new record
AbsolutePosition	Specifies the ordinal position of a **Recordset** object's current record
ActiveCommand	Indicates the **Command** object that created the associated **Recordset** object
ActiveConnection	Specifies to which **Connection** object the specified **Command** or **Recordset** object belongs
BOF	Indicates that the current record position is before the first record
Bookmark	Returns a bookmark that identifies the current record or sets the current record to the record identified by a valid bookmark
Cachesize	Specifies the number of records that are cached locally in memory
CursorLocation	Specifies the location of the cursor engine
CursorType	Specifies the cursor type
DataMember	Specifies the name of a data member to be retrieved from an object referenced by the **DataSource** property
DataSource	Specifies an object that contains data in a **Recordset** object
EditMode	Specifies the editing status of the current record
EOF	Indicates that the current record position is after the last record
Filter	Specifies a filter
Index	Specifies the index name in effect for a **Recordset** object
LockType	Specifies the types of locks placed on records during editing
MarshalOptions	Specifies which records are to marshal back to the server
MaxRecords	Specifies the maximum number of records to return to a record set
PageCount	Specifies the number of pages of data the object contains
PageSize	Specifies the number of records that constitute one page
RecordCount	Specifies the current number of records in the object
Sort	Specifies one or more field names on which to sort a record set
Source	Indicates the source of data or the name of the object or application that generated an error
State	Indicates the object's current state
Status	Indicates the current record's status with respect to batch updates or bulk operations
StayInSynch	Specifies in a **Recordset** object whether the child records changes when the parent row position changes

Table 7.7   Recordset object methods.

Method	Description
AddNew	Creates a new record
Cancel	Cancels a pending asynchronous method call
CancelBatch	Cancels a pending batch update
CancelUpdate	Cancels changes made to the current record or to a new record prior to calling the **Update** method
Clone	Creates a duplicate **Recordset** object from an existing object

(continued)

Table 7.7 Recordset object methods *(continued)*.

Method	Description
Close	Closes an open object and dependent objects
CompareBookmarks	Compares two bookmarks and returns an indication of their relative values
Delete	Deletes the current record
Find	Searches a record set for a row that meets a specified criterion
GetRows	Retrieves multiple records into an array
GetString	Returns the record set as a string
Move	Moves the position of the current record
MoveFirst	Moves to the first record
MoveLast	Moves to the last record
MoveNext	Moves to the next record
MovePrevious	Moves to the previous record
NextRecordset	Clears the current object and returns the next record set by advancing through a series of commands
Open	Opens a cursor
Requery	Updates the record set by reexecuting the query
Resynch	Refreshes the data in the current object
Save	Saves the record set in a file or stream object
Seek	Searches a record set index to locate a row meeting a specified value
Supports	Determines whether a specified object supports a specified type of functionality
Update	Saves changes made to the current record
UpdateBatch	Writes all pending batch updates

Table 7.8 Recordset object events.

Event	Description
EndOfRecordset	Fired when an attempt is made to move past the end of the record set
FetchComplete	Fired after all records in an asynchronous operation have been retrieved
FetchProgress	Fired periodically in a lengthy asynchronous operation to indicate the number of rows currently retrieved
FieldChangeComplete	Fired after the value of one or more **Field** objects has changed
MoveComplete	Fired after the current record set position changes
RecordChangeComplete	Fired after one or more records change
RecordsetChangeComplete	Fired after the record set has changed
WillChangeField	Fired before a pending operation changes the value of one or more **Field** objects in a record set
WillChangeRecord	Fired before one or more records change
WillChangeRecordset	Fired before a pending operation changes the record set
WillMove	Fired before a pending operation changes the position in the record set

The **Parameter** Object

The **Parameter** object represents an argument associated with a **Command** object. It is based on a stored procedure or parameterized query. This object is useful if you want to execute the same command more than one time but change the argument each time. The **Parameter** object has properties, methods, and a collection but doesn't have events.

Table 7.9 lists the **Parameter** object's properties. Table 7.10 lists the **Parameter** object's methods.

The **Parameter** object has only one collection—the **Properties** collection. It contains all the **Property** objects for an instance of an object.

The **Property** Object

ADO objects have built-in and dynamic properties. Built-in properties are standard equipment in ADO. Dynamic properties are defined by the data provider. The **Property** object represents an ADO object's dynamic properties as defined by the provider. The **Property** object has only properties, which are listed in Table 7.11.

The **Field** Object

The **Field** object represents a column of data in a record set. Tables 7.12 and 7.13 list the **Field** object's properties and methods.

The **Field** object has only the **Properties** collection, which contains all the **Property** objects for an instance of an object.

Table 7.9   Parameter object properties.

Property	Description
Attributes	Specifies an object's characteristics
Direction	Specifies whether the **Parameter** is an input or output parameter or both, or if the parameter is a return value from a stored procedure
Name	Specifies the name of an object
NumericScale	Specifies the scale of numeric values in a **Parameter** object
Precision	Specifies the degree of precision for numeric values in a **Parameter** object
Size	Specifies the maximum size in bytes or characters of a **Parameter** object
Type	Specifies the operation type or data type of a **Parameter** object
Value	Specifies the value assigned to a **Parameter** object

Table 7.10   Parameter object methods.

Method	Description
AppendChunk	Appends data to a large binary or text **Parameter** object
Delete	Deletes an object from the **Properties** collection

Table 7.11   Property object properties.

Property	Description
Attributes	Specifies one or more object properties
Name	Specifies the name of an object
Type	Specifies the operational or data type of a **Property** object
Value	Specifies the value assigned to a **Property** object

Table 7.12   Field object properties.

Property	Description
ActualSize	Indicates a field value's actual length
Attributes	Specifies one or more object characteristics
DefinedSize	Indicates a **Field** object's data capacity
Name	Specifies the name of an object
NumericScale	Specifies the scale of numeric values in a **Field** object
OriginalValue	Indicates the value of a **Field** before any changes were made
Precision	Specifies the degree of precision for numeric values
Type	Specifies the operational or data type
UnderlyingValue	Indicates the current value of a **Field** object
Value	Specifies the value assigned

Table 7.13   Field object methods.

Method	Description
AppendChunk	Appends data to a large text or binary data field
GetChunk	Returns all or a portion of a large text or binary data field

The **Error** Object

An **Error** object is created whenever an error occurs that is associated with an ADO object. The **Error** object doesn't contain ADO error information; instead, it contains information on errors generated by a provider. The **Error** object contains only properties, which are listed in Table 7.14.

Table 7.14   Error object properties.

Property	Description
Description	Indicates a short description of the error
HelpContextID	Indicates a context ID for a specific help file topic
HelpFile	Indicates the fully resolved path to a help file
NativeError	Indicates the provider-specific error code
Number	Indicates a number that identifies an **Error** object
Source	Indicates the name of the application or object that generated the error
SQLState	Indicates the SQL state for an **Error** object

The **Property, Field,** and **Error** objects cannot be created separately. They exist only within the context of the parent object.

ADO In Action

Now that you've pored over the ADO objects and their properties, methods, events, and collections, it's time to look at some sample Web pages. The examples that follow continue with the Community Dining Club that was introduced in the preceding chapters. The examples use a Microsoft Access database, Custdb.mdb. You'll find this database on the companion CD-ROM.

The example in Listing 7.1 lists all the Community Dining Club members currently in the database. The rows and columns of data for the members are displayed in an HTML table.

Listing 7.1   A simple listing of all the rows in the member database.

```
<%@ Language=VBScript %>
<HTML>
<HEAD>

<%
Set Conn = Server.CreateObject("ADODB.Connection")
Conn.Open "custdb"
querystring = "SELECT * FROM custinfo "
SET RS = Conn.execute(querystring)
%>

<TITLE>List All Members</TITLE>
</HEAD>
<BODY>
<H2 ALIGN=CENTER>Community Dining Club</H2>
<HR SIZE=5 WIDTH=90%>
<H3 ALIGN=CENTER>Club Members</H3>

<TABLE ALIGN=CENTER BORDER=1>
<TR>
<% For i = 0 to RS.Fields.Count - 1 %>
<TD><B><% =RS(i).Name %></B></TD>
<% Next %>
</TR>
<% Do While Not RS.EOF %>
<TR>
<% For i = 0 to RS.Fields.Count - 1 %>
<TD VALIGN=TOP><% =RS(i) %></TD>
<% Next %>
</TR>
```

```
<%   RS.MoveNext
     Loop
     RS.Close
%>
</TABLE>

</BODY>
</HTML>
```

Consider this code:

```
<%
Set Conn = Server.CreateObject("ADODB.Connection")
Conn.Open "custdb"
querystring = "SELECT * FROM custinfo "
SET RS = Conn.Execute(querystring)
%>
```

The first line creates an instance of the **Connection** object and assigns it to the variable **Conn**. Then, the **Open** method is called to open a connection to the database. An SQL query to retrieve all the rows from the **custinfo** table is assigned to the variable **queryString**, which is then passed as an argument to the **Connection** object's **Execute** method. The query results, a **Recordset** object, are assigned to the variable **RS**.

In the document's **<BODY>** section, server-side script is mixed with HTML to display the results in an HTML table. Various **Recordset** object properties are used to get the number of fields in each row, field names, and values, and to determine whether the end of the record set has been reached. **Recordset** object methods are used to move through the data as well as to close the record set. Actually, quite a bit is going on in this small piece of script, so it might be worth your time to study it until you have a good understanding. Figure 7.2 shows the page in the browser.

The next example uses two listings. Listing 7.2 is an HTML file that is used to collect new member information when people join the Community Dining Club. The information is submitted to the page in Listing 7.3, which adds the new information to the database. Figure 7.3 shows the page.

This HTML page uses an HTML form to collect new member information. The information is submitted to Listing 7.3 when the Submit button is clicked on. The page also uses the ActiveX Label and Timer controls to display a rotating banner to help encourage people to join. Listing 7.3 contains the script to add the record to the database.

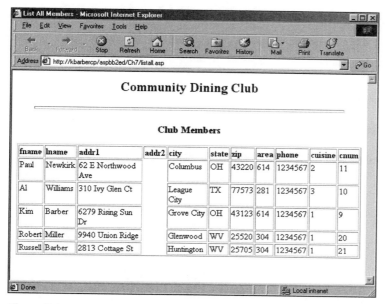

Figure 7.2
The record set in the browser.

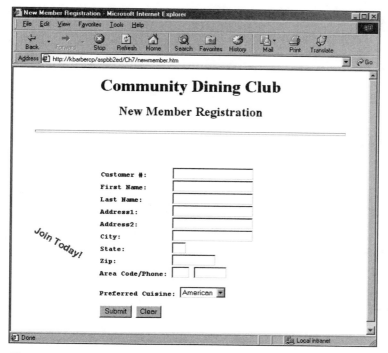

Figure 7.3
The new member registration page.

Listing 7.2   The new member registration page.

```
<HTML>
<HEAD>
<TITLE>New Member Registration</TITLE>
<SCRIPT LANGUAGE=VBScript>
Dim Angle
Dim Message, MsgNo

Randomize
Message = Array("Join Today!", "Fine Dining!", "Impress Friends!", _
      "Save Money!", "Be Cool!")
MsgNo = 0
ColorNo = 1
Angle = 0

Sub IeTimer_Timer
    IeLabel.Caption = Message(MsgNo)
    IeLabel.Angle = Angle
    Angle = Angle + 5
    If Angle > 360 Then
        Angle = 0
        MsgNo = MsgNo + 1
        If MsgNo > 4 Then MsgNo = 0
        ChangeColor
    End If
End Sub

Sub ChangeColor
    IeLabel.ForeColor = Rnd * 16777215
End Sub

</SCRIPT>

</HEAD>
<BODY>
<H1 ALIGN=Center>Community Dining Club</H1>
<H2 ALIGN=Center>New Member Registration</H2>
<HR SIZE=5 WIDTH=90%>

<OBJECT ID="IeTimer" WIDTH=39 HEIGHT=39
 CLASSID="CLSID:59CCB4A0-727D-11CF-AC36-00AA00A47DD2">
    <PARAM NAME="Interval" VALUE="50">
</OBJECT>

<TABLE>
<TD>
```

```
<OBJECT ID="IeLabel" WIDTH=150 HEIGHT=150
 CLASSID="CLSID:99B42120-6EC7-11CF-A6C7-00AA00A47DD2">
    <PARAM NAME="Caption" VALUE=" ">
    <PARAM NAME="Angle" VALUE="0">
    <PARAM NAME="Alignment" VALUE="4">
    <PARAM NAME="Mode" VALUE="1">
    <PARAM NAME="FillStyle" VALUE="0">
    <PARAM NAME="FillStyle" VALUE="0">
    <PARAM NAME="ForeColor" VALUE="#000000">
    <PARAM NAME="BackColor" VALUE="#C0C0C0">
    <PARAM NAME="FontName" VALUE="Arial">
    <PARAM NAME="FontSize" VALUE="14">
    <PARAM NAME="FontItalic" VALUE="0">
    <PARAM NAME="FontBold" VALUE="1">
    <PARAM NAME="FontUnderline" VALUE="0">
    <PARAM NAME="FontStrikeout" VALUE="0">
    <PARAM NAME="TopPoints" VALUE="0">
    <PARAM NAME="BotPoints" VALUE="0">
</OBJECT>
</TD>
<TD>
<PRE>
<FORM NAME="RegistrationForm" METHOD=POST ACTION="7.3.asp">
<B>Customer #:       </B><INPUT TYPE=TEXT NAME="cnum">
<B>First Name:       </B><INPUT TYPE=TEXT NAME="fname">
<B>Last Name:        </B><INPUT TYPE=TEXT NAME="lname">
<B>Address1:         </B><INPUT TYPE=TEXT NAME="addr1">
<B>Address2:         </B><INPUT TYPE=TEXT NAME="addr2" VALUE=" ">
<B>City:             </B><INPUT TYPE=TEXT NAME="city">
<B>State:            </B><INPUT TYPE=TEXT NAME="state" MAXLENGTH=2 SIZE=2>
<B>Zip:              </B><INPUT TYPE=TEXT NAME="zip" MAXLENGTH=10 SIZE=10>
<B>Area Code/Phone: </B><INPUT TYPE=TEXT NAME="area" MAXLENGTH=3 SIZE=3>
                       <INPUT TYPE=TEXT NAME="phone" MAXLENGTH=7 SIZE=7>

<B>Preferred Cuisine: </B><SELECT NAME="cuisine" SIZE="1">
                       <OPTION VALUE="1">American
                       <OPTION VALUE="2">Chinese
                       <OPTION VALUE="3">French
                       <OPTION VALUE="4">German
                       <OPTION VALUE="5">Greek
                       <OPTION VALUE="6">Indian
                       <OPTION VALUE="7">Italian
                       <OPTION VALUE="8">Japanese
                       <OPTION VALUE="9">Other
                       </SELECT>
```

```
<INPUT TYPE=SUBMIT NAME="cmdSubmit" VALUE="Submit">
<INPUT TYPE="RESET" VALUE="Clear">
</PRE>
</FORM>
</TD>
</TABLE>
</BODY>
</HTML>
```

Listing 7.3   The server-side script needed to add the record to the database.

```
<%@ Language=VBScript %>
<HTML>
<HEAD>
<TITLE>Add New Record</TITLE>

<%
set Conn = Server.CreateObject("ADODB.Connection")
Conn.Open "custdb"
set RS = Server.CreateObject("ADODB.Recordset")
Conn.BeginTrans
RS.Open "custinfo",Conn,3,3
RS.AddNew
RS("cnum") = Request("cnum")
RS("fname") = Request("fname")
RS("lname") = Request("lname")
RS("addr1") = Request("addr1")
RS("addr2") = Request("addr2")
RS("city") = Request("city")
RS("state") = Request("state")
RS("zip") = Request("zip")
RS("area") = Request("area")
RS("phone") = Request("phone")
RS("cuisine") = Request("cuisine")
RS.Update
Conn.CommitTrans
RS.Close
Conn.Close
%>

</HEAD>
<BODY>
Member Registered
</BODY>
</HTML>
```

This script creates both a **Connection** object and a **Recordset** object. The **Connection** object's **BeginTrans** method is called to begin a new transaction; then, the **Recordset** object's **Open** method is called to open a record set. The **Open** method's parameters specify the source—**custinfo**, which contains customer information—the active connection, and the cursor and lock types. The **Recordset** object's **AddNew** method is called to create a new record. The next several statements use the **Request** object to get the data values off the HTTP query string and assign them to the record set. The **CommitTrans** method saves the records and ends the transaction, and then the connection and record set are closed.

The next two listings search the database for a specific customer record. Listing 7.4 is an HTML page that has a simple form to enter a customer number. The customer number is sent to Listing 7.5 when the Submit button is clicked on. The code in Listing 7.5 creates and opens a connection to the customer database.

Listing 7.4   An HTML form to get the customer number.

```
<HTML>
<HEAD>
<TITLE>Find A Member</TITLE>
</HEAD>
<BODY>
<H2 ALIGN=CENTER>Community Dining Club</H2>
<HR SIZE=5 WIDTH=90%>
<TABLE>
<TD>
<PRE>

<FORM NAME="RegistrationForm" METHOD=POST ACTION="7.5.asp">
<B>Customer #:      </B><INPUT TYPE=TEXT NAME="cnum">
<INPUT TYPE=SUBMIT NAME="cmdSubmit" VALUE="Submit">
<INPUT TYPE="RESET" VALUE="Clear" id=RESET1 name=RESET1>
</FORM>

</PRE>
</TD>
</TABLE>
</BODY>
</HTML>
```

Listing 7.5   The ASP file to search the database.

```
<%@ Language=VBScript %>
<HTML>
<HEAD>
<TITLE>Member Lookup</TITLE>

<%
Set Conn = Server.CreateObject("ADODB.COnnection")
```

```
Conn.Open "custdb"
queryString = "SELECT * FROM custinfo WHERE cnum = " & _
        "'" & Request("cnum") & "'"
Set RS = Conn.Execute(queryString)
%>


</HEAD>
<BODY>
<H2 ALIGN=CENTER>Search Results</H2>
<HR SIZE=5 WIDTH=90%>
<TABLE>
<TD>
<PRE>
<FORM NAME="RegistrationForm" METHOD=POST ACTION="7.6.asp">
<B>Customer #:       </B><INPUT TYPE=TEXT NAME="cnum"
                        VALUE='<% =RS.Fields.Item("cnum") %>'>
<B>First Name:       </B><INPUT TYPE=TEXT NAME="fname"
                        VALUE='<% =RS.Fields.Item("fname") %>'>
<B>Last Name:        </B><INPUT TYPE=TEXT NAME="lname"
                        VALUE='<% =RS.Fields.Item("lname") %>'>
<B>Address1:         </B><INPUT TYPE=TEXT NAME="addr1"
                        VALUE='<% =RS.Fields.Item("addr1") %>'>
<B>Address2:         </B><INPUT TYPE=TEXT NAME="addr2"
                        VALUE='<% =RS.Fields.Item("addr2") %>'>
<B>City:             </B><INPUT TYPE=TEXT NAME="city"
                        VALUE='<% =RS.Fields.Item("city") %>'>
<B>State:            </B><INPUT TYPE=TEXT NAME="state" MAXLENGTH=2
                        SIZE=2 VALUE=<% =RS.Fields.Item("state") %>>
<B>Zip:              </B><INPUT TYPE=TEXT NAME="zip" MAXLENGTH=10
                        SIZE=10 VALUE=<% =RS.Fields.Item("zip") %>>
<B>Area Code/Phone: </B><INPUT TYPE=TEXT NAME="area" MAXLENGTH=3
                        SIZE=3 VALUE=<% =RS.Fields.Item("area") %>>
                        <INPUT TYPE=TEXT NAME="phone" MAXLENGTH=7 SIZE=7
                        VALUE=<% =RS.Fields.Item("phone") %>>


<B>Preferred Cuisine: </B><SELECT NAME="cuisine" SIZE="1">
                          <% If RS.Fields.Item("cuisine") = "1" _
                          Then %>
                                  <OPTION VALUE="1" Selected>American
                          <% Else %>
                                  <OPTION VALUE="1">American
                          <% End If %>
                          <% If RS.Fields.Item("cuisine") = "2" _
                          Then %>
                           <OPTION VALUE="2" Selected>Chinese
                          <% Else %>
                                  <OPTION VALUE="2">Chinese
```

```
                          <% End If %>
                          <% If RS.Fields.Item("cuisine") = "3" _
                           Then %>
                            <OPTION VALUE="3" Selected>French
                            <% Else %>
                            <OPTION VALUE="3">French
                           <% End If %>
                          <% If RS.Fields.Item("cuisine") = "4" _
                           Then %>
                            <OPTION VALUE="4" Selected>German
                            <% Else %>
                            <OPTION VALUE="4">German
                           <% End If %>
                          <% If RS.Fields.Item("cuisine") = "5" _
                           Then %>
                            <OPTION VALUE="5" Selected>Greek
                           <% Else %>
                            <OPTION VALUE="5">Greek
                           <% End If %>
                          <% If RS.Fields.Item("cuisine") = "6" _
                           Then %>
                            <OPTION VALUE="6" Selected>Indian
                           <% Else %>
                            <OPTION VALUE="6">Indian
                           <% End If %>
                          <% If RS.Fields.Item("cuisine") = "7" _
                           Then %>
                            <OPTION VALUE="7" Selected>Italian
                           <% Else %>
                            <OPTION VALUE="7">Italian
                           <% End If %>
                          <% If RS.Fields.Item("cuisine") = "8" _
                           Then %>
                            <OPTION VALUE="8" Selected>Japanese
                           <% Else %>
                            <OPTION VALUE="8">Japanese
                           <% End If %>
                          <% If RS.Fields.Item("cuisine") = "9" _
                           Then %>
                            <OPTION VALUE="9" Selected>Other
                           <% Else %>
                            <OPTION VALUE="9">Other
                           <% End If %>
                        </SELECT>
<INPUT TYPE=SUBMIT NAME="cmdSubmit" VALUE="Update">
<INPUT TYPE="RESET" VALUE="Clear" id=RESET1 name=RESET1>
</FORM>
```

```
</PRE>
</TD>
</TABLE>
</BODY>
</HTML>
```

The key lines of code for creating and opening a connection are:

```
Set Conn = Server.CreateObject("ADODB.COnnection")
Conn.Open "custdb"
```

The next two statements are the interesting ones:

```
queryString = "SELECT * FROM custinfo WHERE cnum = " & _
      "'" & Request("cnum") & "'"
Set RS = Conn.Execute(queryString)
```

This code dynamically constructs an SQL query using the customer number parameter passed from Listing 7.4. This **SELECT** statement returns all records in the database where the customer number value equals the value passed from the HTML page. You should have no more than one matching record because the customer number is a unique value. Then, the **queryString** variable is passed to the **Connection** object's **Execute** method. The **Execute** method returns a **Recordset** object containing the query results. Further down in the **<BODY>** section, the script binds the record set fields to HTML controls and displays the record in an HTML table.

Now, it's time to see how to update a record. In addition to displaying a record, Listing 7.5 submits record updates to the database. The scenario: You use Listing 7.4 to enter a customer number to search for, and Listing 7.5 searches for the record and displays it in a form. You can then make changes to the record, and the changes are submitted to Listing 7.6.

Listing 7.6   Script to update a database record.
```
<%@ Language=VBScript %>
<HTML>
<HEAD>
<TITLE>Update Record</TITLE>

<%
Set Conn = Server.CreateObject("ADODB.Connection")
Conn.Open "custdb"
Set RS = Server.CreateObject("ADODB.Recordset")
Conn.BeginTrans
queryString = "SELECT * FROM custinfo WHERE cnum = " & _
      "'" & Request("cnum") & "'"
RS.Open queryString, Conn,3,3
```

```
RS.Fields.Item("lname") = Request("lname")
RS.Fields.Item("fname") = Request("fname")
RS.Fields.Item("addr1") = Request("addr1")
If Len(Request("addr2")) = 0 Then
        RS.Fields.Item("addr2") = " "
Else
        RS.Fields.Item("addr2") = Request("addr2")
End If
RS.Fields.Item("city") = Request("city")
RS.Fields.Item("state") = Request("state")
RS.Fields.Item("zip") = Request("zip")
RS.Fields.Item("area") = Request("area")
RS.Fields.Item("phone") = Request("phone")
RS.Fields.Item("cuisine") = Request("cuisine")
RS.Fields.Item("cnum") = Request("cnum")
RS.Update
Conn.CommitTrans
RS.Close
Conn.Close
%>

</HEAD>
<BODY>
Record Updated
</BODY>
</HTML>
```

You're already familiar with this code:

```
Set Conn = Server.CreateObject("ADODB.Connection")
Conn.Open "custdb"
Set RS = Server.CreateObject("ADODB.Recordset")
Conn.BeginTrans
queryString = "SELECT * FROM custinfo WHERE cnum = " & _
        "'" & Request("cnum") & "'"
RS.Open queryString, Conn,3,3
```

This script creates and opens **Connection** and **Recordset** objects. It is the same as in the search example, but it includes a call to **BeginTrans** to begin a new transaction. You'll also notice that the code to assign the new values to the record set is much the same as you saw in the example on adding new records. After the script assigns new values to the record set, it calls the **Recordset** object's **Update** method to save the changes to the record set. Then, a call to **CommitTrans** completes the update and ends the transaction.

So far, you've seen how to add, search, and update. Now, it's time to see how you can delete a record. Listing 7.7 is a slightly modified version of Listing 7.5.

Listing 7.7 A modified file with a delete option.

```
<%@ Language=VBScript %>
<HTML>
<HEAD>
<TITLE>Member Lookup</TITLE>

<%
Set Conn = Server.CreateObject("ADODB.COnnection")
Conn.Open "custdb"
queryString = "SELECT * FROM custinfo WHERE cnum = " & _
        "'" & Request("cnum") & "'"
Set RS = Conn.Execute(queryString)
%>

</HEAD>
<BODY>
<H2 ALIGN=CENTER>Search Results</H2>
<HR SIZE=5 WIDTH=90%>
<TABLE>
<TD>
<PRE>

<FORM NAME="RegistrationForm" METHOD=POST ACTION="7.8.asp">
<B>Customer #:      </B><INPUT TYPE=TEXT NAME="cnum"
                        VALUE='<% =RS.Fields.Item("cnum") %>'>
<B>First Name:      </B><INPUT TYPE=TEXT NAME="fname"
                        VALUE='<% =RS.Fields.Item("fname") %>'>
<B>Last Name:       </B><INPUT TYPE=TEXT NAME="lname"
                        VALUE='<% =RS.Fields.Item("lname") %>'>
<B>Address1:        </B><INPUT TYPE=TEXT NAME="addr1"
                        VALUE='<% =RS.Fields.Item("addr1") %>'>
<B>Address2:        </B><INPUT TYPE=TEXT NAME="addr2"
                        VALUE='<% =RS.Fields.Item("addr2") %>'>
<B>City:            </B><INPUT TYPE=TEXT NAME="city"
                        VALUE='<% =RS.Fields.Item("city") %>'>
<B>State:           </B><INPUT TYPE=TEXT NAME="state" MAXLENGTH=2
                        SIZE=2 VALUE=<% =RS.Fields.Item("state") %>>
<B>Zip:             </B><INPUT TYPE=TEXT NAME="zip" MAXLENGTH=10
                        SIZE=10 VALUE=<% =RS.Fields.Item("zip") %>>
<B>Area Code/Phone: </B><INPUT TYPE=TEXT NAME="area" MAXLENGTH=3
                        SIZE=3 VALUE=<% =RS.Fields.Item("area") %>>
                        <INPUT TYPE=TEXT NAME="phone" MAXLENGTH=7 SIZE=7
                        VALUE=<% =RS.Fields.Item("phone") %>>

<B>Preferred Cuisine: </B><SELECT NAME="cuisine" SIZE="1">
                        <% If RS.Fields.Item("cuisine") = "1" _
                        Then %>
```

```
            <OPTION VALUE="1" Selected>American
  <% Else %>
            <OPTION VALUE="1">American
  <% End If %>
<% If RS.Fields.Item("cuisine") = "2" _
Then %>
  <OPTION VALUE="2" Selected>Chinese
  <% Else %>
            <OPTION VALUE="2">Chinese
  <% End If %>
<% If RS.Fields.Item("cuisine") = "3" _
Then %>
 <OPTION VALUE="3" Selected>French
  <% Else %>
  <OPTION VALUE="3">French
  <% End If %>
<% If RS.Fields.Item("cuisine") = "4" _
Then %>
  <OPTION VALUE="4" Selected>German
  <% Else %>
  <OPTION VALUE="4">German
  <% End If %>
<% If RS.Fields.Item("cuisine") = "5" _
Then %>
  <OPTION VALUE="5" Selected>Greek
  <% Else %>
  <OPTION VALUE="5">Greek
  <% End If %>
<% If RS.Fields.Item("cuisine") = "6" _
Then %>
  <OPTION VALUE="6" Selected>Indian
  <% Else %>
  <OPTION VALUE="6">Indian
  <% End If %>
<% If RS.Fields.Item("cuisine") = "7" _
Then %>
 <OPTION VALUE="7" Selected>Italian
 <% Else %>
 <OPTION VALUE="7">Italian
 <% End If %>
<% If RS.Fields.Item("cuisine") = "8" _
Then %>
  <OPTION VALUE="8" Selected>Japanese
  <% Else %>
  <OPTION VALUE="8">Japanese
  <% End If %>
```

```
                        <% If RS.Fields.Item("cuisine") = "9" _
                        Then %>
                          <OPTION VALUE="9" Selected>Other
                          <% Else %>
                          <OPTION VALUE="9">Other
                          <% End If %>
                        </SELECT>
<FONT COLOR=RED SIZE=4><INPUT TYPE=CHECKBOX NAME="del">
DELETE RECORD</FONT>
<INPUT TYPE=SUBMIT NAME="cmdSubmit" VALUE="Update">
<INPUT TYPE="RESET" VALUE="Clear" id=RESET1 name=RESET1>
</FORM>

</PRE>
</TD>
</TABLE>
</BODY>
</HTML>
```

The highlighted lines in Listing 7.7 add a checkbox control and the text "DELETE RECORD". If the user selects this box, the script will delete the record when the form is submitted to Listing 7.8. Listing 7.8 is a modified version of Listing 7.6. Figure 7.4 shows this page in Internet Explorer.

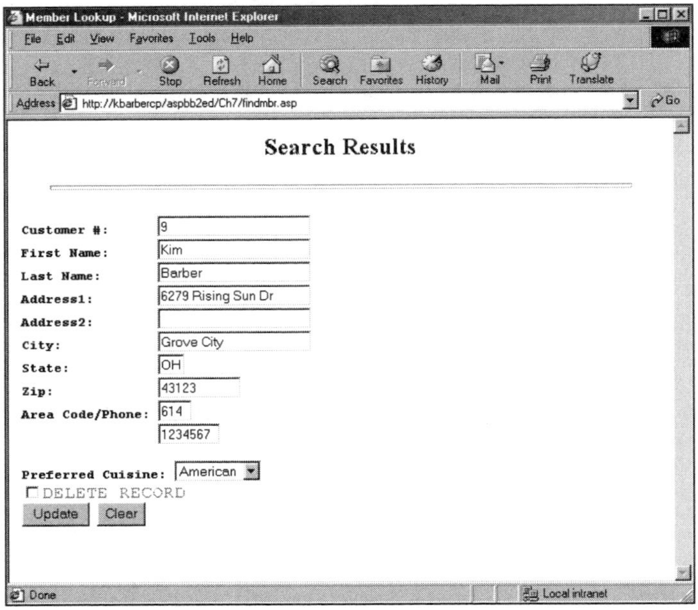

Figure 7.4
Deleting items with Internet Explorer.

Listing 7.8   Adding delete functionality.

```
<%@ Language=VBScript %>
<HTML>
<HEAD>
<TITLE>Update Record</TITLE>

<%
Set Conn = Server.CreateObject("ADODB.COnnection")
Conn.Open "custdb"

Set RS = Server.CreateObject("ADODB.Recordset")
Conn.BeginTrans
queryString = "SELECT * FROM custinfo WHERE cnum = " & _
        "'" & Request("cnum") & "'"
RS.Open queryString, Conn,3,3

If Request("del") = "on" Then
        RS.Delete
        Conn.CommitTrans
        RS.Close
        Conn.Close
Else

RS.Fields.Item("lname") = Request("lname")
RS.Fields.Item("fname") = Request("fname")
RS.Fields.Item("addr1") = Request("addr1")
If Len(Request("addr2")) = 0 Then
        RS.Fields.Item("addr2") = " "
Else
        RS.Fields.Item("addr2") = Request("addr2")
End If
RS.Fields.Item("city") = Request("city")
RS.Fields.Item("state") = Request("state")
RS.Fields.Item("zip") = Request("zip")
RS.Fields.Item("area") = Request("area")
RS.Fields.Item("phone") = Request("phone")
RS.Fields.Item("cuisine") = Request("cuisine")
RS.Fields.Item("cnum") = Request("cnum")
RS.Update
Conn.CommitTrans
RS.Close
Conn.Close
End If
%>

</HEAD>
<BODY>
```

```
Record Updated
</BODY>
</HTML>
```

The highlighted code in Listing 7.8 checks to see whether the user selected the DELETE RECORD checkbox. If so, the script calls the **Recordset** object's **Delete** method to remove the record. **CommitTrans** commits the change and ends the transaction. Finally, the script closes the **Recordset** and **Connection** objects. This is a nice example of how you can use the same files to provide more than one function.

This section is just a brief overview of using ADO, but the examples cover all the basic functions you usually need on a Web site. Visit **http://msdn.microsoft.com/workshop/** to get complete details on ADO.

RDS

The Remote Data Service (RDS) is an ADO service that provides data remoting. In other words, you use it to store and manipulate data on a remote system. Using RDS, you can retrieve a complete record set from the server, process it on the client, and send it back to the server when you're finished. This process requires just one round trip to the server versus one round trip per record. Making just one trip not only improves overall performance, but it also reduces the server's workload. RDS uses client components that run in an ActiveX-enabled browser. At the time of this writing, only Internet Explorer 4 and higher fully support RDS.

RDS uses components on the client and the server. The client-side RDS component sends a query via HTTP to the server. There, the server-side RDS component processes the request and forwards it on to the DBMS. The DBMS performs the requested task and sends the results back to the server. Then, the RDS server component packages the results into an ADO record set and sends it to the client-side RDS component. The browser displays the data using controls bound to the client-side RDS component.

RDS also provides local data persistence by letting you store the data and any changes locally, and then send them to the server later.

RDS uses the Cursor service, which uses data from a rowset. This service stores data locally and exposes that data through rowset interfaces. It caches data on the client and provides a synchronization service, which can send changes back to the server and refresh the local data with data from the provider. When the data consumer requests a local copy of a remote rowset, the Cursor service is invoked. If a consumer requests rowset functionality that isn't provided by the provider's interface, the Cursor service is invoked as well.

RDO consists of three objects: **RDS.DataControl**, **RDS.DataSpace**, and **RDS.DataFactory**.

The RDS.DataControl Object

The **RDS.DataControl** object binds controls to an ADO **Recordset** object. It calls the **RDSServer.DataFactory** object when creating a disconnected record set. A disconnected record set is a record set that no longer is associated with the server but can be reassociated. The **RDS.DataControl** object's properties are listed in Table 7.15, and its methods are listed in Table 7.16.

The RDS.DataSpace Object

The **RDS.DataSpace** object creates a client-side proxy to communicate with server-side business objects. The **RDS.DataFactory** object is the default server-side object, and you can use custom developed business objects as well.

The **RDS.DataSpace** object has one property and one method. The **InternetTimeout** property specifies the HTTP timeout in milliseconds. The **CreateObject** method creates a proxy for the specified business object.

Table 7.15   RDS.DataControl object properties.

Property	Description
Connect	Specifies the database name
ExecuteOptions	Specifies whether asynchronous execution is enabled
FetchOptions	Specifies the type of asynchronous fetching
FilterColumn	Specifies the column on which filtering is to take place
FilterCriterion	Specifies the evaluation operator to be used for filtering
FilterValue	Specifies the value used to filter records
InternalTimeout	Specifies the number of milliseconds to wait before a request times out
ReadyState	Specifies the control's state
Recordset	Indicates the **Recordset** object returned from a business object
Server	Specifies the server name and protocol
SortColumn	Specifies which column to sort on
SortDirection	Specifies ascending or descending sort order
SourceRecordset	Specifies the **Recordset** object to be used
SQL	Specifies the SQL query to retrieve the record set
URL	Specifies a relative or absolute URL

Table 7.16   RDS.DataControl object methods.

Method	Description
Cancel	Cancels a pending asynchronous method call
CancelUpdate	Cancels any changes made to a row in a **Recordset** object
CreateRecordset	Creates an empty, disconnected record set
Refresh	Requeries the data source and updates the query results
Reset	Executes the filter or sort on a client-side record set
SubmitChanges	Submits pending changes to the data source

The RDS.DataFactory Object

The **RDS.DataFactory** object is the default server-side business object that provides read/write data access between the client and server objects. Table 7.17 lists the **RDS.DataFactory** object's methods. It has no properties or events.

Listing 7.9 uses the **RDS.DataControl** to retrieve and display all the records in the Community Dining Club's custdb.mdb database.

Listing 7.9   Using the RDS.DataControl to display a record set.

```
<%@ Language=VBScript %>
<HTML>
<HEAD>
<TITLE>List All Records Using RDS</TITLE>
</HEAD>
<BODY>

<H2 ALIGN=CENTER>Community Dining Club</H2>
<HR SIZE=5 Width=90%>

<OBJECT CLASSID="CLSID:BD96C556-65A3-11D0-983A-00C04FC29E33"
        ID="RDC" HEIGHT=0 WIDTH=0>
</OBJECT>

<TABLE BORDER=1 ALIGN=CENTER DATASRC="#RDC">
<TR>
<TD><SPAN DATAFLD="cnum"></SPAN></TD>
<TD><SPAN DATAFLD="lname"></SPAN></TD>
<TD><SPAN DATAFLD="fname"></SPAN></TD>
<TD><SPAN DATAFLD="addr1"></SPAN></TD>
<TD><SPAN DATAFLD="addr2"></SPAN></TD>
<TD><SPAN DATAFLD="city"></SPAN></TD>
<TD><SPAN DATAFLD="state"></SPAN></TD>
<TD><SPAN DATAFLD="zip"></SPAN></TD>
<TD><SPAN DATAFLD="area"></SPAN></TD>
<TD><SPAN DATAFLD="phone"></SPAN></TD>
<TD><SPAN DATAFLD="cuisine"></SPAN></TD>
</TR>
</TABLE>
```

Table 7.17   RDS.DataFactory object methods.

Method	Description
ConvertToString	Converts a record set to a MIME string
CreateRecordset	Creates an empty, disconnected record set
Query	Uses an SQL query to return a record set
SubmitChanges	Submits pending changes to a record set

```
<INPUT TYPE=BUTTON NAME="Run" VALUE="Run">

<SCRIPT LANGUAGE="VBScript">
Option Explicit
' -- enum values --
Const rdcExecSync = 1
Const rdcExecAsync = 2

' -- enum values --
Const rdcFetchUpFront = 1
Const rdcFetchBackground = 2
Const rdcFetchAsync = 3

Sub Window_OnLoad
        RDC.ExecuteOptions = rdcExecSync
        RDC.FetchOptions = rdcFetchBackground
End Sub

Sub Run_OnClick
        RDC.Server = "http://<%=Request.ServerVariables("SERVER_NAME")%>"
        RDC.Connect = "DSN=custdb;"
        RDC.SQL = "SELECT * FROM custinfo"
        RDC.Refresh
        RDC.Recordset.MoveFirst
End Sub
</SCRIPT>

</BODY>
</HTML>
```

The **RDS.DataControl** resides on a page with the **<OBJECT>** tag and is assigned the ID **RDC**. **RDC** is used in the page to reference this instance of the object. The control is then bound to an HTML table using the following tag:

```
<TABLE BORDER=1 ALIGN=CENTER DATASRC="#RDC">
```

This tag generates an HTML table that displays the complete record set. When the user clicks on the Run button, the **OnClick** event handler is called. The event handler sets some of the **RDS.DataControl** object's properties to define the server, connection, and SQL query. The **Refresh** method causes the query to execute and updates the record set. **MoveFirst** is a **Recordset** object method that points to the first record in the record set. Also, notice that the **Window** object's **OnLoad** event sets a couple of properties as well. Figure 7.5 shows the page in Internet Explorer.

The next example includes a little more functionality. It displays one record at a time in a group of HTML textbox controls. Buttons are included to move forward, backward, and to

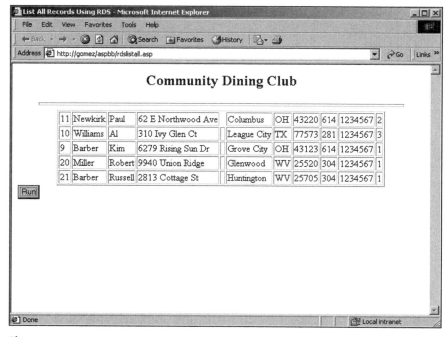

Figure 7.5
Using the **RDS.DataControl** to display a complete record set.

the first and last records in the record set. You also can edit the records and submit the
changes back to the server. Listing 7.10 shows the code.

Listing 7.10   Using RDS to edit a record set.

```
<%@ Language=VBScript %>
<HTML>
<HEAD>
<TITLE>Display, Navigate, and Edit Using RDS</TITLE>
</HEAD>
<BODY>

<H2 ALIGN=CENTER>Community Dining Club</H2>
<HR SIZE=5 Width=90%>

<OBJECT CLASSID="CLSID:BD96C556-65A3-11D0-983A-00C04FC29E33"
        ID="RDC" HEIGHT=0 WIDTH=0>
</OBJECT>

<PRE>
CustNo:      <INPUT TYPE=TEXT DATASRC="#RDC" DATAFLD="cnum">
Last Name:   <INPUT TYPE=TEXT DATASRC="#RDC" DATAFLD="lname">
First Name:  <INPUT TYPE=TEXT DATASRC="#RDC" DATAFLD="fname">
```

```
Address1:    <INPUT TYPE=TEXT DATASRC="#RDC" DATAFLD="addr1">
Address2:    <INPUT TYPE=TEXT DATASRC="#RDC" DATAFLD="addr2">
City:        <INPUT TYPE=TEXT DATASRC="#RDC" DATAFLD="city">
State:       <INPUT TYPE=TEXT DATASRC="#RDC" DATAFLD="state">
Zip:         <INPUT TYPE=TEXT DATASRC="#RDC" DATAFLD="zip">
Area:        <INPUT TYPE=TEXT DATASRC="#RDC" DATAFLD="area">
Phone:       <INPUT TYPE=TEXT DATASRC="#RDC" DATAFLD="phone">
Cuisine:     <INPUT TYPE=TEXT DATASRC="#RDC" DATAFLD="cuisine">
</PRE>


<HR SIZE=5 Width=90%>


<INPUT TYPE=BUTTON NAME="Run" VALUE="Run">
<INPUT TYPE=BUTTON NAME="First" VALUE="First">
<INPUT TYPE=BUTTON NAME="Prev" VALUE="Previous">
<INPUT TYPE=BUTTON NAME="Next" VALUE="Next">
<INPUT TYPE=BUTTON NAME="Last" VALUE="Last">
<INPUT TYPE=BUTTON NAME="Update" VALUE="Update">


<SCRIPT LANGUAGE="VBScript">
Option Explicit
' -- enum values --
Const rdcExecSync = 1
Const rdcExecAsync = 2


' -- enum values
Const rdcFetchUpFront = 1
Const rdcFetchBackground = 2
Const rdcFetchAsync = 3


Sub Window_OnLoad
        RDC.ExecuteOptions = rdcExecSync
        RDC.FetchOptions = rdcFetchBackground
End Sub


Sub Run_OnClick
        RDC.Server = "http://<%=Request.ServerVariables("SERVER_NAME")%>"
        RDC.Connect = "DSN=custdb;"
        RDC.SQL = "SELECT * FROM custinfo"

        RDC.Refresh
        RDC.Recordset.MoveFirst
End Sub


Sub First_OnClick
        RDC.Recordset.MoveFirst
End Sub
```

```
Sub Prev_OnClick
        On Error Resume Next
        RDC.Recordset.MovePrevious
        If Err.number <> 0 Then
                RDC.Recordset.MoveFirst
        End If
End Sub

Sub Next_OnClick
        On Error Resume Next
        RDC.Recordset.MoveNext
        If Err.number <> 0 Then
                RDC.Recordsset.MoveLast
        End If
End Sub

Sub Last_OnClick
        RDC.Recordset.MoveLast
End Sub

Sub Update_OnClick
        RDC.SubmitChanges
        RDC.Refresh
End Sub
</SCRIPT>

</BODY>
</HTML>
```

The individual record fields are bound to HTML textbox controls using the **DATASRC** and **DATAFLD** attributes. This method displays one record at a time. Because the fields appear in text boxes, the user can easily edit them. HTML buttons allow navigation forward and backward in the record set. The **Recordset** object's **MoveFirst**, **MoveLast**, **MoveNext**, and **MovePrevious** methods do the work in response to the appropriate event handlers. When the user clicks on the Update button, changes are submitted with the **SubmitChanges** method. The **Refresh** method refreshes the record set.

Figure 7.6 shows the resulting page in Internet Explorer.

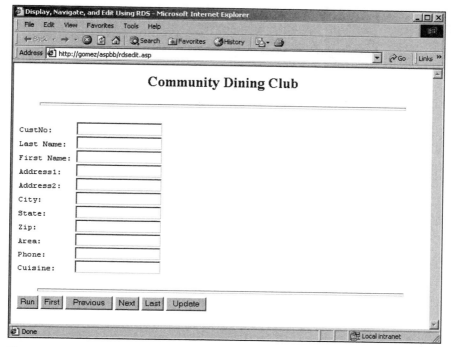

Figure 7.6
Using the **RDS.DataControl** to edit a complete record set.

Chapter 8

Remembering Users

Al Williams

Years ago, I went to a presentation given by a major database company. You know the kind: You show up, and the company's representatives serve a continental breakfast and then regale you with how wonderful its products are. You've probably been to dozens of them.

What made this one different was that the main sales guy met everyone at the door. We tried to make an end run around him, but he very persistently cut us off and introduced himself. After each introduction, he made sure to repeat our names. You know that repeating a name helps you remember it, right?

About 250 people were sitting in the audience. Throughout the presentation, this man kept using people from the audience in his examples. He would say, "Suppose Mark and Al and Beau needed to transfer data from an old database they got from Janet." At each name, he'd point to someone in the audience. It didn't take long to realize he had actually memorized everyone's name!

This amazing feat was great until the end. He was too afraid one person in the crowd might not have figured out his game. So, he went through the audience and named each and every person in one huge example, working from the front to the rear. Naming everyone was a little too much.

Other than that one lapse of judgment, however, this man was on to something. Nothing gets your attention better than someone saying your name. People like to be remembered by name—that's why "Hey, you!" is an insult.

Using people's names is a way to forge a connection with them. Humans have a natural tendency to split into "us" and "them." Anything you can do to put yourself in the users' "us" group—their community—goes a long way toward making them accept your Web page content and probably return again later.

A Web site that fosters the same sense of community is an incredibly valuable resource. The goal of the Microsoft Personalization System (MPS) is to provide this sense of community. You can use MPS to provide a community experience for your users, as it consists of a set of server components that provide support for personalization, opinion sharing, and feedback.

You might know MPS by its older name—the Internet Personalization System. At first, Microsoft provided this system as an installable component. Then, it incorporated the package into Microsoft Site Server and changed the name to MPS.

MPS has three components: User Property Database, User Voting, and Send Mail. You can use these components to provide customized and personalized content, collect the feedback and opinions of your users, and mail feedback to them easily. In this chapter, you'll see examples using these components. You'll also find some more ways to remember data about users without using MPS, in case your server doesn't support it.

The User Property Database Component

The User Property Database (UPD) component helps you remember information about your users. You collect the property information from the users and can use it to personalize the content you provide. You can also collect information from other sources, such as the Browser Capabilities component (introduced in Chapter 5), and store it as user property information.

The GUID

For the UPD component to work, it must be able to recognize when a user returns to a Web site. The first time the user visits a Web application that uses the UPD, the system generates a unique identifier for that user and stores it as a client-side cookie. This identifier is a Globally Unique Identifier, or GUID (as defined by the Open Software Foundation Distributed Computing Environment, or OSF/DCE, specification). The UPD uses the GUID to identify the user later. When the user returns to the Web site, the UPD retrieves the GUID from the cookie and uses it to locate the user's property information in the database.

Because this method relies on a cookie on the client's computer, you need to be aware of a couple of considerations. First, the user's browser might not support cookies, or the user may disable cookie support. Second, the user might use more than one browser or computer. If the user returns to your Web site using another browser or a different machine, the UPD will treat him or her as a different user. Of course, if the user deletes cookies (on purpose or by accident), your site will no longer recognize the user.

If you have an alternate way to authenticate users, you might be able to set your own user IDs and force the UPD to recognize authenticated users regardless of what browsers or machines they use. However, if you authenticate users, you might want to use only the database component to make your own property database and not use the UPD.

Properties

The UPD stores properties as name/value pairs. It can store single or multiple values in each property. You determine the property name and maintain any number of properties for each user. Additionally, the UPD treats all properties as strings.

Assuming that **Props** references an instance of the UPD component (created with **Server.CreateObject**), the following statement assigns a value to the single-value **Cuisine** property:

```
<% Props.Item("Cuisine") = "Chinese" %>
```

Item is a UPD method that assigns a value to a single-value property. The property value is retrieved as follows:

```
<% t_cuisine = Props.Item("Cuisine") %>
```

Item is the default UPD property, so you can also omit **Item** and simply refer to the property as follows:

```
<% Props("Cuisine") = "Chinese" %>
<% t_cuisine = Props("Cuisine") %>
```

This is a nice shortcut that can save you some typing.

The **Append** method, shown here, assigns values to multiple-value properties (similar to a collection):

```
<% Props.Append("favfood") = "pizza" %>
<% Props.Append("favfood") = "cheeseburgers" %>
```

The following statement retrieves the second value of the **favfood** property:

```
<% t_favfood = Props.Item("favfood")(2) %>
```

Alternatively, you could retrieve the same value by using the following statement:

```
<% t_favfood = Props("favfood")(2) %>
```

The UPD component has other properties and methods, as you'll see shortly.

Using The UPD Component

The UPD component is similar to other ActiveX installable components. You create an instance of the component and assign it to an object variable. You then use the object variable to access the UPD. For example, the following statement assigns a UPD component object to the **Props** variable:

```
<% Set Props = Server.CreateObject("MPS.PropertyDatabase") %>
```

One important caveat: The UPD depends on modifying the outgoing HTML document's headers. That means the call to **CreateObject** must appear before you create any HTML. Usually, it is a good idea to create the UPD component in the very first line in your HTML file. It is permissible to precede the line with server-side script but not with HTML.

There are typically three stages to using user properties:

◆ Collecting the information

◆ Writing the properties to the property database

◆ Retrieving and using the properties

Listing 8.1 shows how to use an HTML form to collect two items of data from a user: the first name and a favorite color. Listing 8.2 processes the form submission.

Listing 8.1   Collecting user properties.
```
<HTML>
<HEAD>
<TITLE>Listing 8.1</TITLE>
</HEAD>
<BODY>
<H3 ALIGN=CENTER>Please tell us a little about yourself</H3>
<PRE>
<FORM METHOD=POST ACTION="8-2.asp">
First name:     <INPUT TYPE=TEXT NAME="fname">
Favorite Color: <INPUT TYPE=TEXT NAME="favcolor">
<INPUT TYPE=SUBMIT VALUE="Submit">
</FORM>
</PRE>
</BODY>
</HTML>
```

Listing 8.2 creates an instance of the UPD component and saves the information passed from Listing 8.1.

Listing 8.2   Saving user properties.

```
<%
    Set Props = Server.CreateObject("MPS.PropertyDatabase")
    Props("fname") = Request("fname")
    Props("favcolor") = Request("favcolor")
%>
<HTML>
<HEAD>
<TITLE>Listing 8.2</TITLE>
</HEAD>
<BODY>
<FONT SIZE=4 COLOR=RED>Properties saved.</FONT>
</BODY>
</HTML>
```

Now that the application saves user properties, it needs to retrieve them. Listing 8.3 checks to see whether a first-name property is present. If it is, it reads the properties from the database and uses them.

Listing 8.3   Retrieving and using user properties.

```
<%
    Response.Expires = 0
    Set Props = Server.CreateObject("MPS.PropertyDatabase")
%>
<HTML>
<HEAD>
<TITLE>Listing 8.3</TITLE>
</HEAD>
<BODY>

<% If Props("fname") <> "" Then %>
<FONT SIZE=4 COLOR=<% =Props("favcolor") %>>
Welcome back <% =Props("fname") %>
</FONT>
<% Else %>
<FONT SIZE=4>Hello stranger</FONT>
<% End If %>
</BODY>
</HTML>
```

Another way to determine whether properties are available for the user is to check the **Request** object's **ContentLength** property. If **ContentLength** is zero, no properties exist because no cookie data is present. Of course, a nonzero value doesn't necessarily imply that properties exist because other data may be present. Listing 8.4 checks the **ContentLength** property to determine whether properties exist. If no properties are present, the application displays the form to collect them. If properties are present, the page displays a welcome message and offers the user the opportunity to change his or her properties. Also notice that, in this case, the form controls already contain the existing UPD values.

Listing 8.4 Collecting and using properties in one file.

```
<% Response.Expires = 0 %>
<% Set Props = Server.CreateObject("MPS.PropertyDatabase") %>

<HTML>
<HEAD>
<TITLE>Listing 8.4</TITLE>
</HEAD>
<BODY>

<% If Request("ContentLength") = 0 Then %>
<FONT SIZE=4 COLOR=<% =Props("favcolor") %>>
Welcome back <% =Props("fname") %>
</FONT>
<PRE>
Complete the following form to change your settings.
<FORM METHOD=POST ACTION="8-4.asp">
First name:     <INPUT TYPE=TEXT NAME="fname" VALUE=<% =Props("fname") %>>
Favorite Color: <INPUT TYPE=TEXT NAME="favcolor"
                VALUE=<% =Props("favcolor") %>>
<INPUT TYPE=SUBMIT VALUE="Submit">
</FORM>
</PRE>

<% Else %>
<FONT SIZE=4>Hello stranger</FONT>
<PRE>
<FORM METHOD=POST ACTION="8-4.asp">
First name:     <INPUT TYPE=TEXT NAME="fname">
Favorite Color: <INPUT TYPE=TEXT NAME="favcolor">
<INPUT TYPE=SUBMIT VALUE="Submit">
</FORM>
</PRE>
<% End If %>
</BODY>
</HTML>
```

UPD Component Properties And Methods

The UPD has properties and methods that you use to create, update, and access user properties. A list of the UPD properties is shown in Table 8.1.

Sometimes, it's convenient to set default values for items in the UPD if no entry exists. You use the **Defaults** property to do so. The following example sets the default text color property to green. If the user has set a favorite color, the code uses it. If not, the code uses green. Here's how you do it:

```
<% Response.Expires = 0 %>
<% Set Props = Server.CreateObject("MPS.PropertyDatabase") %>
<% Props.Defaults=("favcolor=GREEN") %>
<HTML>
<HEAD>
<TITLE>Setting Defaults</TITLE>
</HEAD>
<BODY TEXT=<%=Props("favcolor") %>>
<H3>Welcome</H3>
</BODY>
</HTML>
```

Notice that the **Response** object's **Expires** property is set to zero. The **Expires** property specifies the amount of time in minutes before the page expires. If a page is requested before the specified time elapses, it is retrieved from the cache. If it is requested after the specified time elapses, it is reloaded. If you set **Expires** to zero, the page is reloaded every time it is requested. Reloading the page every time is useful when the Web page contents change frequently and you want to use the most current data. You'll probably do this often in your Active Server Pages. Setting **Expires** to zero also prevents older proxy servers from showing one user's custom page to other users who are using the same proxy.

The **ID** property contains the user's GUID. You can also use this property to override the system-selected GUID. The statement

```
<% =Props.ID %>
```

outputs the GUID. For example, it might output the following:

```
66b12ef1d26311d1a00200a024231ce9
```

Table 8.1	General UPD component properties.
Property	**Description**
ID	Specifies the user's ID
ReadOnly	Specifies whether the properties are read-only
PropertyString	Returns the user's current properties as a string

PropertyString returns a string containing the current properties. For example,

```
<%=Props.PropertyString %>
```

displays

```
FAVCOLOR=Blue&ID=66b12ef1d26311d1a00200a024231ce9&FNAME=George
```

You might find the **PropertyString** variable useful if you want to shadow the property database using an SQL database. You could use it to easily manipulate the data or use the same data for groups of users. You also should look at the **LoadFromString** method. Table 8.2 lists the UPD members.

You can use the **Item** property to read from and write to the UPD. You'll find a typical use of the **Item** object earlier in this chapter in the introduction to UPD properties. This property works with both single- and multiple-value properties. Also, its use is generally optional because it is the default property. The **Item** object has the three methods described in Table 8.3.

Assume for a moment that **favcolor** is a multiple-value property. The following statement will append another color:

```
<% Props("favcolor").Append("Purple") %>
```

Also, notice that **Item** isn't specified. The statement

```
<% Props("favcolor").Remove(2) %>
```

removes the second item from the multiple-value property.

The **Item** method has one property, **Count**, which returns the number of items stored in the user property.

Table 8.2   Specialized UPD component members.

Method	Description
Item	Reads and writes user properties
LoadFromString	Loads user properties from a URL-encoded query string

Table 8.3   Item object methods.

Method	Description
Append	Adds items to multiple-value properties
Item	Accesses a single value of a multiple-value property
Remove	Removes items from multiple-value properties

You can use the **LoadFromString** method to load properties directly to the database from the query string. This method is typically used to load the database from data posted from a form, as shown here:

```
<% Props.LoadFromString(Request.Form) %>
```

The User Property Database component is flexible and easy to use. With very little effort, you can maintain user information and preferences and add a personalized touch to your Web applications.

A UPD Example

The following example uses the User Property Database (UPD) component to get a user's dining reservation preferences. The application uses the preferences later when the user makes a reservation online. This example also uses the Send Mail component to send confirmation to the user.

Listing 8.5 contains an HTML form to collect the data. Listing 8.6 processes the form data.

Listing 8.5   Getting the user's preferences.

```
<% Response.Expires = 0 %>

<HTML>
<HEAD>
<TITLE>Listing 8.5</TITLE>
</HEAD>
<BODY>
<FONT COLOR=BLUE>
<H1 ALIGN=CENTER>Community Dining Club</H1>
<HR SIZE=5>
<H3 ALIGN=CENTER>Reservation Preferences</H3>
<PRE>
<FORM METHOD=POST ACTION="8-6.asp">
Smoking?    <INPUT TYPE=RADIO NAME="smoking" VALUE="no">No
            <INPUT TYPE=RADIO NAME="smoking" VALUE="yes">Yes

Best Time: <INPUT TYPE=RADIO NAME="time" VALUE="5-6">5:00 PM to 6:00 PM
            <INPUT TYPE=RADIO NAME="time" VALUE="6-7">6:00 PM to 7:00 PM
            <INPUT TYPE=RADIO NAME="time" VALUE="7-8">7:00 PM to 8:00 PM
            <INPUT TYPE=RADIO NAME="time" VALUE="8-9">8:00 PM to 9:00 PM
            <INPUT TYPE=RADIO NAME="time" VALUE="9">>After 9:00 PM

Email Address: <INPUT TYPE=TEXT NAME="email">

<INPUT TYPE=SUBMIT VALUE="Submit">
</FORM>
```

```
</PRE>
</FONT>
</BODY>
</HTML>
```

Listing 8.6 creates an instance of the UPD and assigns the user's preferences. It then creates an instance of the Send Mail component and sends confirmation to the user.

Listing 8.6   Processing the user's preferences.

```
<% Response.Expires = 0 %>
<% Set Props = Server.CreateObject("MPS.PropertyDatabase")
     Props("smoking") = Request("smoking")
     Props("time") = Request("time")
     Props("email") = Request("email")

     t_smoking = "Smoking"
     If Props("smoking") = "no" Then
          t_smoking = "Non-smoking"
     End If%>

<% Set sm = Server.CreateObject("MPS.Sendmail")
     email = Props("email")
     from = "webmaster@diningclub.com"

     sm.SendMail(from,email,"Reservation Preferences", _
     ("Thank you." & vbCrLf & vbCrLf & _
     "Your reservation preferences are:" & vbCrLf & _
     "Smoking Preference: " & t_smoking & _
     "Preferred Time: " & Props("time")))
%>

<HTML>
<HEAD>
<TITLE>Listing 8.6</TITLE>
</HEAD>
<BODY>
Thank you!
</BODY>
</HTML>
```

The Voting Component

Nothing is as democratic as voting. Of course, many people feel like they should vote even if they don't know anything about what they are voting for! For national elections, voting this way gets the system into trouble, but on the Web, voting is often more innocuous.

Users of your Web applications often have something to say about them, and, equally as often, you are probably very interested in their feedback. Their feedback is useful because you want your users to benefit from visiting your Web site, and you want them to come back. You can use their opinions as input to making improvements. You might also want to collect their feedback on, for example, a restaurant or a movie review so that it can be shared with others. Well, how do you collect your users' feedback? You could create a form to collect the information, write server-side script to collect the data and store it in a database, and write more script to read the database and output the results. Or, you can use the Voting component and let it do all the work.

You can use the Voting component to allow users to provide their opinions and to see the opinions of others. The Voting component does all the work of submitting, counting, and storing the votes. You have very little to do other than create a form to collect the input. Many large sites use this opinion harvesting to further build their sense of community and provide valuable content at little or no cost. For example, if you want to buy a DVD player, you might be interested to see which player other users think is the best.

Using The Voting Component

The Voting component requires an Open Database Connectivity (ODBC) compliant database to store votes. MPS provides a Microsoft Access database (Vote.mdb) that you can use, as well as an SQL script that creates an SQL database. Of course, you can create your own as long as it has the same structure. Usually, however, it's just as easy to use the standard database.

MPS automatically installs and prepares the Access database for use. If you create your own, you need to use the ODBC Data Source Administrator to configure the appropriate driver and other information about the data source. Also, your database must contain the tables with the specified fields shown in Table 8.4.

Table 8.4   Voting component database requirements.

Table	Column Name	DataType	Description
VoteMaster	Name	Character(255)	Ballot name
	VID	Integer	Unique ballot identifier
VoteQuestions	VID	Integer	Unique ballot identifier
	Question	Character(255)	Question name
	Value	Character(64)	Vote submission for the question
	VoteCount	Integer	Number of votes submitted for the ballot, question, and value
	Percentage	Integer	Percentage of total votes for the value
VoteRecord	VID	Integer	Unique ballot identifier
	VoterID	Character(50)	Unique identifier for the user submitting the vote

Votes And Ballots

Votes are organized into ballots that can contain multiple questions, and each question can have multiple values. You can allow users to vote as often as they like or limit each user to one vote. The Voting component has five methods to set ballots and to submit and process votes. Table 8.5 describes each of these methods.

GetVote displays the voting results in an HTML table. The table contains columns for the question, the number of votes per question, and the percentage of votes for each question. **GetVote** uses the following syntax:

```
GetVote([question][,value])
```

question specifies the question name, and *value* specifies the name of the specific value you want to count. Both *question* and *value* are optional, and the output of **GetVote** depends on whether they are specified. **GetVote** returns the following:

- An HTML table of the current ballot and all questions if you omit both *question* and *value*
- An HTML table containing the results for a specific question if you specify the *question* argument
- The vote count for a specific question if you supply both *question* and *value*
- An error message in the event an error occurs

GetVoteCount returns the number of votes per ballot, question, or value. You call it like this:

```
GetVoteCount([question][,value])
```

If you specify only the *question* argument, **GetVoteCount** returns the number of votes for that specific question. If you supply both arguments, the voting component returns the number of votes for the *question* and *value*. If you're keeping track of the users' identities with the **Submit** method and do not specify any arguments, **GetVoteCount** returns the number of people who voted for the current ballot. If you aren't tracking the users' identities and don't specify the arguments, a zero is returned.

Table 8.5 Voting component methods.

Method	Description
GetVote	Displays voting results
GetVoteCount	Returns the number of votes
Open	Opens a connection to the voting database
SetBallotName	Specifies the ballot to vote on
Submit	Submits a vote

Open specifies the ODBC data source where the voting results are stored:

```
Open(source, userID, password)
```

source identifies the data source and is the Data Source Name (DSN) assigned when the data source was configured using the ODBC Data Source Administrator, *userID* specifies the user ID required to log in to the data source, and *password* contains the required password to log in to the data source. **Open** returns **TRUE** if successful and **FALSE** if unsuccessful.

You use **SetBallotName** as follows to specify the ballot to vote on:

```
SetBallotName(name)
```

name is the name of the ballot and is associated with records in the database. **SetBallotName** returns **TRUE** if successful and **FALSE** if unsuccessful.

Submit, which you use as follows, adds a vote to the database:

```
Submit(question, value [,voterID])
```

question specifies the question to vote on, *value* contains the value selected by the user, and *voterID* identifies the user. If you use **Submit**, the system prevents users from voting more than once. Notice that this is often subject to the same limitations of the UPD because you'll usually use the UPD's **ID** property for this argument.

An example is worth a thousand words and is probably more interesting. So, take a look at the following example, which lets users vote on their favorite car or truck. Listing 8.7 contains an HTML form to collect the votes.

Listing 8.7   Collecting user votes.

```
<% Response.Expires = 0 %>

<HTML>
<HEAD>
<TITLE>Listing 8.7</TITLE>
</HEAD>
<BODY>
<H3 ALIGN=CENTER>Vote For Your Favorite Car Or Truck!</H3>
<PRE>
<FORM METHOD=POST ACTION="8-8.asp">
<INPUT TYPE=RADIO NAME="favcar" VALUE="Corvette">Corvette
<INPUT TYPE=RADIO NAME="favcar" VALUE="Dodge Ram">Dodge Ram
<INPUT TYPE=RADIO NAME="favcar" VALUE="Ford F150">Ford F150
<INPUT TYPE=RADIO NAME="favcar" VALUE="Mustang">Mustang
<INPUT TYPE=RADIO NAME="favcar" VALUE="Porsche">Porsche
```

```
<INPUT TYPE=RADIO NAME="favcar" VALUE="Trans AM">Trans AM
<INPUT TYPE=SUBMIT VALUE="Vote">
</FORM>
</PRE>
</BODY>
</HTML>
```

Listing 8.8 accepts the vote and writes it to the database. In this example, users can vote as often as they want because the script doesn't pass the user ID to the **Submit** method. The **Open** method uses a user ID of **guest** with no password. **vehicle** is the name of the ballot (passed to **SetBallotName**). The **Submit** method specifies the question name *Favorite Vehicle* and uses the **Request** object to get the value of the form data. **GetVoteCount** displays the total number of votes for this question, and then the script uses **GetVote** to display the current voting results in a table.

Don't forget to use the **<%=** notation with **GetVote**. If you use only **<%**, the component will generate a nicely formatted table, but you'll end up throwing it away. Of course, you could store the HTML in a variable and further manipulate it, but doing that would doubtless get troublesome rather quickly.

Listing 8.8   Processing votes.

```
<% Response.Expires = 0 %>
<% Set vote = Server.CreateObject("MPS.Vote")
    If vote.Open("Vote","guest","") = TRUE Then
        bal_result = vote.SetBallotName("vehicle")
        vote_result = vote.Submit("Favorite Vehicle", Request("favcar"))
    %>
    Thanks for voting!
    <P>
    Total number of votes is: <% =vote.GetVoteCount("Favorite Vehicle") %>
    <P>
    <% =vote.GetVote %>
    <% Else %>
    The Voting component is not set up correctly.
<% End If %>

<HTML>
<HEAD>
<TITLE>Listing 8.8</TITLE>
</HEAD>
<BODY>
</BODY>
</HTML>
```

I think you will agree that the Voting component does a good bit of work for you. This example uses two documents to collect and process votes. The example in the following section does so using only one page and also limits voters to one vote.

A Voting Example

This example uses the Voting component to let users vote on their favorite restaurant. The **UserPropertyDatabase** component provides a unique identifier for each user. This identifier limits users to one vote each. Also, all processing occurs on a single page. Listing 8.9 contains the script.

Listing 8.9   Collecting and displaying user votes.

```
<% Response.Expires=0 %>
<% Set vote = Server.CreateObject("MPS.Vote") %>
<% Set Props = Server.CreateObject("MPS.PropertyDatabase") %>

<HTML>
<HEAD>
<TITLE>Listing 8.9</TITLE>
</HEAD>
<BODY>
<FONT COLOR=BLUE>
<H2 ALIGN=CENTER>Vote on your favorite Restaurant!</H2>
<HR SIZE=5>
<% If (Request("Content_Length")) = 0 Then %>
<PRE>
<FORM METHOD=POST ACTION="8-9.asp">
<INPUT TYPE=RADIO NAME="favrest" VALUE="Al's Mexican Palace">
    Al's Mexican Palace
<INPUT TYPE=RADIO NAME="favrest" VALUE="Paul's China Garden">
    Paul's China Garden
<INPUT TYPE=RADIO NAME="favrest" VALUE="Kim's Steak House">
    Kim's Steak House

<INPUT TYPE=SUBMIT VALUE="Vote">
</FORM>
</PRE>

<% Else %>
    <% If vote.Open("Vote", "guest", "") = TRUE Then %>
        <% ballot_result = vote.SetBallotName("restaurant") %>
        <% vote_result = vote.Submit("Favorite",
            Request("favrest"), Props.ID) %>
        <% If vote_result = TRUE Then %>
            Thanks for voting!
```

```
                     <P>
                     <% =vote.GetVote %>
            <% Else %>
                     Oops, only one vote please.
            <% End If %>
            <% Else %>
                     The voting component failed...
        <% End If %>
    <% End IF %>
    </BODY>
    </HTML>
```

The Send Mail Component

The Send Mail component enables you to receive email feedback from your users. You can also use it to email information back to them. The Send Mail component is easy to use and, like the Voting component, does most of the work.

To use the Send Mail component, you must have an SMTP mail server available. The component has only one method, **SendMail**:

```
SendMail(from, to, subject, body)
```

from specifies a string that appears in the From field of the message header. It must be a valid email name in the format *name@domain*. *to* specifies a list of recipients. You must separate each recipient in the list with a semicolon. *subject* specifies a string that appears in the Subject field of the message header. *body* specifies the message body. If you want to break the body into paragraphs, you must explicitly embed carriage returns into the message body. You can do so in VBScript by concatenating the constant **vbCrLf** into the body.

SendMail returns **TRUE** if it successfully sends the message or **FALSE** if it is unsuccessful.

Working Without MPS

MPS provides three very interesting functions: persistent user properties, voting, and email. Each of these features allows you to create an online community to attract and retain users.

Is there anything magical about MPS? No. These functions are nothing more than ActiveX controls for the server. However, they are very useful ActiveX controls. Although in theory you could write your own, none of these components is trivial.

For most Web sites, the UPD's limitations are easy to ignore. However, if you are planning on a subscription service or other special site, you must be sure to plan carefully around the UPD's limitations. For example, if I pay to subscribe to your site, I won't be happy if that subscription applies only to one browser on one machine. The UPD ID wouldn't be useful for limiting votes of real importance, either. It's too easy to delete a cookie or to change machines and vote multiple times.

Still, for most sites, these problems are minor in relation to the increased functionality that components like the UPD provide. Customizing content based on user preferences can go a long way to building that all-important surfer loyalty. On the other hand, what if your server doesn't support MPS?

User Properties Without MPS

The UPD component has many potential uses, but what if it isn't available to you? The obvious alternative is to use client-side cookies to store data. However, unlike MPS, cookies don't retain values unless the user accesses the site with the same browser and the browser hasn't decided to delete the cookie for some arbitrary reason.

The answer, then, is to use a database to store user IDs, passwords, and whatever data you need to include for each user. You can refer to the preceding chapter for more details about database access. Storing properties isn't very hard; you simply need a unique way to identify users.

One advantage to using a user ID is that you can restore the user's preferences regardless of where he or she logs in, as long as the user knows his or her ID and password. All that is required is a simple database, a few ASP pages, and the IIS database component.

To illustrate this concept, I put together a simple Web site that allows you to register a user ID and your preferences. The database (see Table 8.6) contains the user's preferred color, name, and email address. It also contains a space that records the last page the user was viewing.

The initial page of the site provides a form to enter a username and password. It also has a link to the registration page. If you are already logged in and you visit the registration page, you can edit your preferences and other information. After you log on, the site returns you to the last page you visited (unless you are a new user; in that case, you arrive at a central default page).

Table 8.6   The Users database schema.

Field	Description
UID	User ID
PW	Password (stored in plain text)
Color	User's color choice
LastPage	Last page user visited
Name	User's full name
Email	User's email address

Logging In

Figure 8.1 shows the first page the user sees. This simple form posts to a separate ASP file (see Listings 8.10 and 8.11). When the user submits the data, the processing script validates the user and then loads the session variable with any information the database contains. The script simply reads every field in the database, so it can accommodate whatever you want to store.

This part of the script loads the session variables:

```
' fill in the user's variables
    for i=0 to RS.Fields.Count-1
      Session(RS.Fields(i).Name)=RS(i)
    next
```

If you have a great deal of data in the database that is not required for the Web site, you might want to customize this code to load only the fields required by the Web site.

Validating the user requires only an SQL **SELECT** statement, as shown here, to search for the user ID requested:

```
Set Conn = Server.CreateObject("ADODB.Connection")
Conn.Open "Users"
SQL="SELECT * FROM Users WHERE UID='" & Request("UID") & "'"
set RS=Conn.Execute(SQL)
if RS.EOF then
  status=0
else
  if RS("PW")<>Request("PW") then
    status=-1
  else
.
.
.
```

If you want only a pass or fail validation, you can rewrite the **SELECT** statement so that the **WHERE** clause includes both the user ID and the password. With the **SELECT** statement as it is, the code can differentiate between a bad user ID and a valid ID with an incorrect password.

The preceding code uses the record set's **EOF** property to determine whether the ID exists. If **EOF** is false, at least one record in the database must match the user ID (and only one record should match). Otherwise, the script checks for a matching password. The **status** variable is 0 or −1 in the event of failure. This variable allows the code in the page's body to determine why the login was invalid.

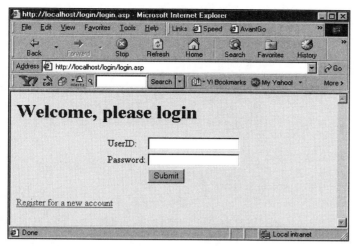

Figure 8.1
The login screen.

The page doesn't do much if the login was incorrect. It would be simple to provide a return link to the login page, or even redirect back to the login page and display an error message there. For now, the page simply warns the user of the invalid login. The user can then click on the Back button and try again.

Listing 8.10 The login page.

```
<HTML>
<BODY BGCOLOR=YELLOW>
<H1>Welcome, please login</H1>
<FORM ACTION=dologin.asp METHOD=POST>
<TABLE ALIGN=CENTER>
<TR><TD> </TD><TD>
<TABLE>
<TR><TD>
UserID: </TD><TD><INPUT NAME=UID VALUE='<%=Session("UID") %>'></TD></TR>
<TR><TD>
Password: </TD><TD><INPUT TYPE=PASSWORD NAME=PW></TD></TR>
<TR><TD> </TD><TD>
<INPUT TYPE=SUBMIT VALUE=Submit></TD></TR></TABLE>

</TD><TD> </TD>
</P>
</TABLE></FORM>
</CENTER>
<A HREF=Register.asp>Register for a new account</A>
</BODY>
</HTML>
```

Listing 8.11 Validating the login.

```
<%
 status=1 'assume success
 Set Conn = Server.CreateObject("ADODB.Connection")
 Conn.Open "Users"
 SQL="SELECT * FROM Users WHERE UID='" & Request("UID") & "'"
 set RS=Conn.Execute(SQL)
 if RS.EOF then
   status=0
 else
   if RS("PW")<>Request("PW") then
     status=-1
   else
     newurl=RS("LastPage")
     if len(newurl)=0 or isNull(newurl) then newurl="memberpage.asp"
' fill in the user's variables
     for i=0 to RS.Fields.Count-1
       Session(RS.Fields(i).Name)=RS(i)
     next
     response.redirect(newurl)
   end if
 end if
%>
<HTML>
<BODY BGCOLOR=YELLOW>
<% if status=0 then %>
<P>Invalid User ID. Please use your back button and login again</P>
<% end if %>
<% if status=-1 then %>
<P>Invalid password. Please use your back button and login again</P>
<% end if %>
</BODY>
</HTML>
```

Registration

The steps you took in the preceding sections assume you have the database populated with some users. Of course, you can seed your table with an initial list of users, but you won't want to manually add users to the database in real life. What you want, of course, is to let the users add themselves to the database using the Web.

The page in Listing 8.12 does just that (see Figure 8.2). It presents a form that allows a user to create a new user ID. If the user is already logged in, or he or she provides the correct password for the ID, the screen provides a means to edit the existing database entry.

The only tricky part to editing is the password. If the form notes that the user is already logged in, it provides a password change field. If the user leaves this field blank, the password

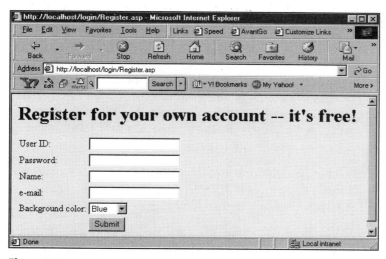

Figure 8.2
The registration page.

remains unchanged. In either case, the user must supply the current password in the appropriate field.

This form submits data back to itself. If the content length is zero, the page displays the form. If a user ID is already in use in this session, the page also displays the change password field, as discussed in the preceding paragraphs. Also, if existing information is available in the user's session, the entry fields show the existing data as the default (with the exception of the password, of course). For example, the **myName** field looks like this:

```
<INPUT NAME=myName VALUE='<%= Session("Name") %>'>
```

Setting the default for the color selection choice is a bit trickier. Instead of duplicating the logic for each color, I wrote a simple function (**selopt**) that requires two arguments: the color in the list and the current color. The function generates the correct **<OPTION>** tag. The code is as follows:

```
<% function selopt(s,ss)
   sout="<OPTION VALUE='" & s & "'"
   if s=ss then sout = sout & " SELECTED"
   selopt = sout & ">" & s
   end function
%>
```

The real tricky part of registration happens when the page detects a form submission. First, the form saves the user's name (not the user's ID, but the name), color choice, and email into the session variables. This way, the form can retain these values even if the registration is not successful. For example, if the user selects an ID that is already in use, the form will remember the entered values when it asks for a new ID so that the user doesn't have to repeatedly enter them.

After saving the information for future use, the script performs essentially the same SQL statement that makes up a login. This action makes sense because you have to make sure the registered ID is new (or it is an old ID with the correct password). If the script finds a matching ID but an incorrect password, it sets the **status** variable to -1. This variable causes the form to be redisplayed with an appropriate error message.

If the requested ID is available, the script uses an SQL **INSERT** command to make a new entry into the database. If this is an edit, an **UPDATE** command handles the transaction. Special logic is required to handle password updates when a new password appears.

If an insert or an update occurs, the page redirects the user back to the original login page. The user can then log in for the first time or use the new password. Going back to the login page also ensures that the most current values appear in the session variables.

Listing 8.12   Registration.

```
<% status=0
  if request("content_length")<>0 then
  ' form submitted
  ' save in case of failure
  Session("email")=Request("email")
  Session("color")=Request("color")
  Session("name")=Request("myName")
  Set Conn = Server.CreateObject("ADODB.Connection")
  Conn.Open "Users"
  SQL="SELECT * FROM Users WHERE UID='" & Request("UID") & "'"
  set RS=Conn.Execute(SQL)
  if RS.EOF then
    ' good to go
    status=1
  else
    ' duplicate
    status=-1
    if Request("PW")=RS("PW") then status=2   ' edit?
  end if
  if status=1 then
  SQL="INSERT INTO Users (uid,pw,name,email,color) values ("
  SQL = SQL & "'" & Request("UID") & "',"
  SQL = SQL & "'" & Request("PW") & "',"
  SQL = SQL & "'" & Request("myName") & "',"
  SQL = SQL & "'" & Request("email") & "',"
  SQL = SQL & "'" & Request("color") & "')"
  Conn.Execute(SQL)
```

```
 response.redirect("login.asp")
 end if
 if status=2 then
 SQL="UPDATE Users SET Name='" & Request("myName") & "',email='"
 SQL= SQL & Request("email") & "', color='"
 SQL= SQL & Request("color") & "'"
 if Request("NewPW")<>"" then
   SQL= SQL & ", pw='" & Request("NewPW") & "'"
 end if
 SQL= SQL & " WHERE UID='" & Request("UID") & "'"
 Conn.Execute(SQL)
 response.redirect("login.asp")
 end if
end if
%>
<!-- no submit so show form -->
<HTML>
<BODY BGCOLOR=YELLOW>
<H1>Register for your own account -- it's free!</H1>
<% if status=-1 then %>
<H3>User ID is already in use. Please select another one.</H3>
<% Session("UID")=""
   end if %>
<FORM METHOD=POST ACTION=register.asp>
<TABLE>
<TR><TD>
User ID:
</TD>
<TD>
<INPUT NAME=UID VALUE='<%= Session("UID") %>'>
</TD></TR><TR><TD>
Password:
</TD>
<TD>
<INPUT NAME=PW>
<% if Session("PW")<>"" then %>  <!-- must be an edit -->
</TD></TR><TR><TD>
New Password:<BR>(Blank for no change)
</TD><TD>
<INPUT NAME=NewPW>
<% end if %>
</TD></TR><TR><TD>
Name:
</TD><TD>
<INPUT NAME=myName VALUE='<%= Session("Name") %>'>
</TD></TR><TR><TD>
```

```
e-mail:
</TD><TD>
<INPUT NAME=email VALUE='<%= Session("email") %>'>
</TD></TR><TR><TD>
Background color:
</TD><TD>

<% function selopt(s,ss)
    sout="<OPTION VALUE='" & s & "'"
    if s=ss then sout = sout & " SELECTED"
    selopt = sout & ">" & s
    end function
%>



<SELECT NAME=Color>
<%= selopt("Blue",Session("Color")) %>
<%= selopt("Yellow",Session("Color")) %>
<%= selopt("Green",Session("Color")) %>
<%= selopt("White",Session("Color")) %>
</SELECT>
</TD></TR><TR><TD> </TD><TD>
<INPUT TYPE=SUBMIT Value=Submit></TD></TR></TABLE>
</FORM>
</BODY>
</HTML>
```

Page Support

Now you can create and modify accounts. You can also log in with a valid account. How can the pages take advantage of the user's properties? Because everything is in a session variable, using the data is quick and easy. For example, the following code starts the main menu page:

```
<BODY BGCOLOR=<%= Session("Color") %>>
<P>Welcome back <%= Session("Name") %>, glad to see you again!</P>
```

Warning

If you use a Web farm—that is, multiple servers that share the same IP address—be aware that you can't use session variables because each server has a separate copy of the variables. In this case, you would need to store the user's ID (and possibly password) in a cookie and extract the data from a database on each page. Each server in the farm would access the same database. Web farms are usually required only on extremely high-volume sites where they help balance the traffic loading for the site.

The page color and user's name are easy to extract and use. The problem, of course, is changing data. Changing data requires changing the database. You could take two approaches. First, you could write a handler in the GLOBAL.ASA file to detect when a session ends and write all the session variables back out to the database. This method is efficient, but it requires modifying the GLOBAL.ASA file when your database structure changes. It also won't save data if your server crashes because you'll lose open sessions.

Another approach is to simply update the database on every change. Obviously, this method requires more database overhead than the first approach. However, for low-volume updates on a relatively fast server, you can get away with it. For example, consider one of the destination pages shown in Listing 8.13. This page sets the **lastpage** field in the database using an SQL **UPDATE** command. The login page therefore can return the user to this page on the next visit.

Listing 8.13   A target page.

```
<%
 Set Conn = Server.CreateObject("ADODB.Connection")
 Conn.Open "Users"
 SQL="UPDATE Users SET lastpage='page1.asp' "
 SQL= SQL &  "WHERE UID='" & Session("UID") & "'"
 Conn.Execute(SQL)
%>
<HTML>
<BODY BGCOLOR=<%=Session("Color")%>>
This is page 1!
<BR><A HREF=memberpage.asp>Home</A>
</BODY>
</HTML>
```

Page Protection

Keep in mind that, as written, the password system doesn't stop a user from accessing pages without a password. It simply allows the user to retrieve his or her properties. It would be a simple matter, however, to change each page so that anyone who did not log in would find himself or herself at the initial login screen.

For example, you might consider placing this code at the start of each page (perhaps using a server-side include):

```
<% if Session("PW")="" then response.redirect("login.asp") %>
```

That would do the trick. When the session expires, or if there was never a session to begin with, the user arrives at the login page. If you want a way for the user to log out explicitly, you could use **Session.Abandon**.

If you use Microsoft Site Server 3, you can set the server to do this type of user ID and password processing for you by using Site Server Personalization and Membership (P&M). Using P&M doesn't require any scripting; you simply use the Membership Authentication tab in the Web site's properties. You can view the properties by using the Microsoft Management Console (MMC).

Other Possibilities

Of course, using an ASP-accessed database is not the only way you can store user preferences. You also can use ActiveX controls, for example, to manage a database and write all the code in Visual C++ or Visual Basic. The key, however, is using some sort of database. You can find out more about custom ActiveX controls in Chapter 11.

You could easily alter this example so that the user would automatically log in from the same computer by storing the user ID and password in a cookie. Then, the login screen would appear only if the cookie were missing or contained incorrect information. Of course, cookies are not very secure, so you wouldn't want to use this method if the password protected critical information.

The other alternative to using a database is to store information on the user's machine by using cookies. One advantage to using cookies is that you don't have to provide space on the server to hold them. On the other hand, the user must use the same browser and computer to access the information. Also, browsers can destroy cookies at their whim.

You can manipulate cookies from within a script in two ways: You can use client-side code exclusively (which is very complicated), or you can use server-side script, which is considerably simpler.

Server-Side Cookie Processing

The key to handling cookies with server-side script is to recognize that the **Request** object has cookies that the browser sent to you (presumably from a previous session). Using the **Response** object, you can set cookies that you can read in the future by using the **Request** object. This approach is easily exemplified by this short Web page (named cookie1.asp):

```
<% if Request("content_length")<>0 then
    Response.cookies("somedata")=request("data")
  end if
%>
<HTML>
<BODY>
Current value is <%= Request.cookies("somedata") %><BR>
<FORM ACTION=cookie1.asp METHOD=POST>
<INPUT NAME=DATA VALUE='<%= Request.cookies("somedata") %>'>
```

```
<INPUT TYPE=SUBMIT VALUE=Submit>
</FORM>
</BODY>
</HTML>
```

Notice that the first part of the file looks to see whether any form data exists. If so, the script uses it to set the cookie. Setting a cookie involves changing the headers sent to the browser, so you must use **Response.cookies** before any HTML output.

When you want to read the value, you can use **Request.cookies**. There is no reason you can't set a cookie on one page and read it back on another. The **somedata** string is just an arbitrary name to identify the data you want. You can store multiple items in the cookie pseudoarray.

You can also set properties on individual cookies. The most common reason to do so is to make the cookie persist beyond the current session. For example, to make a cookie expire at the end of the year 2050, you could write the following:

```
Response.cookies("SomeData").Expires = "December 31, 2050"
```

Another useful property is the domain name property. You use it if you want to share a cookie among multiple subdomains. For example, suppose I have a Web site on **www.al-williams.com** and another at **members.al-williams.com**. Perhaps I have yet another site at **wd5gnr.al-williams.com**. Normally, setting a cookie from any of these Web sites would make that cookie private to the site. If I set a cookie with, for example, your name in the **www.al-williams.com** site, scripts in the **members.al-williams.com** domain could not access the cookie.

However, I can allow the other domains to access the same cookie by using a property, as in this example:

```
Response.cookies("SomeData").domain = ".al-williams.com"
```

Now, any Web site that ends with **al-williams.com** can work with this cookie. There is no easy way to share a cookie with an entirely different domain name. You can, of course, use some scheme in which you redirect to the server that has the cookie value and it redirects back to you with the cookie's data in, for example, the query string. This approach requires script on both your server and the server that has the data.

Cookies With Client-Side Script

Although you can use the **document** object to manipulate cookies in client-side script, it is cumbersome because this object exposes the raw cookie. However, you can use a small JavaScript library, like the one in Listing 8.14, to greatly simplify your interactions with the **document** object.

Listing 8.14   Cookies on the client in JavaScript.

```
<SCRIPT>
<!--
    function getCookieVal (offset) {
      var endstr = document.cookie.indexOf (";", offset);
      if (endstr == -1)
        endstr = document.cookie.length;
      return unescape(document.cookie.substring(offset, endstr));
    }

    function SetCookie (name, value) {
      var argv = SetCookie.arguments;
      var argc = SetCookie.arguments.length;
      var expires = (argc > 2) ? argv[2] : null;
      var path = (argc > 3) ? argv[3] : null;
      var domain = (argc > 4) ? argv[4] : null;
      var secure = (argc > 5) ? argv[5] : false;
      document.cookie = name + "=" + escape (value) +
        ((expires == null) ? "" : ("; expires=" +
          expires.toGMTString())) +
        ((path == null) ? "" : ("; path=" + path)) +
        ((domain == null) ? "" : ("; domain=" + domain)) +
        ((secure == true) ? "; secure" : ""));
    }

    function GetCookie (name) {
      var arg = name + "=";
      var alen = arg.length;
      var clen = document.cookie.length;
      var i = 0;
      while (i < clen) {
        var j = i + alen;
        if (document.cookie.substring(i, j) == arg)
          return getCookieVal (j);
        i = document.cookie.indexOf(" ", i) + 1;
        if (i == 0) break;
      }
      return null;
    }

    function DeleteCookie (name) {
      var exp = new Date();
      exp.setTime (exp.getTime() - 1);  // This cookie is history
      var cval = GetCookie (name);
```

```
        document.cookie = name + "=" + cval + "; expires=" +
          exp.toGMTString();
    }

//-->
</SCRIPT>
```

This library provides three functions of interest. The first, **SetCookie**, allows you to set a named cookie's value. The call also takes up to four additional arguments. The third argument, if present, specifies the expiration time for the cookie. The other arguments allow you to set the path, domain, and security options for the cookie (in that order). You'll rarely use any of them except the expiration date. Remember, without an expiration date, the cookie lasts only for the current session.

Once you set a cookie, you'll want to call **GetCookie** to retrieve it. This function does just what you'd expect, converting a cookie name into a cookie value. When you no longer need a cookie, you can call **DeleteCookie**.

Handling cookies in this way doesn't even require an ASP page; you can use a regular HTML document if you like. One point to keep in mind is that cookies require a server. Even if you are handling cookies with client-side script, you must access the page via a URL and not directly as a local file. If, for example, you point your browser to c:\inetpub\wwwroot\cookietest.htm, you will not find any valid cookies to read.

Voting Without MPS

Voting without MPS is just a matter of designing an appropriate database structure and accessing it. For very simple votes, you might even consider keeping the totals in an application variable.

For example, suppose you have a site aimed at local residents. You want their opinions about what section of your site to expand next. Should you focus on news, weather, or sports? This isn't a world-shattering decision. You don't need to make it more difficult than necessary. A simple form that collects the votes and stores them in an application variable will do fine (see Listing 8.15).

Listing 8.15   Voting with application variables.

```
<% response.expires=0
   if request("show")=1 then
%>
<HTML>
<BODY>
Vote results:<BR>
```

```
News = <%= Application("News") %><BR>
Weather = <%= Application("Weather") %><BR>
Sports = <%= Application("Sports") %><BR>
</BODY>
</HTML>

<%
  else
   if request("content_length")<>0 then
    application.lock
    application(request("Section"))=application(request("Section"))+1
    application.unlock
%>
<HTML>
<HEAD>
</HEAD>
<BODY>
Thanks for voting!
</BODY>
</HTML>
<% else %>
<HTML>
<HEAD>
</HEAD>
<BODY>
<FORM ACTION=vote.asp METHOD=post>
What section would you like us to expand?<BR>
<INPUT TYPE=RADIO NAME=Section VALUE=News>News<BR>
<INPUT TYPE=RADIO NAME=Section VALUE=Weather>Weather<BR>
<INPUT TYPE=Radio NAME=Section VALUE=Sports>Sports<BR>
<INPUT TYPE=SUBMIT VALUE=Vote>
</FORM>
</BODY>
</HTML>
<% end if %>
<% end if %>
```

The disadvantage of using this approach, of course, is that if the server goes down, the results are gone. This single page shows the form, collects the data, and also displays the results. To see the current tallies, you point your browser to **http://localhost/vote.asp?show=1**. Of course, you use your server name instead of **localhost**. Any item that has no votes shows as a blank. You could easily seed each value with a zero one time if that bothers you.

Email Without MPS

If you have the email services from NT Option Pack 4 (or Windows 2000), you already have a powerful email component installed that is just as easy to use as the **MPS.SendMail** component. In fact, it is even more flexible. The object, which is part of the Collaboration Data Objects (CDO) library from Microsoft, is known as **CDONTS.NewMail**.

Assuming you have CDO on your server, sending email is as simple as this:

```
<% set email = server.CreateObject("CDONTS.NewMail")
    email.Send "from@from.com", "to@to.com", "Subject","Message",1
    set email=nothing
%>
```

This component is very similar to the **MPS.SendMail** component. Of course, you would use real email addresses and replace the subject and message strings with the real information. The final argument, 1, is the message priority.

You can also use properties and methods to initialize the object before calling **Send**. A list of the members is shown in Table 8.7. Nearly all the properties are write-only because the component is not often used with a user interface; therefore, you don't need to read the values back from the component.

Table 8.7   CDONTS.NewMail properties and methods.

Name	Type	Usage
Bcc	Property	Specifies blind copy addresses
Body	Property	Contains message body text
BodyFormat	Property	Specifies the format of the message body
CC	Property	Contains copy addresses
ContentBase	Property	Sets the base URL for the message body (used to resolve relative URLs)
ContentLocation	Property	Sets the location of URLs in the message body relative to **ContentBase** (used to resolve relative URLs)
From	Property	Specifies the From address
Importance	Property	Sets the priority of this message
MailFormat	Property	Sets encoding used when sending mail
Subject	Property	Identifies subject text
To	Property	Specifies recipient addresses
Value	Property	Sets headers (for example, Reply-To or Keywords)
Version	Property	Indicates the read-only version number of the component
AttachFile	Method	Attaches a file to the message
AttachURL	Method	Attaches a URL to the message
Send	Method	Sends the message
SetLocaleIDs	Method	Sets language identifiers

Warning

*Each instance of the **NewMail** object is for a single email. You should always create a new copy before sending a new email.*

You can read more about CDO at **www.cdolive.com**. Also, if you don't have CDO or MPS, you might want to check out some of the following free email components on the Web:

- **www.aspemail.com**
- **www.dimac.net/freeasp.asp**
- **www.flicks.com/ASPMail/**

Chapter 9
Advanced Tools

Al Williams

I t is truly amazing how much people can accomplish without using modern tools. The pyramids were built—presumably—without the aid of powered machinery (unless the UFOs really were on hand). Stonehenge is another example. Explorers crossed the North American continent without benefit of Jeeps and Land Rovers. Forests fell without chainsaws.

Not that anyone wants to go back to those days. Who wants to spend weeks or months traveling from one city to the next? Who wants to cut their grass with a hand-held sickle?

Still, doing things the hard way presents some advantages. Calculators are great for crunching numbers, but they don't teach intuition about math. To gain that knowledge, you have to learn the old techniques; there is just no substitute.

No one wants to go back to punching cards and paper tape (well, almost no one; I have a sneaking fondness for paper tape, as do a few other old-timers). However, understanding why things work in computers also presents some advantages. Several tools automate Web page creation; some even generate ASP script for you. But what do you learn? More importantly, do you know what to do when these tools don't generate exactly the code you want?

In this chapter, you'll briefly examine two popular Microsoft tools: FrontPage and Visual InterDev. Of course, you can get whole books on either of these tools. However, if you are accustomed to using similar programs (such as Microsoft Word or Microsoft Visual Studio), you won't have any problem picking up the basics. This chapter focuses on these tools mainly as they relate to scripting tasks.

Available Tools

Microsoft provides two major Web page authoring tool packages: FrontPage and Visual InterDev. Why does Microsoft provide two programs that perform (essentially) the same task? Each program targets a different kind of Web developer. FrontPage is a visually oriented editor that is well-suited for developers who are mainly concerned with the visual appearance and layout of their pages. Visual InterDev caters to programmers who want to write Web pages that incorporate scripts—particularly those that handle database transactions.

Does that mean Visual InterDev doesn't allow you to lay out Web pages or that FrontPage users can't access databases? No. In fact, over time, the two products have converged somewhat so that they each do the other's job to some extent. However, the focus of each product remains on its designated tasks.

The tools do have much in common, and you can use both on the same project—although doing so is cumbersome. For your own peace of mind, you should select one tool and stick with it.

Common Concepts

FrontPage and InterDev have several elements in common. For starters, both rely on the *FrontPage Server Extensions* to some extent. These extensions provide a way for Web publishing tools to communicate with Web servers. Of course, Microsoft's servers support this protocol, but you can usually find these extensions for other servers as well.

Choosing Between InterDev And FrontPage

Microsoft's two tools for creating Web pages are part of other Microsoft bundles: Visual InterDev is part of Microsoft Visual Studio and FrontPage is part of Microsoft Office. As you might expect, each program has features that make it similar to the other programs in the bundle. Visual InterDev, for example, offers features similar to Visual C++—IntelliSense, project management, and the ability to integrate multiple types of projects in a single workspace.

FrontPage, on the other hand, is more like a word processor than a programming tool. Whereas InterDev focuses on programmer functionality, FrontPage concentrates on visual accuracy—WYSIWYG, if you will.

I'm not saying that InterDev is not visual or that FrontPage users can't write script. The two tools have much in common and often share features (for example, themes). Besides, FrontPage comes with a stripped-down version of InterDev (the Microsoft Script Editor), and some versions of InterDev ship with a version of FrontPage.

So, the choice winds up being a personal one. If you already use Visual Studio products, or if you expect to be doing a good bit of scripting, you will probably opt for Visual InterDev. If you are mainly interested in layout and page design, you will probably be happier with FrontPage.

Selecting A Server With FrontPage Extensions

Both Visual InterDev and FrontPage rely on the server implementing FrontPage extensions. Nearly all servers can support these extensions in some way. In their simplest form, FrontPage extensions are simply a way a publishing tool can find out how to post material to the server. This type of extension is pretty easy to handle, and as you might expect, nearly every server can accommodate FrontPage at this level.

For real compatibility with FrontPage, however, the server also needs to support FrontPage's WebBots. Of course, to be fully compatible, you need a server that can handle the ASP script that FrontPage (and InterDev) generates. Because you are reading this book, you are probably already using a server that complies with these requirements, but beware that not all real-world servers support scripting.

Administering FrontPage is often a headache. Several versions of the extensions are available, and if you get them mixed up, the results are usually unpleasant.

If your server does not support FrontPage, you can have the tools publish your finished product using, for example, FTP, but you lose some of the functionality that is possible when you use the FrontPage extensions. If you're using ASP scripting, your server surely supports the full extensions.

FrontPage extensions are notoriously difficult to set up. Luckily, setting up extensions is usually an issue for administrators, not for developers. It is very common for developers to use Personal Web Server (PWS), which is easy to set up, and then publish to an external server (typically, Internet Information Server, or IIS).

Another concept common to both programs is themes. A *theme* is simply a set of graphical design elements that you can apply to a page or to your entire Web site. A theme can set the page background, bullets, horizontal rules, and other design elements. Themes are handy because you can experiment with different looks with almost no effort.

Figure 9.1 shows a Web page using the Blueprint theme. By simply changing the theme to Cypress, you can change the Web page's appearance to look like Figure 9.2. Notice the page banner at the top of each page. It is a good example of an element that combines text and graphics. The program generates these graphics on the fly by combining a base graphic with your text each time you save the page. That means you don't need any special code on the server to produce these graphics.

A similar concept is the *design-time control*. These ActiveX controls generate parts of your Web document when you save it. The controls are necessary only while you're editing the Web page. The final Web page doesn't use the controls; the program remembers them by using special HTML comments. This feature allows you to use special controls to edit parts of your Web page, but not rely on these controls when you deploy your page.

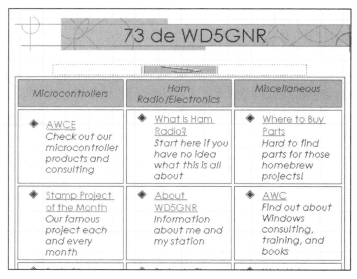

Figure 9.1
A Web page using the Blueprint theme.

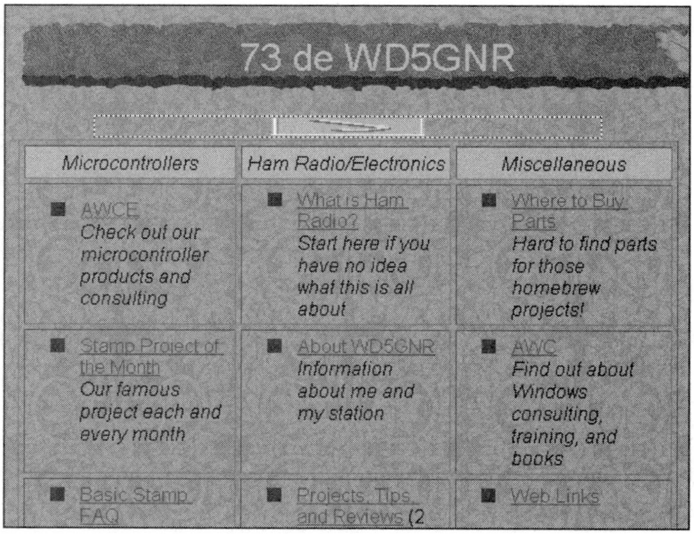

Figure 9.2
A Web page using the Cypress theme.

A good example of a design-time control is the Page Transition Control available with Visual InterDev. This control (see Figure 9.3) provides a nice interface that allows you to change the DHTML page enter and exit effects. Listing 9.1 shows a portion of the generated HTML for this page. Notice that the ActiveX control information appears in the HTML comments. The control creates the required **<META>** tags, which are standard HTML.

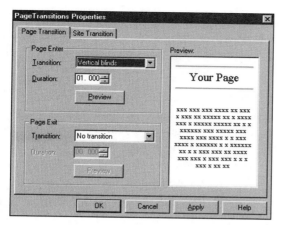

Figure 9.3
The Page Transition Control.

Listing 9.1   A portion of the HTML generated by the Page Transition Control.

```
<HTML>
<HEAD>
<!--METADATA TYPE="DesignerControl" startspan
<OBJECT CLASSID="clsid:8EA785B1-4738-11D1-B47C-00A0C959BB15"
ID=PageTransitions1>
<PARAM NAME="EnterPageDuration" VALUE="1">
<PARAM NAME="EnterPageTransition" VALUE="8">
<PARAM NAME="EnterPageType" VALUE="0">
<PARAM NAME="ExitPageDuration" VALUE="1">
<PARAM NAME="ExitPageTransition" VALUE="-1">
<PARAM NAME="ExitPageType" VALUE="0">
<PARAM NAME="EnterSiteDuration" VALUE="1">
<PARAM NAME="EnterSiteTransition" VALUE="-1">
<PARAM NAME="EnterSiteType" VALUE="0">
<PARAM NAME="ExitSiteDuration" VALUE="1">
<PARAM NAME="ExitSiteTransition" VALUE="-1">
<PARAM NAME="ExitSiteType" VALUE="0">
</OBJECT>
-->
<META HTTP-EQUIV="Page-Enter"
CONTENT="revealTrans(Duration=1.000,Transition=8)">

<!--METADATA TYPE="DesignerControl" endspan-->
```

If you examine Listing 9.1, you'll see what appears to be a normal runtime ActiveX control using the **<OBJECT>** tag. However, closer examination shows that the entire object appears within HTML comments. InterDev interprets these comments, but the browser just ignores everything within them. Another comment appears below the generated HTML so that InterDev knows what part of the HTML corresponds to the control.

Design-time controls provide several of the functions in both FrontPage and InterDev. Although you might shy away from using ActiveX for compatibility reasons, using them at design time doesn't pose any problem because they will run only on your development computer.

It is important to realize that both FrontPage and InterDev are more than just HTML editors. These programs strive to provide a rich editing environment and a way to manage your Web site at the same time. For example, you can generate reports that show broken links. You can publish only the pages that differ from the original Web site to the server. You'll also find that your pages are interrelated. If you move a page, for example, both programs automatically fix any links so that they are correct.

Both products operate on the concept of a project. A *project* is a collection of Web pages, style sheets, and any other files you need to publish your Web site. A document that you'll find in both programs is the site diagram. The *site diagram* defines the relationship between the various pages in your Web site. You create these diagrams graphically (see Figure 9.4). The programs can use these diagrams to automatically generate navigation menus for you.

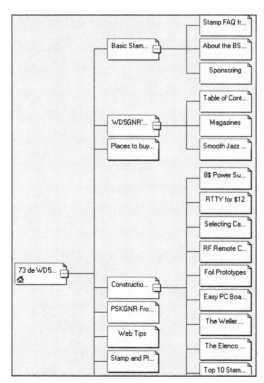

Figure 9.4
A partial site diagram.

Using A Site Diagram

Both FrontPage and Visual InterDev use a site diagram to define the relationships between your pages. With a site diagram, these tools can create automatic navigation bars, page banners, and the like.

In FrontPage, a site diagram is automatically part of any project. With Visual InterDev, you can add a site diagram in the same way you would add an ordinary Web page. In either event, the site diagram consists of small rectangles that represent pages and lines that connect them together.

The site diagram is a tree structure. At the left (or, optionally, at the top) is your home page (the root, if you will), and the branches grow toward the right (or the bottom) of the diagram. Initially, only the home page appears, but you can drag more pages from the list of files into the site diagram. You'll see dotted lines form to show you where the page will go if you drop it at the current location.

When you have your diagram in place (Figure 9.4 shows a completed diagram), you can make modifications. Of course, you can drag and drop pages to new positions in the tree. For example, you might want to change the order of some pages because the order here affects the order on navigation bars.

You can also right-click on the page icons to alter the properties of the particular page. Renaming the page is particularly useful because this name will appear on page banners.

Note that changing the title of a page on the site diagram does not alter the page's HTML title. The same is true for the linking lines on the site diagram. They do not reflect HTML hyperlinks. The names and links in the site diagram are purely conceptual. Only certain components (such as navigation bars and page banners) rely on the site diagram definitions.

Another common piece that Microsoft's Web tools allow is a *shared border*. You can create an area on each page of your site that is shared and contains navigation bars, logos, or anything you want consistently on most or all of your pages.

Using Shared Borders

Shared borders are an interesting and useful feature shared by FrontPage and Visual InterDev. You can define a shared border at the top, left, right, or bottom of a page. The content in this border (typically a navigation bar or a banner) is common among all pages that share the border. Changing the content inside the border changes it for all pages.

In your Web page, shared borders work by using tables. Your page's content resides inside a table cell that separates it from the shared content. When you save the Web site, the editing program saves the shared content into the file; you don't need any special server support to make use of shared borders.

With FrontPage, just right-click on a page and select Shared Borders if you want to manipulate the border setup. You can also choose Format|Shared Borders.

Visual InterDev's shared borders are part of the program's layout feature. To use them, choose Edit|Apply Theme And Layout, and then select the Layout tab. If you want to affect more than one page, you need to select the pages in the Project Explorer.

One factor that makes recent versions of both FrontPage and InterDev simpler to use is that you can always switch to an HTML view of the current document. So, if you want to write script the way it's been written throughout this book, you can do so. You don't need to learn anything new. The editors even color different parts of the HTML source (script in green, comments in red, and so on).

Of course, the whole point to using these tools is to make life simpler. Both programs offer tools that can make scripting easier; you'll learn about them later in this chapter.

FrontPage Fundamentals

Microsoft FrontPage 2000 is part of the Office 2000 family of products. As you would expect, it appeals to Office users. Previous versions had one window for editing and another for managing your Web site. FrontPage 2000 combines all functions into a single user interface, as you can see in Figure 9.5.

When you start FrontPage, you'll see a Views bar on the left that allows you to select what appears in the right-hand window pane. The selections are as follows:

- *Page*—Allows you to view an HTML page for editing
- *Folders*—Allows you to view files and folders in an Explorer-like view
- *Reports*—Allows you to generate reports (for example, broken hyperlink reports)
- *Navigation*—Allows you to define the site diagram that sets the relationship of pages to one another
- *Hyperlinks*—Allows you to see the links into and out of a page
- *Tasks*—Allows you to see the task list that organizes your "To Do" list for this Web site

Many of these items do not do anything unless you have a Web site open. If you open just a single page, you can use only the Page view. If you open a Web site (by choosing File | Open Web), you can use all the views.

If you have used any modern word processor, you should not have much trouble laying out Web pages with FrontPage. You can use the toolbars to set your font, change styles, center text, and perform all the other tasks that you expect. Of course, as usual, you can't rely on all Web browsers to faithfully reproduce your layout. However, the major browsers will work fine, and you can't do much about the lesser-used browsers anyway.

Another Office-like feature that is handy is the automatic spellchecking. FrontPage flags misspelled words automatically, placing a wavy red line beneath them. You can right-click on the word to select from a list of suggestions.

FrontPage 2000 supports themes, of course. However, it also allows you to customize existing themes by changing various colors and graphics elements. You can then save the modified

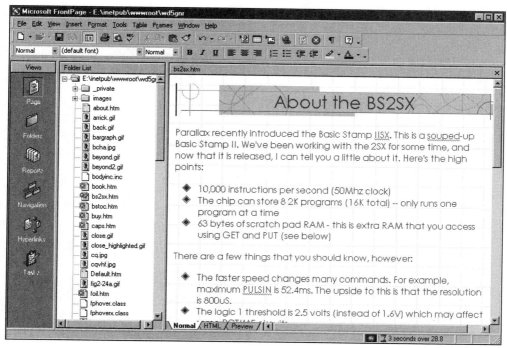

Figure 9.5
The FrontPage 2000 user interface.

theme using a new name to create a new theme. To access this feature, select Format | Theme. Then, select a theme and click on the Modify button near the bottom of the Themes dialog (see Figure 9.6).

Clicking Modify makes five buttons appear. You can use these buttons to modify the colors, graphics, or text styles that make up the theme. When you're satisfied with the result, you can click on Save or Save As. If you modify a standard theme, the Save button forces you to rename the theme anyway.

If you click on the Color button, you can choose from three different methods of changing colors:

♦ *The Color Schemes tab*—Lets you choose color-coordinated sets. These colors work well together, so you can change many design elements simultaneously by choosing one of these sets.

♦ *The Color Wheel tab*—Allows you to change the color scheme, making it brighter, darker, or shifting its hue. Again, these changes apply to the entire scheme.

♦ *The Custom tab*—This is the most flexible option, and also requires the most work. Using this tab, you can select the color for each element separately. Don't forget that each

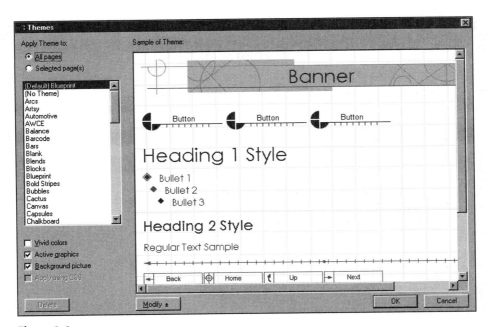

Figure 9.6
The Themes dialog.

theme has two separate sets of colors. One set is for the normal colors, and the other set applies when the designer checks the Vivid Colors checkbox when setting the theme. You have to select which set you want to affect.

By clicking on the Graphics button, you can select each graphic you want the theme to use. Again, you can choose from normal graphics or active graphics and change each individually. You can also select a font for certain graphics. When FrontPage creates, for example, a page banner, it combines text (the page title) and the graphic as you save the page. Using the Font tab, you can select how the text will appear. Early versions of FrontPage 2000 have some trouble with creating custom page banners (the graphic changes, but the text disappears). However, this problem is probably fixed already; just be sure to preview any custom theme carefully in the Web browser (not just in the Preview view) before you use it on a live Web site.

WebBots

FrontPage includes many features designed to prevent you from needing to write script. Collectively, these tools are called *WebBots*. FrontPage inserts them as special comments in your HTML file. The server therefore must implement the FrontPage extensions so that it can read these comments and interpret them properly. From the Insert menu, you can select a variety of special items that you would normally think about writing with script.

Getting The Most From FrontPage 2000

When you're editing in the Design view, you can press Ctrl+/ to view the HTML tags in your document. Let the mouse pointer float over the tags, and you will see the entire tag, including its attributes. Press Ctrl+/ to revert to the normal view.

If you want to format items in the shared borders directly, look for the correct file in the _borders directory. This approach is especially useful if you want to add, for example, DHTML effects to a border element.

You also can drag a page from the folder list into a document to create a hyperlink. If you want to create a hyperlink to a bookmark in the same document, just select the text you want the hyperlink to reference. Then, right-click and drag to the location for the hyperlink. When you release the right mouse button, a menu appears. Select Link Here, and FrontPage automatically creates the bookmark and hyperlink for you.

For example, when you choose Insert | Component, you'll find a hit counter and a way to include a file (using a normal server-side include). Other items on this menu include the scheduled picture and scheduled include file. These components insert a picture (or a file) into your page based on a range of dates and times. During the defined period, the component inserts the specified picture or file. At other times, either the component inserts nothing, or it inserts a default.

Can you include scheduled elements using script instead of a WebBot? Of course. This approach is conceptually the same as writing the following:

```
<% if Now>=StartDate and Now<=EndDate then %>
    <IMG SRC=... ALT="Time-sensitive graphic">
<% else %>
    <IMG SRC=... ALT = "Default graphic">
<% end if %>
```

Changing A Time-Sensitive Graphic In FrontPage

WebBots can often reduce or eliminate the need for scripts. For example, suppose you want to place a graphic next to an element until a certain date. A WebBot might be useful if you want to place a star-burst graphic near new items for two weeks.

You could easily script this graphic using a server-side script, but FrontPage provides an easy way to get the same result with no programming. All you need to do is insert a scheduled picture WebBot. Just select Insert|Component|Scheduled Picture from the main menu to open the dialog shown in Figure 9.7. From this dialog, you can select the image and the range of dates (and times) that you want the picture to appear. You can also optionally specify another picture to use when the scheduled picture does not appear.

Another similar WebBot, the Scheduled Include File, allows you to include another file on schedule instead of a picture. Using such a file is useful when you want to include general HTML—perhaps an announcement of a meeting, a special offer, or a contest that has an expiration date.

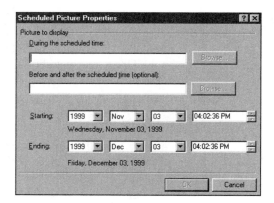

Figure 9.7
Inserting a scheduled picture.

This capability is useful in several situations. For example, you might want to display a NEW! graphic next to new items. Using this component, you don't have to remember to change the graphic when the item isn't so new anymore. Another common use for this type of component is to automatically remove time-sensitive material. For example, if you announce a club meeting or show a link to enter a contest, you can have that message or link disappear after it is no longer valid.

You can also add a substitution component that writes the author's name, the page's URL, or other information that may change. You also can find ways to echo form fields (confirmation fields).

Other WebBots handle form submission. The discussion form WebBot and the registration form WebBot, for example, allow you to create discussion forums or register users. You can select these WebBots by inserting a form and then selecting the form's properties (just right-click inside the form and select Form Properties from the resulting menu). Using the property page that appears, you can send the form results to a file, an email address, a custom script, or a WebBot. If you want to use a custom script, select Custom ISAPI, NSAPI, CGI, or ASP Script in the Send To Other choice of the property page. Then, click on the Options button, and fill in the Action field with the name of your script.

You can even find predefined forms when you create a new page. These templates create an appropriate form connected to a WebBot processor with no real effort on your part.

Field Validation

FrontPage also can replace traditional scripting when you validate fields. If you right-click on a form element (for example, a text box), you can select Form Field Validation from the pop-up menu. Choosing this option makes a validation dialog appear. This dialog's appearance varies depending on what type of element you select. Figure 9.8 shows the dialog for the text box element.

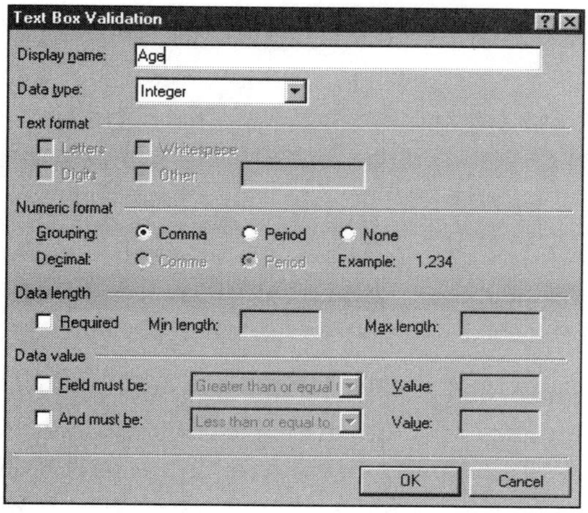

Figure 9.8
The validation dialog for a text box.

Most of the items in the Text Box Validation dialog remain gray until you select a data type. You can select Text for string input, Integer for whole number input, or Number to allow arbitrary numbers.

For a string, you can set the characters allowed and the minimum and maximum length of the string. For integers and numbers, you can select which character groups the number into thousands (usually a comma in the United States), and for regular numbers, which character is the decimal point. You also can specify a minimum and maximum length (just like for strings).

The final option in this dialog allows you to test the input against two values. Usually, you set these rules to define a range of numbers. For example, you might select Greater Than Or Equal To and set the value to 0 for the first rule. The second rule could read Less Than Or Equal To 100. Now, users must enter 0 to 100. You can set tests like this for strings, too, but testing strings is much less common because you usually don't restrict string input in this way.

Tip

Watch out when you're defining validation rules. FrontPage allows you to make up nonsense rules that can never be true. For example, if you set the first rule to read that the input must be equal to 100 and then set the second rule to test that the input is equal to 500, the validation will always fail. After all, the number can't equal 100 and 500 at the same time!

The validation form has an entry for Display Name. Error messages refer to this name when validation fails. Usually, this name matches the name of the text that appears next to the input field.

Scripting In FrontPage

Although FrontPage offers many alternatives to traditional scripting, sometimes you still need to write script. Doing so is easy because you can simply select the HTML view (the tabs at the bottom of the page editor allow you to select Normal, HTML, or Preview). Then, you can enter any type of HTML directly, including client-side or server-side script.

FrontPage offers little in the way of support for scripting. Entering your script in FrontPage isn't much different from using Notepad or some other text editor. Of course, the editor is more capable than Notepad, but it offers no special features to assist you while writing script.

Earlier versions of FrontPage included a Script Wizard. This rudimentary tool kept track of your event handling code. However, FrontPage 2000 doesn't include this wizard. If you install the Web Scripting option, however, you'll find a menu item under Tools | Macros called Microsoft Script Editor. It opens your page in the Microsoft Script Editor, which looks suspiciously like a limited version of Visual InterDev.

One improvement in FrontPage 2000 is that it is much less likely to destroy code you've written by hand (a common problem with earlier versions). In addition, you can select Page Options from the Tools menu and restrict the features you can use. On the Compatibility tab, you can select your target browser and Web server. You can even target Web TV! Depending on what you select, certain FrontPage menus become gray. Also, the code generated by FrontPage differs depending on your choices.

Does the lack of scripting support in FrontPage relegate it to the nonprogrammer? Not at all. Throughout this book, you've created script without using any tools at all. However, if you are writing a lot of script, you might want to consider Visual InterDev, which does have extensive support for scripting. Even then, you might want to use FrontPage to create pages visually and then edit them in Visual InterDev. This approach is tricky, but you can use the Open With selection (right-click on a file to find this menu item) to open a file using a different editor. Of course, if you don't mind opening the separate Microsoft Script Editor, you can simply use that instead.

Visual InterDev Fundamentals

Just as FrontPage resembles Microsoft Word, Visual InterDev resembles Visual C++ and the other members of Microsoft's Visual Studio development tools (see Figure 9.9). If you are familiar with these tools, you'll find InterDev immediately familiar. As you learned previously, FrontPage uses the Microsoft Script Editor, which is somewhat similar.

Visual InterDev's visual editing capabilities are similar to those found in FrontPage, although they do not mimic a word processor to the same degree as FrontPage. Like FrontPage, Visual InterDev's main editing window has three tabs beneath it: Design, Source, and Quick View. Although the names are somewhat different than FrontPage's names (Normal, HTML,

Figure 9.9
The Visual InterDev user interface.

and Preview), the tabs serve the exact same functions. In Design mode, you can see the page in the normal visual editing environment. Source shows you the raw HTML (although certain elements, such as design-time controls, still appear visually). The Quick View mode shows you how the page will look in the browser.

Creating A Web Site

When you create a Web site using Visual InterDev, you have a choice of selecting Master mode or Local mode. In Master mode, changes you make to pages update the project's Web server right away. When you open a file, you can open it for updates (that is, get a working copy) or open for read-only access. When you save the file, it is immediately updated on the project's Web server.

Using InterDev's IntelliSense Features

IntelliSense is the Microsoft feature that lets Visual InterDev offer completions for certain actions while you're entering script. For the most part, you don't need to know anything to use IntelliSense. When you type a function name or an object name followed by a period, InterDev simply offers suggestions. However, for times you want to invoke IntelliSense completely, press Ctrl+spacebar. This feature is useful when you're typing a word and want InterDev to complete it. It can also be handy in cases in which you lose the IntelliSense window as you edit and want to get it back.

Of course, the project's Web server does not have to be the Web server that the public accesses. You may well have the project's server pointing to a development server that you use to stage your Web site. When the site is ready, you can publish the completed work to the actual production server. On the other hand, if you are a brave soul, you can edit your production server live using Master mode (although I do not recommend it).

In Local mode, you can work in isolation on your own private copy of the Web site. This way, you can make changes without affecting a production server. You can also work without interfering with other developers. When you're ready, you can release your changes to the actual Web server. When you do, you may find that someone else has also changed some of the files you have changed. In this case, you are prompted to resolve the conflicts manually.

You can select the mode you want to use when you create a new project. You can also change the mode later if you like (by choosing Project | Web Project | Working Mode).

In addition to using Local and Master mode, you can also do some limited work on your Web site using Offline mode (again, you can set the mode by choosing Project | Web Project | Working Mode). This mode is useful when you want to work, for example, on a laptop when you have no connection to the server. However, you can't make many changes while in Offline mode. For example, you can't move files, release changed files, or get up-to-date copies of your files.

Using Outlines

Visual InterDev relies heavily on Outline views to help you work with your Web pages. The HTML Outline, for example, shows each HTML element in the current document (see Figure 9.10). The Script Outline (shown in Figure 9.11) shows objects and events on both the client and server, allowing you to add and modify the associated scripts. You'll read more about the Script Outline shortly.

Two other important views in Visual InterDev are the Project Explorer and the Toolbox. The Project Explorer is just a view of the files in the current project. The Toolbox contains items that you can drag into the current page.

Choosing Modes

Visual InterDev allows you to work in Local mode or Master mode. As discussed earlier, while you're in Master mode, you make changes directly on the active Web server. When you save a file, the change is made immediately on the server. In Local mode, you make changes on a local copy of the file. You can elect when you want to update the server.

Which mode should you use? The answer depends on your exact circumstances. If you are working with a personal Web server on your own machine, you'll probably want to use Master mode. On the other hand, if you work against a live Web server and have multiple developers, Local mode might be your best choice.

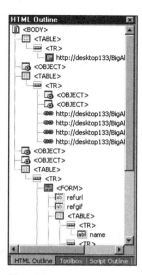

Figure 9.10
The HTML Outline view.

Figure 9.11
The Script Outline view.

By default, the Toolbox has several buttons: HTML, Server Objects, Design-Time Controls, ActiveX Controls, and General. However, you can add more tabs and organize items on the Toolbox as you see fit.

Scripting In InterDev

InterDev has extensive support for scripting. The Script Outline view shows a tree view of all the objects and events in your page. The Script Outline works only when you view your page in Source mode (use the Source tab at the bottom of the editor).

If you want to add or edit code for a particular event, you simply locate it in the Script Outline view. If the event name appears in bold, that event already has a handler. In any

---

Customizing InterDev's Toolbox

Visual InterDev's Toolbox is highly customizable. You can do three distinct things to make the Toolbox work for you:

- Right-click on the Toolbox and select Add Tab to add new tabs. These new tabs can group any items you frequently use.

- Right-click on the Toolbox and select Customize Toolbox to add new ActiveX or design-time controls. By default, the Toolbox does not show every possible ActiveX and design-time control.

- Select an area of a Web page (text, HTML, script, graphics, and so on), and drag it into the Toolbox to create an item that you can drag back into another Web page—almost like a multientry clipboard. Right-click on the item to rename it to something meaningful (or delete it if you decide you don't want it anymore).

---

case, double-clicking on the event name takes you to event handler code, even if InterDev has to write the code for you.

When you are entering the code into the Source view, you'll find that InterDev provides quite a few helpful features. In addition to coloring the parts of your script intelligently, InterDev also suggests what you can type next, when appropriate. For example, if you type an object name and a period, a list of all the possible completions appears. When you enter a function name, you also get pop-up help that shows you the arguments expected. When in doubt, you can force InterDev to suggest a completion to what you are typing by pressing Ctrl+spacebar.

Design-Time Controls

InterDev uses design-time controls to make scripting easier. These ActiveX controls exist while InterDev is running, not on the server or the browser. The idea is that these controls give you, the developer, a handy user interface to control certain parts of your Web page.

As an example of a design-time control, consider adding a fade-in effect to a Web page. Adding such an effect is easy enough to accomplish if you place a special **<META>** tag in the header of the document. Modern browsers interpret this special tag and cause the page to appear using a special effect. For example, consider this line:

```
<META HTTP-EQUIV="Page-Enter"
CONTENT="revealTrans(Duration=1.000,Transition=10)">
```

This will cause the browser to reveal the page using a checkerboard pattern over the span of one second. Creating this effect isn't very hard, but you do have to remember the syntax and that the checkerboard transition is number 10, as opposed to a random dissolve, for example, which is number 12.

Visual InterDev provides a design-time control called a *Page Transition Control*. When you create your page, it is just a simple rectangle that appears in the Design or Source view. If you open the properties for the control (by right-clicking and selecting Properties), you'll see a dialog like the one shown earlier in Figure 9.3. Using this dialog, you can select the duration and the effect for both the page entry and the page exit. In addition, you can even preview the effect.

So, what does this control do? It simply writes the correct **<META>** tag into your Web page when you save. It also saves enough information (in the form of HTML comments) so that InterDev can re-create the design-time control the next time you open the page for editing. Unlike a regular ActiveX control, a design-time control usually doesn't depend on any special features in the browser or on the server. It simply exists to provide a nice user inter-face during development.

If you want to know what a design-time control will insert into your page, you can right-click on it. The context menu shows Always View As Text, Show Run-Time Text, and

Convert To Run-Time Text. These options allow you to selectively view the text that the control will generate. If you convert the control to text, it ceases being a design-time control and behaves like any other text you put in the page.

Of course, some design-time controls might take advantage of particular browser or server features. If the control generates ASP script, for example, then, of course, it will rely on having a server that can interpret that script. However, the control itself runs only while InterDev is running. If the control doesn't create special HTML or script, then it is not dependent on any runtime resources.

Scripting Object Model

You'll notice that most of the design-time controls in the Toolbox mimic HTML form fields. These controls are useful in conjunction with the InterDev scripting object model. When you insert one of these controls on a page for the first time, InterDev prompts you to add the scripting object model to your page.

What does the scripting object model do? Essentially, it turns your entire Web page into a form that submits back to itself. Special scripts, supplied by Visual InterDev, allow you to write code on the server that behaves more like client-side script. You add this script by using the Script Outline. This script, like the client-side script, can react to buttons being clicked or text fields changing. However, your code resides on the server instead of the client.

Another way you can use these scripting object model forms is to include the Form Manager design-time control. This control adds code to your page to create a state machine. Microsoft calls the states of the form *modes*.

For example, suppose you have a form that collects a user's name. If the name field is empty, you can gray out the Submit button. If the name field is not empty, the Submit button

---

Selecting A Control

In previous chapters, you read about the differences between server-side controls and client-side controls. Advanced tools like Visual InterDev and FrontPage add a third type of control: the design-time control.

Of course, client-side controls reside in the Web browser (and therefore require special support in the browser). Server-side controls are executed as part of the server and are not dependent on the browser. Design-time controls, on the other hand, act as part of your development environment. They provide a useful interface for you, the developer. When you save your file, the design-time control writes normal HTML or script to your file. It also writes enough special HTML comments that the development environment can re-create the control when you load the file again.

In general, then, a design-time control does not require special support on the server or the client. Of course, a design-time control might write script that requires some special support, but technically, the control doesn't require special support; the generated script does.

What can you do with design-time controls? You can use design-time controls to set page transition effects, manage forms, and handle other mundane HTML coding tasks.

---

becomes active. This would be easy to do with a client-side script, of course. However, you could also use InterDev's scripting object model. The idea is to define two modes—or states—that the form can be in at any given time. The first state, of course, is when no entry appears in the name field. The other state, just as obviously, is when a name does appear in the name field.

When you insert the FormManager control into your Web page, you can access its Properties page (see Figure 9.12). This page has two tabs. On the first tab, Form Mode, you can define the modes and what actions occur when the mode becomes active. You can also select the default mode for the form.

On the second tab, Action (see Figure 9.13), you can set the rules that govern the transition from one mode to another. You can also define actions that occur when a transition occurs.

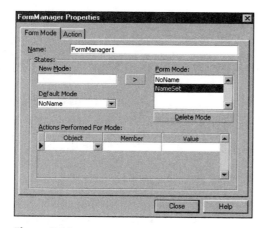

Figure 9.12
The FormManager's Properties page.

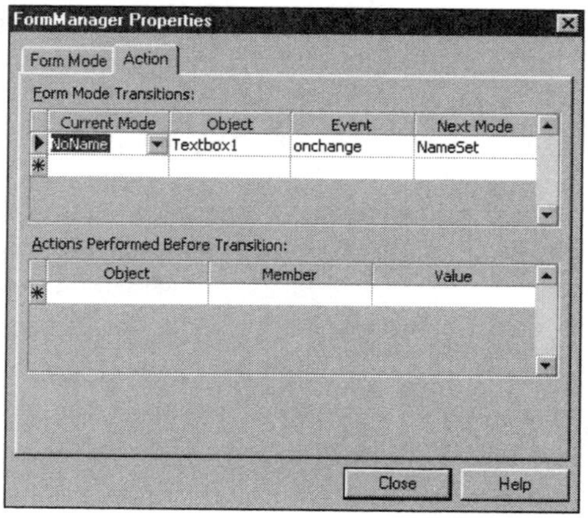

Figure 9.13
The FormManager's Action tab.

Chapter 10
Ideas To Use And Reuse

Al Williams

W hen I was a kid, few things were cooler than a Swiss army knife. It is a classic case of the sum of the parts being greater than the whole. After all, a pair of scissors is no big deal. Who covets a screwdriver or a pair of tweezers? No one cares about any of those things. On the other hand, if you put them all together in a knife, that's something to see!

Did Charles Elsener (the cutler who originally made the Swiss army knives) make better screwdrivers than anyone else? Nope. The power to the Swiss army knife is that, if you're going to carry a knife anyway, it might just as well have a corkscrew, a bottle opener, a magnifying glass, and whatever else you need.

You can think of this knife as a form of reuse—making one tool do the work of many. In software, reuse is the art of fitting a piece of software you already have into a new job. You can usually force just about any tool into a different service. I've hammered nails with the butt of a screwdriver and used a hammer to hold down something I'm soldering. But, the elegance to a Swiss army knife is that it does multiple things *well*.

When you develop software, a certain art is involved in designing components that are easy to reuse. You might be able to force any piece of script to do double duty, but a little forethought will make the process smoother and less painful.

Basics Of Design

Software design can take a lifetime of study. However, you can apply a few simple principles to make developing script for reuse easier. If you are an experienced software developer, you may not even realize you already apply some of these techniques. If you are new to software development, you'll have to apply them until they become habit for you.

Paradoxically, perhaps the most powerful thing you can do is also one of the easiest: plan. Planning your project before you dive into it takes a lot of discipline, but it pays big dividends.

Even simple planning can make a big difference. Take a minute to sketch out the various parts of your project. Try to identify which parts will occur on the server and which parts will be on the client. The more specific you get about the different parts, the more problems you'll find in this planning stage. The more problems you identify now, the fewer changes you'll have to make later.

Simple Object Orientation

Throughout this book, you've seen and used objects. Modern design practice centers around object-oriented principles, so object-oriented design is useful to developers for several important reasons. From a Web scripting point of view, the two main advantages are encapsulation and reuse.

Encapsulation refers to how objects hide their implementation from programs that use the objects. Suppose you create a phone book object that uses a flat file to store its data. It might be appropriate for a small number of entries. However, if the number of entries increases, a flat file does not perform well.

Consider this: The programs that use the phone book object know the object only through its properties, methods, and events. The object's user does not know exactly how the object works. Therefore, the object's designer is free to change any internal operations as long as the changes don't affect the properties, methods, and events. That is encapsulation in a nutshell.

If the phone book changes to use, for example, an Oracle database, it doesn't affect any existing code unless the new object doesn't expose the same properties, methods, and events.

The second major advantage to using objects is the ease of reuse. If you don't have objects, you have to decide what parts of a program you need to cut and paste from project to project. You might also need to duplicate global variables. If you do have an object, all the code for the object is in one place. You can create an instance of the object or even multiple instances in the same program with no fear of conflict.

Of course, object orientation is no panacea. You can write really bad script using whatever method you like. It is possible to define an object so that its internal structure is visible. You can rely on global variables and lose most of the advantage of object orientation as well.

A common misconception is that you need special tools to use object-oriented program-ming techniques. This is not true. You can use object-oriented techniques in virtually any language. Discipline is required to group your code into logical pseudo objects. You also have to limit access to these objects through defined variables and functions. If you follow these precepts, you can use any language to implement objects.

Of course, if you do have special tools, you don't need as much discipline because the tool will help you realize your object-oriented goals. Two major techniques will let you bring a measure of object orientation to Web programming: Java objects and scriptlets.

Creating JavaScript Objects

JavaScript (and JScript, Microsoft's JavaScript clone) is an object-based language that pro-vides several built-in objects. It is no surprise that JavaScript also makes it easy to create your own objects.

The simplest method of creating an object is to declare it using the **Object** object. The statement

```
var myobj = new Object();
```

declares an object variable, but one of little use. Useful objects are collections of methods and properties. The object **myobj** is empty; that is, it has no properties or methods. You can easily add properties to **myobj** by assigning a new property a value, as shown here:

```
myobj.name = "John";
```

Now, **myobj** has a **name** property. You add methods in the same manner:

```
// define the method
function showname() {
   document.write(this.name);
}

// assign the method to the object
myobj.show = showname;
myobj.name = "John";
// now invoke the method
myobj.show();
```

Although creating objects this way is easy, this method poses a slight problem. You must repeat the steps for every object you want to use. So, if you want 10 objects just like **myobj**, you need to repeat the same steps 10 times to initialize each new object. Wouldn't it be easier to define one object and declare objects that would automatically have all properties and methods? You bet, and you can do just that by using a constructor.

Using Constructors To Define Objects

A *constructor* is a function that defines an object's properties and methods and creates and initializes a new object. Constructor functions can take arguments like any other function but do not return a value (technically they can, but they rarely need to). The following statements define a **Loan** object with three properties:

```
function Loan() {
    this.principal = 0;
    this.rate = 0;
    this.periods = 0;
}
```

The keyword **this** is used in the constructor function to refer to the object. It distinguishes constructor functions from ordinary functions.

In the statement

```
var newloan = new Loan();
```

the **newloan** properties are accessed just like properties of built-in objects, as shown here:

```
newloan.principal = 12000.00;
newloan.rate = .18;
newloan.periods = 12;
```

You add methods to the object by defining the necessary functions and then assigning them to object properties. The following example defines a function to calculate a loan payment. The object definition is shown again, but now it includes the method definition:

```
function payment() {
    return this.rate/this.periods * this.principal;
}

function Loan() {
    this.principal = 0;
    this.rate = 0;
    this.periods = 0;
    this.pmt = payment;
}
```

Now that the **Loan** object has a method, you can put it to work like this:

```
var newloan = new Loan();
var loanpmt;
```

```
newloan.principal = 12000.00;
newloan.rate = .18;
newloan.periods = 12;
loanpmt = newloan.pmt();
```

Remember, constructor functions can take arguments that initialize the object's properties. The following is a modification of the **Loan** object constructor that accepts arguments:

```
function Loan(princ, rate, pds) {
   this.principal = princ;
   this.rate = rate;
   this.periods = pds;
   this.pmt = this.rate/this.periods * this.principal;
}


var newloan = new Loan(12000.00, .18, 12);
```

Using The **prototype** Object

Another way of specifying methods and properties is to use the **prototype** object. The **prototype** object defines all the properties and methods for an object, and they become properties and methods of all objects of that type. Prototype properties are shared among all the objects of that type and can be read. However, setting an object property creates a copy of the property for that particular object. The sharing of prototype properties is memory efficient because each object doesn't require a copy.

The following is an example of using **prototype**:

```
// constructor function
function Loan() {
   this.principal = 0;
   this.rate = 0;
   this.periods = 0;
}

// calculate payment function
function payment() {
   return this.rate/this.periods * this.principal;
}

// assign the payment function as a method
Loan.prototype.pmt = payment;

// declare a Loan object
var newloan = new Loan();
var loanpmt;
```

```
newloan.principal = 12000.00;
newloan.rate = .18;
newloan.periods = 12;

loanpmt = newloan.pmt();
```

The next statement adds a default property:

```
Loan.prototype.type = "Auto";
```

You also can override a default property by assigning it a new value, like this:

```
newloan.type = "RV";
```

Scriptlets

A *scriptlet* is an HTML page that contains script that has features normally associated with controls. Scriptlets can expose properties, methods, and events and are used much like ActiveX controls. In addition, they have full access to the DHTML object model. Internet Explorer 4 supports scriptlets, as do Visual Basic and the Active Desktop. Some versions of Netscape Navigator, however, do not support scriptlets.

Scriptlets are easier to write and maintain than controls written in languages such as C, C++, and Java. One of the disadvantages of client-side script is the fact that your script code is visible in the browser. This is not the case with scriptlets. So, if you want to provide rudimentary security to protect your intellectual property, or if you prefer that your users not see your code for some other reason, you might want to use a scriptlet instead of a more conventional script.

Using Scriptlets

You can embed scriptlets into HTML documents by using the **<OBJECT>** tag. Unlike ActiveX controls, scriptlets do not use the **CLSID** attribute. Instead, they are simply assigned an identifier with the **ID** attribute. A special MIME type is also specified using the **TYPE** attribute to inform Internet Explorer that the object is a scriptlet. The **DATA** attribute is used to specify the URL for the page containing the scriptlet's definition.

The following **<OBJECT>** tag inserts a scriptlet contained in the document myscriptlet.htm (which is included on the CD that accompanies this book). The scriptlet used in the example in this section outputs text and uses the identifier **Label1**:

```
<OBJECT ID="Label1"
    TYPE="text/x-scriptlet"
    DATA="myscriptlet.htm">
```

```
     HEIGHT=50 WIDTH=150
</OBJECT>
```

Notice that the object's dimensions are specified using the **HEIGHT** and **WIDTH** attributes. The browser limits a scriptlet's display area to this size. You also can insert a scriptlet this way:

```
<OBJECT ID="Label1" TYPE="text/x-scriptlet" HEIGHT=50 WIDTH=150>
     <PARAM NAME="url" VALUE="myscriptlet.htm">
</OBJECT>
```

Here, the scriptlet's file name appears in a **<PARAM>** tag instead of being part of the **<OBJECT>** tag.

Writing A Scriptlet

Writing a scriptlet is straightforward. You declare the scriptlet by using one of two methods. The first method uses the **public_description** object, which is a JavaScript object providing access to the object's properties and methods defined by its constructor function. The other method uses default interface descriptions. With this method, you must declare the properties and methods that are being exposed by using the prefix **public_**. For example, to declare a public property called **Caption**, you use the following syntax:

```
Dim public_Caption
```

The **public_description** object lets you explicitly declare properties and methods that are exposed and provides one area in the scriptlet where the public interface is declared. Anything declared outside the public description is not accessible outside the scriptlet. This method is used in the following scriptlet example, which contains the declaration for the **Label** scriptlet:

```
<HTML>
<HEAD>
<TITLE> The Label Scriptlet</TITLE>
</HEAD>
<BODY>
<SCRIPT LANGUAGE="JavaScript">

// Declaration
var public_description = new Label();
</SCRIPT>

</BODY>
</HTML>
```

Adding Properties And Methods

The **Label** scriptlet is a simple example that outputs text and provides properties to set the foreground and background colors as well as the text itself. After you declare the scriptlet, you must define the interface for any properties that are exposed to scripting.

You set and retrieve property values with expressions and functions. The code uses the **this** keyword to reference the property. The following example uses a simple expression to set the background color:

```
function Label() {
    this.bgColor = window.document.bgColor;
}
```

Most of the time, you'll use functions to set and get property values. Functions to set property values have the prefix put_, and functions that return property values have the prefix get_. Remember, you don't use the prefixes when referencing the properties in the container (Internet Explorer, in this case). The following statements define the Label scriptlet's properties:

```
function Label() {
    this.put_bgColor = setbgColor;
    this.get_bgColor = getbgColor;
    this.put_fgColor = setfgColor;
    this.get_fgColor = getbgColor;
    this.put_Caption = setCaption;
    this.get_Caption = getCaption;
}
```

Each property in this example has two functions because programs can read and write the property values. However, you can make a property read-only by including only a function with the **get_** prefix. The properties are assigned functions that implement the setting and returning of values. The following code contains the function definitions:

```
function setbgColor(bgcol) {
    window.document.bgColor = bgcol;
    mbgCol = window.document.bgColor;
}

function getbgColor() {
    return mbgCol;
}

function setfgColor(fgcol) {
    window.document.fgColor = fgcol;
    mfgCol = window.document.fgColor;
}
```

```
function getfgColor() {
    return mfgCol;
}

function setCaption(cap) {
    theLbl.innerText = cap;
    mlblCap = theLbl.innerText;
}

function getCaption() {
    return mlblCap;
}
```

The variables **mbgCol**, **mfgCol**, and **mlblCap** are private variables that store the property values. They are declared in script outside the public description. You can find the complete scriptlet in Listing 10.1 at the end of this section if you would like to see where these variables first appear.

The scriptlet now has properties to set and return the background and foreground colors and the text that the scriptlet will display. Now, it's time to add a method. To expose a method called **about** to the rest of the world, you enter the following:

```
this.about = about;
```

The **about** method uses an **alert** box to provide version information. The **about** function implements the method, as you can see here:

```
function about() {
    alert ("My Scriptlet v1.0");
}
```

Adding Events
Scriptlets can notify the container about two kinds of events: standard DHTML events and custom events. Standard DHTML events include the following:

♦ **onclick**

♦ **ondblclick**

♦ **onkeydown**

♦ **onkeypress**

♦ **onkeyup**

♦ **onmousedown**

♦ **onmousemove**

♦ **onmouseup**

The scriptlet notifies the container of a standard event using the event object. DHTML has an event model that "bubbles" events up the object hierarchy. (Event bubbling is covered in Chapter 7.) The following script bubbles an event when the user clicks on the label's caption:

```
<SCRIPT LANGUAGE="JavaScript" FOR="theLbl" EVENT="onclick">
    window.external.bubbleEvent();
</SCRIPT>
```

You use the **raiseEvent** method to notify the container of a nonstandard event. The following is a modification of the **setbgColor** function that raises an event when the background color is changed:

```
function setbgColor(bgcol) {
    window.document.bgColor = bgcol;
    mbgCol = window.document.bgColor;
    window.external.raiseEvent("event_onsetbgColor",window.document);
}
```

You name the event by using the prefix **event_**. The container can respond to the **onsetbgColor** event much like responding to standard events.

Adding A Context Menu

Context menus, which appear when the user clicks the right mouse button over the scriptlet, are used to add functionality. You can easily add them by using the **window** object's **setContextMenu** method. To create a context menu, first define the menu as a series of array elements. Each menu item consists of two array elements: one for the menu selection and one for the function that is called when the item is selected.

The following statements add a context menu to the **Label** scriptlet. The menu has only one selection that displays the **about** box:

```
var menuItem = new Array(1);
menuItem[0] = "&About";
menuItem[1] = "about";
window.external.setContextMenu(menuItem);
```

The ampersand (&) is used to specify a hot key for the menu item (in this case, "a" will be the hot key). When the menu item is selected, the **about** function is called to display the **about** box. This is the same function that the **about** method uses.

The **Label** Scriptlet

Up to this point, you have seen the **Label** scriptlet in small pieces. Now, consider it as one entity. Listing 10.1 contains the complete code for the **Label** scriptlet. Notice the use of the **<SPAN>** tag to display the text. You'll also find a page that uses the scriptlet in Listing 10.2.

Listing 10.1   The Label scriptlet.

```
<HTML>
<HEAD>
<TITLE>The Label scriptlet</TITLE>
</HEAD>
<BODY onload="init()">

<SCRIPT LANGUAGE="JavaScript">
function init() {
    theLbl.innerText = mlblCap;
    window.document.fgColor = "yellow";
    window.document.bgColor = "blue";

    // The context menu
    var menuItem = new Array(1);
    menuItem[0] = "&About";
    menuItem[1] = "about";
    window.external.setContextMenu(menuItem);
}
</SCRIPT>

<SCRIPT LANGUAGE="JavaScript" FOR="theLbl" EVENT="onclick">
// Process a standard event
    window.external.bubbleEvent();
</SCRIPT>

<SCRIPT LANGUAGE="JavaScript">

// Declaration
var public_description = new Label();

var mbgCol = window.document.bgColor;
var mfgCol = window.document.fgColor;
var mlblCap = "I'm a scriptlet!";

// Definition
function Label() {
    this.put_bgColor = setbgColor;
    this.get_bgColor = getbgColor;
    this.put_fgColor = setfgColor;
    this.get_fgColor = getfgColor;
    this.put_Caption = setCaption;
    this.get_Caption = getCaption;
    this.about = about;
}
```

```
// Implementation
function setbgColor(bgcol) {
    window.document.bgColor = bgcol;
    mbgCol = window.document.bgColor;
    window.external.raiseEvent("event_onsetbgColor",window.document);
}

function getbgColor() {
    return mbgCol;
}

function setfgColor(fgcol) {
    window.document.fgColor = fgcol;
    mfgCol = window.document.fgColor;
}

function getfgColor() {
    return mfgCol;
}

function setCaption(cap) {
    theLbl.innerText = cap;
    mlblCap = theLbl.innerText;
}

function getCaption() {
    return mlblCap;
}

function about() {
    alert ("My Scriptlet v1.0");
}

</SCRIPT>

<SPAN ID="theLbl"></SPAN>

</BODY>
</HTML>
```

Listing 10.2   The Label scriptlet container.

```
<HTML>
<HEAD>
<TITLE>The Label scriptlet container</TITLE>
<SCRIPT LANGUAGE="JavaScript">
<!--
```

```
function SetbgColor() {
    Label1.bgColor = "red";
}
// -->
</SCRIPT>
<SCRIPT LANGUAGE="JavaScript" FOR="Label1" EVENT="onclick">
    SetbgColor();
</SCRIPT>

<SCRIPT LANGUAGE="JavaScript"
    FOR="Label1" EVENT="onscriptletevent(name)">
    alert ("Event: " + name + " occurred");
</SCRIPT>

</HEAD>
<BODY>

<OBJECT ID="Label1"
          HEIGHT=50 WIDTH=150
          TYPE="text/x-scriptlet"
          DATA="8-11.htm">
</OBJECT>

</BODY>
</HTML>
```

Setting A Session Debug Flag

One area in which ASP files are badly deficient is debugging. If you have your server set up correctly, you can use server-side debugging. However, most practical servers don't have the correct setup for this type of debugging (because of efficiency and security concerns). I usually resort to writing debugging information in the script using **<%=** or **response.write**. The problem is that the minute you remove the debugging code, you find that you need it again.

A better idea is to set a session variable (perhaps named **Debug**) to control the debugging output. For example, you can use the following:

```
<% For x=0 To 10 %>
<% If Session("Debug")=True Then %>
    <BR>Debug: Current x= <%= x %>
<% End If %>
    . . .
```

Then, you can use any of a variety of methods to set the session variable. I like to use a special file, debug.asp (shown in Listing 10.3), to do the job. Once set, your debugging code is on for your session. Other users don't see it, and the flag resets when your session expires (or when you abandon the session).

Listing 10.3   The debug.asp file.

```
<HTML>
<HEAD>
<TITLE>For internal use only</TITLE>
</HEAD>
<BODY>
<% If Session("Debug")=True Then
        Session("Debug")=False
     Else
        Session("Debug")=True
     End If  %>
Debugging is
<% If Session("Debug")=True Then %>
 On
<% Else %>
 Off
<% End If %>
</BODY>
</HTML>
```

Working With Session Or Application Arrays

Although the **Session** and **Application** objects look like ordinary collections, they are not. For example, you can't enumerate the **Session** variables using **ForEach**. Therefore, it's often handy to store an array in the object. Storing an array in either the **Session** or **Application** object should be simple because these objects contain **Variant** data, right? Wrong.

Look at the code in Listing 10.4. If you execute this code, you'll find that you can read the original data from the array but that you can't alter it. The trick is to copy the session variable array to a local variant, modify it, and then replace the array in the session variable (see Listing 10.5). Although this approach is ugly, it works.

Listing 10.4   An example of a bad array.

```
<HTML>
<HEAD>
<TITLE>Bad Array Code</TITLE>
</HEAD>
<BODY>
<% ' Initialize
   Dim ary(10)
   For i = 0 to 10
     ary(i)=i
```

```
      Next
      Session("Array")=ary
 ' Dump it out to prove it is there
      For i=0 to 10 %>
        <%=Session("Array")(i) %><BR>
      <% Next

  ' Change it
      For i=0 to 10
         Session("Array")(i)=-i
      Next %>
Making Array Negative<BR>

<% ' Dump it again?
      For i=0 to 10 %>
        <%=Session("Array")(i) %><BR>
      <% Next %>

</BODY>
</HTML>
```

Listing 10.5   The proper use of an array.

```
<HTML>
<HEAD>
<TITLE>Good Array Code</TITLE>
</HEAD>
<BODY>
<% ' Initialize
      Dim ary(10)
      For i = 0 to 10
         ary(i)=i
      Next
      Session("Array")=ary
 ' Dump it out to prove it is there
      For i=0 to 10 %>
        <%=Session("Array")(i) %><BR>
      <% Next

 ' Change it
      localary=Session("Array")
      For i=0 to 10
         localary(i)=-i
      Next
      Session("Array")=localary   ' replace old array %>
Making Array Negative<BR>
```

```
<% ' Dump it again?
   For i=0 to 10 %>
     <%=Session("Array")(i) %><BR>
   <% Next %>

</BODY>
</HTML>
```

Of course, you can see the real value to this trick when the array is used in multiple ASP files or is set during one pass and used in another. I can think of no real reason to store the array in the **Session** object other than to illustrate the quirk.

Displaying A Form And Processing Submissions With One File

One thing I never liked about traditional CGI programming is that you need to store forms in one place (an HTML file) and process the data for those forms in another place (typically, a Perl script). You have plenty of opportunities to get the files out of sync with one another.

However, ASP offers a better solution. You can easily detect whether form data is present by examining **Request("Content_Length")**. Even if the form data is blank, the length will still be nonzero because the request will contain the names of the form fields.

Using this bit of information, you can easily put your forms and the related processing in one place (see Listing 10.6). If **Request("Content_Length")** is zero, display the form. Make the form submit its data to the same ASP file. Then, when the content length is not zero, process the data.

Listing 10.6   A self-submitting form.

```
<HTML>
<HEAD>
<TITLE>Form Demo</TITLE>
</HEAD>
<BODY>
<% If Request("Content_Length")=0 Then ' show form %>
<FORM ACTION="ASP3.ASP" METHOD=POST>
Your Name: <INPUT NAME="Name"><BR>
<INPUT TYPE=SUBMIT>
</FORM>

<% Else  ' Process Data %>

Thank you <%= Request("Name") %>.
```

```
<% End If %>
</BODY>
</HTML>
```

At times, using separate form files can be an advantage. Perhaps you have multiple, related forms that submit to the same script, or you might have forms in different languages. On the other hand, you could easily select the correct form on the basis of a query string or session variable and still keep everything in one file.

Using ActiveX To Learn The Screen Size

You can use client-side controls to pass data to your ASP script. For example, wouldn't it be nice to know the exact size of the user's screen in your ASP file? You can do it with an ActiveX control (see Listings 10.7 and 10.8). This trick uses an ActiveX control that you can find on the CD-ROM. Of course, it requires an ActiveX-capable browser to work because it uses a client-side control.

The control works like this: The size.htm file (shown in Listing 10.7) loads an ActiveX control that learns the size of the screen. It also contains an invisible form. When the page loads, some client-side VBScript takes over, stores the screen size in the invisible fields of the form, and submits the form to size.asp (shown in Listing 10.8). Then, the ASP file can read the screen size directly from the **Request** object (just as it can read any form data).

Listing 10.7   Learning the screen size (part 1).

```
<HTML>
<HEAD>
<SCRIPT LANGUAGE="VBScript">
<!--
Sub window_onLoad()
  DataForm.ScrWidth.Value= ScreenMachine.ScreenWidth
  DataForm.ScrHeight.Value=ScreenMachine.ScreenHeight
  DataForm.Submit
end sub
-->
</SCRIPT>
<TITLE>Please wait!</TITLE>
</HEAD>
<BODY>
<H1>Sensing display... please wait</H1>
    <OBJECT ID="ScreenMachine" WIDTH=105 HEIGHT=83
     CLASSID="CLSID:8528EC66-ACC9-11D0-BC98-00400526DBEA"
     CODEBASE="AWC.CAB#version=1,0,0,0">
        <PARAM NAME="_ExtentX" VALUE="2778">
        <PARAM NAME="_ExtentY" VALUE="2170">
    </OBJECT>
```

```
    <FORM ACTION="SIZE.ASP" METHOD="POST" NAME="DataForm">
        <INPUT TYPE=HIDDEN NAME="SCRWIDTH">
        <INPUT TYPE=HIDDEN NAME="SCRHEIGHT">
    </FORM>

</BODY>
</HTML>
```

Listing 10.8   Learning the screen size (part 2).
```
<HTML>
<HEAD>
<TITLE>Main Page</TITLE>
</HEAD>
<BODY>

Greetings!<P>
I see your screen is <%= request("SCRWIDTH") %> X
 <%= request("SCRHEIGHT") %><P>
</BODY>
</HTML>
```

Avoiding Global.asa

Usually, you should avoid placing code in the Global.asa file for two reasons. First, it's difficult to make the server reload the page. Second, because Global.asa doesn't generate HTML,
it's often difficult to see errors that occur.

Sometimes, you can't avoid Global.asa, but with some ingenuity, you can often find a better
answer. For example, suppose you want to set a hit counter to 500 every time your server
starts (or better, read the value from a database). Your first thought might be to initialize in
the **Application_OnStart** event in Global.asa, but you can write this code where you want
to update the hit count:

```
<% if IsEmpty(Application("Hits")) then Application("Hits")=500 %>
<% Application("Hits")=Application("Hits")+1 %>
<%= Application("Hits") %>
```

By testing for an empty variable, you move the initialization from Global.asa to a normal
file where you can see errors and make changes easily.

Creating Reusable Libraries

If you want to make routines that you can reuse, you can place them in a file and include
them using server-side includes (SSIs). For example, you might write the following:

```
<!--#include file="library.inc" -->
```

Don't forget, IIS processes only ASP, STM, and SHTML files for SSIs by default. You can't use them within a regular HTML file without custom settings on the server.

Another idea: Use the **SRC** attribute of the **<SCRIPT>** tag. For example, suppose you have a file named LIB.JS containing these lines:

```
function test_lib() {
  alert("Library code!");
}
```

Then, you could use this file as a library like this:

```
<SCRIPT SRC=LIB.JS>
</SCRIPT>

<SCRIPT>
test_lib();
</SCRIPT>
```

Using Virtual Tags

If you're worried about compatibility with different browsers, you might consider using different tags based on information from the browser capability object (**MSWC.BrowserType**).

For example, consider tables, which some older browsers don't support. Listing 10.9 shows a table using virtual tags. The script creates an **MSWC.BrowserType** object. If the object indicates that the browser supports tables, the script sets up variables named **Table**, **EndTable**, **TR**, **EndTR**, **TD**, and **EndTD**. These variables contain the appropriate HTML tags for tables. If the browser doesn't support tables, the script still sets these variables, but, in this case, it uses characters designed to somewhat mimic the look of a table (see Figure 10.1). Of course, this is just one possible scheme; you could change the look to suit your needs.

Listing 10.9   Virtual tags for tables.

```
<HTML>
<HEAD>
<TITLE>Table Demo</TITLE>
</HEAD>
<BODY>
<% Set bc=Server.CreateObject("MSWC.BrowserType")
   If bc.Tables=True Then
       Table="<TABLE BORDER=1>"
       EndTable="</TABLE>"
       TR="<TR>"
       EndTR="</TR>"
       TD="<TD>"
       EndTD="</TD>"
```

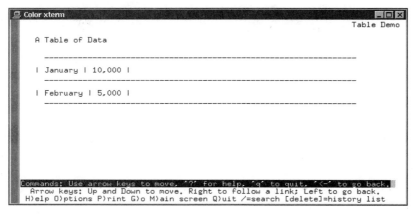

Figure 10.1
A table in a browser that doesn't support tables.

```
    Else
        Table="<BR>"
        EndTable="<BR><HR>"
        TR="<HR>| "
        EndTR=""
        EndTD=" | "
        TD=""
    End If %>


A Table of Data<BR>
<%=TABLE%>
<%=TR%><%=TD%>January<%=EndTD%> <%=TD%>10,000<%=EndTD%> <%=EndTR%>
<%=TR%><%=TD%>February<%=EndTD%> <%=TD%>5,000<%=EndTD%> <%=EndTR%>
<%=EndTABLE%>

</BODY>
</HTML>
```

When you're constructing the table, replace each occurrence of **<TABLE>** with **<%=TABLE%>** and each occurrence of **</TABLE>** with **<%=EndTABLE%>**. Make similar changes for **<TD>** and **<TR>** tags. Now, the table appears formatted properly for all browsers. If you want to test the layout and your browser supports tables, you can temporarily reverse the sense of the **If** statement.

Creating Scripting Buttons On The Server

What do you do when you want to attach server-side script to a button? This procedure isn't trivial because the button is on the client computer. If the buttons are simple push buttons, the process is easy. You can simply make each button a Submit button for a form and use the script to determine which button the user pushed, as in Listing 10.10.

Listing 10.10   Server-processed buttons.

```
<HTML>
<HEAD>
<TITLE>Button Demo</TITLE>
</HEAD>
<BODY>
<% if Request("Content_Length")=0 then %>
   <FORM ACTION=ASP5.ASP METHOD=POST>
   <INPUT TYPE=SUBMIT NAME="Lion" VALUE="Lion">
   <INPUT TYPE=SUBMIT NAME="Tiger" VALUE="Tiger">
   <INPUT TYPE=SUBMIT NAME="Bear" VALUE="Bear">
   </FORM>
<% else %>
   <%  Lion=(request("Lion")="Lion")
       Tiger=(request("Tiger")="Tiger")
       Bear=(request("Bear")="Bear") %>

<% if Lion then %>
  Lion!
<% end if %>

<% if Tiger then %>
  Tiger!
<% end if %>

<% if Bear then %>
  Bear!
<% end if %>

Oh My!

<% end if %>

</BODY>
</HTML>
```

That approach is fine, but what happens if you want something fancier, like radio buttons? A little client-side script can help out in this case (see Listing 10.11). You can simply handle the button's **onClick** event with a small piece of code that submits the form to the server (the **Go** routine in this example). With a little ingenuity, you can adapt this technique to many different types of form controls.

Listing 10.11   Server-processed radio buttons.

```
<HTML>
<HEAD>
<TITLE>Button Demo</TITLE>
```

```
</HEAD>
<BODY>
<% if Request("Content_Length")=0 then %>

   <FORM NAME=aForm ACTION=ASP6.ASP METHOD=POST>
   Lion <INPUT TYPE=RADIO onClick=Go Language="VBScript" NAME="Animal"
   VALUE="Lion">
   Tiger <INPUT TYPE=RADIO onClick=Go Language="VBScript" NAME="Animal"
   VALUE="Tiger">
   Bear <INPUT TYPE=RADIO onClick=Go Language="VBScript" NAME="Animal"
   VALUE="Bear">
   </FORM>
<SCRIPT LANGUAGE=VBScript>
<!--
   Sub Go
   Document.aForm.Submit
   End Sub
-->
</SCRIPT>
<% else %>

<%= Request("Animal") %>

Oh My!

<% end if %>

</BODY>
</HTML>
```

This technique, by the way, is similar to how the design-time controls provided by Visual InterDev work. You can read more about Visual InterDev in Chapter 9.

Using An Image As A Histogram

The whole often is greater than the sum of the parts. This statement is certainly true when you mix the power of script with HTML. Suppose that you want to display some percentages graphically. You might think about using script to create a GIF file on the fly or perhaps using an ActiveX object, but why not use HTML's built-in capability to scale graphics?

Look at Figure 10.2. The code to draw these graphs is surprisingly simple; it's shown in Listing 10.12. The script calculates the percentage of each value and uses it to stretch the width of a five-pixel-wide GIF file (hist.gif). Of course, if you want vertical bars, you could stretch the height instead.

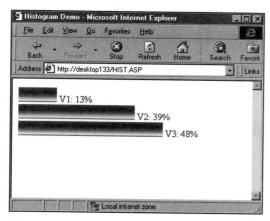

Figure 10.2
An ASP-generated histogram.

Listing 10.12   Histograms.

```
<HTML>
<HEAD>
<TITLE>Histogram Demo</TITLE>
</HEAD>
<BODY>
<% if Request("Content_Length")=0 then %>

    <FORM NAME=aForm ACTION=ASP7.ASP METHOD=POST>
Input three numbers:<BR>
    <INPUT NAME=V1><BR>
    <INPUT NAME=V2><BR>
    <INPUT NAME=V3><BR>
    <INPUT TYPE=SUBMIT>
    </FORM>
<% else %>
    <% total=0+request("V1")+request("V2")+request("V3")
       p1=(request("V1")/total)*100
       p2=(request("V2")/total)*100
       p3=(request("V3")/total)*100 %>

<IMG SRC=hist.gif HEIGHT=25 WIDTH=<%=5*p1%>> V1: <%= CInt(p1) %>%<BR>
<IMG SRC=hist.gif HEIGHT=25 WIDTH=<%=5*p2%>> V2: <%= CInt(p2) %>% <BR>
<IMG SRC=hist.gif HEIGHT=25 WIDTH=<%=5*p3%>> V3: <%= CInt(p3) %>% <BR>

<% end if %>


</BODY>
</HTML>
```

Chapter 11

Custom Server Objects

Al Williams

Have you ever wondered how Microsoft server-side components work? Are they magical parts of Internet Information Server (IIS)? No. Server-side components are simply ActiveX objects that Microsoft ships with IIS. Do you want your own components? If so, you need only write a custom ActiveX object.

Only? Writing ActiveX objects is a tough business, right? It's true that ActiveX programming has a bad reputation, but this reputation is not entirely deserved for several reasons. It's true that general-purpose ActiveX programming for large tasks (such as embedding documents) can be difficult. But, the objects you need to build to make server-side components are much less complex. Besides, with new tools like Visual Basic 6 (VB6), you can create components quite easily. (VB5 also has this capability.)

You can use any tool you like for developing ActiveX. Still, VB6 is probably the most approachable if you're not interested in becoming a full-time ActiveX programmer. When you write client controls (see the next chapter), you might not want to use languages like VB because they require large files that you must download to the client. But on the server side, these files are no problem at all. You just install them on the server, and you're done.

The Anatomy Of A Server-Side Component

A *server-side component* is simply an ActiveX object that implements the **IDispatch** interface. This means that the component is a piece of code that supports a special interface for outside programs. This interface allows another program to set properties and call methods inside the ActiveX object. It also allows the external program to query the object about which properties and methods it supports.

How difficult is it to write an **IDispatch** interface in an ActiveX object? The answer depends on what language you choose. If you're willing to use VB6, writing it is not hard at all. If you use C++ or other languages, the task gets more complex.

Each component resides in a dynamic link library (DLL) file. It is not unusual to make a single DLL that contains more than one component. When a page calls **Server.CreateObject** and passes the name of your component, IIS uses ActiveX to create an instance of your ActiveX object. Because more than one page might be executing at one time, your object might have more than one instance active at any time.

IIS calls a special event in your component immediately after it creates an instance of that component (unless you don't provide a handler for it). It also calls another event when it's ready to delete an instance of your component. Other than these two calls, everything else happens because the ASP script calls a method or accesses a property.

Most high-level languages, including VB6, have special tools that make it easy to add properties and methods to an ActiveX **IDispatch** object. These tools can make it fairly easy to construct simple ASP components. However, because your component might have multiple instances active at once, you need to think about synchronizing between the multiple copies.

A number of ASP components are on the Web, so before you decide to write one, you might want to search to see whether someone else has already written it for you. A good place to start is **www.activeserverpages.com**.

Sometimes, however, you can't find any substitute for rolling your own component. Maybe you need to capture custom business rules or access a special device or database. You can do so by using components. In fact, anything you can do under Windows you can do with a server-side component.

Getting Started

When you decide to write a server-side component, your first step should be planning and designing. Time you spend planning your component now will save you an enormous amount of trouble later.

As with other components, you can have any number of properties and methods. You can't readily support events, however, so don't design them in. Notice that only the ASP built-in objects, such as **Application** and **Session**, support events. The components (like the browser capability or ad rotation objects) also don't support events.

Properties can take several forms. To the ASP script, they always look like simple variables. But your program might see them differently. In their simplest form, properties look like variables to your program as well. Sometimes, though, they look like functions. Why? So you can modify your component's behavior.

Suppose you have a component that reads the temperature from an external sensor. You would like to show the temperature on your Web page, but the sensor reads in Celsius. Because most Web surfers live in the United States, however, you probably will want to use a Fahrenheit display.

Of course, you could just convert the reading to Fahrenheit before storing it in the property. But, what about the Canadian branch office? It might prefer Celsius. You would be converting it once, and the staff there would convert it right back.

In this case, why not make two properties: **TempC** and **TempF**? When the script reads **TempC**, it invokes a function in your component that simply reads the temperature from the sensor. The **TempF** function, on the other hand, calls **TempC** and applies a conversion to the result before passing it back to the script. From the script's point of view, both are only variables.

Because these properties are variables, the script can write to them, which might not be a good idea if the property isn't something the script should change. When you're using functions internally, you can prohibit writing (or reading, for that matter) by returning an error from the appropriate function.

Sometimes, you might want to write to the property. Suppose the component interfaces with a thermostat instead of a thermometer. It would then be reasonable to read and write the temperature value. Again, using a function, you could convert incoming Fahrenheit values to Celsius.

Methods are subroutine, or function, calls that you create with VB6. However, you should consider whether a property would be more effective. Suppose you have a component that breaks a line of text into multiple lines on the basis of a width. You have at least two choices here. The obvious one is to write a method that accepts the text and width as parameters. The method returns the new string.

Another choice is to use three properties. For example, the script sets the **Width** and the **InString** properties, and then it can read the **OutString** property to learn the result. Which method is best? It depends on your needs and your personal preferences. Either way works well.

When you plan your component, remember that you'll have access to all the built-in IIS objects (such as **Application**, **Session**, **Request**, and **Response**). However, you won't have easy access to the other components (such as the ad rotation component). You also can't handle events from the built-in objects. That's up to the script. Of course, if you tell the script author to call your object during an event, you can process events, but it's up to the script author to decide that.

Getting Started With VB6

When you use VB to create a server-side component, you actually create an ActiveX DLL. Technically, IIS can use ActiveX EXEs as well, but doing so can result in performance problems. Unless you know what you're doing and have a very good reason to do so, stick with the DLLs.

When you start VB, you see a dialog like the one shown in Figure 11.1. Simply select ActiveX DLL, and click on Open. Of course, if you're in the middle of a project, you can click on the Recent tab and reopen it instead of creating a new one.

Visual Basic assigns a name to your project and a name to the class module that contains your component. If you want more than one component in a DLL, you can add more class modules. If your project name is **ASPDLL**, and the class module name is **TestComponent**, scripts use the string **ASPDLL.TestComponent** to name your object for **Server.CreateObject**. Therefore, you should first change the default names (unless you really want to use **Project1.Class1**—which is a bad idea).

To change the project name, select the project in the Project Explorer window (see Figure 11.2) and then change the name in the Properties window (see Figure 11.3). If you don't see these windows, use the View menu to open them.

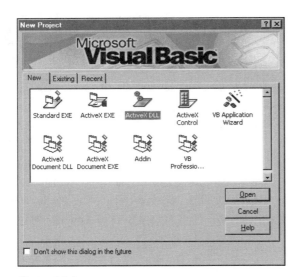

Figure 11.1
Starting Visual Basic.

Figure 11.2
The Project Explorer window.

Figure 11.3
The Properties window.

Changing the class name is just as easy. Just select the class in the Project Explorer window, and change its name in the Properties window. You should not change the other available property—**Instancing**. Leave this value set at 5, which means that your object can service multiple instances at once.

Fleshing Out The Component

If you're an experienced VB programmer, you might want to jump right in and start writing methods and properties in the Code window (see Figure 11.4). Public **SUB**s and **FUNCTION**s become methods, and any public global variables become properties.

However, let me suggest an easier way to proceed. Pull down the Add-Ins menu. Chances are, you won't see an entry there for the Class Builder Utility. If you do, that's great. If you

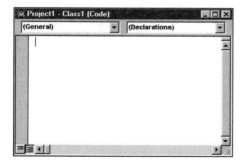

Figure 11.4
The Code window.

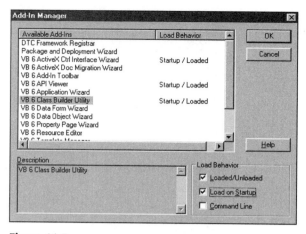

Figure 11.5
Adding Class Builder.

don't, click on Add-In Manager (under the same menu), use the checkboxes to start the
Class Builder Utility (see Figure 11.5), and click on OK. You can check Loaded/Unloaded
to start the Class Builder for this session. If you also check Load On Startup, you won't have
to repeat this step the next time you run VB.

Either way, you should now see the VB6 Class Builder Utility when you pull down the VB
Add-Ins menu. Selecting the utility opens the dialog in Figure 11.6. You might get a warning that the utility found a class already there, but don't worry. By selecting the proper class
in the left-hand portion of the dialog, you can see all the properties and methods for that
class (and events, but then, you can't use events). Right now, you don't have any properties
and methods, so the dialog is blank.

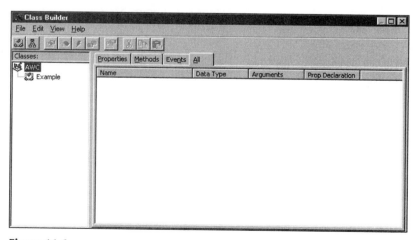

Figure 11.6
Using Class Builder.

Creating Methods

Creating a method is very simple. You can click on the small, green box in the toolbar and select File | New | Method, or you can right-click on the class name and select New | Method. In either case, you see the screen shown in Figure 11.7. Here, you can specify the name of the method, its return value, and any arguments it takes. For the purpose of ASP components, the Declare As Friend? checkbox is meaningless, and you'll rarely use the Default Method? checkbox, because most Web scripting languages don't support default methods in objects anyway.

You can click on the Attributes tab if you want to describe the method and specify a help file ID for it. Specifying an ID and description does not mean a lot for pure ASP scripting, but some development tools might make use of this information.

Creating Properties

Adding properties is just about as easy as adding methods. You either can click on the icon that has a hand pointing to some paper or select File | New | Property. You can also right-click on the class name and select New | Property. Any of these actions make the dialog shown in Figure 11.8 appear.

Again, you need to specify a name and a type. You can also choose whether you want a simple variable or whether you want to use public properties to manipulate the variable. You won't use the Friend Property selection, so don't worry about that.

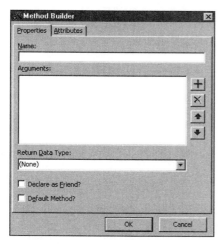

Figure 11.7
Adding a method.

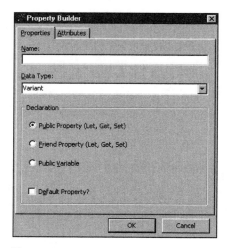

Figure 11.8
Adding a property.

When you pick Public Property as the property type, Class Builder puts two functions in your program. One looks like this:

```
Public Property Let AccessTime(ByVal vData As Date)
'used when assigning a value to the property,
'on the left side of an assignment.
'Syntax: X.AccessTime = 5
. . .
End Property
```

This subroutine assigns the value from the script (passed in as **vData**) to the property.

The other subroutine is as follows:

```
Public Property Get AccessTime() As Date
'used when retrieving the value of a property,
'on the right side of an assignment.
'Syntax: Debug.Print X.AccessTime
 . . .
End Property
```

As you can guess, this piece of code fetches the value of the property and returns it. Class Builder puts sample code in these skeletons to get you started. It's up to you to add any data validation, conversion, or other operations to the basic skeleton.

Finishing Up

After you finish your methods and properties, you can add more classes. Each class is a separate ASP object (but resides in the same DLL file). When you're satisfied, exit the utility, which asks whether you want to update your project. Click on Yes, or it will discard everything you just did.

Now your component has the skeleton for the methods and properties functions. You need to fill in any custom processing (for example, converting Fahrenheit to Celsius).

After you have finished that step, you can save everything (just to be on the safe side) and build your project. You build your project by selecting File | Make *project name* (the actual menu item will have the name of your project on it). Selecting this option saves your project as a DLL file that you can now integrate with an ASP script.

Remember, unless you're developing on your server, you need to put this DLL file on the server, register it (using REGSVR32), and be sure that all the VB support files are present.

How do you know which VB files you need? One way is to run the VB Application Setup Wizard (look for it on the Start menu in the VB group). It creates an entire setup program for you. You can run the setup program on the server, and everything (including the registration) will happen automatically.

You can also ask the program to show you what files you need and then manually copy them over. You need to open a command window first, change the directory to the location where you placed the DLL, and run REGSVR32 with your DLL on the command line. If your DLL is AWCASP.DLL, for example, you would enter "REGSVR32 AWCASP.DLL". Remember, if you're developing on the machine that is also running the Web server, you don't need to do any of this. Just build the DLL, and you're ready to go.

Testing The Component

After you have all the files in place, how can you test your new object? By writing a script, of course. If you're lucky, everything will work the first time. If you're not lucky, you'll need to fix your program.

If you try to rebuild the DLL, you'll find that IIS is holding it open, so you can't rebuild it. Even if you're developing on a different machine, you'll find that you can't copy the new file over the old one because the old one is open.

The solution is to stop IIS and restart it. At one time, restarting meant stopping the W3SVC service. However, the newest versions of IIS still hold your component open when W3SVC shuts down. To completely shut down, you need to stop IISADMIN (which also stops any other IIS services, not just the Web server). Then, you can restart W3SVC (which automatically starts IISADMIN) and any of the other services you want.

You can shut down these services from the Control Panel or a command prompt. From a command prompt, enter "NET STOP IISADMIN" followed by "NET START W3SVC". This command should cause the server to close your component until a page requests it again. I usually rebuild the DLL between the **STOP** and the **START** just to be sure. Obviously, you don't want to develop ASP components on a production server.

Details

As with most things, the devil is in the details. Sure, the Class Builder can put skeletons in for your property functions and methods. It can even add internal private variables for your properties. But, how do you flesh out your code?

A complete treatment of VB is beyond the scope of this book. However, if you have followed the discussion of VBScript in earlier chapters, you probably won't have much trouble anyway.

So the only question left is, "How do I work with IIS?" Luckily, working with the Internet Information Server is not difficult at all. The key is that IIS will call an event in your component every time a page creates or destroys the object. You need not supply code for either of these events, but usually you'll supply **OnStartPage** (the creation event). Why? Because IIS passes this event a magic object (a **ScriptingContext**) that allows you to access the IIS internal objects.

Tip

*The only way to get a **ScriptingContext** object is from the **OnStartPage** event. However, if a script creates an object with Application scope, this event doesn't fire (neither does **OnEndPage**). Therefore, objects that expect to reside at the application level can't really use the internal IIS objects.*

Working With The Events

To know that IIS created your object, you should write a function named **OnStartPage**. Here's how it should look:

```
Public Function OnStartPage(context As ScriptingContext)
. . .
End Function
```

Of course, VB doesn't know what a **ScriptingContext** object looks like, so you must tell it. Select Project | References from the VB menu. Then, locate the entry that says Microsoft Active Server Pages 1.0 Object Library (your version number might be different). Select the checkbox next to this item, and click on OK. Now VB knows about all the objects in IIS (press F2 to open the object browser if you want to examine them). You must take this step one time for each new project you create.

Some components don't care about the scripting context. Suppose your component just wants to write a timestamp to a file. No problem. You could write it from inside **OnStartPage**. Although you still need the **context** argument, you can ignore it.

On the other hand, suppose you want the script to call your **WriteTimeStamp** method to do this work. In this case, you don't need an **OnStartPage** routine at all. However, if you want to work with any of the built-in IIS objects, you must provide an **OnStartPage** routine. You'll probably want to save the **context** argument to some private global variable so that you can use it later.

Using The Objects

Suppose you want a component that writes out a palindrome. Your **OnStartPage** routine would look like this:

```
Public Function OnStartPage(context As ScriptingContext)
context.response.write("A man, a plan, a canal, Panama!")
End Function
```

Of course, this routine is no big deal. You could do the same job in script. But, what if the string came from a database or perhaps a network socket connected to an MOTD (Message Of The Day) server? In this case, using a component that has access to the **Response** object might have some real value.

All the objects you expect are available: **Application**, **Session**, **Response**, **Request**, and **Server**. You can either use them right in place or make copies of them, as in this example:

```
Context.Response.write("Howdy!")
```

Designing A Component

The first step to building a component is to plan (design) it. Before you start, you should have a clear idea of all the properties and methods you'll use.

In addition, you should know whether properties will be read/write, read-only, or write-only. You should also know whether you expect them to be simple variable types or whether they will require public functions.

You should plan which arguments the methods will take and the values, if any, they return. It's also important to have a good idea of what the methods are supposed to do. Often, it's helpful to note which properties a method uses and which properties a method affects.

Finally, you should decide whether you need to write **OnStartPage** and **OnEndPage** event handlers. If you need to know when IIS instantiates your object, or you need to use the built-in IIS objects, you need an **OnStartPage** handler. If you need to clean up anything you created earlier, you need to write an **OnEndPage** handler.

Or, you could write the following:

```
Dim ResponseObj as Response
Set ResponseObj = context.Response
ResponseObj.write("Howdy!")
```

A Complete Project

Now that you've seen what is required to create an object, let's tackle a complete project. To keep things simple yet interesting, let's look at an object that counts page hits and page access times.

Remember: Planning (design) first! Then you can move on to coding and finally testing. Let's discuss these steps in order.

Planning

It's relatively easy to count hits and track access times in regular script, but some problems can occur. One problem is that the counts reset when the server restarts unless you write them somewhere. Tracking time is easy, but you must allocate storage for the time if you want to use it in more than one place.

To make life easier, you can build a component that counts hits and then stores them in the Registry. It will manage different counters by using a unique name for each counter. You should be able to increment the count and retrieve it, or you can simply get the current count. As a by-product, it will also store the time at which you accessed the page. It shouldn't let you change that time, of course. Also, it would be nice if the object could display a preset message with the access time and count nicely formatted.

> **Note**
>
> *It's important to realize that your object might run in a thread that is scheduled with other threads that are working for other clients. This means that if your component depends on sharing a file, a Registry entry, or any other object, it should be prepared to deal with others trying to use it at the same time. This very complex subject requires an understanding of Windows synchronization objects (such as mutexes, semaphores, and events).*
>
> *For many simple components like this one, however, the problem isn't serious. Just be aware of it, and try to think through what would happen if two components were active at the same time.*

To implement these features, I decided to create a read-only property (**AccessTime**), a method named **GetCount**, and another method named **ShowTimeAndCount**. The GetCount method accepts a string and returns the updated count for that string. If you pass an optional second argument as **False, GetCount** doesn't increment the count before returning it. Therefore, assuming that the object is in an object reference variable **obj**, you would write the following:

```
' Assume Count is now 10
x=obj.GetCount("AWC")              ' x=11; count now=11
x=obj.GetCount("AWC",TRUE")        ' x=12; count now=12
x=obj.GetCount("AWC",FALSE)        ' x=12; count now=12
obj.ShowTimeAndCount "AWC"         ' writes formatted string to HTML
```

Getting Started

When you have the design firmly in hand (and in mind), it's time to start a new VB ActiveX DLL project. The first step is to rename the project and class module. The project name is **AWCASP**, and the class name is **ASPDemo1**, meaning that a script that wants to create this object would write the following:

```
<% Set obj=Server.CreateObject("AWCASP.ASPDemo1") %>
```

Next, you must add the ASP Object Library to the project references by choosing Project | References. Then, VB will know about all the IIS objects, including **ScriptingContext**.

This component definitely needs to use the **ScriptingContext** object, so it needs an **OnStartPage** event handler. This handler only has to store away the context and the current time and date for later. The code to do that is as follows:

```
Public Function OnStartPage(context As ScriptingContext)
Set mainContext = context
atime = Now
End Function
```

You also must declare global variables for **mainContext** and **atime**. You can see exactly where to declare these variables in Listing 11.1, which contains the complete listing.

Listing 11.1 The component.
```
VERSION 1.0 CLASS
BEGIN  MultiUse = -1  'TrueEND
Attribute VB_Name = "ASPDemo1"
Attribute VB_GlobalNameSpace = True
Attribute VB_Creatable = True
Attribute VB_PredeclaredId = False
Attribute VB_Exposed = True
Attribute VB_Ext_KEY = "SavedWithClassBuilder" ,"Yes"
Attribute VB_Ext_KEY = "Top_Level" ,"Yes"
' Everything from this point up is automatically put in by VB
' don't type it in!
' From here down is the stuff you type in
Private mainContext As ScriptingContext
Private atime As Date
```

```
Public Property Let AccessTime(ByVal vData As Date)
'used when assigning a value to the property,
'on the left side of an assignment
'Syntax: X.AccessTime = 5
    mainContext.Response.Write ("Error: Can't set Access Time")
End Property


Public Property Get AccessTime() As Date
'used when retrieving value of a property, on the right side of an
'assignment.
'Syntax: Debug.Print X.AccessTime
    AccessTime = atime
End Property


Public Function GetCount(CountName As String, Optional flag)
ct = GetSetting("AWCASP", "Counter", CountName, 0)
If IsMissing(flag) Then flag = True
If flag = True Then
  ct = ct + 1
  SaveSetting "AWCASP", "Counter", CountName, ct
End If
GetCount = ct
End Function

Public Sub ShowTimeAndCount(CountName As String)
ct = GetCount(CountName)
mainContext.Response.Write _
 "<BR><B><I>At " & atime & " you were the " & ct & " visitor!</I></B><BR>"
End Sub


Public Function OnStartPage(context As ScriptingContext)
Set mainContext = context
atime = Now
End Function
```

Starting A Project

To start coding, you need to start a new VB project. Be sure the project is set to be an ActiveX DLL. You can just follow these steps:

1. Start a new project.

2. Rename the project to something meaningful.

3. Rename the class module to something meaningful.

4. Add the ASP Object Library to the project references.

Adding Properties

Using the Class Builder Utility (on the Add-Ins menu), you can add the single property **AccessTime**. If you don't see the Class Builder on the menu, use the Add-In Manager to include it.

At first, you might be tempted to simply use a regular variable for the **AccessTime** property, but that won't do because the property is read-only. Instead, use Public Members for the properties. Then, you can raise an error in the subroutine that attempts to set the value.

Although Class Builder creates a variable to correspond to the **AccessTime** property, you don't need that variable because **atime** already stores the time. After you close Class Builder, you can delete its variable and change the reference in the **AccessTime Get** function to **atime**.

Because this property is read-only, you can get rid of everything in the **Let** function. You can raise a VB error (using the built-in **Err** object) or just write an error out to the HTML using the **Response** object. Usually, writing the HTML error is a better idea.

Adding Methods

Class Builder adds the methods, but it really doesn't know what to do with them. It's up to you to flesh them out with meaningful code.

The **GetCount** function uses several tricks that might not be obvious at first glance. In the argument list, notice that the **flag** argument has the keyword **Optional**. This means that the caller doesn't need to supply it. However, if it's not present and you try to use it, an error will occur.

The trick is to use the **IsMissing** function (see Listing 11.1). If **IsMissing** returns **True**, you can set a default value before proceeding.

The other interesting part of the **GetCount** method is how it manipulates the Registry. Instead of using the Windows API, it uses the ultrasimple **GetSetting** and **SaveSetting** calls. Of course, you can call the Windows API from VB, but that's beyond the scope of this book. Besides, why not use these simple calls? They work very well.

You'll discover one potential problem with the way the object stores counters. If the server is very busy accessing the same page for more than one client, two copies of the object might try to access the count at one time. This can cause small inaccuracies in the count.

For example, suppose I pull up the page with the counter in it at the same time you do. The IIS creates one object for me and another for you. Suppose my object reads the current count from the Registry as 9. The Windows scheduler puts my object to sleep and starts yours. Your object also reads a 9 from the Registry, adds 1 to it, and puts it back. Then, your object sleeps. When my object resumes processing, it will add 1 to the 9 it read before and write the resulting 10 to the Registry. Now, we both think we are the tenth visitor.

This problem is not serious, however, because it's very unlikely to happen unless your site is heavily loaded and often gets multiple simultaneous hits. Even if you do have this problem, it means only that your count is off by 1. If you have a busy site, though, having an incorrect count might be a concern. Also, if you're giving away $1 million to your one-millionth visitor, you sure wouldn't want it to double up on the 1 million count!

In cases in which it matters, you need to use a *mutex*, which is a Windows object that lets one object claim ownership of a resource. This technique is advanced, but you can do it, even in VB. For most people, however, the component is fine the way it is.

The **ShowTimeAndCount** method is very simple because the first thing it does is call **GetCount**. This is a good example of how you can reuse parts of your component. Just because the script calls **GetCount** doesn't mean you, too, can't call it. After **GetCount** returns the correct count, a single line of code formats it and writes it using the **Response** object.

Testing The Component

Using the component is really quite simple. Listing 11.2 shows a simple ASP script that tests the basic functions of the component. Because it's so simple, I didn't even bother making it a proper HTML file. After you view the script, refresh the screen, and you'll see the count increase and the time change.

Listing 11.2   Test script.

```
<% Set obj=Server.CreateObject("AWCASP.ASPDemo1") %> <!-- Sets time string -->
<P>Access time:
<%= obj.AccessTime %>
<P>This page accessed: <%= obj.GetCount("TestCounter") %> times. <P>
Again, that was: <%= obj.GetCount("TestCounter",FALSE) %> times. <P>

-Or-

<% obj.ShowTimeAndCount("AltCounter") %>
```

Debugging Tips

Debugging server components is notoriously difficult. If you're using C++ or other advanced languages, you might be able to run IIS as a debugged program (which has a lot of overhead, as you might expect).

If you're using VB, or you don't want to run IIS as a debugged process, you need to resort to writing debugging information out to the HTML stream or a file. Although this solution is not ideal, you can usually get a handle on things by using this approach.

Another way to approach a VB project is to add an ordinary VB EXE project to your DLL project. Then, you can write simple routines that create your IIS object and call the routines in it. However, if you're using the **ScriptingContext** object, you'll have trouble simulating it and will be stuck, again, with peppering your code with debugging output.

Registration Of Components

Don't forget that you must install the component you write on the Web server. If you're developing on the server, that's fine. If you're not, you need to install the DLL file and any support files the DLL requires and then register the DLL. You can do so manually if you know which files you need. Simply copy them to the server, and run REGSVR32 (on the server) specifying the DLL's file name. Performing these steps will cause the object to make entries in the system Registry so that IIS (and other ActiveX programs) can find it.

What if you don't know which files you need? For a VB program, you can run the Application Setup Wizard (from the Start menu in the VB group). This program can tell you which files a VB project requires and can create a setup program that will do all the installation work (even the registration) for you.

An Advanced Example

Now that you have a taste of what you can do with a custom server-side object, you might be wondering just how far you can go. The answer is as far as you can stomach! To demonstrate the potential power of a custom server component, I decided to write a component that can single-handedly let you edit a Web page on the server and then save it right back to the server live! Imagine—if you see a mistake on your Web page, you can just edit right in your Web browser and save the change immediately.

In principle, this example isn't very hard as long as you can write files to the server. When you create the component, it checks to see whether any form data is attached. If no data is attached, the component creates a form that contains the HTML for the page specified in the query string. If no query string exists, the component creates a form with a generic prototype page.

The form the component creates submits back to another script that contains the same object (actually, it can even be the same script). This time, the component picks up the URL and text data from the form's data (sent via the **POST** method). If you want the component's form to submit to another page, you need to include the **action** query string field to name the script that should process the data.

If the object detects posted form data, it reads the password from the **pw** field. It has to match the object's password (you can set the password in the server's Registry or use the hard-coded default). If the password matches, the object extracts the **url** field and saves the **text** field's data into the appropriate file. Finally, the object redirects the browser to the newly modified or created file.

Of course, you don't have to use the built-in form if you just want to create a Web page or you have your own scheme for loading a text field with the contents of a file. You can create a custom form that has the correct fields. Speaking of files, notice that the object accepts URLs, but it really needs a normal file name. Luckily, the **Server.MapPath** readily does the conversion, and the object can make this call using the **ScriptingContext** object that it receives.

Making The Component Work

You can find the code for this component in Listing 11.3. The object does all its work in the **OnStartPage** function. Because the component generates its own HTML (or redirects to another page), you can use it by writing one line of ASP code:

```
<% set editor = Server.CreateObject("AWC.WebEdit") %C>
```

Suppose the preceding line is in a file named EDIT.ASP. You can create a new page by simply opening EDIT.ASP in a Web browser, filling out the information (see Figure 11.9), and submitting the form. If you want to edit an existing page (say, prices.htm) you could navigate to the following:

```
http://www.al-williams.com/edit.asp?url=prices.htm
```

Of course, you need to substitute your server name for mine.

Listing 11.3   The WebEdit component.

```
VERSION 1.0 CLASS
BEGIN
  MultiUse = -1  'True
  Persistable = 0  'NotPersistable
  DataBindingBehavior = 0  'vbNone
  DataSourceBehavior  = 0  'vbNone
  MTSTransactionMode  = 0  'NotAnMTSObject
END
Attribute VB_Name = "WebEdit"
Attribute VB_GlobalNameSpace = False
Attribute VB_Creatable = True
Attribute VB_PredeclaredId = False
Attribute VB_Exposed = True


Public Function OnStartPage(context As ScriptingContext)
Dim result As String
Dim fn As String
Dim CRLF As String
CRLF = Chr(13) & Chr(10)
If context.Request.ServerVariables("content_length") = 0 Then
  With context.Response
    .Write "<HTML><HEAD><TITLE>Web editor</TITLE>" & CRLF
    .Write "</HEAD><BODY><TABLE WIDTH=320><TR><TD>" & CRLF
    .Write "<FORM ACTION='" & context.Request.QueryString("action") _
        & "' METHOD=POST>" & CRLF
    .Write "Password: <INPUT TYPE=PASSWORD NAME=pw><BR>" & CRLF
    .Write "URL: <INPUT NAME=url"
```

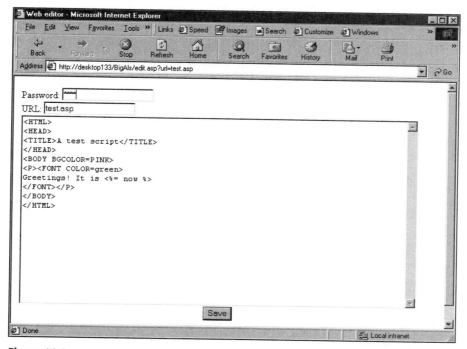

Figure 11.9
The WebEdit component at work.

```
If context.Request.QueryString("URL") <> "" Then
  .Write " VALUE='" & context.Request.QueryString("URL") & "'"
End If
.Write "><BR>" & CRLF
.Write "<TEXTAREA ROWS=20 COLS=80 NAME=Text>" & CRLF
If context.Request.QueryString("URL") <> "" Then
  On Error Resume Next
  Dim l As String
  fn = context.Server.MapPath(context.Request.QueryString("URL"))
  Open fn For Input As #1
    Do While Not EOF(1) And Err.Number = 0
      Line Input #1, l
      context.Response.Write l & CRLF
    Loop
  Close #1
Else
  .Write "<HTML>" & CRLF
  .Write "<HEAD>" & CRLF
  .Write "<TITLE>Untitled Page</TITLE>" & CRLF
  .Write "</HEAD>" & CRLF
  .Write "<BODY BGCOLOR=GREEN>" & CRLF
```

```
            .Write "<P>Your message here</P>" & CRLF
            .Write "</BODY>" & CRLF
            .Write "</HTML>" & CRLF
         End If

       .Write "</TEXTAREA><BR><CENTER>" & CRLF
       .Write "<INPUT Value=Save TYPE=Submit></CENTER></FORM>" & CRLF
       .Write "</TD></TR></TABLE></BODY></HTML>" & CRLF
    End With

Else
    result = "Incorrect password"
    If context.Request.Form("PW") = GetSetting("AWC.WebEdit", "General", "PW", _
      "adgo") Then
      fn = context.Server.MapPath(context.Request.Form("URL"))
      On Error Resume Next
      Open fn For Output As #1
      If Err.Number = 0 Then
        Print #1, context.Request.Form("Text")
        If Err.Number = 0 Then
          Close #1
          If Err.Number = 0 Then
            context.Response.Redirect context.Request.Form("URL")
            Exit Function
          Else
            result = "Can't close file"
          End If
        Else
          result = "File write failed"
        End If
      Else
        result = "Can't open file: " & fn
      End If
    End If
End If
context.Response.Write "<HTML><BODY>"
context.Response.Write result
context.Response.Write "</BODY></HTML>"
End Function
```

This object is one example of how you can move almost an entire Web page into a component. You can decide whether that is a good design principle or a bad one; your decision depends on your overall strategy and what is important to you. I might just as easily have elected to make the component only process the data, forcing you to design the form that collects the data. A simple member function could retrieve the file's text to assist you.

Although this scheme would be very flexible, it would require a lot of work up front so that you can use it. As it is, you can get up and running very quickly, but if you want to customize the form, you can. You can find an example of a custom form in Listing 11.4. This form isn't much different from the default, and it calls EDIT.ASP to save the file. (EDIT.ASP is the simple one-line file described earlier.)

The custom form uses ordinary script to read the contents of the existing file. Of course, you could use the same sort of code to write the file back, too. However, you can see this code is complex; authors who could easily use the WebEdit component might not have as much luck rolling their own code. You could create a second object that performs the read to make the process even easier.

Listing 11.4   Custom form.

```
<HTML>
<HEAD>
<TITLE>Web editor</TITLE>
</HEAD>
<BODY BGCOLOR=GRAY>


<TABLE WIDTH=320>
<TR><TD>
<% if request("content_length")=0 then %>
<FORM ACTION=cedit.asp METHOD=POST>
URL to Edit or Create: <INPUT NAME=url><BR>
<CENTER>
<INPUT Value="Open" TYPE=Submit>
</CENTER>
<% else %>
<FORM ACTION=edit.asp METHOD=POST>
Password (pw): <INPUT NAME=pw><BR>
<INPUT TYPE=HIDDEN NAME=URL VALUE='<%= Request.form("url") %>'>
<TEXTAREA ROWS=20 COLS=80 NAME=Text>
<% set f = Server.CreateObject("Scripting.FileSystemObject")
   set inf = f.OpenTextFile(Server.MapPath(Request.form("url")),1,FALSE,FALSE)
%>
<%= inf.ReadAll %>
<%
  inf.Close
%>
</TEXTAREA><BR>
<CENTER>
<INPUT Value="Save" TYPE=Submit>
</CENTER>
<% end if %>
```

```
</FORM>
</TD></TR></TABLE>
</BODY>
</HTML>
```

Creating More Components

Although the task isn't trivial, you can create your own ASP components. With Visual Basic, creating these components isn't very difficult, and custom components can be the answer to getting just the effect you want in your Web page.

What if you don't like VB? That's okay—ActiveX works with many languages, including C++ and Visual J++ (Microsoft's flavor of Java). If you can build an **IDispatch** interface, you're in business.

You'll discover three major obstacles to creating your own ASP components. First, you need to learn a programming language that supports ActiveX. Second, you need to take multitasking issues into account. Third, and perhaps most frustrating, it's very difficult to debug your code after you have written it.

Note that some languages, such as C++, have debuggers that can attach to IIS and let you step through component code. However, this process isn't trivial, and the extra learning curve that comes with C++ makes this approach of interest mainly to experienced C++ programmers.

ActiveX is a broad topic and has many uses. Writing server-side components is one of them. You can also use ActiveX to create client-side controls, as you'll see in Chapter 12. You'll find many other uses for ActiveX as well.

Time spent learning ActiveX will eventually pay off. Most new features in Windows use ActiveX (including Microsoft Transaction Server, Microsoft Message Queue, and advanced MAPI).

You can also find more information about ActiveX on the Web. My site (**www.al-williams.com**) is one place to start. You might also check out **www.microsoft.com/com** and **www.program.com**.

Chapter 12

Your Own Client-Side Objects

Al Williams

I've been an amateur radio operator for more than 20 years and an electronics hobbyist for longer than that. One odd phenomenon that affects people like me is the do-it-yourself syndrome. I've seen folks like me build their own computers (or televisions or radios) and spend double what it would take to simply buy the thing in the store.

Is this crazy? Maybe. But those of us afflicted with this malady will tell you that we derive a certain satisfaction in doing something ourselves. Besides, after you build something, you know it inside and out. You can also make it just the right size and with just the right mix of features.

You can borrow plenty of ActiveX objects and Java applets from the Web for use on your Web site. On the other hand, there is the satisfaction of making your own. When you make your own objects, you can forge them to best meet your needs.

Surely making your own objects is difficult, right? Well, *difficult* is a relative term, and making objects with Visual Basic really isn't very hard at all. Visual J++ and Visual C++ work as well, but they are a bit harder to use. Even so, I believe that writing an ActiveX control with Visual C++ is easier than writing a complete Windows application.

Downsides

Is there a downside to creating your own control? Unfortunately, yes. Writing your own objects requires you to buy a development tool and learn it. Visual Basic is probably the most approachable, but if you're not a programmer, you need to spend some time getting familiar with it.

Another concern that is true only for ActiveX controls is download efficiency. Sure, VB and Visual C++ (using Microsoft Foundation Classes, or MFC) can make it easy to create ActiveX controls. However, that simplicity depends on large DLLs that the tools use, and most of the code is in those libraries. If the users already have the library for some reason (for example, from downloading someone else's control), that's great. If they don't, they need to wait for a lengthy download before they can see your award-winning control.

Does it have to be this way? For VB, the answer is probably yes. For Visual C++, however, you can write minimalist controls that are much more efficient by using straight C++ or a tool called the ActiveX Template Library (ATL). However, neither of these approaches is simple. You need an advanced understanding of ActiveX and C++ to create controls without the MFC library.

On the other hand, because many people do use these tools to build ActiveX controls, there is a good possibility that the libraries already exist on the users' computers. Also, as connection speeds continue to increase, the penalty for these downloads becomes less important.

Available Tools

Although this chapter is mostly about Visual Basic and Visual J++, many other tools are available to help you build client-side components. Some of them are more visual and some more like traditional programming environments. However, programming in a language you know might be better than learning a new language, even if the new language is easier.

Nearly all C++ compilers can now generate ActiveX, including Visual C++ and Borland's C-Builder. Delphi, also from Borland, can create ActiveX controls as well. C++ allows you to create very efficient ActiveX controls, but with great difficulty. Most compilers also have a simplified approach (MFC, for example), but here the controls are less efficient than they would be had they been properly written without those tools.

Many Java tools are available, ranging from Sun's ultravisual Java Studio to the straight Java JDK (also from Sun). In between are respectable Java tools from Borland (JBuilder), Symantec (Visual Café), IBM (VisualAge for Java), and many others. Visual Studio in particular is very visual and requires almost no programming for many types of applets.

Of course, new tools for both technologies appear every day. You can search the Web or look in one of the many Java resources on the Web (try **www.wdrl.com**).

Using Visual Basic

The skill level required to create your own objects changed with the release of VB5 and later VB6, which allows you to create controls as easily as you currently create form-based applications. It also lets you create ActiveX controls, which, in theory, you can use in VB,

Web pages, C++, Delphi, PowerBuilder, and any other environment that understands ActiveX controls.

If you are already a VB programmer, you'll have little or no trouble creating controls. If you haven't tried Visual Basic, getting started isn't difficult. Also, Microsoft has introduced a new user interface that is more comfortable for programmers who are accustomed to the Microsoft Developer's Studio program.

ActiveX Fundamentals

If you've ever used any kind of component software, you won't be surprised to hear that the fundamental pieces of an ActiveX control are properties, methods, and events. VB-created ActiveX controls are no different.

Properties are similar to variables. They are values that the program using the component (the container) can set or read. In VB, you can place these values in variables or connect them to components that you use to create your component. You'll see how this process works shortly.

Methods are simply functions and subroutines that the container can call. Again, you can define your own, or you can expose methods from components that you use internally.

Events notify the container when something interesting happens. Guess what? You can define custom events or pass events from other components.

Fail To Plan—Plan To Fail

To get the most from an ActiveX control, you should carefully plan which properties, methods, and events it will handle. You can tweak things later, but it helps if you have a good idea from the start about what you want to use. The sample control I'll show you in this chapter is a simple scanning bar of lights (see Figure 12.1)—you know, the sort of thing you see under the view screen on the Enterprise (the original one). It exposes these four properties:

♦ **Delay**—Indicates the number of milliseconds to delay between each lamp turning on

♦ **Direction**—Takes **TRUE** to scan from left to right, or **FALSE** to scan from right to left

♦ **ForeColor**—Specifies the color of lights when they are on

♦ **Hold**—Stops the lights from scanning when **TRUE**

The control also supports a single event, **TICK**, which fires each time the lights change state (that is, once for each period set by **Delay**). The control has no methods.

Laying Out The Control

When you have a plan, you can fire up Visual Basic. From the startup dialog box, select ActiveX Control from the New tab. The program then creates an empty project.

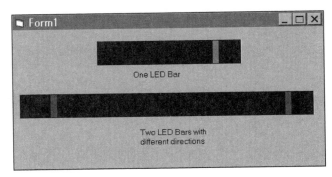

Figure 12.1
The scanning LED bar.

If you start VB (and you have the default screen layout), notice that a property browser window appears. Beneath it is a description window that describes the selected property. When you create a component, you should control what appears in this window when programmers use your component. Even farther down is a layout window that shows where your form will appear when it runs. If you right-click on this window, you can create grid lines to show you the common screen resolutions and select options for the locations where your forms will show up when your program runs.

In the center of the screen are windows that hold forms and Basic code. By default, the code window shows you all the code at once and draws lines between sections. If you prefer the old style, you can click on the small button at the bottom-left corner of the code window. In fact, you can change just about any aspect of the interface and easily move, resize, or hide any of the windows or toolbars. You can customize everything. Right-clicking anywhere brings up interesting menus.

Defining The Interface

To create the LEDBar control (the scanning lights), I used the normal Basic shape component. Each of the 20 lights is a rectangle shape. I created the first one, copied it to the clipboard, and then pasted it to form a control array. Then, I pasted it 18 more times to complete the array. By using a control array, I can refer to each light as an element in an array (or collection, if you prefer). The array's name is **LED0**, and the elements range from 0 through 19.

The control also needs a timer. Each time the timer expires, the control should turn off the current light and then turn on the light to the right or left of the current light (depending on the setting of the **Direction** flag).

At this point, you could start writing code to take care of the logic. However, you'll need some of the properties (for example, **Direction**), and they don't exist yet. To define properties, methods, and events, you can use the Interface Wizard (from the Add-Ins menu). This wizard (see Figures 12.2 through 12.5) allows you to select members (that is, properties, methods, and events) that many controls support (see Figure 12.2). You can also create custom members (see Figure 12.3). On the next screen (see Figure 12.4), you attach the members to corresponding members in the components that the control contains. I attached

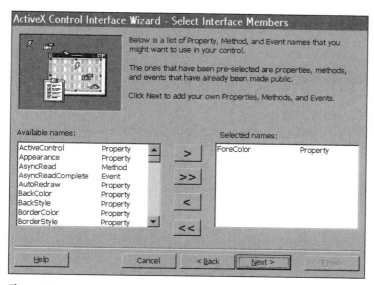

Figure 12.2
The Interface Wizard's first screen.

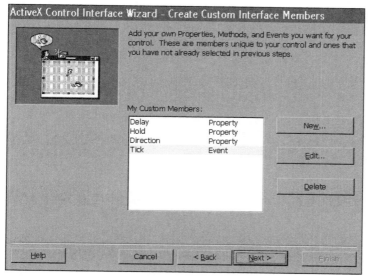

Figure 12.3
Creating custom members.

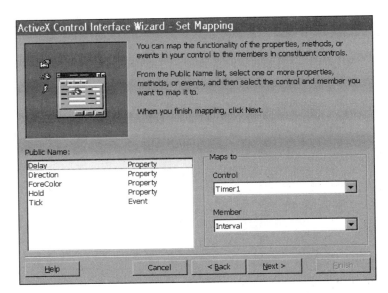

Figure 12.4
Mapping members.

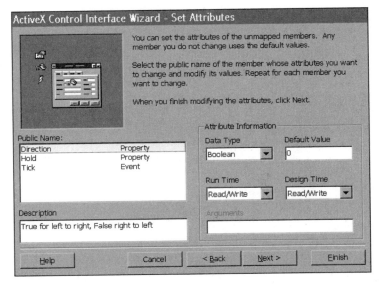

Figure 12.5
Setting member attributes.

the **Delay** property directly to the **Timer** component and the **ForeColor** property to the **UserControl** component. (**UserControl** corresponds to a form in a regular VB program.)

At this point, you might be tempted to attach the **Tick** event to the timer's **Timer** event. You can do so as long as you haven't already put a **Timer** handler in the code.

Warning

If you use the wizard to add a handler and you already have an existing handler, the wizard will write an extra event handler that causes a compile error. You'll have to manually merge the two handlers to resolve the error.

On the final wizard screen (see Figure 12.5), you can define any unattached members. The description text then appears in the design environment (below the property browser). You can also specify types, properties, and so on. The wizard creates variables for your unattached properties. For example, the **Direction** property causes the wizard to create a variable named **m_Direction**. Methods get skeletal function definitions that you must complete. The wizard also handles events. Of course, any members that you connect to other components don't show up on this screen.

After you complete this wizard, all your external members are complete. Of course, you need to write code that handles any custom methods and fires any custom events at the appropriate time. You also need to write all the other code that makes your control work.

VB6 Steps

Using VB to create an ActiveX control takes a few simple steps:

1. Start Visual Basic.
2. Select ActiveX Control from the New tab of the initial dialog box.
3. Add the VB controls you want to use in your ActiveX control (you can even use other ActiveX controls if you like). These are constituent controls.
4. Start the Interface Wizard (from the Add-Ins menu).
5. Select the properties, methods, and events you want to support.
6. Create custom members.
7. Attach your control's members to members of the constituent controls.
8. Define any unattached members.
9. Write code to handle unattached properties and methods.
10. Write code to fire unattached events when appropriate.
11. Write any code that implements logic for the control.
12. Set the **ToolboxIcon** property to set the design-time icon the control displays.
13. If you want a property sheet, run the Property Sheet Wizard.
14. Build your OCX (from the File menu).

You can find the details for this procedure in the examples in this chapter.

Writing The Code

The code to handle the light bar is fairly simple. A **Timer** event handler cycles the lights on the basis of the **m_Direction** flag (see Listing 12.1). Also, the **UserControl_Initialize** event takes care of some setup issues. If you attached the **Tick** event to the **Timer** control, you already have a **Timer** handler. It contains this line:

```
RaiseEvent Tick
```

You can simply add your code in the same handler. If you didn't hook up the **Tick** event, you can now create a **Timer** handler and add the **RaiseEvent** line to raise your custom event.

Listing 12.1   The LEDBar control.

```
VERSION 5.00
Begin VB.UserControl LedBar
   BackColor       =   &H00FFFFFF&
   ClientHeight    =   432
   ClientLeft      =   0
   ClientTop       =   0
   ClientWidth     =   4788
   FillColor       =   &H00FFFFFF&
   PropertyPages   =   "ledbar.ctx":0000
   ScaleHeight     =   432
   ScaleWidth      =   4788
   ToolboxBitmap   =   "ledbar.ctx":001A
   Begin VB.Timer Timer1
      Interval     =   125
      Left         =   4212
      Top          =   0
   End
   Begin VB.Shape LED0
      FillStyle    =   0   'Solid
      Height       =   492
      Index        =   19
      Left         =   4560
      Top          =   0
      Width        =   252
   End
   Begin VB.Shape LED0
      FillStyle    =   0   'Solid
      Height       =   492
      Index        =   18
      Left         =   4320
      Top          =   0
      Width        =   252
   End
```

```
Begin VB.Shape LED0
   FillStyle       =   0   'Solid
   Height          =   492
   Index           =   17
   Left            =   4080
   Top             =   0
   Width           =   252
End
Begin VB.Shape LED0
   FillStyle       =   0   'Solid
   Height          =   492
   Index           =   16
   Left            =   3840
   Top             =   0
   Width           =   252
End
Begin VB.Shape LED0
   FillStyle       =   0   'Solid
   Height          =   492
   Index           =   15
   Left            =   3600
   Top             =   0
   Width           =   252
End
Begin VB.Shape LED0
   FillStyle       =   0   'Solid
   Height          =   492
   Index           =   14
   Left            =   3360
   Top             =   0
   Width           =   252
End
Begin VB.Shape LED0
   FillStyle       =   0   'Solid
   Height          =   492
   Index           =   13
   Left            =   3120
   Top             =   0
   Width           =   252
End
Begin VB.Shape LED0
   BackColor       =   &H00000000&
   FillStyle       =   0   'Solid
   Height          =   492
   Index           =   12
   Left            =   2880
```

```
         Top            =    0
         Width          =    252
      End
      Begin VB.Shape LED0
         BackColor       =    &H00000000&
         FillStyle       =    0   'Solid
         Height          =    492
         Index           =    11
         Left            =    2640
         Top             =    0
         Width           =    252
      End
      Begin VB.Shape LED0
         BackColor       =    &H00000000&
         FillStyle       =    0   'Solid
         Height          =    492
         Index           =    10
         Left            =    2400
         Top             =    0
         Width           =    252
      End
      Begin VB.Shape LED0
         FillStyle       =    0   'Solid
         Height          =    492
         Index           =    9
         Left            =    2160
         Top             =    0
         Width           =    252
      End
      Begin VB.Shape LED0
         FillStyle       =    0   'Solid
         Height          =    492
         Index           =    8
         Left            =    1920
         Top             =    0
         Width           =    252
      End
      Begin VB.Shape LED0
         FillStyle       =    0   'Solid
         Height          =    492
         Index           =    7
         Left            =    1680
         Top             =    0
         Width           =    252
      End
```

```
Begin VB.Shape LED0
   FillStyle       =    0    'Solid
   Height          =    492
   Index           =    6
   Left            =    1440
   Top             =    0
   Width           =    252
End
Begin VB.Shape LED0
   FillStyle       =    0    'Solid
   Height          =    492
   Index           =    5
   Left            =    1200
   Top             =    0
   Width           =    252
End
Begin VB.Shape LED0
   FillStyle       =    0    'Solid
   Height          =    492
   Index           =    4
   Left            =    960
   Top             =    0
   Width           =    252
End
Begin VB.Shape LED0
   FillStyle       =    0    'Solid
   Height          =    492
   Index           =    3
   Left            =    720
   Top             =    0
   Width           =    252
End
Begin VB.Shape LED0
   FillStyle       =    0    'Solid
   Height          =    492
   Index           =    2
   Left            =    480
   Top             =    0
   Width           =    252
End
Begin VB.Shape LED0
   BackColor       =    &H00000000&
   FillStyle       =    0    'Solid
   Height          =    492
   Index           =    1
   Left            =    240
```

```
                    Top                =    0
                    Width              =    252
              End
              Begin VB.Shape LED0
                    BackColor          =    &H000000FF&
                    FillColor          =    &H000000FF&
                    FillStyle          =    0   'Solid
                    Height             =    492
                    Index              =    0
                    Left               =    0
                    Top                =    0
                    Width              =    252
              End
        End
End
Attribute VB_Name = "LedBar"
Attribute VB_GlobalNameSpace = False
Attribute VB_Creatable = True
Attribute VB_PredeclaredId = False
Attribute VB_Exposed = True
Attribute VB_Ext_KEY = "PropPageWizardRun" ,"Yes"

Dim n As Integer
'Default Property Values:
Const m_def_Direction = True
Const m_def_Hold = False
'Const m_def_ForeColor = 255
'Property Variables:
Dim m_Direction As Boolean
Dim m_Hold As Boolean
'Dim m_ForeColor As OLE_COLOR
'Event Declarations:
Event Tick()
'Event Timer() 'MappingInfo=Timer1,Timer1,-1,Timer

Private Sub Timer1_Timer()
If m_Hold = True Then Exit Sub
LED0(n).FillColor = vbBlack
If m_Direction Then
  If n = 19 Then n = 0 Else n = n + 1
Else
  If n = 0 Then n = 19 Else n = n - 1
End If
LED0(n).FillColor = UserControl.ForeColor
RaiseEvent Tick
End Sub
```

```
Private Sub UserControl_Initialize()
n = 0
LED0(0).FillColor = UserControl.ForeColor
Hold = False

End Sub

Private Sub UserControl_Resize()
For i = 0 To 19
  LED0(i).Width = (ScaleWidth \ 20) * 20 / 20!
  LED0(i).Height = ScaleHeight
  LED0(i).Top = 0
  LED0(i).Left = i * (ScaleWidth \ 20) * 20 / 20!
Next i
End Sub
''WARNING! DO NOT REMOVE OR MODIFY THE FOLLOWING COMMENTED LINES!
''MappingInfo=UserControl,UserControl,-1,BackColor
'Public Property Get BackColor() As OLE_COLOR
'    BackColor = UserControl.BackColor
'End Property
'
'Public Property Let BackColor(ByVal New_BackColor As OLE_COLOR)
'    UserControl.BackColor() = New_BackColor
'    PropertyChanged "BackColor"
'End Property
'
'Public Property Get ForeColor() As OLE_COLOR
'    ForeColor = m_ForeColor
'End Property
'
'Public Property Let ForeColor(ByVal New_ForeColor As OLE_COLOR)
'    m_ForeColor = New_ForeColor
'    PropertyChanged "ForeColor"
'End Property

'WARNING! DO NOT REMOVE OR MODIFY THE FOLLOWING COMMENTED LINES!
'MappingInfo=Timer1,Timer1,-1,Interval
Public Property Get Delay() As Long
Attribute Delay.VB_Description = "Returns/sets the timer period in mS"
    Delay = Timer1.Interval
End Property

Public Property Let Delay(ByVal New_Delay As Long)
    Timer1.Interval() = New_Delay
    PropertyChanged "Delay"
End Property
```

```
'Initialize Properties for User Control
Private Sub UserControl_InitProperties()
'     m_ForeColor = m_def_ForeColor
     m_Hold = m_def_Hold
     m_Direction = m_def_Direction
End Sub


'Load property values from storage
Private Sub UserControl_ReadProperties(PropBag As PropertyBag)

'     UserControl.BackColor = PropBag.ReadProperty("BackColor", &HFFFFFF)
'     m_ForeColor = PropBag.ReadProperty("ForeColor", m_def_ForeColor)
     Timer1.Interval = PropBag.ReadProperty("Delay", 125)
     UserControl.ForeColor = PropBag.ReadProperty("ForeColor", &H80000012)
     m_Hold = PropBag.ReadProperty("Hold", m_def_Hold)
     m_Direction = PropBag.ReadProperty("Direction", m_def_Direction)
End Sub


'Write property values to storage
Private Sub UserControl_WriteProperties(PropBag As PropertyBag)

'     Call PropBag.WriteProperty("BackColor", UserControl.BackColor, &HFFFFFF)
'     Call PropBag.WriteProperty("ForeColor", m_ForeColor, m_def_ForeColor)
     Call PropBag.WriteProperty("Delay", Timer1.Interval, 125)
     Call PropBag.WriteProperty("ForeColor", UserControl.ForeColor, &H80000012)
     Call PropBag.WriteProperty("Hold", m_Hold, m_def_Hold)
     Call PropBag.WriteProperty("Direction", m_Direction, m_def_Direction)
End Sub


'WARNING! DO NOT REMOVE OR MODIFY THE FOLLOWING COMMENTED LINES!
'MappingInfo=UserControl,UserControl,-1,ForeColor
Public Property Get ForeColor() As OLE_COLOR
Attribute ForeColor.VB_Description = "Returns/sets the foreground color"
     ForeColor = UserControl.ForeColor
End Property


Public Property Let ForeColor(ByVal New_ForeColor As OLE_COLOR)
     UserControl.ForeColor() = New_ForeColor
     PropertyChanged "ForeColor"
End Property


Public Property Get Hold() As Boolean
Attribute Hold.VB_Description = "Set to TRUE to freeze LEDs"
     Hold = m_Hold
End Property
```

```
Public Property Let Hold(ByVal New_Hold As Boolean)
    m_Hold = New_Hold
    PropertyChanged "Hold"
End Property

Public Property Get Direction() As Boolean
Attribute Direction.VB_Description = "True for left to right"
    Direction = m_Direction
End Property

Public Property Let Direction(ByVal New_Direction As Boolean)
    m_Direction = New_Direction
    PropertyChanged "Direction"
End Property
```

With these two handlers in place, the control will work as advertised. However, you must make the control the exact size of the 20 shape controls—not very programmer friendly. To improve the behavior, you can add a **UserControl_Resize** event handler to resize the shape controls dynamically.

To calculate the new size and position for each shape control, take the **ScaleWidth** of the **UserControl** object, round it so that it is divisible by 20 (the number of shape controls), and then divide it by 20. Given the width of each control, you can easily determine where the left edge of each control should be. You can set the height of the shape controls to the **UserControl**'s **ScaleHeight** property.

Finishing Touches

Now you are almost finished. You can set the **ToolboxIcon** property to a bitmap so that your control shows up with your choice of pictures in toolboxes. You can also edit the project properties and change the name of the control.

If you want a property sheet for the control, you can just run the Property Sheet Wizard. It allows you to select a standard page to select colors (in this case, the foreground color). You can also define custom pages and place properties (such as **Direction** and **Hold**) on them. The wizard automatically creates appropriate pages (see Figures 12.6 and 12.7).

Using The Control

When you are finished, you can test the control. Simply select File | Add Project. When you are prompted, tell the environment that you want an EXE file project. Your control then appears in the Toolbox. Simply grab it, and place it on the form as you would any other component. Use the object browser to set the properties; then double-click on the control to write event handlers. It's easy.

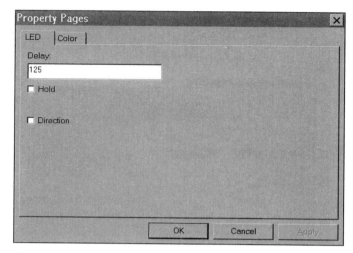

Figure 12.6
A custom property page.

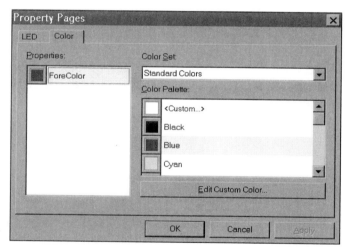

Figure 12.7
A stock property page.

If you want to use the control in a regular VB project or a Web page, you can generate an OCX file (you can find the choice on the File menu). Then, you need to add the component to your toolbox by using the Components command on the Project menu, and you're ready to go. Some other environments might require you to register your control, but that's no problem because VB generates self-registration code automatically. Simply run REGSRVR32.EXE, and specify the OCX file that contains your control.

Packaging Your Control

What happens if you want to distribute your control to other users? To help you create distributions, VB provides a special tool (the Package and Deployment Wizard) that you run directly from the Start menu. You can also install it as a Visual Basic Add-In. It allows you to create setup files for your project or files appropriate to download over the Internet. Simply tell it what project you want to distribute, and it does the rest.

VB Summary

This description sounds too good to be true, right? Well, there is one catch. Your control requires a special runtime DLL before it can run. If you're using your control with conventional programs, this isn't a big problem. However, if you want users to download your control over the Internet, it could be annoying. The good news is that after users download the DLL once, they don't need to download it again; they need only download your control.

You can even use the VB Package and Deployment Wizard (available in the Visual Studio program group on your Start menu) to automatically create a setup program for your control. You can create a conventional setup program or a cabinet suitable for Internet downloading just by filling in a few forms.

Speaking of the Internet, you can even set up asynchronous properties using VB. This advanced technique allows you to load a large property (perhaps a picture) over the network without waiting.

Of course, VB isn't your only choice for creating ActiveX controls (although it might be the easiest way). If you are a C++ programmer, you can use MFC to create ActiveX controls. These controls are nearly as easy to make, but they require the MFC runtime, which is about as big as the VB runtime. If you want to make efficient controls, you can roll them by hand (quite a bit of work), or you can use the ActiveX Template Library (ATL). Although ATL controls can be very lean, they are not nearly as easy to create as VB controls or even MFC-based controls.

The biggest problem with ActiveX controls is that they don't run on a wide variety of browsers. If you want your client-side object to run nearly anywhere, you have to write a Java applet.

Writing A Java Applet

Microsoft offers a Java environment in its Visual J++ product. However, this product is embroiled in legal troubles, and it is not clear whether Microsoft will continue to support it. Earlier versions of Visual J++ provided some support for the visual development of applets. The most recent versions, however, supply virtually no support for developing standard applets. Instead, their visual tools make life easier for those writing Windows-only programs. This is fine if you are writing a Windows program, but applets may run on many different platforms—you usually don't know what operating system the user will have.

In the following sections, I'll show you a calendar applet developed with Java. Along the way, I'll tell you a bit about Java's development philosophy and why you might use Java (and why you might not as well).

About Java

Just in case you've been living in a cave lately, I'll tell you briefly about Java, which is a language similar to C++. As an old-time C and C++ programmer, I think this is probably its chief disadvantage to me. When I use VB or Delphi, it's clear to me, almost immediately, that I'm not using C++. I enter a few too many equal signs once or twice until I shift mental gears; then I don't have any more problems. With Java, I never shift gears. It's very much like C++, so I never get used to the differences (and there *are* differences).

Of course, if you have no predisposition to C++, Java is just another language to learn. It has many nice features, including automatic garbage collection and built-in support for multithreading. However, the overriding question is, "Why another language?"

The answer to this question is one word: portability. Java is typically interpreted by a simple virtual machine, or Java Virtual Machine (JVM). If you can write the relatively simple JVM on your computer, you can run Java programs. Of course, other systems have tried this approach (remember UCSD Pascal?), but Sun (the developer of Java) has made two realizations:

◆ The Web needs a programming language that works on disparate platforms.

◆ Programs that run on the Web should have security constraints to prevent them from harming the system or performing malicious activity over the network.

Because any computer that uses a JVM can run a Java program, the first requirement is satisfied. Because Java runs through an interpreter, you can enforce any security restrictions you like. For example, most Web browsers don't allow Java programs to access local files. They also prohibit programs from opening network connections, unless they're back to the server that provided the program.

If you want to create programs that run on many different platforms, Java is your best chance at doing that. If you want the programs to run on the Web, it's your only chance (for now, anyway). ActiveX works very well on the PC but lacks Java's broad platform support. Even on platforms that support ActiveX, you usually need separate object files for each platform. Because Java is interpreted, a Java class file can run on any computer with a JVM.

Many people think that Java is a major innovation in language design, but it's really just an ordinary object-oriented language that is very similar to C++. The power that people associate with Java is really due to the class library. The same is true for C or C++. C isn't a very sophisticated language. Most of the interesting things you can do in C are really calls to the library. By itself, C (or C++) does very little.

Although Java includes several libraries, the most interesting is the Abstract Windows Toolkit (AWT). This library allows you to create windows, menus, and other user-interface items. If you are accustomed to Windows programming, you'll find the AWT somewhat anemic. For example, the concept of a resource does not exist in a Java program. Dialog boxes and menus require code to create and manage them. Many Windows controls have no equivalent in Java. The newer versions of Java incorporate the Swing classes, which have many more user interface options. However, until major Web browsers support Swing without extra software, most Web developers won't use the library.

On the plus side, Java has some features not readily available in Windows. For example, layout managers control the size and position of other windows. These layout managers allow you to set the position of elements even when you don't know the screen size. For example, you might have a layout manager that resizes all the controls in a user interface when the main window resizes.

Java programs come in two flavors: applications and applets. An application is a standalone program. It has its own main window and behaves like any other program on the target system. An applet doesn't have its own main window. Instead, it relies on another program to contain it. Usually, this program is a Web browser, but it can be any Java-aware program.

When you create a Java applet, you extend the standard **Applet** object. This object (provided by the Java library) contains all the functionality of an applet that does nothing. You only need to write the parts of your applet that don't follow the standard behavior.

Java Development Environments

You can start programming in Java in many ways. If you are comfortable with command-line tools, and you aren't afraid to use your own text editor, you can download the entire Java Development Kit (JDK) from Sun for free (**java.sun.com**). The JDK is available for many different operating systems, but its tools are bare-bones.

If you want to stay low-cost, you can use a variety of add-ons for the JDK that can provide an integrated development environment and better debugging (the JDK's debugger is anemic). IBM's Jikes debugger, in particular, is well worth the download time (**www.alphaworks. ibm.com/aw.nsf/techmain/jikesdebugger**).

If you want to pay for a tool, you can choose from plenty of options. Besides Microsoft, nearly every development tool vendor (including Inprise, Symantec, IBM, and even Sun) has Java suites that include visual development tools, build managers, and all the bells and whistles you expect. You also can choose from many products from lesser-known companies that may or may not be around tomorrow. However, these tools turn out the same class files as the free JDK; you are paying for support and convenience.

Developing The Calendar

To test-drive Java, I decided to develop a simple calendar applet that you can place on a Web page (see Figure 12.8). This simple application doesn't require any dialog boxes, multithreading, or much of anything special. All you need is a simple applet, some code to draw the calendar, and enough smarts to figure out which day of the week corresponds to a given date.

The construction of the calendar object is typical of many Java applets. Because the calendar is simple, I didn't allow for multithreading. For parameters, I added the ones shown in Table 12.1.

The only code that is specific to the calendar applet is the code that handles the specific parameters and the **paint** routine (see Listing 12.2). This code calculates the dimensions for the calendar and then draws it. It also computes the date/day relationship. Instead of writing a standard Zeller's congruence function (the standard way to convert a date to a day of the week) to handle the situation, I relied on a standard Java class, **Date**. The **getDay**

Table 12.1   Calendar parameters.

Parameter	Definition
MONTH	Month (0=January)
YEAR	Year
FGCOLOR	Foreground color (RGB format)
BGCOLOR	Background color (RGB format)

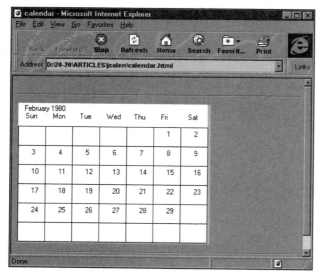

Figure 12.8
The calendar applet.

function for this class knows how to convert a date to a day of the week. My code uses this function to correctly assign the date's position on the calendar.

Listing 12.2   The calendar applet.

```
//*******************
// calendar.java:        Applet
//
//******************
import java.applet.*;
import java.awt.*;
import java.util.Date;


//===================================
// Main Class for applet calendar
//
//===================================
public class calendar extends Applet
{
        // PARAMETER SUPPORT:
        // Parameters allow an HTML author to pass
        // information to the applet;
        // the HTML author specifies them using the
        // <PARAM> tag within the <APPLET>
        // tag.  The following variables are used to
        // store the values of the
        // parameters.
    //--------------------------------

    // Members for applet parameters
    // <type>         <MemberVar>   = <Default Value>
    //--------------------------------
        private int m_month = 0;
        private int m_year = 1980;
        private int m_bgcolor = 16777215;  // white
        private int m_fgcolor = 0;

    // Parameter names.  To change a name of a
    // parameter, you need only make
    // a single change.  Simply modify
    // the value of the parameter string below.
    //--------------------------------
        private final String PARAM_month = "month";
        private final String PARAM_year = "year";
        private final String PARAM_bgcolor = "bgcolor";
        private final String PARAM_fgcolor = "fgcolor";
```

```
    // calendar Class Constructor
    //-------------------------------
    public calendar()
    {
            // TODO: Add constructor code here
    }


    // APPLET INFO SUPPORT:
    // The getAppletInfo() method returns a string
    // describing the applet's
    // author, copyright date,
    // or miscellaneous information.
//-------------------------------
    public String getAppletInfo()
    {
     return "Name: calendar\r\n" +
       "Author: Al Williams alw@al-williams.com\r\n";


    }


    // PARAMETER SUPPORT
    // The getParameterInfo() method returns an
    // array of strings describing
    // the parameters understood by this applet.
    //
// calendar Parameter Information:
//   { "Name", "Type", "Description" },
//-------------------------------
    public String[][] getParameterInfo()
    {
            String[][] info =
            {
             { PARAM_month, "int", "Month" },
             { PARAM_year, "int", "Year" },
             { PARAM_bgcolor, "int",
               "Background color" },
             { PARAM_fgcolor, "int",
               "Foreground color" },
            };
            return info;
    }


    // The init() method is called by the
    // AWT when an applet is first loaded or
    // reloaded. Override this method to
    // perform whatever initialization your
```

```
      // applet needs, such as initializing
      // data structures, loading images or
      // fonts, creating frame windows,
      // setting the layout manager, or adding UI
      // components.
//-------------------------------
      public void init()
      {
        // PARAMETER SUPPORT
        // The following code retrieves the
        // value of each parameter
        // specified with the <PARAM> tag
        // and stores it in a member
        // variable.
        //---------------------------
             String param;

             // month: Month
             //---------------------------
             param = getParameter(PARAM_month);
             if (param != null)
                 m_month = Integer.parseInt(param);

             // year: Year
             //---------------------------
             param = getParameter(PARAM_year);
             if (param != null)
                 m_year = Integer.parseInt(param);

             // bgcolor: Background color
             //---------------------------
             param = getParameter(PARAM_bgcolor);
             if (param != null)
                 m_bgcolor = Integer.parseInt(param);

             // fgcolor: Foreground color
             //---------------------------
             param = getParameter(PARAM_fgcolor);
             if (param != null)
                 m_fgcolor = Integer.parseInt(param);
      }

    // Place additional applet cleanup code here.
    // destroy() is called
    // when your applet is terminating
    // and being unloaded.
    //-------------------------------
```

```
public void destroy()
{
        // TODO: Place applet cleanup code here
}

// calendar Paint Handler
//-------------------------------
public void paint(Graphics g)
{
        FontMetrics fm;
        int margin;
        int i,j;
        // height and width of each cell
        int cellheight,cellwidth;
        String months[]= // names of months
        {
          "January","February","March", "April",
          "May", "June", "July", "August",
          "September", "October", "November",
          "December"
          };
        String days[]= // names of days
        {
                "Sun","Mon","Tue",
                "Wed","Thu","Fri","Sat"
        };
        int len[]= { // 30 days hath September...
         31, 28, 31, 30, 31,
         30, 31, 31, 30, 31, 30, 31 };
        int row=0;  // current drawing row
        String title;  // title at top
        Color fg,bg;  // colors
        Rectangle r;
        r=bounds();
        fm=g.getFontMetrics();
        margin=3*fm.getHeight(); // top portion
        cellwidth=r.width/7;
        cellheight=(r.height-margin)/6;
        fg=new Color(m_fgcolor);
        bg=new Color(m_bgcolor);
        g.setColor(bg);
        // draw header
        g.fillRect(0,0,7*cellwidth,margin);
        Integer yr;
        yr=new Integer(m_year);
        title=months[m_month]+" "+yr.toString();
```

```
        g.setColor(fg);
        g.drawString(title,10,fm.getHeight());
        // draw cells
        for (j=0;j<7;j++)
        {
            g.drawString(days[j],
              j*cellwidth+cellwidth/2-10,
              fm.getHeight()*2); // day names
            for (i=0;i<6;i++)
            {
                g.setColor(bg); // draw inside
                g.fillRect(j*cellwidth,margin+
                  i*cellheight,cellwidth,
                  cellheight);
                g.setColor(fg); // draw outside
                g.drawRect(j*cellwidth,
                  margin+i*cellheight,
                  cellwidth,cellheight);
            }
        }
        j=len[m_month];
        // add one for leap years
        if (m_month==1 && m_year%4 == 0) j++;
        // draw dates
        for (i=0;i<j;i++)
        {
            Date date = new Date(m_year-1900,
              m_month,i+1);
            Integer day= new Integer(date.getDay());
            Integer I= new Integer(i+1);
            g.drawString(I.toString(),
              day.intValue()*cellwidth+cellwidth/2,
              margin+cellheight*row+cellheight/2);
            if (day.intValue()==6) row++;
        }
    }


// The start() method is called
// when the page containing the applet
// first appears on the screen.
// The Applet Wizard's initial implementation
// of this method starts
// execution of the applet's thread.
//------------------------------
public void start()
```

```
        {
                // TODO: Place additional applet start code here
        }


        // The stop() method is called
        // when the page containing the applet is
        // no longer on the screen. The Applet Wizard's
        // initial implementation of
        // this method stops execution of the
        // applet's thread.
        //-----------------------------
        public void stop()
        {
        }



        // TODO: Place additional applet code here


}
```

Using The Calendar

You can use the **<APPLET>** tag to include the calendar applet in a Web page (see Listing 12.3). If you care only about compatibility with Internet Explorer, you could also use the **<OBJECT>** tag to include the applet. The Java JDK also has a program, appletviewer, that accepts an HTML file like this and displays the corresponding applet.

Listing 12.3   Using the calendar.

```
<HTML>
<HEAD>
<TITLE>calendar</TITLE>
</HEAD>
<BODY>
<HR>
<!-- the applet tag appears below (commented out) -->
<!APPLET
    CODE=calendar.class
    NAME=calendar
    ID=cal
    WIDTH=320
    HEIGHT=240>
    <PARAM NAME=month VALUE="1">
    <PARAM NAME=year VALUE="1980">
    <PARAM NAME=events VALUE="">
    <PARAM NAME=bgcolor VALUE=16777215>
    <PARAM NAME=fgcolor VALUE=0>
```

```
</APPLET>
<-- Here is the same applet with an object tag -->
<OBJECT CLASSID=calendar.class HEIGHT=240 WIDTH=320 NAME=cal>
    <PARAM NAME=month VALUE="1">
    <PARAM NAME=year VALUE="1980">
    <PARAM NAME=events VALUE="">
    <PARAM NAME=bgcolor VALUE=16777215>
    <PARAM NAME=fgcolor VALUE=0>
</OBJECT>
<HR>
<SCRIPT>
<!--
 cal.year=1997
//-->
</SCRIPT>
</BODY>
</HTML>
```

Notice the series of **<PARAM>** tags in Listing 12.3. These tags set the initial values for the parameters in the applet. The wizard writes code so that variable **m_month**, for example, gets the value for the **MONTH** parameter. If the HTML doesn't supply a value, the wizard arranges for the default values you specified at design time.

Notice that the code that reads the parameters is in the **init** routine, meaning that after you read the parameters, their value is fixed. This is unlike ActiveX controls, in which you can change properties at any time using script.

Networking With Java

The biggest problem I see with Java is that it's too much like C++. Of course, some people see this similarity as an advantage. I've been programming in C++ (and C) for a long time, so I have two problems. First, because Java is so much like C++, I think I know it better than I actually do. Second, I find it difficult to switch mental gears when I work with Java. If I'm writing, for example, in VB, I can easily change my mindset from C++ to Basic because the two languages are very, very different. However, Java *feels* like C++ enough to prevent me from making the shift. This problem is compounded by the fact that Visual J++ (the Java development system I use) uses the same environment that Visual C++ uses.

My Web page (**www.al-williams.com**) uses a small Java applet to scroll current news at the bottom of the screen (see Figure 12.9). Originally, I used an applet I found on the Web in some library of free applets, but this applet didn't include source code. I didn't like some things about it, but I couldn't change anything because I had only the class file. Eventually, I decided to write my own version of the applet so that I could incorporate the features I wanted. I had written some applets that loaded images across the Web—that's easy. I found that loading text or other document types is a bit more involved. I also found that my commonsense assumptions about double buffering were incorrect.

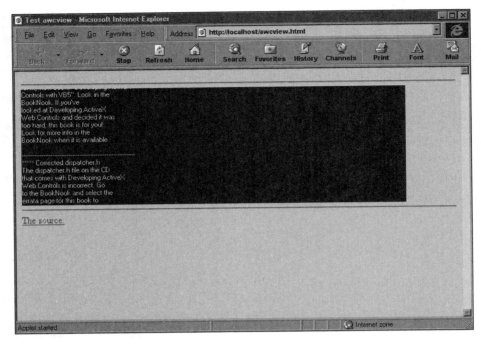

Figure 12.9
The AWCVIEW scrolling text applet.

In the following sections, I'll show you my text-scrolling applet. You'll find out how Java loads data from the Web and how you can customize the process. Along the way, you'll see how to draw off screen (double buffering) and why doing so might not be a good idea.

Java's Library

Like most languages, Java isn't very powerful by itself. The real power comes from the libraries and toolkits that come with Java. These libraries contain classes that do useful things. In this case, the important objects are **URL**, a class that manages Internet connections, and **Thread**, a class that creates an executable thread.

The **URL** class (part of the **java.net** package) really does more than its name implies. It not only stores a URL, but also manages a connection over the network and transfers data.

Of course, if you want a picture or a sound, the **Applet** class automatically loads your file through the **getImage** and **getAudioClip** functions. But what about other types? That's where the **URL** class comes into play. First, you need to construct the object. Usually, you pass the constructor two arguments: the base URL and the URL of the item in question. If the second URL is a full path (for example, **www.coriolis.com/xyz.txt**), the first argument is meaningless. However, if the second argument is not a full path, the constructor uses the first argument to build a full path to the correct name. Where do you get the base URL? The

Applet class provides two handy calls—**getCodeBase** and **getDocumentBase**—to do the trick. The first call returns the URL that corresponds to the location that contains the applet's class file. The **getDocumentBase** function returns the URL that points to the document containing the applet.

After you construct the URL, what do you have? Not much. However, the **URL** object has many functions that you can now use. For example, **openStream** allows you to obtain an **InputStream** object that corresponds to the URL. Armed with this capability, you can create a **BufferedInputStream** or a **DataInputStream**. You can then use these streams as though they were files.

However, an even easier way is to use the **getContent** method, which essentially is shorthand for **openConnection().getContent()**. To establish the connection (a **URLConnection** object), follow these steps:

1. If the application has previously set up an instance of **URLStreamHandlerFactory** as the stream handler factory, the library code calls the factory's **createURLStreamHandler** method, with the protocol string as an argument, to create the stream protocol handler.

2. If the previous step fails (no factory exists or the method returns **null**), the constructor tries to load the class named **sun.net.www.*protocol*.Handler**, where *protocol* is the name of the protocol. If this class doesn't exist, or if the class exists but it isn't a subclass of **URLStreamHandler**, the method throws a **MalformedURLException**.

If you look at your Java source code, you'll see many protocol classes (**http**, **news**, **ftp**, and so on). To actually acquire content, Java looks to another special class:

♦ If the application has set up a content handler factory instance using the **setContentHandlerFactory** method, the **createContentHandler** method of that instance is called with the content type as an argument. The result is a content handler for that content type.

♦ If no content handler factory has been set up yet, or if the factory's **createContentHandler** method returns **null**, the application loads the class named *prefix*.*contentType*. The *prefix* is one of the strings in the system property **java.content.handler.pkgs**; you separate the strings with a pipe character (|). You form *contentType* by taking the content type string and replacing each slash character with a period (.) and all other nonalphanumeric characters with the underscore character (_). If the specified class does not exist or is not a subclass of **ContentHandler**, an **UnknownServiceException** is thrown.

By default, the **java.content.handler.pkgs** property is set to **sun.net.www**. Again, the library contains many appropriate objects for various content types (for example, text/plain, image/gif, and image/jpeg). These collect and return objects of the appropriate type. For example, the **sun.net.www.text.plain** object returns a string.

You can use this knowledge to build your own content handlers. However, for the text scroller, the default plain text handler works fine.

You might wonder why a simple text-scrolling application requires the **Thread** object. The answer is simple. The program requires a periodic nudge to cause the lines of text to scroll. However, you can't just sleep in the main program, as that would prevent the program from functioning correctly. Instead, the main program starts a thread that sleeps for the correct interval; then the thread forces the main program to repaint when it changes the displayed lines.

The Basic Program

Armed with this information, you can easily create the scroller (see Listing 12.4). The basic applet looks a lot like the previous one. The first interesting method, **init**, reads the parameters. It also creates a URL (on the basis of the **m_file** variable) and loads the entire file as a string. Next, the program breaks the string into individual lines and places them in the **lines** array.

Listing 12.4   The scroller applet.

```
//****************************************
// awcview.java:          Applet
//
//****************************************
import java.applet.*;
import java.awt.*;
import java.net.*;
import java.io.*;
import sun.net.www.*;
//=====================================================
// Main Class for applet awcview
//
//=====================================================
public class awcview extends Applet implements Runnable
{
    //-------------------------------------------------

    // Members for applet parameters
    // <type>         <MemberVar>    = <Default Value>
    //-------------------------------------------------
        private String m_file = "";       // file to scroll
        private int m_bgcolor = 65535;    // BG color
        private int m_fgcolor = 0;        // FG color
        private int m_speed = 5;          // speed of scroll in ms
        private int m_step=1;             // size of step
        private URL url;                  // our URL
        private String content;           // string containing text
        private String[] lines;           // array containing text
        private int linect;               // # of lines
```

```java
    private int current=0;          // current line at top
    private boolean first=true;     // first paint pass
    private boolean lock=false;     // don't scroll
    private int offset;             // where to paint 1st line
    private int fonth;              // font height
    private Thread timer;           // timer thread
// Only for double buffering
    private Image img;
// Parameter names.  To change a name of a parameter,
// you need only make a single change.
// Simply modify the value of the
// parameter string below.
//---------------------------------------------------
    private final String PARAM_file = "file";
    private final String PARAM_bgcolor = "bgcolor";
    private final String PARAM_fgcolor = "fgcolor";
    private final String PARAM_speed = "speed";
    private final String PARAM_step="step";

    // awcview Class Constructor
    //---------------------------------------------------
    public awcview()
    {
    }


    // APPLET INFO SUPPORT:
    // The getAppletInfo() method
    // returns a string describing the applet's
    // author, copyright date, or miscellaneous information.
//---------------------------------------------------
    public String getAppletInfo()
    {
            return "Name: awcview\r\n" +
                "Author: Al Williams\r\n" +
                "An applet to scroll text\r\n" +
                "";
    }


    // PARAMETER SUPPORT
    // The getParameterInfo() method returns an array of
    // strings describing the parameters understood
    // by this applet.
    //
// awcview Parameter Information:
//   { "Name", "Type", "Description" },
//---------------------------------------------------
```

```java
        public String[][] getParameterInfo()
        {
                String[][] info =
                {
                   { PARAM_file, "String", "File to read" },
                   { PARAM_bgcolor, "int", "background color" },
                   { PARAM_fgcolor, "int", "foreground color" },
                   { PARAM_speed, "int", "Speed" },
                   { PARAM_step, "int", "Step size"},
                };
                return info;
        }


// Count lines in content
        private int CountLines()
        {
                int n=0;
                int i;
                if (content==null)
                  content="Can't read source file.\n";
                for (i=0;i<content.length();i++)
                {
                        if (content.charAt(i)=='\r'||
                          content.charAt(i)=='\n')
                        {
                                n++;
                                i++;
                                while (i<content.length()&&
                                        (content.charAt(i)=='\r'||
                                        content.charAt(i)=='\n'))
                                           i++;
                        }
                }
        return n;
        }
        // The init() method is called by the AWT
        // when an applet is first loaded or
        // reloaded.
    //-----------------------------------------------
        public void init()
        {
                // PARAMETER SUPPORT
                // The following code retrieves the value
                // of each parameter specified with the
                // <PARAM> tag and stores it in a member
                // variable.
```

```
//--------------------------------------------
String param;
int start,end, i;
char termchar='\n';

// file: file to read
//--------------------------------------------
param = getParameter(PARAM_file);
if (param != null)
        m_file = param;

// bgcolor: background color
//--------------------------------------------
param = getParameter(PARAM_bgcolor);
if (param != null)
        m_bgcolor = Integer.parseInt(param);

// fgcolor: foreground color
//--------------------------------------------
param = getParameter(PARAM_fgcolor);
if (param != null)
        m_fgcolor = Integer.parseInt(param);

// speed: speed
//--------------------------------------------
param = getParameter(PARAM_speed);
if (param != null)
        m_speed = Integer.parseInt(param);

// step parameter
param = getParameter(PARAM_step);
if (param != null)
        m_step = Integer.parseInt(param);

// Read File!
try {
        url=new URL(getDocumentBase(),m_file);
        content=(String)(url.getContent());
    }
catch (MalformedURLException e)
  {
      content="Bad URL: "+url.toString()+"\n"+e.getMessage();
  }
catch (IOException e)
  {
      content="I/O exception: "
```

```
                            + url.toString()+"\n"+e.getMessage();
                }
            catch (Exception e)
              {
                  content="Unknown error: "
                + url.toString()+"\n"+e.getMessage();
              }
            // Break into lines;
            lines=new String[linect=CountLines()];
            start=0;
            if (content.indexOf('\r',0)!=-1) termchar='\r';
            for (i=0;i<linect;i++)
              {
                    end=content.indexOf(termchar,start);
                    if (end==-1)
                            lines[i]=content.substring(start);
                    else
                            lines[i]=content.substring(start,end);
                    start=end;
                    while (start<content.length()&&
                            (content.charAt(start)=='\n'
                            || content.charAt(start)=='\r')) start++;
              }

      }


      // Place additional applet cleanup code here.
      // destroy() is called when
      // your applet is terminating and being unloaded.
      //-------------------------------------------
      public void destroy()
      {
      }

// This routine does the actual painting.
// Since it is here, we can call it from anywhere.
      public void doPaint(Graphics g)
        {
                if (fonth==0) update(g);  // initialize on first try
                Color c;
                int i,ln;
                Rectangle r=bounds();
                c=new Color(m_bgcolor);
                g.setColor(c);
                g.fillRect(0,0,r.width,r.height);
                if (linect==0) return;  // nothing to do
```

```
                c=new Color(m_fgcolor);
                g.setColor(c);
                ln=current;
                for (i=offset;i<=r.height+fonth;i+=fonth)
                {
                        g.drawString(lines[ln++],0,i);
                        if (ln>=linect) ln=0;
                }
        }


// awcview Paint Handler
//----------------------------------------------
public void update(Graphics g)
{

        if (first)  // initial setup
        {
                Rectangle r=bounds();
                Color c=new Color(m_bgcolor);
                FontMetrics fm;
                fm=g.getFontMetrics();
                fonth=fm.getHeight();
                if (m_step<0) m_step=fonth/-m_step;
                if (m_step==0) m_step=1;
                current=0;
                offset=r.height-fonth;
        // The next line is used only for double buffering
                img=createImage(r.width,r.height);
                setBackground(c);
                first=false;
        }
  paint(img.getGraphics());
  // The next line is for double buffering
  g.drawImage(img,0,0,this);
}

public void paint(Graphics g)
{
        doPaint(g);
}

// The start() method is called when the page
// containing the applet first appears on the screen.
//----------------------------------------------
public void start()
{
```

```
                if (timer==null) timer=new Thread(this);
                timer.start();
        }


        // The stop() method is called when the page
        // containing the applet is
        // no longer on the screen.
        // The Applet Wizard's initial implementation of
        // this method stops execution of the applet's thread.
        //---------------------------------------------
        public void stop()
        {
                if (timer!=null) timer.stop();
        }


        public void run()
        {
                Graphics g0;
                while (timer!=null)
                {
                    try
                    {
                        timer.sleep(m_speed);   // wait
                    } catch (InterruptedException e) {}
                    if (first||lock) continue;  // not started yet
                    // advance scroll
                    offset-=m_step;
                    if (offset<=-fonth)
                    {
                        offset=0;
                        if (++current>=linect) current=0;
                    }
                  repaint();
                }
        }




        //---------------------------------------------
        public boolean mouseDown(Event evt, int x, int y)
        {
                lock=!lock;
                return true;
        }


        //---------------------------------------------
        public boolean mouseUp(Event evt, int x, int y)
```

```
        {
                // Nothing for now
                return true;
        }

}
```

The line-breaking logic is a bit odd because I wanted to handle both Windows- and Unix-style files. The code examines the entire string for any **\r** (carriage return) characters. If even one exists, the file is likely to be a Windows text file, so the program splits lines on the **\r** character. If no **\r** characters exist, lines end with **\n** (line feed) characters. In any case, the code skips all **\r** and **\n** characters that it finds grouped together, meaning that the scroller doesn't recognize completely blank lines. If you need a blank line, simply make a line that contains a space or two.

The **paint** routine takes special action the first time you call it. The program needs to know some things about the **Graphics** object it will use, so the **paint** method calculates the font height and other interesting values. Every call to **paint** results in a call to **DoPaint**, which actually calculates the lines to display. This applet does not use double buffering (although it can; see the section "Paint Now Or Later?"). Instead, it draws the lines each time.

The **start** method kicks off the new thread. Notice that the same object that represents the main program also takes care of the thread. It can do so because the object implements the **runnable** interface. Passing **this** to the **Thread** object informs the thread to use the same object.

The code for the thread is in the object's **run** method. This code runs in an endless loop, sleeping most of the time. When it awakes, the thread examines the **first** and **lock** flags. If either is set, the thread goes back to sleep. The first flag indicates that processing hasn't started yet. The second flag tells the thread that the program is paused.

If the thread is active, it alters the **offset** and **current** variables to reflect what line to begin drawing at and where to draw the line on the screen. **DoPaint** uses these variables to draw in response to the **paint** method. Finally, the thread triggers a repaint for the applet and goes back to sleep.

The only other interesting function is the **mouseDown** handler, which toggles the **lock** flag. This allows users to stop scrolling by clicking on the applet. Clicking again resumes the scroll.

Another Way To Load A URL

As usual, you can write a program in more than one way. It's somewhat wasteful to read the entire file as a string and then chop it up into an array. If you prefer, you could use **openStream** on the URL and use the stream it returns to construct a **BufferedInputStream**. You could then construct a **DataInputStream** with the **BufferedInputStream** and use **readLine** to read lines from the **DataInputStream**. This approach is a bit more complicated, but it's more efficient. The only problem is that you can't know how many lines you'll need until you read the entire stream (not a problem if you use a **Vector** object instead of an array). Listing 12.5 shows an excerpt from the same applet that sets up the data input stream object and reads one line at a time.

Listing 12.5   Using a stream.

```
//**************************************
// awcview.java:        Applet
//
//**************************************
import java.applet.*;
import java.awt.*;
import java.net.*;
import java.io.*;
import sun.net.www.*;
import java.util.Vector;
     .
     .
     .
      private Vector lines;
     .
     .
     .


      public void init()
      {
     .
     .
     .


                  try {
                        InputStream is;
                        String s;
                        BufferedInputStream bis;
                        DataInputStream dis;
                        String line;
                        url=new URL(getDocumentBase(),m_file);
                        is=url.openStream();
                        bis=new BufferedInputStream(is);
                        dis=new DataInputStream(bis);
                        do
                        {
                           s=dis.readLine();
```

```
                        if (s!=null)
                        {
                            lines.addElement(s);
                            linect++;
                        }
                    } while (s!=null);   // EOF is s==null
                }
            catch (MalformedURLException e)
            {
                lines.setSize(linect=2);
                content="Bad URL: "+url.toString()+"\n";
                lines.setElementAt(content,0);
                lines.setElementAt(e.getMessage(),1);
            }
            catch (IOException e)
            {
                lines.setSize(linect=2);
                content="I/O exception: " + url.toString()+"\n";
                lines.setElementAt(content,0);
                lines.setElementAt(e.getMessage(),1);
            }
            catch (Exception e)
            {
                lines.setSize(linect=2);
                content="Unknown error: "+url.toString()+"\n";
                lines.setElementAt(content,0);
                lines.setElementAt(e.getMessage(),1);
            }
    }



        .
        .
        .


    public void doPaint(Graphics g)
    {
            Color c;
            int i,ln;
            Rectangle r=bounds();
            c=new Color(m_bgcolor);
            g.setColor(c);
            g.fillRect(0,0,r.width,r.height);
            if (linect==0) return;   // nothing to do
            c=new Color(m_fgcolor);
            g.setColor(c);
            ln=current;
```

```
for (i=offset;i<=r.height+fonth;i+=fonth)
{
        g.drawString((String)lines.elementAt(ln++),0,i);
        if (ln>=linect) ln=0;
}
```
}

.
.
.

Paint Now Or Later?

When I first started this program, I was sure that drawing directly to the screen would result in an annoying flicker. Therefore, I used a technique called *double buffering*. The process is simple. First, the **paint** routine (on its initial pass) creates an **Image** object that is the same size as the applet window. Next, the paint routine simply copies the image to the screen (using **drawImage**). Then, when any portion of the program wants to draw, it can obtain a **Graphics** object from the image, draw to it, and trigger a repaint.

This technique works, but I was surprised at how much flickering occurred when I first used it. The problem is that the **paint** routine is called by the **update** routine, which is part of the default **Applet** class. The **update** code erases the entire drawing area, which is not necessary when double buffering. After all, the buffer will replace the entire drawing area anyway.

Double buffering takes advantage of Java's object-oriented capabilities. The **paint** routine needs only a **Graphics** object. It doesn't know or care where that **Graphics** object originated. When doing ordinary drawing, the **Graphics** object directly refers to the applet's window. When using double buffering, the object refers to an off-screen buffer.

Double buffering is effective because the total time required to copy bits from the off-screen graphic to the screen is less than the time required to render the text (or other graphics). For a simple application like the scroller, this is all that is required. However, you might want to consider a few other ways to optimize Java drawing:

♦ Use the **Graphics** object's **getClipRect** function to determine what area must be redrawn. If you have a complex object, drawing only the visible portion can result in an increase in speed.

♦ If you are writing an animation that requires math, consider calculating as much as possible in advance. Replacing trigonometric functions with lookup tables can also increase speed considerably.

♦ Turn on compiler optimization. For the JDK, the **-O** switch causes the compiler to generate optimized code, which may be faster.

Using The Scroller

Using the scroller could hardly be simpler. You can find a sample HTML file in Listing 12.6 and the parameters you need to set in Table 12.2. The **SPEED** parameter is in milliseconds. The **STEP** parameter, if it is positive, indicates the number of pixels to scroll on each step. If the parameter is negative, it indicates a fraction of the character height. Therefore, when **STEP** is -1, the scrolling is in whole-character increments. When **STEP** is -2, the scrolling is in half-character units, and so on. If the resulting number is 0, the code adjusts it so that **STEP**'s size is 1.

Listing 12.6   Using the scroller.

```
<HTML>
<HEAD>
<TITLE>Test awcview</TITLE>
</HEAD>
<BODY>
<HR>
<APPLET
    CODE=awcview.class
    NAME=awcview
    WIDTH=640
    HEIGHT=200>
    <PARAM NAME=file VALUE="test.txt">
    <PARAM NAME=bgcolor VALUE=0>
    <PARAM NAME=fgcolor VALUE=255>
    <PARAM NAME=speed VALUE=500>
    <PARAM NAME=step VALUE=-2>
</APPLET>
<HR>
<A HREF="awcview.java">The source.</A>
</BODY>
</HTML>
```

Don't forget that the file you supply is a text file, not an HTML file. Java doesn't know how to interpret HTML. You could write an HTML parser in Java, but doing so would be quite a bit of work.

Table 12.2   Scroller parameters.

Parameter	Type	Description
FILE	String	URL (relative or absolute) of file to display
BGCOLOR	int	Background color
FGCOLOR	int	Foreground color
SPEED	int	Delay between scroll steps in milliseconds
STEP	int	Size of scroll steps (see text)

Another thing to watch out for is line width. The applet doesn't wrap your lines, so the lines must fit inside the applet window. Making the lines fit can be a problem if you design your Web page on a 1024×768 screen but your users have 640×480 screens. When developing Web pages, it is a good idea to set your screen resolution down temporarily or to use a laptop to look at the page to get an idea of what users will see if they have small screens.

Future Plans

You could make many enhancements to this text scroller. For example, it would be nice to allow for font effects (bold and italic, for example). It might be nice to allow users to scroll manually with the mouse if the **lock** flag is **TRUE**. None of these additions would be very difficult.

The ultimate, of course, would be to have the applet recognize HTML. However, doing so is a tall order; HTML can be complex to parse and display. Sun provides a Java component that can display HTML, but you must license it to use it (see **www.sun.com/software/ htmlcomponent/index.html**).

A more advanced improvement would use the **URLConnection** object to detect when the source file on the server changes. Then, the program could reload the file and start over again.

The Scroller In Review

If you are a C++ programmer, take heart. You can learn Java with a minimum of fuss. Breaking your old C++ habits just *seems* to take forever. Although Java development tools are still not as nice as some C++ environments, the networking library is quite impressive. If you aren't a C++ programmer, Java is still approachable. Many of the features that make C++ hard to learn are absent from Java.

Don't get me wrong. I still enjoy using C++, but for Internet programming, Java has several distinct advantages. The best way to learn is to dive right in, pick a small project, and write it.

Of course, some programmers won't try a new language no matter what. Maybe we can port the Java library to C++ for them and make a few dollars in the process.

Is using Java as easy as using VB? Not unless you're already a Java or C++ programmer. Even then, VB is very easy to use and learn. However, only Java applets can currently claim to run on a wide variety of platforms.

Java Beans

One area that has received a lot of attention lately is Java Beans. *Java Beans* are simply Java objects that support a particular set of function calls known as the *reflection Application*

Programming Interface (API). By providing this API, programming tools can provide support for the object.

What does this mean to you? A Java Bean—when combined with the right development tools—allows you to do drag-and-drop development similar to what you might expect in Visual Basic, for example. The tools can discover the component's properties, methods, and events and provide ways for you to manipulate them. The object itself can provide custom user interfaces for specialized properties.

If you are accustomed to other visual programming environments, none of these capabilities will be new. The advantage to using Java Beans is that, like Java, they can potentially run on any platform.

Any object that supports the reflection API and adheres to a few simple conventions is a Java Bean. So, an applet might also be a Java Bean. You could also have an ordinary object that is a Bean. In that case, you would have to host the Bean in an applet just like you would use any Java object in an applet. At runtime, the fact that the object is a Bean is usually not important. The real benefit is at development time.

Many companies specialize in selling Beans (for example, see **www.flashline.com**). Browsing through these catalogs of Beans can give you plenty of ideas. Also, you might want to use some commercially available Beans in your own programs.

Client Controls in Review

Using VB enables you to easily create ActiveX controls. Visual J++ simplifies writing Java applets, but that's only part of the story. If you're a C++ programmer, you can certainly write ActiveX controls using C++. Microsoft Foundation Classes (MFC) help out a lot but tend to make large controls. The ActiveX Template Library (ATL), also from Microsoft, makes leaner controls but takes more effort to master.

On the Java side, many environments promise to simplify Java development. Sun and Symantec are both well known for Visual Java tools, and Borland's tools are well respected.

So, if you need client controls or applets, don't be afraid to write your own. With a little practice, you'll find it great fun and maybe even profitable.

You can find a great deal of information on both ActiveX and Java technologies in books and magazines and on the Web. For more information about Java, take a look at the *Java Black Book* by Steven Holzner (The Coriolis Group, 2000). You might also have a look at *Web Techniques* magazine (**www.webtechniques.com**) where my "Java@Work" column appears every month.

Chapter 13
Other Choices

Al Williams

Have you noticed that the old-fashioned main street has all but vanished? Today, most shopping is centered either around a mall or inside a giant all-in-one store like Wal-Mart or Kmart. This evolution in shopping isn't very surprising, if you think about it. People like to have choices.

Technology professionals like choices, too. That's why most people like standards. If you use, for example, a standard database language, you can change database vendors at will. (In real life, changing vendors often isn't this easy, but at least it's true in theory.)

This book focuses exclusively on Active Server Page scripting with Internet Information Server (IIS). Of course, you can't ignore related technologies such as client-side script on the browser, but for the most part, this book's content is strictly Microsoft-related.

Sometimes, it seems as though Microsoft is the only game in town. However, you can do ASP scripting in other ways, and indeed find alternatives to ASP. In this chapter, I'll show you some of those alternatives and provide you with some pointers to get more information.

ASP Tools

With the exception of Chapter 9, this book has focused on a bare-bones approach to ASP. However, you can choose from several tools to create Active Server Pages. In Chapter 9, you read about Microsoft FrontPage and Microsoft Visual InterDev. These tools can create ASP pages—often automatically.

Another tool is Macromedia's Drumbeat 2000 Active Server Pages version. Macromedia—a well-known player in the Web world—touts Drumbeat as a highly integrated solution for developers deploying data-driven sites that require compatibility with a variety of browsers. You can find more information about Drumbeat at **www.macromedia.com/software/drumbeat**. You also can check out a third-party site at **www.drum-machine.com**.

Regardless of which tool you use—Notepad, Visual InterDev, Drumbeat, vi, or Emacs—you still need a good grounding in how the code works. Nothing is more frustrating than trying to figure out why some generated code doesn't work when you have no idea what the tool did for you in the first place.

Popular Web Servers

If you run Windows as your operating system, you probably use IIS as a Web server. Why not? It is essentially free, and it integrates nicely with Windows as you would expect. However, IIS is not the only game in town. Indeed, if you are using a server that runs on another operating system, IIS might not even be an option. Many Web servers run Unix, and a growing number use Linux—the open source Unix-like operating system. Some Web sites even use the Macintosh platform. IIS does not work on any of these platforms.

A dizzying array of choices is available when it comes to Web servers. The following are a few of the most popular choices (other than IIS):

◆ *Apache*—This server is another open source product (in other words, free) and a very popular Web server indeed. You can get this server prebuilt for a variety of platforms (including Windows and Linux). You can also get the source code and build it yourself—in theory—on any platform with a standard C compiler. You can find Apache at **www.apache.org**.

◆ *Netscape Enterprise*—Netscape makes several Web servers primarily aimed at high-volume e-commerce sites. According to Netscape, this server powers Charles Schwab, Lycos, and Excite, among other Web sites. Check out this server at **www.netscape.com/products**.

◆ *Domino*—This Web server is a product of the IBM buyout of Lotus, and it has strong roots in Lotus Notes and IBM technologies (including CGI with Rexx). You can find more details about Domino at **http://domino.lotus.com**.

◆ *Website Professional*—O'Reilly Software makes this Web server, which has a loyal following. This server handles Windows CGI easily (even in Visual Basic). It even supports ASP. Check it out at **http://website.oreilly.com**.

◆ *Commerce Server/400*—This Web server is designed for the IBM AS/400 computer. It is available at **www.inetmi.com**.

◆ *Java Server*—Sun's Java server is cross-platform (because it uses Java) and is well integrated with Java, as you might expect both from its name and its pedigree. You can read more about it at **www.sun.com/software/jwebserver/index.html**.

Plenty of other competitors market servers, too. Of course, like most things on the Internet, the list changes daily. You can find a comprehensive listing at **http://webservercompare.internet.com**.

ASP Without IIS

If you don't use IIS, can you still use ASP? In some cases, you can. The ActiveScripting group (at **www.activescripting.org/html/download.html**) has versions of ASP that run on Apache and Netscape servers for Windows. This group is an open source project, so you can download the source code if you are so inclined. At the time of this writing, the code is a beta test release, but that may change by the time you read this chapter. Also, there may well be more support for other servers and platforms.

Another option is ChiliASP at **www.chilisoft.com**. Although this product is somewhat pricey, it does provide very solid ASP support on a variety of servers and platforms, including AIX, OS/390, Solaris, Linux, and HP-UX. As I mentioned earlier, Website Professional (from O'Reilly) also supports ASP. Another commercial offering from Halcyon Software (**www.halcyonsoft.com/prods/iasp/iasp.htm**) produces iASP, which adds ASP support to any server that can run Java servlets.

Just because you can run ASP with other servers, should you? After all, Microsoft includes IIS with Microsoft Windows, so if you're using Windows, why bother with anything else? Well, another server might be attractive for several reasons.

For example, your company (or client) may stipulate that you use a different server for any of a number of reasons. Perhaps the Web site may move to Unix or Linux at some future date. Perhaps support personnel or a client's staff members are familiar with another server and do not want to learn about IIS.

Of course, using IIS has distinct advantages. It is tightly integrated with Windows, as you would expect. Also, Microsoft supports it—an important consideration if you require assistance.

Other Scripting Options

Many tools try to achieve the same goal as ASP—activating Web content. Many of these tools work on multiple platforms, including some that work with IIS.

Some of the more common solutions include the following:

◆ *CGI*—The Common Gateway Interface allows you to write external programs that supply Web content. Most people use Perl with CGI, although you can use practically any language.

◆ *PHP*—PHP is an open source scripting language that is quite popular (it used to be known as PHP/FI). It is very similar to ASP.

♦ *Servlets*—Servlets are objects you write in Java to produce Web content.

♦ *JSP*—Java Server Pages (JSP) allow you to mix HTML and Java (not JavaScript, but real Java) together. JSP compiles this mix into a servlet that can produce dynamic Web pages.

♦ *ColdFusion*—ColdFusion uses special tags to add scripts and database access to Web pages.

Each of these systems has its proponents and detractors. All of them can perform essentially the same tasks; some make certain jobs easier than others, however.

Perl/CGI

Using CGI is the original way to add features to Web sites. The Common Gateway Interface is a standard way that a Web server can spawn an external program to handle requests. The program can receive its data via a command line or as standard input. The server sets certain environment variables for the external program to read. The program's standard output specifies the data the server will return to the browser.

CGI has several appealing properties. For example, you can use almost any programming language to write CGI programs. In practice, most people use Perl, a common scripting language under Unix, but nearly any programming language can be used. If you write portable programs, your scripts can run on many platforms. Nearly all modern servers support CGI, too, so this may be the most universal solution.

Unfortunately, CGI has its price. Spawning a new program for each user request is not very efficient. For high-volume sites, the overhead of running new programs for every request may be too expensive.

Still, many people do use CGI, and many free and low-cost Perl scripts are available to do everything from counting hits to running online auctions. If you get comfortable with Perl, you can even use it as an ASP scripting language (check out **www.activestate.com/ ActivePerl/** for more details).

PHP

PHP is an open source scripting language similar to ASP that you embed in a Web page. You can find its home page at **www.php.net**. PHP is available for many servers and platforms (including IIS).

Like ASP, PHP uses a special tag to introduce script. The following is a small block of PHP code:

```
<?php
$message = "Howdy, World!";
echo $message;
?>
```

You can even reconfigure PHP to use ASP-style brackets or other tags of your choice. If you are a C or Perl programmer, you'll find PHP's syntax easy to follow. PHP has all the features you would expect; you can read the value of form fields and set cookies—pretty much anything you can do with ASP that doesn't require an external ActiveX control.

This small piece of PHP code sets a persistent cookie:

```php
<?php
$exp = mktime(0,0,0,1,1,2050);
setcookie('name', 'Paul', $exp);
?>
```

The cookie's expiration date is January 1 of the year 2050.

PHP is very similar to ASP and has broad platform support. Because it is open source (and free), you can find it on many commercial Web hosts.

Servlets

Servlets provide a way to create Java objects that the server uses to satisfy requests. This concept is similar to ordinary CGI, except for one important fact: A smart implementation of servlets can create these Java objects once and use them many times. Being able to reuse objects helps the server avoid the inefficiency associated with CGI scripts. Of course, Java runs on many platforms with no changes, so—in theory—a servlet you write on one machine can run on another.

Of course, this increased efficiency is a potential benefit. The original Web server that supported servlets was Sun's Java Server. Because it uses Java, this works quite well. Other servers may or may not be so efficient. In the worst case, a server could use a CGI module to support servlets, which would offer no performance benefit at all.

JSP

Servlets are more similar to Java CGI scripts than anything else. They lack the simplicity of embedding script directly into HTML pages. That's where JSP (Java Server Pages) fills the gap. The following is a simple JSP page:

```jsp
<H1>Does anybody know what time it is?</H1>
<%
java.util.Date datetime =
  new java.util.Date(System.currentTimeMillis());
%>
<%=datetime.getHours()%>:
<%=datetime.getMinutes()%>:
<%=datetime.getSeconds()%>
```

As you can see, this example is little more than ASP, except that the scripting language is full-blown Java, not a subset scripting language.

You'll notice another subtle difference between JSP and most other scripting solutions: The JSP system (for most servers, at least) actually compiles the JSP page and creates a servlet. This servlet creates the HTML output to the browser. This means that after the system compiles the page, it is an efficient servlet, not a piece of script.

Because the system compiles the page into Java, you can, in fact, generate Java compile-time errors in addition to runtime errors. You can even examine the generated Java code, if you like.

ASP relies on ActiveX controls for much of its functionality. Without ActiveX, ASP can't access databases, for example. Where ASP uses ActiveX controls, JSP uses—not surprisingly—Java Beans. Java Beans are analogous to ActiveX controls, except that they use the Java language.

You can find many resources relating to JSP on the Web, including an excellent FAQ at **www.esperanto.org.nz/jsp/jspfaq.html** and an introduction to JSP at **www.esperanto.org.nz/jspbook**.

ColdFusion

ColdFusion (from Allaire) is another popular solution that targets many different servers. If you've ever visited a Web site that uses CFM files instead of HTML files, you've seen ColdFusion at work. Like ASP and PHP, ColdFusion uses special tags to delimit its code. For example, the following line of ColdFusion script changes to another URL:

```
<CFLOCATION URL="/#APPLICATION.RootDir#/login/fail.cfm" ADDTOKEN="No">
```

The special tags begin with **<CF** and end, if they require an end tag, with **</CF**. For example, the following **if** statement is coded in ColdFusion:

```
<CFIF ISDEFINED(SESSION.VALIDATED) IS "No" OR SESSION.VALIDATED IS "No">
<CFLOCATION URL="/#APPLICATION.RootDir#/login/fail.cfm" ADDTOKEN="No">
</CFIF>
```

The **<CFIF>** and **</CFIF>** tags constitute an **if** statement.

ColdFusion supports the notion of application and session variables. It also can create client variables that reside on the user's computer. These variables provide a good place to store data that pertains to a specific user when you are using a Web farm (that is, multiple load-balancing servers).

Which To Use?

This book is about ASP, so it's no surprise that I do prefer ASP over these other systems. If I had to choose one system other than ASP, it would probably be JSP. Although the compilation step is cumbersome, JSP offers the simplicity of scripting, combined with the power and portability of Java.

Although PHP is comparable to ASP, it lacks an easy facility to use external components, which is where ASP (and JSP) derive so much power and flexibility.

Of course, you may not be lucky enough to pick what you use, anyway. As a consultant, I often have to use whatever is thrust upon me by the job at hand. At least now, ASP is available on more platforms, which makes it that much more likely I'll be able to use it in some form.

Chapter 14
ASP Cookbook

Al Williams

When I was a kid, my family drove through Murfreesboro, Arkansas, on a family vacation. If you haven't been in that part of the country, it is the location of the Crater of Diamonds State Park. This park is a diamond field where—for a small fee—you can wander around looking for diamonds. The problem with diamonds, of course, is that every diamond is surrounded by several tons of dirt and rocks.

We prospected for a few hours with our rented pans and shovels to no avail. I hear about 600 diamonds are found each year, including one that was nearly 9 carats found as late as 1981 (many years after I had been there). Apparently, finding diamonds is like winning the lottery. That's something that happens to other people, but not me. The first diamonds were found in 1906, and I suspect any diamonds lying around have been picked up since then.

Many ASP tricks have been presented in this book. Your job, sometimes, is reduced to extracting the diamonds from all the dirt surrounding them. Although the bulk of this book is good for garnering understanding, this chapter is little more than a cookbook of code you can cut and paste into your own pages. I hope that you'll uncover a diamond or two you can take home with you.

You'll find some of the techniques in this chapter in other parts of the book, but most of them are unique. Many are just short snippets of code; however, you'll find some major items you can cut and paste as well (for example, the message board system).

Accessing All Session/Application Variables

Sometimes—especially when you're debugging—you'll find it useful to search all the variables in the **Session** object (or the **Application** object). You can do so by using this simple script:

```
<%
for i = 1 to Session.Contents.count
   response.write Session.Contents.Key(i)
   response.write ":"
   response.write Session.Contents.Item(i) & "<br>"
 next
for i = 1 to Application.Contents.count
   response.write Application.Contents.Key(i)
   response.write ":"
   response.write Application.Contents.Item(i) & "<br>"
 next
%>
```

You might not be accustomed to seeing the **Contents** member of the **Session** and **Application** objects. You normally don't need these members, but in this case, they are essential because they provide access to the **Key**, the **Item**, and the number of elements in the array.

If you set **Session("name")="Al"**, for example, then the **Key** portion of this item is **name** and the **Item** portion is **Al**.

Date Formatting

People around the world format dates in many different ways. Luckily for you, you can handle date formatting in script in several ways as well. For example, suppose you want to display the date in DD/MM/YYYY format instead of the usual (for the United States) MM/DD/YYYY format. To do so, you can just manually create the date format you want like this:

```
Function DDMMYYYY(datein)
M = Month(datein)
D = Day(datein)
Y = Year(datein)
DDMMYYYY = D & "/" & M & "/" & Y
End Function
```

You can also use the **MonthName**, **Weekday**, and **WeekdayName** functions to extract portions of dates. Of course, you also can use some other functions to simplify your task. The **DatePart** function is very versatile. For instance, you could rewrite the preceding example like this:

```
Function DDMMYYYY(datein)
M = DatePart("m",datein)
D = DatePart("d",datein)
Y = DatePart("yyyy",datein)
DDMMYYYY = D & "/" & M & "/" & Y
End Function
```

The **DatePart** function can even extract weekdays and quarters if you pass it the correct arguments.

Using **DatePart**, you can do any formatting you might imagine. However, for common formatting, you might consider using **FormatDateTime**. This function requires a date and time as the first argument, and the second argument is an optional formatting code (see Table 14.1).

Replacing Strings

Often, replacing one string with another can be useful. This is especially true when you're dealing with database data. For example, suppose you want to write an **INSERT** statement like this:

```
SQL="INSERT INTO atable (id,message) values "
SQL=SQL & "(" & id & ", '" & msg & "') "
```

This **INSERT** statement doesn't quote the **id** variable because it is a number. However, the **msg** variable is a string and requires quotes. So, if **msg** contains the string "**Danger Will Robinson!**", the resulting SQL statement is as follows:

```
INSERT INTO atable (id, message) values (1, 'Danger Will Robinson!')
```

Table 14.1   FormatDateTime format codes.

Constant	Value	Description
vbGeneralDate	0	Displays a date and/or time. If you have a date part, it is displayed as a short date. If you have a time part, it is displayed as a long time. If both are present, both parts are displayed.
vbLongDate	1	Displays a date using the long date format specified in your computer's regional settings.
vbShortDate	2	Displays a date using the short date format specified in your computer's regional settings.
vbLongTime	3	Displays a time using the time format specified in your computer's regional settings.
vbShortTime	4	Displays a time using the 24-hour format (hh:mm).

This statement is, of course, perfectly legitimate. However, what about a case in which the string contains an apostrophe? If **msg** contains "**Don't turn around**", the statement reads as follows:

```
INSERT INTO atable (id, message) values (1, 'Don't turn around')
```

Needless to say, this statement generates an error because the apostrophe in "**Don't**" ends the string, and the SQL interpreter determines the remaining text is just an error.

The answer to this problem is to replace the apostrophe with two apostrophes, which is the way to escape a quote in SQL. You can easily do so by using the **replace** function, as in this example:

```
SQL=SQL & "(" & id & ", '" & replace(msg,"'","''") & "') "
```

Now, the generated insert looks like this:

```
INSERT INTO atable (id, message) values (1, 'Don''t turn around')
```

You need the preceding line to get the correct insertion.

This technique is also useful when you retrieve data that contains carriage returns. Suppose you want to display a message from a database that contains multiple lines separated by carriage returns. In VBScript, **Chr(13)** represents a carriage return, but in most HTML, the browser will replace the carriage return with a space, destroying the formatting. Of course, you could place the message inside a tag that respects white space (such as **<PRE>**), but that approach also affects other formatting. A better idea would be to replace each carriage return with a **
** tag. Doing so is also easy when you use **replace** like this:

```
s = replace(s,Chr(13),"<BR>")
```

If the text originated on Unix, you might have better luck using **Chr(10)**, which is a line feed. Extra carriage returns or line feeds don't matter because the browser will ignore them anyway.

Employing Simple Password Protection

Using session variables, you can provide rudimentary password protection easily to individual files using ASP. You can devise any number of schemes to validate users with passwords (see Chapter 8 for some ideas). When you are sure a user is bona fide, you can simply set a session variable, as in this example:

```
Session("authenticated") = 1
```

Then, you can include a script like this at the beginning of each page:

```
<%
if Session("authenticated") <> 1 then Response.Redirect "badpw.asp"
%>
```

Of course, you have to put this script at the beginning of each page you want to protect. This is a good place to use a server-side include. Users can't modify their own session variables, so an incorrect setting in the authenticated session variable will effectively prevent execution of the page.

This scheme protects only ASP pages and is certainly not bullet-proof, but it is adequate for many uses. Internet Information Server (IIS) provides other ways you can password-protect files so that users must have Windows accounts to access them (although that solution can be a problem if you don't want to make many accounts on your Windows server).

Forcing A Start Page

Sometimes, you might like to force users to a particular start page (perhaps a login page) even if they have another page bookmarked. You can do so easily enough, because each new user gets a new session. By writing some script in the GLOBAL.ASA file to handle the **Session_OnStart** event, you can redirect the users to any page you like:

```
<SCRIPT RUNAT=Server LANGUAGE=VBScript>
Sub Session_OnStart
    ' Force start page

    homePage = "/login.asp"
    currentPage = Request.ServerVariables("SCRIPT_NAME")

    ' don't send user to same page!
    if strcomp(currentPage,homePage,1) then
       Response.Redirect(homepage & "?page=" & Server.URLEncode(currentPage))
    end if
End Sub
</SCRIPT>
```

This script simply makes certain that a user is not already loading the login page. If the page about to appear is the login page, nothing happens. If it isn't, the redirection sends the user to the correct starting page. Notice that the comparison uses **strcomp**, which is not case sensitive. This point is important because IIS does not distinguish between upper- and lowercase.

A few caveats apply to this code. First, browsers that don't support cookies will execute this code for each page request! That means the browser must have cookies enabled. Depending on your circumstances, you might want to put a notice on the login.asp page that informs users they must have cookies enabled. You could also use the **BrowserCapabilities** object (see Chapter 5) to determine whether the users' browsers support cookies and inhibit the redirection if no cookie support is available. However, using this object doesn't help with users who simply have cookies turned off. You can, however, determine that information with a bit of subterfuge (see the next section in this chapter).

Another point to remember is that any code in this function that follows the **Response.Redirect** call will not execute. When the server encounters the redirection, it goes on to the new page and does not execute any more code from the original page. Be sure to do whatever you need to do before calling **Response.Redirect**.

The redirection code modifies the URL so that the login page can determine the original page a user attempted to load by examining a query string variable (**page**). Don't forget the old URL must be encoded (using **Server.URLEncode**) for this technique to work properly. The login page can then redirect the user back to this page after validating the user's credentials.

Another possible use for this technique is to catch pages that no longer exist or that have moved and cause a redirection to occur. For example, suppose your company used to make a particular product. At some point, another company bought that product, and now the new company is responsible for it. You could use a similar script to determine whether a user is loading a page relating to that product and redirect him or her to the other company's Web site.

Determining Whether Cookies Are On

The techniques presented in the preceding section lead to another interesting idea: determining whether cookies are enabled. You can easily do so because a browser that does not store cookies has a different session ID for each page. You can make your default.asp page (or any other page for that matter) contain a single line like this:

```
<% Response.Redirect "main.asp?PageOID=" & Session.SessionID %>
```

Then, main.asp can perform a simple test to see whether cookies are available:

```
<% if Request("PageOID")=Session.SessionID then %>
<!-- Cookies on -->
<% else %>
<!-- Cookies off -->
<% end if %>
```

If cookies are not available, you won't have any way to use session variables or cookies. That means you can't really store any state about these users. Many Web sites simply redirect the users to a page telling them that they must enable cookies to visit the site.

Processing Radio Buttons On The Server

Typically, the only way a user can initiate server-side code is through a hyperlink or form submission via a submit button. However, if the browser supports client-side script, you can effectively make any item a submit button.

The idea is to use JavaScript to force a form submission when the client-side event you want occurs. For an example, consider Listing 14.1, which shows a set of radio buttons. When a user clicks on any radio button, the **onClick** event handler causes the form to submit to the associated script.

Listing 14.1   Server-side radio buttons.

```
<HTML>
<% if request("content_length")=0 then %>
<P>Pick your background color
<P>
<FORM NAME=f1 ACTION=radio.asp METHOD=POST>
<INPUT TYPE=RADIO NAME=B1 VALUE=Red onClick='f1.submit();'>
<FONT COLOR=RED>Red</FONT><BR>
<INPUT TYPE=RADIO NAME=B1 VALUE=Blue onClick='f1.submit();'>
<FONT COLOR=BLUE>Blue</FONT><BR>
<INPUT TYPE=RADIO NAME=B1 VALUE=Green onClick='f1.submit();'>
<FONT COLOR=GREEN>Green</FONT><BR>
</FORM>
<% else %>
<BODY BGCOLOR=<%= request("B1") %>>
You picked: <%= request("B1") %>
<% end if %>
</BODY>
</HTML>
```

You can use this same technique with virtually any client-side event. For example, the following hyperlink triggers server-side script when the user's mouse pointer floats over the link:

```
<FORM NAME=f1 ACTION=script.asp METHOD=POST>
<A HREF=. onMouseOver='f1.submit();'>Don't touch this spot!</A>
</FORM>
```

Creating Image Histograms

You can use a little script to coerce the Web browser into making nice histograms (bar graphs) for you very easily. First, create a small graphic that represents 1 percent of your bar graph. Make sure that when you multiply the width of the image by 100 it will still fit on most screens. For example, 4 pixels wide is usually a good choice. The image's height will be the height of your bars, so whatever you want there will be fine.

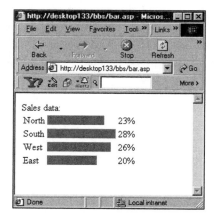

Figure 14.1
Sales data shown as a histogram.

This trick takes advantage of the way the browser stretches graphics to fit the size you specify in the **<IMG>** tag. Suppose your company has four sales regions (north, south, west, and east). You want to present the sales data in graphical form (see Figure 14.1).

In Listing 14.2, you can see the data is simply coded in the page, but in real life, you would probably get it from a database. Regardless, it is simple to compute the total (the **t** variable in the listing). Then, you can compute the percentages using simple mathematics. In the sample code, the variables **p1**, **p2**, **p3**, and **p4** hold the percentage data.

Listing 14.2   Computing the sales data.

```
<%
  iwidth = 4    ' image is 4 pixels
  north = 2500
  south = 3000
  west =  2800
  east =  2200
  t = north+south+east+west
  p1 = north/t*100
  p2 = south/t*100
  p3 = west/t*100
  p4 = east/t*100

%>
<P>Sales data:
<TABLE>
<TR><TD>North</TD>
<TD><IMG SRC=bar.gif HEIGHT=16 WIDTH=<%=p1*iwidth%>></TD>
<TD><%=Int(p1)%>%</TD></TR>
<TR><TD>South</TD>
```

```
<TD> <IMG SRC=bar.gif HEIGHT=16 WIDTH=<%=p2*iwidth%>></TD>
<TD><%=Int(p2)%>%</TD></TR>
<TR><TD>West</TD>
<TD> <IMG SRC=bar.gif HEIGHT=16 WIDTH=<%=p3*iwidth%>></TD>
<TD><%=Int(p3)%>%</TD></TR>
<TR><TD>East</TD>
<TD> <IMG SRC=bar.gif HEIGHT=16 WIDTH=<%=p4*iwidth%>></TD>
<TD><%=Int(p4)%>%</TD></TR>
</TABLE>
```

If your prototype bar image is in the bar.gif file, you can create a simple **<IMG>** tag, as follows, to display the bar:

```
<IMG SRC=bar.gif HEIGHT=16 WIDTH=<%=p1*iwidth%>>
```

The width will be the percentage multiplied by the width of the graphic. Using this approach is probably the simplest way to create a graphical presentation of data without resorting to a Java applet or other external program.

Writing Random Links

Using script, you can easily select a random item from a list and use it as a link, an ad banner, or a quote of the day, or you can use it in any other situation where you need a random piece of text or HTML.

With VBScript, the way to generate a random number is to use the **rnd** function. However, you need to know two facts about **rnd** to successfully use it. First, **rnd** generates a number between 0 and 1. So, calling **rnd** might return 0.125321, for example. If you want a number between 0 and some maximum, you can multiply the result by the maximum. To generate a number from 1 to some maximum, you multiply by the maximum minus 1 and then add 1. In general, if you want to create an integer number between **n** and **m**, you can write the following:

```
r = CInt(rnd * (m-n)) +n
```

Second, **rnd** requires a seed number. This seed allows you to generate the same sequence of random numbers. If you start with the same seed, you get the same numbers. This seems odd, but it is important in certain math problems in which you want a random distribution of numbers, but you want to repeat it for different cases.

The default seed is 0 each time you load a page, so if you simply call **rnd** in your script, you always get the same number. For example, if your script uses the following, the **rnumber** variable will always be 6:

```
rnumber = CInt(rnd * 9)   ' 0 - 9
```

Most people using **rnd** really want unpredictable numbers. In that case, you can set the seed to a value derived from the system clock by using the **randomize** statement. Then, the user can't guess the first (or subsequent) numbers. This next example shows how to select a link at random and transport the user there:

```
<%
   dim links(10)
   links(0)="http://www.coriolis.com"
   links(1)="http://www.al-williams.com"
   links(1)="http://www.alltheweb.com"
   links(2)="http://www.webtechniques.com"
   links(3)="http://www.planetit.com"
   links(4)="http://www.aj.com"
   links(5)="http://us.imdb.com"
   links(6)="http://www.tricksandtrinkets.com"
   links(7)="http://www.thefreesite.com"
   links(8)="http://station.sony.com"
   links(9)="http://www.thehungersite.com"

   randomize ' very important
   rnumber = CInt(rnd * 9)   ' 0 - 9
   ritem = links(rnumber)
   response.redirect ritem
%>
```

This code stores the possible choices in an array. After you set **ritem**, you can do anything with it. For example, the array could contain banner advertisements, and this script could do banner rotation. You could easily provide a random tip this way also.

Creating A Hit Counter

You can easily track a variety of statistics using nothing more than some simple ASP code and some **Application** object variables. Counting at the page level is as simple as placing this script on each page:

```
<% Application.Lock
   Application("Hit")=Application("Hit")+1
   Application.Unlock
%>
```

You do have to consider a few factors with this simplistic approach. First, the count resets every time the application reloads. Also, the counter increases every time a user views the page. If one user refreshes the page 10 times, that counts as 10 hits.

The first problem requires that you save the count somewhere more durable than an application variable. You could store the count in a file or a database. The problem here is when to write the count to the persistent storage. Ideally, you would write it in the **Application_OnEnd** event (in the Global.asa file). Then, you would read it in during **Application_OnStart**, and you wouldn't have much overhead. The problem is that **Application_OnEnd** is unreliable. You may or may not get a chance to execute that code. On top of that, there are limits to what you are allowed to do during the **Application_OnEnd** handler.

The hit counter presented in Appendix A reads the count during **Application_OnStart** from a file. Then, it rewrites the file every time it records a page view. This approach is not very efficient, but it does allow the counts to remain accurate when the server restarts.

The other problem, counting the same user multiple times, is easy to correct. If you want to count unique users, you can do the counting in the **Session_OnStart** event handler. This way, you count all users who visit your site no matter which page they view. You count a visitor only once per session unless the user doesn't handle cookies.

This sample Global.asa file provides support for several forms of counting:

```
<SCRIPT LANGUAGE=VBSCRIPT RUNAT=SERVER>
Sub Application_OnStart
Application.Lock
Application("Start")=Now
set ifile=Server.CreateObject("Scripting.FileSystemObject")
set file=ifile.OpenTextFile("gnrcount.txt",1,TRUE)
s=file.ReadLine
if s<>"" then
  Application("TCount")=CInt(s)
else
  Application("TCount")=0
end if
file.close
ifile.close
'file=nothing
ofile=nothing
Application.Unlock
End Sub

Sub Session_OnStart
Application.Lock
Application("UCount")=Application("UCount")+1
Application("Sessions")=Application("Sessions")+1
set ofile=Server.CreateObject("Scripting.FileSystemObject")
set file=ofile.CreateTextFile("gnrcount.txt",TRUE)
file.WriteLine CStr(Application("TCount"))
```

```
file.Close
ofile.Close
file=nothing
ofile=nothing
Application.Unlock
End Sub

Sub Session_OnEnd
Application.Lock
Application("Sessions")=Application("Sessions")-1
Application.Unlock
End Sub
</SCRIPT>
```

With this Global.asa file in place, you have access to several **Application** variables:

♦ **Start**—The time of the last server restart

♦ **UCount**—The number of sessions processed

♦ **TCount**—The total number of users (stored in a file)

♦ **Sessions**—The total number of active sessions

Redirection Counting

It is often useful to know how many times someone clicked on a link. Why not just count the page hits? Perhaps the page points somewhere offsite? For example, you might want to know how many users are clicking on ads for another Web site.

The simplest way to count the number is to change the links to point to a redirection script. This script can then do the appropriate counting and complete the surfer's journey.

Suppose you have this link:

```
<A HREF=http://www.coriolis.com>Coriolis Books</A>
```

You could rewrite it to read:

```
<A HREF=xlink.asp?counter=coriolis&url=http://www.coriolis.com>
Coriolis Books</A>
```

The xlink.asp file need not be complex. This example keeps the count in an **Application** object variable:

```
<%
Application.Lock
Application(Request("counter")) = Application(Request("counter"))+1
```

```
Application.Unlock
Response.redirect Request("URL")
%>
```

You can easily write a page to show the counts for any particular link or set of links. Of course, you can make different links increment the same counters, by setting the **counter** argument for xlink.asp to the same string for both links.

In real life, you might want to keep these counts in a database. Keeping them there would be a good idea because the **Application** object variables will reset on each server restart.

Keeping FrontPage From Altering Code

If you use FrontPage, you might be worried that the program will modify your code. Older versions were especially bad about changing code you had written. Even the latest versions don't appreciate tags with script embedded within.

You can add a special pair of WebBot comments by hand, or you can use the Insert I Advanced I HTML menu item to insert the same comments. Anything you place between these comments, FrontPage will ignore:

```
<!--webbot bot="HTMLMarkup" startspan -->
Whatever is here will remain untouched
<!--webbot bot="HTMLMarkup" endspan -->
```

Testing NULL Vs. Empty Strings

Dealing with empty strings and null values—especially from databases—can be maddening. The problem is that, conceptually, programmers tend to think they are equivalent, but in fact they are different. A field that contains **NULL** is empty. A field that holds an empty string is not empty itself. It contains a string that has no characters.

The classic way to test whether a field is **NULL** is to use **IsNull**. If you really want to distinguish between a **NULL** and other values, using **IsNull** is certainly the right way to do it. However, you might frequently want to treat **NULL** and an empty string as the same thing. You can do so by appending an empty string to the value that might be **NULL**. If the value is **NULL**, adding an empty string results in an empty string. If the value is an empty string, adding another empty string still produces a single empty string. If the value is not an empty string, the result is the same as the original string.

The following example sets a default value in a variable named **ucolor** that might be **NULL**:

```
if ucolor & "" = "" then ucolor="blue"
```

Mapping And Encoding Paths

As a Web developer, you are probably painfully aware that your pages are located in some strange place on your server. What the Web surfer thinks is your root directory may really be a deep, dark subdirectory of your server's hard drive. Typically, but not always, your Web site will be in a directory under c:\inetpub\wwwroot.

However, it is a bad idea to count on this directory location. What if the server runs out of space, and the administrator moves Web sites to the E: drive? What if you use one location on your development server and another on the actual server you use to deploy your site?

The answer is to use **Server.MapPath**. Several of the examples in this chapter use this handy function to find file names for databases and other purposes. This function takes a normal file name, relative to the root of your Web site, and translates it into a proper Windows NT name. Presumably, the server knows where your files are supposed to be, so even if the administrator changes the location, this function will work.

Server.MapPath doesn't check to see whether the file you specify exists. That makes sense, because you might be creating the file. Just remember that the call does not ensure the file exists or that you have rights to access it in any way.

Two other useful **Server** functions allow you to encode strings suitable for use in a URL or within HTML. These functions, **Server.URLEncode** and **Server.HTMLEncode**, handle all the problems with converting characters such as < and / into acceptable equivalents, as in this example:

```
<%
 s1="http://www.al-williams.com"
 s2="<good job>"
 Response.Write(Server.URLEncode(s1))
 Response.Write("<BR>")
 Response.Write(Server.HTMLEncode(s2))
%>
```

The first encoding results in the following string:

```
http%3A%2F%2Fwww%2Eal%2Dwilliams%2Ecom
```

The second string encodes to the following:

```
&lt;good job&gt;
```

These odd-looking characters, of course, cause the correct display in the browser.

Using Databases Without DSNs

Sometimes, you might like to access a database on the server, but it doesn't have an ODBC Data Source Name (DSN) associated with it. Perhaps it is just a test database, or perhaps you are not allowed to create new DSNs on your server.

Luckily, you can easily create a connect string that allows you to open a database directly by using the file name and the name of the driver you want to use. Here's how:

```
<%
Set Conn = Server.CreateObject("ADODB.Connection")
Set RS = Server.CreateObject("ADODB.Recordset")

openstring = "DBQ=" & Server.Mappath("mydata.mdb")
openstring = openstring & ";Driver={Microsoft Access Driver (*.mdb)};"
Conn.Open openstring
SQL = "SELECT * FROM mytable"
RS.Open SQL, Conn , 2, 3
%>
```

The key here is the **Server.Mappath** function. It transforms the name of your database (relative to your Web application) into a proper NT file name. Interestingly, the function doesn't really check to see whether the file exists, so a successful mapping does not imply that the file is readable or even that it exists.

Another way to accomplish this task is to create a file that describes the database. It is known as a *file DSN*. You can create this type of file from the Windows ODBC Control Panel. Using a DSN file is not very different from using the preceding method, except that most of the parameters are in the file instead of in the **openstring** variable. However, if you have a high-volume Web site, you should avoid using file DSNs because some overhead is involved in each visitor opening the ASCII file that contains the parameters.

Suppose you create a file DSN using the ODBC Control Panel on your local machine. It refers to a database, bbs.mdb, in the root of your C drive. The resulting DSN file might look like this:

```
[ODBC]
DRIVER=Microsoft Access Driver (*.mdb)
UID=admin
UserCommitSync=Yes
Threads=3
SafeTransactions=0
PageTimeout=5
MaxScanRows=8
MaxBufferSize=2048
```

```
FIL=MS Access
DriverId=281
DefaultDir=C:\WINDOWS\
DBQ=c:\bbs.mdb
```

Of course, the last two lines point to a specific file, and the database's location on the server is sure to be different. In that case, you can delete these last two lines. You also might need to change other items (such as the **UID**), depending on your particular circumstances. Suppose you save this file as bbs.dsn and save it and bbs.mdb to the root of your Web site. Now, the script to work with this database looks like this:

```
<%
DBname = "bbs.mdb"
Dir = Request.ServerVariables("SCRIPT_NAME")
' cut off at last slash so we just get the directory name
Dir = StrReverse(Dir)
Dir = Mid(Dir, InStr(1, Dir, "/"))
Dir = StrReverse(Dir)
Path = Server.MapPath(Dir) & "\"
f = "bbs.dsn"
DSN = "filedsn=" & Path & f & ";DefaultDir=" & Path
DSN = DSN & ";DBQ=" & Path & DBname & ";"
SQL = "SELECT * FROM bbs"
Set rs = Server.CreateObject("ADODB.Recordset")
rs.Open SQL, DSN
%>
```

Interestingly, using a direct connect string may result in better performance, depending on your database and server setup. As usual, you have to measure the performance on your own hardware. You can read all about database connect strings at **http://support.microsoft.com/support/kb/articles/q193/3/32.asp**.

Searching A Database

Have you ever wanted to implement a keyword search on a database? Performing such a search is not hard if you know a little bit about SQL, the language used to write queries. When you write the **WHERE** clause of a **SELECT** statement, you usually provide specific criteria to indicate a match.

Another way to specify a match, however, is to use the **LIKE** operator. Using this approach, you can perform a matching operation with wildcards. SQL on an ASP page uses the % character as a wildcard. Suppose you have a form that allows the user to submit a **keyword** field to the following script:

```
<%
Set Conn = Server.CreateObject("ADODB.Connection")
Conn.Open "MsgBoard"

SQL = "SELECT * FROM BBS WHERE Message LIKE "
SQL = SQL & "'%"  & Request("keyword") & "%'"

Set rs = Conn.Execute(SQL)
do while not rs.eof
%>
<p>
<%=rs("Message")%>
<!-- put code here to display results -->
<p>

<%
rs.MoveNext
Loop
rs.Close
Conn.Close
set Conn = Nothing
%>
```

If the **keyword** were, for example, "active", the script would return messages containing that word, as well as entries that contained "activated", "reactivated", and "deactivated". The search string formed, "%active%", would match any of these strings.

You can also use **NOT LIKE** to reverse the sense of the search. Of course, you could also add other conditions using **AND** to further limit the search to a specific date range or other criteria.

Displaying Data In An HTML Table

A common need when you're working with databases is to display an SQL table or query in an HTML table. You can easily write a single piece of code to display any record set's data, regardless of the specific table and field names involved. Listing 14.3 shows the code.

Listing 14.3   Displaying a table from a record set.

```
<%
Sub ShowTable(RS)
Response.Write "<TABLE BORDER=1><TR>"
' write heading
for i=0 to RS.Fields.Count-1
 Response.Write "<TD><B>" & RS(i).Name & "</B></TD>"
next
```

```
Response.Write "</TR>"
Do while not RS.EOF
  Response.Write "<TR>"
  for i=0 to RS.Fields.Count -1
    Response.Write "<TD>" & RS(i) & "</TD>"
  next
  Response.Write "</TR>"
  RS.MoveNext
  Loop
  Response.Write "</TABLE>"
End Sub
%>
```

This straightforward subroutine simply loops through each field once, retrieving the name of the field (**RS(i).Name**). The code uses this name to form the headings for the HTML table.

After the heading is complete, the script loops through each field again. This time, it retrieves the actual data, placing each data item in an HTML table cell. It then repeats this step for each row in the record set.

One problem to watch for is whether your data might be blank or empty. Most browsers do not show the border around an empty cell, which makes your table look strange. If you expect to have empty or blank cells, and you want the table to appear with full borders, you can write a simple function to convert empty or blank data into an ** **. Then you can use this function to process the data before placing it in each cell. Consider this example:

```
Function bdata(s)
bdata=s
if s & "" = "" then bdata = " "
End Function
```

Armed with this function (which converts empty strings and null values), you could rewrite the name **Response.Write** statement in Listing 14.3 like this:

```
Response.Write "<TD>" & bdata(RS(i)) & "</TD>"
```

If you are worried about strings that contain actual blanks, you can add a call like the following to **trim** inside **bdata** to remove leading and trailing blanks before making the test:

```
if trim(s) & "" = "" then bdata = " "
```

If you have version 2 or higher of Active Data Objects (ADO), and you don't want to do any special processing, you can use **GetString** to retrieve the entire database in one fell swoop:

```
Response.Write "<table border='1'><TR>"

'make header
for i = 0 to RS.fields.count-1
    Response.Write "<TD><B>" & RS(i).name & "</B></TD>"
next
Response.Write "</TR><TR><TD>"
Response.Write RS.getstring(,, "</TD><TD>", "</TD></TR><TR><TD>", "n/a")
Response.Write "</TD></TR></table>"
```

Displaying A Fixed Number Of Records

Sometimes, you might want to display a particular number of records. Sure, you could re-trieve all the records and output only a certain number, but that approach is inefficient. Instead, you can limit the number of records you obtain from the database.

You can limit the number by setting the **maxrecords** property of the **Recordset** object. However, that means you have to use **Recordset** directly instead of using the **Connection** object's **Execute** method to create a record set. Check out this sample code:

```
set RS=Server.CreateObject("adodb.Recordset")
RS.maxrecords=10
DSN ="DSN=test;uid=tester;pwd=trek"
RS.open "select * from thetable",DSN,3
```

As you might expect, this example limits the results to 10 records. If you combine this example with selections (**WHERE**) and sorting (**ORDER BY**), you can answer questions such as "What were the top 10 revenue-producing products last month?"

Displaying Data In Pages

For large databases, you might like to show your data in pages that contain a fixed number of records. You can do so easily enough if the database driver you are using supports paging in the **Recordset** object. For Microsoft Access, for example, if you set the record set's cursor location to client, you can use the **pagesize**, **pagecount**, and **absolutepage** members to break the data into page-sized chunks.

Keep in mind that, although the cursor is a "client-side cursor," it is not on the user's browser. In this context, client-side means the ODBC client, which is your ASP page. You might be tempted to store the record set in a **Session** object variable so you could avoid issuing a query for each page. This technique sounds like a good idea, but it places an extraordinary strain on the server if there are a large number of users.

You can see an example of how this technique works in Listing 14.4. After the script sets the **pagesize** property, the record set reports how many pages are available (in the **pagecount** property). The script selects a specific page using **absolutepage**.

Listing 14.4 Page display.

```
<HTML>
<BODY>
<%
pg=request("pg")
If  pg="" then
   pg=1
end if
psize=request("psize")
If  psize="" then
   psize=10
end if
SQL="SELECT * FROM test"
openstring="provider=MSDASQL;driver={Microsoft Access Driver (*.mdb)};DBQ="
openstring=openstring & Server.MapPath("database\test.mdb")


set RS=Server.CreateObject("ADODB.Recordset")
RS.cursorlocation = 3   ' client cursor
RS.open SQL,openstring
RS.pagesize=psize
maxpages=int(RS.pagecount)
maxrecs=int(RS.pagesize)
RS.absolutepage=pg
recct=0
Response.Write "Page " & pg & " of " & maxpages & "<br>"
Response.Write "<table border='1'><tr>"

'Put headings on the table of field names
FOR i=0 to RS.fields.count -1
   Response.Write "<td><b>" & RS(i).name & "</b></td>"
NEXT
Response.Write "</tr>"

' Now loop through the data
DO  UNTIL RS.eof OR recct>=maxrecs
   Response.Write "<tr>"
   FOR i = 0 to RS.fields.count -1
      value=RS(i)
      If value & "" = "" THEN value=" "
      response.write "<td valign='top'>"
      response.write value
      response.write "</td>"
   next
   response.write "</tr>"
```

```
      RS.movenext
      recct=recct+1
LOOP
Response.Write "</table><p>"

' close, destroy
RS.close
set RS=nothing
%>


<HR>
<% if pg<>1 then %>
<A HREF=page.asp?pg=<%=pg-1%>&psize=<%=psize%>>Previous</A>
<% end if %>
<% if pg-maxpages<>0 then %>
<A HREF=page.asp?pg=<%=pg+1%>&psize=<%=psize%>>Next</A>
<% end if %>
</BODY>
</HTML>
```

Populating A List Box From A Recordset

Another common thing you might want to do with a set of database records is to place them in a drop-down box on a form. Populating a list box is essentially the same as (or perhaps easier than) filling in an HTML table:

```
<FORM ACTION=processform.asp METHOD=POST>
<SELECT NAME=dbselect>
<OPTION SELECTED>Choose one:

<% Do While not rs.EOF %>
<OPTION VALUE="<%=rs("ValueField")%>">
<%=rs.fields("NameField")%>

<%
rs.MoveNext
Loop
rs.Close
%>

</SELECT>
</FORM>
```

In the preceding code, you should replace **ValueField** and **NameField** with the appropriate names from your database. In many cases, they will be the same field names anyway.

Developing A Message Board System

Many ASP programmers want to develop message board systems. You know what message boards are—a set of Web pages that manage a discussion group. Ideally, you could look at the various topics of discussions, read individual items, and post follow-up messages. If you have the right password, it would be nice to be able to delete items as well. Searching for particular messages would be another nice feature.

Obviously, you need some sort of database in which to store the information. I created a simple database with the following fields:

- **Name**—Name of the user entering the message
- **Email**—Email address of the user
- **Posted**—Date and time the user posted the message
- **Subject**—Message subject
- **Message**—Actual message text (memo field)
- **Next**—ID of message that this message is in reply to (long integer)
- **ID**—Message ID (long integer)

Microsoft Access (and many other databases) allow you to create fields that automatically increment so that each record gets a unique ID. The **ID** field uses this feature. The system really doesn't care what the ID is as long as it is unique for each message.

The entire BBS system requires four pages. The bbs.asp file (see Listing 14.5) shows the top-level messages and offers the user a way to post a new message (using postnew.asp from Listing 14.6). The view.asp file (see Listing 14.7) shows a message with a particular ID number. It also shows any replies to the message and offers a form that allows the user to reply as well.

Because two forms post messages (postnew.asp and view.asp), I placed the actual posting logic in a separate file (post.asp in Listing 14.8). Posting and viewing are straightforward, except for the maintenance of the **ID** and **Next** fields.

Messages fall into two classes: top-level messages and replies. Top-level messages appear on the first page and have zero in the **Next** field. Messages that are replies have the **ID** of the main message in their **Next** field. So, to find the top-level messages, you can use the following SQL statement:

```
SELECT ID,Name,Posted,Subject FROM BBS WHERE next=0 ORDER BY posted DESC
```

This statement selects top-level messages and sorts them by the **posted** field in descending order. That way, the newest messages appear first.

If you want all the immediate replies to a message with an **ID** of 33, you can write the following:

```
SELECT ID,Name,Email,Posted,Subject,Message FROM BBS WHERE ID=33
```

The main page (Listing 14.5) is simple if you know how the queries work. Each top-level item becomes a hyperlink to the view.asp page (Listing 14.7). The hyperlink contains a query string that contains the **ID** of the message, so the view.asp scripts can extract the correct message.

Listing 14.5   BBS main page.

```
<HTML>
<HEAD>
<TITLE>The BBS</TITLE>
</HEAD>
<BODY BGCOLOR=#008080>
<H1>Welcome to the message board</H1>

<TABLE BORDER=1 WIDTH=75%>
<TR><TD WIDTH=50%><B>Subject</B></TD><TD WIDTH=20%><B>by</B></TD>
    <TD WIDTH=80%><B>Posted</B></TD></TR>

<!-- display all the top-level items -->
<%
 Set Conn = Server.CreateObject("ADODB.Connection")
 Conn.Open "MSGBoard"
 SQL="SELECT ID,Name,Posted,Subject FROM BBS WHERE NEXT=0 ORDER BY Posted DESC"
 set RS=Conn.Execute(SQL)
 do while NOT RS.EOF
%>
 <TR><TD><A HREF=view.asp?ID=<%= RS("ID") %>><%= RS("Subject") %></A>
 </TD><TD><%= RS("Name") %></TD>
 <TD><%= RS("Posted") %></TD></TR>
<%
 RS.MoveNext
 loop
 RS.close
 Conn.close
%>
</TABLE>
<BR><A HREF=postnew.asp>Post a new message</A>

</BODY>
</HTML>
```

The posting of a new message is little more than a form that submits its data to post.asp. The form (see Listing 14.6) contains a hidden field named **nextid** that contains a zero. This is the value post.asp will use for the **next** database field.

Listing 14.6   Posting a new message.

```
<HTML>
<HEAD><TITLE>New Post</TITLE>
</HEAD>
<BODY BGCOLOR=#008080>
<TABLE BORDER=1>
<TR><TD>
<!-- this form creates a new post -->
<FORM ACTION=post.asp METHOD=POST>
<P><B><I>New Post:</I></B></P>
<P>From: <INPUT NAME=From>
Email: <INPUT NAME=EMAIL></P>
<P>Subject: <INPUT NAME=SUBJECT></P>

<P>Message:</P>
<P><TEXTAREA COLS=80 ROWS=10 NAME=msg>
</TEXTAREA></P>
<P><INPUT TYPE=SUBMIT VALUE=Post></P>
<!-- next is zero because this is top level -->
<INPUT TYPE=HIDDEN NAME=NEXTID VALUE='0'>
</FORM>
</TD></TR></TABLE>
</BODY>
</HTML>
```

The view.asp file (Listing 14.7) allows you to reply with a similar form that has several hidden fields—one for the **nextid** and another for the **Subject**. In this case, however, the values are not constant. Instead, the values depend on the displayed message. Which message does the page display? That depends on the **ID** query string. The form submits to the same post.asp script that a new posting uses.

The portion of the viewing script that shows the current message replaces carriage returns in the message with a **
** tag. However, it does not replace any other characters such as < or >. You therefore can place HTML tags in the message, but you can't reliably process messages that contain these characters for real (unless the user types "<" or ">", for example). Processing the message using **Server.HTMLEncode** would be easy enough, but that would prevent HTML entry into the message.

Listing 14.7   Viewing and replying to a message.

```asp
<!-- view a message based on the passed-in ID -->
<HTML>
<HEAD>
<TITLE>Message View</TITLE>
</HEAD>
<BODY BGCOLOR=#008080>
<%
 Function crlf(s)   ' expand cr's into <BR>
 crlf = replace(s,chr(13),"<BR>")
 end function


 Set Conn = Server.CreateObject("ADODB.Connection")
 Conn.Open "MSGBoard"
 SQL="SELECT ID,Name,Email,Posted,Subject,Message FROM BBS WHERE ID="
 SQL=SQL & Request("ID")
 set RS=Conn.Execute(SQL)
 %>
<!-- make header -->
<H1><%=RS("Subject")%></H1>
<TABLE BORDER=1 WIDTH=75%>
<TR><TD><P>From: <%=RS("Name") %> (
<A HREF='mailto:<%=RS("Email")%>'><%=RS("email")%>
</A>)
Posted at: <%=RS("Posted")%></P></TD></TR>
<TR><TD>
<!-- show message -->
<!-- If you don't want to allow HTML, consider using Server.HTMLEncode here -->
<P>
<%= crlf(RS("Message")) %>
</P>
</TD></TR>
<TR><TD>
<!-- this is the form that lets you post a reply -->
<FORM ACTION=post.asp METHOD=POST>
<P><B><I>Reply:</I></B></P>
<P>From: <INPUT NAME=From>
Email: <INPUT NAME=EMAIL></P>
<P>Message:</P>
<P><TEXTAREA COLS=80 ROWS=10 NAME=msg>
</TEXTAREA></P>
<P><INPUT TYPE=SUBMIT VALUE=Post></P>
<INPUT TYPE=HIDDEN NAME=NEXTID VALUE='<%=Request("ID")%>'>
<INPUT TYPE=HIDDEN NAME=SUBJECT VALUE='RE: <%=RS("Subject")%>'>
</FORM>
</TD></TR>
```

```
<TR><TD>
<!-- this section shows any follow-ups -->
<%
 SQL="SELECT ID,Name,Posted FROM BBS WHERE next="
 SQL=SQL & Request("ID") & " ORDER BY posted DESC"
 set RS=Conn.Execute(SQL)
 if RS.EOF then response.write("<P>No replies</P>")
 do while NOT RS.EOF
 %>
 <P>
 <A HREF=view.asp?ID=<%=RS("ID")%>>Reply from
 <%=RS("Name")%> posted at <%=RS("Posted")%></A>
 </P>
 <%
 RS.MoveNext
 loop
 RS.Close
 Conn.Close
 %>
</TD></TR>
</TABLE>
<P><A HREF=bbs.asp>Back to the message board</A></P>
<% if request("password")="startrek" then %>
<FORM ACTION=delmsg.asp METHOD=post>
<INPUT TYPE=HIDDEN NAME=pw VALUE=<%= request("password") %>>
<INPUT TYPE=HIDDEN NAME=ID VALUE=<%= request("id") %>>
<INPUT TYPE=SUBMIT VALUE=Delete>
</FORM>
<P>Be sure to delete replies first!</P>
<% end if %>
</BODY>
</HTML>
```

The script that posts the actual message is straightforward (see Listing 14.8). It simply creates an **INSERT INTO** SQL statement. You don't need to insert the **ID** field because the database automatically sets this field anyway.

The only tricky part is getting the quotes right. Because the **INSERT INTO** statement uses apostrophes to quote the value strings, any embedded apostrophes require doubling to prevent syntax errors. You can do so easily by using the VBScript **replace** function.

Listing 14.8   Posting a message.

```
<%
' This file posts a message from another form
' The view and postnew scripts call this one
```

```
Function dblq(s) ' double quotes
dblq = replace(s,"'","''")
End Function


Set Conn = Server.CreateObject("ADODB.Connection")
Conn.Open "MSGBoard"
quote=39
SQL="INSERT INTO bbs (Name,Email,Posted,Subject,Message,Next) values ("
SQL=SQL & chr(quote) & dblq(Request("From")) & chr(quote)
SQL=SQL & "," & chr(quote) & Request("email") & chr(quote)
SQL=SQL & "," & chr(quote) &  Now  & chr(quote)
SQL=SQL & "," & chr(quote) & dblq(Request("subject")) & chr(quote)
SQL=SQL & "," & chr(quote) & dblq(Request("msg")) & chr(quote)
SQL=SQL & "," & Request("nextid")
SQL=SQL & ")"
' Response.Write(SQL)   ' debugging
set RS=Conn.Execute(SQL)
RS.Close
Conn.Close
%>
<HTML><HEAD>
<TITLE>Thanks for posting your message</TITLE>
</HEAD>
<BODY BGCOLOR=#008080>
<P>Thank you for posting your message.</P>
<P><A HREF=bbs.asp>Back to the message board</A></P>
</BODY>
</HTML>
```

One last script is rarely, if ever, used by ordinary users. If you use the view.asp script directly, you can add a password to the query string. For example, if you want to see message number 100, you might use this URL:

```
http://desktop133/bbs/view.asp?ID=100&password=startrek
```

The password, "startrek", appears in the ASP file, which is secure enough for this purpose. When the viewing script sees the correct password, it adds a button to delete the message. This button submits a form that contains only hidden fields. One field passes the password on to the deleting script. The other passes the message ID. The deleting script appears in Listing 14.9.

Because this page is strictly for internal maintenance, I didn't spend time making it pretty. It simply uses an SQL **DELETE FROM** statement to wipe out the message in question. I didn't make it recursively seek out replies, so you should be careful to delete replies first. Otherwise, you'll have messages stored in the database that users can't readily find.

Listing 14.9 Deleting a message.

```
<%
' delete a record -- requires a hardcoded password
 if request("pw")<>"startrek" then response.redirect "bbs.asp"
 Set Conn = Server.CreateObject("ADODB.Connection")
 Conn.Open "MSGBoard"
 SQL="DELETE FROM BBS WHERE id="
 SQL=SQL & Request("ID")
 set RS=Conn.Execute(SQL)
 Conn.close
%>
<HTML><BODY>Deleted...</BODY></HTML>
```

One simple addition to the message system is a keyword search. Listing 14.10 shows a page that accepts a single keyword and searches for it (using the **LIKE** clause in an SQL **SELECT**) in the message and subject of each message.

The resulting display is similar to the top-level message display. It presents the titles of the matching messages as links to the view.asp script. If no records match, an appropriate message appears instead of the list.

This search is simplistic, but you could add more fields to match more keywords. You could also add fields that allow searching on date ranges, names, or any other criteria.

Listing 14.10 BBS search form.

```
<HTML>
<BODY BGCOLOR=#008080>
<% if request("content_length")=0 then %>
<FORM ACTION=bbssearch.asp METHOD=POST>
Keyword: <INPUT NAME=keyword><INPUT TYPE=SUBMIT VALUE=Search>
</FORM>
<% else %>

<%
Set Conn = Server.CreateObject("ADODB.Connection")
Conn.Open "MsgBoard"

SQL = "SELECT * FROM BBS WHERE Message LIKE "
SQL = SQL & "'%" & Request("keyword") & "%' or Subject LIKE"
SQL = SQL & "'%" & Request("keyword") & "%'"
Set rs = Conn.Execute(SQL)
if rs.eof then %>
<P>No messages found. <A HREF=bbssearch.asp>Try again</A>
<% else %>
<TABLE BORDER=1 WIDTH=75%>
```

```
<TR><TD WIDTH=50%><B>Subject</B></TD><TD WIDTH=20%><B>by</B></TD>
    <TD WIDTH=80%><B>Posted</B></TD></TR>
<%
do while not rs.eof
%>
 <TR><TD><A HREF=view.asp?ID=<%= RS("ID") %>><%= RS("Subject") %></A>
 </TD><TD><%= RS("Name") %></TD>
 <TD><%= RS("Posted") %></TD></TR>

<%
rs.MoveNext
Loop
rs.Close
Conn.Close
set Conn = Nothing
%>
</TABLE>
<% end if %>
<% end if %>
</BODY>
</HTML>
```

Improving ASP Performance

You can employ several tricks to improve the performance of ASP pages. Some of them involve common sense, and others are somewhat specialized. However, the exact timing of a piece of script depends heavily on factors that may be unique to your site. Therefore, you should always test to see what parts of your scripts are taking the longest to run and then test different methods for making them run faster.

You can time script execution in several ways. However, you can also store time markers in your scripts, repeat a sequence of code multiple times, and then determine how long the operations took. If you divide the total time by the repeat count, you'll have a good idea how long a single operation takes. You might also find the capacity-testing tools at **http://msdn.microsoft.com/workshop/server/toolbox/wcat.asp** useful.

Session State

One way to speed up an ASP page is to disable the session state for that page. Of course, that assumes the page doesn't require **session** variables or the Microsoft Personalization System (MPS). You can disable the session-tracking logic from a page by placing this line at the top of the ASP file:

```
<%@ enablesessionstate=false %>
```

Buffering Output

You can often get better performance by setting **Response.buffer=true** so that the system caches all your **Response.Write** calls until the end of processing. This call modifies the page's headers, so you must put it before any HTML output.

If you don't turn on buffering, you can still gain some benefit by batching your writes as much as possible. In other words, instead of using

```
<%= x %>
<BR>
<%= y %>
<BR>
<%= z %>
<BR>
```

you might try

```
<% s = x & "<BR>" & y & "<BR>" & z & "<BR>" %>
<%= s % %>
```

Read Properties Once

Reading ActiveX object properties is more expensive than reading an ordinary variable. So, you should read properties once and then reuse the value where possible. Consider this example:

```
for I = 1 to RS.Count
    Response.Write RS(I) & "<BR>"
next
```

The preceding script will probably execute more slowly than the following:

```
n = RS.Count
for I=1 to n
    Response.Write RS(I) & "<BR>"
next
```

Do Not Store Objects At The Session Or Application Level

Storing objects (not variables, but objects) within a **Session** or **Application** object variable is usually a bad idea. Storing them this way is a drain on system resources; unless you have a compelling reason to do so, don't create objects with extended scope.

This same principle applies, of course, to data in collections like **request**. The **server.mappath** variable is especially expensive, so you should cache it if you need the results more than once.

Use **Response.IsClientConnected**

If you are generating a long output page, you might find it useful to make sure the browser is still there to hear what you are saying. If the **Response.IsClientConnected** function returns **false**, the client is no longer listening, so there is no need to continue processing.

This function can be very useful in a loop displaying a long data table:

```
do while NOT RS.EOF
  if NOT response.IsClientConnected then exit do
.
.
.
RS.MoveNext
loop
```

Set **ProcessorThreadMax** And Other Registry Entries

If you administer your own server, be sure to examine all the performance tuning that is possible. For example, setting **ProcessorThreadMax** sets the maximum number of threads IIS will use to handle requests.

A related parameter, **ThreadCreationThreshold**, determines how many requests must be pending before IIS will create another thread. This number is confusing because it is really part of a formula that determines how many threads IIS will use (subject to the maximum, of course). IIS takes the number of pending requests and divides it by **ThreadCreationThreshold** to determine how many threads to use. So, decreasing **ThreadCreationThreshold** actually increases the number of threads in use. If you set **ThreadCreationThreshold** to 1, each request will spawn a new thread (up to the maximum allowed). For especially busy sites on dedicated servers, this technique may be a viable option.

Use **Option Explicit**

Using **Option Explicit** in your ASP pages requires you to use the **Dim** statement to declare all variables. However, using this statement can significantly speed up your pages. Besides, explicit declaration of variables can also help you avoid many common programming bugs.

You should try to declare variables inside functions and subroutines instead of at the page scope. Declaring them this way is also more efficient and will speed up your pages.

Remove Comments

Although using comments is a great idea for maintaining your scripts, they can slow down your page in production.

SELECT * Is Generally Slower Than EXPLICIT SELECT

You can tune database performance in many ways. However, most of these methods depend on the type of database you're using. One approach that is very likely to slow you down is using * in a **SELECT** statement. Even if you need all the columns, it is still more efficient to ask for a specific set of columns.

Of course, any time you can narrow your selection, you'll improve performance. Depending on how the database indexes tables, slight variations in queries (such as the order of items in the **WHERE** clause) can have an enormous effect on performance.

Chapter 15
Where To On The Web?

Al Williams

In my lifetime, nothing has so radically altered the fabric of society as the Internet and the World Wide Web. I imagine that living through this time is similar to how it must have been to live during the migration to the New World or the widespread use of moveable type printing. Of course, the obvious parallel to the Web is twentieth century mass media, such as radio, movies, and television.

Early television hardly resembles what we know today. When I was a kid, my family had a single black-and-white TV set. Cable was something I had dimly heard about but had never seen. Today, my house has six sets (including a 53-inch behemoth). I get nearly 100 channels (although it still seems like nothing of value is playing). A far cry from Uncle Miltie and Ernie Kovacs.

The Wild, Wild Web

The Web of tomorrow will resemble today's Web about as much as David Letterman's show resembles the old Ernie Kovacs show— some remnants of influence, but hardly recognizable. You might like to think that the changes are an improvement, but not everyone agrees. Still, the very worst of television eventually falls victim to poor ratings and popular pressure. Ernie Kovacs himself said, "Television is often called a medium because it's so rarely well done."

Many factors will combine to change the face of the Web. Although the media would have you believe that everyone is on the Web, the truth is that only a small fraction of the world is connected to the Internet. It will be a long time before the Internet can boast the simultaneous reach of television, where over 31 million people watched the last episode of *Seinfeld* and well over 125 million watch the Super Bowl.

Of course, the number of people using the Web increases every day. Estimates vary, but at the beginning of the year 2000, NUA Internet Surveys estimates about 201 million users worldwide. That number is not even 5 percent of the world's population. As more and more people join the Web, the Web will change, too.

Another factor is bandwidth. As more people have high-speed access to the Net via ISDN, DSL, cable modems, or even high-speed wireless connections, they will expect to do more. A 56Kbps connection is barely adequate to make choppy phone calls. A 250Kbps connection allows you to make high-quality phone calls. Even higher speeds will make the videophone a reality.

Combining high-speed multimedia with a mass market will make some parts of the Web look something like television. But, the good thing about the Web is that it has virtually limitless channels. Just as cable TV brought small, specialized networks (such as the Food Channel or Home and Garden Television) into their own, the Web will still provide plenty of space for applications that don't look like television, even though television-like services may dominate the Web's revenue generation.

Another player to watch is the embedded Internet. Already, several vendors produce tiny Internet-capable computers that can reside in a car, a refrigerator, or a cell phone. Forgot to record a movie? Log in to your VCR (using your car phone), and set it. If your freezer overheats, it can send you an email.

Who Will You Be?

The point is, big changes are coming. Some of the changes are obvious. Making predictions is always dangerous. Compare Arthur C. Clarke's *2001: A Space Odyssey* to the reality now that we are nearly at the year 2001. Clarke was conservative; he imagined only lunar colonies and picture phones. Other prognosticators assured us we would fly to work in personal helicopters and heat our homes with nuclear energy. Even if you know change is coming, it doesn't always help you figure out what that change will look like.

Among the people working in the Internet business today, who will be the next Ted Turner or Rupert Murdoch? Probably someone who can guess the future better than I can. However, one point is clear: A strict television model, in which the same content is just beamed at everyone at once, will not work on the Web. Because of the way the Web works, it can be an interactive medium, and that is what truly differentiates it from ordinary broadcast media.

This entire book has focused on how to make interactive Web sites. Sure, the Web sites you create today will be as quaint in the year 2050 as old episodes of *Sky King*. Still, the formula—interactivity and content—will remain constant even if the presentation and the tools you use change.

ASP In The Future?

This book, of course, is mainly about Active Server Pages. Will ASP survive all the mutations that are in store for the Web? I suspect it will in some form or another. Microsoft is heavily invested in ASP, and ASP does enable a wide range of programmers to create Web-based interactive content.

I'm not saying that I think ASP will remain just as it is today. Far from it. It seems, at least in the computer business, that each generation reinvents the things that have gone before and thinks it has found something new. Do you think PC and workstation operating systems invented virtual memory? No—mainframe computers employed that technique a decade or more earlier. How about arrays of disk drives? No, again the mainframe computers had them long before most PCs even had hard disks.

Even in software, we see certain recurring themes. When two professors at Dartmouth developed Basic, they wanted something easier than FORTRAN to use in class. They never dreamed people would actually use it. When the PC burst on the scene, Basic stood for some time as the language of choice for developers. When people started to get serious about PCs, however, real developers chose C over Basic. C is compiled and promotes structured programming practices.

For a while, it looked like Basic was all but dead. Then, Visual Basic became popular and started a renaissance of Basic programming. Visual Basic could be compiled (sort of, at first—it took awhile for it to become fully compiled); it had the same structured constructs that C had and even some that you would associate with C++.

Now people use Basic for everything from Windows applications to Excel spreadsheet macros to Web page scripting. At one time, you could have found many people to tell you Basic was dead. Now it thrives again—but in a different form.

If you are accustomed only to Visual Basic, you might not even recognize an old-fashioned Basic program. In those days, Basic used line numbers instead of labels. Most Basics required you to use the dreaded **GOTO** statement because they didn't support structured programming.

Of course, FORTRAN remained popular with the scientists and engineers. I've heard the quote, "I don't know what language scientists will use to write programs in the twenty-first century, but I know it will be called FORTRAN!" The same might be said for ASP. In 2050, you'll probably still use ASP, but you might not recognize what you are writing today as the same thing.

Conclusions

I have always been a believer in function over form. If it's usable on all possible clients, that's a passing mark. If it's spectacular on some sites and unusable on others, the end result is a failing mark, regardless of how spectacular it would have been *if only they could have seen it.*

Public speaking guru Bert Decker always says, "You've got to be believed to be heard." On the Web, you might well turn that statement around to be, "You've got to be seen to be believed." To start with, then, the best design solution is to keep it simple and functional. From there, you can add the bells and whistles. On top of that, although it might sound contradictory, the better *looking* sites are often more believable than the most authoritative sites. So, you have to keep that point in mind.

It really is a tough game, knowledgeably weighing the different technologies (VBScript or JavaScript), tools (Internet Explorer or Netscape), and areas of emphasis (pretty or usable). One goal of this book is to help you make those decisions.

It's hard to tell what conclusions to draw from this book or the state of the industry at the time of this writing because everything is changing so fast and so much can change in a short time. I don't know when that will not be the case, but, to play it safe, I've included things closer to facts here and left things closer to speculation to the following "Prognostications" section.

Security

In terms of guaranteeing the safety of active content, the security model of the Internet and Web is insufficient for the demands that will be placed on it. "What are you talking about?" some people might ask. It has to become seamless, unobtrusive, and foolproof. You don't worry about security when you change channels on your TV, nor should you do so on the Web. The current models offer more or less security with corresponding better or worse performance. Although Microsoft is the unstoppable train, my bet is on Java and JavaScript until someone comes out with a better security model.

Of course, security can also mean the encryption of user data (such as credit card numbers). With the relaxation of export restrictions on encryption technology, I expect to see this become a nonissue for most users. Today, e-commerce buzzes happily along with only a few cases of credit card fraud reported. You are probably safer transmitting your credit card number over the Net than you are giving it to the kid who brings your dinner at the local Pizza Hut—not to mention much safer than reading it to someone over a cordless or cellular phone.

Browsers

Some time ago, I would have said that at some date in the future you could stop worrying about Netscape and its browser. Now, I'm not so sure. This is not a comment on the relative quality of the browsers. It's just that Microsoft is a huge company that makes a lot of money, and Netscape is a company for which I have yet to figure out how it generates cash to validate its stock price other than by stock sales. Microsoft can afford to give away a browser because it has other sources of income, but how can Netscape make money when everyone gets the browser free? Yet, several other players are in that game, such as the Justice Department, AOL, Sun, and IBM, so who knows?

On the other hand, AOL bought Netscape and doesn't seem to have a great commitment to the browser itself. Perhaps the day when you can assume users are running Internet Explorer is close at hand.

Today, Netscape has at least enough market share that you have to consider both browsers when designing your site (unless you work in a closed system, such as an intranet, where all software can be specified top-down). The safest bet for all is either Java and client-side JavaScript, or server-side scripting and controls. This bet is not necessarily the fastest or the easiest, but it is the choice that accommodates the most users.

Server Or Client?

Do you create scripts and applets for the server or for the client? A lot depends on what kind of environment you expect (intranet or Internet). By default, I think the answer is server, unless you write your client-side applications so that they have the capability to punt if the browser doesn't support what you're trying to do. Server-side technology (be it Active Server Pages or other server-side techniques such as JSP [Java Server Pages], servlets, or PHP) allows you the maximum control over the entire process. No one can know for sure what system the user has, but you can, potentially, control every aspect of the server and the software it runs.

Speed

What's the fastest speed? After the initial download of a control, ActiveX wins in terms of performance. If you depend on that performance, its other shortcomings diminish. Of course, depending on how you write the control, the download time might be incredible, based on a variety of factors.

HTML 4, Scriptlets, Applets, JScript, ActiveX, And VBScript

By now, all these terms should no longer seem like a confused mess of alphabet soup. Furthermore, you should know how to make decisions regarding using the technologies and be well informed about their strengths and weaknesses. However, you should also realize that no one answer is always best.

Combination Of Technologies

If you should walk away from this book with one thing, it is this realization: You'll often need a combination of techniques to produce the results you want. You might be tempted to go with the tools you know, but you need a big enough tool set to get the job done. You wouldn't build a house with only a screwdriver, so why create a Web site with only one tool?

Prognostications

This section is almost a freebie for an author, like being an economist or a weathercaster. Maybe that's a cheap shot, however, because they supposedly keep their jobs only when they make more right guesses than wrong ones. Like a tabloid psychic, I can gloat over my correct predictions and conveniently ignore when I've missed the mark.

I've seen the online world go from scrolling ASCII text to pretty front ends with graphics and sounds. I've seen the Internet go from ASCII news and mail readers to fantastic-looking Web applications. I heard the sound of the waves going by as the Web lapped the online world, and I watched the online (information service) world groan and creak and wobble to attempt to catch up to a business that it had been doing for years. I've also seen the thrashing of the whole computer and business world as everyone tried (and is still trying) to figure out what to make of the Web. Will e-commerce destroy the brick-and-mortar retail store? Or, will the two combine into some new synergistic entity?

Bell Labs displayed a prototype videophone many years ago. It was a great idea. It had three views you could use, displaying your face, the table in front of it (to show a document that both sides of the conversation could look at), and the view from the other person's camera. It was definitely ahead of its time. In those days, there wasn't enough bandwidth in the copper lines or enough computing power to make up for that lack of bandwidth.

Many futuristic ideas grew out of Xerox's Palo Alto Research Center (PARC). The mouse, the folder metaphor, desktops, and icons all grew out of PARC (the old Star workstations were virtually indistinguishable from Macintoshes unless you looked at the size of the CPU or the price tag). Apple borrowed ideas from PARC and then unsuccessfully waged legal wars on Microsoft for also borrowing the same ideas.

All this goes to show you some important points. Having the best product doesn't always matter. Being first doesn't always matter. Having 20 years' worth of great products and high standing in the industry doesn't guarantee you a place for life (the examples in the past few years are numerous).

What should be exciting (or frightening) for everyone reading this book is the potential for profit and change and the explosive development of exciting new technologies. At the 1997 Professional Developers Conference, a Microsoft executive showed a chart that compared the technological life cycles of radio, television, and microwave ovens. According to my understanding of what was said, all these products have similar growth curves. These curves grew slowly at first (early adopters), steadily climbed for so many years, and then leveled off. For example, either you or your parents (or, heaven forbid, your grandparents) remember when the first family on the block got a television set (perhaps a Dumont with a tiny, round screen). Then, it seemed like everyone had a television, and now everyone has two or three. Of course, many of them are huge and almost always in brilliant color, if not stereo sound.

The curve that Microsoft's exec showed indicated that we in the Internet/Web world are past the early adopter's stage and at the bottom of a staggeringly upward rise during which time every household will soon come to own a multitude of Web-enabled devices. I fully expect the telephone, television, and computer to completely consume each other and merge into one class of device.

Certainly, we will leave behind the hardware and network limitations we faced yesterday and even today. Cable modems are promising exciting new speeds, some communities are going fiber-optic, and parts of the old copper-wire network are being replaced by (or are at least competing against) fiber. Then, we also must consider satellites and other wireless technologies.

Sitting on our desktops—everyone's desktop—are not the junky old 8088s, 386s, or 486s, but faster processors with more RAM, bigger hard drives, CD players, speakers, sound cards, and bigger and better-quality monitors. I looked into buying a new PC recently and had to ask myself whether I was buying a PC or a home entertainment system. I mean, you have to have the upgraded speakers, the television and radio tuner, and the bigger and better monitor, don't you? Wait a minute. This PC now is a major purchase and has more gadgets than the rest of my house. I'll have to upgrade my house to keep up!

But the prices will come down (as they always do), and everyone will have not only a PC but a multimedia PC. Furthermore, I think the revolution will go way beyond that. I'm talking about a browser in every room of every building, on every toaster and bank machine, in every booth in restaurants and bars, and as an interface to vending machines. Many vendors are already shipping tiny Internet-enabled computers for just this purpose (see **www.ibutton.com**, for example).

At one time, Bill Gates may have dreamed that Windows would be that interface—the interface to the modern world. But, he has since realized something different, which is why I think he doesn't want to divorce Internet Explorer from the Windows operating system. Browsers are not just another piece of commodity software to be sold on the shelf like compilers, word processors, and sound editors. They likely will be the front end to the entire computer. In many people's minds, browsers will probably be as important or indistinguishable from what people like us understand as the operating system. This is especially true as your computer lives less and less on (or under) your desk and more throughout your home (or even your community) over the network.

Imagine Internet Explorer (or Netscape Navigator or some other browser) on every soda machine, toaster, and TV in the world. Imagine the power you would have if you controlled that front end and the power you wouldn't have if you couldn't. On the one hand, you have to define the direction; on the other, you have to follow it and hope to keep up. This sounds like the kind of power any company would enjoy, at least until the Department of Justice steps into the fray.

Mr. Gates—certainly an astute predictor of the future—gave the keynote address at the 2000 Consumer Electronics Show in Las Vegas. There, he showed an array of devices embedded in a mockup of a living room and a den. These devices used a form of Windows to check email, control music throughout the house, and even answer the door remotely. Gates envisions each home as a private little Internet with a Windows PC at the hub and a plethora of Web-enabled devices (also running Windows, of course). With or without Windows, imagine connected intranets that are as common as electric lighting or television.

What does this coming technology mean for the Web hacker writing scripts? It means that if you are a programmer, a graphic artist, or a technical writer, you will have ample opportunity to make your mark in any number of these new areas. The explosion from 10 Web surfers on every block to dozens of Web-surfing tools in every home means an explosion in opportunity; and, although the technology gets more complex, the tools for delivering it are becoming easier to use. The best way to stay on top of it and be a part of it is to keep your hands in the business and, wherever possible, take advantage of other people's homework, like you did with this book.

You also will have to select among the competing technologies and tools as they continually develop. Keep your learning hat on, and hold on tight.

Whatever the future, I want to wish you luck in this exciting new age. And, when you see the first toaster with a Web browser on it, with clickable regions for light, medium, dark, and bagel, let me know.

Links And Resources

The following are some good resources on Active Server Pages, and other related online topics:

- **www.netscape.com**—Netscape is currently one of the Big Three (with Sun and Microsoft) setting the directions of the industry. If you are looking for information or want to stay current, it never hurts to check out Netscape's site. You can find references on technology, tips, and information about its browser and JavaScript. You especially should head to the areas for developers (**http://developer.netscape.com/index_home.html**). Because Netscape was bought by AOL, it isn't clear just what Netscape's future holds, but the site is full of useful information.

- **www.sun.com**—Currently the only credible competitor to Microsoft, Sun is the developer of Java and holding tightly onto it. This is another site that you should check out if you are looking for information or trying to stay abreast of new technology. Look for developer areas. Also check out the free office suite (StarOffice), which includes usable HTML creation tools.

- **www.microsoft.com**, **msdn.microsoft.com**—Regardless of what some people say about Microsoft, it has become very good at what it does, and it does almost everything. It has a lot of information, and it is a great site to use to stay current on Microsoft technology. Microsoft is the leader in tools and technology, and the wealth of information on its Web site is considerable (that is, assuming you're running some version of Windows). For the good stuff, you currently have to register, but it doesn't cost anything, and you have to hand over only an email address and some other harmless information. When the system is up, it really provides a lot of information, such as documentation, articles, and so on, that you can quickly search.

- **www.cnet.com**—Along with technology news, CNET is the best place to find browsers (such as Internet Explorer and Netscape Communicator)—even better than Microsoft's or Netscape's site.

- **www.w3.org**—If Microsoft, Sun, and Netscape have their slants, the standards body World Wide Web Consortium (W3C) heralds back to the old Internet days, when semi-academic bodies were responsible for standards. The W3C is vendor-neutral, and it works with the global community to "produce specifications and reference software that is made freely available throughout the world." In other words, if you want to find the latest HTML specifications, you go here.

- **www.learnasp.com**—Formerly **www.activeserverpages.com**, this site contains a wide variety of lessons, ASP-related downloads, and other information.

- **www.4guysfromrolla.com**—This ASP site has many original articles apparently by the four guys.

- **www.15seconds.com**—Another online ASP resource, this site includes a consultant registry.

- **www.asphole.com**—Despite the name, this site also has many good ASP articles and reviews.

- **www.webtechniques.com**—You probably qualify for a free subscription to this print magazine, which really keeps you abreast of the entire Web industry.

- **www.planetit.com**—This major site is for computer-related news that affects industry professionals. You'll find news, commentary, and roundtable discussions.

- **www.builder.com**—Another news-oriented site for Web developers, this one is from CNET, which is known for general technology news.

- **www.wdvl.com**—The Web Developer's Virtual Library is one of my favorite vendor-neutral sites for information about Web technology. If you can use it to create Web content, you'll find detailed technical information about it here.

One question that people frequently ask me is where they can get free ASP Web hosting. There are many Web providers that offer free space, such as GeoCities, Tripod, and VirtualAve. They usually make their money by placing ads on your Web site. Unfortunately, most of these sites don't support ASP.

Recently, several providers have started offering free ASP Web sites. However, these providers tend to fill up quickly and then they stop taking new members. Also, free Web hosts tend to disappear if they are not successful. Here are a few that offer ASP hosting for free:

♦ **www.webhostme.com**

♦ **www.exine.com**

♦ **www.ewebcity.com**

♦ **www.domaindlx.com**

If you can find a free ASP host that is accepting members it's a great way to get some practice using ASP live on the real Internet with real users.

Appendix A
A Case Study

Al Williams

Building a Web site is like building a house. None of the parts is overly difficult, but taken together, it's a major undertaking. In this appendix, I'll show you a Web site I've used in training classes for several years. On it, you can read about sightings of "The King," a near-mythical figure who seems to pop up everywhere. You'll find lots of little pieces in this project to borrow for your own sites. Here, I'll focus less on the details of each piece and more on how the pieces go together. You'll find all of these techniques covered in detail in the main portion of this book.

In the beginning, the Web site is fairly typical—just some static pages and a few images. In several steps, you'll see how to convert the pages to use VBScript on the client and server sides. The site also uses the Microsoft Personalization System (MPS, a part of Site Server) and has many interesting features, including:

♦ Access to a live database (updates and queries)

♦ Registration and user preferences (for example, graphics)

♦ Ad rotation

♦ Random content selection

♦ Rudimentary security to lock out certain users

♦ Hit counting

♦ Email notification and logging of user registrations

Figure A.1 shows the basic home page at the beginning of the project. Although certainly no paragon of site design, this page is typical of the kind of site you might inherit. Also, it has a simple layout, so it will be easier to work with. The only advanced feature

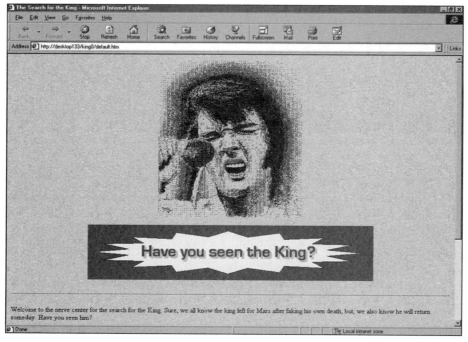

Figure A.1
The original King home page.

is an image map for navigation. However, many of the pages have inconsistent backgrounds and other design flaws.

The original site has 17 files (see Table A.1). You'll also find the starting site in the KING0 directory for this appendix on the CD. The final Web site is in the KING1 (no MPS) and KING2 (MPS) directories.

Table A.1   The original King site.

File	Description
AL_SM.GIF	GIF file of yours truly
DEFAULT.HTM	Main page
FACE.GIF	Picture of the King's Martian monument
FIND.HTM	Reports of sightings (statistics)
HISTORY.HTM	The history of the King
KAUFMAN.JPG	A picture of a man who did a pretty good King
KING1.GIF	The King's picture
KINGBAN.GIF	The King's site banner
KINGBAR.GIF	Navigation bar
LARROW.GIF	The usual left arrow graphic

(continued)

Table A.1   The original King site (continued).

File	Description
MEN.HTM	One of these men may be the King?
PBML03.GIF	Used for some backgrounds
QUOTE.HTM	Read the quote of the day
REPORT.HTM	Report your sightings (not really functional yet)
TU.WAV	"Thank you very much"
VOTE.HTM	Nonfunctional voting page
WHO.GIF	Question graphic

Converting To ASP

Converting the site to utilize ASP is relatively straightforward. At first, you might try simply renaming the HTM files to ASP files. However, this approach doesn't work because the links between pages must also change.

A common mistake at this point is to copy the HTM files so that you have two versions of each file: one with an .HTM extension and another with the .ASP extension. Everything would appear to work. However, the links then take you to the HTM files, which do not support script. Changing your ASP file but never seeing any changes in the browser can be very frustrating.

If you are in control of your server, you'll probably want to change the default page to DEFAULT.ASP. However, if some people still have DEFAULT.HTM bookmarked, you might want to supply a simple jump page (see Listing A.1), which is a bridge that vectors users to the ASP file. Notice that you can't use **Response.Redirect** here because, to use it, you would have to be in an ASP file. The entire point to the bridge is that it is an HTM file.

Listing A.1   Bridging the old and the new.

```
<HTML>
<HEAD>
<META HTTP-EQUIV="REFRESH" CONTENT="1" URL="default.asp">

</HEAD>
Whoops...you probably meant to go to <A HREF="default.asp">HERE.</A>
</HTML>
```

Making Simple Enhancements

After you convert the files to ASP format, you can make some quick enhancements fairly easily. For example, the quote feature is easy to enhance.

In the basic pages, the King's quote is always the same. Why not make the quote change at random? You can find a server-side solution in Listing A.2. Of course, you could get the same effect with client-side script as well, as shown in Listing A.3.

It is interesting to see how the **rnd** function works. Two aspects make this function odd. First, it employs a seed value. Given the same seed, **rnd** will always produce the same sequence of numbers. That's fine if you want repeatable random numbers, but you usually want numbers that are unpredictable, in which case, you should be sure to call **Randomize** first. This call sets the seed to an unpredictable value based on the current time.

The other oddity about **rnd** is that it generates a number between zero and one. So, if you want to generate integers between 1 and 100, you need to compute the following:

```
x=Int(rnd*99)+1
```

Next, you might add rotating advertisements. The **MSWC.AdRotator** component does so, but it is somewhat cumbersome to use. Why not roll your own? It isn't much different than picking a random quote.

Listing A.2   Server-side quotes.

```
<HTML>
<HEAD>
<META HTTP-EQUIV="REFRESH" CONTENT="15">
<TITLE>King's Quote for the Day</TITLE>

</HEAD>
<BODY <!-- #include file="stdbody.inc"-->>

<H1>The King's Quote of the Day</H1>

<HR>
<P>
&quot;
<%
  dim qt(10)
  qt(0)="Thank you very much!"
  qt(1)="Blue suede shoes"
  qt(2)="Uhhh huh huh...huh huh huh...yeah!"
  qt(3)="Man...that sucker's huge!"
  qt(4)="TCB!"
  qt(5)="If you play my records backwards, you can hear SIVLE!"
  qt(6)="They said they were just vitamins"
  qt(7)="I like sequins...a lot!"
  qt(8)="Can't get enough of them jumpsuits!"
  qt(9)="If they make a movie about me, don't let Roseanne play Priscilla!"
  qt(10)="One word: Hips!"
  Randomize
  n=Int(11*rnd)
%>
```

```
<%= qt(n) %>
<% if request("Debug")="1" then
    Response.Write(" Debug=")
    Response.Write(n)
    end if
%>
&quot;
</HTML>
```

Listing A.3   Client-side quotes.

```
<HTML>

<HEAD>
<META HTTP-EQUIV="REFRESH" CONTENT="15">
<TITLE>King's Quote for the Day</TITLE>


</HEAD>
<BODY <!-- #include file="stdbody.inc"-->>

<H1>The King's Quote of the Day</H1>

<HR>

<P>
&quot;
<SCRIPT LANGUAGE=VBScript>
<!--
  ' Client side quote script
  dim qt(10)
  qt(0)="Thank you very much!"
  qt(1)="Blue suede shoes"
  qt(2)="Uhhh huh huh...huh huh huh...yeah!"
  qt(3)="Man...that sucker's huge!"
  qt(4)="TCB!"
  qt(5)="If you play my records backwards, you can hear SIVLE!"
  qt(6)="They said they were just vitamins"
  qt(7)="I like sequins...a lot!"
  qt(8)="Can't get enough of them jumpsuits!"
  qt(9)="If they make a movie about me, don't let Roseanne play Priscilla!"
  qt(10)="One word: Hips!"
 'Randomize
  n=Int(11*rnd)
  document.Write(qt(n))
<% if request("Debug")="1" then %>
```

```
    document.Write(" Debug=")
    document.Write(n)
<% end if %>
-->
</SCRIPT>
&quot;
<P>
</HTML>
```

Listing A.4 shows an ad rotation using the built-in component. Listing A.5 shows an alternate scheme based on files. This code assumes that the ad banners are GIF files named Ad1.GIF, Ad2.GIF, and so on. You also can create a corresponding SPONSORx.ASP file (where *x* is a number). This file should use the **Response.Redirect** call to vector the user to the correct page. The sponsor file might take other actions, too. For example, you could record the click in a file or a database. The sample files don't do anything but pop up an alert box.

The custom rotation code is in the ROTATE.INC file. You can easily include it anywhere you want a rotating advertisement. You can find ROTATE.INC in Listing A.5. You'll see some similarity between this code and the random-quote-generation code you looked at earlier.

Listing A.4   Standard ad rotation (excerpt from DEFAULT.ASP).

```
<% set ad=Server.CreateObject("MSWC.AdRotator") %>
<hr>
Please visit our sponsors:
<CENTER>
<%= ad.GetAdvertisement("ads.txt") %>
<hr>
</CENTER>
```

Listing A.5   Custom ad rotation.

```
<!-- Rotate Ads -->
<%
  maxads=2    ' Set to maximum # of ads
  Randomize
  n=Int(maxads*rnd)+1
%>
<A HREF=SPONSOR<%= n %>.ASP><IMG SRC=AD<%= n %>.GIF></A>
```

With this simple scheme, it's trivial to have your ASP file pick a number and call up the right files. By placing the code in an include file, you can use it from many places easily.

Another simple enhancement is to allow the user to disable most graphics. You can do so by setting a session variable with a flag indicating whether graphics are off. (The absence of the flag should mean that graphics are on, as this will be the default case.) Then, you can bracket every nonessential graphic with an **if** statement so that it doesn't appear when the flag is set. Listing A.6 shows GOFF.ASP, which turns graphics off. Listing A.7 shows an optional graphic.

Listing A.6   GOFF.ASP.

```
<% Session("Graphics")="N" %>
<SCRIPT Language=VBScript>
location.pathname="default.asp"
</SCRIPT>
```

Listing A.7   Making a graphic optional.

```
<CENTER>
<% if Session("Graphics")<>"N" then %>
<IMG Have you seen the King?  SRC="kingban.gif">
<% end if %>
</CENTER>
```

Of course, you shouldn't disable all graphics for this site. The original site design depends on the graphics navigation bar for users to jump from the home page to the other pages on the site. Unless you add text-based navigation, you should leave the bar visible. Doing so should be no problem because it will always appear unless you bracket it with an **if** statement.

An interesting effect is to use an **else** clause with an optional graphic. You could display some text or provide a link to turn graphics back on. You could even make the graphics flag select a level of graphics. Perhaps a value of 0 means no graphics, 1 selects low-resolution images, and 2 turns on everything.

As it stands, the graphics flag survives only for the user's session because it's in a session variable. However, you could store the flag in the user property database if you are using the Microsoft Personalization System.

Although most users likely won't notice that the original site had inconsistent backgrounds, you can easily fix this problem by filling in each **<BODY>** tag with a server-side include. Using the STDBODY.INC file (shown in Listing A.8), you can easily change the background for each page.

Listing A.8   STDBODY.INC.

```
BACKGROUND="pmb103.gif"
```

Another way to change it is to place the entire **<BODY>** tag in the STDBODY.INC file. This approach has the advantage of allowing you to put other HTML or script in the STDBODY.INC file, but the disadvantage of not allowing you to customize the **<BODY>** for individual pages.

Debugging

Debugging ASP is notoriously difficult because it all takes place on the server. Every programmer must debug sometimes, and a few tricks can help make your life easier.

In the QUOTE.ASP file (shown in Listings A.2 and A.3), notice the debugging statements that print out key values for inspection (the ordinary user never sees these values).

The key is a session variable named **Debug**. The main page checks to see whether there is a query string named **Debug**. If one exists, the value of the session variable becomes the value of this query string, and then any page that wants to print debugging information checks the state of the session variable first. If the variable is not **True**, the page skips the debugging code.

Hit Counting

Sometimes it seems as if creating hit counters was the reason Web scripting was invented. You can easily create a counter by using ASP. You simply increment the count in an application variable (see Listing A.9). Be sure to lock the **Application** object before accessing it.

Listing A.9   Hit counting.
```
<BR>
<% application.Lock
   application("Count")=application("Count")+1
   n=application("Count")
   application.Unlock
   set ofile=Server.CreateObject("scripting.FileSystemObject") '
   set file=ofile.CreateTextFile("kingcount.txt",TRUE) '
   file.WriteLine CStr(n)
   file.Close
 %>
You are visitor number <%= application("Count") %>
<P>
```

The catch here is that the server resets all application variables each time you restart the server, and you need a way to make your hit count persistent. Of course, you could read the count from a file when the application starts (in the GLOBAL.ASA file, as shown in Listing A.10), but you can't write out the count when the application shuts down. By the time ASP informs you that the application is shutting down, most variables are already gone. Also, what happens if the server doesn't shut down in an orderly fashion?

Listing A.10   Reading the hit count (excerpt from GLOBAL.ASA).
```
<SCRIPT Language=VBSCRIPT RUNAT=Server>
   Sub Session_OnStart()
   End Sub
```

```
Sub Application_OnStart()
set ifile=Server.CreateObject("Scripting.FileSystemObject")
set file=ifile.OpenTextFile("kingcount.txt",1,TRUE)
s=file.ReadLine
if s<>"" then
  application("Count")=CInt(s)
else
 application("Count")=0
end if
End Sub

Sub Application_OnEnd()
' Can't write out here because everything is shut down!
End Sub
```

```
</SCRIPT>
```

The solution, then, is to write out the hit count when you update it, as Listing A.9 does. Although this approach is reliable, it isn't as efficient because each hit produces a file write.

If you have several pages a user can visit directly, and you want to keep track of unique visitors, try incrementing the hit count in the **Session_OnStart** event handler.

Content Linking

Often, it's useful to imagine your Web pages having a particular order (like the pages in a book). Although having pages in a sequence is often a good thing in terms of usability, it can be a real nightmare in terms of maintenance.

The **MSWC.NextLink** component can be a real help in this case. This component uses an ordinary text file that contains the URLs in their correct order. When you ask the component to give you the next (or previous) URL, it locates the current URL in the list and returns the appropriate string.

Each line in the file consists of a URL, a tab character, a description, a tab character, and an optional comment. Although the description is optional, the tab preceding it is not (at least until Microsoft fixes this obvious bug). Also, you have to be careful that the text editor you use doesn't replace tabs with spaces.

You'll use this component mainly to generate hyperlinks, using the URL as the link's target and the description as the display portion. You can put a set of Previous and Next links in an include file (like the one in Listing A.11) and easily place them on each page. Notice that each page ends with an include of a standard copyright file. This copyright file also contains the include file that handles the Next and Previous links. (See BROWSE.INC in Listing A.11.)

Listing A.11   Using MSWC.NextLink.

```
<% set seq=Server.CreateObject("MSWC.NextLink") %>
<PRE>
<A HREF=<%=seq.GetPreviousURL("/index.txt")%>>Previous Page </A>
<A HREF=<%=seq.GetNextURL("/index.txt")%>>Next Page </A>
<A HREF=index.asp>Goto Index</A>
</PRE>
```

The **MSWC.NextLink** component also allows you to step through the entire list. This way, you can easily generate an index (see Listing A.12 and Figure A.2). Armed with these tricks, you can easily maintain the index and the Next links. Simply make an entry in the text file to add the new page to the list, and the scripts take care of the rest.

Listing A.12   Automatically generating the index.

```
<HTML>
<HEAD>
<TITLE>The King's Page Index</TITLE>
</HEAD>
<BODY>
<% set link=Server.CreateObject("MSWC.NextLink")
    for i=1 to link.GetListCount("/index.txt") %>
<A HREF=<%= link.GetNthURL("/index.txt",i) %>>
```

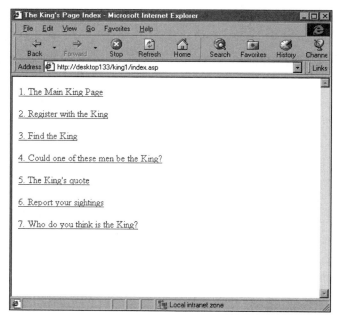

Figure A.2
The index page is automatically generated.

```
    <%= CStr(i) + ". " %> ]
    <%= link.GetNthDescription("/index.txt",i) %>
</A><P>
<% next %>
</BODY>
</HTML>
```

Using More Advanced Techniques

Using the User Property Database (UPD, part of the Microsoft Personalization System), you can make many other enhancements to the Web site. In Listing A.13, notice that the page greets the user by name, if it knows the user's name. If it doesn't, the user sees a link to a registration page. Because registration relies on cookies, the code doesn't present the registration option unless the browser capability object indicates that the browser supports cookies.

Listing A.13   Excerpt from DEFAULT.ASP.

```
<% set prop = Server.CreateObject ("MPS.PropertyDatabase")
. . .
<P>
Welcome
<% if prop("Name")<>"" then %>
<%= prop("Name") %>
<% end if %>
to the nerve center for the search for the King. Sure,
we all know the king left for Mars after faking his own death,
but, we also know he will return someday. Have you seen him?
<P>
. . .
<% set binfo=Server.CreateObject("MSWC.BrowserType")
    if prop("Name")="" and binfo.Cookies<>"FALSE" then %>
    <A HREF=register.asp>Click here to register!</A>
    <% end if %>
<P>
```

When the user registers using the form in Listing A.14, the script logs the entry in a file and sends email to the Webmaster. In this case, the registration is the user's name, but it could be anything.

Listing A.14   Registration (REGISTER.ASP).

```
<% set prop = Server.CreateObject ("MPS.PropertyDatabase")
  response.Expires=0 %>
<HTML>
<HEAD>
<% if request("Content_Length")<>0 then %>
```

```
<!-- Client pull is OK, but leaves this page in the
     history. Better to use redirection. Try it! -->
<META HTTP-EQUIV="REFRESH" CONTENT="5" URL="default.asp">
<% end if %>
<TITLE>Register with the King</TITLE>
<BODY <!-- #include file="stdbody.inc" -->>
<% if request("Content_Length")=0 then %>
<H1>Tell us your name!</H1><P>
<FORM NAME="Register" Action="register.asp" METHOD="POST">
Enter your name: <INPUT NAME="Name" Value= "<%= prop("Name") %>"
   MAXLENGTH="60" SIZE=60>
<INPUT TYPE=SUBMIT NAME="Enter" VALUE="Enter">
</FORM>
<% else
  prop("Name")=request("Name") %>
  Thanks for registering <%= prop("Name") %>

<!--Mail to Webmaster -->
<%  set mailer=Server.CreateObject("MPS.SendMail")
  mailer.SendMail "web1","bigdummyal@coriolis.com",
  "Registration",prop("Name")+" registered!" %>

<!-- Text log -->
<% set file=Server.CreateObject("Scripting.FileSystemObject")
   set tfile=file.OpenTextFile("register.log",8)
   tfile.WriteLine prop("Name")+" registered."
   tfile.Close
%>

<% end if %>
<!-- #include file="copyright.inc" -->
```

Another interesting effect of the UPD is allowing for the King pages to lock out unwanted users. If you ask for the King's history, the HISTORY.ASP file chastises you (see Listing A.15) and sets a flag in the UPD. If the main page detects this flag, it redirects you to a page (see Listing A.16) where you can redeem yourself and clear the flag.

Listing A.15   Banishing the user.

```
<% set prop = Server.CreateObject ("MPS.PropertyDatabase")
  response.Expires=0 %>
<% prop("Banish")=1 %>
<HTML>

<HEAD>

<TITLE>History of the King</TITLE>
```

```
</HEAD>
<BODY <!-- #include file="stdbody.inc"-->>

<H1>About the King</H1>

<P>
You don't know every detail about the King? What shoe size did
he wear? What was odd about his ears? How many cars did he buy?
How many sequins were on his favorite jump suit?<BR>

<H2>WHAT!? You don't know these things? Then go away and never
return! You are banished from these pages forever!<BR>
<BR>
</H2>

</BODY>
</HTML>
```

Listing A.16   Redeeming the user.

```
<% set prop = Server.CreateObject ("MPS.PropertyDatabase")
  response.Expires=0
  if request("Answer")=2 then
    prop("Banish")=""
    response.redirect("default.asp")
  end if
%>
<HTML>
<HEAD>
<TITLE>Your Chance to Redeem Yourself!</TITLE>
<BODY <!-- #include file="stdbody.inc"-->>
<H1>You blew it!</H1>
Yes, you blew it, sport. You don't know beans about the King.
Well, here is your one chance to make good. If you can
answer the following question, we will forget all about
this unfortunate incident:
<P><P>
Pick the correct answer:<P>
The King was a burnin' burnin' hunka<P>
A. <A HREF=trivia.asp?Answer=1>Tire rubber</A><P>
B. <A HREF=trivia.asp?Answer=2>Love</A><P>
C. <A HREF=trivia.asp?Answer=3>Rubbish</A><P>
</BODY>
</HTML>
```

This trick isn't bulletproof, however, because a smart user can just delete your cookie to regain access. If you authenticate users, though, you could make a more secure system.

Adding Database Access

Adding live access to a database is one of the most powerful features you can add to a Web site. The King pages allow you to enter and view sightings right from the Web site.

The first step to adding access is to create your database and install it as a system DSN (using the ODBC control panel). You can find the "sighting" database table on the CD and in Table A.2.

Assuming that you want to display only data, the steps are simple. The code in Listing A.17 converts any database table into an HTML table. It even labels the columns automatically. Often, this is all you need. The King pages modify this code just a little so that the last column isn't displayed (see Listing A.18).

Listing A.17   Generic database table display.

```
<% Set Conn = Server.CreateObject("ADODB.Connection")
 ' Use your database info on the next 2 lines
   Conn.Open "MyDB","guest",""
   SQL="Select * from SomeTable"
   set RS = Conn.Execute(SQL)
%>


<P>
<TABLE BORDER=1>
<TR>
<% For i = 0 to RS.Fields.Count - 1 %>
     <TD><B><%= RS(i).Name %></B></TD>
  <% Next %>
</TR>
<% Do While Not RS.EOF %>
  <TR>
  <% For i = 0 to RS.Fields.Count - 1 %>
      <TD VALIGN=TOP>
      <%= RS(i) %>
      </TD>
  <% Next %>
  </TR>
<%
  RS.MoveNext
  Loop
  RS.Close
  Conn.Close
%>
</TABLE>
```

Table A.2   The "sighting" table.

Field	Description
Date	Date and time of sighting (not the entry date and time)
Before	True if user has seen the King before this sighting
Location	Where was the King?
Name	User's name
Comment	User's comments
subtime	System-generated submission time and date stamp

Listing A.18   The King database display.

```
<% set prop = Server.CreateObject ("MPS.PropertyDatabase")
  if prop("LastQuery")="" or request("RESET")=1 then
    prop("LastQuery")="01/01/80"
    noreset=1
  else
    noreset=0
  end if
  response.Expires=0
%>
<!--#include file="adovbs.inc" -->
<HTML>

<HEAD>

<TITLE>Find the King</TITLE>

</HEAD>
<BODY <!-- #include file="stdbody.inc"-->>

<H1>Recent King Sightings: </H1>

<% Set Conn = Server.CreateObject("ADODB.Connection") '***
   Conn.Open "KingSight","guest",""
   SQL="Select * from Sighting where "
   SQL= SQL & "subtime > CDate('"
   SQL= SQL & prop("LastQuery")
   SQL= SQL & "') or isnull(subtime) order by date desc"
   set RS = Conn.Execute(SQL)
   prop("LastQuery")=now
%>

<P>
<TABLE BORDER=1>
```

```
<TR>
  <!-- last field is hidden -->
  <% For i = 0 to RS.Fields.Count - 2 %>
     <TD><B><%= RS(i).Name %></B></TD>
  <% Next %>
</TR>
<% Do While Not RS.EOF %>
  <TR>
  <% For i = 0 to RS.Fields.Count - 2 %>
     <TD VALIGN=TOP>
   <% if RS(i).Name<>"Before" then %>
      <%= RS(i) %>
   <% else %>
      <% if RS(i)=0 then %>
        N
      <% else %>
        Y
      <% end if %>
   <% end if %>
     </TD>
  <% Next %>
  </TR>
<%
  RS.MoveNext
  Loop
  RS.Close
  Conn.Close
%>
</TABLE>


<P>
<% if noreset=0 then %>
This page only shows sightings reported after <%= prop("LastQuery") %>
<A HREF="find.asp?RESET=1">Click here to see all sightings</A>
<P>
<% end if %>
Be sure to add your sightings by clicking <A HREF="report.asp">here</A>.

<P>
<A HREF="default.asp"><IMG SRC="larrow.gif" ALT="home"> Back to home page</A>
</BODY>
<!-- #include file="copyright.inc" -->
</HTML>
```

Why not display the last column? In this case, the last column stores the date and the time a user entered a sighting (not the date and time of the sighting). The code in Listing A.18 remembers the time of the user's last query (using the UPD) and doesn't show data entered before that date and time. Presumably, the user already saw this data. However, setting the query string to **RESET=1** overrides this behavior and forces a complete display.

Note

*The display code in Listing A.18 differs somewhat from that in Listing A.17 in another way: It converts the Boolean value in the **Before** field more meaningfully.*

Entering data is straightforward (see Listing A.19). The code automatically fills in the entry timestamp.

Notice that the display code uses an SQL query but that the data entry form uses a record set. Which is better? The answer to that question depends. It's often more efficient to use an SQL statement to work with the database, but it can be very difficult to formulate a mix of HTML, SQL, and VBScript. Keeping the quotes straight is a major headache. In the end, you can use either method, or you can use both, as the example in Listing A.19 does.

Listing A.19   Data entry.

```
<!--#include file="adovbs.inc" -->
<HTML>

<HEAD>

<TITLE>Report Your Sightings!</TITLE>

</HEAD>
<BODY <!-- #include file="stdbody.inc"--»>

<% if Request("Content_Length")=0 then %>
<H1>Report Your King Sightings Here!<BR>
</H1>

<FORM NAME="KingForm" ACTION="report.asp" METHOD="POST">

<PRE WIDTH=132>
<FONT SIZE=2>Date:      </FONT><INPUT NAME="KDate" VALUE="" MAXLENGTH="8"
 SIZE=8><FONT SIZE=2 FACE="Courier New">       I've seen the King before:
</FONT><INPUT TYPE="CHECKBOX" NAME="Before">

<FONT SIZE=2 FACE="Courier New">Location: </FONT><INPUT NAME="Loc" VALUE=""
 MAXLENGTH="128" SIZE=64><FONT SIZE=2 FACE="Courier New">
```

```
<FONT SIZE=2 FACE="Courier New">Your name: </FONT><INPUT NAME="Name" VALUE=""
 MAXLENGTH="128" SIZE=64><FONT SIZE=2 FACE="Courier New">


Comments:

</FONT>
<TEXTAREA NAME="Comment" ROWS=3 COLS=80>
</TEXTAREA>
</PRE>
<CENTER><INPUT TYPE=SUBMIT NAME="Enter" VALUE="Enter" >
</CENTER>
</FORM>
<%else %>
<% ' Using record set, which is easy, but an Insert would
   ' have better performance (see FIND.ASP)
   Set Conn = Server.CreateObject("ADODB.Connection") '***
   Conn.Open "KingSight","guest",""
   set RS=Server.CreateObject("ADODB.RecordSet") '***
   Conn.BeginTrans ' start a unit of work
   rs.Open "Sighting", Conn, adOpenStatic, adLockOptimistic ' static open ***
   rs.AddNew ' new record
   rs("Date")=CDate(Request("KDate"))
   if Request("Before")="on" then
     rs("Before")=-1
   else
     rs("Before")=0
   end if
   rs("Location")=Request("Loc")
   rs("Name")=Request("Name")
   rs("Comment")=Request("Comment")
   rs("subtime")=now
   rs.Update
   Conn.CommitTrans
   rs.Close
   Conn.Close
%>


<H1> Thanks for your report </H1>
<% if Session("Debug")="1" then %>
Debug:<%= Request.Form %> <P>
<%end if %>
Your name is <%= Request("Name") %> and you saw the King
<% if Request("Before")="" then %>
for the first time
```

```
<% else %>
again
<% end if %>
on <%= Request("KDate") %> at <%= Request("Loc") %>
<P>Thank you very much!
<A HREF=find.asp>Click here to view recent sightings!</A>
<% end if %>
<P>
<A HREF="default.asp" ><IMG SRC="larrow.gif" ALT="home"> Back to home page</A>
</BODY>
<!-- #include file="copyright.inc" -->
</HTML>
```

Voting

Another part of the Microsoft Personalization System is the voting component. This component makes it simple to ask users questions and to have them reply. The component keeps a record of the vote in a database. You can ask the component to retrieve the results in a variety of ways. You can even ask the component to make a nicely formatted HTML table.

The voting component is very handy. If you want to do something fancier (for example, create a graph), you can ask the component for the raw data. Usually, you don't care exactly how or where the component stores its data.

A downside of the voting component is that you can't easily preload the choices without voting for them. So, if the question is "How much income tax would you be willing to pay?" and you don't preload any choices, the results will show only numbers that someone has already voted for. On the other hand, suppose you set a single vote at each 10 percent mark from 0 through 100. Then, a user might look at your results and think that someone really voted for 100 percent and 0 percent.

Another problem with the voting component is the lack of security. If your script supplies a unique user ID (such as the MPS UPD ID) during voting, the component makes sure that the user did not previously vote. However, this makes the database grow quickly because it has to store each ID. Also, savvy users can delete cookies, start other browsers, or change computers if they want to vote more than once.

VOTE.ASP (see Listing A.20) shows how easily you can integrate a form for voting and the voting component into one file. The script checks the content length. If the length is zero, the script shows the voting form. Otherwise, the script creates a vote object, opens the default voting database, sets the ballot name, and submits the question and the vote (this ballot has only one question). Next, the script shows the user the results obtained so far. Of course, you don't have to display the results to the public if you don't want to.

Listing A.20   Voting.

```
<HTML>

<HEAD>

<TITLE>Vote for the King</TITLE>

</HEAD>
<BODY <!-- #include file="stdbody.inc"-->>

<% if request("Content_Length")=0 then %>
<!-- get vote -->
<H1>Vote for the King</H1>
<% set vt = Server.CreateObject("mps.vote") %>
<form action="vote.asp" method="post">
    Which of these men is the King: <BR>
    <input type=radio name=king value="Williams">Al Williams<BR>
    <input type=radio name=king value="Kaufman">Andy Kaufman<BR>
    <input type=radio name=king value="Simmons">Richard Simmons<BR>
    <input type=submit value="Vote">
    </form>
<% else %>
<!-- record and show votes -->
<% set vt=Server.CreateObject("mps.vote")
    if vt.Open("vote", "guest", "") = TRUE then
    ballotresult = vt.SetBallotName("King")
    voteresult = vt.Submit("King", Request("King")) %>
    Here are the results so far:
    <%= vt.GetVote("King") %>
    <% else %>
    Error! The Voting system is down. Please contact the web master!
    <% end if %>
<% end if %>
<P>
<A HREF="default.asp"><IMG SRC="larrow.gif" ALT="home"> Back to home page</A>
</BODY>
<!-- #include file="copyright.inc" -->
</HTML>
```

What If I Don't Have Site Server?

The enhanced site assumes that you have Site Server installed. However, Site Server doesn't work with the current version of Personal Web Server. If you still want to work with most of the examples, you can look in the KING1 subdirectory. This is a lite version of the final site that has most (but not all) of the features in the KING2 version.

If you want the advantages of the user property database without having Site Server, you can create a simple system that allows users to log in and have values associated with them using a custom database. You can find an example of this type of system in Chapter 8. Although this system isn't exactly like the UPD, in some ways it's better because you don't have to rely on cookies.

Summary

This appendix gave you an inside look at converting an existing Web site into an ASP-based site. You've probably noticed that you can perform the same tasks in more than one way. For quotes, you can use server-side or client-side script. For ad rotation, you can use an ActiveX component on the server or just write some script.

The best approach is to start with an idea of what you want to do and then let the solution suggest the way to do it. Of course, you can have too much of a good thing, so be sure to use active features only where they make sense.

Introduction To HTML

Paul Newkirk

Have you ever dealt with people who don't speak your language but have one of those little books that supply common phrases in your language and theirs? Very frustrating, isn't it? Of course, those with the book usually have no idea how to pronounce what they want to say, and the book's phrases often aren't exactly what they want to say anyway.

The British comedy troupe Monty Python has a hilarious sketch about a man with a phrase book that was purposely wrong. Instead of asking a store clerk for matches (or something), he exclaims, "I will not buy this record; it is scratched!" Eventually, the conversation deteriorates to the point that the man is arrested, and the publisher of the book winds up on trial for deliberately misprinting the book.

This sketch reminds me of computers. Each program has its own unique file format. In the old days, trying to interchange data was especially frustrating. I once worked for a firm that was completely sold on WordPerfect (version 3 or 4). Too bad I was a firmly entrenched WordStar user (back from CP/M days, even). There was no end to the frustrations that caused. Sure, WordPerfect had a phrase book for WordStar (well, a conversion filter), and WordStar came with a program that could export and import WordPerfect, but somehow they never worked exactly right. Too bad we couldn't put those software publishers on trial.

Interchanging across platforms is even worse. Even if the same program is on a PC and a Mac, good luck trading data between them. This is a central issue with the Web. The Web consists of many different kinds of computers: Unix workstations, minicomputers, PCs, Macs, Power PCs, and there is probably even a Commodore 64 out there somewhere. How can you trade anything other than plain text among all these machines?

HTML (Hypertext Markup Language) is the *lingua franca* of the Web. Web content, ranging from the simplest personal home page to a state-of-the-art virtual reality extravaganza, uses HTML to define the appearance of the page. All Web browsers are supposed to understand HTML. Also, HTML is forgiving so that, if someone sends you something you don't understand, you can just skip it and hope for the best. This capacity allows older browsers to display some content even if the document is for newer browsers.

Of course, HTML by itself isn't powerful enough to build virtual reality venues, but it is powerful enough to contain objects (such as ActiveX objects or Java applets) that can do anything you can dream up.

Entire books have been written on how to create HTML, but this appendix shows you enough HTML to get started and try a few things. You can use this appendix as a reference, or you can use it to refresh your understanding of some of the finer points. More advanced topics appear in Appendix C, and you'll find Dynamic HTML in Appendix D.

Many tools create HTML for you without much effort on your part. Still, if you want to do anything out of the ordinary, you need to know HTML, so you might as well dig right in and get started. Even the best tools won't do everything you need. Also, it isn't unusual to have to tweak automatically generated HTML to get the results you want.

By the way, HTML started as a subset of SGML (Standard Generalized Markup Language), which was designed to transfer documents between systems. If you know SGML, you might find that you practically know HTML already.

The Basic Structure

HTML files are really just ASCII text files. By convention, they use the .HTML extension unless DOS is involved, in which case the .HTM extension is the standard.

Ordinary text in an HTML file appears as ordinary text in the produced document. What could be easier? The magic comes into play when you add tags to produce special formatting. Most tags come in pairs so that they affect the text between them. For example, to indicate boldface, you use the **<B>** and **</B>** tags like this:

```
<B>This is bold text</B> This is not!
```

The starting tag has no slash, but the ending one does. In a few special cases, you can omit the ending tag, but usually you need it. For example, the preceding line needs the **</B>** tag so that the remaining text is not in bold. By the way, tags are not case sensitive. You could just as well use **** and **** in the preceding example.

Note

If you have looked at other chapters in this book, you might have noticed that we use uppercase for HTML tags in the text of this book. There are a couple of reasons for this, but mostly it's because it makes reading HTML easier (your eyes can more easily separate tags from content). Using uppercase tags, although not required, is a good coding practice.

Some tags take parameters that appear *inside* the angle brackets. Others are required by the HTML specification but not required by common browsers. Like most other things involving computers, HTML is subject to some interpretation.

An HTML Document

An HTML document has several standard elements. Some of these elements are optional in some cases, but all of them are available if you want to use them. The structure of a correctly formatted HTML document looks like this:

```
<!DOCTYPE HTML PUBLIC "-//W3C//DTD HTML 3.2//EN">
<HTML>
<!-- A comment - these can go anywhere -->
<HEAD>
<!-- Header information (e.g., the page title)-->
</HEAD>
<BODY>
<!-- Main text, consisting of headings, paragraphs, and images -->
</BODY>
</HTML>
```

The first line is technically a comment and is frequently left off. If it is present, it informs newer browsers about which version of HTML the document uses (3.2 in this case).

Notice that the entire visible content appears between the **<HTML>** and **</HTML>** tags. Although using these tags is officially correct, most browsers display any file with an .HTM or .HTML extension as HTML, even if it doesn't contain these tags.

The first portion of the HTML document appears between the **<HEAD>** and **</HEAD>** tags. This section contains special information pertaining to the entire document. You can use the **<TITLE>** tag in the **<HEAD>** section, for example, to set a title for your page. Keep it 64 characters or fewer if you expect it to be visible in its entirety.

Another tag that can appear in the **<HEAD>** section is the **<BASE>** tag. This tag has no closing tag; it appears by itself. You can use it to specify the address of the page. Knowing the address is helpful if someone copies your page (such as to a local machine). If someone tries to follow a link, and the browser can't find it, it will search relative to the address specified in the **<BASE>** tag. Any time you need to specify a URL in a tag, you use the **HREF** parameter, as in this example:

```
<BASE HREF=http://www.coriolis.com/made_up.html>
```

In between the **<BODY>** and **</BODY>** tags is where most of the work is done, and where most of the things that actually show up on a Web page come from. See "Inside The Body" later in this section for more details.

Some pages place an **<ADDRESS>** tag pair after the **</BODY>** tag, but doing so isn't strictly necessary. The intent of this tag is to place information about the page's authorship, revision date, and so on at the bottom of the page. When you see a line at the bottom of the page that reads

```
Last modified: December 15, 1999. Send comments to webmaster@coriolis.com
```

that text is probably inside a pair of **<ADDRESS>** tags.

Tools For Creating An HTML File

Today, you have many choices for editing HTML files. Quite a few traditional Web authors who write a lot of low-level HTML simply use Notepad or some other text editor. However, most people will want a slightly higher-level interface. Microsoft makes several HTML editors, including Visual InterDev (aimed at software developer-level HTML authors) and FrontPage (for everybody else). FrontPage allows you to work with a page as it will look when it is done or to work directly with HTML. Internet Explorer 4 and 5 also include FrontPage Express, a stripped-down version of FrontPage.

Several other tools are also available from other vendors. HoTMetaL Pro (from SoftQuad) and HotDog (from Sausage Software) are just two examples. In addition, many other products can now generate HTML, even though that is not their primary function. For example, many word processors can now work with Web pages directly. Most of the Microsoft Office suite (Word, PowerPoint, and the other similar products) now have options that let you "Save As HTML." PowerPoint, one of Microsoft's better products, is quite good at this. Word (at least the 97 version I'm using), makes a pretty rough job of it and automatically generates ugly and hard-to-read HTML source code, although Word 2000 does a better job. But, in the right circumstances, using these products can save you time. For example, hand coding tables in HTML is pretty cumbersome if you are dealing with big tables. It's pretty easy to forget a tag, which requires you to slowly read line by line to find out why your table is two by eight cells instead of four by four. And you have to hand code each table cell because the properties you define don't carry from table cell to table cell. If you use Word, for example, you can make a table and format and position all the elements in it probably 10 to 50 times faster than doing it by hand. Word still makes very ugly HTML out of the table, but it is worth putting up with for the time you save.

Another interesting way to create HTML is to use Sun's free office suite, StarOffice. If you can tolerate the 65MB download, StarOffice is free (**www.sun.com/staroffice**). Otherwise, you can pay about $10 for a CD-ROM version. Along with a complete HTML editor, StarOffice also has word processing, presentation graphics, and more, and it can save everything to HTML. It also reads and writes Microsoft Office-compatible files. Not bad for free. However, the Help leaves something to be desired, and because it is a free product, support is spotty—at least for now. Maybe in the future Sun will let you buy support and improve the user documentation.

Inside The Body (With Apologies To Asimov)

Within the body of the document, the browser wraps all untagged words in the file into one long paragraph—unless you tell it otherwise. This makes sense because you can't know how big the users' monitors are or how large they've sized their browsers. It is a bad idea, but if you put one word on each line of your HTML source file, the browser will take care of wrapping all the words into a paragraph for you.

To break out of this autowrap feature, you use tags to set off different kinds of text in a file. When you want to start a paragraph, you use the **<P>** tag to start the following text on a new line (and break from any preceding text). Technically, you use this tag to start a paragraph and the **</P>** tag to end it. However, very few people actually use the **</P>** tag because it is optional.

Sometimes, you might want a line break inside the same paragraph. To add it, you use the **
** tag to start a new line. This tag has no corresponding ending tag. For example, to format an address, you might write the following:

```
Coriolis Group Books<BR>
14455 North Hayden Road #220<BR>
Scottsdale, AZ 85260<BR>
```

Formatting Text

You can format text in a variety of ways. The best way is to use a logical formatting attribute. You tell the browser what you want to do, and it figures out how to represent that format. For example, if you tell the browser you want strong emphasis (using the **<STRONG>** tag), it will probably render the text in boldface. Table B.1 shows the common logical attributes and the standard ways in which browsers render them. Notice that the browser may elect to show different items in different colors or use a user-defined style, so don't count on the appearance of these items to be consistent. Naturally, all these tags have a corresponding closing tag.

Table B.1   Common logical attributes.

Tag	Name	Use	Often Rendered As...
<CITE>	Citation	References to books	Italic
<CODE>	Code	Source code	Monospace
<DFN>	Definition	Definition of a word	Italic
<EM>	Emphasis	Special emphasis	Italic
<KBD>	Keyboard	Text the user should type	Bold/monospace
<SAMP>	Sample	Sample output	Monospace
<STRONG>	Strong	Strong emphasis	Bold
<VAR>	Variable	Placeholder text	Italic

Table B.2   Physical attributes.

Tag	Name	Description
<B>	Bold	Heavy-face text
<I>	Italic	Italic typeface
<U>	Underline	Line drawn beneath text
<TT>	Teletype	Monospace text

Sometimes, you might want more control over the appearance of your text. To get this control, you use the physical attribute tags shown in Table B.2. They allow you to specify exactly how the text should look, if the browser is capable of producing the effect you want.

You can even nest attributes. For example, if you want bold underlined text, you might use the following:

```
Try <B><U>ActiveX</U></B>
```

Be sure to place the closing tags in the reverse order of the starting tags. Otherwise, some browsers may get confused. Again, you can't be sure the browser will respect your wishes. A text-based browser on Unix, for example, might not be able to show bold text (or it may elect to put it in reverse video). It is hard to know exactly what each browser might do.

In addition to normal paragraphs, HTML has tags for six different styles of headings that you can use for different sections of a document. Actually, you can use them for anything you like. You also can use them in any order, or you don't have to use them at all. The tags are **<H1>** through **<H6>** (and, of course, the usual closing tags).

Horizontal Rules

Among people who design pages, there is debate over rules (horizontal lines that break up sections of text). Respected print designers think that you should never use rules. Others think that rules are acceptable on the Web. You can decide for yourself. However, if you want to create a rule, simply use the **<HR>** tag (with no closing tag). This tag sets a thin line across the entire width of the page. Using this tag is better than drawing a line with ASCII characters (or even a graphic) because you don't know how wide the user's screen is and the line could be too short or too long (whereas a rule will automatically resize to the screen's width).

A nice effect is to make the line smaller than the page and center it. You can create this effect with the following code (assuming you want the rule to be 80 percent of the page width):

```
<CENTER>
<HR WIDTH=80%>
</CENTER>
```

You can also use a graphic for a rule (see the next section), but, again, you won't know how wide the browser's screen is. You must either set a particular size or scale the graphic. Scaling often ruins the graphic's appearance (it depends on the graphic). If you decide to set a certain size, you can at least center the graphic so that it will look acceptable on larger screens.

In addition to the header styles, HTML also provides the **<BLOCKQUOTE>** and **<PRE>** paragraph tags for formatting text. The **<BLOCKQUOTE>** style sets off text in some way (usually by using indentation and italics). The **<PRE>** style implies that the text is preformatted. The browser does *not* wrap text in a **<PRE>**-style paragraph but shows it exactly as it is in the HTML file. These tags are useful for source code or for exact placement of text on a page (such as for crude tables). Usually, a **<PRE>** paragraph appears in monospace type. You can specify the width of the text in characters by using the **WIDTH** parameter to the **<PRE>** tag. Don't forget the closing tags **</BLOCKQUOTE>** and **</PRE>**.

Inserting Special Characters

Because HTML interprets many characters in a special way, you must have an escape mechanism to allow you to insert any character without it having any special meaning. For example, suppose you want to compose a line that looks like this:

```
Is 10<20?
```

The problem is that the browser will assume that the < character is the start of a tag and it won't display it on your Web page. To solve this problem, you need to use an escape sequence (in this case, **<**) to tell the browser to display the special character.

Escape sequences are especially important for the less-than (<), greater-than (>), and ampersand (&) characters because they have special meaning to the browser. Escape sequences are also important for currency and other non-ASCII characters that you might not be able to easily enter from the keyboard.

Special characters always begin by using an ampersand (&). You can then use a letter name followed by a semicolon. For example, **<** is the less-than (<) character, and **>** is the greater-than (>) character. Alternatively, you can use the sequence **&#*nnn*;**, where *nnn* is a decimal character code from the ISO Latin-1 character set.

For example, an uppercase A is code 65, so you could write the following:

```
&#065;
```

Using this sequence is the same as placing an uppercase A in your HTML document. Of course, there isn't much reason to do this for an A, but you might want to specify some characters this way.

Sometimes you just have to have a real space. HTML usually consumes multiple white space into a single space, but what if you really want a legitimate space? One answer is to use the special escape sequence ** **.

Tip

*Remember that another way to control spacing is to enclose your text in one of the tags that doesn't reformat your text (such as **<PRE>** or **<PLAINTEXT>**). Of course, using these tags also changes the appearance of that text, which may not be desirable.*

Table B.3 shows a list of common character names.

Images And Objects

Of course, the big selling point of the Web is graphics. Using the **<IMG>** tag is the ordinary way to insert a graphic in your document. However, the **<OBJECT>** tag also inserts graphics (among other things). But because the **<OBJECT>** tag is relatively new, most pages still use the **<IMG>** tag for simple graphics.

Each **<IMG>** tag requires a **SRC** parameter to name the file that contains the image. This file name can be a full-blown URL or just a file name if the file is in the same location as the Web page (or its base address). Because some browsers don't show graphics (or users turn graphics off), it is a good idea to also specify the **ALT** parameter, which specifies showing some text in case the image does not display. A typical image statement looks like this:

```
<IMG SRC="PIX1.GIF" ALT="The first picture">
```

Normally, an image acts like a single character in your text. If you don't want things to appear after your image on the same line, you need a **
** or **<P>** tag following it. You can also control the alignment of text around the image by using the **ALIGN** parameter. This parameter can take one of three values: **TOP**, **BOTTOM**, or **MIDDLE**. If you don't use an **ALIGN** parameter in your **<IMG>** tag, the text lines up with the bottom of the image.

Table B.3   Common character names.

Name	Character
<	Less than (<)
>	Greater than (>)
&	Ampersand (&)
©	Copyright (©)
	Nonbreaking space
"	Quotation mark (")
®	Registered trademark (®)
­	Soft hyphen

Of course, you could also insert the same image with the following:

```
<OBJECT DATA="PIX1.GIF">
</OBJECT>
```

The **<OBJECT>** tag is more flexible because it can insert typed data (like a GIF file) or an object. Table B.4 shows a summary of parameters the **<OBJECT>** tag accepts.

Scaling Graphics

Using the **WIDTH** and **HEIGHT** parameters, you can specify the desired size in pixels (which need not match the actual size). This way, you can scale up a small image (which transfers faster).

You should always supply the **WIDTH** and **HEIGHT** for every image. This allows the browser to correctly lay out the page right away. If you don't supply a size, the browser reserves a very small place for the graphic and then recomposes the page when it actually loads the picture. Recomposing causes the page to jump around and is very distracting to users.

The size you provide to the **<IMG>** tag need not match the actual size of the graphic. If it doesn't, the browser scales the image to match the selected size. This capability can be useful if you want to use a graphic as a rule, for example.

Suppose you create a graphic 20 pixels high by 1 pixel wide that has a variety of shades of red in it. You could transform it into a nice-looking rule with this HTML:

```
<IMG SRC="redrule.gif" HEIGHT=20 WIDTH=100% ALT="Section Break">
```

Table B.4   <OBJECT> parameters.

Parameter	Description
ALIGN	Alignment properties
BORDER	Size of border (0 = no border)
CODEBASE	Location to download object from
CODETYPE	Type of object
DATA	Data to use with object (object may be implied by type)
DECLARE	Don't create object until referenced
HEIGHT	Height of object
HSPACE	Horizontal space around object
ID	Name of object
NAME	Name used in forms
SHAPES	Use client-side image map to create anchors
STANDBY	Message to display while loading
TYPE	Type of data (if not implied by file extension)
USEMAP	Use an image map to create anchors
VSPACE	Vertical space around object
WIDTH	Width of object

You might want to scale a graphic for other reasons. For example, you might load a large image but display it only as a thumbnail. Of course, the large image will still load more slowly than a real thumbnail, but then the image will be completely in the browser's cache, making subsequent display faster.

Lists

HTML supports several types of lists. They are similar to paragraph styles. The most common types of lists use the **<LI>** tag to denote the beginning of each list element. To create a numbered list, you use the **<OL>** (ordered list) start tag, as in this example:

```
<OL>
<LI> Item 1 </LI>
<LI> Item 2 </LI>
</OL>
```

This example produces what you see in Figure B.1.

If you prefer a bulleted list, use the **<UL>** (unnumbered list) tag (see Figure B.2). You can also get a more compact list with some browsers by using **<MENU>** or **<DIR>**. Items in a menu list should not exceed one line of text. The **<DIR>** list items shouldn't exceed 20 characters so that the browser can form columns, if it has that capability.

HTML also supports another kind of list: the description list. This type of list uses text instead of a bullet and can be used for lexicons or encyclopedia-style entries. The **<DL>** tag starts the list. You begin each text "bullet" with the **<DT>** tag. After the text, you place a

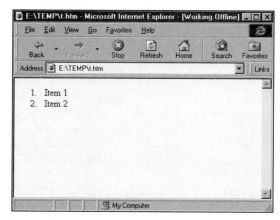

Figure B.1
A numbered list.

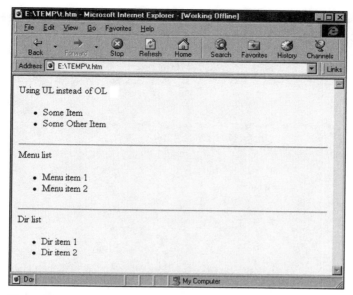

Figure B.2
Some unnumbered lists

<DD> tag (not a **</DT>** tag). Then, you follow with the text that goes with that pseudo-bullet. There is no **</DD>** tag; just start another **<DT>** entry or end with **</DL>**. Some browsers attempt to place short text bullets on the same line as the other text if you specify the **COMPACT** parameter to the **<DL>** tag.

For example, suppose you have the following HTML:

```
<DL>
<DT>Megatarts<DD>Stratagem spelled backwards
<DT>Yoodoo<DD>Popular person in songs ("no one can love me like yoodoo")
<DT>Neutron bomb<DD>Bomb that kills people, while leaving property intact
(see also, mortgage)
</DL>
```

This example would create a display like the one shown in Figure B.3.

Hyperlinks

The *H* in HTML stands for *hypertext*, and the Web wouldn't be the same without links, would it? Each link has two parts: a presentation part (text or graphics) and an invisible part (the *anchor* that specifies where to go).

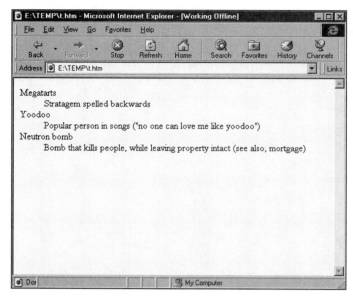

Figure B.3
A definition list.

The **<A>** tag inserts anchors. The presentation portion can be any mix of text or graphics you like. Using this tag, you can create very sophisticated links because you can use any text or HTML commands you like in the presentation. The following is a simple link:

```
To continue click
<A HREF="http://www.coriolis.com/nextpage.htm">here</A>
```

When you click the word *here* (which, because it's between the anchor tags, is the only thing on the line that the browser actually displays), the browser jumps to the correct URL. Of course, many people think it is amateurish to create a link that says "click here," but this is just an example. Style-wise, it would be better to have this link read "You can continue" and assume the user will understand by the text's appearance that it can be clicked. Usually, the browser shows the link word underlined (and possibly in a special color). Of course, you can also use graphics as the presentation portion, as in this example:

```
<A HREF="http://www.coriolis.com/pl.htm"><IMG SRC="clickme.gif"></A>
```

Defining And Linking To An Anchor

You can define a particular spot in your document by using the **<A>** tag in conjunction with the **NAME** parameter. Hyperlink anchors can refer to the named anchors to navigate to a specific portion of your document. Consider this example:

```
<A NAME="Summary">My Conclusions</A>
```

You can link to named anchors in the current page or link to an anchor on a different page. Suppose you have a page that has information for three years: 1998, 1999, and 2000. Your document might look like this:

```
Navigation:<BR>
<A HREF="#YR1998">1998</A>
<A HREF="#YR1999">1999</A>
<A HREF="#YR2000">2000</A><BR>
<!—begin 1998 data —>
<A NAME="YR1998"></A>
<H1>1998</H1>
.  .  .
<!—begin 1999 data —>
<A NAME="YR1999"></A>
<H1>1999</H1>
.  .  .
<!—begin 2000 data —>
<A NAME="YR2000"></A>
<H1>2000</H1>
```

You can also link to one of these anchors from outside the document. Suppose the data is in the file YEARDATA.HTM. From another document, you could write the following:

```
<A HREF="http://www.al-williams.com/YEARDATA.HTM#YR2000">
View 2000 Projections
</A>
```

Image Maps, Forms, And More

There is much more to HTML. For example, you can divide a single graphic into multiple anchors or use a background graphic. You can use tables and multiple windows (frames). You can create forms and process them on your server. You can also add sounds, scrolling marquees, and—well, you get the idea.

With each new browser release comes new HTML features. One of the best ways to get information about HTML is from the Web itself. Technical specifications, tutorials, and even software are available to help you create HTML. For the latest specifications for HTML, check out **www.w3.org**. After all, what better place to find information about the Web than on the Web? Remember to also check out the Appendix C for more information on image maps, forms, and so on.

Appendix C
Advanced HTML

Paul Newkirk

If you read Appendix B or are familiar with the information it contains, you should know that basic HTML is little more than a system for formatting text for display by a browser. From that appendix to this one, you will now leap to the core of using more-advanced HTML tags as well as some tricks that are still the bread and butter of much of the Web.

Almost anyone with some computer background has worked with something that looked and worked like HTML. If you have experience in Unix, you used NROFF or TROFF. You might be familiar with SGML, of which HTML is a subset. What is modestly different are the specific tags used, and they take only a little bit of learning. What is exceptionally different are the new tag attributes and techniques that allow you to operate in and take advantage of the graphically aware, interactive, Internet-connected environment, rather than formatting for print.

Using Arguments With Tags

With most HTML tags, you use arguments to further expand their capabilities. For example, from the simple **<HR>** tag, you can expand to **<HR SIZE=4 WIDTH=70% ALIGN=LEFT NOSHADE>**. In paired tags, such as the **<H1>...</H1>** tags, arguments are enclosed in the first of the paired tags. For example, **<H1 ALIGN=CENTER>My Heading</H1>** shows how attributes are included in the first of a tag pair.

As you try to do more with HTML, you'll notice that most of the fun, control-type stuff happens within the argument area of the

Cheap Trick For Finding Hex Color Values

You have probably seen tags such as **<COLOR="#FF0000">**. If you are a hex gearhead, you know exactly what this tag means. If you aren't, this discussion is for you.

The number in the tag is the hexadecimal representation of the RGB (Red, Green, Blue) values for a color. To find these colors (assuming you're a Windows user), open Paint (an often useless program that comes with the operating system) by choosing Start|Programs|Accessories (you can also use the Run menu and type "MSPAINT" or type "MSPAINT" in a DOS window). Next, click on Options|Edit|Colors, and then click on Define Custom Colors. In the lower-right corner of Paint's screen, you should see Red, Green, and Blue. After you pick a color (by clicking on one), the RGB decimal values for that color appear. For example, if you click on that sort of yellowish-greenish-brown color, you see the RGB values change to 128, 128, 0. To convert those values to hexadecimal, open the Calculator, select the Scientific view, enter a number, and change the radio button setting from Dec to Hex to convert. In this case, you'll learn that 128 decimal is 80 hex and that 0 decimal is 0 hex. So, if you want to use that color in HTML, you can use **<COLOR="#808000">**. Because there are two values for each number, just fill in an extra zero for the zero value.

As mentioned earlier, you can now use actual color names, such as **<COLOR="RED">**, but it is unclear how different browsers will handle these names (as opposed to the specific hex values). Stay tuned; maybe striped avocado mousse will become one of the standard colors you can specify by name (in addition to red). More than likely, if the browser cannot handle the color, it will try to fake it in some way.

tags. Although an exhaustive list of tags and arguments is not included in this book, you can find one online in a variety of places, including **www.w3.org**. One I found useful recently was **www.december.com/html/**.

If you want to do something in HTML using a tag, an argument likely exists that will let you do it. As tags and HTML specifications evolve rapidly, you have to read the latest news about them practically every day to keep up with them all. However, the newer tags and arguments continue to make your life easier and your pages more fun. For example, when specifying colors, you once had to find the hex RGB values for the colors. Now, you can use an argument such as **COLOR="RED"** inside the **<FONT>** tag (instead of **COLOR= "#FF0000"**).

Making Your Pages Prettier (Bargain Shopper Overview)

Almost anything is more attractive than plain text on a Web page. You can use some fundamental tricks to make more stylish Web pages that even the most graphically challenged Web apprentice can understand.

Changing Page Backgrounds

Backgrounds were one of the first features to add pizzazz to Web pages. Backgrounds began as gray, then parchment colored, then pebbles in a stream, and so on. Everyone was well-versed in using ASCII menus, so these new backgrounds looked amazing. In fact, you can still use these techniques (in the **<BODY>** tag), which are described later in this appendix, but you should use them with caution. Most professional or large corporate sites shy away from using funny backgrounds, and with good reason. For one, these backgrounds often make text more difficult to read. For another, some browsers let you override the backgrounds and colors of a page. This can create problems, for example, if you use a black, star-field background with white text, and users decide to override all backgrounds to make them white on their browsers (leaving white text on a white background).

Microsoft Internet Explorer 4 does not allow you to override the backgrounds, whereas Netscape Navigator 4 still does. The final word is that using backgrounds is an easy way to make your page look nice with very little effort, but you should use them with the knowledge of their limitations and pitfalls. Of course, you can still get into trouble with the star field and Internet Explorer if the users change the text to black.

Although gray is the default color for backgrounds, you can use the following techniques to create other backgrounds. You can use a graphic (for example, a GIF, JPEG, or BMP file), set the background to a color, or even do a trick that gives you a colored bar or pattern down the side of the page (maybe to put navigation tools on). The action happens inside the **<BODY>** tag.

Using A Graphic As A Background

To use a graphic as a background, enter **<BODY BACKGROUND="*file.gif*">**, where **"*file.gif*"** (or .JPG, .BMP, and so on) is the name of the graphic you want to use as a background.

Using A Color As A Background

To use a color as a background, inside the body tag, enter **<BODY BGCOLOR= "#808000">**, where **"#808000"** is the hex value of the color you want.

Using The Bar-On-The-Side-Of-The-Page Trick

It's quick, it's easy, it's useful, and it takes almost no bandwidth whatsoever. What is it? You've seen this bar on the side of the page all over the Internet. To use this trick, take a very small, colored line (say, light blue or gray, about the width of a paper clip laid flat), and extend that line with a white, transparent, or parchment-colored line farther than any browser on any huge monitor could ever display. Then you can use this image as your background. Browsers automatically repeat this very small image down the page, so the line appears as long as is necessary. For very little bandwidth, you get a nice tool to divide your page.

Suppose you have this **<BODY>** statement:

```
<BODY BACKGROUND="file.gif">
```

Figure C.1 shows what the GIF looks like by itself. Figure C.2 shows the result of using this image as a background. Notice that the page is now divided nicely for text and navigation

Figure C.1
The border GIF.

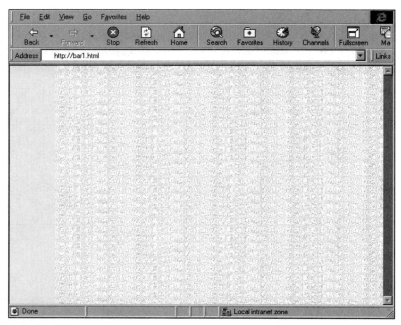

Figure C.2
The border GIF on a page.

buttons. To take advantage of this setup, you can use tables without borders to place the items on your page on the right part of the background.

Tip

Make sure you go back and check your page's appearance once in a while. I created a neighborhood Web page for my homeowner's association a few years ago. Back then, 17-inch monitors were not available for home users, so users could open their browsers only so big. When I revisited the site, 17-inch or better monitors were the norm, and the bar on the side of the page trick broke and gave me two bars, which ruined the page. I had to go back and adjust the graphic to account for the larger screens that were now the norm.

Using Fancier Bullets, Rule Lines, And Buttons

Previously, you saw how to make bulleted lists (using **<UL>**), rule lines (**<HR>**), and images (**<IMG SRC="file.gif">**). You can fairly easily combine them for some nice effects, and you can make your own or find thousands of free samples on the Web.

Plain old bullets are fine for paper, but for the Web, you can use marbles, smiley faces, or pretty much anything. Just throw away your unordered list tags, and instead use the **<IMG SRC>** tag, text or links, and breaks to get some fancy-looking buttons.

For fancier rule lines, you can throw away the **<HR>** tag and use the **<IMG SRC>** tag. With rules, as with buttons, you can create your own rule line images or get some of the thousands available on the Web. You can discard your plain old rule lines and find ones with marble textures, wild colors, and even movement (if your graphic is an animated GIF file).

It does not take much to extrapolate from using graphics as bullets to set off a text list or a bunch of links to figuring out how to effectively use the graphics themselves as links (or buttons). You can make your own button graphics using tools that almost every computer has natively (such as Microsoft Paint), using inexpensive shareware (such as LView), or using an Internet search engine with the words *icons* and *buttons*.

One major caveat for these tricks: Use graphics over text when possible (a picture paints a thousand words), but avoid using gratuitous or incomprehensible graphics. For example, I once found a great button of a dog with tread marks from a car across its sprawled body. I was amused by its "roadkill on the information superhighway" meaning but decided it was both gratuitous and unintuitive (what sensible thing would *that* link to without words to explain it?), so it did not make the cut.

Using Graphics For Bullets And Rule Lines

Listing C.1 (see also Figure C.3) shows the use of standard HTML techniques to create bullets and rule lines. Listing C.2 (see also Figure C.4) shows the use of graphics to do the same. In both, note also the use of a nested list and some list arguments. The list arguments **TYPE=I** and **START=5** for the ordered list give you large Roman numerals and start the list counting at 5. Also, note that the indents on the nested list have no effect on the indents on the Web page's list. They are indented automatically on the Web page for readability.

Good Places To Look For Web Graphics

The Web is full of pages that have graphics you can use for bullets, lines, icons, and backgrounds. The following are a few of my favorites:

- **http://snaught.com/JimsCoolIcons/**
- **www.iconbazaar.com**
- **www.aplusart.com**

Because any of these links could be dead by the time you read this appendix, you might also check out the Yahoo! list of Web graphics at **http://dir.yahoo.com/Arts/Design_Arts/Graphic_Design/ Web_Page_Design_and_Layout/Graphics/**. Be sure to read and follow any conditions that the site places on using its graphics.

Listing C.1   A nested, nongraphical menu.

```
<CENTER>
<HR SIZE=4 WIDTH=65% NOSHADE>
<OL TYPE=I START=5>
<FONT SIZE=5><LI>Shrimp in white wine, garlic, butter and dill</FONT>
<UL>
<LI>rice medley
<LI>vegetable of the day
<P>
</UL>
<FONT SIZE=5><LI>Shrimp in Cajun Alfredo sauce</FONT>
<UL>
<LI>linguini or roti
<LI>vegetable of the day
<P>
</UL>
</OL>
<HR SIZE=4 WIDTH=65% NOSHADE>
</CENTER>
```

Notice that whereas some tags have an **ALIGN=** attribute, others do not. Therefore, you must improvise with the **<CENTER>** tag to center the list. Note the font change outside the list item (**<LI>**) tags. If you place the tag on the other side of the list item tag, the Roman numerals appear small. Note also that you use paragraph tags (**<P>**) for spacing instead of break (**
**) tags. To see what happens, try the same code with break tags to see whether your browser does what you expect.

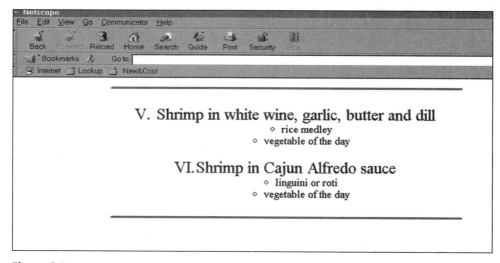

Figure C.3
The nested menu list.

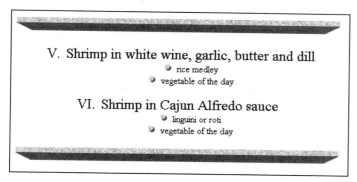

Figure C.4
An example using graphics as bullets to add pizzazz.

Listing C.1 is not a bad example, as it is better than just text, but look at Listing C.2. It creates some unique buttons and rule lines using simple tools to add some pizzazz. Remember that you can find thousands of buttons and rule lines on the Web.

Listing C.2   Adding pizzazz to pages by using graphics as buttons or bullets.

```
<CENTER>
<IMG SRC="RULE1.GIF">
<OL TYPE=I START=5>
<FONT SIZE=5><LI>Shrimp in white wine, garlic, butter and dill</FONT>
<BR>
<IMG SRC="BALL1.GIF">
rice medley <BR>
<IMG SRC="BALL1.GIF">
vegetable of the day
<P>
<FONT SIZE=5><LI>Shrimp in Cajun Alfredo sauce</FONT>
<BR>
<IMG SRC="BALL1.GIF">
linguini or roti <BR>
<IMG SRC="BALL1.GIF">
vegetable of the day
<P>
</OL>
<IMG SRC="RULE1.GIF">
</CENTER>
```

Note the difference in look. The first example did not look bad originally, but it looks awful next to the second one.

Creating Graphics

You can create simple graphics in many ways using tools that you already have or that are nearly free. You don't have to buy a $600 program. Believe it or not, one of my favorite graphics tools is Microsoft Word, which most people already have. You can use its drawing capabilities to create graphics and move them around on the page (easier than in Paint because the images are clickable objects that can be dragged). Then, you can capture the window (using any graphics program), crop it, make the background transparent (so you don't have a rectangular box around an image), and save it in GIF 89a format. This approach is quick and easy, although you can use many other drawing programs to do the same thing.

If you are interested in doing screen captures, you can also use the ubiquitous Print Screen (or PrtSc) key instead of a dedicated program. Pressing this keyboard button captures your whole screen to the clipboard. If you press Alt+Print Screen, you capture the contents of the current window. You can then paste the picture into any graphics program.

If you are looking for some inexpensive image editors, search the Web for Paint Shop Pro, LView, or Ulead PhotoImpact. StarOffice (free from Sun) has some credible graphics tools (**www.sun.com/staroffice**). There is also GIMP (GNU Image Manipulation Program—known as the GIMP by those in the know), which is a powerful free program. You can find more details at **www.gimp.org** and specifically at **www.gimp.org/~tml/gimp/win32/**.

You can also find image manipulation programs that run completely on the Web (although they disappear when they get popular and expensive to maintain). One example that is currently working is located at **http://newbreedsoftware.com/webfx**. Another very impressive effort is at **www.gifworks.com**. Most of these programs focus on modifying existing GIF files instead of creating them from scratch.

If you are looking for more exciting examples of making Web pages more attractive, read the following sections. It is sometimes hard to distinguish between techniques that make navigation easier and ones that just make the pages prettier. For that reason, you'll find features such as image maps, which make pages more eye-appealing but are used mostly for navigation. An ardent disclaimer: This book is about programming. Using some of the techniques here (frames, for example) is considered bad form by Web design professionals. You'll have to make up your own mind about that. I'm just showing you how HTML works; I'm not passing judgment.

Improving Navigation, Ease Of Use, And Layout

Making pages prettier goes hand in hand with making them easier to use. You have to walk a fine line between making pages more attractive and making them more navigable, and, in doing one, you often step back and forth across that line and do the other.

The curse of the Web medium is that you must work with only one page at a time. A gift of the Web is that you can use hypertext links to leave that one page and go to a large number of places and do a large number of things. With print media, such as books, magazines, and manuals, you have some control of the path your users will take. You also have a few helpers, such as indexes, tables of contents, and page and chapter numbers. Regardless of the path users choose to read your book or selected parts thereof, you hope they will always know which book they are in and roughly where they are in relation to the rest of the book.

Within the Web medium, you have a few more obligations:

◆ Maintaining site continuity in a medium in which page numbers and beginnings and ends can have no meaning whatsoever

◆ Ruthlessly judging every potential tenant on your page's real estate for economy, clarity, and effect because surfers can easily zip off to another Web page (click!) if this one does not let them find what they want

◆ Meeting or exceeding the expectations of surfers whose expectations span not only a variety of historical media but also the ever-changing developments in this new one

Image Maps

To maintain continuity, you can carry a map with you onto each page of your site. At its simplest, your map could be a group of hypertext links repeated at the bottom of every page on the site. No matter where the user is, he or she can use these links to navigate back to the top of the site or the top of certain sections.

From this humble beginning, you can go many places. You can use images as hypertext links instead of just textual links. Better yet, you can arrange the images so they look like a nice row or column of buttons. You can create image maps that act as navigational tools. Image maps divide one graphic into multiple clickable regions. With creativity, you can make an image that represents in pictures or text the topography of your site and repeat that image map on all your pages as a navigational aid.

For example, you can create an architect's view of a mall where you click on each store to navigate. A simpler approach is to create a textual, hierarchical view of a site with colored lines drawn between the top and the current pages, the other sites being either unlined or having lines of a different color. A more button-ish use of image maps is to create the effect of a series of buttons or menu items in which the button for the page you are on is set off in some way.

Image maps take a graphic and define multiple regions on the graphic as hypertext links. There are two types of image maps, and each operates on the same principles but has different implementations. The first is server-side image mapping, and the second is client-side image mapping. Each lets you take an image and map out areas on the image as clickable regions. When a region is clicked on, some action occurs, usually a hypertext link to another page or to a picture.

Server-Side Image Maps

Server-side image mapping, so called because all the work is done by a gateway application residing on the server, requires these four elements to work:

- ◆ A graphic
- ◆ A Web page with the correct set of image map tags
- ◆ A Web site with a gateway application (such as imagemap.dll, usually in the cgi-bin directory)
- ◆ A separate map file (which maps out the graphic by providing coordinates and the corresponding actions to be taken when a region is clicked on)

You know what a graphic is (any image will do). The correct tags in a Web page look like this:

```
<A HREF="http://www.server.com/cgi-bin/imagemap/mapdir/file1.map">
  <IMG SRC="file1.gif" ISMAP></A>
```

These tags are confusing, but let me give you a quick explanation: The first part you know—the anchor tag. It is followed by a URL, a link to a graphic, and then a closing anchor tag. What's different here is the **ISMAP** part of the **<IMG>** tag, which is a flag that says this line is different—that it's an image map. The URL is also different. If the browser were thinking out loud as it processed this line, it might say something like this:

- ◆ Oh, this is a hyperlink.
- ◆ Plop file1.gif on the page as a picture.
- ◆ I see **ISMAP**, so this picture is an image map.
- ◆ When the user clicks, I'll send the coordinates to a gateway application on the server.

A server-side image map file looks like this:

```
#This is an image map for Darlene's Big Hair Salon
rect        http://www.hair.com      0,0 35,48
circle      http://www.nails.com     66,24 85,40
poly        /pics/customers.htm      99,45 140,2 144,55
default     http://www.hair.com
```

Here, note that, unlike the rest of HTML, comments in map files are preceded by a number symbol (#). Comments in map files help remind you where links are going, so you should use them liberally. You can see the types of regions you can define in the code (I neglected to include *point*, which is also valid).

From left to right, you're defining a region, a destination, and Cartesian coordinates that define the region. The destination can be either a local file on the server or a full URL on another server. For coordinates, a point is the easiest to define (you just need one x and one y coordinate), although a point is probably the most useless (unless you're playing a game in which you drag your mouse around on the page until you find the secret link). It takes two coordinates to define a rectangle or a circle, but with a polygon, you can define as many as you want. This gives you the best chance to be most accurate and detailed because all the areas within the collection of *x* and *y* coordinates become hot. The default takes care of clicks that occur on undefined areas of the map. It is considered good practice to set the default to reload the same page. This usually causes clicks to be more accurate.

Client-Side Image Maps

Client-side image maps are a horse of another color (or shade at least). To create client-side image maps, you need the following:

♦ A graphic

♦ A Web page with the correct set of image map tags and mapped coordinates on the same page

♦ A Web browser that supports client-side image mapping

Again, you know what a graphic is (any image will do). The correct tags and mapped coordinates in a Web page look like this:

```
<IMG BORDER=0 SRC="/graphics/zippo.gif" USEMAP="#mapfile1">
<MAP NAME="mapfile1">
<AREA SHAPE="RECT" COORDS="7,5,168,139" HREF="http://www.wacky.com" >
<AREA SHAPE="RECT" COORDS="171,4,426,137" HREF="http://www.zany.com">
<AREA SHAPE="RECT" COORDS="430,5,612,141" HREF="http://www.wow.com">
</MAP>
```

The first line is an **<IMG>** tag with a few extras. The first extra is **BORDER=0**, which turns off the default blue border around image maps. Turning off the border is a good idea because it's unnecessary. (A few years ago, when no one knew that you could click on images, the blue border helped the feeble-minded among us by saying, "Pssst, hey, you. This thing is clickable!" Nowadays, you assume that almost anything is clickable, so the blue border looks lame.) The next extra simply specifies the location of the graphic file. The last part of this line is like the **ISMAP** argument, except for the client side you write **USEMAP** and then give internal directions on where to find the map in the same document (instead of in a different file). In this case, the browser looks in the file for a map with the same name (for example, MAPFILE1). Note that the names must be exact matches. Also, note that case matters because you could have several **USEMAP**s and maps in one document, and the browser has to be able to connect the right ones.

You don't need a gateway application because the browser does the work here. The downside is that the browser has to support client-side image maps (although most modern browsers will support them, there are some browsers that can't handle client-side maps). Therefore, server-side maps are more general because they work with any browser. Note that the layout of client-side maps is also different, with quotes and all (although, to be honest, they look more HTML-like).

When it comes to client-side and server-side map files, the advantages of using one are almost the disadvantages of using the other, and vice versa (see Tables C.1 and C.2).

Table C.1   Advantages and disadvantages of server-side maps.

Advantages	Disadvantages
They work with all browsers.	You must have a gateway application (like imagemap.dll).
Map files remain hidden from surfers.	To port to another server, you have to find an appropriate gateway application for each new server.
	They're slower if the network is slow.
	You must maintain more files.
	Some server sites don't provide for gateway applications.

Table C.2   Advantages and disadvantages of client-side maps.

Advantages	Disadvantages
They have reduced bandwidth and increased speed (mapping is done on the client without repeated trips back to the server to resolve clicks).	They work only with some browsers.
It's easier to maintain a single file.	Your map file is viewable.
They're portable, so it doesn't matter which server or platform is being used.	

Getting Map Coordinates

You can get map coordinates in a number of ways. For me, the easiest way is by hand, using nearly free tools that almost everyone has access to. Paint, a program that most people would admit has very limited usefulness as a graphics tool, nevertheless does the trick here. "But," some of the wise grasshoppers say, "Paint, evil incarnate that it is, does not read GIFs (for some unfathomable or sinister reason)." Yes, that is true. The workaround to this problem is to open your graphic with your Web browser, right-click on it, and choose the Save As option to save it as a BMP file. No, you don't have to use the file as a BMP; you can simply use the BMP to map the coordinates in Paint.

After you open the file in Paint, notice that as you drag your mouse cursor across it, coordinates appear in the lower-right corner of the screen. Say you're trying to map the ABC checkboxes shown in Figure C.5.

To map these checkboxes, put your mouse cursor over the top-left corner of the A box to see the two coordinates. Put it on the lower-right corner of the A box, and you have two more

Figure C.5
An image for you to map.

(enough to define a rectangle). Repeat the process for B and C, and you can now define three regions. At this point, you don't have to worry if it's not exact. Most people will click somewhere around the letter, and that area is not hard to define.

Are there easier ways? Yes. Some free programs do this job, but they take almost as much time to learn as the pencil-and-paper way shown here. You can find several sites on the Web that will help you calculate image maps (for example, **www.pangloss.com/seidel/ClrHlpr/ imagemap.html**). You also might want to check out a site that will convert your server-side maps to client-side format: **www.popco.com/popco/convertmaps.html**.

Tables

In their simplest form, tables allow you to organize sets of data on a page (using the **<TABLE>** tag). For example, putting lists or categories of links into a table makes for a nice arrangement on a Web page (better than a bunch of unending left-justified text). Also, many sites use tables without borders to create newspaper-style layouts. You can use tables within tables within tables (and so on) to provide finely detailed page layouts. Just remember that the more complex you get, the more you need to leave yourself a healthy dose of comments to help you remember which table contains which part of the page.

Using Tables For Page Layout

If you have experimented with simple HTML, you have no doubt been frustrated by the tendency of every piece of text or graphic to not go exactly where you want it to go. If you don't have a tool, creating complex layouts (for example, multicolumns) can seem difficult. Tables to the rescue!

You can use tables without borders to set up a layout for your Web page and then use tables within tables to define the layout even more. Listing C.3 offers a simple two-column example (you can see the resulting page in Figure C.6).

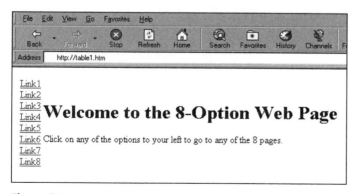

Figure C.6
What a two-column table looks like.

Listing C.3   A two-column layout.

```
<TABLE BORDER=0>
<TD>
<!--This is the left cell of the table, the left column of the two.-->
<A HREF="http://www.linkone.htm">Link1</A><BR>
<A HREF="http://www.linktwo.htm">Link2</A><BR>
<A HREF="http://www.linkthree.htm">Link3</A><BR>
<A HREF="http://www.linkfour.htm">Link4</A><BR>
<A HREF="http://www.linkfive.htm">Link5</A><BR>
<A HREF="http://www.linksix.htm">Link6</A><BR>
<A HREF="http://www.linkseven.htm">Link7</A><BR>
<A HREF="http://www.linkeight.htm">Link8</A>
<TD>
<!--This is the right cell of the table, the right column of the two.-->
<H1>Welcome to the 8-Option Web Page</H1>
<P>
Click on any of the options to your left to go to any of the 8 pages.
</TABLE>
```

Although this example is rather simple, you can see where it's going. Say that you use the same table template on all eight pages, but you change the text in the second cell for each page. Then, to make it more visually different, you put a long line down the side of the page, as described earlier (using the **<BODY>** tag). This way, all the navigational items on each page appear on a colored bar.

To add a little more flair, you can make another table in the second cell of each page, as shown here:

```
<TABLE BORDER=0>
<TD>
<!--This is the top of the page, for banners and graphics.-->
Fancy banner stuff and graphics
<TR>
<TD>
<!--This is the bottom of the page, for most the text.-->
Lots of text and more text
   .
   .
   .
</TABLE>
```

The complete package gives you a menu bar down one side, a large page display area to the right with a newspaper-size header on top (if that's the size of the stuff you stuck in there), and a larger text display area on the bottom. A newspaper-style layout gives you greater control over your pages. Unless you specify otherwise, tables are automatically sized to their contents.

Frames

What about frames? Well, for as many people who hate them, there seems to be as many who use them religiously. I think tables offer a cleaner-looking approach. However, frames are uniquely suited to catalog-type sites, where you want to keep some kind of navigational menu on the screen and where, from clicks on the navigational area, you have only one target window change (again and again and again).

If there is a more controversial HTML feature than frames, I don't know what it is. Frames allow you to split the browser's windows into portions and display different data in each piece independently. Using frames, you therefore can create very convenient interfaces. For example, Figure C.7 shows a frame that keeps a menu visible at the top of the screen at all times. Other sites use similar ideas to create permanent navigation bars on one side of the screen (see Figure C.8).

However, using frames has a downside—mainly that they chew up screen space. Your framed Web site might look great on your 1,024×768-pixel screen, but it might not look as good at 640×480. Also, some browsers don't support frames at all.

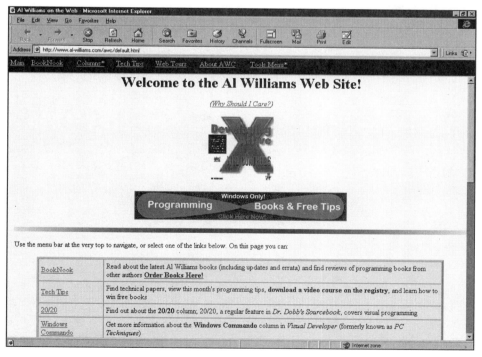

Figure C.7
A menu bar.

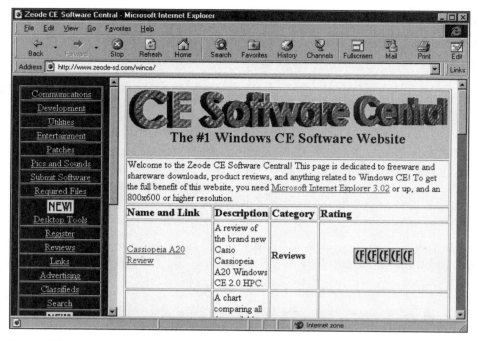

Figure C.8
A navigation pane.

Another problem with frames is that some browsers treat them differently. Suppose you do a search on AltaVista and end up viewing the site shown in Figure C.7. You click on BookNook, read a bit, and click on the Back button. What happens? The answer depends on your browser. Internet Explorer takes you back to the page in Figure C.7. Netscape returns you to AltaVista (you would have to right-click and select Back In Frame to go to the first page).

My last major complaint with frames is bookmarking. When you bookmark a framed page, the bookmark always returns to the initial page, regardless of the particular frames that are visible when you create the bookmark (you'll see why shortly). Some designers see this aspect of frames as an advantage because it forces users to enter the site at the front door.

In the end, only you (and perhaps your users) can decide whether frames are right for your site. But, you still should know how to make them if you want to use them. If you simply hate frames, you might consider skipping the following sections.

The document that displays frames doesn't contain any HTML pages itself; it merely defines the frames. The HTML comes from other documents. You can define a set of frames with the **<FRAMESET>** tag and individual frames with the **<FRAME>** tag.

Creating Framesets

The HTML document that creates a framed page (a frameset) doesn't contain any of the actual display data. Instead, it simply defines the size and shape of each frame. The initial content of each frame comes from separate URLs. Hyperlinks (or scripts) can change the contents of each frame later. In fact, a link in one frame can change the contents of another frame (see Figure C.7 for an example).

Here is a simple frameset:

```
<HTML>
<HEAD>
<TITLE>A simple example</TITLE>
</HEAD>
<FRAMESET ROWS="35,*">
<FRAME NORESIZE SCROLLING=NO NAME=MENU MARGINHEIGHT=0 MARGINWIDTH=0
  FRAMEBORDER=0 FRAMESPACING=0 SRC="menu.htm">
<FRAME NAME=BODY MARGINHEIGHT=0 MARGINWIDTH=0 FRAMEBORDER=0
  FRAMESPACING=0 SRC="main.htm">
</FRAMESET>
</HTML>
```

This example is simple, but it works. By setting options in the **<FRAMESET>** and **<FRAME>** tags, you can get different effects. Notice that each frame has a name. Using a name makes it easy to work with the frame in other hyperlinks and scripts. The **MENU** frame is 35 pixels high, and the user can't resize it (**NORESIZE**). It also has no margins or border. The actual content of the frame is in MENU.HTM.

Notice that the **<FRAMESET>** and related tags don't go in the **<BODY>** section. Some browsers allow you to put a frameset inside a **<BODY>** tag, but others don't. Besides, you can't really have a body with a frameset anyway, so why bother?

Here is another simple example:

```
<HTML>
<HEAD>
<TITLE>Another example</TITLE>
</HEAD>
<FRAMESET ROWS="50%,50%">
<FRAME NAME=TOP SRC="frame1.htm">
<FRAME NAME=BOTTOM  SRC="frame2.htm">
</FRAMESET>
</HTML>
```

This example splits the screen in two, leaving one portion along the top and one along the bottom. If you want three areas, you can simply add another argument to the **ROWS** parameter. You can use **COLS** instead of **ROWS** to split the screen vertically instead of horizontally.

You can set the size of the rows and columns using any of the conventional measurement units. Often, percentage is useful (as in the preceding example). If you have a graphic or a menu, you might prefer to use pixels (the default). Another useful measurement is the asterisk (*), which tells the browser to allocate all remaining space to the frame. For example, if you want a 30-pixel-high graphic at the top and bottom of the screen, you can write the following:

```
<FRAMESET ROWS="30,*,30">
```

Nesting Frames

Sometimes, you might want to subdivide a frame into another frame (for an example, see Figure C.8). You can do so by nesting framesets. Usually, you nest in one file (although you can use a frameset file as the content for a frame). Frames that you nest inside another frame inherit many of the outer frame's properties. For example, if the outer frame doesn't have a border, and you don't specify the border width in the inner frame, the inner frame doesn't have a border either.

The following HTML creates the layout in Figure C.8:

```
<HTML>
<HEAD>
<TITLE>Example</TITLE>
</HEAD>
<FRAMESET ROWS="50%,50%">
<FRAME NAME=TOPFRAME SRC="top.htm">
  <FRAMESET COLS="50%,50%">
  <FRAME NAME=LEFTFRAME SRC="left.htm">
  <FRAME NAME=RIGHTFRAME SRC="right.htm">
  </FRAMESET>
</FRAMESET>
</HTML>
```

Changing Frame Contents

You can change the contents of a frame easily by using a hyperlink. To do so, simply specify the name of the frame using a **TARGET** argument, as in the following example:

```
<A HREF="left2.htm" TARGET=LEFTFRAME>
```

If you don't use the **TARGET** argument, the link replaces the document in the current frame, as you would expect. There are several twists on this approach, though. First, in the **<BASE>** tag (part of the **<HEAD>** section), you can specify a default target to use if a link in that document doesn't explicitly name a target. This approach is useful when you have a menu bar that almost always links to another frame. The following example creates a simple navigation bar that sits to the right of a frame named "PAGE" and lets the user change pages:

```
<HTML>
<HEAD>
<BASE TARGET=PAGE>
</HEAD>
<BODY>
<A HREF="p1.htm">Page 1</A><BR>
<A HREF="p2.htm">Page 2</A><BR>
<A HREF="p3.htm">Page 3</A><BR>
</BODY>
</HTML>
```

Another problem arises when you want to wipe out the entire set of frames and load the new document in its own window. Of course, the new document may supply its own frameset, or it may be a simple document. You can load a new document outside of the current frame by using the predefined target name **_top**. You can use **_blank** instead to open a completely new browser window with the new document. You then can replace your parent frameset by using the **_parent** target. The final predefined target name is **_self**. It is useful when you are using **BASE** to set a default target, but you want a link to act like it normally would. Instead of naming the current frame explicitly, you can simply use **_self**.

Floating Frames

Internet Explorer (but not Netscape Navigator) supports a different type of frame called a *floating frame*. It is simply a window that can appear at any place containing HTML (a feature reminiscent of Microsoft Word Help files). Unlike a regular frame, a floating frame can appear anywhere in your document. It therefore is ideal for displaying elements (such as advertisements) that you want to change without disturbing your document.

For example, imagine that you want to display a news file in a scrolling window. To do so, you could enter the following:

```
<HTML>
<BODY>
<P>Welcome to the WizzBang Web Site!</P>

Today's news:
<CENTER>
    <IFRAME HEIGHT=50 WIDTH=200 SRC="NEWS.HTM">
    <A HREF="news.htm">View the News</A></IFRAME>
</CENTER>

</BODY>
</HTML>
```

Dealing With Browsers Without Frames

How do you handle browsers that don't support frames in general? Some Windows CE Web browsers don't handle frames, and neither do text-based browsers.

The answer is to use the **<NOFRAMES>** tag inside the frameset. Frame-aware browsers skip everything between **<NOFRAMES>** and **</NOFRAMES>**. Other browsers ignore the tags themselves and process the items between them.

What do you put in the **<NOFRAMES>** section? That's a difficult question to answer. If you use frames as an auxiliary navigation aid, you might put a link to your main page here along with a message explaining that the site will look different without frames. If you just can't live without frames, you can explain that, too. Some sites maintain completely separate sets of pages for browsers that don't handle frames (certainly enough of an argument for some people to stay away from frames entirely).

Notice that a hypertext link (**<A HREF="news.htm">**) appears between **<IFRAME>** and **</IFRAME>**. This tag causes browsers that don't understand **<IFRAME>** to display the link instead of the floating frame. Browsers that understand the **<IFRAME>** tag ignore what is between the two **IFRAME** tags.

Style Sheets

For the ultimate control in page layout, you can use *cascading style sheets* (CSS), sometimes simply called *style sheets*. This powerful standard lets you control the appearance and position of everything in your document. Of course, many browsers don't support CSS yet (or they support it poorly). However, you can develop pages that look great in CSS-capable browsers and passable in other browsers.

A very stylish page with lots of effects and tricks can be very difficult to create by hand. For example, if you want all level-one heads (**<H1>**) to look a certain way, why can't you simply specify that information in a list and have all the files on your site read it in from that one list? Then, if you want to change the appearance of your site, you can make the change in one place. This is exactly how style sheets work.

Using style sheets, you can apply styles to a specific element (for example, a paragraph) or to all elements of one type. In other words, you can set a particular paragraph to use green text, or you can set all paragraphs to use green text.

You can also specify classes of elements. For example, you might mark certain paragraphs "urgent." You could arrange it so that all the urgent paragraphs appear in bold red type.

The *cascading* part of CSS occurs when your commands conflict with one another. For example, you mark a paragraph as urgent, but you also directly specify that the paragraph should appear in green. Because the direct command is more specific, it wins. The browser displays the text in green (although it uses the other styles that were afforded urgent paragraphs, if any).

Using Style Sheets To Affect A Particular Element

Any element, such as **<B>** or **<H1>**, can accept a **STYLE** parameter to affect the element. For example, suppose you want a link to a help file. If so, you might write the following:

```
<A STYLE="cursor:help" HREF="help.htm">Help!</A>
```

This line causes the hyperlink to display a help cursor (that is, an arrow with a question mark).

The advantage of this method is that it specifically overrides any other styles in effect. However, maintaining it is also a problem because your styles are scattered about each element. If you want to apply the same style to multiple elements, you'll have a lot of ugly repetition.

Using <SPAN> And <DIV>

Sometimes, you want to affect more than one element with the same style. That's what the **<SPAN>** and **<DIV>** tags are for. You can use them, along with a style parameter, to group parts of your document together. The **<SPAN>** tag affects all the text from where it occurs to the **</SPAN>** tag, but doesn't affect text flow. The **<DIV>** tag affects everything from the tag to the corresponding **</DIV>** tag and places the affected text in its own paragraph.

For example, consider this HTML fragment:

```
<P>I am on one line and not green!
<DIV STYLE="color:green">I'm green on my own line!<BR>
I'm green too
</DIV>
```

The text "I'm green on my own line!" indeed appears on a separate line. In a way, the **<DIV>** tag acts like a paragraph tag. If you use **<SPAN>** instead, the text simply flows as it would have flowed had you not used style tags.

Naming A Style Sheet Element

To prevent confusion when you're using styles, you can name an element. By doing so, you can embed the style information in the **<HEAD>** section of the document, where it is easy to find and change. For example, suppose you want to call attention to a special offer. In this case, you might write the following:

```
<HEAD>
<STYLE>
<!--
#Special { color:salmon; font-size:33pt; }
-->
</STYLE>
```

```
</HEAD>
<BODY>
<P ID=Special>A Special Offer</P>
```

The comments in this example are for the benefit of browsers that don't understand style information. The comments cause these browsers to skip the style data. The ID must begin with the number sign (#), but you don't use it when you reference the ID (as in the **<P>** tag). There is nothing to stop you from having more than one element with the same ID, but, usually, you think of an ID as referring to some particular element. If you want to have a group of elements with the same style, you can use a class (see "Using One Style For Multiple Elements").

Applying A Style To An Element Type

You can use the same syntax you use for a style ID to set the style for a particular type of element. Suppose you want all bold text to be in red. To add this color, you could write the following:

```
<STYLE>
<!--
B { color:red; }
-->
</STYLE>
```

Now, all the bold elements will appear in red. You can also override a particular bold item like this:

```
<B STYLE="color:black;">
```

Style Classes

If you want to group a bunch of elements together, you can assign them to a class. A class is similar to an ID except that you usually think of a class as having more than one item. The following is an example:

```
<STYLE>
<!--
.JanuaryItems { color:salmon;}
.FebruaryItems { color:blue;}
-->
</STYLE>
<BODY>
<H1 CLASS=JanuaryItems>January Specials</H1>
<H1 CLASS=FebruaryItems>February Specials</H1>
```

Again, notice that the class name must start with a period but that you don't use the period when you reference the class.

Using One Style For Multiple Elements

If you want to apply the same style to multiple elements, list the elements and separate them with commas. For example, to make first- and second-level heads blue, you write the following code:

```
<STYLE>
<!--
H1, H2 { color:blue;}
-->
</STYLE>
```

Nested Styles

You can nest styles when you define them by listing them with a space between them. Nesting means that the element will have a certain style only when it appears within another element. Consider this example:

```
<STYLE>
<!--
H1 B { color:red;  }
H2 B { color:yellow; }
B { color:orange; }
-->
</STYLE>
</HEAD>
<BODY>
<H1>What is <B>HTML</B></H1>
<H2>An Introduction to the <B>Web</B></H2>
<P>Here is some <B>bold</B> text.</P>
```

Now, bold items that appear in **<H1>** tags are red, bold items in **<H2>** tags are yellow, and ordinary bold items are orange.

Using External Style Sheets

The biggest problem so far with style sheets is that they are integrated into your document. Wouldn't it be nice if you could have a single style sheet apply to all the pages in your site? Of course, you could use server-side includes, but some servers don't offer them. It would be better if the style sheets themselves could take care of the problem.

This problem has two answers. First, you can link the style sheet to the document by using the **<LINK>** tag in the header of your document. In this case, the contents of the style sheet are all the lines you would have normally put between the **<STYLE>** and **</STYLE>** tags (except for the comment lines). Don't include the comments, and don't include the **<STYLE>** tags. If your style sheet were named MYSTYLE.CSS, for example, you would put a **<LINK>** tag like this in each document:

```
<LINK REL=stylesheet HREF="MYSTYLE.CSS" TYPE=text/css>
```

Another option is to use the **@import:** style. You put it as the first line in a style block or style sheet, as in this example:

```
<STYLE>
<!--
@import:url(dept.css);
H1 { font-size=44pt;}
-->
</STYLE>
```

The styles you set have priority over imported styles as long as you import them before making any other definitions.

Resolving Style Sheet Conflicts

In general, if you specify more than one style for an element, the most specific style takes precedence. For example, suppose you have this line:

```
<H1 CLASS=BigHeader STYLE="font-size:33pt;">
```

If the **BigHeader** class defines a font size, it isn't used (for this header at least). The 33-point directive takes priority. However, the browser observes the other attributes for the **BigHeader** class (color perhaps).

If you really want to be sure that a style takes hold, you can suffix it with **!important**, and some browsers will respect it. For example, suppose you want to make sure that a certain style of text is always red, no matter what. In this case, you can write the following:

```
{color:red!important; }
```

Available Styles

For your reference, Table C.3 shows many of the styles you can use in a style sheet. Of course, they are subject to change, and not all browsers support everything in the same way, so beware. You can find a great deal of information about style sheets at **www.w3.org/Style/css/**.

Table C.3   Selected styles for cascading style sheets.

Style	Description	Typical Values	Applies To	Inherited During Cascading?	Notes
@font-face	Specifies downloadable font		All	Yes	Allows you to specify a font and where to download it from
background	Combines all background attributes		All	Yes	
background-attachment	Used to create watermarks	Scroll, fixed	All	No	
background-color	Background color	Black, white, transparent	All	Yes	
background-image	Background image	bkgnd.gif	All	No	
background-position	Positions background	Top, center, none, right	All	No	
background-repeat	Controls tiling of background	Repeat, repeat-x, repeat-y, no-repeat	All	No	
border-style	Border style	None, solid, double, groove, ridge, inset, outset	Block-level elements	No	
color	Element color	Red, blue, orange	All	Yes	
cursor	Sets cursor shape	Auto, crosshair, default, hand, move, text, wait, help	All	Yes	
font	Completely specifies font	Bold 12pt Times	All	Yes	Combines other font styles together into one style
font-family	Font name	MS Sans Serif	All	Yes	Separate alternative font names with commas
font-size	Type size	12pt, large, larger	All	Yes	Can specify size as percentage or absolute or relative size
font-style	Font style	Italic, normal	All	Yes	

(continued)

Table C.3 Selected styles for cascading style sheets (continued).

Style	Description	Typical Values	Applies To	Inherited During Cascading?	Notes
font-variant	Indicates regular or small-cap face	**Normal, small caps**	All	Yes	
font-weight	Bold	**Normal, bold**	All	Yes	
letter-spacing	Spacing of letters	**Normal, 2pt**	All	Yes	
line-height	Line spacing	**Normal, 5pt, 10%**	All	Yes	
margin	Sets unified margin	**5px, 2pt, auto**	Block-level elements	No	
margin-bottom	Bottom margin	**5px, 2pt, auto**	Block-level elements	No	
margin-left	Left margin	**5px, 2pt, auto**	Block-level elements	No	
margin-right	Right margin	**5px, 2pt, auto**	Block-level elements	No	
margin-top	Top margin	**5px, 2pt, auto**	Block-level elements	No	
text-align	Alignment	**left, right, center, justify**	Block-level elements	Yes	
text-decoration	Text effects	**None, underline, line-through**	All	Yes	
text-indent	Indentation	**10px, 2pt, 5%**	All	Yes	
text-transform	Shifts case	**Capitalize, uppercase, lowercase, none**	All	Yes	
vertical-align	Sub- and superscripting	**Sub, super**	Inline elements	No	

Forms

Forms are usually used for collecting and submitting data, but they can also be used for navigation (although this use crosses over into scripting). For example, you can use selection lists in a form (and other list elements for that matter) to help provide a concise area for selecting links on a site. Selection lists give you the functionality of a pull-down menu on a Web page, which means that, by having little in the way of an original real estate outlay, you can provide a lot more hidden punch and still stay on the same, single page.

Using Forms

HTML forms give you a way to allow users to input text; make choices from checkboxes, radio buttons, and selection lists; and submit the data to an application to process it. Although HTML forms give you a nice, predefined way of putting up boxes and so on to collect data, they are useless without some application to process the form. Listing C.4 provides a sample form to give you an idea.

Listing C.4   A sample form.

```
<FORM METHOD=POST ACTION="/cgi-bin/foo.exe">
<H3>Gourmet Dining Club Membership Form</H3>

<PRE>
<B>Membership Options:</B>

        <INPUT TYPE="radio" NAME="MembershipType" CHECKED
          VALUE=1> 1 Year Prestige Membership ($29.99)
        <INPUT TYPE="radio" NAME="MembershipType"
          VALUE=2> 2 Years Prestige Membership ($49.99)
        <INPUT TYPE="radio" NAME="MembershipType"
          VALUE=3> 1 Year Ambassador Membership ($39.99)
        <INPUT TYPE="radio" NAME="MembershipType"
          VALUE=4> 2 Years Ambassador Membership ($59.99)

        <INPUT TYPE="checkbox" NAME="SendBroch"
          VALUE="Yes"> Please send me more information on
          the different valuable membership options.

<B>Your Mailing Address:</B>

      Name:<INPUT NAME="FirstName" size=16> <INPUT NAME="LastName" size=27>
   Address:<INPUT NAME="Address1" size=43>
          <INPUT NAME="Address2" size=43>
      City:<INPUT NAME="City" size=15> State:<INPUT NAME="State" size=2>
       Zip:<INPUT NAME="PostalCode" size=10>
   Country:<INPUT NAME="Country" size=20>

<B>Your Credit Card Information:</B>

      Type:<SELECT NAME="CardType">
        <OPTION SELECTED>Visa
        <OPTION>MasterCard
        <OPTION>Discover
      </SELECT> Name:<INPUT NAME="CardName" size=25>
    Number:<INPUT NAME="CardNumber" SIZE=20>
   Expires:<INPUT NAME="CardExpDate" SIZE=7>

      <INPUT TYPE="submit" VALUE="   Send    ">
      <INPUT TYPE="reset" VALUE="Clear Form">
</PRE>
</FORM>
```

The first line is the beginning form tag. The first argument specifies that the name-value pairs of the form will be passed (posted) to the application by way of **stdin**. **ACTION** specifies the URL of the application that will process the data, and **foo.exe** stands for any program.

Next, notice the preformatted text tags (**<PRE>**) around this form. They may seem crude, but using such tags is one way to get the form to line up on the page. (If you are trying to use this example, also notice that the breaks made to fit the 80-character limit of code examples in this book may cause your output to appear slightly different.)

Next, notice the tags that say **INPUT** followed by arguments. The **INPUT** element is used for single-line text entry boxes, radio buttons, checkboxes, and two predefined buttons (**SUBMIT** and **RESET**). Notice that the type is specified in each case except for text entries (**TYPE="TEXT"**) because text is the default. Also, notice that the size of the submit and reset buttons is determined by the size of the text within. If you want the buttons to be the same size, you can pad the **VALUE** arguments with spaces. Figure C.9 shows the resulting form.

Other tags you might see are the **TEXTAREA** element for entering multiple lines of text (not in this example) and the **SELECT** element for selection and scrolling lists.

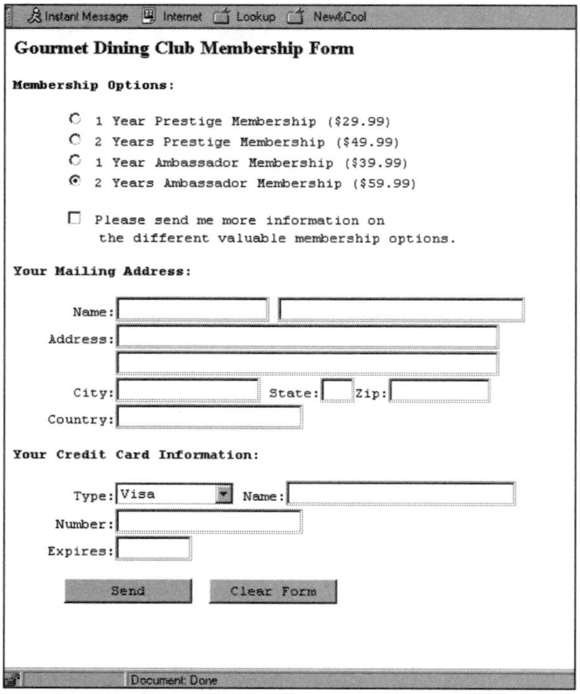

Figure C.9
What the form looks like.

Earlier in this book, you learned how scripts, applets, and controls are used with these same predefined form tags.

Putting Your Page To Work

HTML forms give you a prepackaged way to create forms and enter data—the foundation of business interactions—that you will want to shoot off across the Web to some application. Do you want prize-seeking suckers to fill out personal information pages on themselves so that you can inundate them with junk mail? Do it with a form. Do you want to sell anything? Let the surfers fill out a form that indicates their names, sizes, mailing addresses, and so on. Do you want to pay your taxes, sign up for life insurance, make a bank deposit, or get your driver's license renewed? Fill out some forms.

Now, however, the forms are not paper; they are on the Web. A limitation is that forms can do practically nothing by themselves, so they need to be hooked up to a helper or gateway application or a script that can do something with the information entered on the forms. In the early days, these helper applications were usually Perl programs known as CGI scripts. Today, they are more often Visual Basic or Java scripts.

As with all other HTML, you will find the tags and attributes for forms used in conjunction with all the other HTML and non-HTML tools. Many Web scripts use forms as the front end for gathering input. Now that you know how to make forms, it pays to look at how forms transmit data to the server, and how the server replies. Understanding this underlying communications protocol is crucial to developing interactive Web sites.

Inside HTTP

Hypertext Transfer Protocol, or HTTP, is the networking protocol that makes Web pages work. It is really quite simple. The client (usually the browser) sends a request. The request may contain data (such as form data), and it will contain request headers. These headers provide information about the browser and its current state. For example, the browser may tell the server what kinds of files it will accept.

The server returns a response. You hope this response contains data (the Web page). It also contains headers that contain information about the response (for example, the kind of data the response represents).

Headers can hold all kinds of information. For example, a browser might ask the server to send the document only if it has been modified after a certain date. The browser also sends the user-agent string by way of the header, which is how the server can identify which browser and operating system are in use.

If you want to see the action firsthand, fire up a Telnet client (Windows comes with one). Next, connect to a Web server, but instead of using the standard Telnet port, use port 80.

When you connect, you probably won't see anything. Then, if you connect to AltaVista, for example, type the following:

```
GET http://www.altavista.com/HTTP/1.0
```

Then, press Enter and Ctrl+J (line feed). Depending on how your system is set up, you might not see what you typed. However, you will see the Web page's raw HTML appear on your Telnet screen. If you can scroll back, you'll see that the first few lines are the response headers that were sent to you.

This is essentially how the Web browser accesses your server. It logs in and requests a certain page. Each request can have a header that contains information about the browser (for example, the acceptable languages or cookies the browser holds for this server). The request can also have a body (or content) that is often data from a form, for example.

When the server replies, it also has two portions in its response. The headers contain information about the reply. For example, the header might indicate when the page was modified. Some headers instruct the browser to perform certain actions (for example, redirect to another page). After the headers, the response body appears and contains the actual Web page.

The following is an example from The Coriolis Group's Web site. I entered the following command:

```
telnet www.coriolis.com 80
```

Then, I typed the following:

```
GET http://www.coriolis.com/default.asp
```

In the response, you'll see the headers, followed by a blank line and then the actual Web page content:

```
HTTP/1.1 200 OK
Server: Microsoft-IIS/4.0
Date: Thu, 23 Dec 1999 15:52:45 GMT
Content-Type: text/html
Set-Cookie: ASPSESSIONIDGGGQGRSH=OFIDIFCCHCEHIHLMGGHLHLEN; path=/
Cache-control: private

<HTML>

<HEAD>
<META NAME="Keywords" CONTENT="Books,Exam Cram, Exam Prep,
    .
    .
    .
```

Client Pull

Sometimes, it is useful to have a page update after a certain amount of time. You might want to show something that changes frequently (for example, a stock quote). You might also display a message that redirects the user to another page automatically. Although you could use redirection on the server, you wouldn't get to display a message.

Client pull is the way to accomplish these tasks. Actually, client pull is a special HTTP header (**REFRESH**) that informs the browser (the client) that it should reload in a certain number of seconds. You can ask the browser to load a different page or simply reload the current page. With this header, as with all headers, you use the **<META>** tag to insert it. To find more details about headers and HTTP, you might start at **www.w3.org/Protocols/** or **www.ics.uci.edu/pub/ietf/http/rfc1945.html**.

Because **<META>** tags insert new headers into your document, they must occur in the **<HEAD>** section. After you close the **<HEAD>** tag (or start the **<BODY>** tag), you can't write any more headers.

Suppose that you want to reload a page every 30 seconds. You can put the following statement in the **<HEAD>** section of the page:

```
<META HTTP-EQUIV="REFRESH" CONTENT=30>
```

What if you want the page to go somewhere else? The syntax to do so is straightforward but odd looking:

```
<META HTTP-EQUIV="REFRESH" CONTENT="5;URL=http://www.newplace.com">
```

This isn't a typo; the quotation marks go before **5** and after **.com**. The meaning here is that the content of the **<REFRESH>** header is literally "**5;URL=http://www.newplace.com**".

By the way, some old browsers don't support this tag, so putting an equivalent link on the page is a good idea, as in this example:

```
<P>We've moved</P>
<P>If your browser doesn't go to our new site, use this link:
<A HREF="http://www.newplace.com">http://www.newplace.com</A></P>
```

If you set the **CONTENT** portion to 0, the page will refresh as soon as possible (which, despite the implication, will not be instantaneous).

You'll often see the **<META>** tag used to redirect a user to a new page. This allows you to display a message before causing the browser to load the new page. It also doesn't require any special access to the server because the browser does all the work.

However, if you are using ASP pages, you might prefer to use **Response.Redirect** to vector the browser to the new page. For example:

```
<% Response.Redirect("anotherpage.asp") %>
```

This approach does not leave any reference to the old page in the browser's history list, nor does it afford you the opportunity to display a message before redirecting. It also requires that your page handles ASP script. So, you can use this method on non-ASP servers. However, you can't use it in HTM or HTML files on most servers.

Using mailto To Send Email

A nice feature of the major browsers is the capability to click on a link and automatically pop open an email program (usually without having to set MIME types and so on like you once had to). It's a nice way to let users send you feedback. At the bottom of your pages, consider adding the following line:

```
<A HREF="mailto:bs@bscompany.com">Bill Smithers</A>
```

When users click on Bill's name, their browsers should pop open an email program with Bill's email address already tucked into the To field.

The following are a few tricks that might not work on all browsers:

♦ You can separate multiple email addresses with commas.

♦ You can use a query string with **SUBJECT=** to set the email's subject.

♦ You can place **BODY=** in the query string to set the default message text.

So, you could write the following:

```
<A HREF=
"mailto:alw@al-williams.com,
 paul@al-williams.com
?SUBJECT=Greetings&BODY=Hello">
Say Hello
</A>
```

Remember, any spaces or other special characters require quoting. For example, if you want the subject to be "ASP Book", you need to use a hyperlink like this:

```
<A HREF="mailto:alw@al-williams.com?SUBJECT=ASP%20Book">
Book comments
</A>
```

Using <META> For Search Engines

The **<META>** tag can help boost your image with search engines. Have you ever noticed how some search engine displays read like a hackneyed chop list of words? They use their own criteria for automatically pulling out a descriptive "paragraph" from your site. You can help most search engines by using the **<META>** tag. Inside the **<HEAD>** tags, consider using the **<META>** tag like this:

```
<META NAME="Keywords"  CONTENT="clacker store,
dangerous amusements, clackers">
<META NAME="Description"  CONTENT="Remember
those two plastic balls on a string back in the '70s that kids smacked
together and were rumored to kill kids who used them near their temples?
Bill's clacker page has them for sale, in 454 colors!">
```

The first **<META>** tag marks relevant words the search page can index. The second tag provides a paragraph for the search engine to display.

If you need help on using these tags, a neat site is **http://vancouver-webpages.com/META/ mk-metas.html**, which generates the tags for you and points you to documentation. Most Web sites derive much of their traffic from search engine hits, so anything you can do to increase and improve exposure on these sites is crucial.

Note

This appendix is certainly not an exhaustive reference on HTML. Plenty of references are available in other books and on the Web. You can think of this appendix as more of a cookbook that allows you to cut and paste items of interest into your own Web pages.

Before you tackle scripting, the major focus of this book, you really do need to understand forms and form processing because nearly all server-side scripts work with forms in some way. Style sheets also are important if you are interested in Dynamic HTML (see Appendix D).

Appendix D
DHTML In Depth

Paul Newkirk

To obtain the results you want on your Web page, you'll probably have to turn to Dynamic HTML (DHTML). Server-side script is great for processing, but if you want to change some element after the browser has loaded the page, you'll need to use DHTML.

Does this mean that DHTML should replace ASP? Not really. Like most things, DHTML is good at certain tasks. ASP is still the choice for supporting many browsers, handling server-side databases, and performing other tasks that DHTML can't really handle. On the other hand, DHTML allows animation of page elements and client-side access, for example, which would be cumbersome, if not impossible, to do with ASP. The best Web sites use a synergy of DHTML and ASP (and indeed, of other technologies as well).

This appendix provides an explanation of what DHTML is and why it is important. It then introduces the following features of DHTML (with example code):

- Dynamic style
- Dynamic content
- Dynamic positioning
- Filters and transitions
- Data binding

> **Note**
>
> *If you have not done so already, you might want to read or skim the latter two-thirds of Chapter 6 before reading this appendix. There, you can read about the Dynamic HTML Object Model and see how Internet Explorer uses it to expose documents to scripting. You can also read about specific objects and find quick references for their properties.*

What Is DHTML?

For a few years, DHTML has been a cutting-edge technology. This statement is interesting because it is difficult to be cutting edge on the Web for years. In the case of DHTML, it is true both because of its inherent capabilities and the fact that DHTML is still evolving.

The breakthrough represented by DHTML comes from several different capabilities it allows beyond plain HTML. In the not-so-old days of Web page development, you had to make all changes to a displayed Web page at the server. For example, if you wanted to change text color, the browser had to fetch a new page from the server. In another case, let's assume you created a Web page to read data from a database and display it in an HTML table. In the past, enabling your users to sort the data in the table would require another request to the server and quite possibly an additional HTML document. With DHTML, you can implement both of these examples without additional server requests.

Using DHTML, you can develop Web pages that have application-like behavior not typically found in HTML pages. You can change content and text styles, such as color, font face, and font size, on the fly. You can explicitly position HTML elements and later reposition them. Doing so repetitively can create simple animation. You can apply a variety of visual filters and transitions to create interesting effects. Additionally, you can bind data from a data source to HTML elements, allowing your users to access and manipulate data on the client without making numerous requests to the server (as described in the table-sorting example in the previous paragraph).

Further, you can use most of DHTML's functionality without adding ActiveX controls or Java applets to your Web pages. One exception to this general rule is data binding, which uses an ActiveX control that is installed with Internet Explorer.

Thus, DHTML allows you to change the contents or even the look and feel of a page after it has loaded (without another trip to the Web server). This is obviously an advantage because it can give the appearance of a fairly quick site when network latency might otherwise make your site seem sluggish. And, DHTML gives you scriptable access to elements in Web pages.

OK, you've read through examples and explanations, but, truth be told, you still might be asking, "What exactly is DHTML? Is it a language? Is it a tool? Is it a standard or a protocol?" In return, you might get many different answers. For brevity, though, let me just say that DHTML is a way you can use scripting to access built-in features provided by Microsoft and Netscape in version 4 or higher browsers.

Does DHTML pose any problems? Well, of course. Although DHTML has been around since 1997, corporate buddies Microsoft and Netscape decided to implement DHTML differently. Thus, when you want to use DHTML, you need to understand the differences because you might be forced to check not only which browser you have, but also which version.

Both Internet Explorer 4 and Netscape Navigator 4 support DHTML, but, as you might expect, the implementations are different. Both, however, support the World Wide Web Consortium's (W3C) proposed HTML 4 and cascading style sheets (CSS) standards and plan to implement the eventual standards set by the consortium. Because this area changes rapidly, you might check a few Web sites for current information on the proposed standard and the leading implementations:

- *W3C*—**www.w3c.org/TR/REC-html40**
- *Microsoft*—**msdn.microsoft.com/workshop/author/default.asp** and **msdn.microsoft.com/workshop/author/dhtml/dhtmlovw.asp**
- *Netscape*—**developer.netscape.com/one/dynhtml/dynhtml.html**

I can think of two good sides to the infant-like state of DHTML. One, checking for browsers has gotten easier. And, two, if you are an optimist, you can hope that the disparate sides will eventually converge in a common and honestly followed standard.

Dynamic Styles

By using dynamic styles, you can change the formatting and appearance of HTML elements without reloading the page. DHTML accomplishes these changes through a combination of the exposed object model, styles and cascading style sheets (CSS), and client-side scripting.

For styles, you usually use the **<STYLE>** tag or the inline **STYLE** attribute, which assigns a style to an HTML element. In either case, you can change the style settings dynamically in response to an event or via script logic.

Listing D.1 shows how to use the **<STYLE>** tag to define two styles. The **<STYLE>** tag uses CSS attributes to set various style properties and is usually placed in the **<HEAD>** section. Here, two styles are defined: **style1**, which sets the text color to blue, and **style2**, which sets the text color to red and the font size to 36 points. A level 2 header is defined and assigned **style1** with the **CLASS** attribute. When the mouse pointer is moved over the header, the **onmouseover** event fires, and the style is changed to **style2** in response. The style is reset to **style1** when the mouse pointer is moved away.

Listing D.1   Dynamic styles with the <STYLE> tag.

```
<HTML>
<HEAD>
<TITLE>Listing D.1 Dynamic Styles</TITLE>
<STYLE>
     .style1 {color:blue}
     .style2 {color:red;font-size:"36"}
```

```
</STYLE>
</HEAD>
<BODY>

<H2 CLASS=style1 onmouseover="this.className='style2'"
onmouseout="this.className='style1'">DHTML is flexible!</H2>

</BODY>
</HTML>
```

Listing D.2 also shows how to change the font color in response to events, but calls JavaScript functions to get the job done. Also, notice that the functions use the DHTML event model (see Chapter 6).

Listing D.2   Changing style with script.

```
<HTML>
<HEAD>
<TITLE>Listing D.2 Script with style</TITLE>
<SCRIPT LANGUAGE="JavaScript">
<!--
function TurnRed() {
     window.event.srcElement.style.color = "red";
}

function TurnBlue() {
     window.event.srcElement.style.color = "blue";
}
// -->
</SCRIPT>
</HEAD>
<BODY>

<H2 STYLE=color:blue onmouseover="TurnRed()"
onmouseout="TurnBlue()">DHTML is flexible!</H2>

</BODY>
</HTML>
```

Even browsers that don't understand DHTML will display the headings; they just won't change colors. This is an example of how you can jazz up your Web page without worrying about compatibility (if you are careful).

Listing D.3 shows a more complex example. This page uses dynamic styles to change the appearance of selected elements. Four styles are defined in the **<HEAD>** section. The page applies these styles to various elements in the **<BODY>** by assigning them via the **CLASS** attribute. It also defines a **<SPAN>** that contains underlined text. When the user moves the mouse pointer over the text, the **onmouseover** event handler changes the style. The new style changes the font color and size and changes the mouse pointer to a hand, giving the appearance of a hyperlink. When the user moves the mouse pointer away, the **onmouseout** event fires, and the code restores the style to its previous setting. Also, notice that as the text gets larger, the document layout changes with it. When the user clicks on the text, the event handler calls **OpenModal**, which opens a modal dialog window to display another document. You'll read more about the function of the new document in the "Tabular Data Control" section later in this chapter.

Further down in the document, you'll see another **<SPAN>** with an **ID** of **free**. When the document loads, the **onload** event handler calls **init**. This function calls **setInterval** so that the browser will call **blink** every 200 milliseconds. The **blink** function causes the text in the span to blink red and blue.

Finally, the page defines a hyperlink and assigns it the style **hot**. When the mouse pointer moves over the hyperlink, the link changes color and size.

Listing D.3   Using dynamic styles.

```
<HTML>
<HEAD>
<TITLE>Listing D.3 Community Dining Club</TITLE>
<STYLE>
     .s1 {color:blue;text-align:center}
     .s2 {color:red;font-size:"36";text-align:center}
     .normal {color:blue;font-size:"16"}
     .hot {cursor:hand;color:red;font-size:"18"}
</STYLE>

<SCRIPT LANGUAGE="JavaScript">
<!--
function blink() {
     if (free.style.color == "red")
          free.style.color = "blue";
     else
          free.style.color = "red";
}

function init(n) {
     setInterval("blink()", n);
}

function OpenModal() {
     window.showModalDialog("D-3.htm");
}
```

```
//-->
</SCRIPT>
</HEAD>
<BODY onload="init(200)">
<H1 CLASS=s1 >Welcome To The</H1>
<H1 CLASS=s1 >Community Dining Club!</H1>
<HR SIZE=5>
<P CLASS=normal>The Community Dining Club is for those who enjoy
dining out and the convenience of the online world!</P>

<P CLASS=normal>As a visitor, you can
<SPAN CLASS=normal onmouseover="this.className='hot'"
onmouseout="this.className='normal'" onclick="OpenModal()">
<U>see the many fine participating restaurants.</U></SPAN>

As a member, you will enjoy the following benefits:</P>
<UL class=normal>
<LI>Online Reservations
<LI>10% Discount On All Meals
<LI>Special Discounts
<LI>Submit and Read Member Restaurant Reviews
<LI>Coolness
<LI>and More!
</UL>

<P CLASS=normal>Best of all, membership is <SPAN ID=free class=hot>
FREE!</SPAN>

So why not <A CLASS=normal onmouseover="this.className='hot'"
onmouseout="this.className='normal'"HREF="D-2.htm">
join today?</A></P>

</BODY>
</HTML>
```

Positioning And Animation

You can explicitly place an HTML element at a specific location in a document by using *positioning*. Positioning is an extension of CSS; therefore, you specify an element's position by using the **STYLE** attribute. You can also specify the position by using the **STYLE** object (see Chapter 6), which allows you to position elements with script and even create animation effects.

Elements are positioned either *absolute* or *relative*. When you specify absolute positioning, the browser positions the element with respect to the top-left corner of the container, which is the document body by default. When you specify relative positioning, the browser places the element relative to its flow within the HTML document.

Elements are also positioned using x and y coordinates as well as a z-index. The *z-index* specifies how the element "stacks up" with other elements. The element with the largest z-index is on top, and the element with the smallest z-index is on the bottom. Imagine it like a pile of papers on your desk. You can use both positive and negative values for the z-index.

Consider the following:

```
<H3 STYLE="color:yellow">Using Positioning</H3>
<IMG STYLE="position:relative;top:0;left:0" SRC="turkey.gif">
```

The preceding HTML displays a header followed by an image. The image follows the header because the document specifies relative positioning. The top and left coordinates are relative to the header. In contrast, the following HTML displays the image over the header:

```
<IMG STYLE="position:absolute;top:0;left:0" SRC="turkey.gif">
```

You can control the overlapping and force the image under the header by specifying a z-index of -1, as shown here:

```
<IMG STYLE="position:absolute;top:0;left:0;z-index:-1" SRC="turkey.gif">
```

You can produce some interesting effects by combining script, positioning, and dynamic style. In the section "Using The Transition Filter Control," later in this chapter, you'll learn how to display a billboard in various locations.

Dynamic Content

By using dynamic content, you can change the content of a Web page after it is loaded. Before the advent of DHTML, you had to request a new page from the server to reflect content changes. Now, you can manipulate a set of properties and methods to change the content of many HTML elements. Some of these features operate only on the text within an element; others operate on the text and the appearance of the element.

You'll use four properties to modify an element's contents. Assigning a string to them replaces the associated element's contents. You'll find these properties in Table D.1.

Listing D.4 shows how to define a level 2 header with an **ID** of **aTag**. The **onload** event handler calls the function **ChangeHTML** to change the contents of the header.

Table D.1 Dynamic content properties.

Property	Description
innerHTML	Replaces the contents of the existing element and renders any included HTML tags as HTML
innerText	Replaces the contents of the existing element and renders any included HTML tags as text
outerHTML	Replaces the entire element using HTML
outerText	Replaces the entire element as text (may change the element type)

Listing D.4 The innerText property.

```
<HTML>
<HEAD>
<TITLE>Dynamic Content</TITLE>
<SCRIPT LANGUAGE="JavaScript">
<!--
function ChangeHTML() {
     document.all.aTag.innerText = "Dynamic HTML is <I>dynamic!</I>";
}

// -->
</SCRIPT>
</HEAD>
<BODY onload="ChangeHTML()">

<H2 ID=aTag>DHTML is flexible!</H2>

</BODY>
</HTML>
```

Because the **innerText** property renders included HTML tags as text, the new header is as follows:

```
Dynamic HTML is <I>dynamic!</I>
```

You might prefer using the **innerHTML** property in this case. Then, the header looks like this:

```
Dynamic HTML is dynamic!
```

Using the same header, you could modify the **outerText** property instead:

```
document.all.aTag.outerText = "<H1>Dynamic HTML is <I>dynamic!</I></H1>";
```

This code changes the header to the following:

```
<H1>Dynamic HTML is <I>dynamic!</I></H1>
```

Setting **outerHTML** results in the following:

```
Dynamic HTML is dynamic!
```

Notice that using the outer properties, you can change the type of the element. The inner properties preserve the element's type. If you change the **outerHTML** property, you probably should set the **ID**. Otherwise, the previous **ID** is no longer valid. You can also position text and HTML at the beginning or end of elements using the methods described in Table D.2.

These methods take an argument that specifies where the new content is placed relative to the element:

+ **BeforeBegin**—Inserts the text before the beginning tag
+ **AfterBegin**—Inserts the text after the beginning tag
+ **BeforeEnd**—Inserts the text before the ending tag
+ **AfterEnd**—Inserts the text after the ending tag

Continuing with the heading defined in Listing D.4, you can change the statement in the **ChangeHTML** function to read:

```
document.all.aTag.insertAdjacentHTML("BeforeBegin", "<I>Wow!</I> ");
```

This statement produces the following:

```
Wow!
DHTML is flexible!
```

Changing the argument to **AfterBegin** produces the following result:

```
Wow! DHTML is flexible!
```

Table D.2   Dynamic content methods.

Method	Description
insertAdjacentHTML	Inserts text and HTML at the beginning or end of an element
insertAdjacentText	Inserts text at the beginning or end of an element

A Dynamic Example With Timeouts

The capability to change things after the fact is quite useful, especially when combined with a timeout. For example, consider this simple page:

```
<HTML>
<HEAD>
<SCRIPT>
var i=0;
var msgs;

function onTick() {
  setTimeout("onTick();",2500);
  document.all.spot.innerText=msgs[i];
  i++;
  if (i==6) i=0;
  }

function init() {
  msgs=new Array();
  msgs[0]="Every Day";
  msgs[1]="We Do";
  msgs[2]="Our Part";
  msgs[3]="To Make Your Face";
  msgs[4]="A Work of Art";
  msgs[5]="Burma-Shave";
  setTimeout("onTick();",1); // first timeout
  }
</SCRIPT>
</HEAD>
<BODY onLoad='init();'>
<CENTER>
<H1 ID=spot></P>
</CENTER>
</BODY>
</HTML>
```

This page displays a different part of its message every 2.5 seconds (like an old-fashioned Burma-Shave sign). Achieving this nice effect with DHTML is trivial. Without DHTML, however, you would have to load a new page for each message (or at least reload a page that contains script).

Another nice effect you could achieve here is to replace the **onTick** code with the following:

```
function onTick() {
    if (i==6) {
```

```
      document.location="http://www.burmashave.com";
    }
  else {
    setTimeout("onTick();",2500);
    document.all.spot.innerText=msgs[i];
    i++;
    }
  }
```

This example moves the browser to the Web site after showing the display one time. The previous page showed the message over and over again.

The **TextRange** Object

The properties and methods described in the preceding sections are used with a specific element. You can also manipulate page contents using an entire range of text. Using the **TextRange** object, for example, you can reference a part of the document. This object doesn't actually hold any content; it just provides a reference to that content. You can use the **TextRange** object to move through text and perform searches, select specific portions of text, and copy portions of text.

You create a **TextRange** object by calling the **createTextRange** method of **<BODY>**, **<BUT-TON>**, **<TEXTAREA>**, and text **<INPUT>** elements. Using **createTextRange** with the **<BODY>** element returns a reference to the entire document.

The **TextRange** object has several properties and methods that provide information about the range, move through the text, compare selections, set text ranges, and more. Table D.3 describes the **TextRange** object properties. **TextRange** object methods are described in Table D.4.

Listing D.5 shows the use of the **TextRange** object to search a text range for a specified string. The function **SetRange** creates a text range consisting of the contents of the **<BODY>** section. It then moves the element with the **ID** of **theText** into the text range. The **doSearch**

Table D.3   TextRange object properties.

Property	Description
boundingHeight	Returns the height of the rectangle that bounds the range
boundingLeft	Returns the left coordinate of the rectangle that bounds the range
boundingTop	Returns the top coordinate of the rectangle that bounds the range
boundingWidth	Returns the width of the rectangle that bounds the range
htmlText	Returns the text ranges as an HTML fragment
offsetLeft	Returns the left position of the rectangle that bounds the range
offsetTop	Returns the top position of the rectangle that bounds the range
text	References the text contained in the range

Table D.4   TextRange object methods.

Method	Description
collapse	Moves the insertion point to the beginning or end of the range
compareEndPoints	Compares two end points
duplicate	Returns a duplicate of the range
execCommand	Executes a command over the specified range
expand	Expands the range so that partial units* are completely contained
findText	Searches for text
getBookmark	Returns a bookmark specifying a position
inRange	Returns whether one range is contained within another
isEqual	Returns whether the specified range is equal to the current range
move	Moves the start and end points a specified number of units
moveEnd	Moves the end position of the range
moveStart	Moves the start position of the range
moveToBookmark	Moves to a bookmark
moveToElementText	Moves the text range so that the start and end positions encompass the text in a specified element
moveToPoint	Moves the start and end positions of the range to the specified point
parentElement	Returns the parent element of a specified range
pasteHTML	Pastes HTML and/or text into the current range
queryCommandEnabled	Returns whether the specified command can be executed
queryCommandIndeterm	Returns whether the specified command is in the indeterminate state
queryCommandState	Returns the current state of a specified command
queryCommandSupported	Returns whether a command is supported on the current range
queryCommandValue	Returns the current value of a specified command
scrollIntoView	Scrolls the range into view at either the top or bottom of the window
select	Makes the active selection equal to the current text range
setEndPoint	Sets the end point of one range based on the end point of another

*A unit is a character, word, sentence, or textedit.

function prompts the user to enter a search string and then calls the **Find** function. If the search string is found, it is highlighted within the text range.

Listing D.5   Using the **TextRange** object.

```
<HTML>
<HEAD>
<TITLE>Listing D.5 The TextRange object</TITLE>
<SCRIPT LANGUAGE="JavaScript">
<!--
var theRange;
var fndText, searchStr;
```

```
function SetRange() {
    theRange = document.body.createTextRange();
    theRange.moveToElementText(theText);
}

function Find(s) {
    if (theRange.findText(s)) {
        fndText = "<FONT STYLE="+"COLOR:WHITE;BACKGROUND:BLACK" +">" +
            theRange.text + "</FONT>";
        theRange.pasteHTML(fndText);
    }
}

function doSearch() {
    searchStr = prompt("Enter search string:")
    Find(searchStr);
}

// -->
</SCRIPT>
</HEAD>
<BODY onload="SetRange()">

<H2>The TextRange Object</H2>
<DIV ID=theText>You create a TextRange object by calling the createTextRange()
method of BODY, BUTTON, TEXTAREA, and text INPUT elements. Using
createTextRange() with the BODY element returns a reference to
the entire document.</DIV>

<INPUT TYPE=BUTTON VALUE="Search" onclick="doSearch()">
</BODY>
</HTML>
```

The **Selection** Object

Another way to create a text range is to use the **Selection** object. A *selection* is a portion of text that has been selected by the user. The **Selection** object contains information about the current selection and provides methods to create a **TextRange** object and to clear and delete the selection.

The following statement creates a **TextRange** object using the **Selection** object:

```
theRange = document.Selection.createRange();
```

The preceding statement could be included in an event handler that is called when the user releases the mouse button after making a selection.

You can also create selections in script by calling the **select** method of **TextObject**.

Filters

Filters add special visual effects to elements. DHTML supports two types of filters: *visual* and *transition*. You use visual filters to change an element's appearance, such as flipping an image, adding a shadow, or adding a blur effect. You use transition filters when you want to change the display of an element gradually, such as fading from one image to another.

Filters are extensions to CSS. You implement them by setting style properties within a **<STYLE>** tag or by using an element's **STYLE** attribute. You can add filter and transition effects without using script, but if you need to control these effects with script, you can do so by using the **filters** collection. Each HTML control has a **filters** collection that provides script access to the filters. Also, filters have properties, methods, and events that control their appearance and behavior.

Filters can be used only with HTML elements that are controls. Control elements define a rectangular area in the display. You can add filters to the following controls:

♦ **<BODY>**

♦ **<BUTTON>**

♦ **<DIV>** (with a defined height, width, and absolute positioning)

♦ **<IMG>**

♦ **<INPUT>**

♦ **<MARQUEE>**

♦ **<SPAN>** (with a defined height, width, and absolute positioning)

♦ **<TABLE>**

♦ **<TD>**

♦ **<TEXTAREA>**

♦ **<TFOOT>**

♦ **<TH>**

♦ **<THEAD>**

♦ **<TR>**

Visual Filters

Visual filters modify a control's appearance. For example, you can use visual filters to add a shadow to text, flip an image horizontally or vertically, and apply other special effects. Table D.5 describes the visual filters supported by Internet Explorer 4.

Filters are applied as filter strings, and you can apply multiple filters at the same time. For example, the following HTML flips text vertically:

Table D.5 Internet Explorer visual filters.

Filter	Description
alpha	Sets a transparency level
blur	Creates a movement effect
chroma	Makes a specified color transparent
dropshadow	Creates an offset silhouette
fliph	Creates a horizontal mirror image
flipv	Creates a vertical mirror image
glow	Creates a glow effect
grayscale	Removes color information from an image
invert	Reverses hue, saturation, and brightness values
light	Projects a light source onto the object
mask	Creates a transparent mask from the object
shadow	Creates a silhouette of the object
wave	Creates a sine wave distortion of the object
xray	Shows only the edges of the object

```
<SPAN ID="mySpan" HEIGHT=20 WIDTH=50
STYLE="position:absolute;top:0;left:0;font-size:24;color:blue;filter:flipv">
Using filters is easy</SPAN>
```

Some visual filters take arguments to specify how the filter will be applied. The **glow** filter takes up to two arguments to specify the color and strength. For example, the following HTML adds a red glow effect to the text:

```
filter:glow(color=red)
```

Listing D.6 shows how you can add filters using script. When the user moves the mouse pointer over the text, an event handler adds the glow effect.

Listing D.6 Adding visual filters with script.

```
<HTML>
<HEAD>
<TITLE>Listing D.6 Visual Filters</TITLE>
<SCRIPT LANGUAGE="JavaScript">
<!--
function addGlow() {
    mySpan.style.filter = "glow(red)";
}

// -->
</SCRIPT>
</HEAD>
<BODY>
```

```
<SPAN ID="mySpan" HEIGHT=20 WIDTH=50
onmouseover="addGlow()"
STYLE="position:absolute;top:0;left:0;
font-size:24;color:blue">
Using filters is easy</SPAN>

</BODY>
</HTML>
```

Transition Filters

You can use transition filters when you want to change a control's appearance over a period of time or gradually hide and reveal a control. This kind of transformation is commonly used in slide show presentations in the transition from one slide to another.

The two types of transition filters are *blend* and *reveal*. Blend causes the control to gradually fade in and out. Reveal causes the control to gradually appear and disappear in one of 24 predefined patterns.

The **blendTrans** filter is very easy to use and takes one argument, **duration**, to specify the length of time the transition should take to complete. At the time of this writing, **blendTrans** doesn't work exactly as documented on all browsers. You can, however, coerce it into working by using script. The following HTML uses the blend transition to fade in text over a three-second period:

```
<SCRIPT LANGUAGE=JavaScript>
<!--
function doTrans() {
    mySpan.filters.blendTrans.Apply();
    mySpan.innerText="Filters are easy!";
    mySpan.filters.blendTrans.play();
}
//-->
</SCRIPT>

<SPAN ID="mySpan" HEIGHT=20 WIDTH=50
STYLE="position:absolute;top:0;left:0;font-size:24;color:blue;
filter:blendTrans(duration=3)" onclick="doTrans()">
Click here to see blendTrans work!</SPAN>
```

The **revealTrans** filter causes the control to transition in and out using one of 24 patterns. This filter accepts two arguments to specify the duration in seconds of the transition and the transition pattern. Table D.6 describes the available transition patterns.

A few transition filter methods affect the transitions. The **apply** method applies a transition to the specified object, **play** causes the transition to happen, and **stop** stops the transition play.

Table D.6   Reveal filter transition patterns.

Transition Pattern	Value	Transition Pattern	Value
Box in	0	Box out	1
Circle in	2	Circle out	3
Wipe up	4	Wipe down	5
Wipe right	6	Wipe left	7
Vertical blinds	8	Horizontal blinds	9
Checkerboard across	10	Checkerboard down	11
Random dissolve	12	Random	23
Split vertical in	13	Split vertical out	14
Split horizontal in	15	Split horizontal out	16
Strips left down	17	Strips left up	18
Strips right down	19	Strips right up	20
Random bars horizontal	21	Random bars vertical	22

Listing D.7 shows how to use the **revealTrans** transition filter to cycle through a series of images. An image is inserted into the document, and the **revealTrans** filter, with the random dissolve effect, is assigned. The **duration** property is set so that the transition occurs over a two-second period. When the document **onload** event fires, a call is made to the function **initTrans**, which uses the **setInterval** method to call the **doTrans** function every three seconds. The **doTrans** function cycles through the series of images. The **apply** method applies the specified transition filter to the image element. The next image is assigned to the image element, and then the **play** method is called to play the transition. The **play** method can take an argument to specify the duration, which would override the initial setting.

Listing D.7   Using transition filters.

```
<HTML>
<HEAD>
<TITLE>Listing D.7 Transition Filters</TITLE>
<SCRIPT LANGUAGE="JavaScript">
<!--
var picNum = 0;
var pics = new Array("turkey.gif",
  "tbone.gif","beef.gif",
  "dessert.gif","fish.gif","tacos.gif",
  "hotdog.gif");

function doTrans() {
    pic.filters.revealTrans.apply();
    picNum++;
    if (picNum > 6)
        picNum = 0;
    pic.src = pics[picNum];
    pic.filters.revealTrans.play();
}
```

```
function initTrans() {
    setInterval("doTrans()", 3000);
}
// -->
</SCRIPT>
</HEAD>
<BODY onload="initTrans()">

<IMG NAME="pic" SRC="turkey.gif"
STYLE="filter:revealTrans(duration=2, transition=12)"
WIDTH=100 HEIGHT=100>

</BODY>
</HTML>
```

Using The Transition Filter Control

Listing D.8 contains the code for the familiar Community Dining Club New Member Registration page. The page is a bit different than before because it uses a visual filter and a transition filter with dynamic positioning to display the billboard. The billboard consists of an array that contains the messages to display. When the document's **onload** event fires, the handler calls **startBillboard**. The billboard is in the **<SPAN>** with the **ID** of **msg1**. The function applies the **blur** filter and the random dissolve transition and sets the billboard's starting position.

The **startBillboard** function applies the transition using the **apply** method. Then, it sets the first message in the sequence using the **innerText** property. Next, the call to the **play** method causes the transition. Finally, the function uses **setInterval** so that the browser will call **cycle** every 2,500 milliseconds (2.5 seconds).

The **cycle** function displays the appropriate message on the billboard. Assigning a value to the **top** property sets each message position. When the cycle is complete, the code resets the property to the initial position.

Listing D.8   Using the transition filter control.

```
<HTML>
<HEAD>
<TITLE>Listing D.8 Member Registration</TITLE>
<STYLE>
    .s1 {color:blue;font-size:"18pt"}
    .s2 {color:blue;font-size:"12pt"}
    .s3 {color:red;font-size:"18pt"}
</STYLE>
<SCRIPT LANGUAGE=JavaScript>
<!--
var MsgNo, MsgTop;
```

```
var Message = new Array("Join Today!", "Fine Dining!",
                        "Impress Friends!", "Save Money!", "Be Cool!");

MsgNo = 0;
MsgTop = 125;

function startBillboard() {
    msg1.filters.revealTrans.apply();
    msg1.innerText = Message[MsgNo];
    msg1.filters.revealTrans.play();

    setInterval("cycle()", 2500);
}

function cycle() {
    MsgNo++;
    MsgTop += 35;
    if (MsgNo > 4) {
        MsgNo = 0;
        MsgTop = 125;
    }
    msg1.innerText = "";
    msg1.style.top = MsgTop + "px";
    msg1.filters.revealTrans.apply();
    msg1.innerText = Message[MsgNo];
    msg1.filters.revealTrans.play();
}

//-->
</SCRIPT>

<SCRIPT FOR="cmdSubmit" EVENT="onclick" LANGUAGE=JavaScript>
<!--
    // data validation here
// -->
</SCRIPT>
</HEAD>
<BODY onload="startBillboard()">

<SPAN ID=msg1 class=s3 style="position:absolute;top:125;left:0;
    filter:blur(add=1,direction=45,strength=3)
    revealTrans(transition=12 duration=8)"></SPAN>

<H2 class=s1 Align=Center>New Member Registration</H2>
<HR SIZE=5 WIDTH=90%>
```

```
<P ALIGN=CENTER>
<TABLE>
<TD>
<PRE>
<FORM NAME="RegistrationForm">
<B>First Name:        </B><INPUT TYPE=TEXT NAME="firstname">
<B>Last Name:         </B><INPUT TYPE=TEXT NAME="lastname">
<B>Address1:          </B><INPUT TYPE=TEXT NAME="addr1">
<B>Address2:          </B><INPUT TYPE=TEXT NAME="addr2">
<B>City:              </B><INPUT TYPE=TEXT NAME="city">
<B>State:             </B><INPUT TYPE=TEXT NAME="state" MAXLENGTH=2 SIZE=2>
<B>Zip:               </B><INPUT TYPE=TEXT NAME="zip" MAXLENGTH=10 SIZE=10>
<B>Area Code/Phone: </B><INPUT TYPE=TEXT NAME="code" MAXLENGTH=3 SIZE=3>
                        <INPUT TYPE=TEXT NAME="phone" MAXLENGTH=7 SIZE=7>

<B>Preferred Cuisine: </B><SELECT NAME="cuisine" SIZE="1">
                        <OPTION VALUE="1">American
                        <OPTION VALUE="2">Chinese
                        <OPTION VALUE="3">French
                        <OPTION VALUE="4">German
                        <OPTION VALUE="5">Greek
                        <OPTION VALUE="6">Indian
                        <OPTION VALUE="7">Italian
                        <OPTION VALUE="8">Japanese
                        <OPTION VALUE="9">Seafood
                        <OPTION VALUE="0">Other
</SELECT>

<INPUT TYPE=BUTTON NAME="cmdSubmit" VALUE="Submit">
<INPUT TYPE="RESET" VALUE="Clear">
</PRE>

</FORM>
</TD>
</TABLE>
</P>
</BODY>
</HTML>
```

Data Binding

By using data binding, you can develop Web pages that display and manipulate data on the client. Without data binding, if the user needs to manipulate the data (for example, search or sort) on your Web page, doing so would require a trip to the server. Also, if your page displays data one record at a time, then each time the user moved forward or backward in the data, it would result in a request to the server. With data binding, you can cache a record set on the client and allow the user to navigate, search, and sort the data without making repeated requests to the server. Additionally, some elements can update the data if the data source supports updates.

Data binding binds database fields to HTML elements. The data binding architecture consists of four components:

♦ Data source objects (DSOs)

♦ Data consumers

♦ The binding agent

♦ The table repetition agent

Data source objects provide the data to the page. Internet Explorer provides two DSOs: the Tabular Data Control and the Remote Data Service. The Tabular Data Control is useful for delimited text files, such as comma-delimited files, and does not support updates. The Remote Data Service uses OLE-DB and ODBC data sources and supports updates. This appendix covers the simplest data source object: the Tabular Data Control.

Data consumers are HTML elements that display the data. The binding agent and table repetition agents take care of synchronizing the data provider with the data consumer. The binding agent binds single-value elements to data, and the table repetition agent binds the entire record set to multiple-value elements, such as HTML tables.

The Tabular Data Control

The Tabular Data Control is used to bind single-value elements, such as **<INPUT TYPE=TEXT>** or **<SPAN>**, to data. It can also bind multiple-value elements, such as **<TABLE>**, to data. You can embed data source objects in a page by using the **<OBJECT>** tag as follows:

```
<OBJECT ID="restData" WIDTH=0 HEIGHT=0
CLASSID="CLSID:333C7BC4-460F-11D0-BC04-0080C7055A83">
     <PARAM NAME="DataURL" VALUE="restaurants.txt">
     <PARAM NAME="FieldDelim" VALUE=",">
     <PARAM NAME="UseHeader" VALUE=True>
</OBJECT>
```

The **DataURL** parameter specifies the URL of the data source. In this case, it is restaurants.txt, a comma-delimited file that contains restaurant information. **FieldDelim** specifies the character that separates the records. **UseHeader** specifies whether the data source contains field names in the first row.

Now, the data is ready to be bound to elements. The restaurant database consists of the following fields:

◆ **Name**

◆ **Cuisine**

◆ **Hours**

◆ **Address**

◆ **Phone**

Single-value elements are bound at design-time as follows:

```
<INPUT TYPE=TEXT ID=restName DATASRC="#restData" DATAFLD="Name">
```

This statement binds the **Name** field of the **restData** data source to the input text control. The attribute **DATASRC** is assigned the ID of the data source object. The hash mark (#) is required. The attribute **DATAFLD** is assigned the name of the field being bound to the element.

Single-value elements can also be bound at runtime, as shown here:

```
<SCRIPT LANGUAGE="JavaScript">
. . .
restName.dataSrc = "#restData";
resName.dataFld = "Name";
. . .
</SCRIPT>

<BODY>
<INPUT TYPE=TEXT NAME=restName>
</BODY>
```

Navigating With The Tabular Data Control

The data source has a **Recordset** object that contains all the records in the data set. The **Recordset** object has the following methods that let you move around in the data:

◆ **MoveFirst**

◆ **MoveNext**

◆ **MovePrevious**

◆ **MoveLast**

The **Recordset** object also has properties that indicate whether the record pointer is at the beginning or the end of the record set. **BOF** is **true** if it's at the beginning, and **EOF** is **true** if it's at the end.

Listing D.9 shows how to bind single-value elements to records in a database. It also has buttons that let the user move forward and backward through the data.

Listing D.9   Using single-value elements with the Tabular Data Control.

```
<HTML>
<HEAD>
<TITLE>Listing D.9 Single-Value Data Binding</TITLE>
<SCRIPT LANGUAGE="JavaScript">
<!--

function BindData() {
    restName.dataSrc = "#restData";
    restName.dataFld = "Name";
    restCuisine.dataSrc = "#restData";
    restCuisine.dataFld = "Cuisine";
    restHours.dataSrc = "#restData";
    restHours.dataFld = "Hours";
    restAddress.dataSrc = "#restData";
    restAddress.dataFld = "Address";
    restPhone.dataSrc = "#restData";
    restPhone.dataFld = "Phone";
}

function next() {
    if (restData.recordset.EOF)
        restData.recordset.MoveFirst();
    else
        restData.recordset.MoveNext();
}

function gotoEnd() {
    restData.recordset.MoveLast();
}

function prev() {
    if (restData.recordset.BOF)
        restData.recordset.MoveLast();
    else
        restData.recordset.MovePrevious();
}

function gotoBegin() {
    restData.recordset.MoveFirst();
}
// -->
</SCRIPT>
```

```
</HEAD>
<BODY onload="BindData()">

<OBJECT ID="restData" WIDTH=0 HEIGHT=0
CLASSID="CLSID:333C7BC4-460F-11D0-BC04-0080C7055A83">
     <PARAM NAME="DataURL" VALUE="restaurants.txt">
     <PARAM NAME="FieldDelim" VALUE=",">
     <PARAM NAME="UseHeader" VALUE=True>
</OBJECT>

<INPUT TYPE=TEXT ID=restName><INPUT TYPE=TEXT ID=restCuisine>
<INPUT TYPE=TEXT ID=restHours><INPUT TYPE=TEXT ID=restAddress>
<INPUT TYPE=TEXT ID=restPhone><BR>
<INPUT TYPE=BUTTON onclick="next()" VALUE=">">
<INPUT TYPE=BUTTON onclick="gotoEnd()" VALUE=">>">
<INPUT TYPE=BUTTON onclick="prev()" VALUE="<">
<INPUT TYPE=BUTTON onclick="gotoBegin()" VALUE="<<">

</BODY>
</HTML>
```

When the document is finished loading, the function **BindData** is called to bind the first record to the text controls. The page provides four buttons to allow the user to move to the next and previous records as well as to the first and last records. If the record pointer is at the first record and the Previous button is clicked, the page displays the last record. Conversely, if the pointer is at the last record and the Next button is clicked, the page shows the first record.

An example of using the Tabular Data Control with multiple-value elements appears in the next section.

Data Binding With The Tabular Data Control

Listing D.10 does a lot of work with surprisingly little script or HTML. It uses the Tabular Data Control to bind a comma-delimited data source to an HTML table. Notice that the table definition has only one **<TR>** tag (table row) defined. The Tabular Data Control and the table repetition agent take care of binding each record to this one definition. The code sets the **DATAPAGESIZE** attribute to 5 to limit the number of rows displayed at a time. Two navigation buttons appear at the top of the table for moving forward and backward a page at a time. Additionally, the **Name** and **Cuisine** columns have buttons that, when clicked, cause the page to sort the data.

Listing D.10   Data binding with the Tabular Data Control.
```
<HTML>
<HEAD>
<TITLE>Listing D.10 The Tabular Data Control</TITLE>
```

```
<SCRIPT LANGUAGE="JavaScript">
<!--

function sort(fld) {
     restData.sort = fld;
     restData.reset();
}

function fwd() {
     restSet.nextPage();
}

function back() {
     restSet.previousPage();
}
// -->
</SCRIPT>
</HEAD>
<BODY>

<OBJECT ID="restData" WIDTH=0 HEIGHT=0
CLASSID="CLSID:333C7BC4-460F-11D0-BC04-0080C7055A83">
     <PARAM NAME="DataURL" VALUE="restaurants.txt">
     <PARAM NAME="FieldDelim" VALUE=",">
     <PARAM NAME="UseHeader" VALUE=True>
</OBJECT>

<INPUT TYPE=BUTTON VALUE="<" onclick="back()">
<INPUT TYPE=BUTTON VALUE=">" onclick="fwd()">

<TABLE ID=restSet BORDER=1 DATASRC="#restData" DATAPAGESIZE="5">
<THEAD>
<TH><INPUT TYPE=BUTTON VALUE="Name" onclick="sort('Name')"></TH>
<TH><INPUT TYPE=BUTTON VALUE="Cuisine" onclick="sort('Cuisine')"></TH>
<TH>Hours</TH>
<TH>Address</TH>
<TH>Phone</TH>
</THEAD>
<TBODY>
<TR>
<TD><SPAN DATAFLD="Name"></SPAN></TD>
<TD><SPAN DATAFLD="Cuisine"></SPAN></TD>
<TD><SPAN DATAFLD="Hours"></SPAN></TD>
<TD><SPAN DATAFLD="Address"></SPAN></TD>
<TD><SPAN DATAFLD="Phone"></SPAN></TD>
</TR>
```

```
</TBODY>
</TABLE>

</BODY>
</HTML>
```

A Few Words About Scriptlets

DHTML is what makes Web pages powerful enough to stand alone as objects. That's the whole idea behind using scriptlets. A *scriptlet* is a Web page that behaves like an object, exposing properties, methods, and events to other Web pages.

You can find a sample scriptlet in Chapter 10. Without DHTML, Web pages could not alter themselves dynamically, which would make scriptlets almost worthless. For example, the Label scriptlet in Chapter 10 uses DHTML to modify a **<SPAN>** element, replacing the text inside to match a property.

Most of the time, scriptlets have properties, methods, and even events. However, some scriptlets just encapsulate some functionality that you want to reuse (or would like others to reuse). These scriptlets are very easy to create.

For example, consider Listing D.11, which contains the Burma-Shave sign Web page re-written as a scriptlet. This scriptlet is nothing more than a JavaScript object that contains the Burma-Shave sign logic. If the scriptlet is in the file toscript.htm, you can easily add it to another Web page (like that in Listing D.12), as follows:

```
<OBJECT ID="Burma" HEIGHT=50 WIDTH=450 TYPE="text/x-scriptlet"
      DATA=toscript.htm>
```

Of course, adding properties to make the component even more useful is easy enough. For example, you could set a property to alter the speed at which the sign changes. First, you would need to change the constant 2500 to use a variable instead. Then, you could add the property code, as in Listing D.13.

Listing D.11   The Burma-Shave scriptlet.

```
<HTML>
<HEAD>
<SCRIPT>
var i=0;
var msgs;

var public_description = new Burma();
```

```
function onTick() {
  setTimeout("onTick();",2500);
  document.all.spot.innerText=msgs[i];
  i++;
  if (i==6) i=0;
  }

function Burma() {
  msgs=new Array();
  }


function init() {
  msgs[0]="Every Day";
  msgs[1]="We Do";
  msgs[2]="Our Part";
  msgs[3]="To Make Your Face";
  msgs[4]="A Work of Art";
  msgs[5]="Burma-Shave";
  setTimeout("onTick();",1); // first timeout
  }

</SCRIPT>
</HEAD>
<BODY onLoad='init();'>
<H1 ALIGN=CENTER ID=spot></P>
</BODY>
</HTML>
```

Listing D.12   Using the Burma scriptlet.

```
<HTML>
<HEAD>
</HEAD>
<BODY>
<TABLE BORDER=1><TR><TD>
<OBJECT ID="Burma" HEIGHT=50 WIDTH=450 TYPE="text/x-scriptlet"
        DATA=toscript.htm>
</TD></TR>
</TABLE>
</BODY>
</HTML>
```

Listing D.13   Adding a property.

```
<HTML>
<HEAD>
<SCRIPT>
```

```
var i=0;
var msgs;
var dly=2500;

var public_description = new Burma();


function onTick() {
  setTimeout("onTick();",dly);
  document.all.spot.innerText=msgs[i];
  i++;
  if (i==6) i=0;
  }

function setDelay(d) {
  dly=d;
  }

function getDelay() {
  return d;
  }

function Burma() {
  msgs=new Array();
  this.put_delay=setDelay;
  this.get_delay=getDelay;
  }


function init() {
  msgs[0]="Every Day";
  msgs[1]="We Do";
  msgs[2]="Our Part";
  msgs[3]="To Make Your Face";
  msgs[4]="A Work of Art";
  msgs[5]="Burma-Shave";
  setTimeout("onTick();",1); // first timeout
  }

</SCRIPT>
</HEAD>
<BODY onLoad='init();'>
<H1 ALIGN=CENTER ID=spot></P>
</BODY>
</HTML>
```

Links

One of the interesting things you'll find on the Web is Web-based games that people have created by using DHTML:

- The following is a link to a DHTML video poker game: **www.insideDHTML.com/games/poker/video.asp**.
- To find free DHTML scripts to use, check out the following: **www.dynamicdrive.com**.
- For more information about DHTML, go to this site: **www.dhtmlzone.com/index.html**.

Notice that the constructor sets the **this.put_delay** and **this.get_delay** variables to point to the names of the functions that handle the **delay** parameter. Therefore, the container could set the speed by setting the parameter. For example, suppose you change the **<BODY>** tag in Listing D.12 to read:

```
<BODY onLoad='Burma.delay=100;'>
```

At 100 milliseconds, it will look like you are driving very fast indeed. Other properties could set text color, size, or even the text elements themselves.

DHTML In Review

In this appendix, you learned what you can do with DHTML. By combining the many features and functions of DHTML with script, you can create interesting and highly functional Web pages. Additionally, you can put much of the work on the client and, thereby, reduce the load on the server and provide a better experience for the user.

Although this book is about ASP, which by definition is on the server, you'll often find it necessary to combine client-side techniques and server-side techniques. Even if you don't have to, pushing some processing off to the client allows your server to be more responsive and handle larger loads. DHTML gives you more opportunities than ever to move processing to the client computer.

Appendix E
Design Considerations

Paul Newkirk

D o you remember the trend some years back toward "generic" groceries? The idea was that you could get a better price on, say, canned corn if you bought a can with a white label printed with the word "CORN" in big black letters. If you bought the name brand, you were paying for the color label and the picture of the corn, not to mention the advertising and other overhead costs. This marketing ploy was mildly successful for some products, but you don't see much of it anymore. Why? People have a natural inclination to believe their impressions. Something that looks better must be better in some way. After the infamous Nixon-Kennedy debates, a poll found that people who heard the debate on radio thought Nixon had won. Those who watched on TV, who saw Nixon squirm and sweat, thought Kennedy had won. As you can see, whether you like it or not, function is nothing without form.

The bulk of this book is about how to create interactive Web sites—the function. This appendix covers some steps you should be taking before you fire up your favorite editor to crank out your Web site so that it also has some form. Although you can find any number of sources telling you how to design a Web site, few take the holistic approach that you will get in this appendix, looking at the design issue from several different perspectives and disciplines.

Why You Need Design

A couple of the questions you might ask yourself when deciding to build a Web site—whether you are the developer, the manager, the marketing team, or whatever—are who should design your Web site and how should you do it?

The act of designing a site is often left to some kind of mutual agreement and loose arrangement based on personal ties. "Well, Joe said he could do it, and he did a good job on that other project." Even when a more formal approach is undertaken, with well-written plans, the results can be less than spectacular. For example, if only one group, such as engineers, is involved in creating and reviewing the plans, you can fall into a trap I call "validity without veracity." You can test whether whatever conditions you set out to meet are valid without checking outside the loop you set up to see if they are universally true. For example, you might set certain guidelines for the speed of operation of each part of the Web site. To meet these guidelines, you scrupulously watch the size of your graphics, and you avoid using scripts and applets that take a long time. If you finish your design, and your site meets all the specs, you might feel proud that you met your goals. However, the truth may be that although your users can easily navigate through your whole site in a reasonable amount of time, they can't easily find anything they want.

The First And Second Steps

The problem highlighted in the preceding section is one of the primary problems people face when trying to present information to other people. Most people are fully prepared to take the first step—dumping out all they know about whatever they are doing. Some are even prepared to organize the information they are presenting. But, fewer than one in ten (in my experience) understands what I call the second step. That second step is preparing data in a way that makes it accessible to all the people who may be trying to use it.

Most people think that after they have done the data dump, they're done. However, the real work (and value) comes in the second step—organizing the data.

Again and again, I look at sites and when asked to comment, say, as nicely as I can, "Yikes." The developers are all obviously smart people. The scripts they have coded work well. They have put a lot of thought into capturing all the data. They have even organized it in some way or another. However, they rarely have gone through the second step of organizing it for the types of people who might want to use it. They have done only half of the work. The sad part is, regardless of their hard work and good intentions and good coding, the site may be a failure because they didn't take the second step.

At my day job, I often hold mini-classes to impart the basics of design. This appendix draws from these sessions and some real-life examples.

Design: Who Can Help?

Before I describe design more fully, I think it is good to understand who can help in the design process, and further, what strengths and weaknesses they bring. The following categories of professionals can help in design:

- Software developers
- Technical writers
- Marketing specialists
- Users or user advocates
- Usability specialists
- Graphic designers/artists

Of course, you probably can think of many other occupations or titles, but most fit into the preceding categories. The professionals in each category have their strengths and weaknesses. I must admit that the following descriptions are generalizations based on my experience, but Table E.1 shows some strengths and weaknesses these people bring to a design effort.

Table E.1   Strengths and weaknesses of Web professionals.

Category	Strengths	Weaknesses
Software developers	Understand the technology of delivery Are inventive Are detail-oriented Are consistent Understand the limitations of technology	Often are not visually artistic Often are not very good with the written word (despite this, some vehemently feel the reverse, which leads to nonsense or ambiguous words becoming undeletable parts of systems) Are often weak at appreciating other groups' viewpoints
Technical writers	Can organize data hierarchically Can use words concisely Possess empathetic user advocacy skills Have some design skills	Often may not be visually artistic May not understand technology May place emphasis on form to the detriment of function
Marketing specialists	Usually know what the customers want Usually know what is "hot" or will sell Often clearly see the point (to sell more widgets), in contrast to engineers (who see building the widget as the goal)	Might not be technically adept May harm development and quality (for example, picking dates without asking engineering) May base decisions on instinct instead of data
Users or user advocates	Possess first-hand information Provide important data (via surveys or detailed interviews) Are the ultimate judges of success	Can provide accurate but perhaps useless information (you could create a product that does everything your users asked, but it still does not sell) Have no idea of what they want until they see it

(continued)

Table E.1 Strengths and weaknesses of Web professionals (continued).

Category	Strengths	Weaknesses
Usability specialists	Are trained to make Web sites more usable Use scientific methodology	Use time, manpower, and resources (may require a lab, equipment, several staff, and the time to collect and analyze the data) Provide worthwhile support, although some may find it hard to justify resources to management and to trace benefits to dollar figures
Graphic designers/artists	Are very good at the visual medium Use buttons, layout, and color dramatically better than others Believe that a picture can be worth a thousand words	May not be technical May not be good with words May go overboard with pointless graphics (as on many Shockwave sites)

Note

You also might wonder about a Web wizard. Well, it has been my experience that most Web wizards fit more or less into one of the preceding categories, with the same strengths and weaknesses.

As you can see in Table E.1, you might need to address many potential design pitfalls, depending on the composition of your design team. Keep this table in mind when you're building your team. You can also use the information in this table to try to make sure you balance the strengths and weaknesses of your team and are not caught unaware when a weakness turns up a flaw in your design. The following sections give additional information that might help you create a good design for your Web site.

Designing A Web Site: Some Preparatory Steps And Design Rules

Before you begin to build your site, take some time to write down your basic requirements. Listing your requirements doesn't have to take months. Writing down the basic requirements performs two functions: It forces you to think through what you're doing in a fairly systematic and complete way and it gives you the chance to have your requirements reviewed by others before you go to the design or construction phase. Why is this good? Fixing a misunderstanding is easy and cheap at the requirements phase. At that point, the fix requires only a change in a word processor, not recoding hundreds of lines of code or more.

Whom do you collect requirements from? Ideally, the first answer is always the users. But you also collect requirements from marketing, sales, field service personnel, and telephone support people—anyone who might have an idea. You can find whole books on requirements collection and different techniques for doing so. For the purposes of this appendix, simply collecting them and putting a priority by them would be a good start.

How Do You Collect Requirements?

You can collect requirements in many ways. As you can see from the preceding section, it is important you collect them from the appropriate people. When you decide to collect them, one way that works well is to get all the people involved in a room and just have them spit out their requirements. This approach allows some synergy between the groups who might not get together much, and it also allows some realtime prioritizing. For example, the engineering team might think that one requirement is really neat and a high priority, but if the marketing team says, "Nah, nobody cares about that," then it's good to know that information. In many cases, you might give the marketing team's votes more weight than the engineering team's because the marketing staff presumably know what the customers want.

I have been surprised in requirements-gathering sessions when a feature I would have planned to work on with some industry as a "must have" turned out to be a "luxury" item according to the marketing team. Finding out that information not only saves me the time I would have otherwise spent, but it also saves misunderstandings when I deliver something I'm proud of and the marketing staff say, "Yeah, so, what about the other features?"

Because this chapter is about design, I won't go into much more detail on requirements-gathering techniques. As a rule, though, you should take the time to collect and organize the requirements up front. You will find that this step takes a bit of extra time (sometimes up to several hours just to collect the raw requirements from one meeting), but it is well worth the effort. Generally, you should keep the requirements short and refrain from providing specific solutions. Answer the "what" and avoid the "how." Later efforts can describe how to meet the requirements. For example, "It should have an SQL database on an NT server using ASP Web pages to access the data" describes the "how." "Users need to be able to search from a Web page through 1,000 data sets" describes the "what." Now, when you are building Billy Bob's T-Shirt Web site, with over 500 T-shirts available for ordering, you might very well implement this requirement using SQL, NT, and ASP. But, in most cases, that is not a requirement.

You must be able to test requirements. Here is an untestable requirement: *The Web site should be attractive.* Who is to say what is attractive? A better requirement might be: *The Web site should appeal to the majority of our target demographic.* That is at least somewhat testable. An even better requirement is: *The Web site's main page will allow single-click access to all pages identified as major sections in the design document.* That, you can test.

Any requirement you can't objectively test is not a requirement at all. Remember, the two parts to this step are testing and objectivity. I might think the site is attractive, but I might just have offbeat tastes.

Changing Requirements

Changing requirements also is a big hang-up for some people. Maybe it is a fixation on the notion that "once it is on paper, it must be permanent" that makes changing requirements so difficult. Others might need to know all the requirements before beginning. Whatever the reason, if creating a requirements document is a hang-up, give yourself a break and don't take it so seriously. Requirements change, and sometimes you won't figure out half of your requirements until you've nearly finished development (as a process of discovery). Whatever the case, take your best shot at creating a requirements document, and you will be the better for it.

If you change your requirements and try to keep your requirements document up to date (as you should), you should keep all your old requirements in the document. Don't delete the ones you kill. Even better, try to put a date by your changes, and mark who made the decision (many Word processors, including Microsoft Word, have a revision-tracking feature—learn how to use it). If any confusion occurs during the development process, you can go back and easily figure out how you got to that point. Further, though you will probably delete a bunch of requirements along the way, the deleted and amended ones could make a very good source for the next version of your site. You could also use the progression of changes in a post-development analysis to see how the way you received and handled requirements made your jobs easier or harder; that way, you can make changes for the next time.

Surveying Other Sites Before Design

I suggest that you refrain from ever starting to design a site from scratch or in the dark. Before you begin your design, and before you pick your colors, graphics, and navigation methods, look around the Web to see what the competition is doing, what the experts are doing, or both. If possible, don't forget to check out your own company. It is amazing how many different kinds of Web sites exist in companies, each isolated group reinventing the wheel repeatedly.

There is an old saying that you are the sum total of everyone you've ever met in your life. In other words, everyone you meet has some effect on who you are. What people tend to forget is that some people add to you, and others subtract. Although you want to emulate sites you admire, you'll also want to learn from the sites you don't like. If you can quantify why you don't like a particular site, you can avoid making the same mistakes in your own design.

Creating A Design Document And Having It Reviewed

It also is well worth your time to create a design document, like the requirements document. At first, it will not be a final design document with screen shots and details of everything that will happen (though creating such a document may be worth your time later). To start, grab a huge white board, collect all the data you have to provide on your Web page, and write it all down. I use a circling technique, in which I circle different blobs of data. After you've written all the data or functionality on the board, you can start to group it. Most of the data on the board will lend itself to some association with other sets of data. Major groups will start to creep to the top.

For example, if you were creating Billy Bob's T-Shirt Site, the main categories that would float to the top might be "ordering," "catalog," "search," and "feedback/about." All other data or functionality you think of would probably fit under one of these categories. For example, if you wrote down "company history" and "company guarantee," they would both go under "feedback/about." If you wrote down "long sleeve" and "decals," they might require more thought. Often, you'll see a difference between the design of the user interface and the design of underlying components—what happens in front of the curtain and what happens behind. If you find yourself banging your head while trying to create your design, thinking of both at once, break these design elements apart.

I normally design the interface first, deciding how to best present the data and how it all logically fits together. Then, I decide how to make the design of the software that supports it work underneath the hood. You can document both of these components to great advantage. For one, documenting the process makes you carefully think out your plans. The mere exercise of doing this often reveals data and associations you might not have found otherwise until months into development. For another, writing down this information documents it for others who may benefit from it.

Basic Design Rules

The following sections provide a basic list of design rules I verbally give to newer Web developers in one form or another. They are practical hints to keep in mind while you're designing a Web site.

Keep It Simple

"Keep It Simple" is a shortened form of the well-known KISS rule. Simple really is best most of the time, and you can reach a point where too much cleverness is simply too much. If you are spending time with a troubling design element, and it keeps causing trouble, think about getting rid of it or treating it in a much simpler manner. You would be surprised how often this technique works or leads to a solution.

Navigation Bars/Aids

Most sites use a common navigation mechanism that is repeated throughout the site, or at least to the top-level pages of a site. You should take the time to design this element correctly. If you do, your users will not only know where they are in the context of your site, but also where else they can go and how to get there.

Designing this navigation mechanism can take a lot of time. This step requires that you do your homework for your users. Web sites are not like books, in which it is clear which direction is forward and which direction is back. In a book, it is immediately obvious where you are in relation to other locations in the book. In a generation or so, this sense of location may not matter. But, for the current generation of Web users raised on books, knowing and having a sense of where you are and how the information all fits together are very important from both a usability and a comfort standpoint. The only way you can provide this sense of location is through a structured effort at design and working with the data you have to display. You need to understand not only the relationships in the data, but the importance of these relationships to your users. Figure E.1 shows part of Yahoo!'s mechanism.

Notice that no matter how far down a path you go at Yahoo!, you have a simple contextual map to show you where you are. Not only that, but you can click on any of the words in the map to go back to the level you want (which is faster than one-level-at-a-time Back button progression).

Figure E.2 shows Amazon.com in action. Notice the index card–like approach here. No matter where you are on Amazon.com, you can see where you are on the site and quickly click to another part of the site by using this card approach.

An approach that is much simpler to develop uses just a colored bar down the side or across the top of a page, with the main links for the whole site listed there. You repeat it on each main page of your site. Then, you can use tables to place the navigation items on the bar. See Appendix C, which covers HTML, for information on one way to create a colored bar on your page.

Determine A Maximum Number Of Items Per Page

You also should figure out some maximum number of items per page. On some sites I have seen lately, the designers have gone overboard stuffing more and more data on one single page. The effect, to my mind, is grating. The ultimate number you should use is somewhere between 6 and 16 items, depending on how you count and how well you design and stuff your data.

Consider Yahoo!, for example. Its main categories of "Arts Humanities," "Reference," and so on include 14 divisions of data. If you have too many divisions on your site, your users will reach a point where they would find it hard to intuitively tell whether what they want is in division A or one of the other three or four divisions that sound similar. If your users are

Figure E.1
Yahoo! exemplifies a useable, structured navigational design.

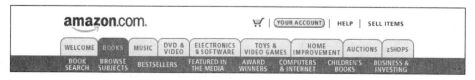

Figure E.2
Amazon.com uses an index-card approach.

confused or find themselves having to guess, you haven't done your job properly, and you might lose customers. I think Yahoo! has done a good job of dividing its data because I usually can sort my way through the pages without feeling lost, confused, or even stupid.

Here's one point to keep in mind: Try never to have what I call "miscellaneous" sections. You probably know what they are. You're dividing the data, and you have some leftover pieces. So, you come up with a term that covers all the stuff you can't figure out where to put but which, in itself, means nothing intuitively. It really means that, if all else fails, look here. Such a section is a shining example of poor design and what is more likely than not a bit of laziness. Take the time. Figure out where the data goes and what to call it, and your users will be the happier for your efforts.

No Scrolling (Long Pages)

Having to scroll is a pet peeve of mine, but I see it violated a lot and quite often without any good reason. Simply stated, try to avoid making your users scroll down your page to see important information on your Web site. Try to keep your sites to one screen. Recently, I went to a truck site (see the examples later in this appendix), and the very important Next button was scrolled off the edge of my screen. I clicked on more than a few things on the page trying to figure out how to go on, but nothing worked. Finally, by chance, I scrolled down and saw the Next button. A wise designer would have put it at the top of the page. I think that in very few instances (other than listings of features and catalogs in which you expect a long page) should main pages require you to scroll down. If you do have a long page, make sure you take that fact into account when you design your site (for example, consider what happens if the bottom half is cut off).

Reuse Items Such As Graphics

A well-designed site can take advantage of a sort of graphics pool. These graphics are used for dividing pages, providing navigation, and so on. You can store them all in the same graphics directory. You then can pull them from that same directory when you create your Web pages. Later, when you want to update your Web site, you know where to go (one place). And, if your company colors change from red and black to green and white, you can change a few graphics in one place and essentially update your entire site.

Create A Directory And Naming Scheme

Before you begin building your Web site, you should think about (and even design and write down) a basic naming scheme and even a directory scheme for the site. This tip might seem obvious to you. However, if you do not come up with a naming scheme, you might be in the middle of editing the files in your second directory, naming them all differently than the first, because you thought of an even better naming scheme. Four weeks later, when you go back to find a file, you'll have to re-create the logic you used at the time you created the files (logic made up on the fly) instead of using a scheme that is predictable and repeatable.

I once created a directory for certain types of files, and the first one I called file.ext. The next one I called file2.ext and then file3.ext, and so on. This naming scheme is messy because you have to figure out that the unnumbered one is the first. So, on my next directory, I used file01.ext, file02.ext, and so on. This scheme works better until you get to 100 files. But even something as simple as deciding on using .html or .htm consistently can save time later. Having wisely named directories also helps if you name them correctly up front.

Provide A Standards Document

If it is appropriate and you have a corporate intranet site (as opposed to an extranet site), you might be wise to create a standards document for your site as you design and build it. In many intranet sites, one person or group may maintain the top layers of the site, but other groups often maintain sublayers or subsites. Providing a standards document with naming schemes, assumptions on graphics and navigation, and so on may help reduce confusion and even save these other groups time in developing their sites.

No New Paradigms

Sound like a famous politician who likes lip reading? In this case, "no new paradigms" is a promise worth keeping. What does it mean? People have expectations about how they surf the Web. Over time, those expectations slowly change and evolve. But, whatever you do, you should avoid making your site radically depart from those expectations to do something really neat and cool (just because you like it). If you do, you do so at your own risk.

If you remember your basic HTML, you remember that pictures turned into hypertext links, by default, have a blue border. That's because, at one time, no one would have expected that you could click on a picture (back then, surfers were used to pretty much ASCII everything). Now, you hide that blue border because it looks old, and everyone knows to click on pictures (some might even say, "what, there was a time we couldn't?"). But, I have seen quite a few Web sites ruined, in my opinion, because the designers decided to give the sites a Notes or Windows (or other specialized) type of look. Most of the people used to surfing the Web in its standard form were left scratching their heads at these sites, while trying to figure out an unfamiliar user interface. I find it irritating when I am forced to learn a new paradigm at somebody's site. One of the nicest aspects of the Web is its near universality of operational paradigms. You should think twice before subverting that, no matter how clever you think you are (see also "Keep It Simple").

Three-Color Rule

I got my three-color rule from a house painter. I know what I think is pretty, but I have very little intuition about why some colors go together to make a beautiful effect. And, although I might hunt and peck my way along to some success, that success is a long way off from what the artistically inclined are usually able to create in short order. These people can not only make the site succeed but make it say "wow." One such person gave me a rule about house painting. He had recently painted a historic house that was hardly noticeable, and afterward, it was stunning. He said to never use more than three colors in a room or on a house. Believe it or not, this rule works. I apply the same principle to the Web. Go to any big site on the Web, and count the colors. You will find most often that the predominant color is white (which doesn't count in most cases if it represents the background of the page), and the site usually has three or fewer theme colors throughout. You can see some bleeding over this line, for example with the use of dark or light versions of one of the colors or several shades of gray. But, keep the three-color rule in mind. Using only three colors can make your site look a lot better than if it has colors all over the place.

The Résumé Rule (Five Seconds)

When you're designing your site, think of it as a résumé. You have maybe five seconds and five bullet entries on your résumé before a hiring manager decides to look deeper into your résumé or go on to the next (he or she probably has 30 or so to look at each week). If you have meticulously organized your data as described in the preceding sections, you should be okay. However, you should test your Web site with this rule in mind. Can users get to what they want in five or so clicks? They want to read only a few lines, and not even whole lines at that. Don't presume anyone wants to read your site or to sort through the stuff on your page to find the meat. Put it out for them, and make it easy to find.

An example from the résumé world helps. I've seen many résumés that highlight where people worked, the dates, the addresses of the companies, followed by blocks of text describing what they did. You have to read these résumés carefully to see what the titles were and what these people did. Using the five-second rule, an interviewer might say, "Worked at Smith Industries, did something," and go on. A person might have been the vice president of engineering and created 57 patents, but that information wasn't on top of the résumé or easy to find, although the company name and address was.

The same rule applies for Web page design. One of the reasons sites fail and one of the reasons I never go back to them is that they contain pointless animations and folderol that may have been neat to build and may look neat the first time through but mostly make it hard to find what I want in five seconds or less.

If It Isn't Broke, Don't Fix It

I used to use Lycos extensively. At one time, it was the fastest search engine, and I preferred the way it presented its data. I could easily sift through and find the meat. I don't recall when I switched (sometime in 1999), but Lycos seemed to have been made over (probably to generate more revenue), and it seemed to get much slower and had a higher noise-to-signal ratio. I had used Lycos for years, but the design change led to enough flaws to frustrate me into investigating other options. Make sure you don't fall into the same trap—redesigning a perfectly acceptable site. Don't make changes for the sake of the change.

Try It Out On Multiple Browsers And Screen Resolutions

Finally, you should be sure to try your Web page on multiple browsers and screen resolutions. This point might seem obvious, but I see problems from people not checking their pages all the time. A Web page doesn't fit right, colors are rendered differently, scripts don't work the same way on different browsers—all these problems combine to make a colossal "oops." Most people develop and test with the browser of their choice on the screen resolution and size they have. They don't think to resize the graphics display options on their PCs to see what happens. Or, they don't fire up another browser or minimize the browser or even maximize it.

I used a graphic that worked for years, and then all of a sudden, it started doing things I hadn't intended. When I developed it, people did not have, for the most part, anything bigger than 15-inch monitors. Now, people mostly have 17-inch monitors, so you need to take these factors into consideration when you're creating a design.

If you design a table that works well on your 17-inch monitor, but most of your users use a laptop, should you make the table smaller, or is it okay for them to have to scroll to get all the data? I think scrolling is sloppy, but in some cases, it is inevitable.

In any case, when you're designing a site, you should take these issues into consideration before you release your pages.

Sales Letter Tips

It is surprising how similar Web pages are to sales letters and advertisements. When a junk mail envelope appears in your mail box, it has to entice you to open it, and then it has just a matter of seconds to hook you into reading the contents. Even then, the eventual goal is to get you to call a toll-free number, return a response coupon, or plunk down some cash.

As you might expect, writing sales letters is a well-known art. Let me share a few tips that copywriters know:

♦ Use power words such as *you, free, discovery, guaranteed,* and *secret.*

♦ Use bullet lists to attract attention. (You're reading this one, aren't you?)

♦ Use action verbs rather than passive ones. Say, "Make a fortune," not "A fortune can be made by you."

♦ Use subheadings to attract readers who skim.

♦ Use white space to break up copy.

♦ Make sentences and paragraphs as short as possible.

♦ Ask for what you want the readers to do.

♦ Put yourself in your readers' place.

An old rule of thumb is to achieve AIDCA: Attention, Interest, Desire, Conviction, Action. Your copy should accomplish these objectives. It should command attention, hold interest, evoke desire, generate conviction, and then spur the readers to the desired action.

You might think these tips apply only to Web pages that sell products, but every Web site sells something—even if it is only itself. Do you want the users to return on another day? Perhaps you want to influence the readers' opinions about something. Maybe you want the readers to enjoy some subject you are passionate about. In all these cases, you are selling ideas that are just as much a commodity as products.

A Tale Of Four Web Sites

What better way to show some design do's and don'ts than by example? Because some of these sites may change radically in the time that this book goes to and stays in print, I've taken a few screen shots so that the examples I explain stay relevant to the site being described.

Site One: Yahoo!

One of my favorite examples of how to do things right is at Yahoo!. The Yahoo! staff manages to cram a ton of stuff on each page, as shown in Figure E.3, but it is all nicely organized and hierarchically divided, with several ways for you to navigate and approach pages (all of

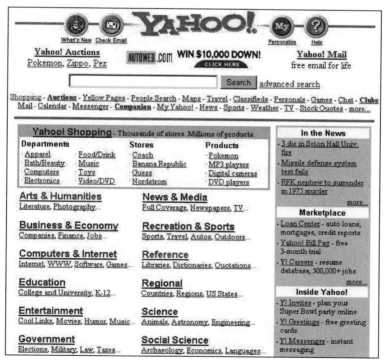

Figure E.3
A typical Yahoo! page contains plenty of information.

them good). The page has some graphics, to give it an appealing look. You'll notice that almost all the graphics are very tiny, so although the site uses graphics and color to nice effect, none of it takes very long to load. The site loads quickly, whether you use a T-1 line or a 28.8Kbps modem.

If you use the résumé rule, what are the most important things you want to do at Yahoo!? You want to find something, of course. What stands out most prominently on the page? The search tool is prominently displayed at the top where you can find it. What else? Sets of data are grouped. The first group contains more references to specific types of data resources (shopping, yellow pages, maps, weather, quotes), and the next group contains types of Web pages you might be looking for (reference, entertainment, business and economy). In case you can't tell the difference at the higher level (for example, between Recreation and Entertainment), further clarification is provided at half the size.

One last nod to Yahoo!'s good design: It clearly segregates the data as you move down in the hierarchy. When you search, you don't find all 5,000 entries on a particular topic on the Web, which would be hard to go through 20 or 50 at a time.

Site Two: Amazon.com

Another site to look at is Amazon.com, as shown in Figure E.4. Notice the three ways to get around this site at the top level. You can use the tabbed section at the top, the search mechanism at the top left (where all Western readers look first), and the Browse section. The middle thing seems kind of a waste, but it really doesn't matter because the site is otherwise so accessibly designed.

Figure E.4
Amazon's top-level page.

Sites Three And Four: Newspapers (latimes.com And CNN.com)

Another place to look for examples of good and bad design is newspapers. You can take your choice and see how they do or do not live up to the loose set of rules I outlined earlier. The *Los Angeles Times* recently redid its site (see Figure E.5). I would include it on a list of how not to design a site. More often than not, the Java working behind the scenes takes awhile to load the page. And lately the site went to a split-page look, with one side being a custard yellow background with blue text on top. I find the layout and colors hard to take, though I generally like the paper.

The middle of the page (where the yellow and white meet)—where, for some reason, I want to look—is mostly blank. And, because I have to look left or right to see anything, instead of where I want, I am immediately put off by the site (refer to the "no new paradigm" rule).

Other papers, such as the *Washington Post*, the *New York Times*, or CNN.com, have taken a more traditional approach. And, though most of them break the one-page rule, I don't mind because the data is fairly well organized as I go down the page into sections, and I am used to papers being long.

For another example, look at CNN.com's page, which is shown in Figure E.6. As you scroll down this page, as shown in Figure E.7, notice the nicely divided sections for quick browsing.

Figure E.5
The *Los Angeles Times* has great content, but poor design.

Figure E.6
CNN's page is too long to view all at once on most monitors.

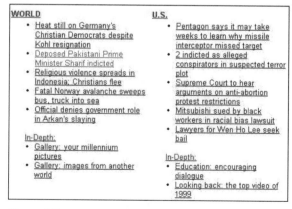

Figure E.7
CNN's page has easy-to-navigate sections.

A More Detailed Look (Putting Four Sites To The Design Test)

Another way to improve and even rate your design is to put it to some kind of roughly objective test. Throughout the rest of this appendix, I will tell a little story, to give the tests a background. Then, I will describe my goals. Finally, I will describe several sites to see how they measure up.

To illustrate this part of the design do's and don'ts, I decided to take a look at some sites from more traditional businesses that do not really make money from their sites but provide them more as customer service or some sort of extended advertising. I chose to visit some automotive sites.

I never thought I would be a truck person. However, a couple of years ago, a friend loaned me the keys to his truck (to use whenever I needed it). When he upgraded to a newer model, I bought his old truck. A nice way of saying it is that my truck is a classic. It's paid for, it runs dependably, and I can haul plywood, lumber, and landscaping stones any time I want (which is a must for a person owning an old house).

Recently, my wife's car was in the shop, and I borrowed my friend's newer truck (she didn't want to drive a full-sized pickup with a stick, so she borrowed my truck). Although I had never been unhappy with my classic (the "beast"), you can imagine what happened. Driving the newer truck got me thinking—not seriously, but enough to go out to the Web sites and have a look. After all, isn't that what most marketing and advertising people live for? They live for the chance that somebody will come into their store, with "maybe" on his mind, and while they have him there, whatever magic their profession gives them will turn that maybe into a buying decision.

I don't want to go into great detail on my needs, but they help to illustrate the points later. I currently have simple needs. If I were to upgrade my truck, I would want a full-sized pickup with a full-sized bed and likely a big enough engine (V-8). That's it. Of course, I would like the extended cab and four-wheel drive and aluminum wheels and V-10 and moon roof—I would just never for an instant consider paying for them. So, my rough needs are a full-sized pickup with a V-8 engine. I might be enticed into some extra features such as an extended cab or air conditioning or a towing package, but probably not.

Because I have never owned a truck prior to this one, and neither has anyone in my family, I have scant idea what the different models are for each manufacturer. I don't intuitively know the difference between an F-150 and an F-250 or the Rams and Sonomas and so on. I have only a rough idea that I can choose a full-sized one or a little one.

My goal, then, was to go to the big three auto makers and find out the cost to buy a basic, full-sized pickup at each. I wanted to see the basic model at Ford and Dodge, and at GM I wanted to learn the difference between a Chevy and a GMC.

Half the value of the Web for surfers is that it provides the ability to find information quickly and easily. No trips to the library, no asking four friends, no finding out from this or that esoteric source, no more being at the mercy of car salespeople. You can find the raw, unvarnished data for yourself to make your own decisions. Or, can you?

Again, to be fair, maybe some car makers have decided that they don't want you to have that information. Maybe they want you to have to go to the car salesperson and the show-room to find out anything intelligent in five questions or fewer. However, that seems somewhat unlikely, because in the Web age, you are just as likely to go to another site to find your data (and the spin there, they have no control over). So, you can presume car makers intend to give you the information you want in a reasonable time and reasonably enjoyably.

Ground Rules

For each of the sites I'll describe, I'll provide a couple of screen shots and comments on the design of each. At the end of this appendix, I'll provide a design test table based on my stated needs.

For the first trip, I went to GM. I already drive a Chevy truck, and when I was growing up in a steel town, my family always drove GM. (I think most of the steel was sold to GM.) So, my first goal was to figure out what the basic Chevy and GMC trucks are called, what features they have, and what are the basic costs.

Chevrolet

The Chevrolet home page is shown in Figure E.8. What I don't like about this page is that it looks more like an advertisement than a Web page. It's pretty, but it breaks the paradigm, so I had to figure out how to use it. For a minute or so, I was waiting for it to go away (like an intro video) and take me to the real page. After a while, it didn't, so I had to figure out how to get around.

I saw the truck, and when I moved my mouse pointer over it, "Chevy Trucks" came up to light the way—sort of. So, I clicked. The next page, shown in Figure E.9, was worse.

Better than half of the page is either pictures or advertising fluff. The only three pieces of real data I could see (and where it told me to click) were in the lower-left corner. I couldn't figure out why those three things were the top items on the page, but because I didn't want a commercial vehicle, nor did I care about partners, I clicked on the confusing third item, "Deals" (by process of elimination).

This item turned out to have been the wrong place to click. Here's an important lesson: Whenever you're designing a site, you never want your users to have to choose by trial and error or by a process of elimination. This is poor design.

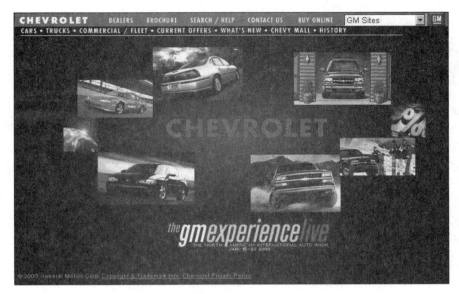

Figure E.8
The Chevrolet page looks like a print advertisement.

Figure E.9
The Chevrolet site has a confusing navigation scheme.

When I finally decided "Deals" was not the place I wanted to go, I went back to the top of "Trucks" to look at it again. I was on the truck page and thinking, while looking at the top, "I don't have to click on 'Trucks' again do I? I am already on the trucks page." But, I guessed again by process of elimination and clicked on "Trucks".

The menu bar at the top listing the truck models (shown in Figure E.10) would be a nice touch if it weren't for the rest of the page. When I moved the mouse pointer over the truck names, I got the picture of each model. Still not knowing which truck was which, I had to guess. I knew that C/K Pickup, S-10 Pickup, and Silverado were pickup trucks, but again I was left to guess which was which. So, I guessed C/K and went to a page with a cowboy on it.

By now, I just wanted to know what a basic model cost, so I clicked on "Pricing" and saw that the basic model cost around $20,000. The cost made me think that the C/K wasn't a plain old truck model. I tried to figure out what it would cost with air conditioning, just in case, but it was very hard to tell with all the "this or that" package group nonsense.

Next, I tried S-10, and although this page had lots of graphic doo-dads, I quickly realized the S-10 was not a full-sized pickup and decided to go to the Silverado page (and yet another graphics-laden intro). By now, I just wanted to see the price on a basic truck but felt I was on the right track because this page compared the Silverado to Ford's and Dodge's best-selling full-sized trucks. But, alas, there was no price on this page. Not only that, no features were listed on this page. I found only the options shown in Figure E.11.

In which of these selections, I wondered, could I find truck options or price? I had no clue. Once again, because no other options were listed, I chose by process of elimination. I clicked on "Performance," then clicked on "Pricing," and then I had to guess to click on "STD" (from a bunch of acronyms that meant nothing to me). I had to wait for another picture to come up; then I saw a base price of roughly $16,000. That was more like it. Dare I try to

Figure E.10
This Chevrolet page has an interesting navigation scheme, but is still too confusing.

Figure E.11
Price is conspicuously absent on this Silverado page.

figure out what it would cost to add AC and a V-8? Should I risk more graphics swashing across my page when all I wanted was a simple list? No.

GMC

After visiting the Chevrolet home page, I turned to the GMC home page, which is shown in Figure E.12. From the first look, I felt this was an excellently designed site. It is clean, it is simple, and it looks like a Web page. When I moved the mouse pointer over the models, instantly a picture of each model appeared with a useful description (full-size or mid-size). The information appeared all on one page, and I could figure it out without having to do one click or search.

I clicked on Sierra, and at the second page (see Figure E.13), I was again amazed. Right where I wanted it, I found a price for a base model (roughly $17,000), and I saw buttons that I wanted to see, such as Engines and Features. At that point, the design falls down a bit because I had to figure out the model and so on, and the site didn't easily show prices for each. It did have a fairly nice comparison feature, in which I could compare a model to other manufacturers' models. This comparison is a brave feature, especially if the manufacturer you're checking doesn't come out on top. But, in the vehicle comparison feature and the comparison pricing feature, I saw what I wanted to see a step or two up (like how much it would cost to get AC). What a great use of an application to enhance a site.

Figure E.12
GMC's page is clean and follows standard Web conventions.

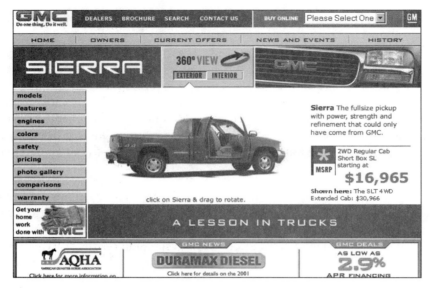

Figure E.13
The Sierra's price is readily accessible.

Dodge

The next site I visited, Dodge's site, was nice although it is hard to find because somebody else seems to own dodge.com. When I figured out it is **www.4adodge.com** (see Figure E.14), I was ready to test its design.

This site uses only a few colors—red and variations on white or black. The design is very crisp, clean, and small. When I moved the mouse pointer over the models listed, I got instant pictures—a very nice feature.

Here, I clicked on Ram Pickup and went to a page that was mostly a picture and one option—Create Your Ram Pickup (see Figure E.15). Again, this design is an example of sending your users to places where they have to guess how to get where they want to go.

To me, "Create Your Ram Pickup" sounded like many extra mouse clicks, so I clicked on "Price". Well, I didn't save any time. Clicking on this option took me to the same place that "Create Your Ram Pickup" does.

I had to select a state and a model year. Then, I went to a six-step page (shown in Figure E.16) for which the design is confusing.

First, I didn't know whether I wanted to go through six pages of stuff. Second, I didn't know what any of these terms meant, such as *club* or *quad*. So, deciding to ignore it all and just take the defaults, I looked for how to go on. I clicked on "Step Two" (nothing happened), I clicked on the picture of the truck (nothing happened), and finally I realized I needed to scroll down until I saw the Next button.

Figure E.14
This Dodge page has a pleasant and easy-to-follow appearance.

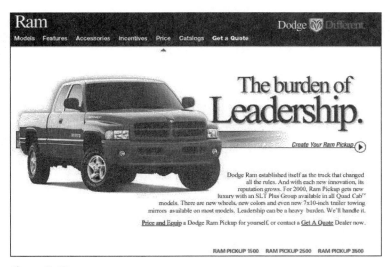

Figure E.15
The links on this page are not very meaningful.

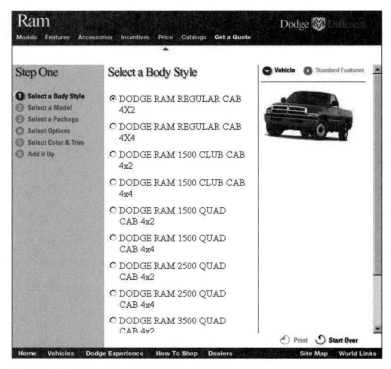

Figure E.16
Confusing steps to create a truck.

I could see what the items in the radio button list were by scrolling down the box below the picture of the truck. But, the textboxes were not as large as they could be, so I was forced to read the information five lines at a time. At each step, I was forced to find the Next button at the bottom of the page (off my screen). At first, I couldn't figure out how to move to the next step! It wouldn't have hurt to put it at the top. That would have made it more obvious, and would also allow it to be in the same position for each step.

I eventually found a rough price and options list, so I was happy with that. However, maneuvering through this site could have been easier.

Ford

One of my friends owns an F-150. I always thought Fords had the worst interiors on the planet. But, that is my memory from the early 1980s, and my friend's new F-150 is as luxurious as any sedan on the inside.

Because I liked my friend's truck, I decided to check out the Ford site. Ford has a fairly clean Web site, as you can see in Figure E.17.

Figure E.17
The Ford Web site's main page.

Features are listed in order of likely importance from left to right, and they prominently display a search mechanism. I selected "Browse Our Products" and went to the page shown in Figure E.18.

This page is nice. Like Amazon.com, it offers several ways to go. I could use one of several pull-down lists, or I could use the list on the left side of the page. To avoid being unfair to the other companies, because I already knew what an F-150 was, I chose Trucks from the menu at the left. On the generic truck screen, it was hard to tell which one was which, but going left to right, I guessed that the Ranger is smaller and the F-250 looks like a moose. So, without knowing it, I might have deduced what I probably wanted is the F-150.

When I clicked on this truck, I went to the page shown in Figure E.19. I clicked around, but my only options on this huge page seemed to be the ones shown in Figure E.20.

Here, I selected "Build It Online." The design got pretty bad at this point, because I had already made a bunch of decisions, and when I got here, it didn't remember any of them. I had to start again from scratch. So, I went back to the page shown in Figure E.21.

Figure E.18
Browsing the Ford catalog.

Figure E.19
Ford's model-specific page.

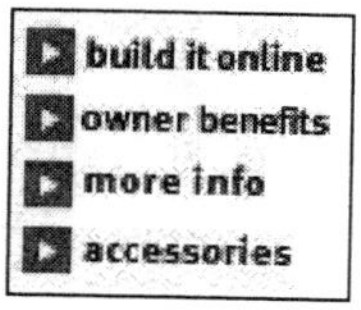

Figure E.20
More confusing options.

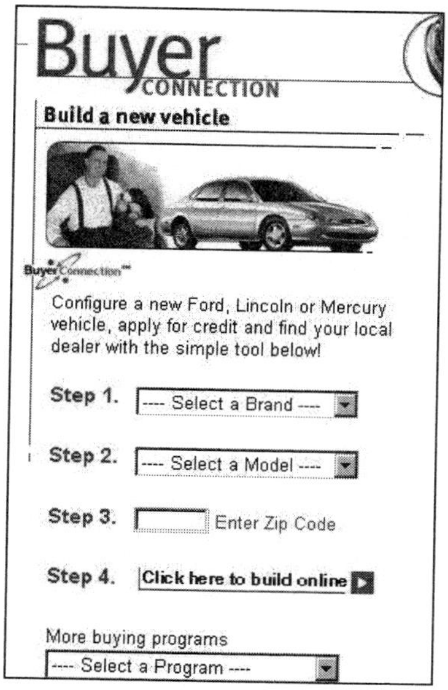

Buyer
CONNECTION

Build a new vehicle

Buyer Connection™

Configure a new Ford, Lincoln or Mercury
vehicle, apply for credit and find your local
dealer with the simple tool below!

Step 1.   [---- Select a Brand ---- ▼]

Step 2.   [---- Select a Model ---- ▼]

Step 3.   [   ] Enter Zip Code

Step 4.   [Click here to build online ▶]

More buying programs
[---- Select a Program ---- ▼]

Figure E.21
Reentering information for Ford.

At this point, I entered "Ford", selected F-150 (both for the second time), and entered my ZIP code (which I didn't want to do). Unfortunately, from there, I went to a useless page (see Figure E.22).

Once again, I had made choices, and here I got a picture that had nothing to do with what I wanted (even though I had made several selections), a bunch of text I didn't want to read, and a button I had to guess to find (it's the triangle). So, I had to click on "Start Building" again.

From this point on, however, the system was fairly well designed. In fact, I think it was very easy to use to do what I wanted to do after I figured it out. I wanted to add AC and a V-8, and I wanted to see a basic price. I didn't want to figure out anything else. So, I clicked on "Power" and added a V-8, and the page said these options cost more and added some option package or another (see Figure E.23).

Figure E.22
This picture really didn't match what I had selected.

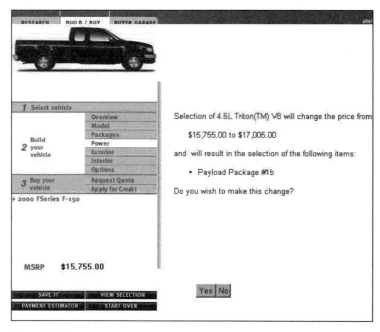

Figure E.23
Price information—finally.

I said, "Okay." I clicked on "Interior", found out that section didn't hold the checkbox for AC, and then clicked on "Options" (which did). At the top of this page was AC with a price! How nice. I clicked on "AC" and immediately got a new price, as shown in Figure E.24.

From the "Configure A Vehicle" part down, the site was very easy to read and the easiest to get what I wanted (after getting past the top few pages).

Final Ratings

So, after reading my descriptions (or better yet, visiting the sites yourself), how do you rate the Web sites on design? Some had good and bad features mixed together; some had more of one than the other. To rate the sites, you must define your design criteria.

In the preceding examples, my goal was to find out how much a basic, full-sized truck with a V-8 and air conditioning would cost. In doing that, I realized I might have to figure out which vehicles were the full-sized trucks. I didn't want to become a genius on any one company's model names or feature sets. Ideally, I would have liked to learn everything I wanted to know in five or fewer clicks. Plus, I had hoped to have an overall nice experience in which I didn't waste clicks getting lost or waiting for a bunch of graphics to bop around for no reason.

Based on the sites examined in this appendix, I created a table (Table E.2), giving a rating of 0 to 10, with 10 being the highest rating. You can do the same. After you fill out your table for your own site based on your own criteria, you will know where to make improvements.

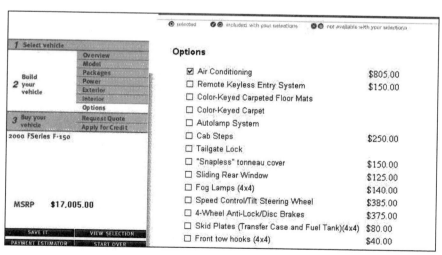

Figure E.24
Adding the air conditioning.

Table E.2 My final ratings for the Big Three.

Test	Chevrolet	GMC	Ford	Dodge
First impression, topmost page	5 (graphical but confusing)	10 (clear and concise)	6 (reasonable but nothing special)	8 (nice, but un-related "noise" on page; for example, a huge presence for NASCAR dwarfing the primary parts of the page)
Some navigation mechanism on top page (such as a bar)	6 (page below made it confusing)	8 (visually crisp, nice on models, but top bars do not provide fully intuitive snap-shot of site; for example, what does clicking on "Owner" get you?)	0 (down one level)	8 (nice)
Evident search button on top page	7	7	10	0
Multiple paths to destination from top page (not including Search)*	5 (not intuitive)	0 (but okay because so clearly done at top of page)	0 (pretty much one path from top, not even clear which one)	5 (nice, but tiny in relation to rest of page)
Graphics annoyance factor or pointless advertising junk	10	1	2	1
Satisfaction with number of clicks to goal**	0	4	4	4
Mis-clicks rating (got lost or had to guess direction)	8	1***	6	4
Data successfully found	2	6	9	8
Exit/completion satisfaction rating	1	4	7	6

*Two or more menus or navigation bars were available on the same page.

**On GMC and Dodge, I don't know that I ever really felt like I reached my goal, and though I did on Ford and liked the tail end of it, the front end was not very good.

***To be fair, GMC has far fewer product lines and models, so its site should be easier.

Conclusion On The Truck Site Designs

Based on my descriptions and the preceding table, you will notice that some groups started great and finished badly; others started badly and finished pretty well. Chevrolet seems to have put more of its design money into graphics and snazzy-looking features to the utter detriment of its site's users. To me, this approach is an absolute waste of money, especially if all the users walk away annoyed. It is okay to have a snazzy and pretty site, but you must have a good design underneath it first.

On the sites for some companies, such as Ford, I had to enter data several times at the beginning, which is a poor design strategy. However, later the presentation of the data, options, and prices was very simple and clear. These sites made good use of the medium. Dodge came in close in some ways; however, its tables and navigation were unwieldy at the option selection level (and for some reason didn't use the entire screen available), and the typefaces in some parts looked clunky.

If I had to go out and buy a truck at this point, I don't know which one I would buy. But, none of these sites (sponsored by deep-pocketed companies) made it exceedingly appealing for me to choose them. Better design would have prevented some of my indecision. For the record, you would probably be better off going to a car shopping site like **cars.yahoo.com**, anyway.

Design Wrap-Up

The point behind this appendix was mostly to give you some ideas to think about before you build a Web site. You should consider these points for many reasons, but the primary ones are:

♦ Carefully designing the site will likely make it much easier for your users to use your Web site.

♦ Taking the time up front makes it much easier to maintain your site over time.

Failing to make things easy for users causes you to lose customers; failing to make your site maintainable costs you a lot of money whenever you have to update or change your site. A well-thought-out design is easier to change over time, whereas a hacked design becomes increasingly more cumbersome to hold together, especially as a site grows. Creating a design test table might help you validate your design and site.

Final words? Design early and design well. Doing so will make everything go much more smoothly and make your site more effective.

Index

H

Related Coriolis Technology Press Titles

Active Server Pages Solutions

By Al Williams, Kim Barber, and Paul Newkirk
ISBN: 1-57610-608-X
Price: $49.99 US • $74.99 CAN
Available Now

Explores all the components that work with Active Server Pages, such as HTML (including Dynamic HTML), scripting, Java applets, Internet Information Server, Internet Explorer and server-side scripting for VBScript, Jscript, and ActiveX controls. Offers practical examples using commonly used tools.

HTML Black Book

By Steven Holzner
ISBN: 1-57610-617-9
Price: $49.99 US • $74.99 CAN
Available: May 2000

Explores HTML programming thoroughly, from the essentials up through issues of security, providing step-by-step solutions to everyday challenges. This comprehensive guide discusses HTML in-depth, as well as covering XML, dynamic XML, JavaScript, Java, Perl, and CGI programming, to create a full Web site programming package.

Java Black Book

By Steven Holzner
ISBN: 1-57610-531-8
Price: $49.99 US • $74.99 CAN
Available Now

A comprehensive reference filled with examples, tips, and solved problems. Discusses the Java language, Abstract Windowing Toolkit, Swing, Java 2D, advanced java beans, the Java Database Connectivity Package, servlets, internalization and security, streams and sockets, and more.

XML Black Book

By Natanya Pitts-Moultis and Cheryl Kirk
ISBN: 1-57610-284-X
Price: $49.99 US • $73.99 CAN
Available Now

Covers everything from markup and Document Type Definition (DTD) design, to the most popular XML-based markup applications, to best practices you can put to work right away. Demonstrates successful implementation of XML projects. A comprehensive reference for XML designers and content developers.

Visual Basic 6 Black Book

By Steven Holzner
ISBN: 1-57610-283-1
Price: $49.99 US • $69.99 CAN
Available Now

Completely explains the crucial Visual Basic tool set in detail. Jam-packed with insight, programming tips and techniques, and real-world solutions. Covers everything from graphics and image processing, to ActiveX controls, database development and data-bound controls, multimedia, OLE automation, Registry handling, error handling and debugging, Windows API, and more.

Visual Basic 6 Core Language Little Black Book

By Steven Holzner
ISBN: 1-57610-390-0
Price: $24.99 US • $36.99 CAN
Available Now

Provides a detailed reference on all Basic control structures, data types, and other code mechanisms. Includes step-by-step instructions on how to build common code structures in VB, from simple if statements to objects and ActiveX components. Not merely a syntax summary, but a detailed reference on creating code structures with VB6 code and data elements.

THE CORIOLIS GROUP, LLC   Telephone: 1.800.410.0192 • www.coriolis.com
Coriolis books are also available at bookstores and computer stores nationwide.

What's On The CD-ROM

The *Active Server Pages Solutions* companion CD-ROM contains elements specifically selected to enhance the usefulness of this book, including:

◆ *Halcyon iASP*—Allows you to run ASP on any server that supports Java.

◆ *Summit Software Open ASP*—An open source implementation of ASP for Win32 Apache and Netscape servers.

◆ *CtrlSoft QuoteBoy*—Obtains realtime stock quotes for free. (Registration is required if you want support.)

◆ *Visual ASP Component Pack*—Allows you to add several useful ASP components, including progress bars, tree views, and a calendar.

◆ All the example code, including several versions of the King Web site, along with the example ActiveX controls and Java applets.

Be sure to check out the Coriolis Web site at **www.coriolis.com** for any updates to the book or CD-ROM.

System Requirements

Software

◆ You may run many of the examples in this book using Windows 95, 98, or above. However, a few of the examples may require Windows NT Server or Windows 2000 Server.

◆ You will need a Web server that supports Active Server Pages for nearly all of the examples in this book. Personal Web Server (from Microsoft) is adequate for all but a few examples. Some of the examples require Site Server, or another server that supports Microsoft Personalization System.

◆ All the examples require a Web browser. Many examples utilize VBScript, which means you should have Internet Explorer. Version 5 or above is recommended.

◆ Several chapters have programming examples that require Microsoft Visual Basic 6 or above and the Sun Java Development Kit (JDK) version 1.2 or above.

◆ The chapter regarding FrontPage and Visual InterDev requires FrontPage 2000 and Visual InterDev 6.

Hardware

◆ Any PC capable of running the required Windows operating system should be adequate to run the examples in this book. A separate server is not required.